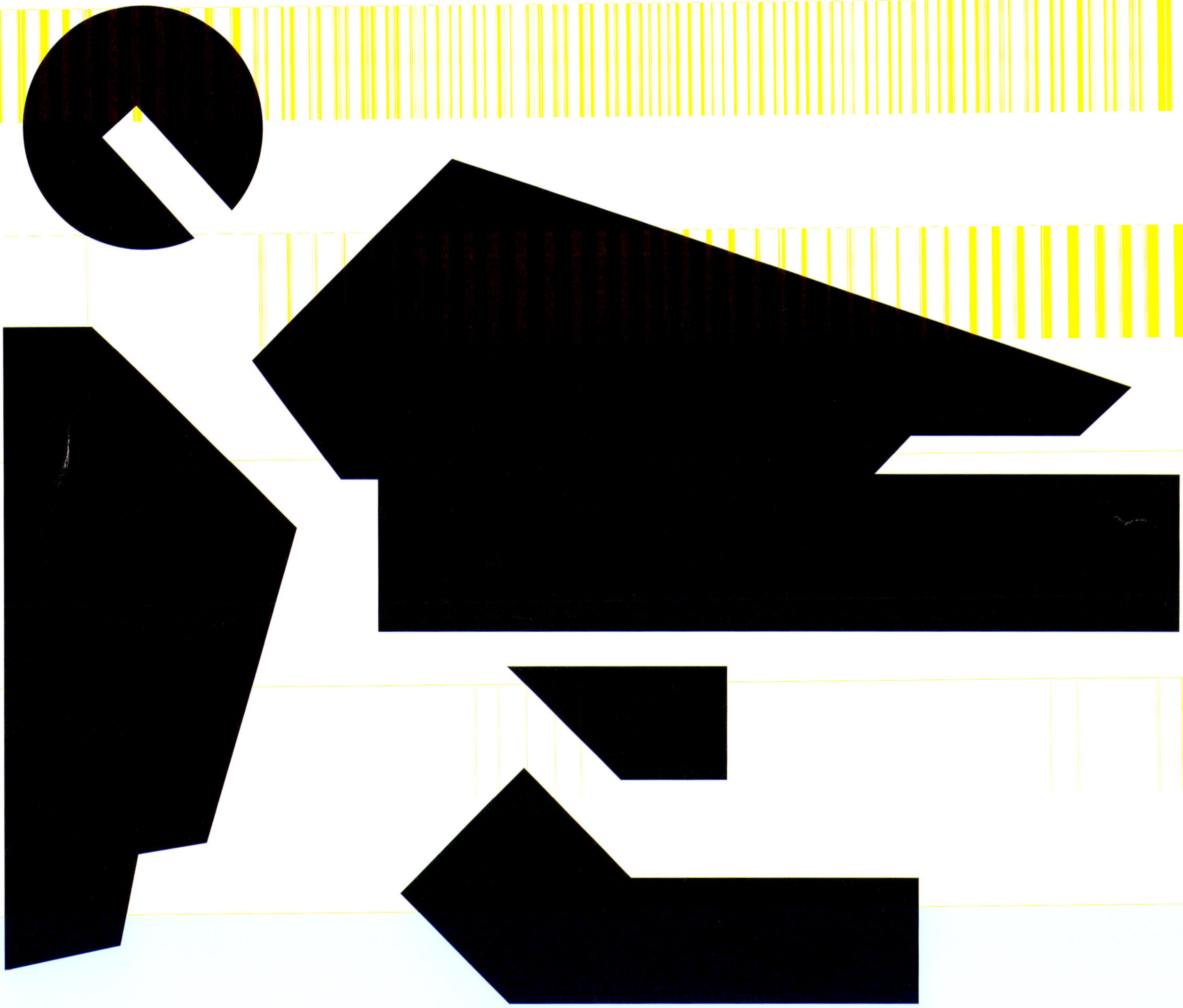

DKV

Conceived by
Dr. Ute Chibidziura, Bundesamt für Bauwesen und Raumordnung
Dr. Constanze von Marlin, schmedding.vonmarlin.

Bundesministerium des Innern, für Bau und Heimat

Bundesamt für Bauwesen und Raumordnung

70 YEARS

IN GERMANY

OF ART IN ARCHITECTURE

DEUTSCHER KUNSTVERLAG

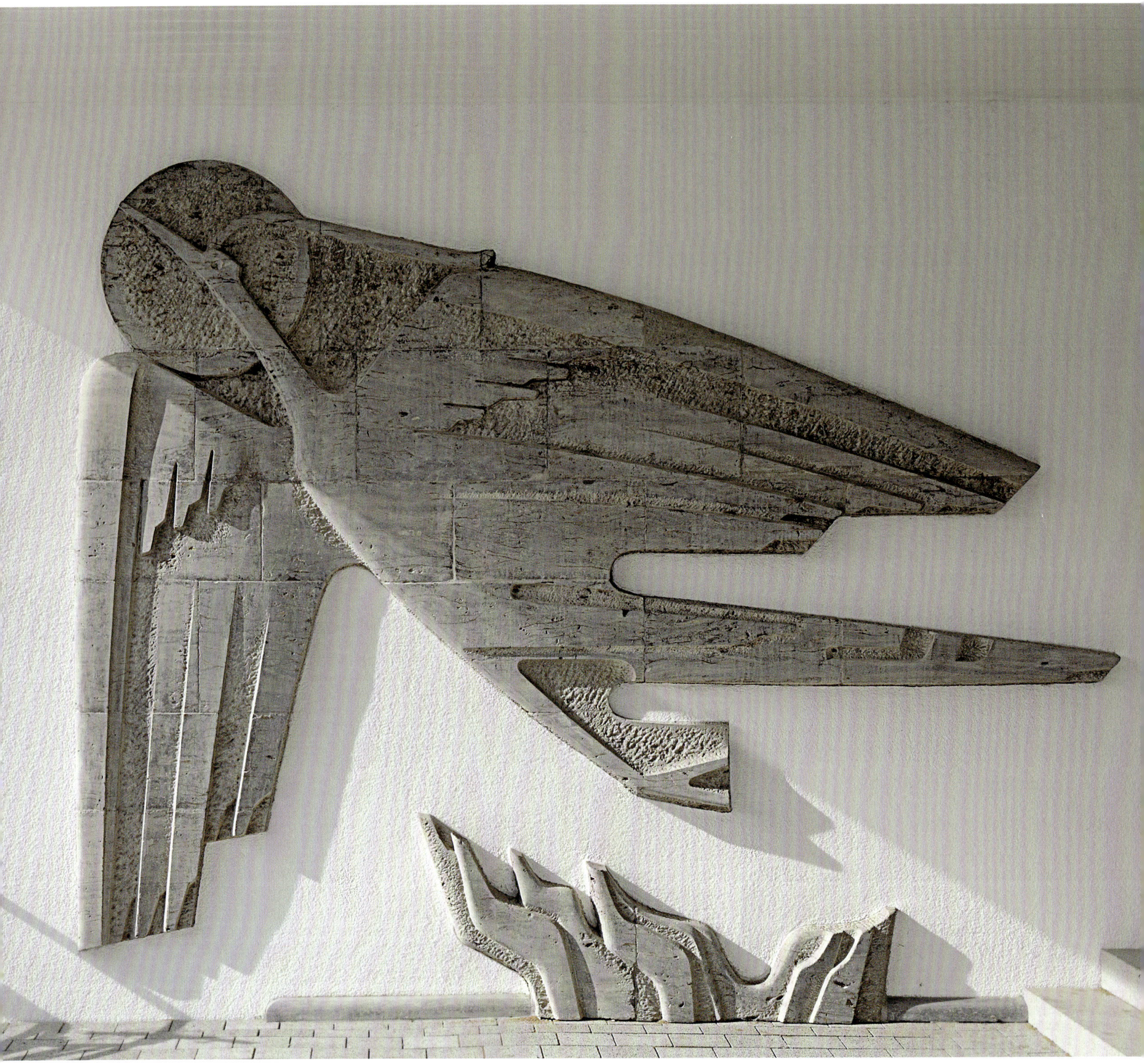

Hannes Schulz-Tattenpach,
“Aufsteigender Phönix”, 1953,
Bundeshaus, Bonn

CONTENTS

PREFACE

Art in architecture has been an integral element of German building culture for 70 years. Both German states already committed to involving artists in state building projects in 1950.
Since the adoption of art in architecture regulations, artworks have always accompanied our building measures, mostly following a competition process. As a result, many renowned artists have enhanced the building culture of the Federal Government with their work.
Today, the Federal Republic of Germany is responsible for around 10,000 artworks, both inside and outside federal buildings, demonstrating an extremely wide range of forms and materials. We take the preservation of these pieces very seriously.
Art in architecture exists in a special field of tension with the building and the grounds it is intended for: the architecturally related framework stipulates clear boundaries and is equally a challenge for free artistic expression. The artworks reflect the artistic engagement with the political and social history of Germany, as is excellently presented by our website "Museum der 1000 Orte" ("Museum of 1000 places"). The website already provides comprehensive presentations of around 200 artworks from both German states up to the most recent past.
This anniversary publication entitled "70 Years of Art in Architecture in Germany" presents the different facets of art in architecture and discusses selected artworks in detail. I would like to thank everyone who has contributed to the production of this extensive volume, especially the artists, whose works have brought us lasting joy and enriched the cultural diversity of Germany.

I hope you enjoy reading this book.

Horst Seehofer
Federal Minister of the Interior, Building and Community

ART IN ARCHITECTURE: THE FORM OF SELF-CANCELLATION

Horst Bredekamp

THE NECESSITY OF ART

One of the most surprising results of research on late pre- and early history lies in the discovery that from the very earliest human production of artefacts, the function by no means preceded the form. Instead, both values were inseparably connected and produced simultaneously. Aesthetics are an element of human evolution and part of what defines humanity. Another, perhaps even more astounding insight from the above research is that a significant number of pre- and early historical "handicrafts" were never intended for use at all and were exclusively produced for the inherent qualities of their form, as demonstrated in the hand axe containing a fossil of a sea urchin, which was found in Swanscombe (Fig. 1).[1] From that fundamental perspective, the history of "adornment" is a narrative of necessity and not simply an added feature. The rule has applied throughout, except during Modernity, an infinitesimally short period compared to the enormous historical time spans.

Since the oldest cultures such as the 80,000 year-old Blombos cave dwellings in South Africa, numerous pieces of evidence have shown that almost all communities regarded art and artistic design as an essential part of their identities.[2] From despotism to democracy, all social structures have followed that principle. It is not the existence itself, but the character of the formal distinction that determined the significance of the respective manifestation.

The formula of *art in architecture* was established in the Weimar Republic on June 20, 1928. Its aim was to counteract the separation of the building sector from the general interrelationship of the visual arts, which began as a long-term consequence of the 19th-century conviction that form should follow function. All knowledge of human nature suggests that the notorious formula of "form follows function", established by the architect Louis Henry Sullivan in 1896, can equally be inverted into "function follows form",[3] but it has nevertheless enjoyed a long, seemingly uninterrupted history of dominance and been upheld like a dogma due to Adolf Loos's perception of "ornament as crime" (1908).[4] A fixation on steel and glass, apparently renouncing the principle of a holistic, artistic shaping of the environment, has characterised the contemporary perception of "Neues Bauen". The grandest examples of Modernity, such as Mies van der Rohe's German Pavilion at the Barcelona Expo in 1929 or the Villa Tugendhat in Brno, regarded themselves as a *Gesamtkunstwerk* that integrated painting and sculpture as spatially formative constituents of the architecture. However, minutely budgeted suburban housing estates led to the horrors that were countered during the Weimar Republic by the principle of *art in architecture*. It was subsequently renewed almost without amendment during the National Socialist period and again after the war,[5] the result of the realisation that life without ornamentation and adornment is not viable in the full sense of the word. Thus *art in architecture* compensates for an insoluble deficit. The negation of that flaw remains marked by the problem needing a solution. In the best sense, *art in architecture* has managed to transcend architecture and achieve

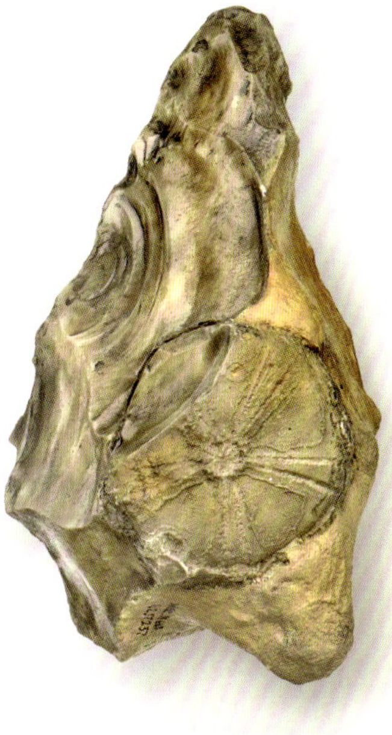

Fig. 1
Hand axe with sea-urchin fossil, Swanscombe, approx. 400,000 years old, World Museum, Liverpool

a new, conceptually enhanced experience; by contrast, its negative examples create an addendum that reveals the artificiality of a supplement. On that premise, the principle of *art in architecture* is to belong to elements that aspire to render themselves unnecessary in the long run by becoming self-evident through the continuous education of general awareness.

THE "IN" OF *ART IN ARCHITECTURE*

Furthermore, the limiting formulation of art "in" architecture should be dropped since it implies that the design is merely applied to architecture, as if backing it up. The historical examples since 1950 show that this conceptual limitation was at times regarded as motivation to oppose it.[6]

Once again, an example from pre- and early history sheds light on the underlying problem. In 2016, the stalagmite rings in Bruniquel Cave, which are over 175,000 years old, attracted considerable attention, since they undoubtedly interacted with the warmth and light of the fire.[7] The rings were designed in a cave that is a natural structure, but can also be grasped as architecture, since it was chosen and adapted for habitation by humans. Thus, the rings represent *art in architecture*, but they also outline an area, assuming the function of spatially definitive art, which could in principle also be installed in front of the dwelling. In that sense, *art in architecture* has no fixed applicatory location and instead has a spatially definitive purpose that can be developed in front of the building, on the building and in the building.

1 M.-H. Moncel, L. Chiotti, C. Gaillard, G. Onoratini and D. Pleurdeau: "Non-utilitarian Lithic Objects from the European Paleolithic", in: *Archeology, Ethnology & Anthropology of Eurasia*, Vol. 40, No. 1, 2012, p. 24–40. Re. the hand axe: Kenneth J. McNamara: *The Star-Crossed Stone. The secret Life Myths, and History of a Fascinating Fossil*, Chicago and London 2011. Cf. in general: Horst Bredekamp: *Art History and Prehistoric Art. Rethinking their Relationship in the Light of New Observations* (trans.: Mitch Cohen), Groningen 2019.

2 Christopher Henshilwood, Francesco d'Errico: "Being modern in the Middle Stone Age", in: Clive Gamble, Martin Porr (Eds.): *The Hominid Individual in Context. Archeological investigations of Lower and Middle Palaeolithic landscapes, locales and artefacts*, New York 2005, p. 244–264.

OUTSIDE: THE ATHENS AGORA

The timeless question of the extent to which democracy can be specifically defined by art has been answered in various ways. The Greek Polis was a space that was meticulously designed down to its structural pores, never requiring the principle of *art in architecture*. Perhaps the most impressive example of an attempt to present visual art and democracy in a mutual relationship is the pair of bronze figures of the Athens citizens Harmodius and Aristogeiton, who assassinated the tyrant Hipparchus in 514 BC. Four years later, two statues were dedicated to them, which were reproduced in 477/476 BC and became, in that form, the archetypal image of the struggle for democracy. It was possible to recreate the lost original statues from ancient reproductions, such as the pair of statues in Naples and other finds (Fig. 2).[8]

The elder, bearded, naked Aristogeiton, a chlamys over his arm, holds a scabbard in his left hand, from which he has drawn a sword with his right hand, his arm behind his body, preparing to strike. The younger, beardless Harmodius, also naked, holds his sword over his head, poised to attack. While the younger man embodies action, the elder expresses latency before the deed, preparation; both represent different characters who complement each other equally. They thereby contrast with the tyrant, who combines both in a single entity. Democracy had found its symbol. The fact that the group of statues was installed on the political marketplace, the Agora, was entirely based on a decision by the citizens' assembly to let the statues define the key public space of Athens democracy. There was a firm conviction that the community required such symbols to ensure that internal cohesion was strong enough to regulate and steer social interaction

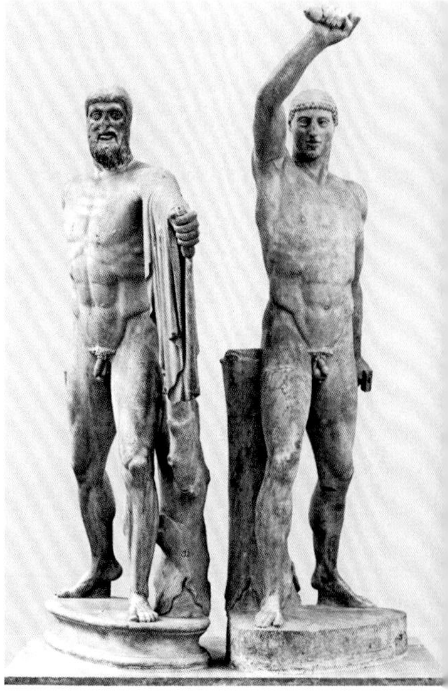

Fig. 2
Harmodius and Aristogeiton, known as the "tyrant slayers", 477/476 BC, plaster reconstruction of the Greek bronze original, Museo dell'Arte Classica, Rome

3 It has been notoriously misunderstood as a call to functionalism, cf. *Ákos Moravánszky (Ed.): Architekturtheorie im 20. Jahrhundert. Eine* kritische Anthologie, Vienna and New York 2003, p. 397–401.
4 Adolf Loos: *Trotzdem* 1900–1930 (Adolf Opel, Ed.), Vienna 1982, p. 79–80, 83–86.
5 Ute Chibidziura: "Kunst am Bau beim Bund – Geschichte, Regularien, Beispiele", in: *In situ*, 5, 2013, p. 249–266, here p. 251.
6 Museum der 1000 Orte. Kunst am Bau im Auftrag des Bundes seit 1950, https://www.museum-der-1000-orte.de.

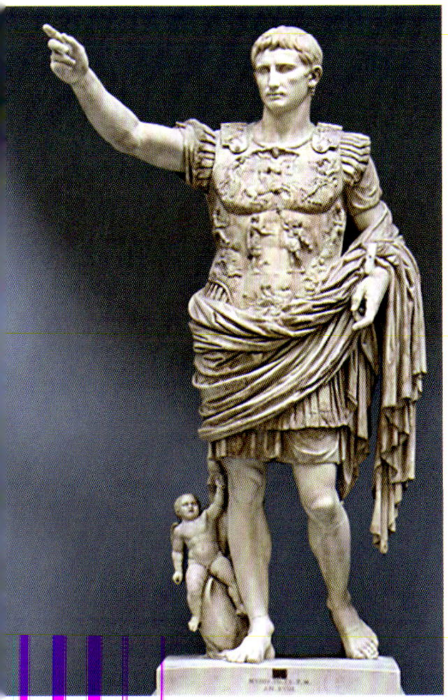

Fig. 3
Augustus of Primaporta,
1st century AD, marble,
Musei Vaticani, Vatican City

along peaceful lines. Discourse on the validity of such visual symbols continues to this day with the controversial debate on the Berlin Monument to Freedom and Unity.

In ancient Rome, statues of honour depicting Emperor Augustus were installed throughout the empire (Fig. 3), referring to the proverbial claim that he transformed his urbs from wood into marble.[9] The conviction that a community needed specific visual points of reference to ratify the actions of its members and thereby allow it to evolve to a higher level was a key element of its internal cohesion.

INSIDE: SIENA

Probably the most complex presentation of a form of government and its effects are the frescoes on the Town Hall in Siena, produced by the artist Ambrogio Lorenzetti around 1300 as a monumental art project in the interior space. On the left, the deterrent outcome of bad government is shown, while the opposite wall presents good government's beneficial effect on the city and country. The centre depicts an allegory of good government.[10]

The panorama of the city of Siena (Fig. 4) seems almost inexhaustible with its squares in the foreground, working and trading people, a ring of dancing girls at the centre, who move to the music of a tambourine, a speech by two private lecturers in the front building and finally the hubbub of houses with high-rise noble towers, one of which is still under construction. The impression is of diligent, peaceful activity.

In the central allegory of wise rule (Fig. 5), the towering regent is enthroned as the incarnation of city government, holding a sceptre in his right hand and the shield of the city in his left hand. The embodiments of the cardinal virtues of Faith, Love and Hope hover around

7 Jacques Jaubert, Sophie Verheyden et al.: "Early Neanderthal constructions deep in Bruniquel Cave in southwestern France", in: *Nature*, No. 534, May 2016, p. 111–114 (DOI:10.1038/nature18291).
8 Burkhard Fehr: *Die Tyrannentöter. Oder: Kann man der Demokratie ein Denkmal setzen?*, Frankfurt am Main 1984, p. 6–8.
9 Paul Zanker: *Augustus und die Macht der Bilder*, Munich 1987.
10 The classical study stems from Quentin Skinner: "Ambrogio Lorenzetti: The Artist as Political Philosopher", in: *Proceedings of the British Academy*, Vol. 72, 1986, p. 1–56.

his head, while the she-wolf sits with Romulus and Remus at his feet, implying that Siena is the "New Rome". The six women either side of him embody further virtues, including Justice on the outside right, the head of an executed man beneath her upright sword. The 24 people looking up to the regent on the opposite side hold the Concordia band of unity, consisting of different coloured threads, indicating that the divergent factions of Siena must be intertwined to strengthen the republic through unity. The rope leads up to the ruler's sceptre, which the citizens can pull down with a single tug: this is the republican element of the band of unity. Further to the left, it leads to the embodiment of democracy. She is holding a plane on her knee, with which to smooth over any irregularities. The rope is provided by the second incarnation of Justice, seated upon a throne on the left-hand edge of the image. The embodiment of Wisdom hovers above Justitia to maintain the balance of justice, the scales suspended beside her. Equality and justice are imposed with the extreme clarity and toughness of the Roman Republic. The visualisation of the relationship between Security, Justice, Equality and Prosperity requires the letter of the law, but the foundations upon which they are based can be experienced almost without words. Perhaps never before or afterwards has a commissioned piece delivered so much more than the task at hand through its implementation, presenting the utopia of an inwardly and externally fortified republic.

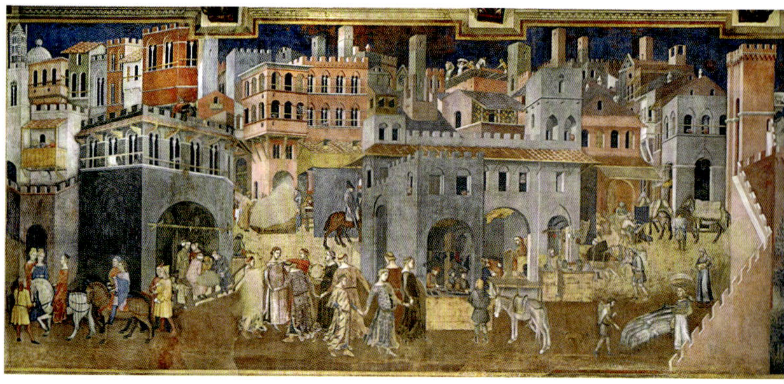

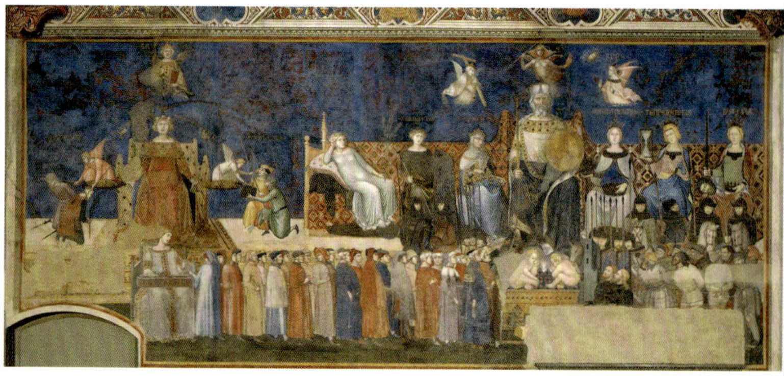

Fig. 4
Ambrogio Lorenzetti, "Effects of good government in the city and the country", 1338/1339, fresco, Palazzo Pubblico, Siena

Fig. 5
Ambrogio Lorenzetti, "Allegory of good government", 1338/1339, fresco, Palazzo Pubblico, Siena

Fig. 6
Piazza della Signoria with the sculptures "David", 1501-1504, by Michelangelo, and "Hercules and Cacus", 1525-1534, by Baccio Bandinelli, Florence

OUTSIDE AND INSIDE: FLORENCE

Two hundred years later, a comparably paradigmatic attempt was made in Florence to design the transition from the square to the

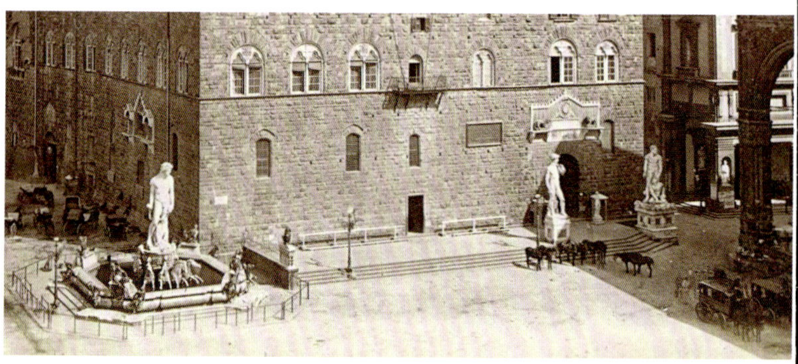

façade and on to the interior space: the interaction between Michelangelo's David with the frescoes in the grand council hall of the Palazzo Vecchio. Michelangelo's marble figure was initially conceived as ornamentation for Florence Cathedral, to decorate the ambulatory chapels with sculptures in a way that would be visible from afar. Various terracotta figures provided such an appealing example that the community conceived a plan to display both its artistic prowess and technical skill in implementing artworks by placing marble figures of a similar size on the dizzying heights of the buttresses. However, the attempts failed until Michelangelo managed to master one of the enormous marble blocks, which had been considered unworkable. When he presented the crowning achievement of his younger years to the municipal authority commission, it decided to transform the work into the emblem of the republic by placing it in full view in front of the Town Hall, rather than on the elevated centres of the cathedral ambulatory chapels (Fig. 6). Just as David defeated Goliath, so the republic would use its courage and skill to overcome enormous kingdoms and duchies, such as Milan and Naples.

This David, a naked, unprotected youth, is not a born hero; instead he overcomes his fear, transforming his weakness into strength (Fig. 7). He turns his panic into a distant fixation on the overwhelming power of the Goliath, in political terms, to oppose the despotic strength of duchies and kingdoms. As the weaker party who is able to defeat the overpowering giant though self-sacrifice and guile, David is an early incarnation of the people's army. He became the symbol of the Florentine Republic due to his character and intelligence, rather than his physical strength.

This can be seen in a painting by Francesco Granacci, on which a young man is presented as a member of the people's army. Both the government palace and the figure of David in front of it are depicted in the background as equal symbols of society's backbone (Fig. 8). The victorious republic had its new symbol, its new cult image. Some contemporaries even called for the introduction of a new calendar after the David statue was installed.

David embodies the city's democratic self-perception. It is why the statue was controversial from the outset. While it was transported from the cathedral workshop to the Town Hall, a process that took days, supporters of an autocratic political system threw stones at it. However, all critics were silenced once the work was unveiled, its radiance overpowering their censure. In that respect, Michelangelo's David can be regarded as the unsurpassed symbol of a commission that can be connected to the concept of *art in architecture*.

After the statue's completion in 1504, Michelangelo was commissioned to paint a mural in the grand council hall of the government palace, thereby entering into an electrifying competition with Leonardo da Vinci, who was commissioned to paint the other wall with the motif of the battle of Anghiari. The latter addressed a heroic moment, the battle for the standards (Fig. 9). By contrast, Michelangelo focused not on heroism, but on an internal struggle; instead of combat, he portrayed a false alarm that enabled a later triumph. The picture was never actually applied to the wall and Michelangelo's preparatory study was only preserved in copies, but it is nevertheless sufficiently expressive (Fig. 10).

During the war against Pisa, the leader of the Florentine army caught a severe fever and was forced to rest in a military camp near Cascina. In view of the scorching sun, his soldiers also withdrew to rest or go bathing. Concerned about poor discipline, their General Donati staged a false alarm. Michelangelo shows how the Florentines suddenly transform from relaxing men at leisure into warriors. He chose a moment that, taken by itself, appears ridiculous in terms of its details: negligent soldiers who are unable to put on their trousers and breastplates quickly enough because they were either asleep or still wet from bathing. However, a comparison with David shows that it is precisely this moment that Michelangelo believed to be a precondition of heroism.

While Leonardo had chosen an action-packed combat scene on horseback from the Battle of Anghari for his opposite wall in the Florence Council Hall, Michelangelo selected the foot soldiers, like David, who was similarly a shepherd. The biblical hero is naked, like the warriors in Cascina. Neither the enemy nor the battle is portrayed, only the preparation: the same is presented in the resilient statue of David. One can also see fear in David's eyes, which, however, is channelled into a focused assessment of the duel. The soldiers equally overcome their reticence, expressing all possible emotions, from resignation to angry haste. Michelangelo's battle painting does without blood, celebrating the supremacy of the local soldiers not in the form of a general, but by focusing on foot soldiers, abandoned by their sick leader, readying themselves for battle. Seismographically, Michelangelo picked up on the defence strategy of his home city, which was building up an army of citizens, without any mercenaries, at the time when he was preparing his Cascina fresco.

Michelangelo's design was never painted because he was sent on a commission to Rome, but nevertheless, his concept inspired by the frescoes of Siena was regarded as an outstanding piece of republican political iconography.

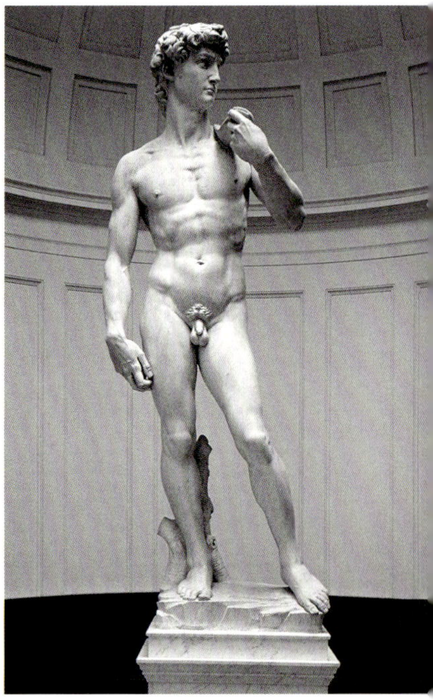

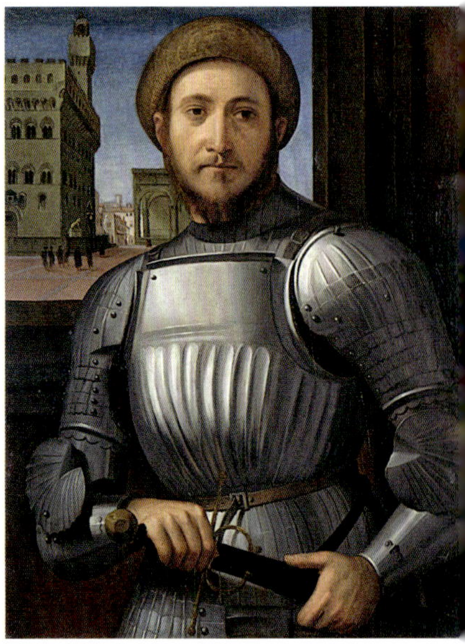

Fig. 7
Michelangelo, "David", 1501-1504, marble, Galleria dell'Accademia, Florence

Fig. 8
Francesco Granacci, "Portrait of a man in armour", around 1510, oil on wood, National Gallery, London

Fig. 9
Leonardo da Vinci, Tavola Doria, preparatory study for the "Battle of Anghiari", 1503, oil on poplar wood, private collection

Fig. 10
Aristotile da Sangallo, copy of Michelangelo's "Battle of Cascina", 1542, Grisaille, Holkham Hall

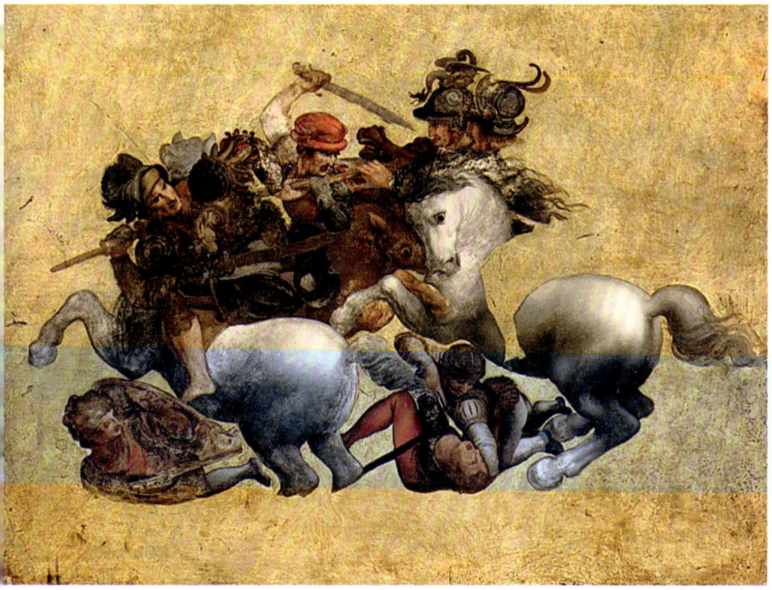

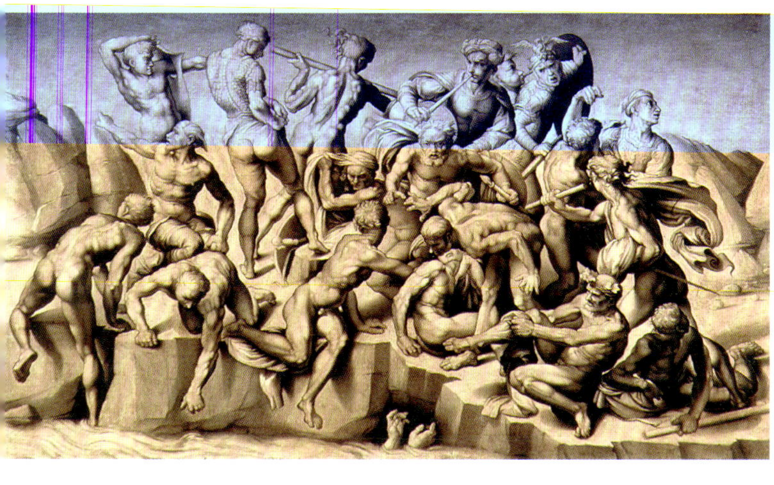

Using today's vocabulary, both Leonardo da Vinci and Michelangelo had been commissioned to produce *art in architecture*. Notions on the content of their work, the free Republic of Florence, were as precise as the expectations regarding their implementation. However, the city government by no means intended pure propaganda, giving the artists a free rein. Michelangelo enjoyed a leeway stemming from the insight that the artist can only achieve his greatest heights if he is free, using that freedom in a way that had been inconceivable until then. He created icons for the republic because he renounced all one-dimensionality. This set the standard for all subsequent commissioned artworks. Generally, the commissioning client fails if he wishes to see his own ideas directly implemented. *Art in architecture* can only be art for art, not art for the funding authority.

The legally defined necessity, the principle of regulating and implementing *art in architecture*, poses the question of the extent to which democracy can appear as the commissioning body of art at all. Art is subjective and every vote by elected representatives entails the danger of undermining the extremes of subjectivity, forcing it into the mainstream of general agreement. This is why the processes of decision-making are so difficult and often controversial. The conflict can never be resolved, but it can be managed if it is a conscious process and, as the Florentine example magnificently shows, if the art retains its autonomy within its framework of a commission.

THE MODERN STATE

Following the destruction of the republic in 1530, Baccio Bandinelli's "Hercules and Cacus" was established as an opposing symbol of raw power, thereby representing autocracy

(Fig. 6). The age of absolutism adopted the model of a powerful male brute. Hardly any other community has used the expressive, intimidating and memorable form of political communication through artworks to a comparable extent. The France of Louis XIV, with its Versailles palace grounds, can be regarded as a form of governance that stages the principle of visualised rule down to the smallest elements of daily life, as a form of surveillance and simultaneously as the rapture of overcoming one's own boundaries.[11]

The alternative to a non-personal representation of a state that could be perceived both as an autocracy and as a communal form of governance, which however certainly took the wishes of society into account, but only did so at the price of disarming society in the spirit of the state's monopoly of violence, was based on the image of the state in the eyes of Hobbes' Leviathan. It became the quintessential image of modern society: a body with cells consisting of its citizens (Fig. 11).

Shaping society by means of visual staging and artworks that merged with the buildings was such an opposing image for the French Revolution, and above all subsequent democratic societies, that the question arose whether public artworks and images were detrimental to democracy per se. The question remains unresolved today. The former President of the United States, John Quincy Adams, coined the radical formula as follows in reaction to Baroque absolutism: "Democracy has no monuments. / It strikes no medals. / It bears the head of no man on a coin."[12]

The iconoclastic variety of the definition of democracy as a purely intellectual society, like the imageless community of the original Christians, remained an exception that was perhaps most similarly reflected by the Federal Republic after 1945, to distance itself from

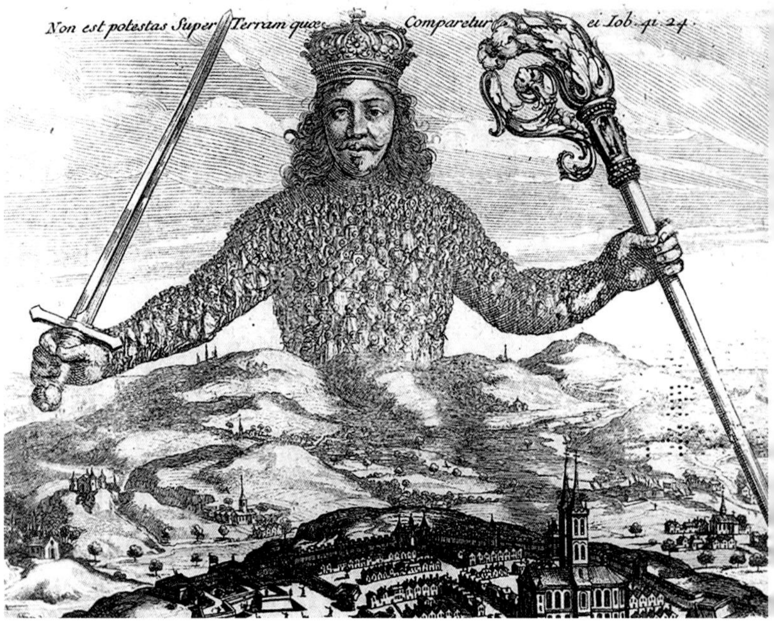

Fig. 11
Thomas Hobbes, "Leviathan", frontispiece detail, 1651

11 Louis Marin: *Le portrait du roi*, Paris 1981; Stefan Germer: *Kunst – Macht – Diskurs. Die intellektuelle Karriere des André Félibien im Frankreich von Luis XIV.*, Munich 1997; Pablo Schneider: *Die erste Ursache. Kunst, Repräsentation und Wissenschaft zu Zeiten Ludwigs XIV. und Charles Le Bruns*, Berlin 2011.
12 Marion G. Müller: *Politische Bildstrategien im amerikanischen Präsidentschaftswahlkampf* 1828–1996, Berlin 1997, p. 23.
13 Horst Bredekamp: "Politische Ikonologie des Grundgesetzes", in: Michael Stolleis (Ed.):

the visual propaganda with which the National Socialists so forcefully imposed their rule. But that very principle led to a state style that preferred a reserved stance, in the hope of being readmitted to the international community.[13]

Today, the problem is a global phenomenon. *Art in architecture* represents the fundamental insight that the absence of visual art weakens the conditio humana. In doing so, it stakes a claim that enables the thought experiment of applying this principle to any field revealing a similar deficit.[14] Should humanity truly have arrived in the so-called Anthropocene, in which the traces of human design have inscribed themselves upon the geological formation of the Earth,[15] then it is only consistent to grasp the goal of *art in architecture* as a global responsibility. That means no intellectual excesses, since the goal of *art in architecture* remains its own dissolution. Design must retain an artistic character that does not require additive ornamentation, instead using the principle to pursue the single goal of rendering this very additive principle superfluous, and to design on, in and in front of the buildings of the entire world, as was equally achieved in Bruniquel Cave, in Siena and in Florence.

Herzkammern der Republik. Die Deutschen und das Verfassungsgericht, Munich 2011, p. 9–35; Elisabeth Plessen: Bauten des Bundes 1949–1899. *Zwischen Architekturkritik und zeitgenössischer Wahrnehmung*, Berlin 2019.

14 Martin Warnke: "Kunst unter Verweigerungspflicht", in: Volker Plagemann (Ed.): *Kunst im öffentlichen Raum. Anstöße der 80er Jahre*, Cologne 1989, p. 223–226.

15 Paul J. Crutzen, Eugene F. Stoermer: "The 'Anthropocene'", in: *Global Change Newsletter*, No. 41, May 2000, p. 17–18.

CULTURAL TRANSFER BETWEEN EAST AND WEST DURING THE COLD WAR

Sigrid Hofer

Since the mid-1990s, the Federal Government's move from Bonn to Berlin has required a large number of new building and conversions. Thus, arts committees and experts have been developing concepts to complement those measures on the level of visual art. It plays a key role in the process of the democratic formation of opinion – despite or perhaps due to the fact that it can raise unpleasant questions and make antagonisms visible: because art encourages discourse that goes beyond pure functional rationalism, and because sensorial and aesthetic perception are essential stimuli of individual development. Furthermore, its focus lies on a critical reflection upon overall social developments. Bernhard von Loeffelholz put it succinctly: "Every power system needs resistance to ensure it does not become totalitarian and inhumane."[1] Whether produced by commission, through competitions or as purchases, the choice of artworks for federal buildings focused both on internationalism, as a reflection of Berlin policy, and on highlighting renowned German artists who were regarded abroad as representatives of contemporary aesthetics. Local specifics and historical references often provided the theme for the content as it addressed German history, giving the artworks a symbolic effect.

With respect to German reunification, the state had to fulfil its mandate from an overall social perspective by equally involving representatives from the former East and West Germany. In 1999, the so-called "Bilderstreit", a dispute on the value of the two systems of art and the integrity of their respective protagonists,[2] made such parity extremely important. The selections made over the years demonstrate the diversity of modern art forms, as well as their interweaving and points of contact, which had also existed during the years of separation. Thus the artworks are not fundamentally different from each other, since the East was by no means cut off from international trends. Exchange, communication, travel, participation in exhibitions and competitions were all possible, although their concrete forms were affected by fluctuations in inner-German relations.

Since art from the GDR was only perceived in the FRG to a limited degree, this section focuses on the former and its relationship with the FRG. Starting with pieces in the parliamentary buildings, it covers a broader thematic field, including inner-German cultural exchange viewed from the perspective of principles. In this context, examples are preferable to an overview. They stand for specific developments, typical biographical stages and non-conformist aesthetics, against which the State Security repeatedly intervened, as well as for self-will and self-assertion. However, they also stand for artists that held official posts in the GDR and wavered between striving for independence and conformity. This section therefore focuses on artists from the GDR in order to add nuances to the narrative on the GDR to date. They make the complexity of the arts system visible, although the actions of the dictatorial surveillance system should by no means be trivialised.

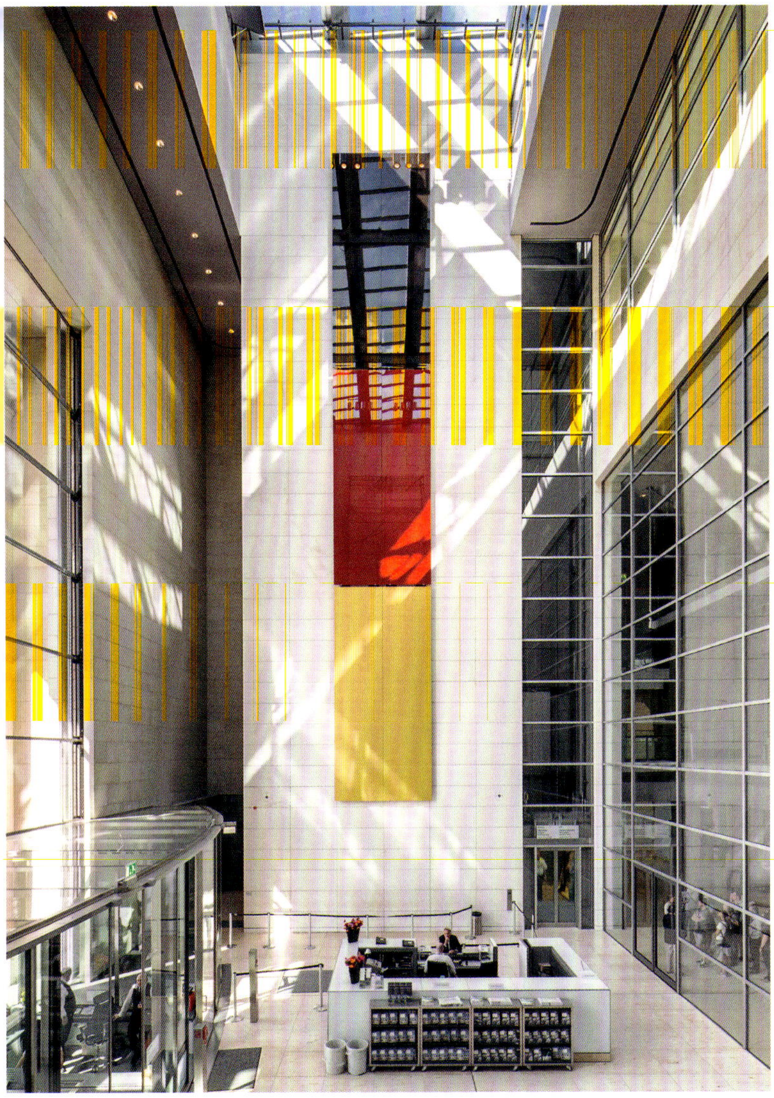

Fig. 1
Gerhard Richter, “Schwarz, Rot, Gold”, 1998, German Bundestag/ Reichstag building, Berlin

THE GDR IN YOUR SUITCASE

The honour of the first example goes to Gerhard Richter (born in 1932), perhaps the most well known contemporary German artist, also due to his multipart tabular pieces in the main entrance hall of the Reichstag building (Fig. 1). He represents a generation of visual artists who emigrated from the East to the West and whose life and work are characterised by the themes of new beginnings and engagement with the western art scene.[3] Richter, who moved from Dresden to Düsseldorf in 1961, joined with Konrad Lueg (1939–1996) and others to establish what they called Capitalist Realism. By referring in this way to Socialist Realism, the guiding doctrine of visual art in the GDR, and combining it with a critical distance to the dogmas of western economics, the artists used the style to examine their current experiences, reacting to the phenomena of the time with constantly new forms of presentation.

In the Rhineland region, which quickly established itself as the centre of contemporary art in the new FRG, Richter was joined by a large number of emigrants from the GDR. Some of them began studying again and later held professorships. One example is Gotthard Graubner (1930–2013). He entirely dedicated his piece “… die rosenfingrige Eos erwacht ...” (“… the rose-fingered Eos awakes…”, 1989/1999) to the intrinsic value of colour, which he applied in many layers to large, cushion-like image media. They thereby lose their hard edges – as is the case in the protocol room of the Reichstag building – and radiate into the surroundings. Günther Uecker (born in 1930), who left the GDR in 1953, should also be mentioned in this context. For the Reichstag building, he designed a non-denominational commemoration room that uses laterallyinduced, blue light to create a

1 Bernhard von Loeffelholz: “*Wechselwirkungen zwischen kultureller und wirtschaftlicher Entwicklung*”, in: Walter Grasskamp et al. (Eds.): Mäzene, Stifter und Sponsoren. Ostfildern-Ruit 2001, p. 205–212, here p. 209 [trans.].

2 See Karl-Siegbert Rehberg: *Bilderstreit und Gesellschaftsumbruch*, Berlin 2013.

3 For an overview of the many artists who left the GDR from 1949 onwards, see Werner Schmidt (Ed.): *Ausgebürgert, Berlin 1990.*

spiritual effect, while his nail art, which is placed against the walls, invites meditative contemplation (Fig. 2). Like many artists who were considered "staatsfern" (literally "distanced from the state"), Georg Baselitz (born in 1938) was expelled from university. In 1957, he switched from the Kunsthochschule Berlin-Weissensee to the Akademie der Künste in the western part of the city. From the 1960s onwards, he shocked viewers with taboo subjects that discredited the bourgeois code of norms. From 1961, the construction of the Berlin Wall made it impossible to emigrate as those artists had done, but emigration especially increased again after the expatriation of the singer-songwriter Wolf Biermann in November 1976. Fluctuating between state concessions and restrictions, it was impossible for a climate to evolve in the GDR that supported autonomous artistic development. Thus in 1984, Lutz Dammbeck (born in 1948) breached state regulations in a targeted way by joining with colleagues in initiating the inaugural Leipzig Herbstsalon ("Leipzig Autumn Salon") at the Leipzig Messehaus – without the required authorisation and under false pretences. His "Herakles-Notizen" ("Heracles Notes"), presented on the parliamentary-party level of the Reichstag building, is part of a major cyclical multimedia project he pursued from 1977 to 1987. After moving to Hamburg in 1986, he continued working on it as the theme of his life, with diverse connotations including the fight against fascism, criticism of the system and questions of self-respect.

In addition to émigrés, there are also references to a number of old masters who had remained in the GDR and were forbidden to exhibit their works or carry out their profession, or were kept under observation by the State Security. They included the visual

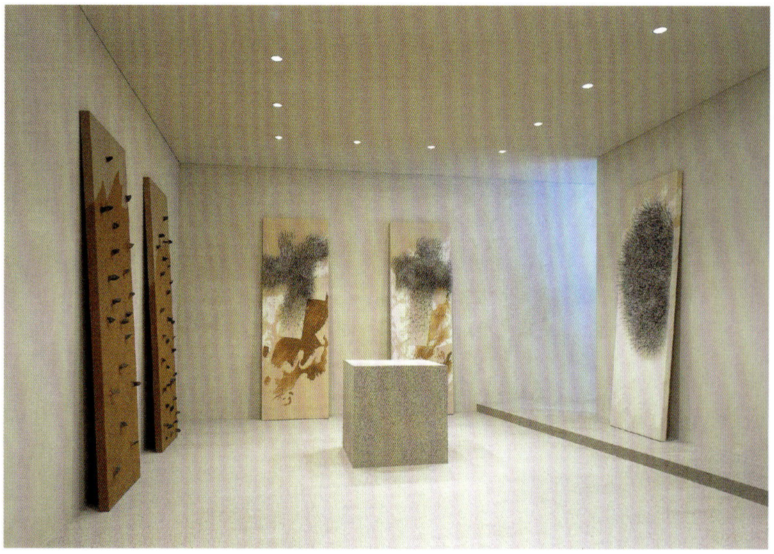

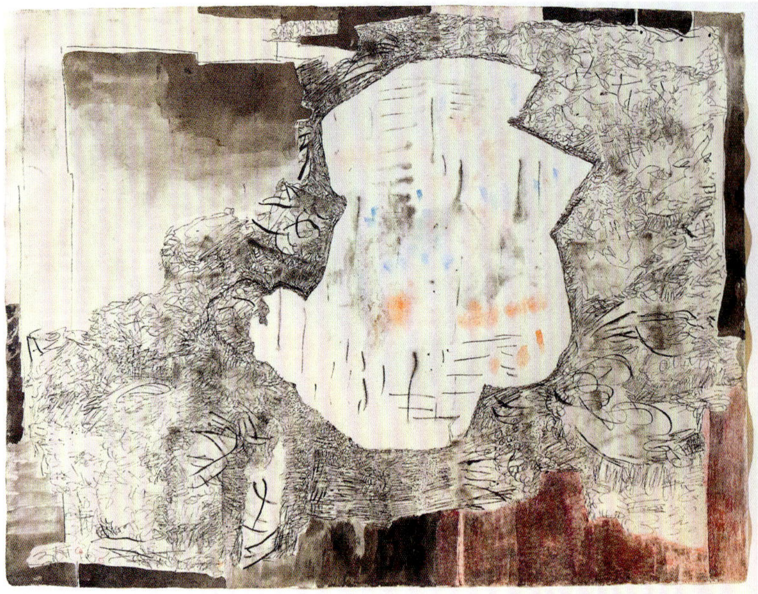

Fig. 2
Günther Uecker, commemoration room, 1998/1999, German Bundestag/Reichstag building, Berlin

Fig. 3
Gerhard Altenbourg, "Große Landschaft", 1953, German Bundestag/ Reichstag building, Berlin

Fig. 4
Carlfriedrich Claus, "Aurora-Experimentalraum", 1977/1993, German Bundestag/ Reichstag building, Berlin

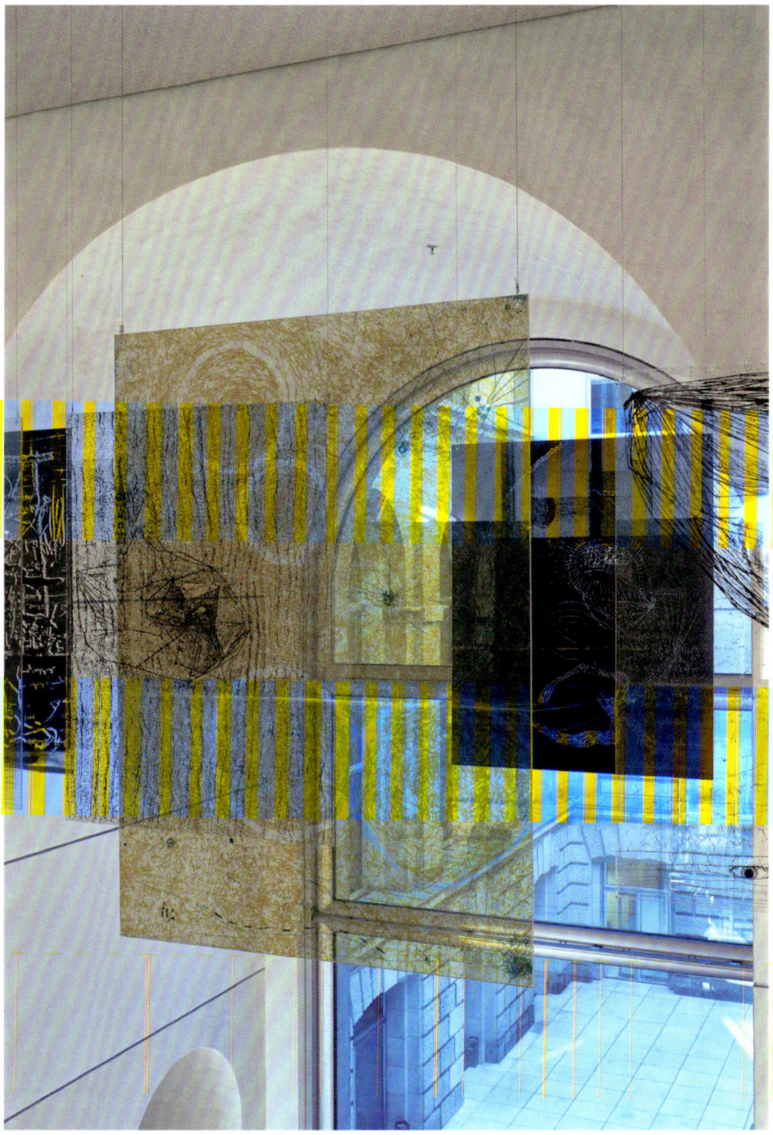

artists Gerhard Altenbourg (1926–1989) and Carlfriedrich Claus (1930–1998), as well as Hermann Glöckner (1889–1987), whose constructivist, informal work was only officially recognised in the GDR on his 95th birthday. Altenbourg's paper work "Große Landschaft" ("Great landscape"), which is exhibited in a showcase in front of the parliamentarians' lobby in the Reichstag building, had already been produced in 1953 (Fig. 3). In front of an abstract background, it presents a light field, its outlines combining to form the external borders of the FRG and GDR. Today, it can be interpreted as both a visionary and a utopian work that anticipated historical developments. One important artwork by Carlfriedrich Claus also stems from the GDR period. The artwork "Aurora-Experimentalraum" ("Aurora experimental space", 1993) is installed in front of the parliamentarians' lobby in the Reichstag building (Fig. 4). The artist produced a paper piece as early as 1977 and later transposed it onto large acrylic boards. Throughout his life, he produced what he called "Sprachblätter" ("language papers") that tread a fine line between drawing and text, containing legible and illegible elements, as well as landscape motifs. With exceptional concentration and inner contemplation, he penned the finest lines to draw his philosophical reflections on mysticism, the Kabbala and Marxism. The transparency of his image media and his characteristic treatment of the front and rear sides of paper pick up on the method of dialectic materialism, which approaches the multifaceted nature of a situation by means of theses and antitheses.

Moritz Götze (born in 1964) was one of the few artists whose Pop Art style was permitted to flourish during the GDR period. His enamel plates at the Jakob Kaiser House of the German Bundestag focus on historical figures and events that were key to the development of German parliamentarianism (Fig. 5). Angela Hampel (born in 1956), whose work often addressed gender issues, which were discussed with equal intensity in the GDR and the FRG and have not been sufficiently resolved to this day, arranged eight "artists" over each other in the Federal Ministry of Economics. The work can be interpreted as an appeal to uphold an essential sense of balance and foresight in all decision-making (Fig. 6). On the ground floor of the Bendlerblock, which is used by the Federal Ministry of Defence, the "Roter Teppich" ("Red carpet") by Via Lewandowsky (born in 1963), who belonged to the rebellious "autoperforation artists" in Dresden during the late 1980s, refers back to the procedure of diplomatic ceremony, combining it with German history (→ p. 170). The war-damaged Tiergarten district that is visible on the carpet recalls the crimes of the National Socialists and also the attempted assassination of Adolf Hitler, for which Claus von Stauffenberg paid with his life: he was executed at that very location.

As the above examples show, the majority of artists developed pieces that sought to engage with German history. For example, Baselitz explicitly referred to Caspar David Friedrich in both of his works, thereby recalling the Romantic movement, which was so important to German intellectual life. Richter's tripartite piece "Schwarz, Rot, Gold" ("Black, Red, Gold", 1999) is by no means a replica of a political symbol, as the title may suggest. Instead, he uses the means of art to create a confusing interplay of image and reflection: it is clear that the coloured, enamelled glass he uses cannot be interpreted as the image of a textile flag and is rather an autonomous artwork. Personal preconceptions, standard iconography and the aesthetic perception of the image surface interact with each other and leave the interpretation to the observer. However, it is

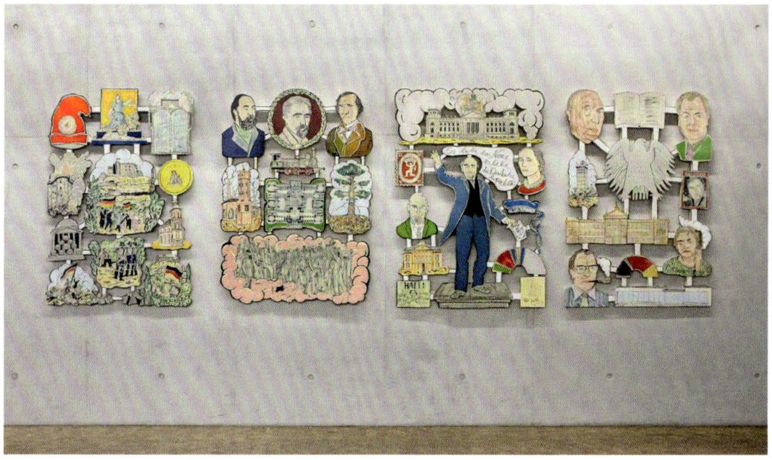

Fig. 5
Moritz Götze, "Vier Emaille-Tableaus zur Geschichte des Deutschen Parlamentarismus", 2016, German Bundestag/ Jakob-Kaiser-Haus, Berlin

impossible to overlook the fact that the plates express a challenge to engage with the political past when perceiving the opposite wall. A cycle of images has been installed there, focusing on one of the darkest chapters of German history. The artwork "Birkenau", produced by Richter in 2014, pays homage to those murdered in the concentration camp of the same name. Richter refrained from realistic portrayal in attempting to capture the unspeakable horror that the people experienced in the concentration camp. Instead, he decided to use abstract presentation based on photographs that are no longer recognisable. Multiple overpainting and removal of the previous colour layers communicate the fallacy of the belief that one can approach such a theme by concrete means. The formal metaphorical power of creating and destroying is an impressive solution.

Fig. 6
Angela Hampel, "Artisten", 2000/2001, Federal Ministry for Economic Affairs and Technology, Berlin

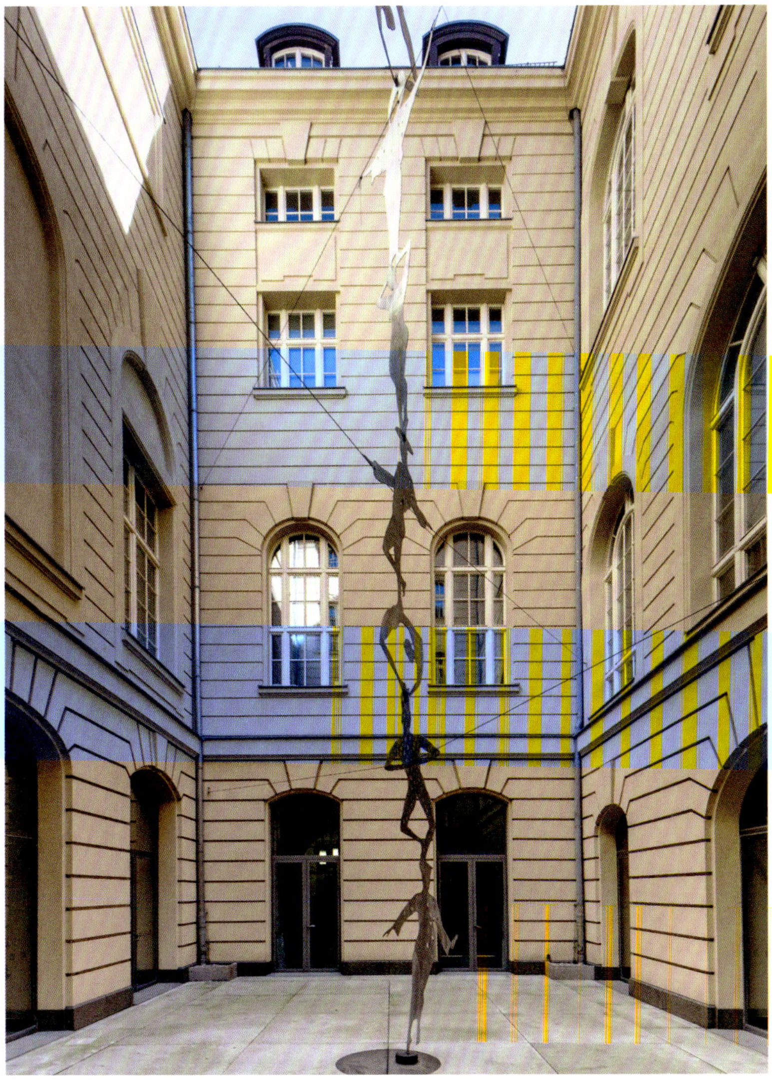

Not only artists who openly expressed their distanced stance towards the GDR were noticed. Others who held important positions in the GDR system were also invited to contribute. For instance the Leipzig School was represented by Bernhard Heisig (1925–2011) and Wolfgang Mattheuer (1927–2004). The inclusion of Heisig, the former Dean of the Leipzig College of Art and Vice President of the GDR Association of Visual Artists, even took the "Bilderstreit" inside the walls of the Reichstag building. The subsequent, contentiously argued public debate offered the advantage of discussing commissioned and state art in an in-depth and differentiated manner: because, as already mentioned above, hasty verdicts do not do justice to the arts system of the GDR, with its many discrepancies. In this context, the historian Mary Fulbrook spoke of a "partizipativer Diktatur" ("participatory dictatorship"),[4] as artists weighed up concessions to state power with the question of self-preservation, as well as the desire and ability to visibly contribute to society through their work. For instance in 1964, Heisig was removed from his position as College Dean following his criticism of the state's cultural policy, later giving up his work as a lecturer altogether due to the strict arts doctrine. After his professional rehabilitation, he continued his career as a cultural functionary in the 1970s, working towards greater freedom of expression for his students. In his painting "Zeit und Leben", ("Time and life", 1998/1999) commissioned by the Bundestag (Fig. 7), he presents the hardships and horrors of tyranny, but also uses the Icarus motif, which was regarded in the GDR as a symbol of failed utopian ideals, thereby creating a plethora of ethical value notions.

In the context discussed above, the federal institutions accommodated in buildings that had previously served the GDR state should not be forgotten. In 1950, the same year as the FRG enacted a law on "art in architecture", the GDR also undertook to award the same kind of commissions, calling them "building-related art". Various examples of such works still exist, such as the porcelain frieze "Aufbau der Republik" ("Development of the republic", 1953) by Max Lingner (1888–1959) for the then Haus der Ministerien ("House of Ministries")(→ p. 74). Today, it accommodates the Federal Ministry of Finance. Naturally, the respective works had to fulfil a political function and communicate the Socialist vision. However, as the architectural historian Thomas Topfstedt explains, "many of the pieces... were coded with much more multifaceted significance, so it would be a rather crude over-simplification to label them all as merely 'SED propaganda art'."[5] Furthermore, like all artworks, the same applied to this genre: party-political briefs were not always, or could not always be enforced or implemented.

4 Cit. Johannes Hürter, Hermann Wentker: "Diktaturen im 20. Jahrhundert. Überlegungen zu einem zeithistorischen Forschungsfeld", in: id. (Eds.): *Diktaturen*, Berlin et al. 2019, p. 7–29, here p. 25.

5 Thomas Topfstedt: "Baubezogene Kunst in der DDR", in: Bundesministerium für Verkehr, Bau und Stadtentwicklung (Ed.): *60 x Kunst am Bau aus 60 Jahren*, Berlin 2010, p. 28–39, here p. 28 [trans.].

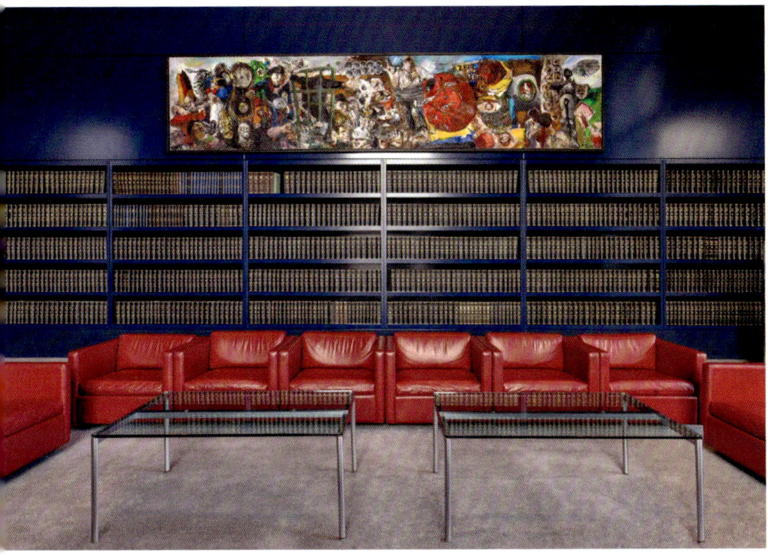

Fig. 7
Bernhard Heisig, "Zeit und Leben", 1998, German Bundestag/Reichstag building, Berlin

ART AND STATE REPRESENTATION

The fact that for a long time, the general public in the Federal Republic did not perceive the artistic production in the GDR is essentially due to the contrasting political systems, which encouraged or demanded specific art forms in each part of Germany. After the end of World War II, the formation of blocs led, to a greater or lesser extent, to the instrumentalisation of the arts and culture for propaganda purposes. The western zone and later the new Federal Republic pursued a strategy of western integration under Federal Chancellor Konrad Adenauer, taking a decisive step towards a policy of alliance with the USA. Individual freedom in the artistic working process was therefore regarded as an inalienable asset. On the political stage, this was equated with a regained democracy and these new values were to be empathically demonstrated to the world, especially by means of aesthetics. The Federal Government saw itself suitably reflected in an abstract visual language that resisted any appropriation in terms of the content and favoured the artist's subjective design intentions. Thus it is not surprising that, following initial controversial debates in the late 1950s, the Kulturkreis der deutschen Wirtschaft im BDI e.V. (an industrial association supporting the arts) became an advocate of the avant-garde, since it welcomed "the free pathos of autonomous art".[6]

While visual artists in the West were not immune to such instrumentalisation, the phenomenon was far more severe in the East. The SED regarded state-imposed Socialist Realism to be an appropriate form to implement their political credo in all areas of life. The themes of the paintings, graphic designs and sculptures had to glorify the achievements

6 Walter Grasskamp: "Auftragskunst und Gestaltungsfreiheit", in: id. et al. (see Footnote 1), p. 11–25, here p. 15 [trans.].

and future goals of Socialism, while also calling upon the population to actively support the state. To ensure clear visual statements, a figurative mode of presentation was obligatory, with a pleasing, popular character. And naturally, Socialist Realism was an adequate response to and explicit rejection of abstraction, which apparently served the class enemy. Insofar as this could be called the official arts policy of the GDR (the existence of counter-movements that were critical of the state have been mentioned above), this meant that only shortly after 1945, art forms established themselves in the East and West that were diametrically opposed to each other. For a decade, they dominated the cultural-political discourse and public reception in the two parts of Germany. The West took hardly any notice of the counter-cultural movements in the GDR. However, the following sections discuss examples of the many ways in which the Iron Curtain was nevertheless overcome, as well as the levels on which and intentions with which this was achieved.

TRAVELLING ARTISTS AND ARTWORKS. FROM EAST TO WEST AND VICE VERSA

After the end of the National Socialist dictatorship, there was an enormous appetite for cultural sustenance. Very quickly, the first galleries and museums reopened and were joined by theatre and concert performances. In Dresden, a group of art historians and artists worked on developing a stock-take of contemporary art, while rehabilitating those who had been ostracised during the Nazi period. It was clear that this could only occur within the framework of an all-German event. Thus the first Deutsche Kunstausstellung ("German Art Exhibition") was organised in 1946 (Fig. 8). Although the majority of jury members were from the Soviet Occupation Zone, Karl Hofer and Max Pechstein from West Berlin were also involved. Will Grohmann (Dean of the Dresden Hochschule für Werkkunst) and Hans Grundig (Dean of the Dresden Hochschule für Bildende Künste) were commissioned to survey the studios in West Berlin and make a preliminary selection. Avant-garde positions were represented by Karl Otto Götz (1914–2017), Ernst Wilhelm Nay (1902–1968), Heinz Trökes (1913–1997) and Fritz Winter (1905–1976), enabling the exhibition to fulfil its role as an important communicative platform. The programme was only changed symptomatically for the Deutsche Kunstausstellung in 1953. From then on, the official aim was to permanently impose Socialist Realism, which had not been practised by the artists as instructed. Unlike the exhibition in 1946, the event in 1953 was to explicitly stress the class contrasts compared to the West. However, despite this dictum, the number of artists from the FRG was still significant.

Idiosyncrasies such as this characterise the GDR's cultural-political activities until the end of its existence. Depending on the respective domestic and foreign policy constellations, the government was repeatedly forced to change course, thereby principally influencing East-West contacts. This particularly affected travel to non-Socialist countries. Although it was forbidden even before the Berlin Wall was constructed, artists did travel nevertheless. Hermann Glöckner repeatedly participated in exhibitions by the Deutscher Künstlerbund, which was refounded in Cologne in 1950. For example, at its West Berlin exhibition in 1957, Herbert Kitzel (1928–1978) from Halle a. d. Saale and the Dresden artists Ernst Hassebrauck (1905–1974), Josef

Hegenbarth (1884–1962), Hans-Theo Richter (1902–1969) and Helmut Schmidt-Kirstein (1909–1985) were all exhibited. Furthermore, several artists from East Germany attended the *documenta* exhibition in Kassel, including Glöckner, Helmut Schmidt-Kirstein (1909–1985), Hans Christoph (1901–1992), Herbert Kunze (1913–1981) and Wilhelm Müller (1928–1999), who also repeatedly visited the West Berlin Haus am Waldsee.[7] A catalogue with original drawings by Gerhard Altenbourg was even presented at the *documenta* in 1959.

Trips to the West were also essential for the exhibition programme of gallery operators. For example, the Galerie Eduard Henning in Halle a. d. Saale was committed to avant-garde art, with a special focus on French Modernism. Until 1961, it was possible to maintain intensive contacts with Paris and import works directly .[8] When the border was closed and private trade in art was gradually forbidden, international exchange naturally suffered significantly. Nevertheless, it did not die out completely. For instance, at least on the western side, three galleries pursued a programme that was explicitly dedicated to artists from the GDR: Rudolf Springer (from 1948) and Dieter Brusberg (from 1958) represented Altenbourg, Baselitz, Heisig, Tübke, Mattheuer and Harald Metzkes, among others. From 1978, the Galerie Döbele became specialised in artists from Dresden. Exports were always the subject of control by the Staatliche Kunsthandel (State Art Trading Authority), which had been founded in 1955 and handled the GDR's hard-currency transactions. The importance of such income for the East German economy can be seen in the fact that the Galerie Döbele received permanent visas for the GDR from 1982 onwards.[9]

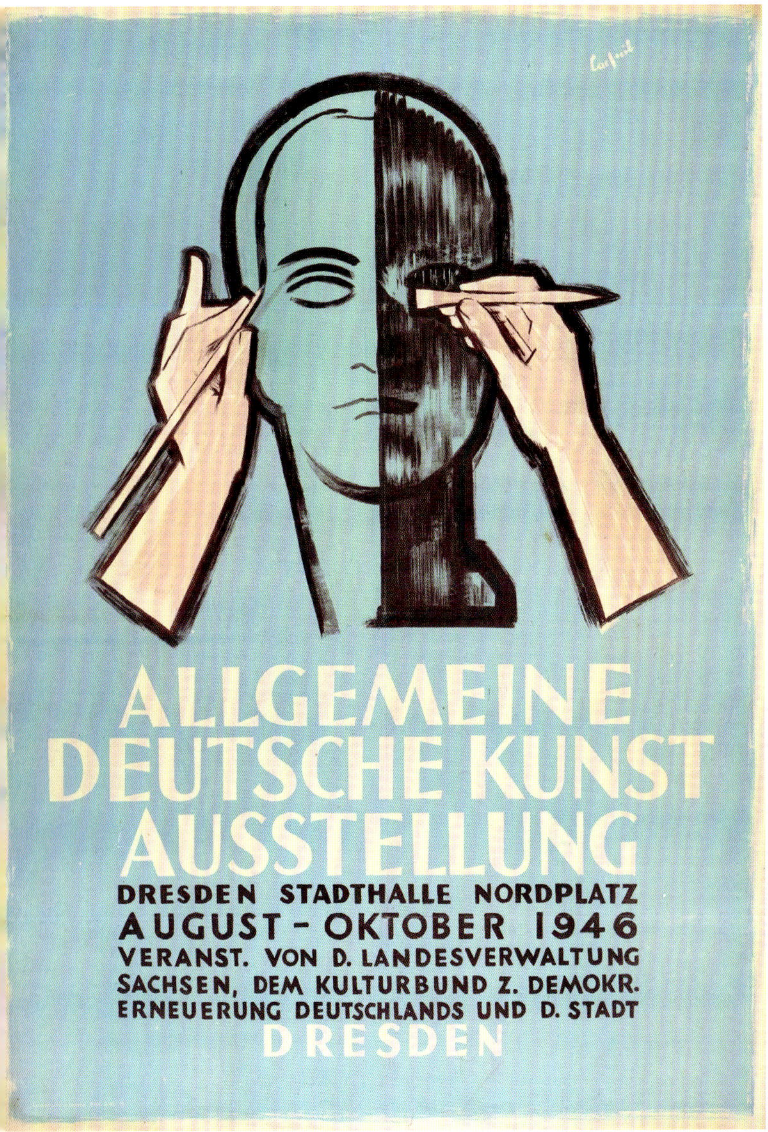

Fig. 8
Wilhelm Lachnit, poster, "Allgemeine Deutsche Kunstausstellung", Dresden, 1946

7 Sigrid Hofer: "Wider die Kunstdoktrin", in: id. (Ed.): *Gegenwelten*, Frankfurt a. M. 2006, p. 9–36, here p. 22–24.

8 Yvonne Fiedler: *Kunst im Korridor*, Berlin 2013, p.100f.

The activity of these galleries was also made possible by a significant shift in the foreign cultural policy of the GDR in the 1970s. This was the result of concerted efforts by the SED to achieve recognition under international law, in order to expand its international relations beyond the Warsaw Pact countries, as well as neutral and friendly governments, thereby consolidating their *raison d'être* as a sovereign state and appearing on the international stage alongside the FRG as an equal partner. The arts and the foreign travel played a key role in the GDR's struggle to achieve those goals, since the GDR needed to "present itself as a communicating society [that] was not closed to encounters beyond the Iron Curtain".[10] Signed in 1972, the Basic Treaty between the GDR and FRG opened a new chapter that permitted contacts with the West going far beyond what had been allowed before. Travel statistics from those years reflect this growing trend.[11] At the same time, the number of diplomats, journalists and tourists entering the GDR also increased. This led to complications since the spread of western ideologies accelerated correspondingly. The historian Ulrich Pfeil spoke in this context of a "tightrope walk between opening and separation".[12] The SED attempted to counter the dilemma by further expanding its network of informants.

From that period onwards, the number of visits to exhibitions and museums in the West also grew and, surprisingly, were frequently recorded as part of everyday professional life. Similarly, the obligatory letters of support that the GDR Association of Visual Artists had to fill out were often very terse. When Peter Sylvester (1937–2007) and Rolf Münzner (born in 1942) wished to travel to the 5th International Graphics Biennale in Frechen near Cologne, the 1978 travel directives merely stipulated that: "… colleagues participate in numerous international exhibitions, especially renowned and important graphics biennales. Therefore direct, expert exchange is essential for their further creative work."[13]

In the late 1970s, not only cultural functionaries such as Walter Womacka (1925–2010) and Werner Tübke (1929–2004), but even the graphic designer Otto Möhwald (1933–2016), who had been prohibited from working for some time, were permitted to attend the Francis Bacon exhibition in West Berlin. It is also remarkable that a whole series of artists received travel permits to learn about the avant-garde, the art of the class enemy. Broad knowledge of artistic developments from first-hand experience was now regarded as sensible and helpful, while also involving trips to other European countries. In 1978, the designer Hans Brockhage (1925–2009) was permitted to spend three weeks in the south of France, while the sculptor Volker Beier (born in 1943) spent time in Rome, Bologna, Modena and Treviso. Even Eberhard Göschel (born in 1943), who was considered a critic of the state, was allowed to travel to

9 Thanks to Mr. Döbele for providing this information to the author, 1.7.2020.
10 Ulrich Pfeil: "Dreiecksbeziehungen sind immer schwer", in: Nicole Colin et al. (Eds.): *Lexikon der deutsch-französischen Kulturbeziehungen nach 1945*, Tübingen 2013, p. 60–68, here p. 67 [trans.].
11 See file documents in the Akademie der Künste (AdK), Berlin, Verband Bildender Künstler der DDR (VBK), VBK-Zentralvorstand, Personalangelegenheiten, Reiseangelegenheiten.
12 Pfeil (see Footnote 10), p. 66 [trans.].

Italy for ten days in 1985.[14] In 1978, he and his colleagues had founded an autonomously operative printing workshop in Dresden called the Obergrabenpresse, which subtly undermined the GDR's printing regulations and was therefore under constant observation by members of the Ministry of State Security.

Another indicator of inner-German relations is the fact that the East German state sent many artists abroad on its own accord. They were assigned missions going beyond their specific tasks. For instance in the autumn of 1978, after the Ministry of Culture had established "the extent to which [...] contacts" at the University of Groningen could be relevant to foreign policy, the painter Horst Jährling was commissioned to present a lecture there on the "Restoration and colour design of the urban centre of Weimar and the Anger square in Erfurt".[15] Since these were prime prestige locations, Jährling not only had to describe monument preservation aspects, but also highlight, in passing, the capability of the Socialist economy. Karl-Georg Hirsch, a jury member of the exhibition "Graphica Creativa" by the Finnish Association of Artists, also received an explicitly ideological instruction. He was ordered, "to represent the realistic positions of visual art [...] and, when discussing with international guests, inform them on the development of contemporary Socialist art in the GDR."[16] In addition to visual artists, architects for instance studied the "systems of orientation [...] in new development areas and public buildings".[17] In this context, Klaus Aukner (name illegible in the document) produced a critical survey of the Märkische Viertel and Gropiusstadt districts. In view of the major prefabricated housing estates with which the GDR addressed its acute housing problem, the adopted approaches were welcomed by other cities. Thus "Aukner" derived "a number of remarkable inspiring aspects on the variable use of prefabricated slabs" from the Gropiusstadt, nor did he shy away from praising the Märkische Viertel's "diverse design of its open spaces between the buildings using standardised means".[18]

International competitions provided an important forum of state self-presentation. In 1976, Thomas Ranft (born in 1945) and Dieter Tucholke (born in 1934) represented the GDR at the 2nd Graphics Biennale in Mulhouse, France (Fig. 9). Two years later, nine artists from the GDR were admitted, followed by another seven artists after a further two years.[19] The annually published report by the GDR Zentrum für Kunstausstellungen ("Centre for Art Exhibitions") recorded participation at the respective Graphics Biennales. They included event locations in the West: Frechen/FRG, Frederikstad/Norway, Ibiza, Mulhouse, Nuremberg, Visby/Gotland and Jyväskylä/Finland. Furthermore, Jürgen Schieferdecker (1937–2018) was permitted to attend the XI. International Graphics Biennale in Tokyo (1978/1979). Since his socially critical work

13 Direktive ausgestellt durch den 1. Sekretär des VBK Dr. Horst Kolodziej am 25.10.1978. AdK, Berlin, VBK, VBK-Zentralvorstand 1701/5, R-S [trans.].

14 See Sigrid Hofer: "Die DDR im Westen", in: Andreas Tacke et al. (Eds.): *Künstlerreisen*, Petersberg 2020, p. 233–245, here p. 233f.

15 Cit. ibid., p. 234 [trans.].

16 Cit. ibid [trans.].

17 Report by Klaus Aukner (name illegible), undated, no address. AdK, Berlin, VBK, VBK-Zentralvorstand 290, Reiseberichte S-T [trans.].

was clearly not aligned towards the GDR system, his attendance must be regarded in the context of political divergences that were observed on several occasions. When Schieferdecker won a prize for his submitted piece "Beuys macht Licht" ("Beuys makes light"), it was even worth a report in the GDR's daily press (Fig. 10). The title of the artwork was omitted, to avoid its subversive connotations.[20]

The above-described, relatively tolerant approach to travel regulations and the number of artists who were permitted to travel although they did not represent the official canon of the GDR policy, are extraordinary. On the level of discourse, the doctrine remained that the arts had to, "contribute to the consolidation of the Socialist community of states and present a combative stance towards imperialism."[21] This contradiction should probably be regarded in connection with the above-mentioned foreign-policy efforts of the GDR, which forced it into the dilemma of, on the one hand, signalising ideological loyalty to the Warsaw Pact states and, on the other, taking international requirements into account to avoid undermining the state's new image.

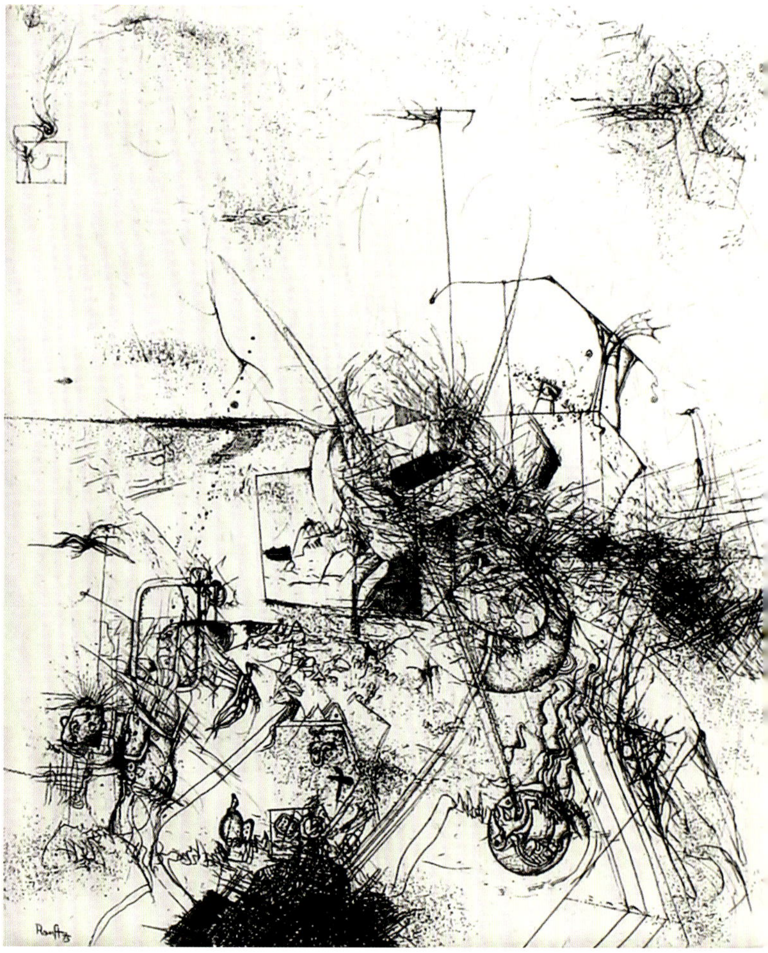

Fig. 9
Thomas Ranft, "Geburt des Ikarus", 1975

INNER-GERMAN SERVICES: THE METAL DESIGNER FRITZ KÜHN

Even during the years when the GDR policy of distancing was strictly applied, there were individual cases of intensive exchange. One of the artists who worked on both sides of the border was the East Berliner Fritz Kühn (1910–1967). Due to his mastery of craftsmanship and art, he enjoyed a high degree of respect in the FRG. He had contacts with modern architects and even with the industrial company Krupp. In 1958, his network gained him a commission by the FRG for the Brussels

18 See Footnote 17 [trans.].
19 See Hofer (see Footnote 14), p. 237.
20 Jürgen Schieferdecker interviewed by the author on 9.10.2015 at his studio in Dresden.
21 Pfeil (see Footnote 10), p. 64 [trans.].

Expo. Together with Fritz Koenig (1924–2017) and Bernhard Heiliger (1915–1995), he was contracted to present elite performance in metalworking craftsmanship at the German pavilion. Koenig and Heiliger produced sculptures that were later installed in the garden of the Kanzlerbungalow, the Chancellor's residence in Bonn. In addition to various small objects, Kühn especially produced a ten-metre long geometrically perforated lattice wall that was freely suspended between two supports (Fig. 11). In view of the fact that the GDR did not yet enjoy any international diplomatic recognition at the time, and was therefore not represented in Brussels, Martin Damus stated that, "politically, in times of the Cold War, the commission [...] was a veritable sensation."[22] By contrast, Kühn's executor described it as a consciously unpolitical procedure. For instance, Kühn's place of residence was officially stated as Berlin-Grünau, so that only people with local knowledge would realise that this was in the East.[23] Brussels further enhanced Kühn's reputation in the West. A total of 28 commissions from churches and public bodies are documented, all of which were completed without problems. Presumably, once again, the government's interest in hard currency encouraged such activities.

Fig. 10
Jürgen Schieferdecker, "Beuys macht Licht", 1987

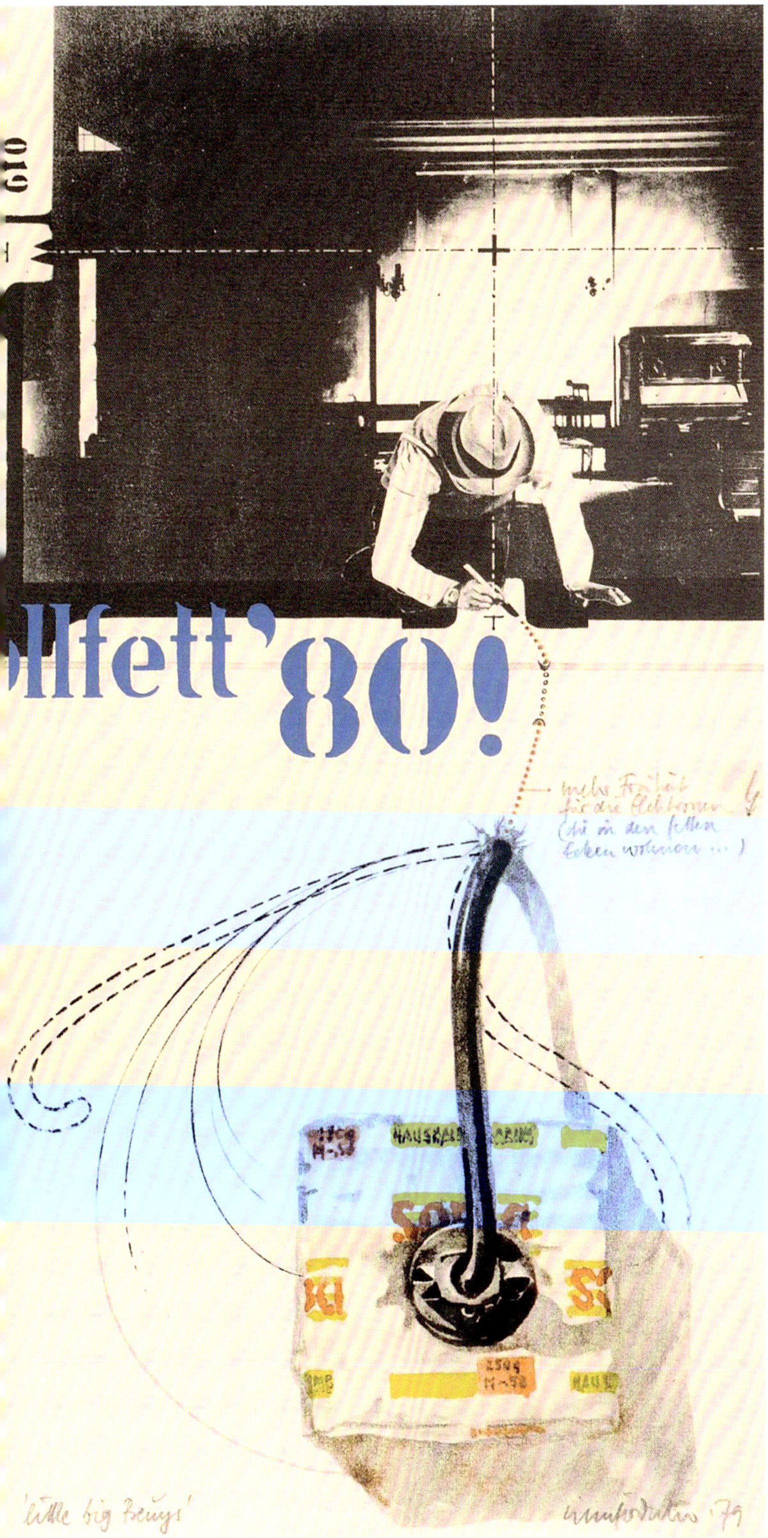

In 1964, Kühn, who had not yet been awarded any important official commissions in the GDR, was finally asked to design the so-called Akustikwand (Acoustic wall) in the meeting room of the Staatsrat building. Over an impressive area of 42 square metres, he was to implement a political statement with the theme of "The economy of the GDR under the sign of peace" ("Die Wirtschaft der DDR unter dem Zeichen des Friedens"). Apparently, only Kühn was capable of doing justice to the theme, which the artist would have been unable to resist even if he had wished to. The wall with figurative motifs served as a stately background for political leaders. Kühn thereby made a name for himself among the general public. In this piece, even the strategic political message was outshone by the artist's virtuosity.

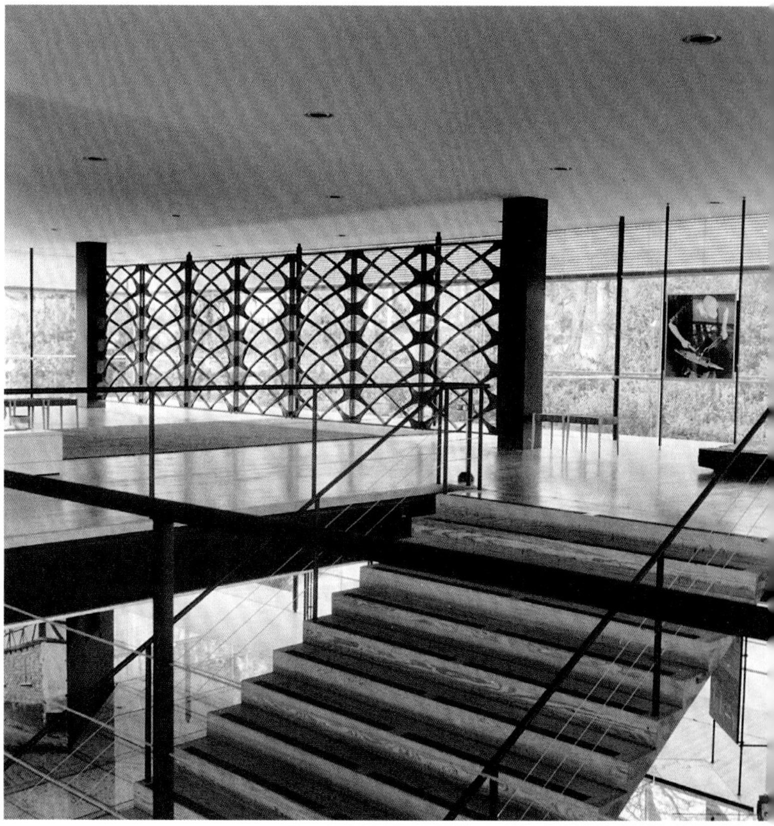

Fig. 11
Fritz Kühn, lattice wall, German Pavilion, Brussels Expo, 1958

VISIT FROM THE WEST

During major arts festivals and "Pleinairs" in East Germany, in between all the other events, it was often possible to exchange information on the latest developments in the West (Fig.12). These Pleinairs were usually two-week working get-togethers involving representatives from the fields of the visual arts, literature and music. They were warily monitored by informants of the state apparatus and protocolled in detail. This was also due to the fact that guests from non-Socialist countries often attended and their participants were all considered to be critical of the state. For instance in 1977, a land-art project was carried out in Leussow (Fig. 13). According to the State Security report, there was evidence that Gregor Torsten Schade (later Kozik, born in 1948) from Karl-Marx-Stadt (today's Chemnitz) had intensive contact with Joseph Beuys (1921–1986) and Wolf Vostell (1932–1998).[24] One highlight of the Pleinair was a report by the East Berlin Art Historian Lothar Lang on the *documenta 6*. On another occasion in Groß-Zicker (Rügen) in 1982, Klaus Werner, who ran the Galerie Arkade in East Berlin, which had developed into a centre of the avant-garde scene, reported on the new radicals in Western Europe and the USA. In 1983, he also presented a lecture on Joseph Beuys in Gager (Rügen).[25] In 1981, Wolf Biermann from Hamburg and the poster artist Klaus Staeck (born in 1938) from Heidelberg

22 Martin Damus: "Fritz Kühn 1910–67", in: Sigrid Hofer (Ed.): *Grenzgänge zwischen Ost und West*, Dresden 2006, p. 27–40, here p. 33 [trans.].
23 Thanks to Helgard Kühn for providing this information to the author, 23.7.2020.
24 BStU, MFS, BV KMSt (Der Bundesbeauftragte für die Unterlagen des Staatssicherheitsdienstes der ehemaligen Deutschen Demokratischen Republik, Ministerium für Staatssicherheit,

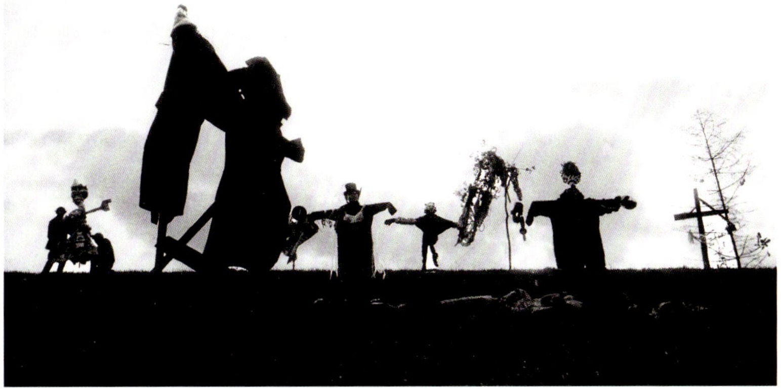

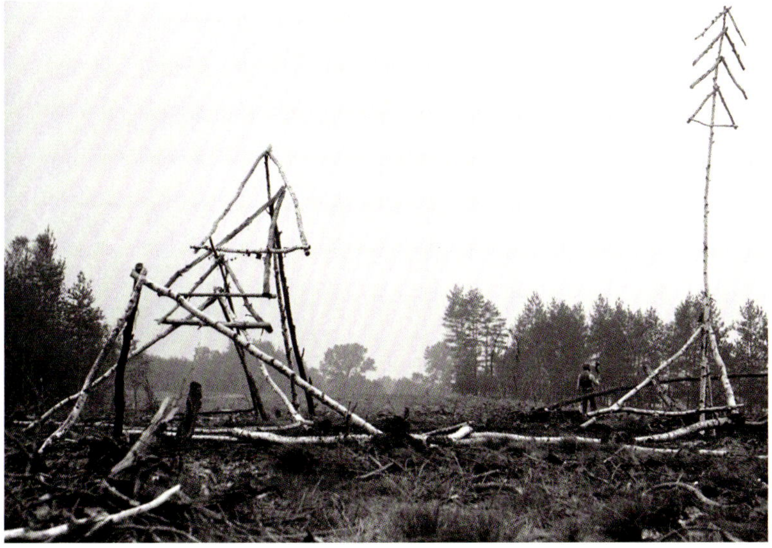

Fig. 12
Clara Mosch,
"Vogelscheuchenfest",
1983, Chemnitz/Adelsberg

Fig. 13
Clara Mosch,
"Leussow-Recycling",
1977, Pleinair in Leussow,
wooden sculpture
by Michael Morgner

were among those who joined the East Berlin writers Christa and Gerhard Wolf in Gallentin (near Lake Schwerin).[26] Those present spoke of producing an "all-German portfolio of works by 10 artists from the FRG and the GDR respectively […] who are committed to peace". These meetings were organised thematically in a way that made it difficult for officials to ban them for ideological reasons.[27] "Artist celebrations" also provided opportunities for contact with the western scene. In 1980, when the Galerie Clara Mosch celebrated its third anniversary in Adelsberg (near Chemnitz), around 400 people attended, including Georg Girardet, Cultural Advisor at the Permanent Representation of the FRG in the GDR. As was reported to the Ministry of State Security, he even had "personal" contact with the artists.[28]

At the Permanent Representation, whose specific tasks included inner-German exchange, Günter Gaus and his cultural attachés developed a network and exchange forum. The large receptions in their official apartments were also frequently used to establish contacts between the recognised and non-conformist scenes.[29] Artists from the Gallentin Plenair were explicitly invited to the Beuys exhibition. To prevent the state from obstructing their attendance, Klaus Staeck proposed disguising the exhibition opening as an official reception and having the BRD State Secretary, Klaus Bölling, send out the invitations – which was apparently standard procedure at the time.[30] In addition to Beuys, whose show "Multiplizierte Kunst 1965–1981" ("Multiplied art 1965–1981") was attended by around 400 people (Fig. 14), there were exhibitions in other years by artists including Horst Janssen (1929–1995), August Sander (1876–1964), Bernd and Hilla Becher (1931–2007 and 1934–2015), as well as "the wild young generation" in 1982, represented

Bezirksverwaltung Karl-Marx-Stadt). SVG XIV 1000168, Nr.1661, Blatt 30f.
25 Ibid. Reg. 1184/68, Bd.II/V, Blatt 37 u. 229.
26 Ibid. AKG-2267, Blatt 50f.
27 Ibid. Blatt 52.

by Rainer Fetting (born in 1949) and Salomé (born in 1954). However, not only artists belonging to the sub-cultural milieu gathered in the "StäV", as the Permanent Residence was known. Even Willi Sitte, Bernhard Heisig and Hermann Raum, the Vice President for Foreign Affairs of the GDR Association of Visual Artists, were occasional visitors.[31]

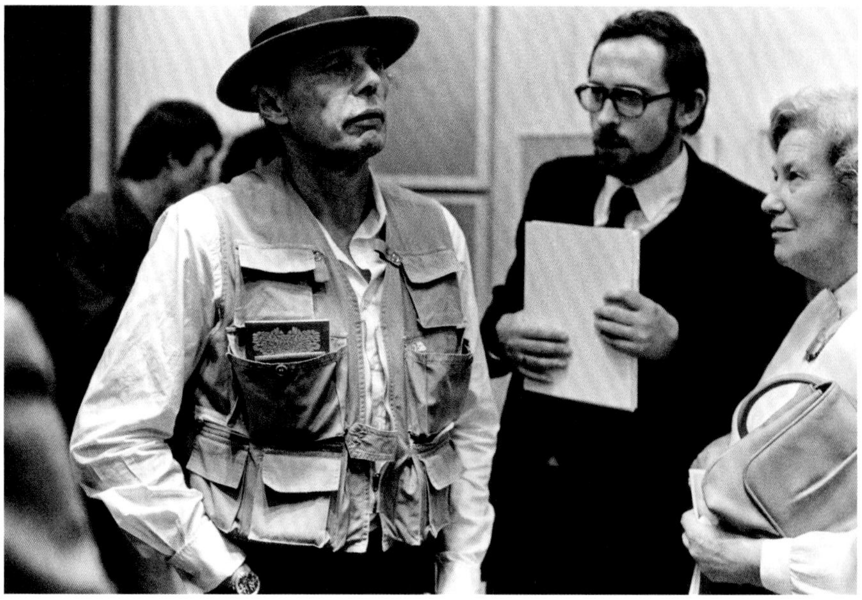

Fig. 14
Joseph Beuys at the opening of his exhibition "Multiplizierte Kunst 1965-1981", 1981, Permanent Representation of the Federal Republic in East Berlin

THE MUSEUM'S ROLE AS A HUB

Time and again, the state control system in arts management was also undermined by museum professionals who used their official contacts with the West for informal meetings. One of their most prominent protagonists was Werner Schmidt, who managed the Kupferstich-Kabinett in Dresden from 1958 onwards and became its General Director in 1990. He often travelled to the West as his museum's courier. Whenever he could, he sought artists and art dealers to ask them to provide works for his museum's collection. Using methods that recall a spy film, he hid these gifts in a suitcase with a false bottom to conceal them from inspection by the GDR border guards.[32] Over time, he compiled an impressive collection in this way, thereby benefiting study in his own country.

The extent of efforts by the GDR to present itself in capitalist countries, despite contradictory ideological diction and attacks on the class enemy, was again revealed in 1970. At an exhibition entitled "Dialoge" ("Dialogues"), Schmidt investigated the transfer and transformation of subjects and motifs over the centuries. Since the project required a European perspective, a wide range of works were presented that the GDR regarded as examples of western decadence. There was a liberal tone

28 See Footnote 27. AKG-11555, Blatt 126f.
29 Paul Kaiser et al.: *Boheme und Diktatur in der DDR*, Berlin 1997, p. 94.
30 BStU, MFS, BV KMSt (see Footnote 24). AKG-2267, Blatt 52.
31 See Jacqueline Boysen: *Das „weisse Haus" in Ost-Berlin,* Berlin 2010, p. 146f.
32 See Werner Schmidt: "Das Kupferstich-Kabinett in Dresden und seine Sammlungen zur Kunst

at the opening ceremony, which was attended by representatives of the western collections. However, immediately afterwards, works by Paul Klee and Pablo Picasso were removed from the walls. Schmidt's defiant exhibition had its consequences. He was required to make a self-critical public declaration and feared for his position. However, the fact that Albrecht Dürer's grand 500th anniversary was imminent and could not be implemented without Schmidt's competencies led to a grotesque turnaround. Instead of being disciplined, he was awarded the GDR Medal of Merit.[33] In addition to cultural-historical insight, his audacious project had offered the general public the chance to see works that were otherwise inaccessible and also encouraged cross-border interaction between art historians and artists.

The cooperation and communication efforts only briefly outlined in this article were by no means limited to the sector of the visual arts. They also occurred in the fields of music, literature and theatre. The examples provide evidence on the one hand of foreign-policy strategy, while on the other – and essentially – revealing the will of artists to resist being limited in their own development potential by political boundaries, thereby contributing to international understanding.

in der Moderne", in: Hofer (see Footnote 7), p. 37–53, here p. 44.

33 See Sigrid Hofer: "Die Historisierung der Moderne", in: Christiane Kruse et al. (Eds.): *Fassaden? Zeigen und Verbergen von Geschichte in der Kunst*, Munich 2017, p.138–158, here p.152–154.

ART IN ARCHITECTURE

IN GERMANY

Art in architecture is a key element of democratic culture. As commissioned art, it must balance out the diverse interests of art, architecture, urban planning and policy, taking the locations, specific architecture, history, utilisation and users of the buildings into account. This makes art in architecture a "matter of negotiation". In addition to artists, the client, building administrations, architects, expert committees, art consultants and jurors all play key roles in the production of art in architecture.

It is reasonable to fear that the many cooks involved in art in architecture might spoil the broth and that the numerous external factors are even detrimental. However, the opposite is the case. While collectors, museums and art shows see the character of free art in its uncompromising nature, art in architecture is defined by its ability to compromise. The challenge, goal and attraction of art in architecture is to be "art for all" on a high, and in ideal cases, the highest artistic level. In that respect, it is the legitimate successor of building sculptures, murals and ceiling art that decorated not only palaces and private villas, but also publicly accessible prestigious buildings and churches.

Whether art justifies itself through religion, magic, psychology, artistry or aesthetics: since it has existed, art has been an anthropological necessity and a way of appropriating the world, turning things and spaces that people initially regard as alien or even frightening into things that are not only familiar, but also more beautiful, more liveable and more significant. Art in architecture is complex. It engages with the themes of our time and is an especially sustainable way of humanising our environment and enhancing it in the spirit of contemporary building culture.

ART IN ARCHITECTURE IN GERMANY

Martin Seidel

The term "art in architecture" is often understandably connected to the idea of art that is actually "in" a building. However, "art in architecture" is a term for art that is created on the occasion of and in connection with a building measure. Thus, "art in architecture" should really be called "art because of architecture", especially since many thousands of implemented works are not only "in" the building, i.e. on the surface of a building element, but also in front of, behind, above and even beneath it.

The guideline on art in architecture produced by the Federal Ministry of Building defines it as the commitment, above all by public, but also private builders to spend a specific percentage of a building measure's costs on art. With respect to federal construction in Germany, that specifically means: if the Federal Government acts as the building client in construction, conversion, extension or renovation measures on a building, the costs of the actual construction and the structure's technical facilities are extrapolated from of the building measure's overall costs and a proportion of the resulting sum is assigned to art in architecture. If a building costs up to € 20 million, 1.5 percent are budgeted; costs between € 20 million and € 100 million result in a 1-percent allocation; projects with a budget of over € 100 million lead to 0.5 percent invested in art in architecture. That is essentially the official understanding of federal art in architecture. Several federal states, including Baden-Wuerttemberg, Bavaria, Mecklenburg-West Pomerania, Rhineland-Palatinate and Saxony – as well as municipalities such as Düsseldorf and Munich, have also adopted the rule and apply it to their state and municipal building projects. The federal states of Hamburg and Bremen have long replaced their art in architecture activities with engagement in the field of art in public spaces. On a municipal level, Dresden invests in art in public spaces exclusively from funds that are independent of the building sector. Munich and Düsseldorf combine art in architecture and art in public spaces, including civil engineering in their programmes.

As in many countries with architecturally related art programmes, art in architecture in Germany is usually implemented with percentage funding. Several municipal programmes in Germany (but especially in Austria and Switzerland) replace percentage funding, which is linked to an individual building project, with fixed or variable art in architecture budgets. In this way, the available means can be distributed according to needs over individual or several building projects. Experience of this method has been gathered on a state level in North Rhine-Westphalia and on a municipal level in Munich. Public-private partnerships, sponsorship and donation funding are also regularly used for art in architecture projects. Private companies often own mobile art collections and artworks that are essentially "art in architecture"; naturally, they are at liberty to fund art according to their means, as they wish, and at any desired time during the process of a building's construction and use, or decide against any funding for art at all.

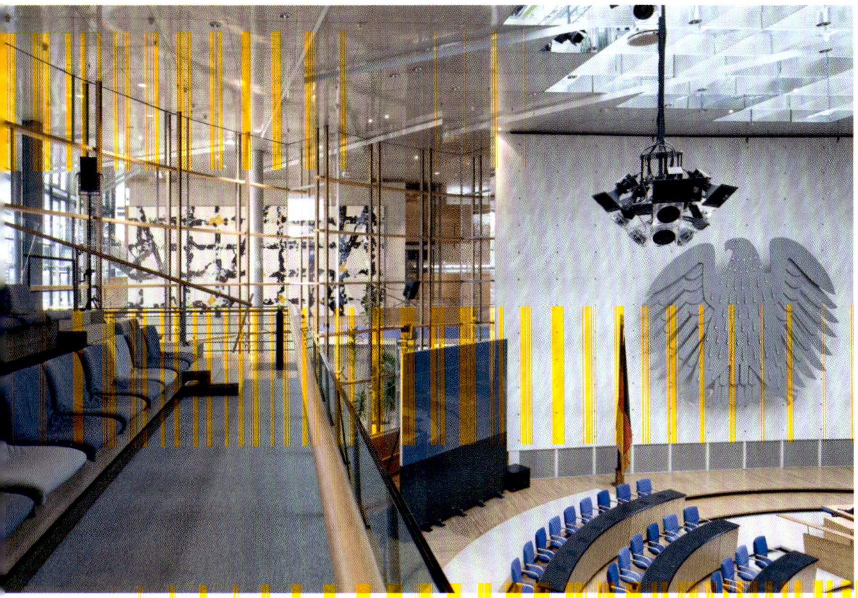

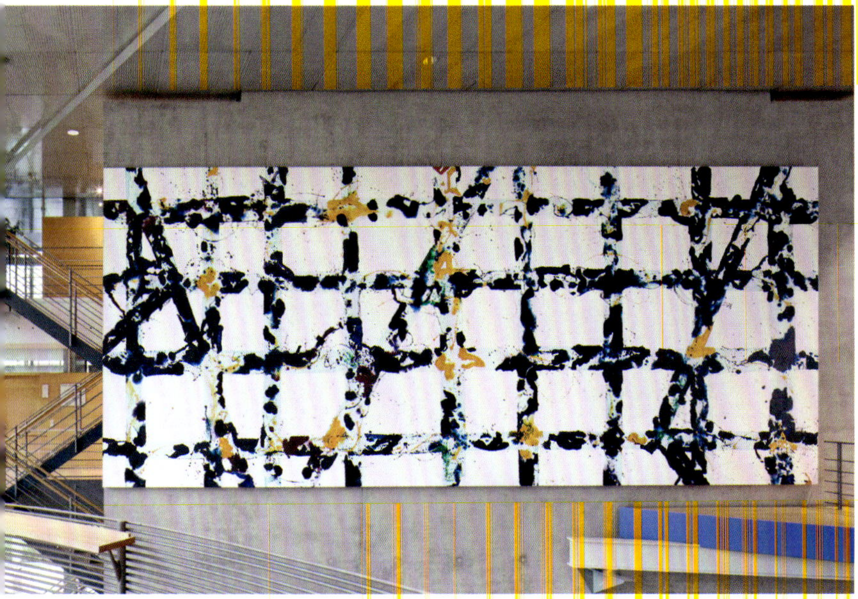

UNDERLYING PRINCIPLES AND INTENTIONS

The fact that in 1950, only a year after their foundation, both German states decided to involve artists in state building tasks is because "art in architecture" had its predecessors in the Weimar Republic and the "Third Reich". The GDR enacted the "Law to develop an advanced democratic culture for the German people and to further improve the working and living conditions of the intelligentsia", also known as the "Kulturverordnung". It was supplemented in 1952 by the "Law on the artistic decoration of administrative buildings", stipulating that designs of "buildings of particular social importance" were to be coordinated with the State Commission for Cultural Affairs, and that artists were to be selected by the commissioning committee – using a competition in the case of major projects. The law not only permitted works that were produced for the building and connected to them, but also mobile pieces of visual art or handicrafts. Requiring "down-to-earth, realistic art" naturally meant figurative art in the doctrinal style of Socialist Realism.

The German Bundestag pursued three aims with its decision on art in architecture on January 25, 1950. The first objective was to revive the cultural life that had run into a cul-de-sac during Nazi rule. Secondly, it aimed to provide economic support for artists during the especially difficult post-war years. Thirdly, the Bundestag was aware of the developing and sensitising potential of "artworks of the highest rank". The responsible officer reporting to the Committee for Cultural Policy emphasised the necessity of art in architecture with the words: "Art should be among the people, where people come together." In the Federal Republic, preliminary implementation orders in 1953 were followed four years later by the

Sam Francis, "Dynamic Symmetry", 1978/1995, German Bundestag, Plenarsaal, Bonn underlying principles that still apply today, namely the "Guidelines for federal building tasks within the field of responsibility of the financial construction administrations" (RBBau), including Section K 7 on the "Participation of visual artists". Naturally, the regulations remained general. However, the "Guideline on art in architecture" developed in 2005 by the Ministry of Building, the Federal Office for Building, and the Ministry of Finance, which was updated in 2012, is more specific. It regards art in architecture as an integral part of building culture. Furthermore, it makes a statement on the nature and appearance of such art by stipulating that the "prior determination of a specific artistic genre [...] should be avoided". Otherwise, "the artworks should be an autonomous contribution to the building task, referring to the architecture or the building's function, while reacting to the surroundings and impressing through the artistic quality and power of expression. Thus, art in architecture should be newly produced for the respective context."

FIGURATION AND ABSTRACTION

With respect to the artistic genre, there have not been any limitations in Germany. The GDR permitted architecturally related and mobile art. The Federal Republic also allowed art in architecture to be produced in all forms of expression and genres. The GDR did stipulate its position with respect to styles and stances, particularly the cardinal artistic question of "figuration or abstraction". Its decision in favour of Socialist Realism supported content as opposed to western-style abstract art, which was denigrated as "formalism". The artistic installations of the major prestigious GDR buildings – notably the Staatsrat building (1962–1964) (→ p. 102), the Chancellery of the Embassy in Budapest (1965–1968) (→ p. 268), the Palace of the Republic (1973–1976) (→ p. 108) and the Neue Gewandhaus Leipzig (1977–1981) (→ p. 208) – combined with the abstract murals of the prefabricated housing developments of the 1970s and the sculptural "Formstein" brick walls, show that the GDR at least occasionally adopted a more relaxed policy. In 1971, Erich Honecker himself argued, albeit rather unconvincingly, in favour of the famous slogan for "Weite und Vielfalt" ("Breadth and diversity").

In debate prior to the introduction of art in architecture in the Federal Republic, traditionally minded politicians also spoke out against abstract art, instead preferring the practicality and popular education uses of sgraffiti, mosaics and wire reliefs with figurative motifs and scenes from nature, school, sport, work and the family. However, it was easier to avoid such instrumental figurative art in the West than the Socialist Realism of the East. Many proponents of non-ideological figurative and certainly (at least apparently) non-ideological, non-figurative art regarded the art form as an expression of freedom that the Nazi dictatorship had consistently suppressed. In doing so, they consciously positioned abstract art as a sign of freedom and artistic autonomy in times of the Cold War, thereby countering the doctrine of Socialist Realism. This was repeatedly revealed at Expos, the 1972 Munich Olympic Games and many foreign buildings with art in architecture that was aimed at demonstrating the freedom and openness of the young Federal Republic. Even after German reunification and the government's move to Berlin, abstract art was able to be more than just an artistic avowal. Since 1992, the new Plenarsaal in Bonn, which was used by the Bundestag between 1992 and 1999, has not

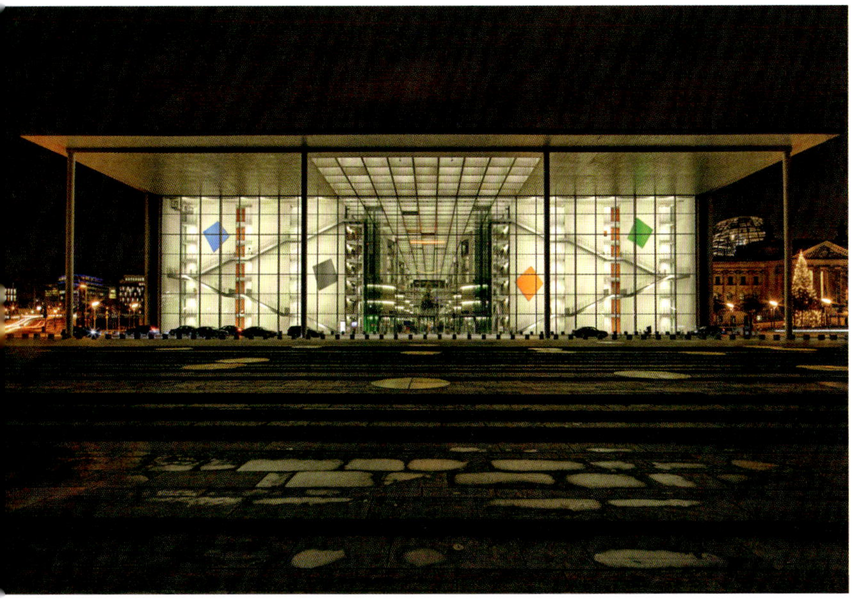

only been decorated by the large-scale Federal Eagle by Ludwig Gies (1887–1966), but also by the highly visible, net-like structures and the definitive fluent colours of the enormous painting "Dynamic Symmetry" by Sam Francis (1923–1994). In 2000, the German Bundestag installed four coloured aluminium panels on the western façade of its Paul Löbe House. Entitled "Berlin Panels 2000", the artwork in blue, black, red and green was produced by Ellsworth Kelly (1923–2015). Four neon garlands by François Morellet (1926–2016) are suspended in the hall behind it. They are all autonomous colour-and-form objects; their non-hierarchical aesthetics are ideally suited and specifically intended to symbolise democratic principles of freedom and the equal status of neighbours. When the former Prussian House of Lords in Berlin was renovated for use by the Bundesrat in 2000, the sculptor Per Kirkeby (1938–2018) created eight abstract sculptures for the parapet zone of the entrance portal and the head-end buildings. The sculptures complement and relativise the Wilhelminian visual programme of the tympanum (→ p. 140). In the same year, the painter Michael Wirkner (1954–2012) covered Nazi and GDR symbols in the historical building of the Finance Ministry (→ p. 146), adding an aspect of exorcist meaning to his abstract plates.

THE ART – ARCHITECTURE RELATIONSHIP

When it was introduced during the Weimar Republic, art in architecture was a political construct that was unusual for its time. It was intended to benefit artists with a commissioning apparatus, but had not kept abreast with art-historical developments. Only a few decades lie between the architectural sculpture of

Elsworth Kelly, "Berlin Panels 2000", 2000, German Bundestag/Paul Löbe House, Berlin historicism and the beginnings of art in architecture, yet from a stylistic perspective, they are worlds apart, representing unbridgeable differences: the paths of art and architecture had separated. In the vocabulary of Adolf Loos, the architecture of Modernity considered ornament to be a "crime", following the architects Louis Sullivan and Ludwig Mies van der Rohe's ideas of function and the aesthetics of "less is more". Visual arts, which had developed out of the subordinate function of decoration, had long been present as mobile sculptures or panels in salons, galleries and museums, but now strived for even greater autonomy. While the first art in architecture programmes were initiated in the 1920s, the "White Cube", a new venue, was constructed specifically for art. Painted all in white, the cuboid museum space itself was reserved, allowing the newly autonomous art to appear even more independent and auratic.

It is not the case that art and architecture no longer had any reference to each other, but that architects initially planned without art, and artists, when painting or producing a sculpture, did not immediately consider architecture. Thus a typical and very plausible quality of art in architecture continues to be defined by its independence from architecture. One prototype of this is the unornamented Barcelona pavilion by Ludwig Mies van der Rohe from 1929, with its bronze sculpture by Georg Kolbe (1877–1947) placed in a pool. Kolbe, an important figurative sculptor and a key witness of the emerging art in architecture, spoke out against the appropriation of sculptures as a "decorative element of architecture". He accepted that "Neues Bauen" and sculptures were very compatible – as long as artists were not just given a wall surface, but also received space, thereby allowing sculpture to remain an "autonomous artwork". In addressing the wall, Kolbe also criticised the key aspect of the many art in architecture murals and wall pieces that continue to be produced to this day. In 1925, the Hamburg Chief Director of Building Fritz Schumacher initiated the programme "24 murals in Hamburg state buildings", representing a precursor of "art in architecture". It was initially managed by a committee called the "Council for the Support of Visual Artists". As a result, the programme was aimed more at artists in need than the quality of the art; it sought to commission artists who were especially in need of support and even those who had no references to show for themselves. Under those remarkable circumstances, the hierarchical superiority of architecture was undisputed and the art was initially defined as an addendum that served artists with commissions, thus hardly requiring any consideration from the architects during the planning or construction stages.

After World War II, the regulations of the FRG and the GDR consolidated this marriage of convenience between art and architecture. The GDR was more interested in visual programmes with a broad effect that were, by order, applied to the largest possible space on the façades of administrative buildings, rather than a stringent synthesis of art and architecture. In the Federal Republic, the interests, especially aesthetic and artistic, had a greater range and the forms of expression and appearance were more diverse. But even so, public commissioning bodies regarded art and architecture as separate entities: first the building, then the art. This becomes apparent in the awarded commissions. Until the enactment of the RBBau in 1975, competitions were regarded as an equal alternative to direct commissions when acquiring art in architecture. In the case of direct commissions, the architect had a greater influence. For instance,

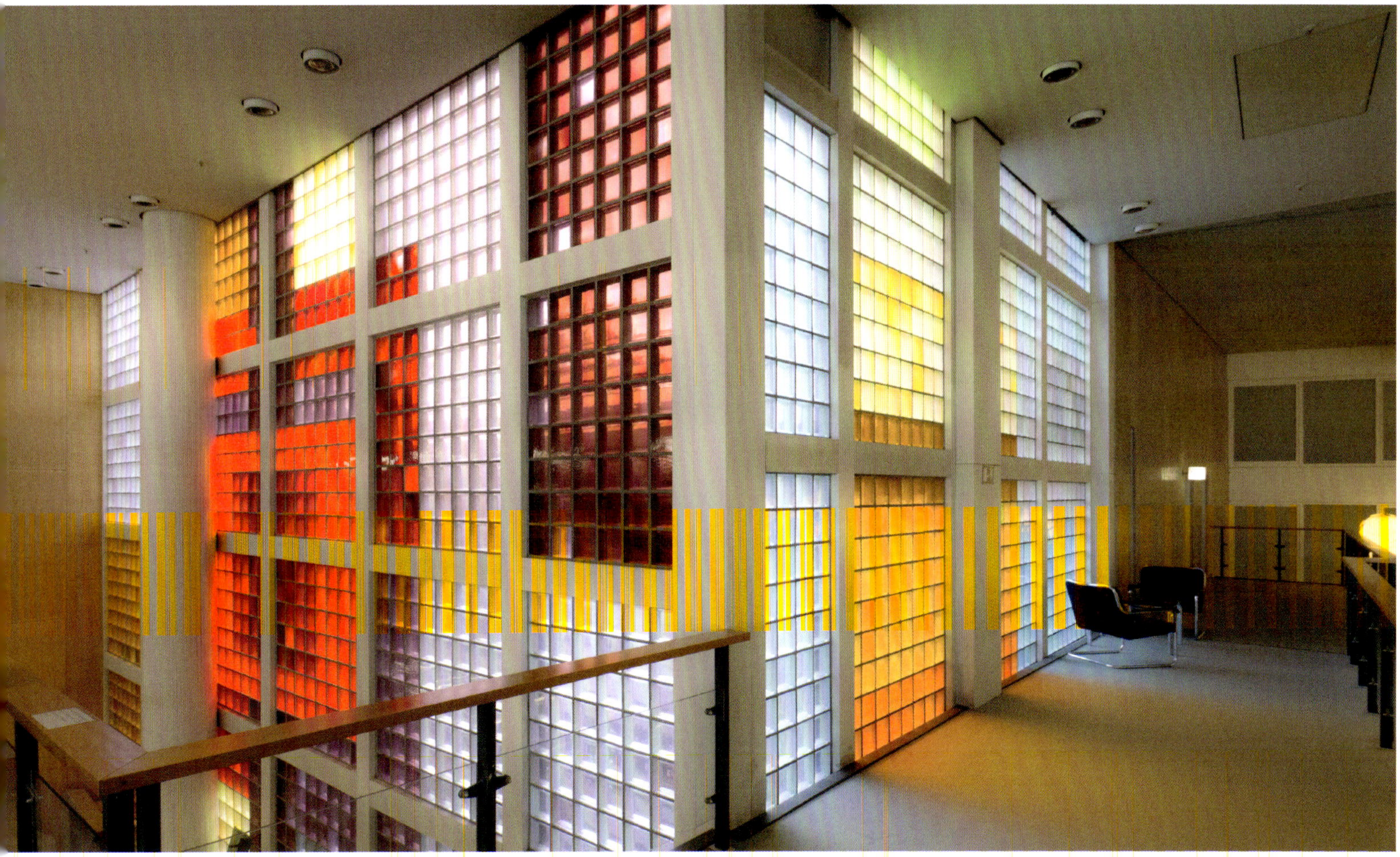

Alexander Camaro, coloured glass brick window, 1974/1975, Berlin State Library, Potsdamer Strasse, Berlin

Hans Scharoun, the architect of the Berlin Philharmonic, the State Library at Potsdamer Platz and other important federal buildings, was decisively involved in art in architecture plans by defining their locations and recommending artists (→ p. 204). In the mid-1960s, Egon Eiermann encouraged contracting the artists Karl Hartung, Fritz Koenig and Erich F. Reuter for the new chancellery building in Washington. They had previously contributed works for his German Pavilion at the 1958 Brussels Expo.

Even after the RBBau in 1975, which determined that competitions should be the general rule for commissioning artworks, architects continued to be highly influential because the competitions for architecture and art are always separate and announced consecutively; thus, artists generally need to engage with the architecture more often than architects with the art. Occasionally, direct

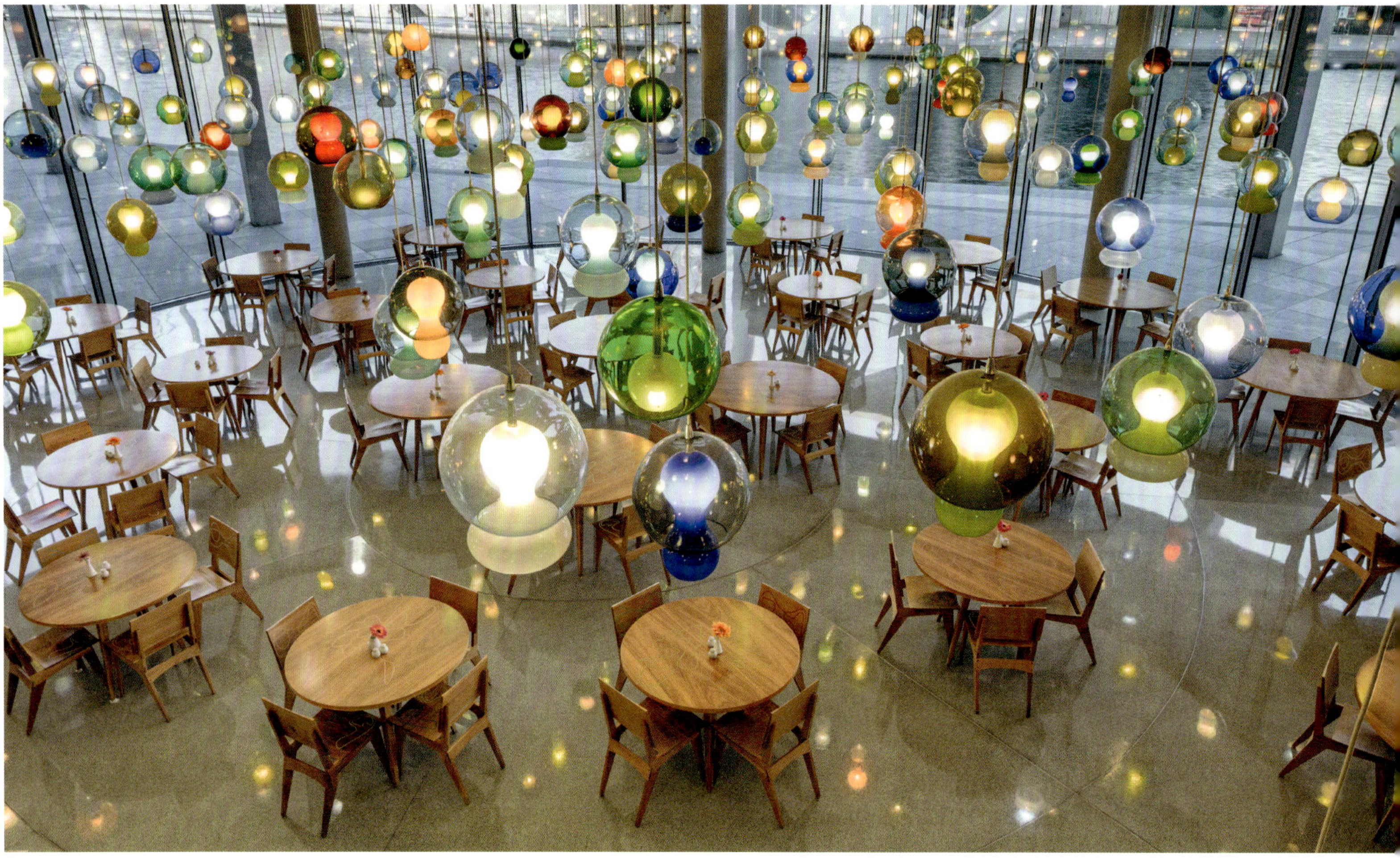

commissions continue to be awarded, as in the past. For example, Oswald Mathias Ungers made it a condition of his plans for the embassy residence in Washington, which was completed in 1994, that he exclusively decided on the facility's artistic installations, single-handedly awarding the art commissions.

In the classic-modern duality of architecture and art, many freely positioned sculptures impress to this day, which artists have created without a commission and produced for no specific location. They all assume important art in architecture functions by standing in front of or beside building entrances, or on the green spaces around the buildings, thereby giving them a specific address. They also add a characteristic and unmistakeable profile to edifices whose uses are otherwise unrecognisable or to buildings with no striking appearance. Thus the artworks are also a feature of building culture that the general public can

Jorge Pardo, "untitled (restaurant)", 2002, German Bundestag/Paul Löbe House, Berlin perceive. Often, builders and users of the buildings adopt such free-standing artworks as symbols of sovereignty or as logos, appropriating them for their image policy. Above all sizeable, free-standing sculptures have the potential of becoming hallmarks and, on a larger scale, emblems of entire cities. Even in the urban-planning jungle of Berlin, the Federal Intelligence Service managed to make its mark not only with the enormous size of its architecture, but also through two almost 25-metre high palm trees by the artist Ulrich Brüschke (born in 1959), made of steel and plastic.

The important role such artworks can play for individual buildings and its contribution to building culture can be seen in the former Federal Chancellery in Bonn, with the sculpture "Large Two Forms" by Henry Moore (1898–1986). Initial plans for the organically formed, two-part bronze sculpture date back to 1966, even before plans for the Chancellery had been conceived (→ p. 114). Although Moore had not designed his work for a specific place and it exists in four moulds, it achieved a worldwide media presence due to its location – and to this day, the former Chancellery is associated more with this magnificent artwork by Henry Moore than with the pavilion architecture by the Stieldorf Planning Group, which was constructed between 1969 and 1975.

EXPANSIONS

In 2005, the amended "Guidelines for federal building tasks" allowed art in architecture to be expanded into the public space in so far as it acknowledged that, as an exception, "artistic designs [...may] extend beyond the property boundary and occupy the surroundings of the planned building measure." Even before then, however, dense urban situations had already led to the installation of large-scale, free-standing sculptures that had a direct effect on the urban space or were even installed in it. For instance, when the chancellery of the German Embassy in London was extended between 1972 and 1978, the Federal Building Authority organised a competition for six artists with the task of, "formulating an artistic expression [for the competition] that does justice to the building, denotes the new entrance and is therefore eye-catching to as many visitors as possible." This desire to be seen was comprehensively fulfilled by Fritz Koenig (1924–2017) with his unmissable, six-metre tall bronze sculpture "Große Flora" ("Large flora"), which was installed on the pavement.

For a long time, artists have been rejecting the "mere applicative character" of art in architecture. They question the historically ascribed allocation of roles and are freeing the artworks from the constraints that the architecture places upon them. They are opening up their art to installations, integral concepts and staged scenes, which reach out towards the furniture from the walls, ceilings and floor. Numerous works are striking in the claim they stake for a holistic aesthetic experience; one such example is the work by the Cuban-US artist Jorge Pardo (born in 1963) for the Berlin Bundestag's Paul Löbe House (2002): a restaurant furnished with a terrazzo floor, orb-shaped lamps, chairs and tables. An example of artistic expansion of a different kind has existed since 2012 in the MRT Research Building of the Max Delbrück Centre in Berlin; the artist Robert Patz (born in 1981) applied a wallpaper design for all three of the building's levels, depicting a graphic novel, the fictional story of an apprentice at the institute.

Even bulky installations are establishing themselves at prominent locations. The labyrinthine iron grid by Franka Hörnschemeyer (born in 1958) in one of the courtyards of Paul Löbe House no longer treads the path of aesthetically enhancing and "decorating" courtyards and squares with sculptures or fountains; instead, it uses second-hand building materials to outline the overlapping ground plans of the GDR's border-guard buildings along the former Berlin Wall and today's Bundestag building. Other works use their design and use-potential to enhance the quality of stay. The list of such works is long, including the over 2,500 square-metre "Platzartikulation" ("Spatial articulation", 1976) by the artist Otto Herbert Hajek (1927–2005) for the Bonn Ministry of Agriculture (→ p. 110). It reaches deep into the building and includes coloured paths, floor designs and fountains. Another example is the sound installation on the square behind the Martin-Gropius-Bau in Berlin, which was jointly developed by the artist Ina Geißler (born in 1970) and the architect Fabian Lippert (born in 1972), and was completed in 2009. The pavilion sculpture by Beat Zoderer (born in 1955), which was produced in 2012 for the green inner courtyard of one of the Bundestag buildings in Berlin, not only looks attractive, but is also walkable and used as an exterior space; it is perhaps telling that the design was preceded by an art in architecture competition that supported such breaking down of boundaries from the outset, since it was announced for groups consisting of landscape architects and artists.

Like any art, the K 7 guideline of the RBBau, which regulates art in architecture practice, affords art in architecture the almost complete freedom to develop, change, renew and expand its appearance, forms of expression and intentions. Thus art in architecture has long become mobile; it works with wind, light and water. It uses new materials for innovative aesthetics, as well as so-called "new

Franka Hörnschemeyer, "BFD - bündig fluchtend dicht", 1998/2001, German Bundestag/Paul Löbe House

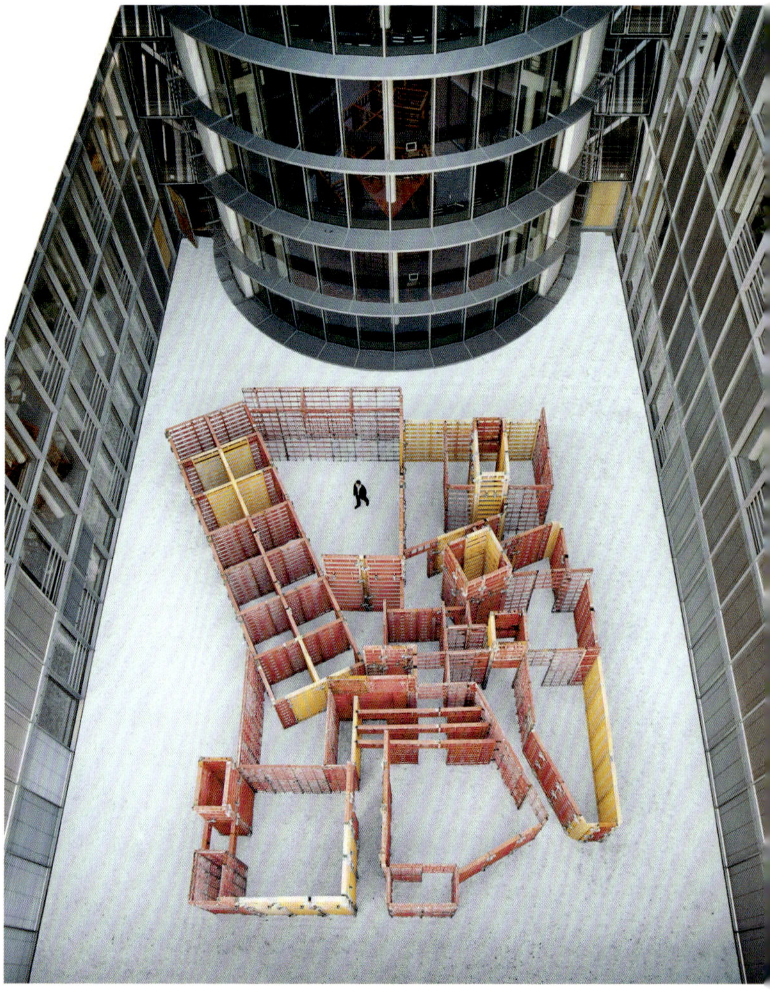

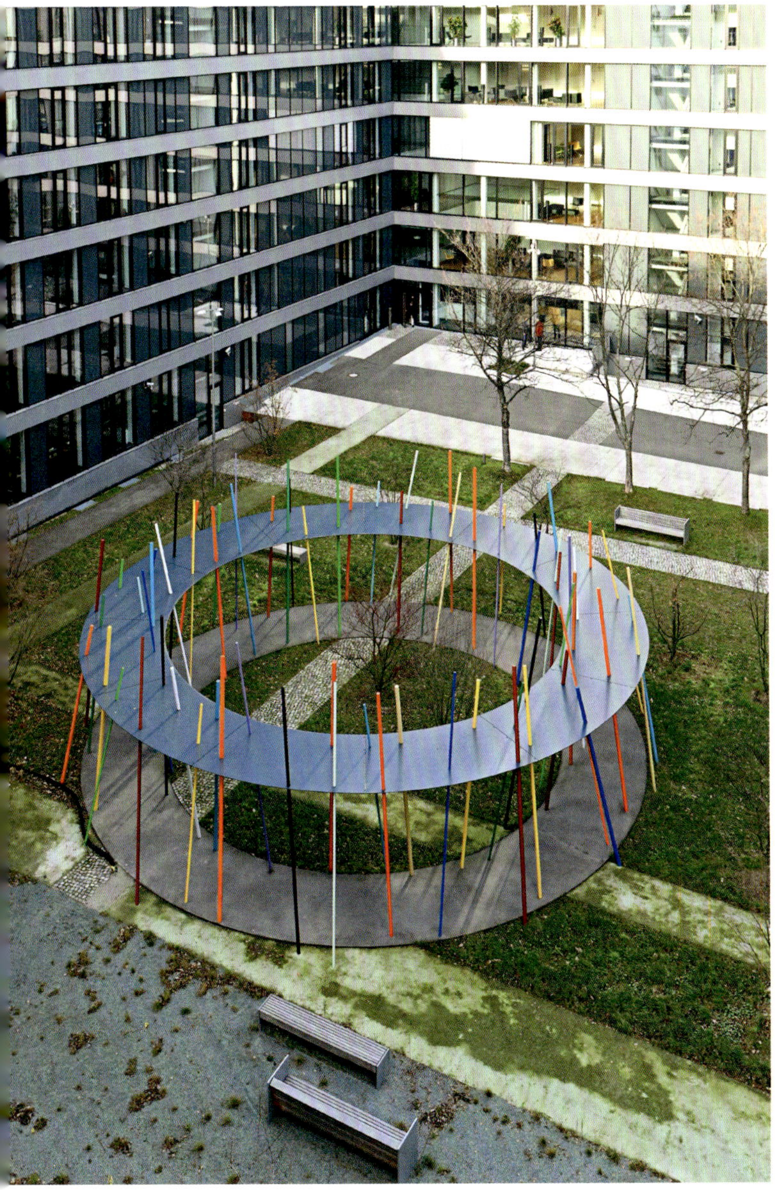

media" that had not yet existed when art in architecture was introduced, including video, computer-controlled interactive light sculptures and high-tech LED walls. For a long time, photography generally enjoyed little or no recognition as an art form. By now however, art in architecture projects for the Bundestag building at Unter den Linden 50, the Transport Ministry and the Ministry of Food and Agriculture in Berlin have been implemented with a focus on photography series and photo installations. Artistic approaches presented at the *documenta*, biennales and other ambitious exhibitions are also reflected in art in architecture. For example the artist Josefine Günschel (born in 1960) placed live bee populations in the garden of the Centre for Microsystems and Materials in Berlin, as well as a wall piece in the foyer, presenting the age-old natural principles on which the rapidly developing field of microsystems technology is based (2012). While on a federal level, the durability of the art in architecture is binding, programmes on a state and municipal level regularly fund temporary art projects, such as the design of building-site fences.

NEW COMMITMENT

Not only the GDR was interested in "down-to-earth, realistic art". There were similar tendencies in the Federal Republic and regular demands for art with content-based "messages". Ironically, the conservativism of the Adenauer era and the will to reform as a result of the protests in 1968 provided a fairly stable front. Thus, in the 1970s, there was vociferous criticism of the geometric, abstract large and free-standing sculptures, which were often accused – with little foresight and a certain narrow-mindedness – of lacking emancipatory

Beat Zoderer, "Pavillon-Skulptur No. 2/12", 2012, German Bundestag/ Wilhelmstrasse 65, Berlin

or enlightening potential. To this day, abstract art is often disparaged as "l'art pour l'art" or for its "merely attractive appearance", communicating no tangible or educational value or otherwise "useful" content. In fact, there were often shifts in the focus of art in architecture. The emerging desire to replace abstract art, which was regarded as decorative and uncommitted, with a critically engaged figurative art, was based on postmodern thought and the artistic ideals of the "New Figuration" movement. This development was combined with a new understanding of the tasks of art in architecture, derived from Germany's new role on the international stage after regaining full sovereignty in 1990, as well as the conditions of the government's move to Berlin and the new use of buildings that were historically burdened. Not least, it was important to demonstrably integrate artists from the former GDR into art in architecture activities, especially in the new/old capital Berlin, and their artistic background continued to be figurative and characterised by narrative.

Since the 1990s, there has been a very large number of art in architecture pieces that engage with their locations in a critical, avowing, promising or contradictory way to their nature and history: since 1999, the "Archiv der Deutschen Abgeordneten" ("Archive of the German members of parliament") by Christian Boltanski (born in 1944) has symbolised the foundations of democracy in the cellar of the Reichstag building; since 2002, Dani Karavan (born in 1930) has reminded us of the articles of fundamental human rights defined in the constitution by applying them to the panes of glass in the outer courtyard of Jakob Kaiser House along the Spreepromenade; the biotope by Hans Haacke (born in 1936) entitled "DER BEVÖLKERUNG" ("TO THE POPULATION", 1999/2000) in the atrium of the

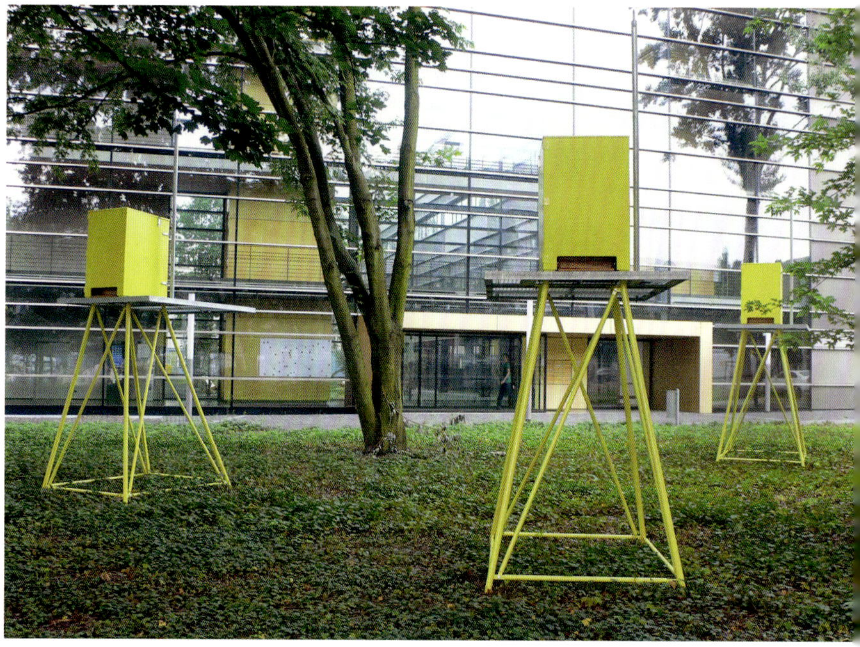

Josefine Günschel, "Smart Systems", 2012, Centre for Microsystems and Materials, Berlin

Christian Boltanski, "Archiv der Deutschen Abgeordneten", 1999, German Bundestag/ Reichstag building, Berlin

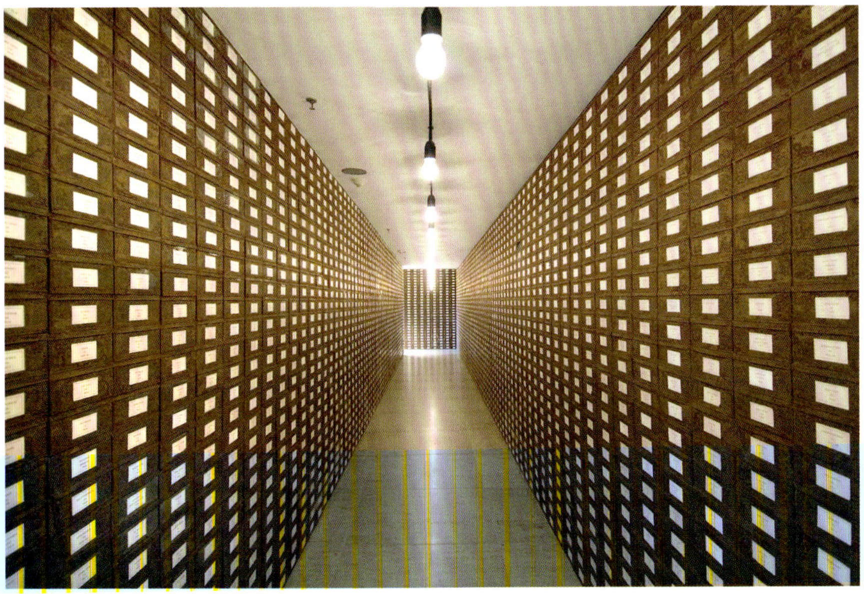

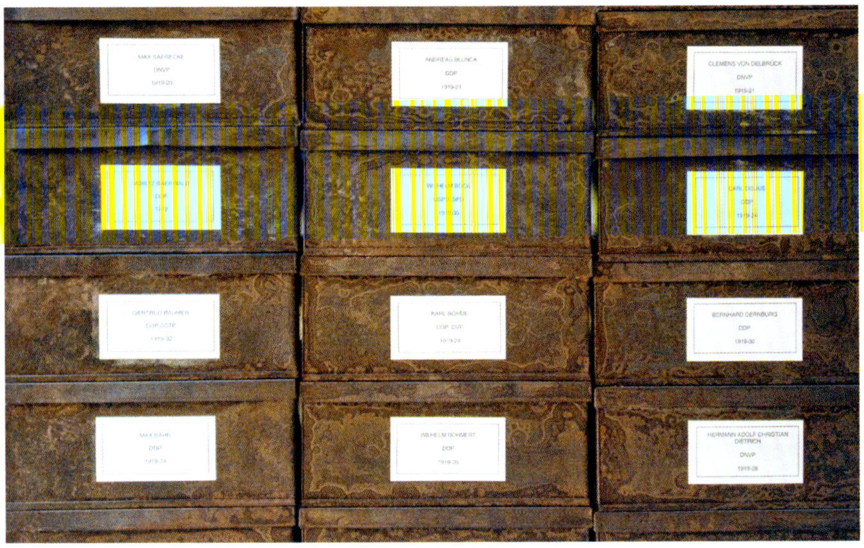

Reichstag building updates the declaration inscribed on the building's western portal "DEM DEUTSCHEN VOLKE" ("TO THE GERMAN PEOPLE") on its western portal (→ p. 168). In 2009, the artist Gabriele Obermaier (born in 1957) counteracted the architecture of the Federal Social Court of Germany in Kassel, which was built during the Nazi period, with the travesty of an aluminium sculpture entitled "Weiches Haus" ("Soft house"). In 2011, the Berlin network collective raumlaborberlin marked the forecourt, canopy and main roof of the former Stasi building in Berlin-Lichtenberg with the revealing facsimile of a stamp reading "Eingegangen am ..." ("Registered on...") (→ p. 172); such visual exposition of the formerly concealed place legitimises the building's subsequent use. Since 1990, the building has presented exhibitions on the theme of the State Security, while the permanent exhibition "Staatssicherheit in der SED-Diktatur" ("State Security during the SED dictatorship") was opened in 2015.

In terms of its underlying nature, art in architecture is not an art movement that can be openly combined with current political discourse. Nevertheless, there are certain approaches in this respect. The photo collage by J&K (Janne Schäfer, born in 1976, and Kristine Agergaard, born in 1975), which was installed in 2016 at the Goethe Institute in Cairo, is dedicated in a direct visual way to the 2011 Arab Spring in Egypt (→ p. 276). The artist Sunkoo Kang (born in 1977) works on a symbolic level. In 2020, he installed the bronze sculpture "Statue of Limitations" in the two-storey staircase of the Humboldt Forum in the Berlin Palace. It presents half of a black flag at half mast, while the title, which alludes to the "statute of limitations", recalls Germany's colonial past. The contemporary and controversial quality of this art in architecture

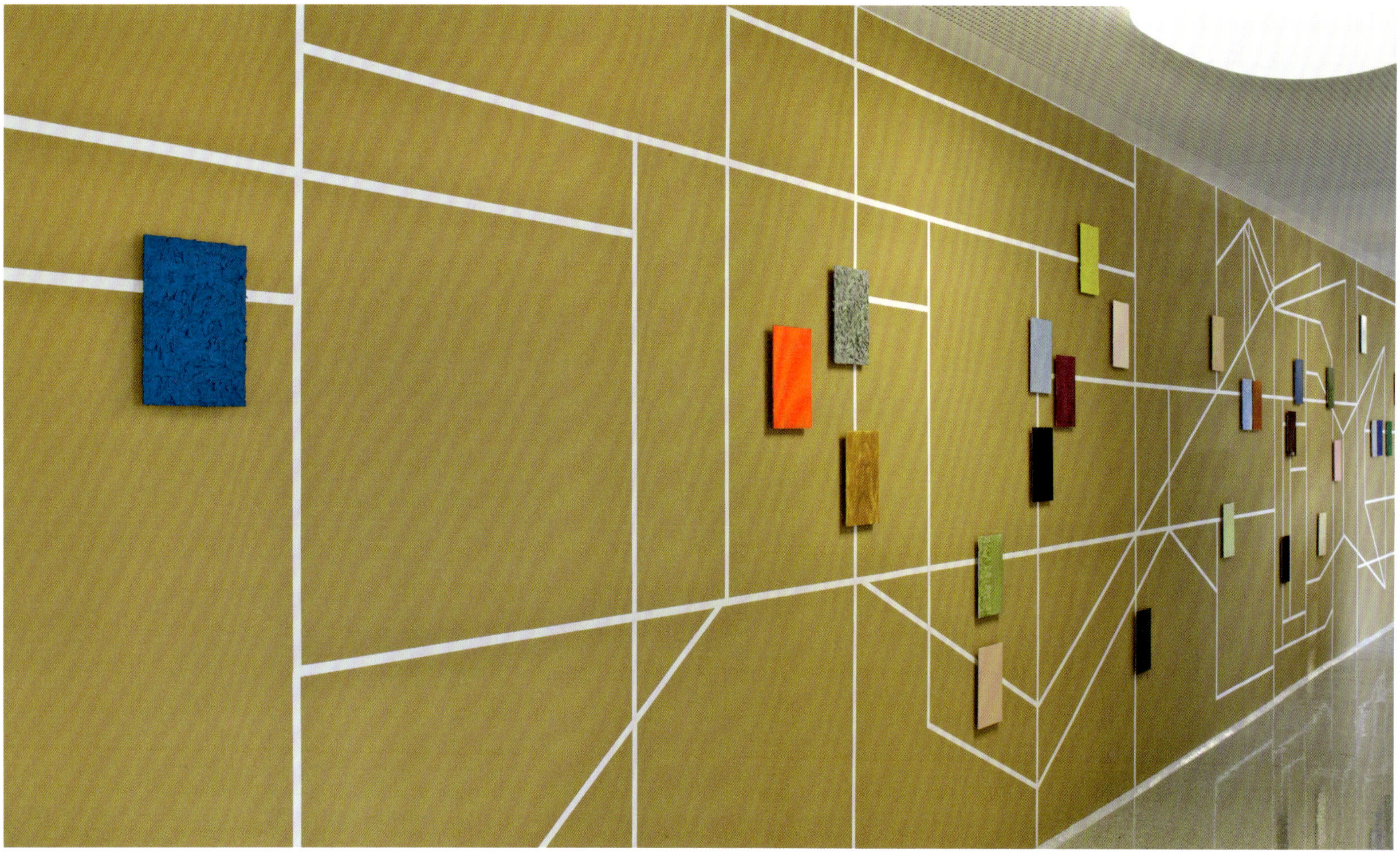

can firstly be grasped in the fact that the Humboldt Forum is itself the subject of criticism due to its colonial heritage, and secondly in the special aspect that the second, upper part of the critical, cautionary flag will be temporarily set up in an open public space on Nachtigalplatz in the "African Quarter" of Berlin-Wedding.

Art in architecture is no longer merely a visual object. It also involves the viewers as active participators or co-designers. In 2011, the Cologne painter Michael Jäger (born in 1956) designed a wall of the federally funded Laboratory for Battery Technology in Ulm, with over a hundred monochrome image panels, allowing the institute's employees to personally appropriate the area again and again by creating new formations. On a state and municipal level, there are examples of artists who, for instance, involve prison inmates in art in architecture projects, or design a school building together with the pupils. One particularly participatory and interactive project was the design of the large entrance area of the Berlin Ministry of Finance. The Arts Council of the Federal Government therefore decided against a competition and directly commissioned the concept artist Jochen Gerz (born in 1940), who is renowned for his participatory memorials. In 1999, Gerz created a complex laser projection and video installation that involved the ministry employees in the form of an interview on the theme of "Money, love, death, freedom – what counts in the end?". Passers by on the busy Wilhelmstrasse are also involved, since from the pavement, they can activate the screens integrated into the gateposts of the inner forecourt.

Michael Jäger, "Ulmer Farblabor", 2011, Center for Solar Energy and Hydrogen Research Baden-Württemberg, battery technology laboratory, Ulm

Jan Hendrik Theissen, "Pinnwand", 2000, Federal Ministry of Education and Research, Berlin

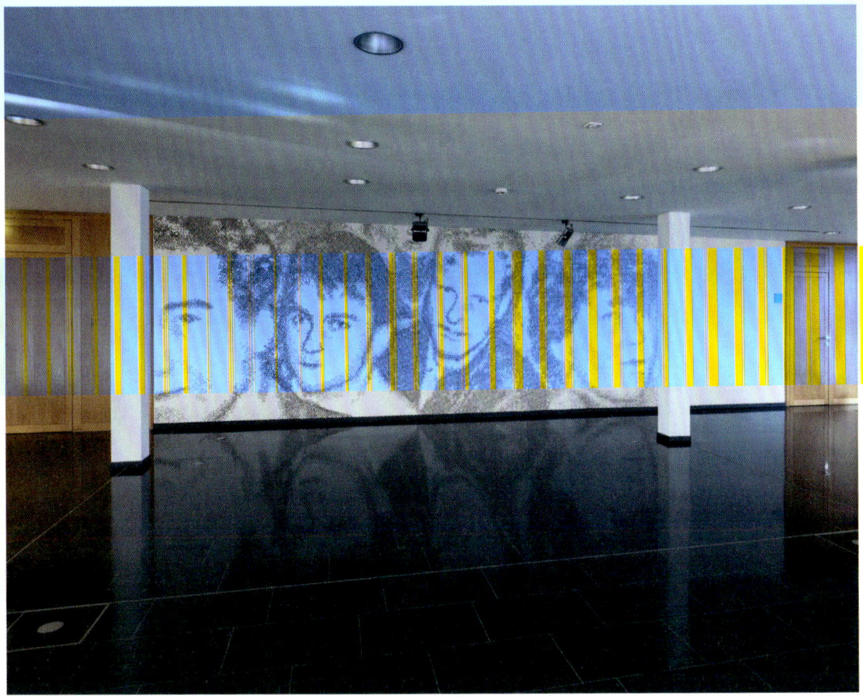

FROM SUPPORTING ARTISTS TO SUPPORTING ART

The old idea of support for artists, which led to the introduction of art in architecture, is not an empty promise. To this day, it has its role – not least in a very tangible way when art in architecture competitions are limited to artists with a biographical connection to a specific federal state or region, or in the case of student competitions, which are even occasionally organised on a national level. Such competitions were used for the former Berlin headquarters of the Federal Ministry of Education and Research (1999) and for the Federal Institute for Materials Research and Testing in Berlin-Adlershof (2009).

In the period following the decision in 1991 to restore Berlin as the capital, involving many extremely important building projects, the commitment to art in architecture can also be seen in the fact that, in an effort to maximise the number and quality of the artworks, the art in architecture funds for the Reichstag building were increased to 3 percent. However, the specific artistic and overall cultural value of art in architecture lies in the continued funding of advanced artistic positions located not in the protected spaces of the art world, but "where people come together" – as reported by the Council for Cultural Policy in 1950 when art in architecture was introduced. The 1949 constitution was reserved in this matter, but the 1990 unification contract between the Federal Republic and the German Democratic Republic, which dissolved the GDR, describes the importance not only of political and social tasks, but also the cultural obligations for a state's self-perception. It now stresses the need to protect and support the arts and culture. That supportive duty had long been implemented by art in architecture. Since 1961, the two-metre high, abstract steel sculpture by Hans Uhlmann (1900–1975), which was heavily criticised to begin with, has stood in front of the Deutsche Oper in Berlin. In the 1970s, there was a flood of large-scale sculptures made of Corten steel (→ p. 206), stainless steel and aluminium, which have written a highly important chapter of German and international art history. It is not difficult to imagine what would have become of such art if art in architecture had not taken it on board and – despite the scepticism and accusations from the population – established it in the public world. An emblematic example of arts and cultural support is the design of the exclusive location in front of the Plenarsaal of the Bundestag in Bonn, which was completed in 1992. Established in the early 1990s, the newly introduced Arts Council of the Bundestag, consisting of ten members of parliament in proportion to party representation, awarded a direct commission in 1993, without a prior competition, to the sculptor Olaf Metzel (born in 1952), who subsequently produced the famous sculpture of a bicycle stand entitled "Meistdeutigkeit" ("Maximum ambivalence"). This treasure for the art world was a delicate matter from a political perspective: only a few years earlier, another piece by the artist in Berlin, entitled "Randale-Denkmal" ("Memorial to riots") had been removed from the Kurfürstendamm sculptural boulevard: protest from parts of the population and the press against such art had simply become too loud and aggressive.

Although it sometimes takes years or even decades, art in architecture indeed becomes one of the most effective instruments of support for the arts, thereby fulfilling the aspirations it has always upheld in the seventy years of its existence, namely to create "art for all" that – unlike the merely likeable decoration in some pedestrian precincts and shopping malls – truly deserves to be described as "art".

Hans Uhlmann, untitled, 1960/1961, Deutsche Oper, Berlin

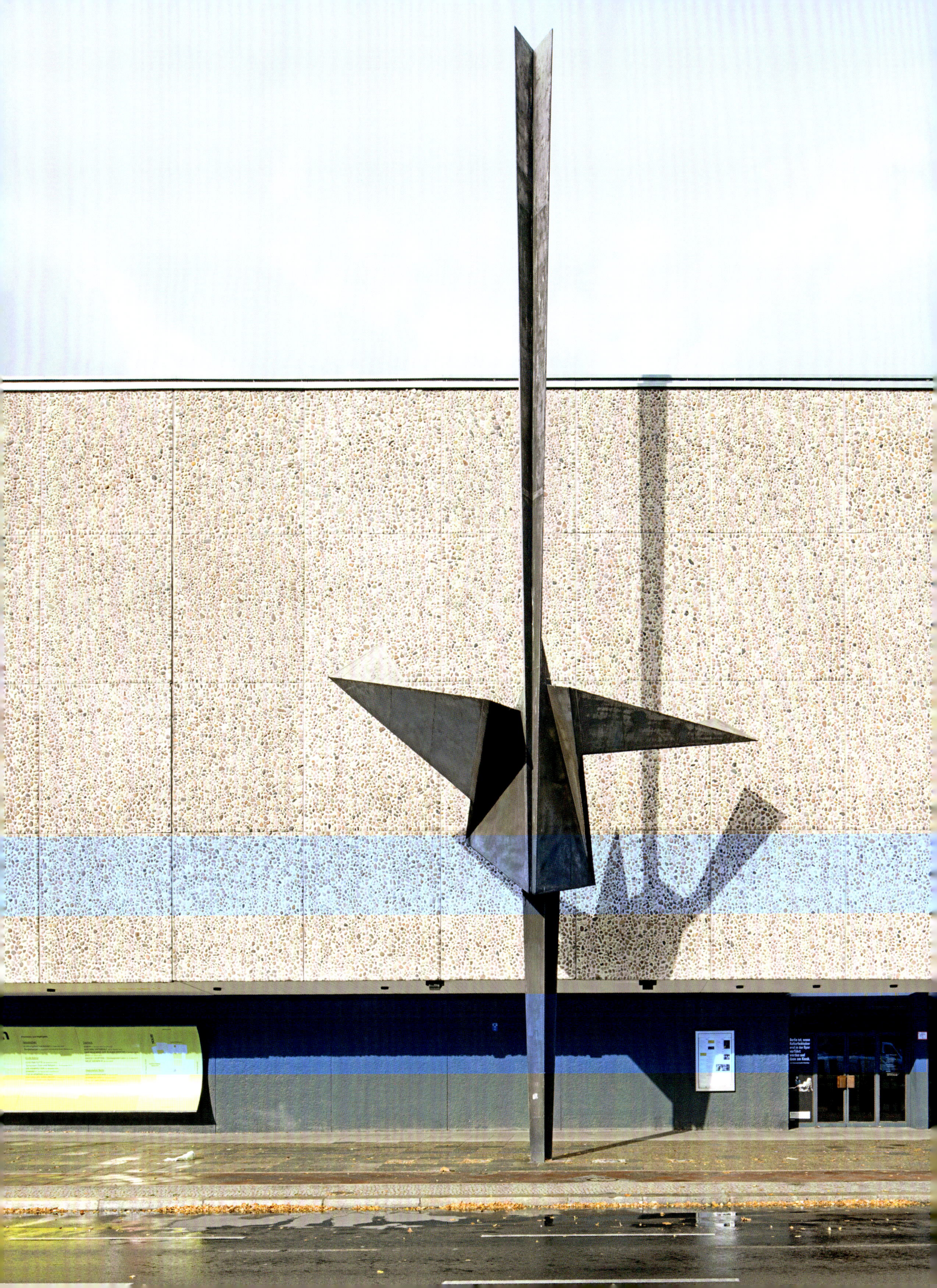

NEW ART FOR

ART IN ARCHITECTURE FROM WORLD WAR II TO THE CONSTRUCTION OF THE BERLIN WALL IN 1961

NEW STATES

In 1950, a year after the two German states were founded, regulations on the participation of artists in state building measures were introduced both in the Federal Republic of Germany (FRG) and the German Democratic Republic (GDR). For both states, commissions were aimed at supporting artists, but the more important cultural-political intention was to bring art out of museums and into the midst of society. The purpose of art in architecture was to give the respective buildings a special means of identification and add an independent level of interpretation. Methods of representing art in architecture developed in highly contrasting ways in the competing political systems: on the one hand, the Socialist workers' and farmers' state under the hegemony of the Soviet Union, and on the other, the Federal Republic of Germany, which was dedicated to a free, democratic basic order and aligned towards the West. Yet both systems explicitly rejected the methods of heroification applied during the National Socialist period.

In the GDR, artists were used as co-shapers of a social transformation process. Above all, down-to-earth murals in the style of Socialist Realism were seen as an appropriate means to accomplish a positive propaganda image of the state's historical and contemporary achievements. Thus the interaction between the presented theme of architecturally related art and the tasks of the respective institution only played a subordinate role. By contrast, art in architecture in the young Federal Republic was characterised by the tendency to avoid ideological presentation and symbolism. Moreover, the Federal Republic's constitution guaranteed the freedom of art. Nevertheless, the first decade was dominated by figurative and realistic artworks, their style based on pre-war Modernity, although some abstract pieces were also produced. For federal building tasks, they served decorative purposes and as a comment on the building's institutional or public fields of operations. This level of interpretation, which the artists developed independently, fulfilled non-material, building-cultural and representational tasks.

NEW ART FOR NEW STATES

Constanze von Marlin

The occupation of Germany between 1945 and 1949 was an interim period between the end of the National Socialist state and the foundation of the Federal Republic of Germany and the German Democratic Republic, which belonged to two opposing power blocs during the Cold War. The four victorious powers, Great Britain, France, the USA and the Soviet Union, had divided the country into one eastern and three western occupation zones. In 1949, the three western zones became the democratic Federal Republic of Germany, which was aligned towards the West, while the eastern zone became the Socialist German Democratic Republic under Soviet hegemony. The post-war period was characterised by enormous construction efforts, initially to establish Bonn as the temporary capital of the Federal Republic, and to appropriately accommodate the GDR government in the war-ravaged East Berlin. In addition to the focus on building measures in the two capital cities, reconstruction work quickly began throughout Germany.

Despite all the political and social differences in the two German states, support for culture through state commissions became part of the new arts policy in both systems. One of the first important projects in East Germany was the reconstruction of the badly damaged German National Theatre in Weimar in 1946, with the support of the Soviet military administration. The measure was aimed at commemorating the national assembly of the Weimar Republic, where on July 31, 1919, delegates had adopted the first democratic constitution of Germany in its final form. The architects commissioned to carry out the reconstruction, Kurt Hemmerling and Werner Harting, convinced the artists Hermann Kirchberger (1905–1983) and Bruno Quass (1904–1972) to design a mural and the columns in the theatre foyer (→ p. 70). Both artists chose actors, harlequins and mask motifs from the performing arts, which they strongly abstracted and developed in forms and colours that were almost Expressionist.

Even before the establishment of a state regulation on art for building measures in 1950, this direct collaboration between architects and artists created a decorative solution that related to the building's use. In the context of the state criticism of Formalism, a term the Socialist Unity Party of Germany (SED) used to accuse artists of placing form above content and therefore "falsifying reality", art in the GDR became entirely subordinate to Party requirements from 1949 onwards. Socialist Realism was considered an appropriate style. It had been developed in the Soviet Union and was regarded as the only style that was able to communicate political messages to the people. Within this discourse, the *National-Zeitung*, a central instrument of the of the National Democratic Party of Germany, was among the first to call for the removal of the Weimar Theatre's mural by Herman Kirchberger, deeming it to be Formalist. When the Thuringia SED state newspaper *Das Volk* also argued against the artwork, it was removed in 1950.

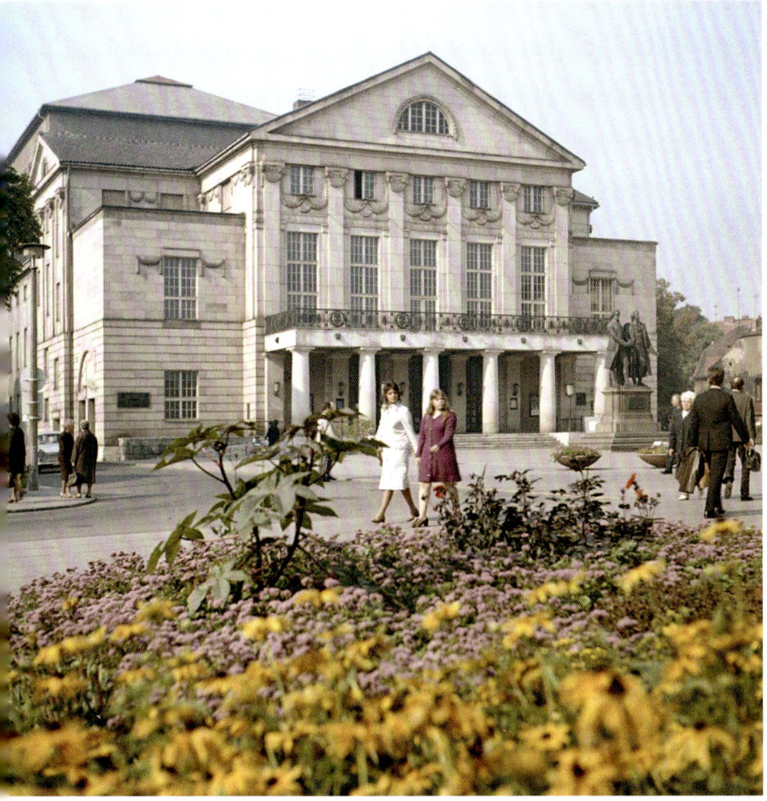

German National Theatre, Weimar

LEGAL BASIS FOR ART IN ARCHITECTURE

The parliamentary initiative for artistic commissions on buildings was debated by the German Bundestag on November 2, 1949. After only a two-month discourse, which essentially focused on whether the regulation should primarily support artists or be an educational initiative in the spirit of "art for all", the German Bundestag adopted the following decision on January 25, 1950: "To support the visual arts, the Federal Government has been requested, in so far as the character and framework of the individual building measure justifies it, to commit to all federal building tasks (new construction and conversions) an investment in works by visual artists to the amount of at least 1 percent of the building-contract sum. Artists from all German states should be taken into account in awarding commissions. An expert committee is responsible for the selection of each individual artwork. It is recommended that the professional association of visual artists should be consulted with respect to the awarding of commissions."

In accordance with a decision on March 17, 1950, the newly founded federal building authority in Bonn, known as the Bundesbaudirektion, assumed responsibility for the building tasks relating to the Federal President, the Bundesrat (the federal upper house), the Bundestag (the federal lower house), the Federal Chancellor and the Federal Ministries, as well as federal representations abroad. All other building tasks were carried out by the respective building authorities of the individual federal states, while the Deutsche Bundespost (federal post office) and the Deutsche Bundesbahn (national rail) had comparable, regionally structured building authorities. As early as in 1951, an art in architecture competition was

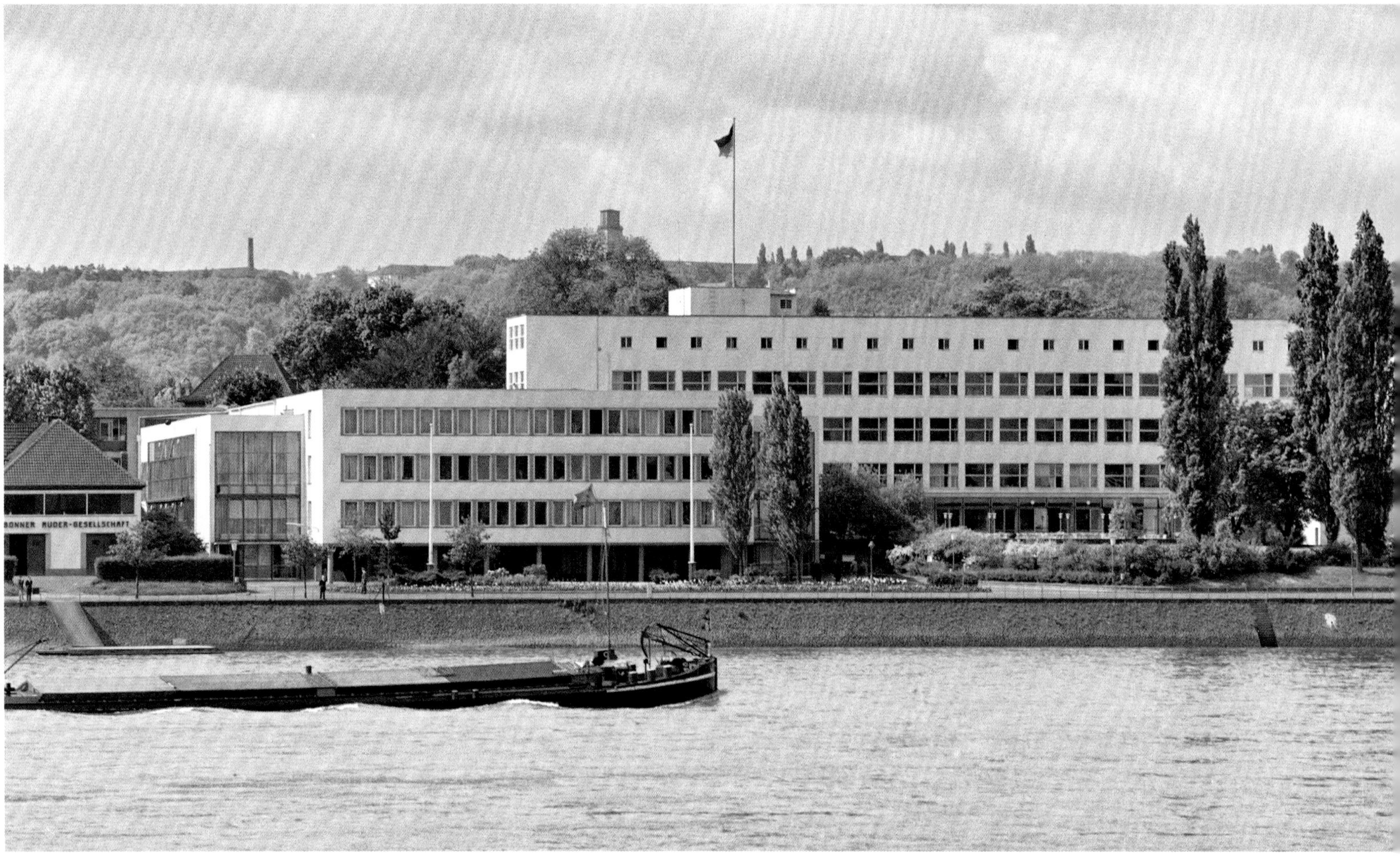

announced for Munich's Central Station, which was won by Rupprecht Geiger (1908–2009) with his design for a plate mosaic (→ p. 72). The implemented artwork was not only the first art in architecture commission for a federal building, but is also remarkable in combining an abstract mosaic form with integrated fluorescent tubes.

The 1950 resolution by the Bundestag was followed on August 1, 1953 by the first "Preliminary guidelines for the implementation of federal buildings", which also regulated commissions to visual artists. They prioritised the competition process instead of direct commissions, as well as the involvement of experts in the selection process. Furthermore, with respect to building measures for which art in architecture was intended, it defined the proportion of costs for art, the art forms and the responsibility of expert committees for making selections, as well as compulsory annual

Bundeshaus Bonn

reporting on commissions and their costs. The first final guidelines for federal building tasks under the auspices of the Federal Financial Construction Offices (RBBau) were enacted by the Federal Minister of Finance on January 2, 1957. They listed both competitions and direct awards as processes to commission works of art in architecture.

In the Soviet occupation zone, support for art was part of Socialist cultural policy from the outset. The 1949 constitution of the GDR promised to respect the freedom of art, but in practice, artists often experienced conflicts with their state contractor with respect to implementing thematic and stylistic briefs. This was due to socio-political demands for monumental murals, which were regarded as a means of communicating the achievements and advances of Socialist society to the people using images that were easy to grasp.

The Kulturfonds (cultural fund) was founded as early as in September 1949, forming the basis of state commissioning of artists in the Soviet occupation zone. Its budget was funded by a cultural tax. On March 16, 1950, following the foundation of the GDR, Prime Minister Otto Grotewohl established a second pillar for awarding commissions: "All measures to build new and restore existing administrative buildings must include between 1 and 2 percent of the authorised building budget to be invested in the artistic design of the rooms, consisting of works of down-to-earth, realistic art." A programmatic alignment was thereby clearly assigned to art in architecture in terms of its style and statement. The Chairman of the SED party, Walter Ulbricht, saw special potential in the field of culture to strengthen the alliance between the working class and the intelligentsia. At the 3rd Party Assembly in 1950, he stressed the importance of cultural work in supporting the freedom and unity of Germany. Thus, efforts to communicate culture to the "working masses" and the rural population were considered essential. As a consequence of the so-called 1951 Formalism Plenary, where the SED aimed to impose a cultural policy that was analogous to the Stalinist example, the "Directive for the artistic design of administrative buildings" was enacted in August 1952. It required the clients of major building projects to use 1 to 2 percent of the planned building costs for artistic design. In addition to the Kulturfonds, the newly founded State Commissioning Committee assumed responsibility for awarding contracts, which were to be decided by competition in the case of major projects. The committee examined and approved sketches and designs for their implementation, which meant that at times, politicians and functionaries directly influenced the visual programme of the artworks.

ART IN THE SERVICE OF THE GDR STATE

During the drive to establish Socialism in the early 1950s, the Party and state massively influenced arts policy – going as far as giving direct orders on the design of thematic murals. One of the most important such commissioned works from this period is the mural "Aufbau der Republik" ("Building the Republic", 1953), by Max Lingner (1888–1959) on the House of Ministries in Berlin, the former Reich Aviation Ministry (→ p. 74). Like the Olympic Games facility, the administrative building is one of the few major architectural projects completed by the National Socialists in Berlin. It was erected in 1935/1936 according to plans by Ernst Sagebiel. In 1941, the year of the attack on the Soviet Union, an over 20-metre long mural relief was installed in its northern columned hall.

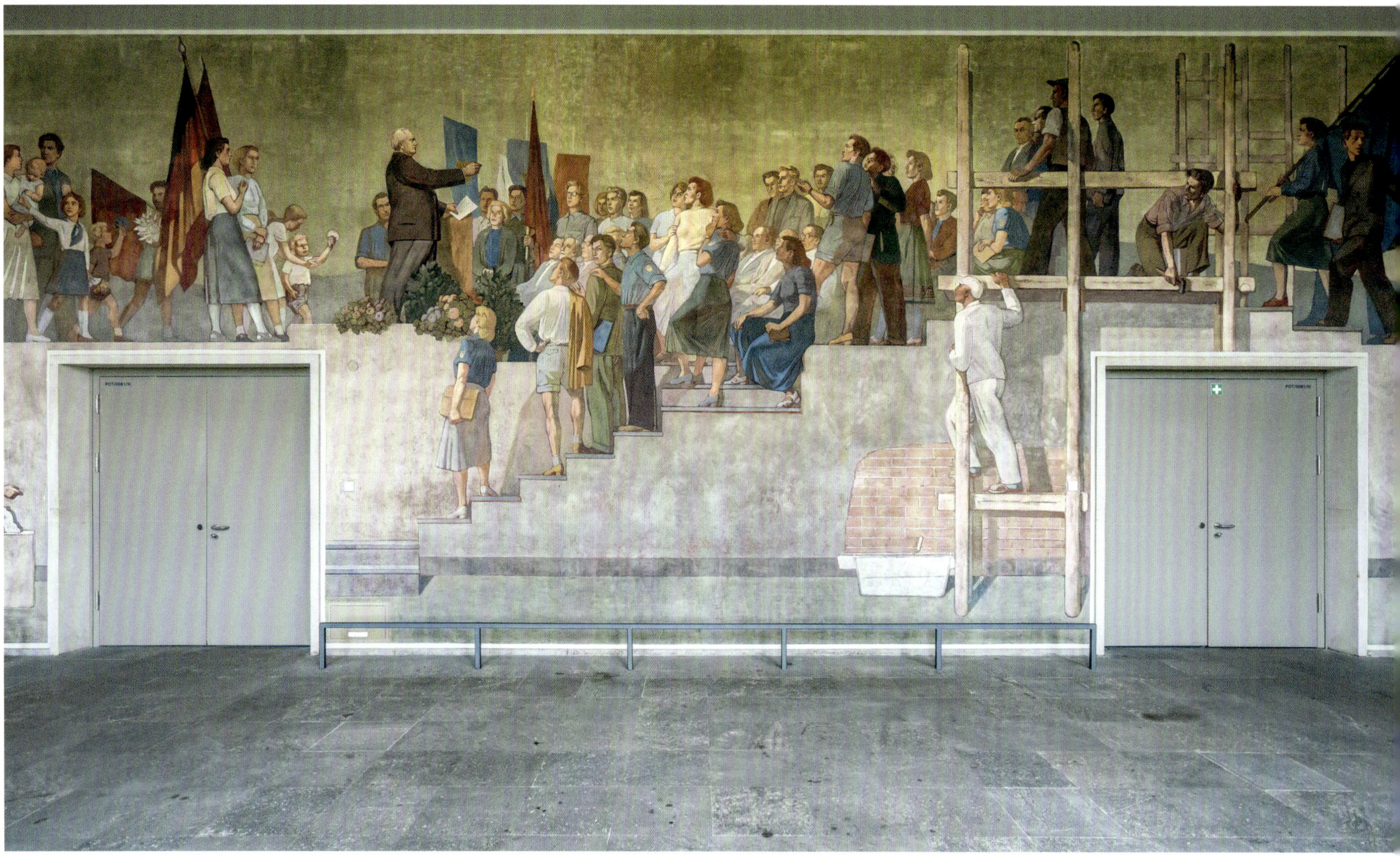

Entitled "Soldatenfries" ("Soldier frieze"), the mural by Arnold Waldschmidt (1873–1958) served to glorify the German Wehrmacht. Initial measures to denazify the architecture were carried out immediately after World War II, removing the artistically designed "Reichsadler" ("Imperial Eagle") and symbols of National Socialist sovereignty. During restoration work on the ideologically laden building to convert it into the seat of the GDR government and accommodate its ministries, the SED had to interpret the architecture in a new way. The wall area used for the removed mural relief by Waldschmidt was a suitable location for that purpose. In August 1950, a competition was announced for a mural on the theme of "The importance of peace for the cultural development of humanity and the necessity to fight for it", in which Carl/Charles Crodel (1894–1973), Kate Diehn-Bitt (1900–1978), Hermann Kirchberger, Max Lingner and Wilhelm Lachnit (1899–1962) participated. The competition's aim was to give the building complex an externally visible, political reinterpretation in the spirit of Socialist development. Otto Grotewohl, Prime Minister and the chief occupant of the building, ordered the winning design by Lingner to be amended several times until the composition conformed to the political programme of the Party. This process of collaboration between the contractor and the artist was documented as a prime example in the catalogue entitled *Vom Auftrag zum Wandbild* (trans.: *From a commission to a mural*), which was published in 1953.

The mural was programmatically presented on January 3, 1953, the birthday of President Wilhelm Pieck. Only six months later, in June 1953, the forecourt of the House of Ministries of the GDR became the central location of nationwide protests and demonstrations. It is where the uprising of June 17

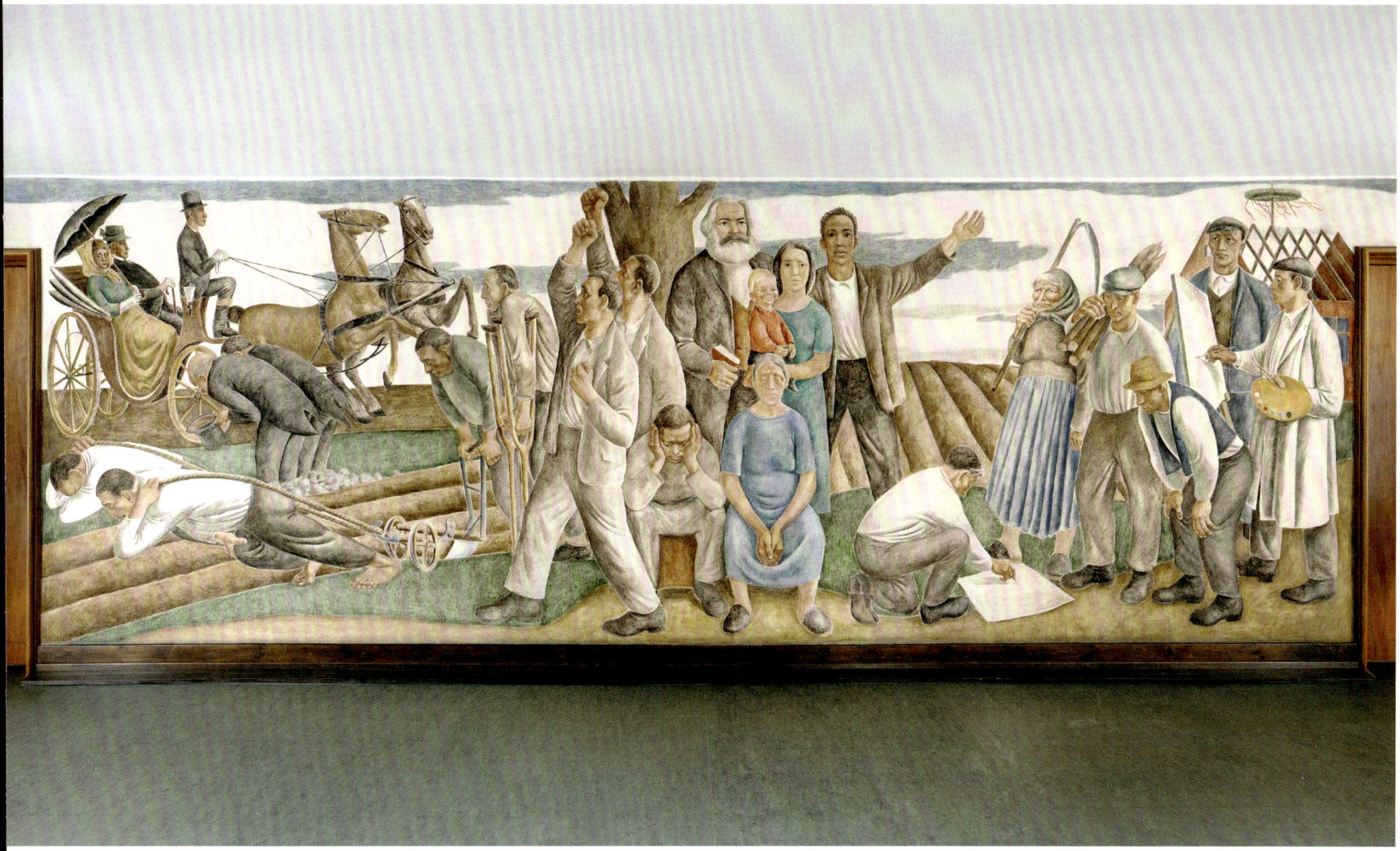

Alfred Hesse, Erich Gerlach, "Wilhelm Pieck spricht zu den Studenten", 1954, University of Transportation, Dresden

Arno Mohr, "Wendepunkt Deutschlands", 1956, University of Visual and Applied Arts, Berlin-Weissensee

was crushed by the Soviet military with the help of the Volkspolizei. The main addressees of SED policy, the working class, which was so prominently depicted on the mural by Lingner, had withdrawn their trust in the Party on a massive scale.

In the following years, architecturally related art in the GDR also revealed the state's attempt to use art for politic goals, propagating the harmonisation of society in all age groups, social strata and professional fields. Universities were considered as suitable forums for this purpose, since the primary goal of education was to create a "Socialist intelligence", which was mainly to be derived from the workers' and farmers' families. Completed in 1954, the mural "Wilhelm Pieck spricht zu den Studenten" ("Wilhelm Pieck speaks to the students") by Alfred Hesse (1904–1988) and Erich Gerlach (1909–2000) for the foyer of the main lecture theatre of the University of

Transportation in Dresden, fulfilled precisely that function. In view of the thematic brief of "education for awareness of the state in connection with transport and technology", the artists chose the lecturing President of the GDR, Wilhelm Pieck, as the centrepiece of the artwork. The students, workers, members of the Pioneer movement and intellectuals gathered around him refer to the state's efforts to achieve harmony between the different classes in society, as well as addressing the themes of collaboration between urban planning, architecture and art, which was intended to have a positive effect on a new working ethos.

Due to a lack of prestigious new state buildings in the Soviet occupation zone, the University of Visual and Applied Arts in Berlin Weissensee was selected as a public forum to implement the important theme of land reform in 1945/1946 as a propaganda image. The positive presentation of a new social order in Arno Mohr's (1910–2001) mural "Wendepunkt Deutschlands" ("Germany's turning point"), which was painted in 1956, contains symbolic references to the foundation of agricultural cooperatives, which therefore also seemed appropriate for a college of art. The cultural policy of the GDR, the workers' and farmers' state, regarded art as a "symbolic solution" to social contradictions. Thus, art played a key role in implementing Marxist-Leninist historical interpretation and was used for the moral, political and aesthetic education of the population.

The designs of art in architecture in the GDR were to be aligned towards the style known as Socialist Realism. Themes for public commissions in the 1950s included the working class, peace, international friendship, close ties with the Soviet Union, transformation and defence. Sports and the military were also used as a means of strengthening the state's identity. State commissions for architecturally related art were assigned politically motivated content that declared the advances and aims of the workers' and farmers' state, as well as the education of the people – at times regardless of the buildings' functions. In the process of finding themes and developing the content of the artworks' visual programme, the politicisation of art demanded close collaboration between state commissioning, the Party and the designing artists.

ENDOWING THE NEW FEDERAL CAPITAL BONN WITH ART IN ARCHITECTURE

Following the decision in 1949 to make Bonn the new Federal Capital, at least on a temporary basis, the most important building tasks of the early 1950s consisted of converting and extending the University of Education to create the Bundeshaus as the seat of the Bundestag and the Bundesrat (1949–1953), as well as refurbishing the former barracks for various federal ministries, and new buildings for both the Foreign Office (1953–1954) and the Federal Ministry of Finance (1955) in Bonn. Furthermore, important federal institutions were established in the individual states, some of which required new buildings, such as the Bundesrechnungshof (the federal auditing authority) in Frankfurt am Main (1951–1953), the Federal Statistical Office in Wiesbaden (1952–1956), the German Patent and Trade Mark Office in Munich (1954–1959) and the Federal Court in Karlsruhe (1958–1960).

Based on the art in architecture regulations adopted in 1950, the Federal Building Authority announced the Federal Republic's first open art competition for one of its buildings in 1952, namely the Bundeshaus. 333 designs for a wall area of four by six metres at its main

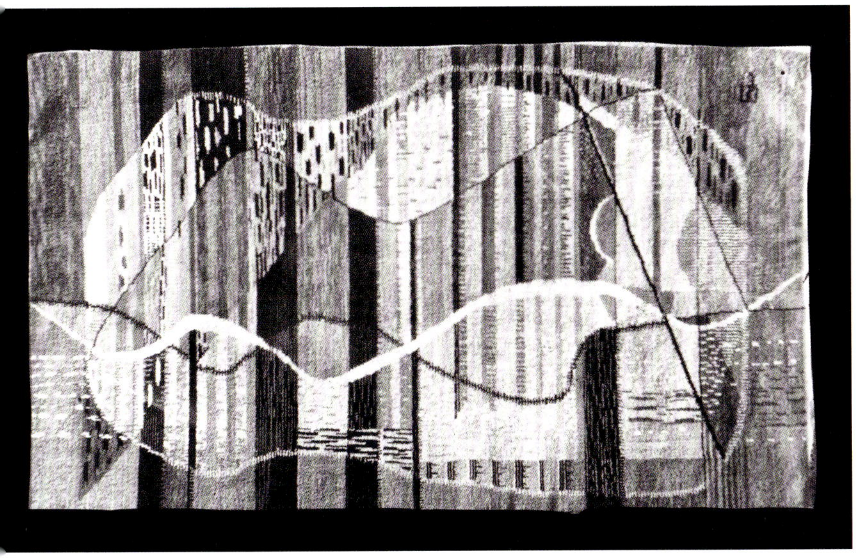

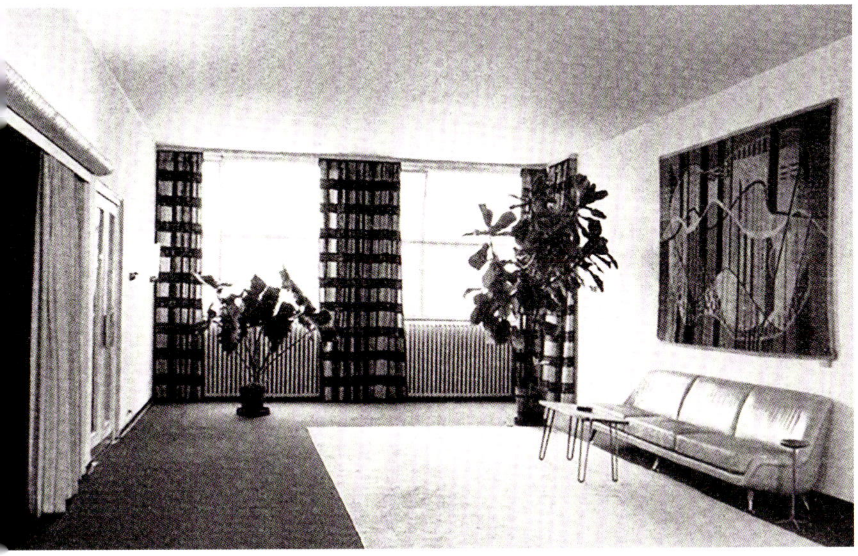

Edith Müller-Ortloff, "Farbfuge", 1957, Bundeshaus, Bonn

entrance were submitted for the "Competition for sculptural ornamentation on the extension building of the Bundeshaus in Bonn". For the prestigious entrance area, the prize jury chose an abstract figuration of an ascending phoenix by Hannes Schulz-Tattenpach (1905–1953). The artwork "Aufsteigender Phönix", 1953, immediately became a symbol of the will to make a fresh start and a new beginning for the Federal Republic (→ p. 76). The mythological, metaphorical choice of a phoenix motif replaced the National Socialist cult of heroes and Teutons with a new, ideologically unburdened visual language, which nevertheless remained universally understandable. The identity-shaping quality of this art in architecture was confirmed in the design of a special stamp on the 25th anniversary of the Federal Republic, which presented the ascending phoenix in front of the colours of the national flag.

In 1957, when the Bundeshaus was extended to accommodate the Bundesrat, a limited, anonymous competition was announced for a tapestry on the theme of "The Law". In view of the submitted sketched proposals, the prize jury recommended the production of an abstract textile piece by Edith Müller-Ortloff (1911–1995), rather than adhering strictly to the content brief. The non-figurative composition "Farbfuge", 1957, ("Colour fugue" or "Colour joint"), with its powerful colours, strong contrasts and amorphous forms, only very remotely recalls the competition theme, namely a symbolic balance of powers and forms.

Unlike the GDR, there was no defined visual programme and no direct influence by high-ranking politicians, parties or building administrations in the FRG. In practice, this meant finding compromises between the constitutionally guaranteed freedom of art and demands for the art to deliver a prestigious, image-strengthening expression of the state's

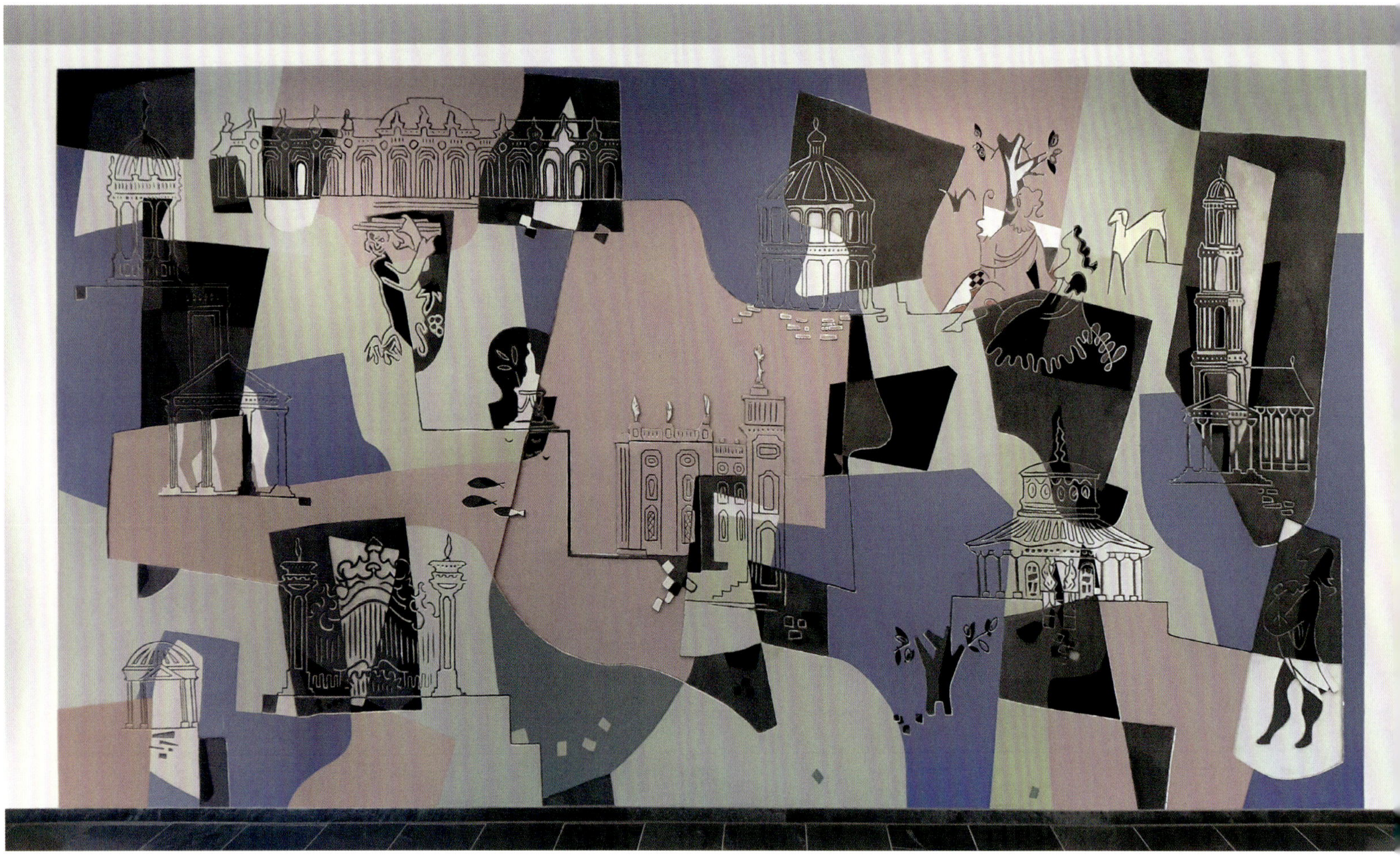

democratic self-perception. However, there were occasional thematic briefs relating to the history and tasks of the relevant institution. For instance, in the case of the project for art in the new Bundesrechnungshof building in Frankfurt am Main, its President Josef Mayer, the State Building Authority in Frankfurt and the architects Werner Dierschke and Friedel Steinmeyer all contributed concrete proposals for the content and placement of the art in architecture. In the foyer, a mural with motifs of the city of Potsdam was meant to reflect the location of the predecessor institution. Following a limited competition process, Eberhard Schlotter (1921–2014) was commissioned with his design "Potsdam". The President's publicly expressed criticism of a narrative group of figures, instead of purely topographical motifs, merely led to a slight modification of the sgraffito design, which was completed in 1953.

In the 1950s, a bitter struggle developed within the Federal Republic's art scene concerning the dominance of abstraction compared to figurative art, which had its roots in Modernity. At the first Kassel *documenta* in 1955, apart from artists whose works had been denounced as "degenerate" by the National Socialists, most other exhibited artists chose an abstract formal language. Thus, one of the most important exhibition series of international post-war art provided the reference for contemporary art in the Federal Republic, which was clearly orientated towards abstract art. The Federal Republic's art in architecture of the 1950s includes the full stylistic spectrum of artistic work, picking up on the artistic movements of early 20th-century Modernity, however without disconcerting the respective buildings' users with excessively avant-garde forms of expression.

The Federal Republic's building administrations sought new, innocuous motifs on

Eberhard Schlotter, "Potsdam", 1953, Bundesrechnungshof, Frankfurt am Main

Will Sohl, untitled, 1955, Federal Ministry of the Interior, Bonn

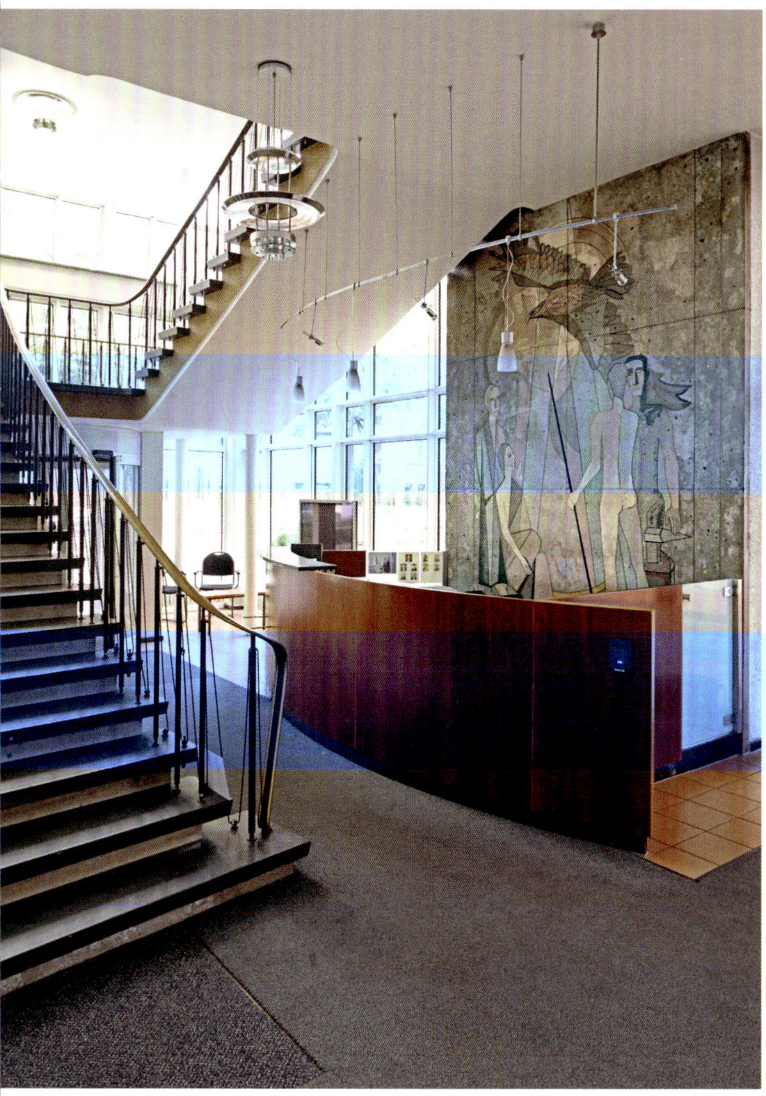

murals and sculptures for façades and entrance areas, in order to set themselves apart from the visual vocabulary of the National Socialists. In addition to rarely implemented symbols of sovereignty, such as the Federal Eagle on a stele (1953) by Hans Oskar Wissel (born in 1925) for the Bundesrechnungshof in Frankfurt am Main, and the cartouche with the Federal Eagle by Hans Wimmer (1907–1992) on the façade of the Federal Ministry for Post and Telecommunications in 1955, predominantly figurative representations of animals and people were conceived, for instance in the well that was produced in the same year by Fritz Melis (1913–1982), entitled "Bären" ("Bears"), for the Federal Ministry of the Interior in Bonn. In 1955, Will Sohl (1906–1969) designed the directly commissioned mural of polished natural stone for the foyer of the Main Federal Treasury at the Federal Ministry of the Interior in Bonn. In this case, the dominant eagle figure seems less a symbol of sovereignty than a freely flying creature. Sohl's mural has both a figurative representation and an abstract background, thus managing to bridge the divide of the time, between, on the one hand, clients in building administration, with their relatively conservative outlooks, particularly in matters of art, as well as the users of the public buildings, and, on the other, an art scene in which many artists were orientated towards pre-war Modernity and developing new forms of expression. Abstract pieces such as the plate mosaic by Rupprecht Geiger for Munich Central Station, or the mosaic at the Federal Statistical Office in Wiesbaden by Bernd Krimmel (born in 1926), which was produced in 1956 (→ p. 78), remained the exceptions.

The Federal Ministry for Post and Telecommunications, which was completed in 1954, was the first new ministry building in Bonn. In its simple, reserved appearance, it reflects

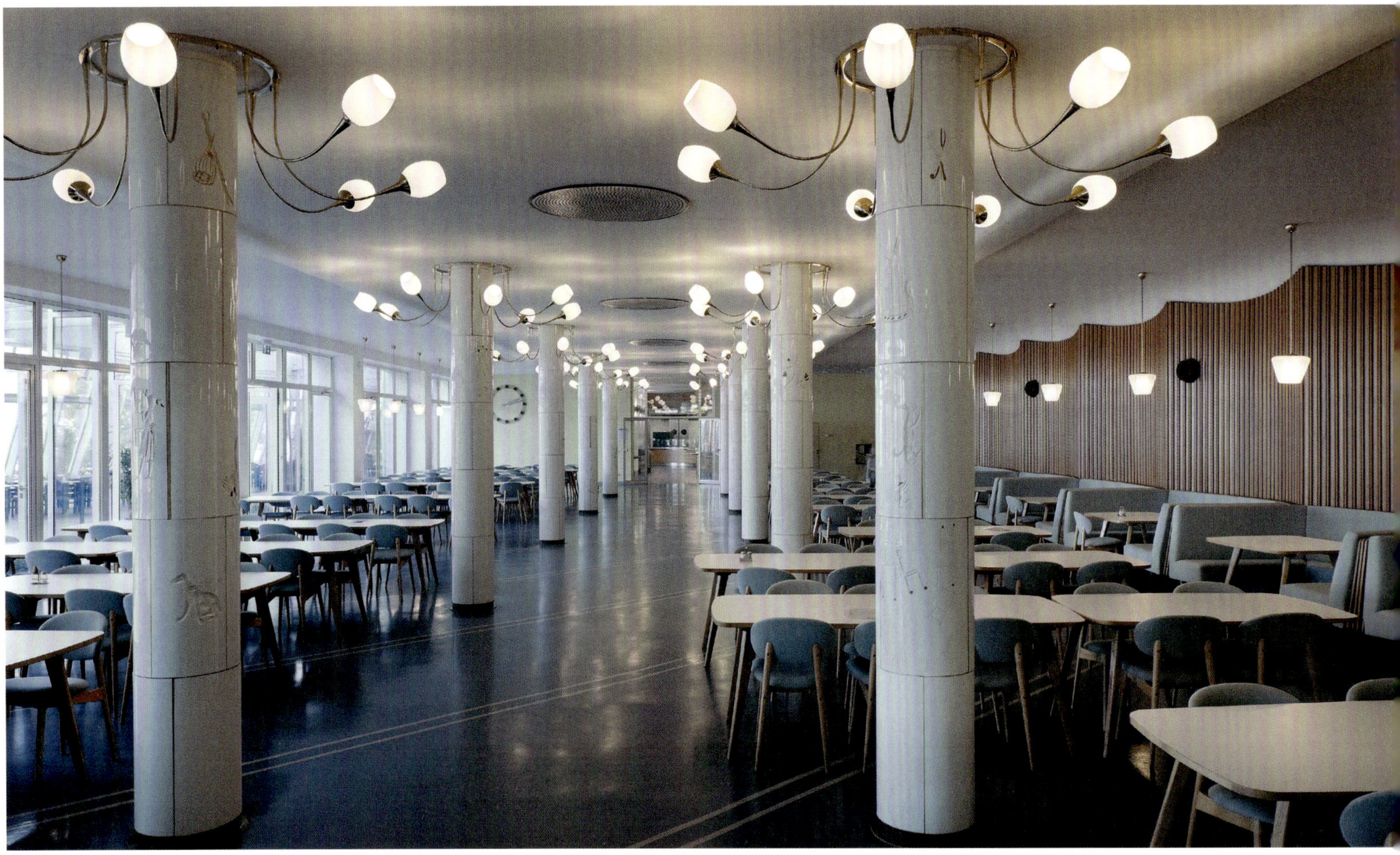

both the character of the temporary capital Bonn and also the expression and self-perception of the young Federal Republic, as opposed to the "Third Reich's" dictatorial claim to power. In 1957, Hans Wimmer was invited by the architect Josef Trimborn to design the sculpture "Fünf Erdteile" ("Five Continents", → p. 80) for the Rhine-facing head-end of the lecture theatre. Wimmer, like his sculptor colleague and friend Gerhard Marcks (1889–1981), whose piece "Soldanelle" was installed in the inner courtyard of the Federal Ministry of the Interior in 1954, was dedicated to figurative sculpture, thereby resisting abstract tendencies in post-1945 sculpture. This circle also included Charles Crodel, who was himself a friend of Gerhard Marcks and was commissioned to design the canteen of the Ministry for Post and Telecommunications. In 1954, Crodel created ten column-cladding elements in glass ceramics, with ornamental polishing,

Charles Crodel, untitled, 1954, Federal Ministry of Post and Telecommunications, Bonn

which rhythmically structure the space. Above all depending on the light conditions, it is possible to recognise motifs such as landscapes, small genre scenes, stylised plants and everyday objects.

COMMISSIONS IN BOTH PARTS OF GERMANY

Until the watershed in inner-German relations with the construction of the Berlin Wall in 1961, it was not uncommon for artists to produce commissioned artworks in both East and West Germany. Even after that time, artists' careers did not simply come to an end. For instance Carl/Charles Crodel, who had participated in the competition for the mural at the East Berlin House of Ministries in 1950 and had moved from Halle an der Saale to Munich in 1951, continued to work in both states. He collaborated with the Monument Preservation Office in Halle and, between 1950 and 1973, created stained glass windows for churches in Bernterode, Delitzsch, Erfurt, Halberstadt, Merseburg, Sangerhausen and Schmalkalden. However, he focused his stained glass artworks and exhibition activities on the artistic centres of West Berlin, Hamburg, Cologne and Frankfurt am Main. Another artist who worked both in the East and West was the metal sculptor Fritz Kühn (1910–1967), who was based in East Berlin and received prestigious state commissions from both German states until his death. In 1958, the Federal Republic of Germany invited him to exhibit alongside artists such as Bernhard Heiliger (1915–1995) and Fritz Koenig (1924–2017) at the German pavilion of the Expo in Brussels. Other commissions included works for the Lower Saxony State Parliament in Hanover (1962) and the State Council Building in East Berlin (1964). Waldemar Grzimek (1918–1984) taught in the West Berlin University of the Visual Arts between 1948 and 1952, but was fired for simultaneously working with the GDR Association of Visual Artists and exhibiting works with them. Between 1956 and 1961, Grzimek was Professor at the Weissensee Academy of Art in East Berlin. During that period, he produced art in architecture pieces for the animal testing facility on the island of Riems near Greifswald (1960) and the mural reliefs on the Kino International in East Berlin (1962) in collaboration with Hubert Schiefelbein and Karl-Heinz Schamal. In 1961, while attempting to cross the border between East and West Germany, Grzimek was deported to West Berlin and he ultimately decided against returning to the East, without however breaking his ties with sculptor colleagues in the GDR. He also remained a member of the GDR Academy and retained his official titles, as well as continuing to participate in exhibitions in East Germany. At the same time, his sculptures were presented at the 1964 *documenta III* in Kassel in the Federal Republic – also in public spaces.

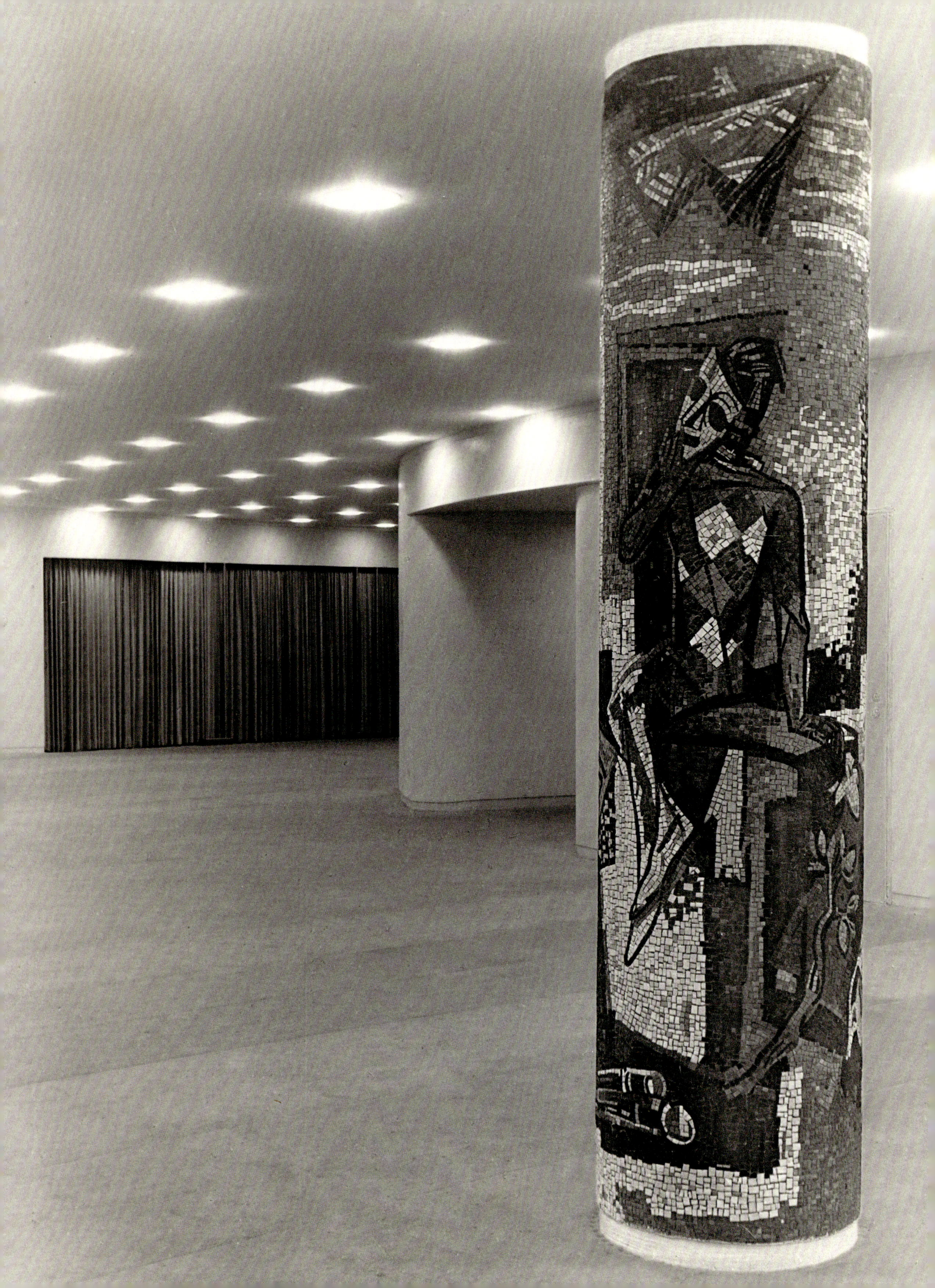

GERMAN NATIONAL THEATRE WEIMAR

Address:
Theaterplatz 2
99423 Weimar

Architecture:
Max Littmann, 1906–1908
Reconstruction:
Kurt Hemmerling and
Werner Harting, 1946–1948

Art in architecture:
Hermann Kirchberger
and Bruno Quass

The Neoclassicist new building of the Weimar Theatre was built according to plans by Max Littmann and opened in 1908. After World War I, it also served as a political stage: in 1918, the Weimar Republic was officially declared in the theatre and it was also the scene of the 1919 vote on the German National Assembly, which defined the constitution, as well as serving as the venue for the parliament's first sessions. When the building was reconstructed in a reserved, modern style after World War II, the architects Kurt Hemmerling and Werner Hartnig chose Hermann Kirchberger (1905–1983) and Bruno Quass (1904–1972) for its artistic decoration.

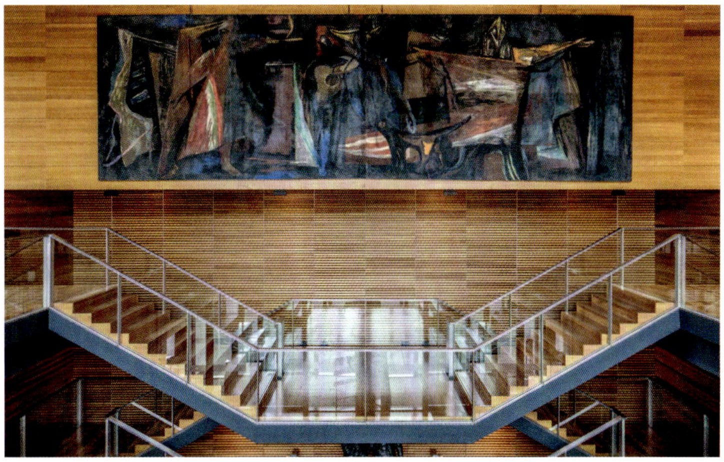

In 1948, Kirchberger produced a glass mosaic column for the main foyer, as well as a mural for the upper foyer. The architects considered the first version of the mural to be inappropriate for modern interior architecture, due to its depiction of an illusionistic space with theatrically presented stage figures, and therefore rejected it. They preferred an abstract style that was more in line with international artistic developments. In 1949, Kirchberger painted a second version on canvas, consisting of an almost Expressionist group of figures, their style, two-dimensionality and powerful outlines recalling paintings by Pablo Picasso. However, the Professor of Mural Art was publicly criticised by the College of Architecture and Fine Arts for his Weimar mural. The criticism referred to the style, which was branded as Formalist, decadent and impossible for the working public to decipher. As a result of the cultural-political campaign that eventually led to the mural's removal in 1950 (it remained in storage for decades), as well as the college's new ideological alignment, Kirchberger resigned from his professorship in 1951 and returned to West Berlin. The mural eventually found a new home in the Weimarhalle, where it has been presented since 2003.

HERMANN KIRCHBERGER
Untitled, 1949
Mosaic column
Mural (since 2003 in the Weimarhalle)

CENTRAL STATION MUNICH

Address:
Bayerstrasse 10a
80335 Munich

Architecture:
Federal Railway
Construction Authority, Munich
Reception hall opening in 1953

Art in architecture:
Rupprecht Geiger

The hallmark of the reception hall at Munich Central Station, which was demolished in 2019, had been the broadly projecting, sweeping flying roof that spanned the forecourt at the main entrance. The hall's glass façade ascended above it, its rhythm defined by vertical rods. To the right and left of the reception hall, functional administration buildings with grid façades were added, their top floors structured by aluminium slats. The design of the plate frieze, which won the art in architecture competition announced in 1950 and covered the entire length of the reception-hall façade and integrated the station clock, was conceived by the Munich architect and artist Rupprecht Geiger (1908–2009). His use of anodised aluminium plates in different shades of grey and blue picks up on the colours and materiality of the façade elements of the adjoining administrative buildings. The square, small-scale basic grid of the plate mosaic gained further dynamism through the diagonally running shifts in colours and asymmetrically positioned plates, making the lines distantly recall an Alpine landscape. Above all at night, the artwork revealed its spectacular effect, as the sweeping fluorescent lighting almost concealed the façade's vertical structure, playfully assuming the form of the flying roof.

As a founder-member of the "Zen 49" group, Geiger played a key role in repositioning art in post-war western Germany. The group of artists regarded abstract art as an appropriate response to the heroic, nationalist representations of art during the "Third Reich". In making his plate mosaic out of aluminium, a material that was still alien to art at the time, Geiger combined this stance with a clear proximity to architecture, since he not only trod new ground in terms of materials and colours, but also by using neon tubes, which had already became a symbol of urban life through advertising.

RUPPRECHT GEIGER
Untitled, 1953
Anodised aluminium plates,
fluorescent lighting tubes
6.5 x 30 m
(in storage until its reinstallation)

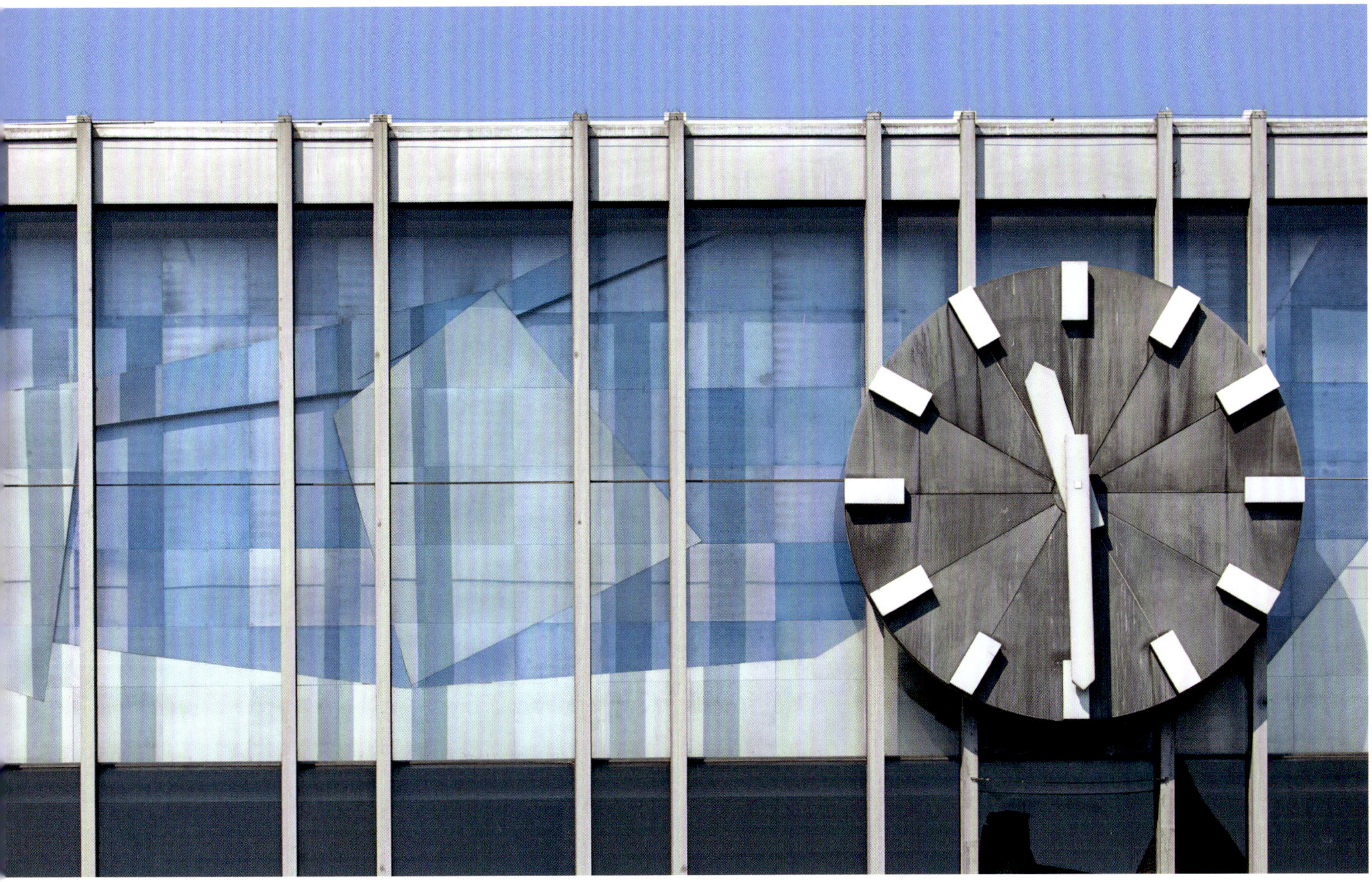

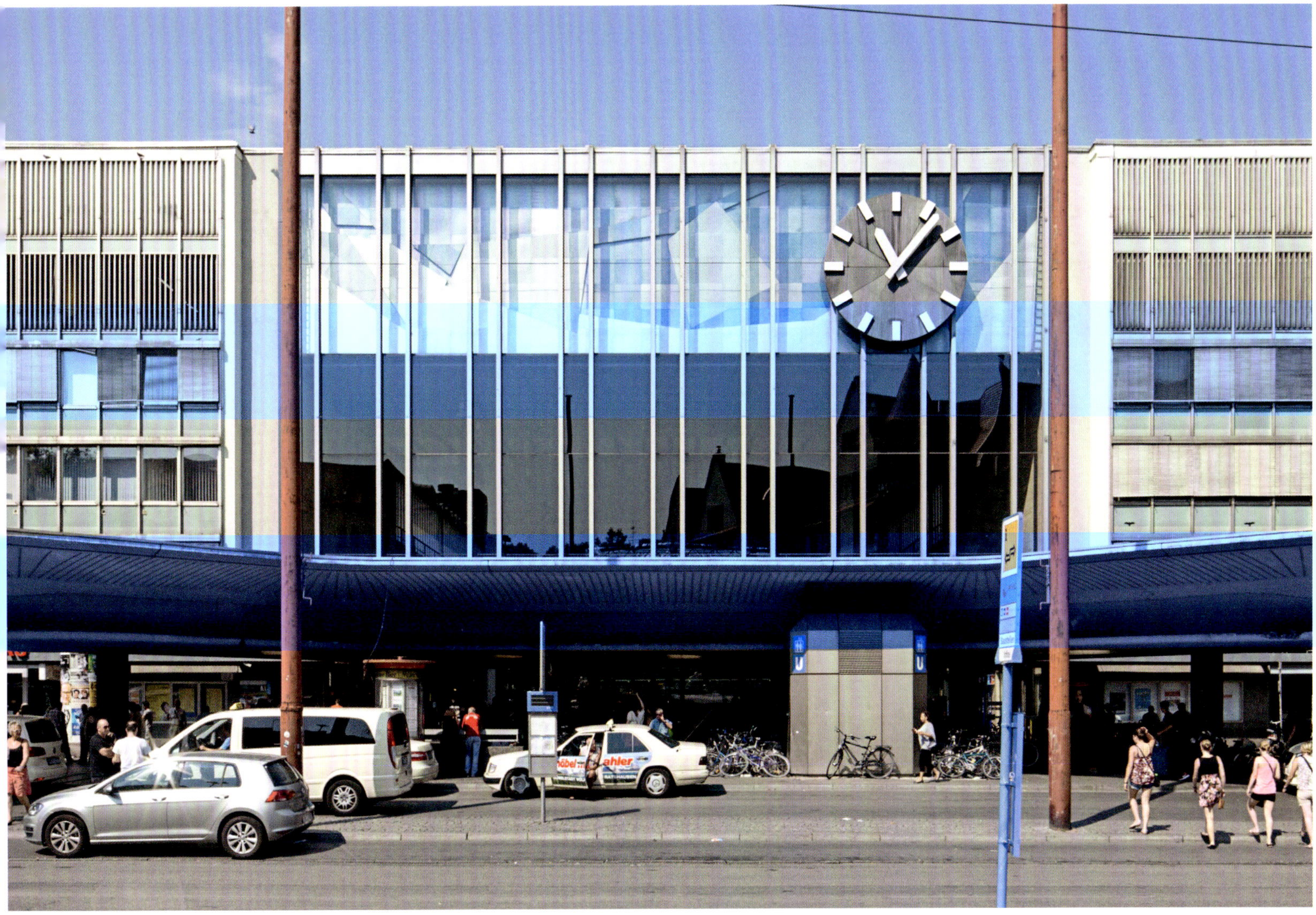

HOUSE OF MINISTRIES BERLIN

TODAY FEDERAL MINISTRY OF FINANCE

Address:
Wilhelmstrasse 97
10117 Berlin

Architecture:
Ernst Sagebiel, 1935/1936

Art in architecture:
Max Lingner

One of the most important commissioned works of the new GDR state was the mural entitled "Aufbau der Republik" ("Building the Republic", 1953), by Max Lingner (1888–1959) on the House of Ministries in Berlin. The seat of the GDR's government in the former Reich Aviation Ministry building required a symbolic transference of the ideologically burdened Nazi architecture, for which the area of the removed relief of a soldier by Arnold Waldschmidt (1873–1958) was suitable in the northern column hall. Lingner's design for the limited competition announced in 1950, which had the theme of "The importance of peace for the cultural development of humanity and the necessity to fight for it" had to be amended six times on the instructions of the Chairman of the State Council Walter Ulbricht and the Prime Minister Otto Grotewohl, in order to do justice to the intended political message. The intellectual at the centre of the first composition had to be replaced by workers and farmers as the driving

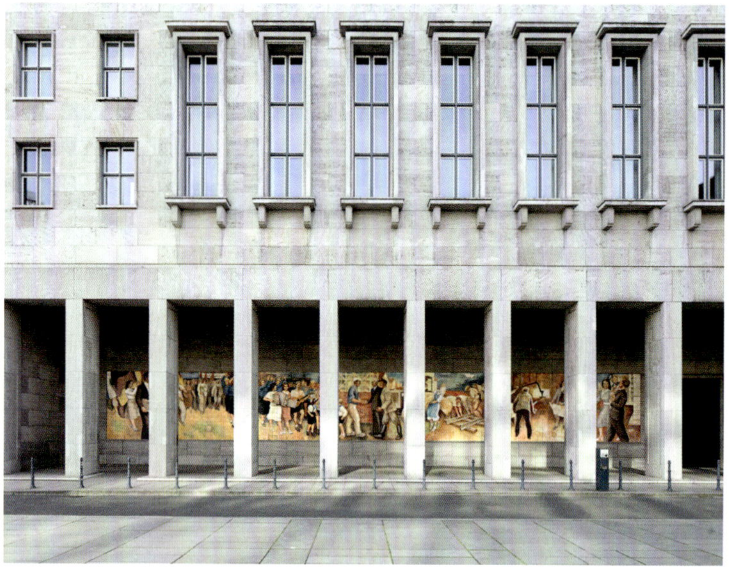

MAX LINGNER
"Aufbau der Republik"
("Building the Republic"), 1953
Meissen porcelain
3 x 24 m

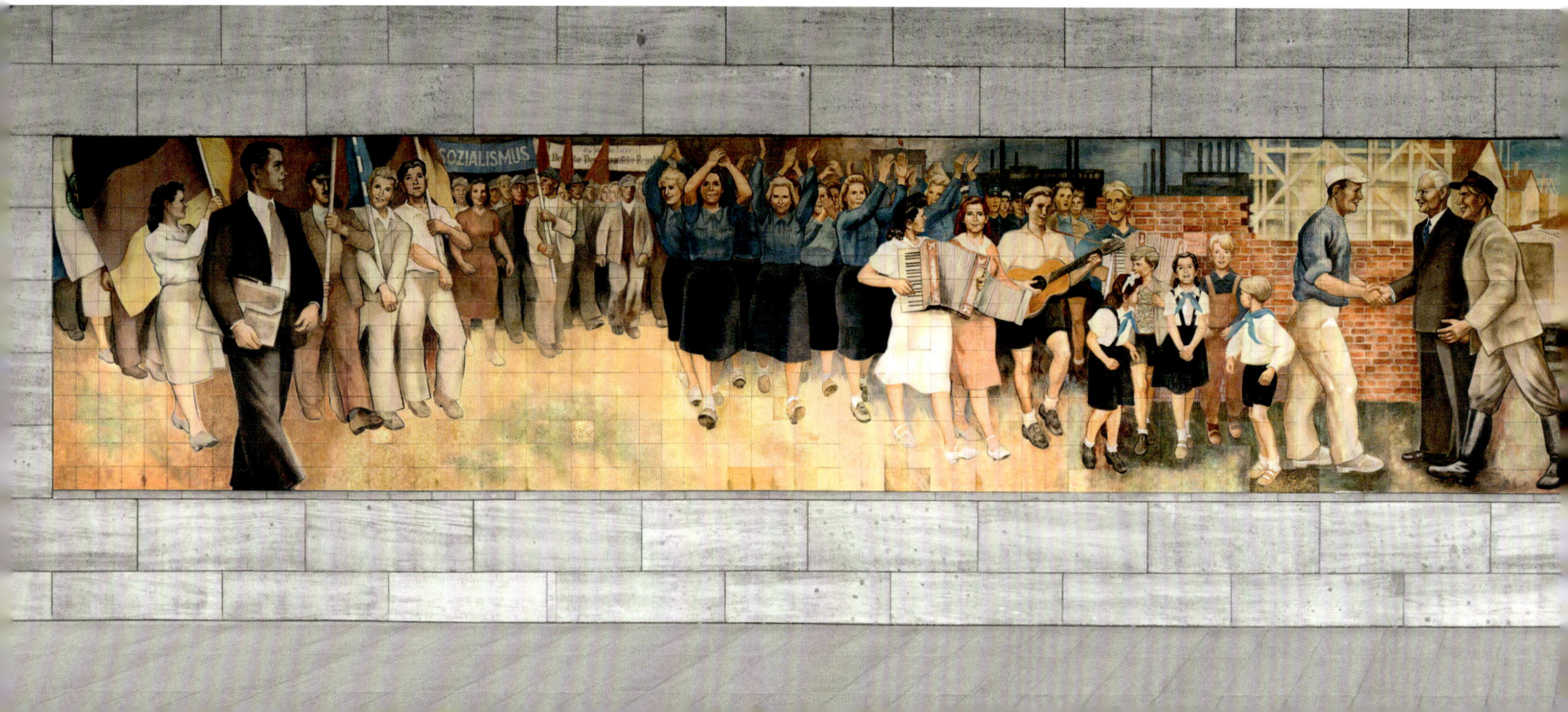

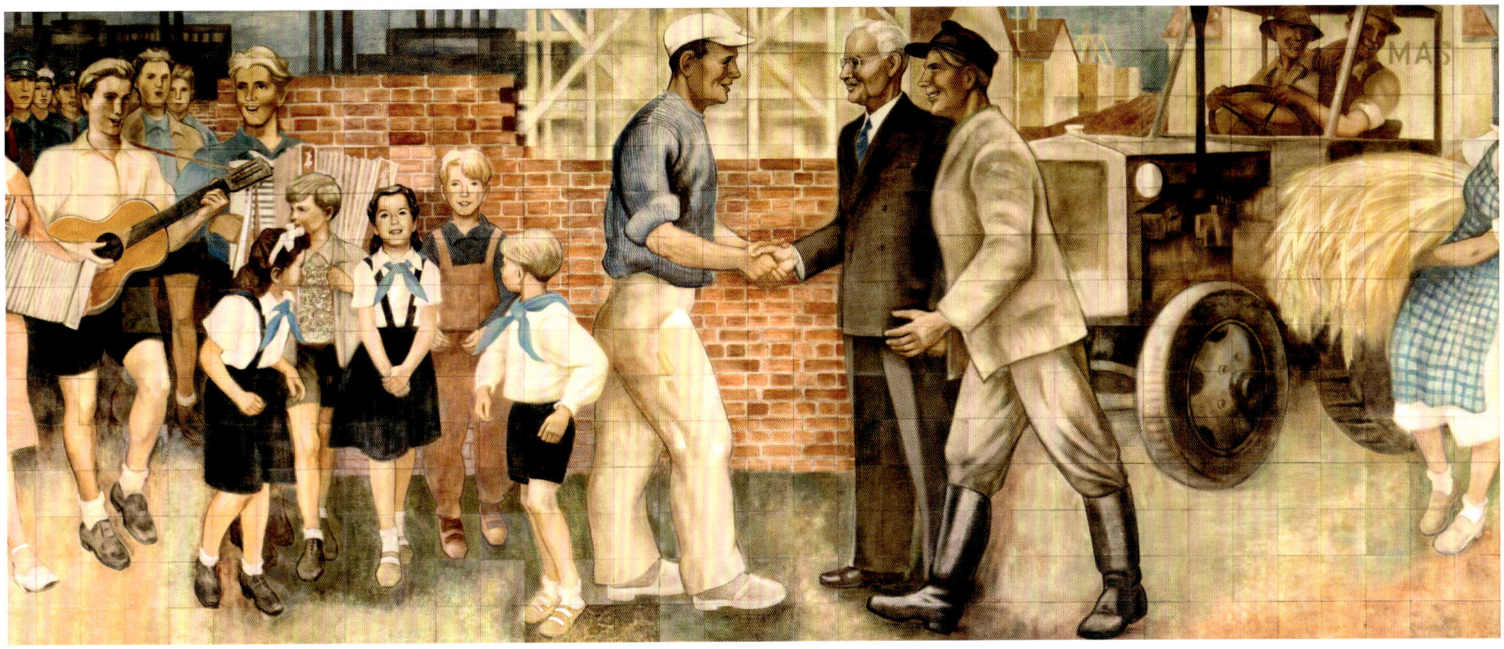

forces behind the development of Socialism. Furthermore, industry had to be presented more prominently and the participation of the entire population in advancing the peace process had to be evident, as represented by politically motivated groups of people, members of the working class, the agricultural class and the intelligentsia, as well as the happy family. The mural was made of Meissen porcelain tiles and provided an answer to the heroic Nazi "Soldier frieze" with a down-to-earth, easily grasped propaganda image in the style of politically mandated, idealised Realism.

After training to become a painter and graphic designer in Dresden, Lingner had initially developed his style in France during the 1930s, where he worked as a press illustrator and poster designer. Following his return from exile in 1949, the Free German Trade Union rewarded his left-wing political commitment with a major commission for the festive decoration of the 1950 May Festival, which later served as inspiration for the mural "Aufbau der Republik".

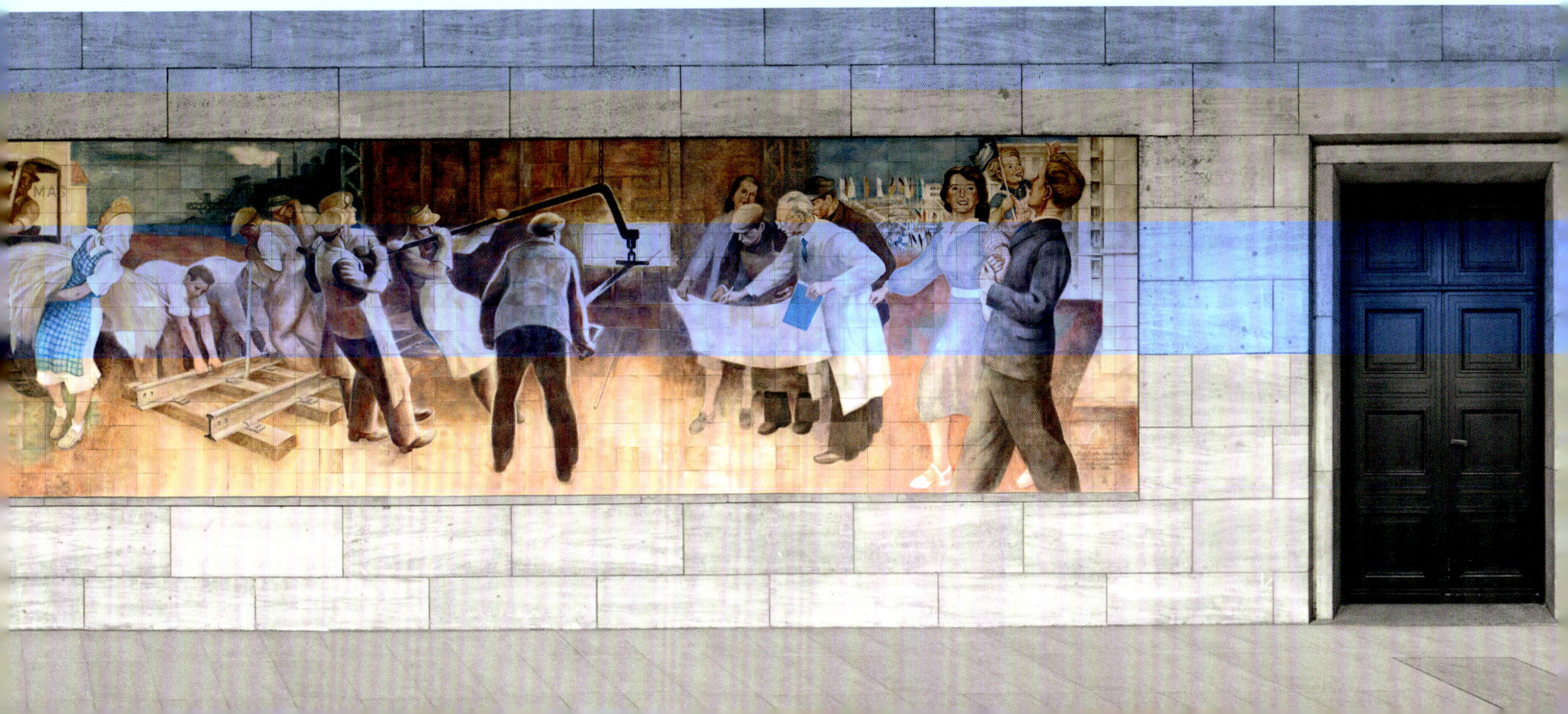

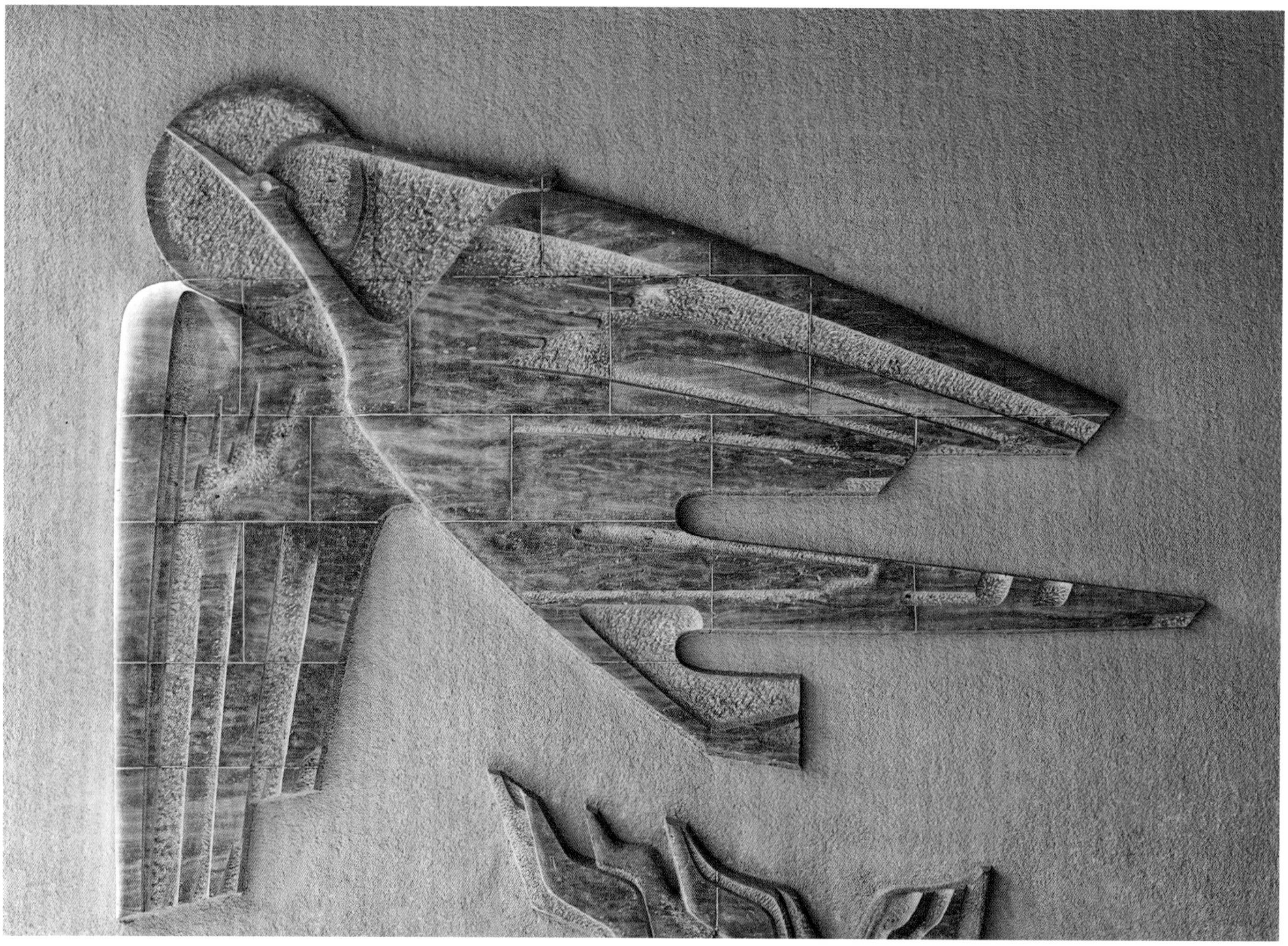

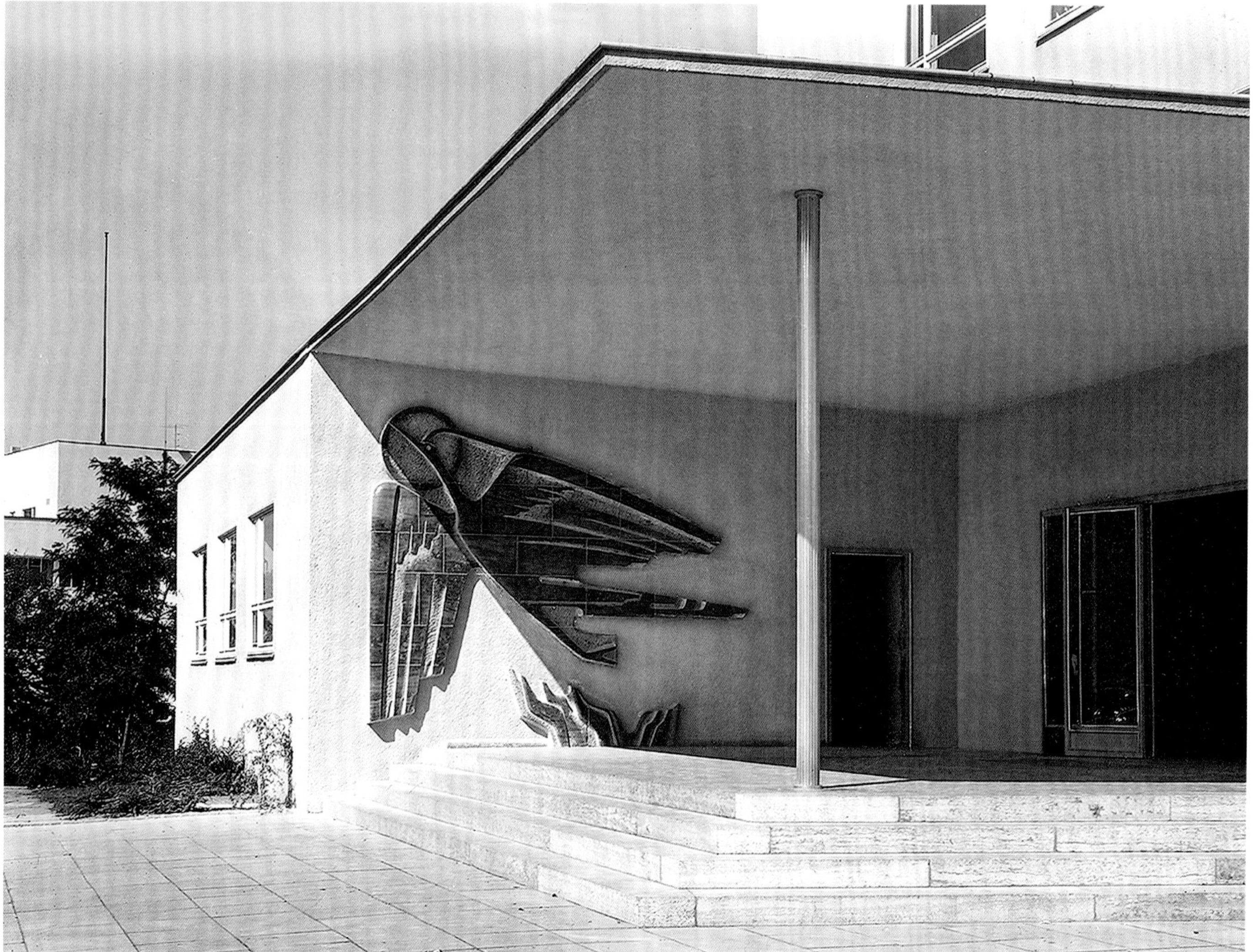

GERMAN BUNDESTAG BUNDESHAUS / PARLIAMENT BUILDING BONN

TODAY
SECRETARIAT OF THE UNITED NATIONS FRAMEWORK CONVENTION ON CLIMATE CHANGE (UNFCCC)

Address:
Hermann-Ehlers-Strasse 10
53113 Bonn

Architecture:
Martin Witte, 1930–1933
(Academy of Education)
Conversion:
Hans Schwippert,
Düsseldorf, 1948/1949
Extension:
Federal Building
Authority 1951/1952

Art in architecture:
Hannes Schulz-Tattenpach

In 1949, the Academy of Education, which was built in 1933 according to designs by Martin Witte in the style of New Objectivity, formed the core of the Bundeshaus complex after the decision to make Bonn the capital. It was converted to become the provisional seat of the Bundestag and the Bundesrat. Hans Schwippert added a connected assembly hall in 1949 and extended the building by two wings. Then in 1951, the Federal Building Authority added an intermediate wing, followed by a building for the parliamentary parties in 1952. During that building measure in 1952, the first open competition was organised for art in the prestigious entrance area. The design by Hannes Schulz-Tattenpach (1905–1953) was initially only selected for a purchase from among the 333 competition participants, since the jury criticised its elegant lines for being contradictory to the artistic seriousness of the task. However, the artwork eventually managed to impress with its modern, abstract figuration of an "Ascending Phoenix" and its symbolic content.

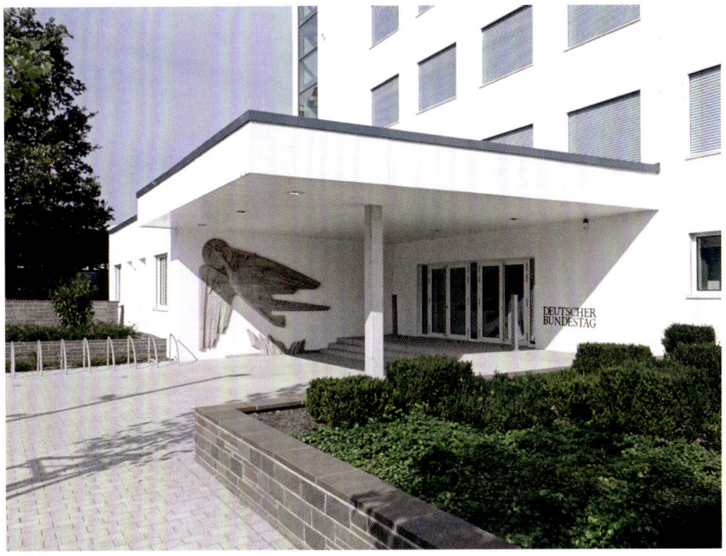

Since ancient times, the phoenix has been a symbol of transformation, change and resurrection, as it is first destroyed by fire before being reborn from its own ashes. In Christianity, the phoenix stands for the resurrection of Christ. The painter Schulz-Tattenpach was closely linked to the Catholic Church and had designed church windows in Berlin, Jüterbog, Leipzig and Rahnsdorf in the 1930s. The limestone relief on the Bundeshaus, with its elegantly sweeping representation of the bird in front of a solar disk, quickly acquired the status of a signet for the new Federal Republic, as it regained its strength and vitality after rising from the rubble of World War II.

HANNES SCHULZ-TATTENPACH
"Aufsteigender Phönix"
("Ascending Phoenix"), 1953
Limestone

FEDERAL STATISTICAL OFFICE WIESBADEN

Address:
Gustav-Stresemann-Ring 11
65189 Wiesbaden

Architecture:
Paul Schaeffer-Heyrothsberge, Oberfinanzdirektion Frankfurt, 1953–1966

Art in architecture:
Bernd Krimmel
and Fritz von Graevenitz, Werner Kump, Erwin Spuler

In 1948, the Federal Statistical Office was set up in the Bizone of the US and British occupation zones. Following the foundation of the Federal Republic of Germany in 1949, the new authority was transferred to the auspices of the Federal Government and, in 1950, it received the name by which it is known today. The 14-storey new building by Paul Schaeffer-Heyrothsberge, with its window bands and tiled balustrades in different blue tones, defines the urban image of Wiesbaden. The artists Werner Kump (1896–1989) and Erwin Spuler (1906–1964) were directly commissioned to produce the mural artwork, while Fritz von Graevenitz (1892–1959) was also directly contracted to create a major sculpture. The fourth artist, Bernd Krimmel (born in 1926), won the limited competition with his design for the elongated entrance hall.

The Darmstadt painter conceived a monumental mosaic mural with a total length of almost 20 metres. The large-scale, abstract composition was produced with alternating black natural stone and larger tiled wall surfaces, into which irregular small "image fields" made of stained glass were integrated at irregular intervals. The large areas recall letters of the alphabet or numbers, whereby a tilting effect makes either the black plates or the lighter wall surfaces come to the fore, as figures or the background. The surface gains additional dynamism through the freely spread coloured mosaic areas, their distribution and geometric development conforming to the zeitgeist of the times by highlighting the materials and emphasising their high quality. In addition to numerous art in architecture works for schools, kindergartens and children's clinics in the 1950s and early 1960s, Krimmel organised the 1955 exhibition "Kunst am Bau" at the Mathildenhöhe in Darmstadt in his capacity as Director of the Neue Darmstädter Sezession.

BERND KRIMMEL
Untitled, 1956
Natural stone tiles, stained glass
3.5 x 4.5 m and 3.5 x 15 m

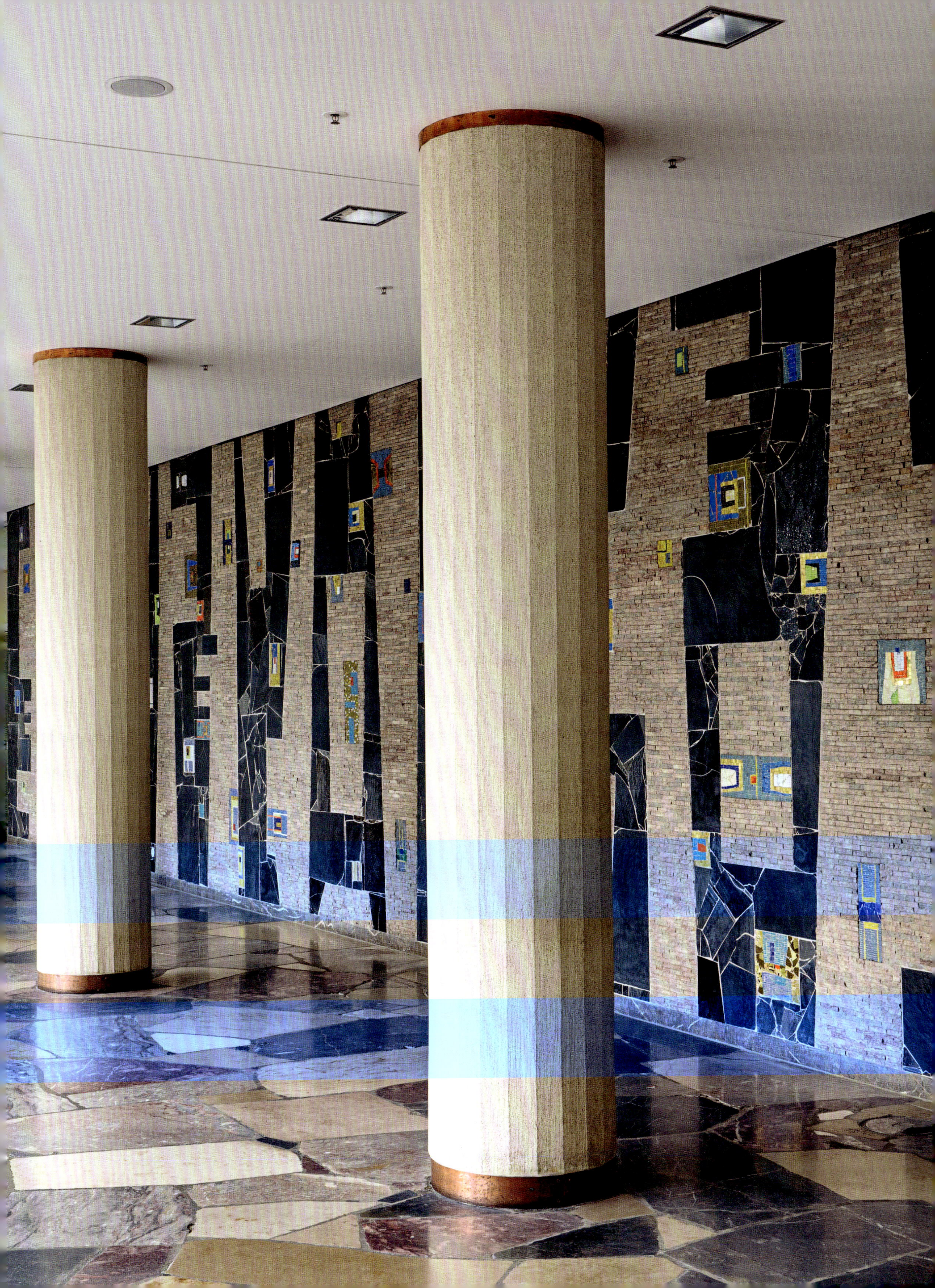

FEDERAL MINISTRY FOR POST AND TELE-COMMUNICATIONS BONN

TODAY BUNDESRECHNUNGSHOF

Address:
Adenauerallee 81–83
53113 Bonn

Architecture:
Josef Trimborn, 1953/1954

Art in architecture:
Hans Wimmer
and Charles Crodel,
Gerhard Marcks

The Federal Ministry for Post and Telecommunications, which is situated on the bank of the River Rhine in Bonn and was completed in 1954, was the first ministry building in the new capital. The architect Josef Trimborn designed it as a four-winged, self-enclosed complex on a square ground plan, with three or five floors. For the event hall projecting towards the Rhine, he used brickwork with bands of the locally typical basalt stone, while the main building is simply covered in white plaster.

Hans Wimmer (1907–1992) was commissioned on the architect's recommendation to design the Rhine-side façade of the event hall. Wimmer developed a group of sculptures entitled "Five Continents", which were mounted in 1957. They consist of five naturalistically reduced animal sculptures in bronze attached to metal struts. The animals symbolise the five continents: the bull stands for Europe, the eagle for America, the elephant for Asia, the lion for Africa and the kangaroo for Australia. In this respect, the work refers to the task of the Ministry for Post and Telecommunications, connecting Germany to the rest of the world through communication. The animals are enthroned high above, where they can be seen from afar despite their relatively small size, which seems fitting for the theme. The Munich-based sculptor, who produced many pieces for public spaces and is above all renowned for his animal depictions, participated in the *documenta I* and is among the most important representatives of post-war figurative art.

HANS WIMMER
"Fünf Erdteile"
("Five Continents"), 1957
Bronze
Each approx. 60 cm high

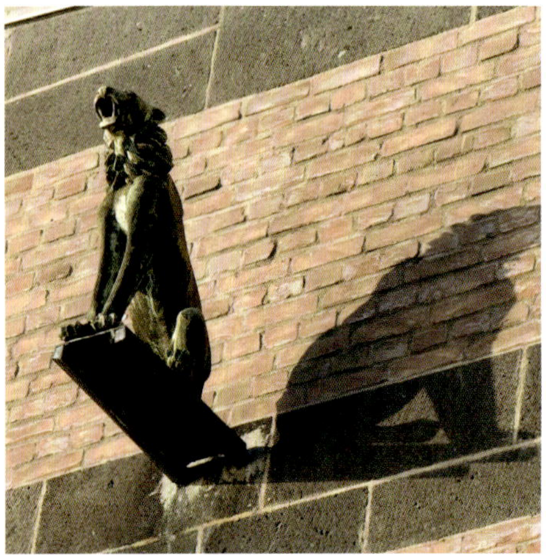

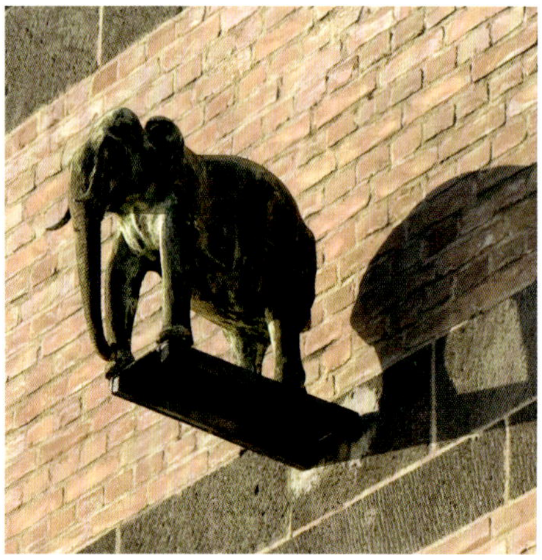

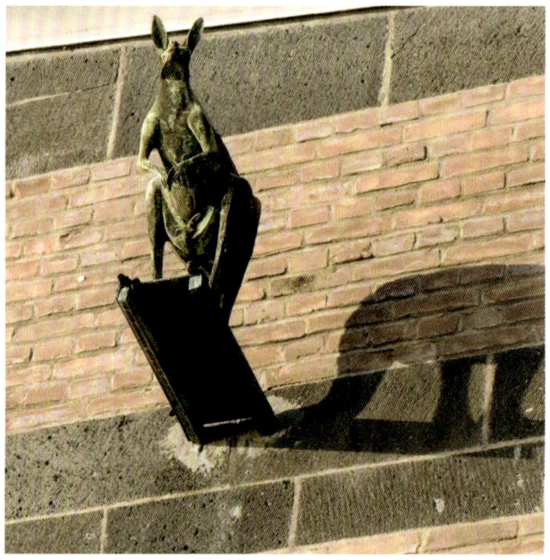

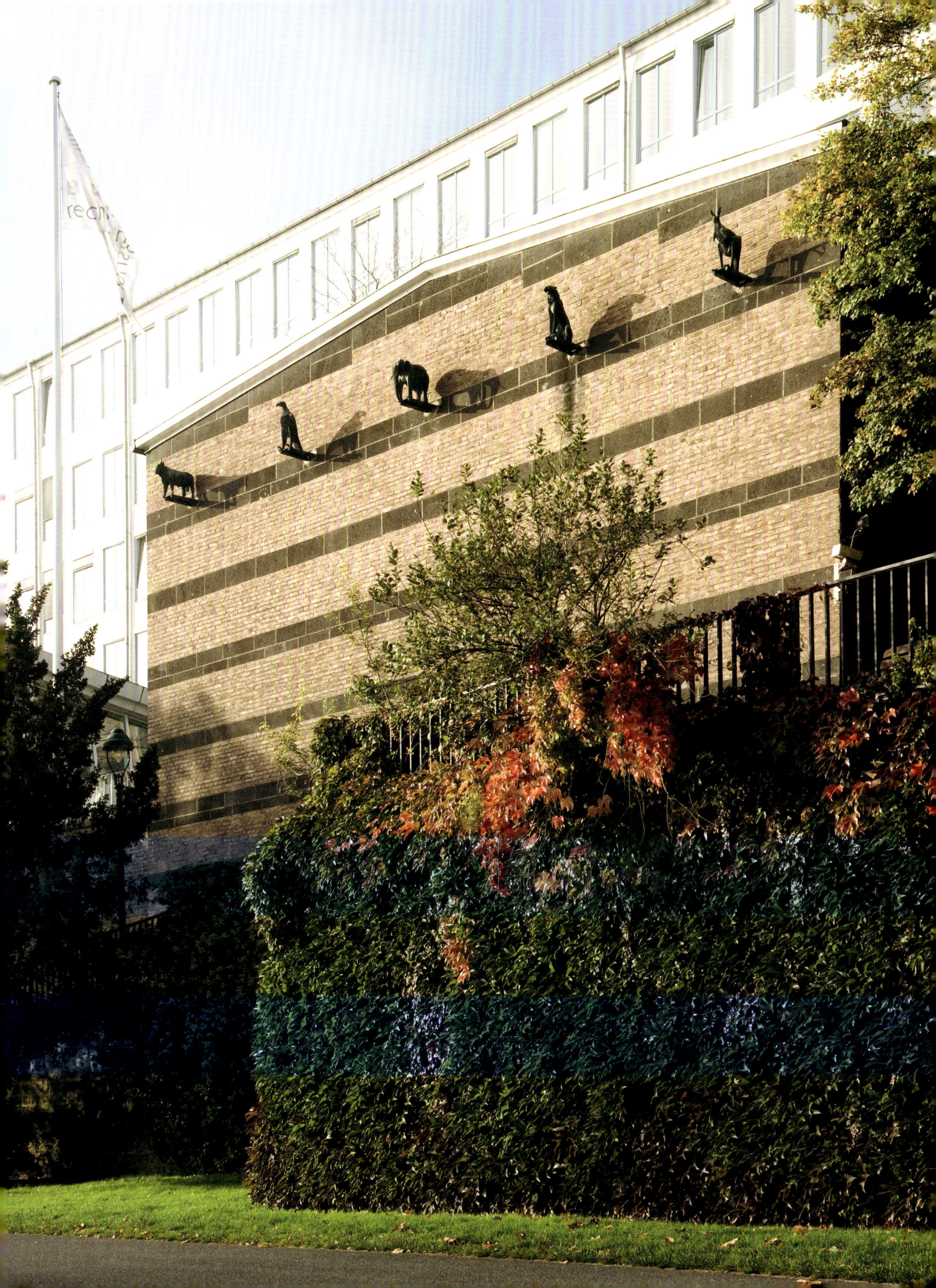

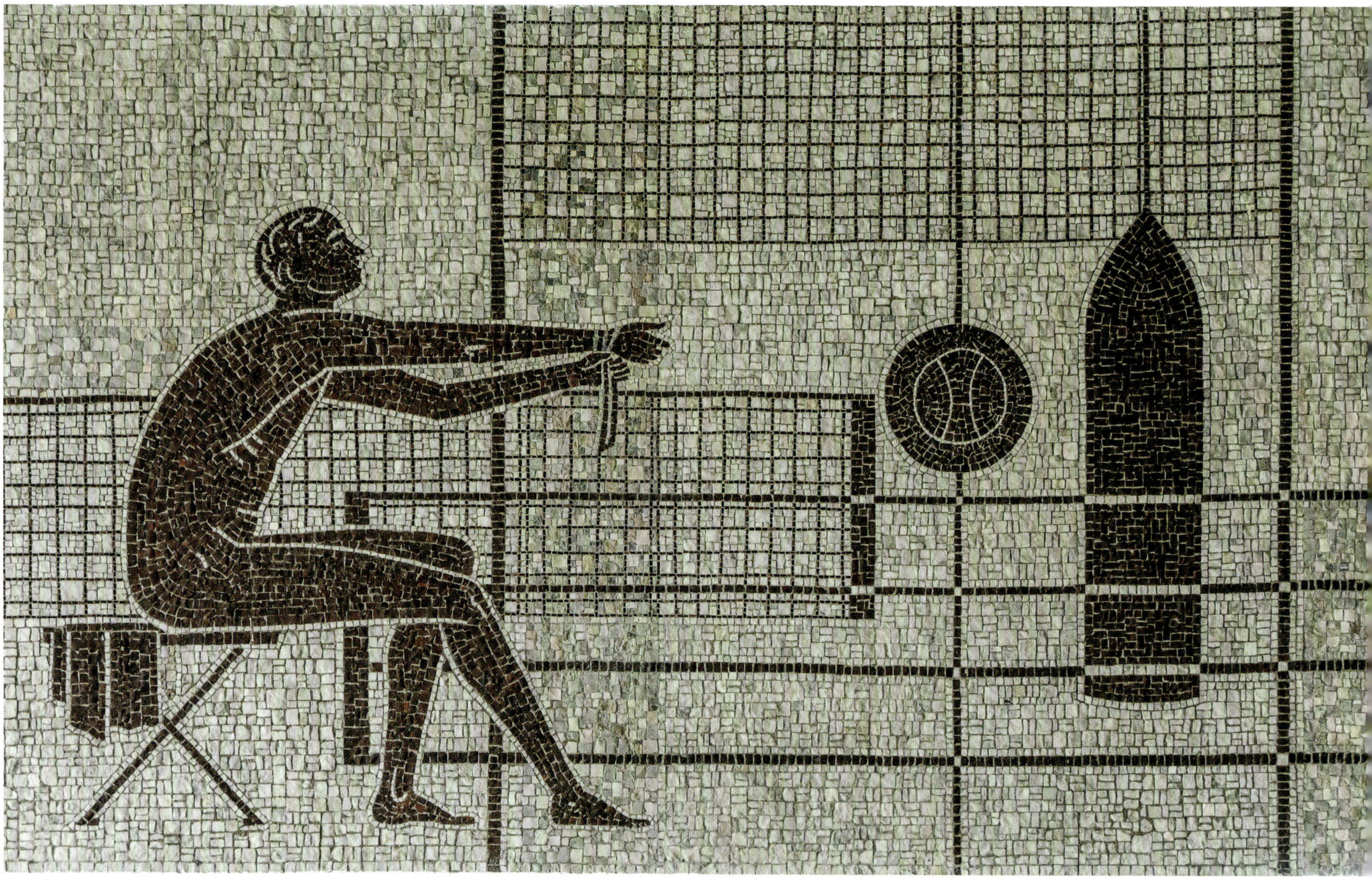

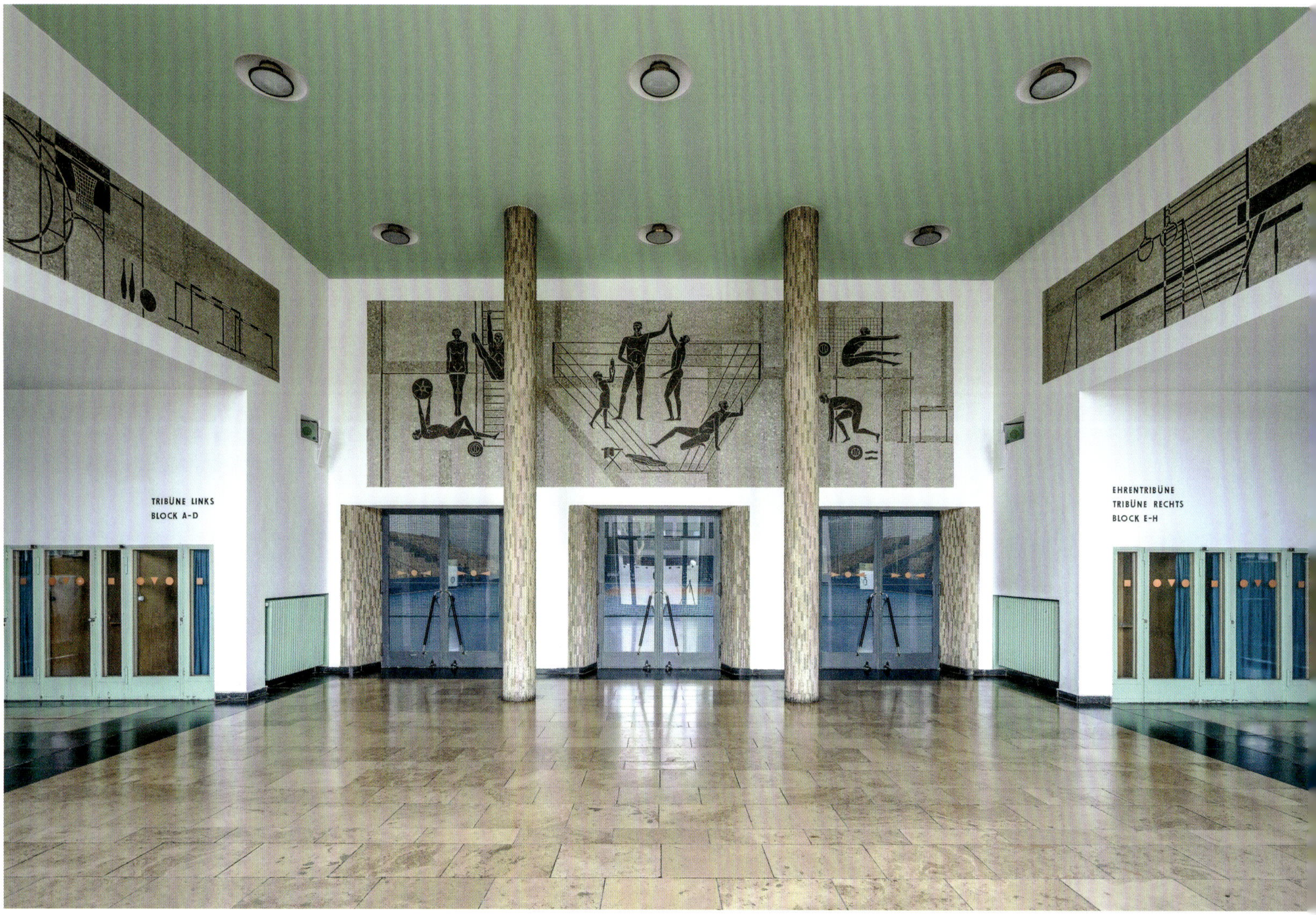
TRIBÜNE LINKS
BLOCK A-D
EHRENTRIBÜNE
TRIBÜNE RECHTS
BLOCK E-H

DYNAMO SPORTS HALL BERLIN

TODAY SPORTFORUM HOHENSCHÖNHAUSEN

Address:
Weissenseer Weg 53
13053 Berlin

Architecture:
Kollektiv W. Schmidt
& Scharlipp, 1955–1959

Art in architecture:
Wolfgang Frankenstein

Sport in the GDR was controlled and supported by the state, since the GDR tried to use exceptional results in high-performance sports to enhance its international reputation. The Sportforum in Berlin-Hohenschönhausen was one of its elite sports centres for training Olympic disciplines. The Ministry of the Interior and the Ministry of State Security were the official clients of the Dynamo Sports Hall construction project. It was inaugurated in 1958 in the presence of Erich Mielke and Walter Ulbricht. The painter Wolfgang Frankenstein (1918–2010) was commissioned to conceive the artistic decoration, having previously produced murals in the style of Socialist Realism in Hessenwinkel for barracks of the East Germany armed forces, for a "Jugendwerkhof" (youth re-education centre) and for the VEB Holzwerk timberworks in Berlin-Hohenschönhausen.

In 1959, Frankenstein produced several overdoor mosaics in a predominantly abstract style for the design of the entrance-hall. The representation of sporting activities, including gymnastics on the rings and vault, ball sports, the long jump and boxing, forgoes genre scenes and ornamental additions. The athletes and sports equipment are partially represented as stylised pictograms, while the colours are reduced to light and dark contrasts. The presentation lacks all pathos and educational content, instead referring solely to the function of the location. Together with the interior architecture, which reveals the stylistic influence of the Federal Republic in the mid-1950s, this represents an example of architecturally related art that attempts to connect with trends in international aesthetics.

WOLFGANG FRANKENSTEIN
Untitled, 1959
Natural stone mosaic

BUILDING FOR

BETWEEN PRESTIGE AND FREEDOM FROM 1961 TO 1989

THE STATE

When the Berlin Wall was built in 1961, a period of political consolidation began in both German states. After the closure of the border, the population in East Germany was to be permanently aligned towards the ruling system of the Socialist Unity Party (SED). To communicate this state ideology, thematic murals initially became politically expedient during the 1960s. In 1959, East Germany had originally decided to pursue what was known as the "Bitterfeld Way", a programme supporting an autonomous "Socialist national culture", but this was discarded again in 1965. As a result, architecturally related art became increasingly prevalent, since it still addressed the theme of class struggle, but gave the artists greater freedom in their formal development than had been possible with "realistic" depictions in the style of Socialist Realism. From 1972, the desired integration of urban planning, architecture and art in architecture as part of the national housing development programme led to the complete pervasion of art in all fields of life, including public spaces.

While the GDR developed a state-controlled planned economy, the social market economy was introduced in the Federal Republic. From the 1970s onwards, there was considerable building activity in Bonn and elsewhere to cover the growing spatial requirements of the federal ministries and the increasingly differentiated federal administrations, as well as nationally relevant institutions. This was combined with commissions for internationally renowned architects and artists, with whom the Federal Republic intended to demonstrate its desire for integration into the western world. Competition processes to select art in architecture also became more common. During this period, there was a trend towards integrating sculptural ensembles and ground sculptures in large designs for open spaces. These concepts focused less on implementing individual artworks than on the new idea of holistically shaping the surroundings. The Plenarsaal ("Plenary Hall", 1986–1992), which was built according to plans by Günter Behnisch, represented the conclusion of construction work for the German Bundestag in Bonn.

BUILDING FOR THE STATE

Constanze von Marlin, Anna-Sophie Laug

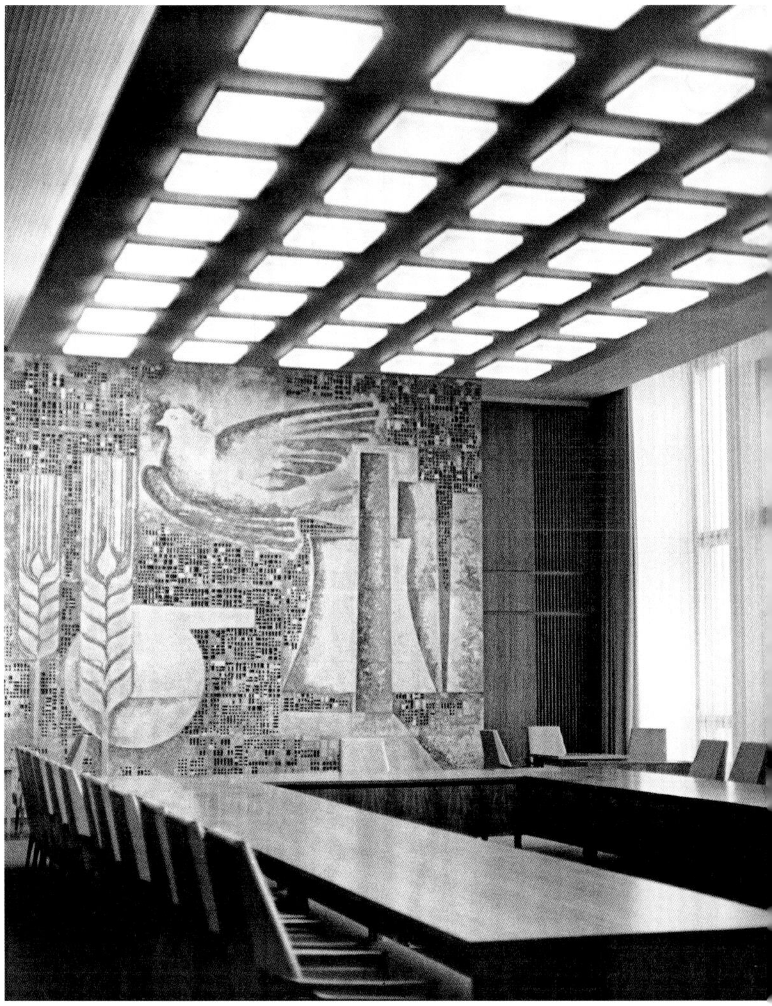

Fritz Kühn, "Die Wirtschaft der DDR unter dem Zeichen des Friedens", 1964, Staatsrat building, Berlin

In the 1960s, the different structures of the East and West German state systems influenced the building tasks and architectural styles on both sides of the border. The transformation in the building policy of the GDR was combined with the Moscow-induced industrialisation of the building sector. This meant an end to the doctrine of Stalinist Neohistoricism, of which the Stalinallee housing development in East Berlin is a prime example. It was replaced by a dedication to more functional post-war Modernity, which was also applied to new buildings for the GDR government. A year after the Berlin Wall was built, the Staatsratsgebäude ("State Council Building", 1962–1964) represented the first new GDR government building in the historical centre of the capital Berlin. By contrast, major new construction projects were not discussed in the Federal Republic until the mid-1960s due to the decision in 1949 to make Bonn only the provisional seat of parliament and government. To be prepared for the desired reunification of Germany and a move to Berlin as the capital of the Federal Republic, building work was interrupted in Bonn in 1956 and only resumed in 1966 with the new construction of the high-rise representatives' house known as the "Langer Eugen". It was followed by a wide range of new buildings for federal ministries, including the so-called "Kreuzbauten" ("Cruciform Buildings") and the Federal Chancellery in Bonn. Due to the federal structure of West Germany, federal authorities were established throughout the country, including the Federal Constitutional Court in Karlsruhe and the Federal Labour Office in Nuremberg.

BETWEEN THE PAST AND THE FUTURE: THE SYMBOLISM OF THE HISTORICAL

In 1955, the Bundestag decided to completely reconstruct the Reichstag building in West Berlin, although the way it should be used in a divided Germany was uncertain. However, restoring the historical building also symbolically demonstrated the claim to the old centre of government and stressed the fact that all options were being kept open. In 1961, following a limited competition, the architect Paul Baumgarten was commissioned to plan and supervise the reconstruction, which was concluded in 1973. Three of the most important German post-war sculptors, Bernhard Heiliger (1915–1995), Hans Uhlmann (1900–1975) and Karl Hartung (1908–1967), who had participated in the *documenta II* and had already contributed art in architecture to the German embassies in Paris and Washington, as well as exhibiting at the 1958 Expo in Brussels, were commissioned to produce artworks for the Reichstag building.

In the GDR as well, fundamental political decisions had a direct influence on building tasks. In 1960, the death of the first and only President of the GDR, Wilhelm Pieck, led to the foundation of the Staatsrat (GDR State Council) as the officially highest state body. This further aligned the GDR's state structure towards the Soviet role model. In 1964, to underline the importance of the new government body, the Staatsrat moved from its first headquarters at Schloss Niederschönhausen to an architecturally programmatic new building at Marx-Engels-Platz 1, in the historical centre of Berlin. Built between 1962 and 1964 in the style of "Ostmoderne" by the architectural collective led by Roland Korn and Hans-Erich Bogatzky, the new Staatsrat building, which now houses the European School of Management and Technology, was the first new government building in East Berlin since the end of World War II. The façade cladding with high, rectangular banner-like fields of red granite was intended as a reference to the red flag, the political symbol of identification with the Socialist and Communist movements. Its highly symbolic features also included the installation of a historical portal from the Berlin Palace, which had been demolished in 1950, commemorating Karl Liebknecht's declaration of a Socialist Republic on November 9, 1918. The selection of the art in architecture for the building was also highly programmatic. In the foyer, a building-high, coloured glass window was installed with scenes "Aus der Geschichte der deutsche Arbeiterbewegung" ("From the history of the German workers' movement") by Walter Womacka (1925–2010) (→ p. 102), presenting a positive picture of the living conditions in the GDR and the SED leadership, while creating a thematic bridge to the palace portal with portraits of Karl Liebknecht and Rosa Luxemburg. Dedicated to Socialist Realism, Womacka was a leading artist in the field of art in architecture in the GDR. In the 1960s alone, he produced several large-scale murals, including pieces for the Haus des Lehrers (1961–1964) (→ p. 196), the GDR Ministry for Foreign Affairs (1964–1967) and the Ministry for Building (1968).

The rich decoration of the Staatsrat building also includes the mural frieze "Das Leben in der DDR" ("Life in the GDR") by Günther Brendel (born in 1930), which is made of

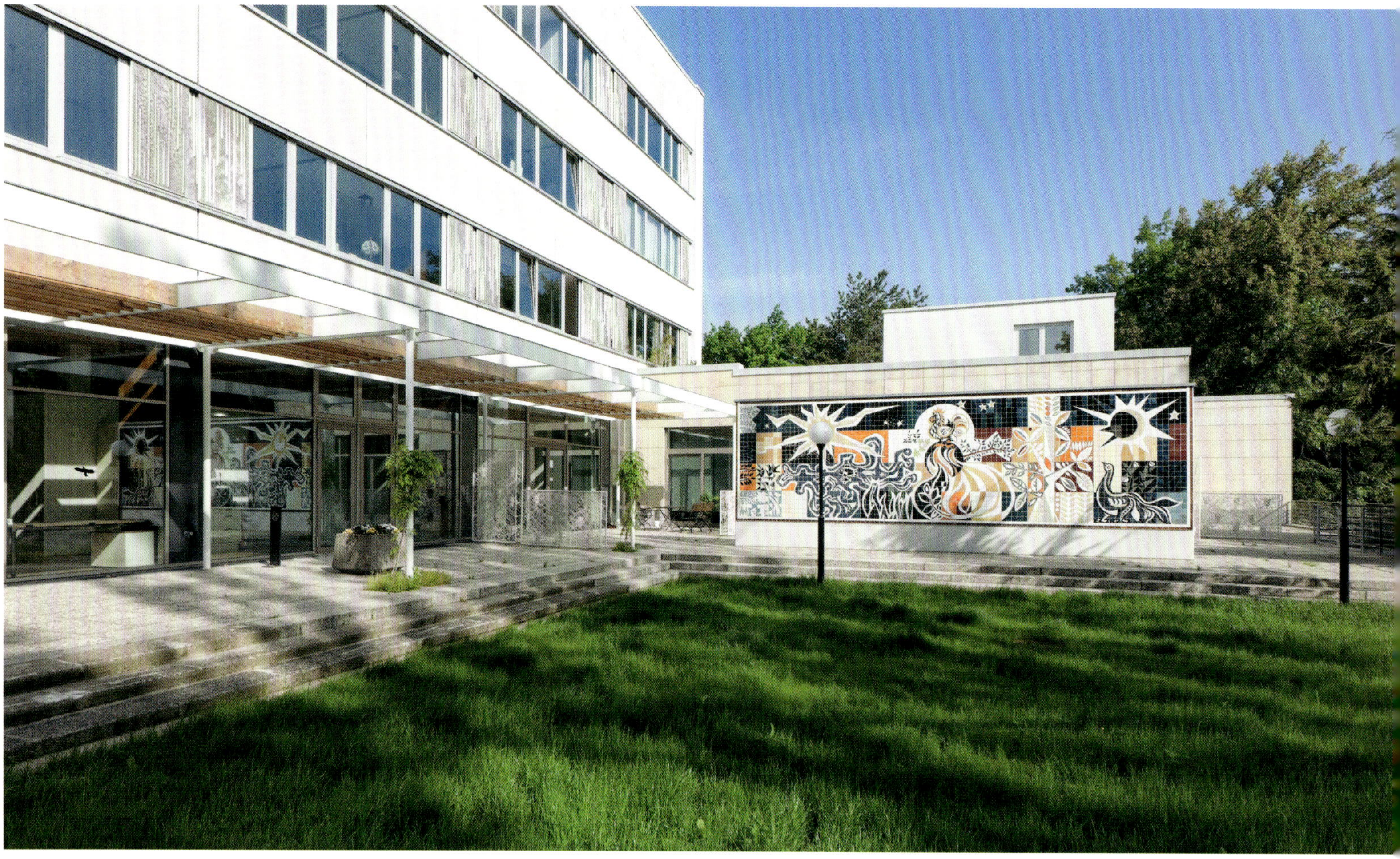

Meissen porcelain and located in the banquet hall, as well as "Die Wirtschaft der DDR unter dem Zeichen des Friedens" ("The economy of the GDR under the sign of peace") by Fritz Kühn (1910–1967), which was installed in the meeting room. The same artist also produced the metal work for the doors of the diplomats' hall, the heating cladding and the banisters in the staircase hall. The East Berlin-based metal artist and sculptor was one of the few visual artists of his time who was highly regarded and received state commissions in both German states. In the 1960s, the SED reformulated its German policy, encouraging selected visual artists to use their contacts with the West. By contrast, it became very difficult or indeed illegal for other artists in the GDR to engage in such exchange.

When the Staatsrat moved out of the building, the Baroque palace in the Berlin district of Niederschönhausen was converted into the GDR government's house for guests of state. To accommodate the ministers, employees and visitors' staff, an apartment building was constructed in the western part of the palace park between 1966 and 1968. The architecture of this guest accommodation, which was built according to plans by Walter Schmidt, is orientated towards the principles of the International Style. The façade above the basement level, which is clad in dark slate, radiates in white, while the windows are framed together in a band using darker aluminium panels produced by the workshop of Fritz Kühn. The horizontal structure of the façade is interrupted by the vertical aperture of the staircase window, with a stained glass design by Walter Womacka, who also produced the mural mosaic "Erde, Feuer, Wasser, Luft" ("Earth, fire, water, air") in the garden and the supraporte "Tauben und Weltkugel" ("Doves and globe") above the entrance doors.

Walter Womacka, “Erde, Feuer, Wasser, Luft”, 1967/1968, GDR house for guests of state, Berlin

Bert Heller, “Friedensfries”, around 1964-1970, GDR Ministry for Foreign Affairs, Berlin

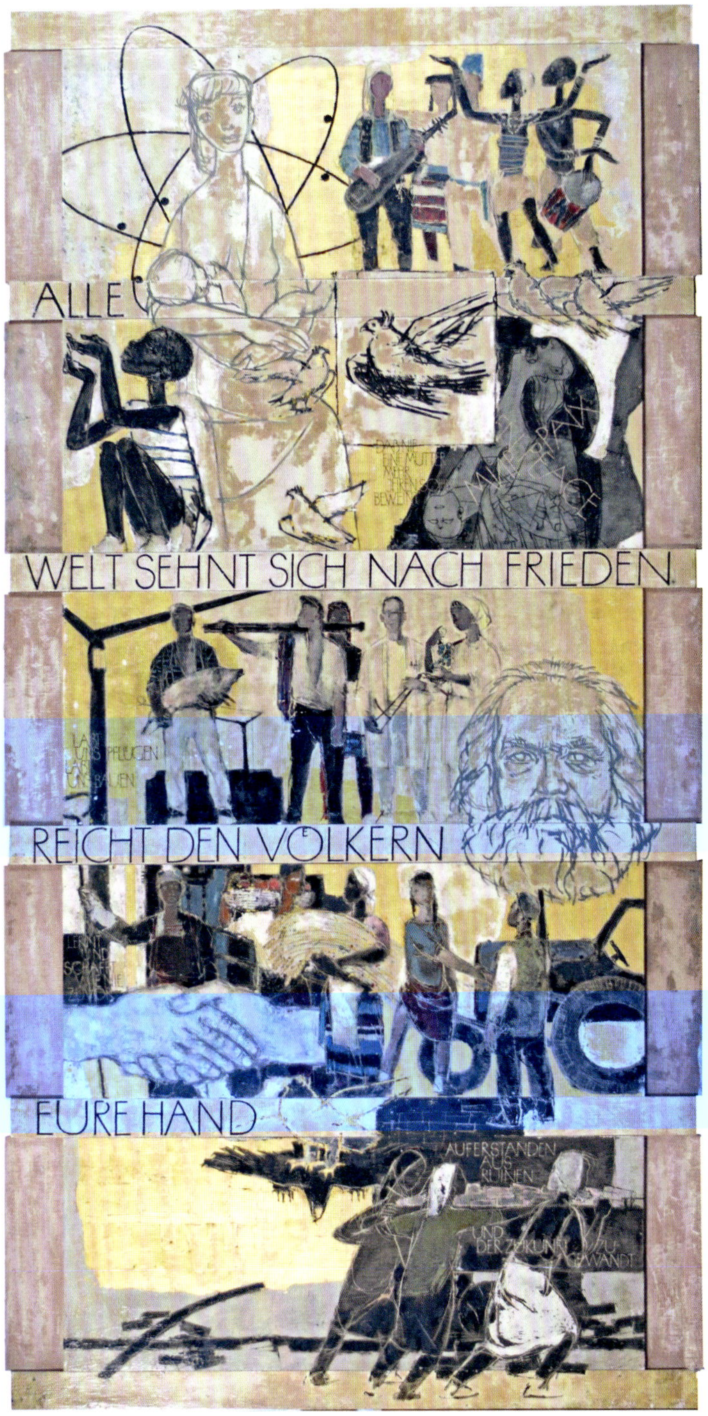

Between 1964 and 1967, a prestigious high-rise building was constructed for the GDR Ministry for Foreign Affairs, which had been founded in 1949, in the direct vicinity of the Staatsrat building. The 145-metre long and 44-metre high new building designed by Josef Kaiser’s architectural collective had a curtain wall above a recessed ground floor that consisted of white lightweight metal elements with a pilaster-strip structure that achieved a strongly sculptural effect. The façade was perforated on the second floor by two ornamental bands. The rich architecturally related features included three large-scale murals by Walter Womacka, as well as a visual frieze for the White Salon, the reception room on the ministerial level, produced by Bert Heller (1912–1970). The second verse of the GDR’s national anthem provided the thematic motif for the artwork. Heller produced a wide-ranging visual programme for the words “All the world yearns for freedom. Reach your hand out to the peoples”, including a portrait of Karl Marx, a symbolic handshake representing the merger of the KPD and the SPD, a visual reference to the dove of peace by Pablo Picasso, as well as people of various nationalities. The artistic strength of the artwork lies in its emphasis on the sketch-like quality of the painting. Heller almost compiled the visual elements like a comic and structured the narrative with bands of text, inserting additional words to individual drawings, as well as Latin, English and Russian translations of the word “peace”. In doing so, Heller served the peace propaganda of the GDR, its “peaceful” foreign policy going hand in hand with promotion of the state’s antifascist character.

INCREASED SPATIAL REQUIREMENTS IN BONN

As the partition of Germany deepened following the construction of the Berlin Wall in 1961, there was an increasing will in West Germany to expand the Bonn government district. Thus in 1962, the President of the Bundestag, Eugen Gerstenmaier, established a planning committee that was to work together with the Federal Building Authority in developing proposals to reorganise the government district. One result of that work was the idea of building a high-rise block for all the required offices of the members of parliament, including meeting rooms. Following tense political wrangling over the building plans, the thirty-storey building was ready for use by 1969.

This first high-rise building on the banks of the Rhine was known as the "Langer Eugen", representing a further visible sign of the new self-confidence of the young democracy. The internationally renowned architect Egon Eiermann, who stood for International-Style Modernity, was commissioned with the design. The art in architecture concept for the parliamentarians' tower was to commission avant-garde art by renowned German artists, reflecting the desire to express West Germany's membership of the community of democratic states. Twelve direct art in architecture commissions were awarded as a result of the design concept developed by Eiermann, in collaboration with the Federal Building Authority, namely to Angelika Baasner-Matussek (born in 1941) (→ p. 104), Alexander Camaro (1901–1992), HAP Grieshaber (1909–1981), Hans Kaiser (1914–1982), Fritz Koenig (1924–2017), Norbert Kricke (1922–1984), Georg Meistermann (1911–1990), Günter Ferdinand Ris (1928–2005), Lothar Schall (1924–1996), Emil Schumacher (1912–1999),

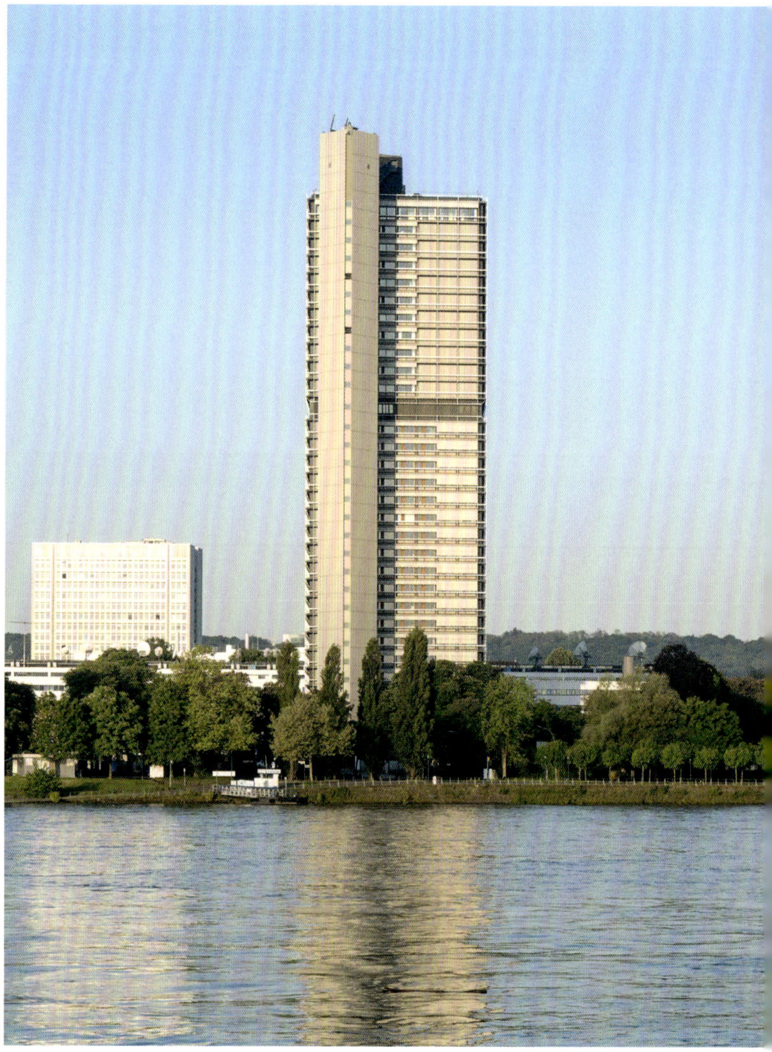

German Bundestag, "Langer Eugen" parliamentarians' tower, Bonn

HAP Grieshaber, "Weltgericht (Inferno des Krieges)", 1970, parliamentarians' tower, Bonn, closed panels

HAP Grieshaber, "Weltgericht (Inferno des Krieges)", 1970, parliamentarians' tower, Bonn, open panels

Woty Werner, untitled, 1971, parliamentarians' tower, Bonn

Günther Uecker, untitled, 1970, parliamentarians' tower, Bonn

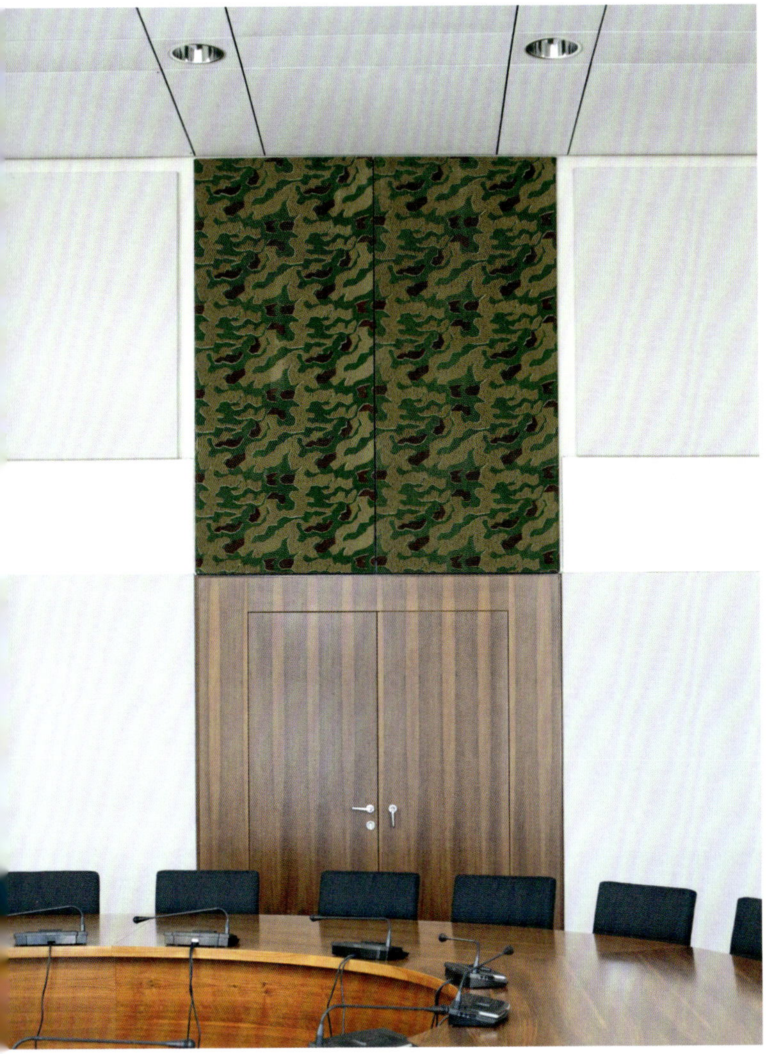
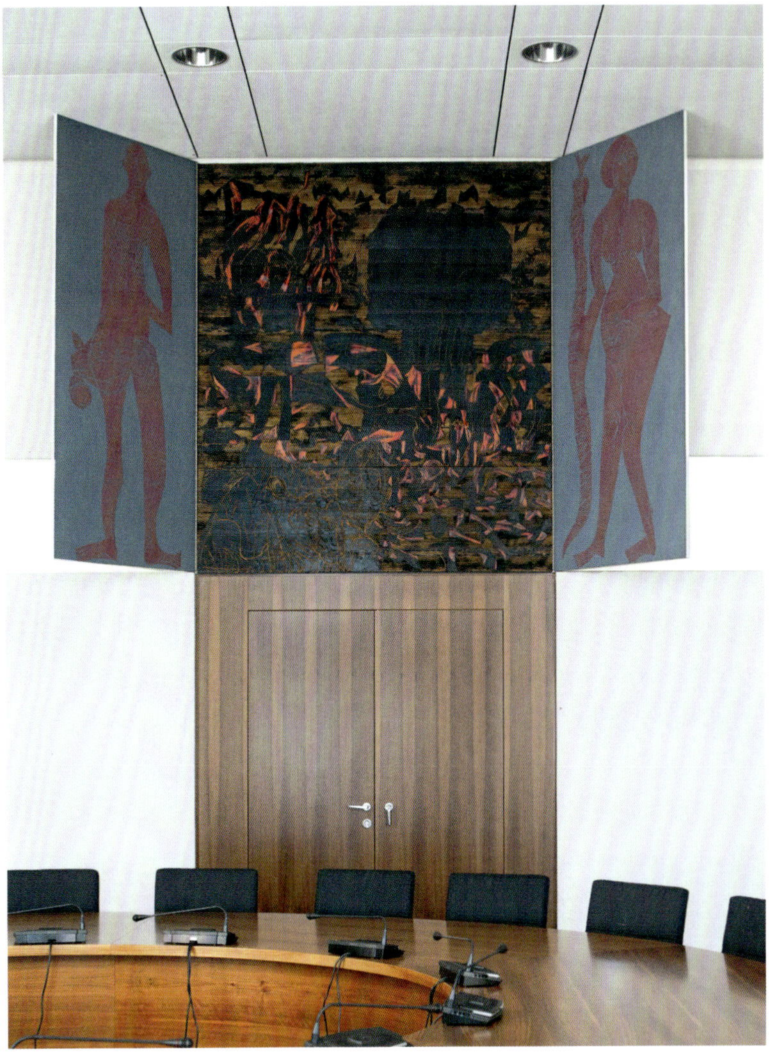
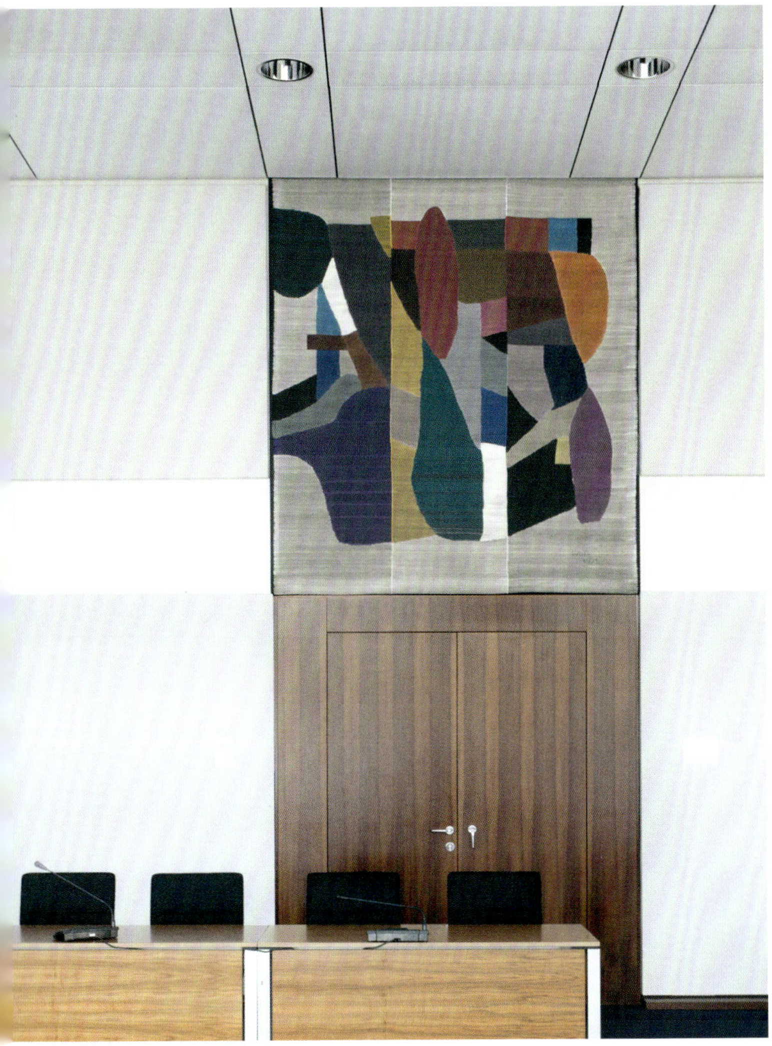
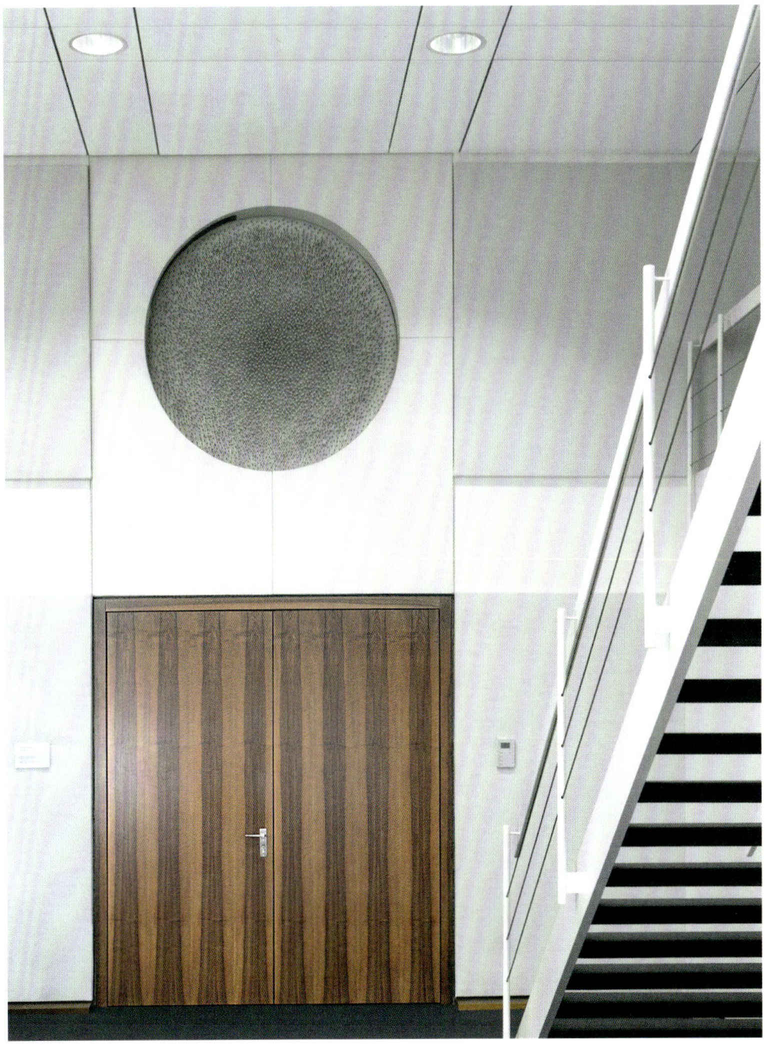

Günther Uecker (born in 1930) and Woty Werner (1903–1971), for the design of the supraportes, meeting rooms, foyers and common rooms. Apart from Baasner-Matussek and Schall, all selected artists had taken part in one of the three first *documenta* exhibitions in 1955, 1959 or 1964. For the "Langer Eugen", they produced art in architecture that was dedicated to all contemporary artistic movements, such as informal, concrete and kinetic art, as well as op art, thereby further opening art in architecture practice to new artistic forms of expression.

While the parliamentarians' building by Eiermann was being constructed, plans were also developed for a new ministerial district between Bonn and Bad Godesberg to provide new buildings for the federal authorities, which were rapidly growing and still accommodated in provisional quarters. Urban-planning competitions for ideas, building competitions and parliamentary committees produced numerous urban-planning designs in Bonn by the end of the decade, on both sides of the Rhine.

One result was the development of cruciform buildings, the "Kreuzbauten" (1969–1973), by the Stieldorf planning group. However, only two of the planned buildings, with eleven and fourteen storeys respectively, were ultimately constructed on a broad green area. In 1973, the Federal Ministry of Justice and the Federal Ministry of Research and Technology moved into the high-rise buildings with their characteristic cruciform floor plans and façades made of tinted glazing, as well as continuous balconies and concrete staircases. An extensive art in architecture concept was already developed during the planning stage, resulting in around thirty artworks being installed in the exterior grounds and inner courtyards. The pieces were selected through limited competitions or commissioned directly. They include abstract sculptures with figurative echoes such as those by Rolf Szymanski (1928–2013) and the artist couple Brigitte Matschinsky-Denninghoff (1923–2011) and Martin Matschinsky (1921–2020), concrete-constructive sculpture such as the works by Victor Bonato (1934–2019) and Ansgar Nierhoff (1941–2010) (→ p. 112), as well as the "Pavillon der Elemente" ("Pavilion of the Elements") by the artist group Haus-Rucker Co (founded in 1967 by Laurids Ortner, Günter Zamp Kelp and Klaus Pinter, disbanded in 1992), which was intended as an entrance gate. The artistic interventions structure the expansive open space and, in their entirety, constitute an open-air museum of important artistic positions of the time.

Aside from the measures in the new capital Bonn, new authority buildings were being constructed and others expanded throughout the republic during the 1960s and 1970s, since important federal institutions were established such as the Federal Labour Office in Nuremberg (→ p. 200), the Deutsche Wetterdienst (German Weather Service) in Offenbach, the Federal Archives in Koblenz and the Federal Motor Transport Authority in Flensburg. The same applied to the Federal Constitutional Court, which had been founded in 1951, for which a new building was constructed between 1965 and 1969 by the State Civil Engineering Authority according to plans by the West Berlin architect Paul Baumgarten, since the Prinz-Max-Palais in Karlsruhe no longer provided sufficient space to operate efficiently. Instead of focusing the building's mass on a single major volume, Baumgarten distributed it over five pavilions that he structured through enveloping window bands. He also designed the large meeting room with glazing on both sides to communicate democratic transparency through architectural means.

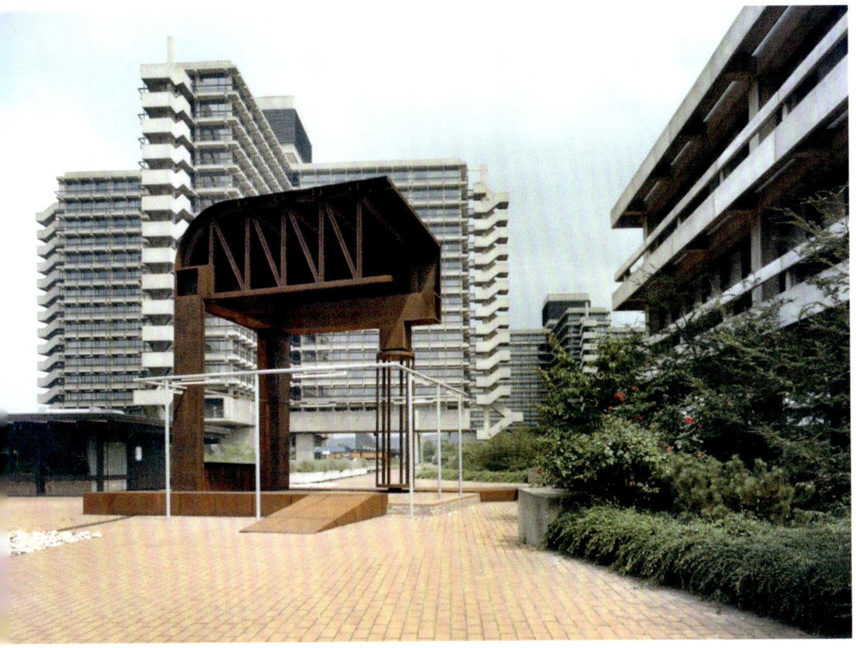

The curtain façade for the buildings, which are up to four storeys high, is a fitting contrast, for which Baumgarten ordered hand-crafted cast aluminium plates. The art in architecture for the courtroom building was produced by the sculptor Hans Kindermann (1911–1997) and the graphic designer HAP Grieshaber (1905–1981), who regarded the Federal Eagle as an appropriate motif for the institution, since its task of protecting German law made it more than a symbolic guarantor of federal German democracy.

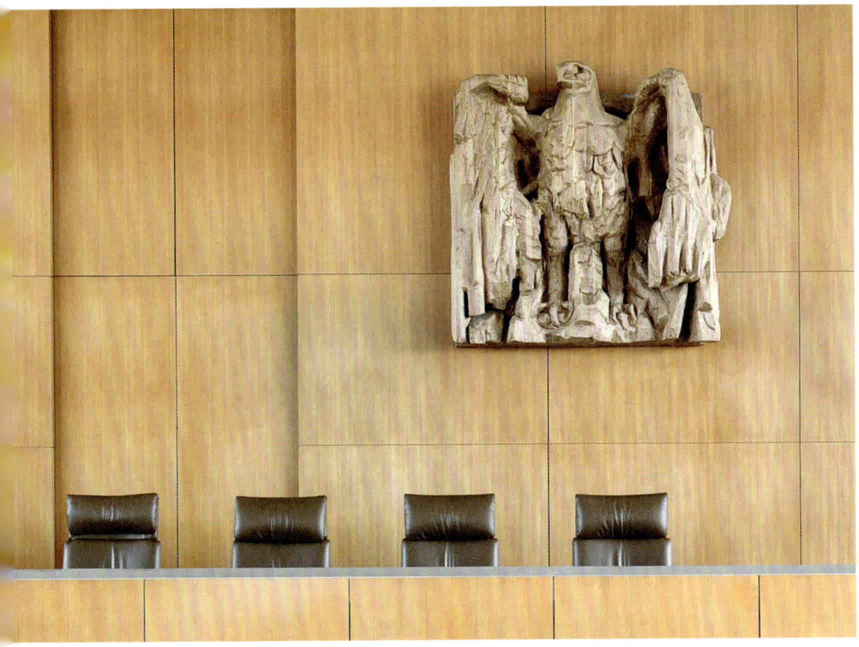

REPRESENTATIONS OF POWER: THE PALACE OF THE REPUBLIC IN EAST BERLIN AND THE FEDERAL CHANCELLERY IN BONN

The Palace of the Republic in East Berlin was completed in 1976. It was the first large-scale, prestigious building project after Erich Honecker became First Secretary of the Central Committee of the SED. As Honecker had already declared at the topping out ceremony in 1974, it was intended as a people's building and a place of vibrant political and cultural life. The architect Heinz Graffunder was responsible for its planning. Together with his colleagues, he developed a glass building structure that could be looked into from all sides and – uniquely for both parts of Germany – combined the centre of power with an entertainment centre in a single building. Like the major popular venues of the turn of the century, the Palace of the Republic included a public multifunctional facility with theatres, youth clubs, a bowling alley and gastronomic services, as well as acting as the seat of the GDR parliament, known as the Volkskammer. The building closed an urban-planning gap created in the centre of Berlin

Haus-Rucker Co, "Pavillon der Elemente", 1980, Federal Ministries of Justice, Education and Science, and for Research and Technology, Kreuzbauten, Bonn

Hans Kindermann, "Adlerrelief", 1969, Federal Constitutional Court, Karlsruhe

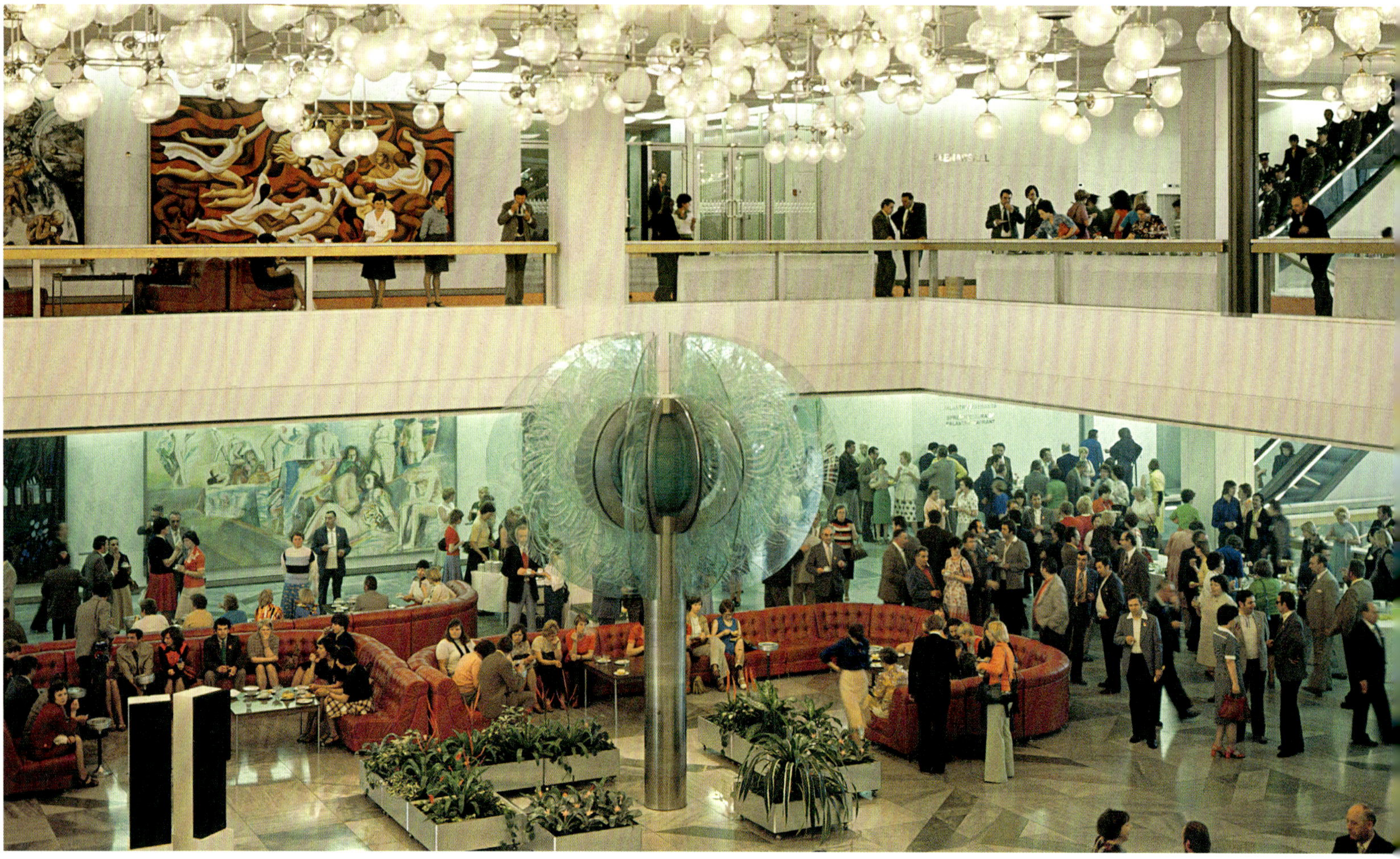

by the demolition of the Hohenzollern palace in 1950, while also combining with the Staatsrat building (1964) and the Ministry for Foreign Affairs (1967) to complete the political state forum of the GDR on Marx-Engels-Platz, establishing a prestigious location for the state's self-presentation.

The art in architecture for the project played a special role in view of the intended integrative interaction between architecture and art: the planners of art in architecture for the Palace of the Republic led by the sculptor, graphic designer and visual artist Fritz Cremer (1906–1993) developed a diverse overall concept of various figurative and pictorial pieces, including the "architecturally formative" object entitled "Gläserne Blume" ("Glass Flower") by Reginald Richter (born in 1931) and Richard Otfried Wilhelm (born in 1932) for the large foyer. After Honecker's accession to power, a certain opening of GDR cultural policy was confirmed at the VIII. Party Congress in June 1971, affording greater freedom for the artistic interpretation of political content within the overall formal language of Socialist Realism. When choosing artists, the influence of Cremer therefore made it possible to select paintings for the palace foyer gallery that broke with the uniform stylistic presentation of Socialist Realism, delivering a more subjective formal perspective. During efforts to find a common theme that would be accepted by the party and state leadership, as well as by the artists, the original motto of "The struggle and victory of Socialism" was replaced by a reference to Lenin: "Are Communists allowed to dream?".

The sixteen commissioned artists included Bernhard Heisig (1925–2011), Arno Mohr (1910–2001), Willi Neubert (1920–2011) and Willi Sitte (1921–2013), as well as Wolfgang Mattheuer (1927–2004), who generally did not accept state commissions that

Reginald Richter, Richard O. Wilhelm, "Gläserne Blume", 1975/1976, Palace of the Republic, Berlin

Federal Chancellery, Bonn

Adolf Luther, ceiling lights, 1975/1976, Federal Chancellery, Bonn

highlighted the "potential achievements and effects of Socialism" (→ p. 108). The sculptor Jo Jastram (1928–2011) was commissioned to produce a piece for the entrance hall of the Volkskammer. His bronze relief "Lob des Kommunismus" ("In praise of Communism") already indicated the importance and dignity of the Volkskammer through the sheer cost of the material itself. Peter Guth commented on the architecturally related art, which he programmatically called "Walls of promise", as never calling the GDR state into question, instead continuing to support the state while expressing a reformative intention. He believed this had been especially successful in the artworks for the Palace of the Republic.

Almost in parallel with the completion of the Palace of the Republic in East Berlin, the new Chancellery building was constructed in Bonn between 1973 and 1976. The administrative building designed by the Stieldorf planning group comprises a three-storey complex with a reserved, sober appearance, its staggered volumes forming a forecourt with a drive for official purposes. In 1974, in view of the importance of the building task, the Federal Building Authority announced the Federal Republic's second open art in architecture competition for the Chancellery, with the aim of finding an integrative design. Out of the 173 entries, a lighting installation by Günther Ferdinand Ris (1928–2005) for the driveway, a six-part ground sculpture by Erich Hauser (1930–2004) for the drive and a kinetic orb by Hans Dieter Bohnet (1926–2006) for the forecourt designed by the landscape architect Hans Luz (1926–2016) were chosen. However the forecourt design failed to impress, both aesthetically and functionally, so by 1979, it had been replaced by a large green area, on which the sculpture "Large Two Forms" by Henry Moore (1898–1986) was installed at

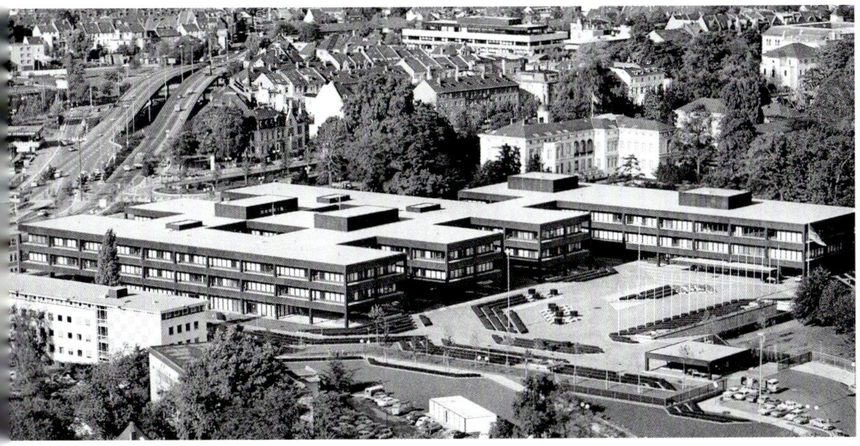

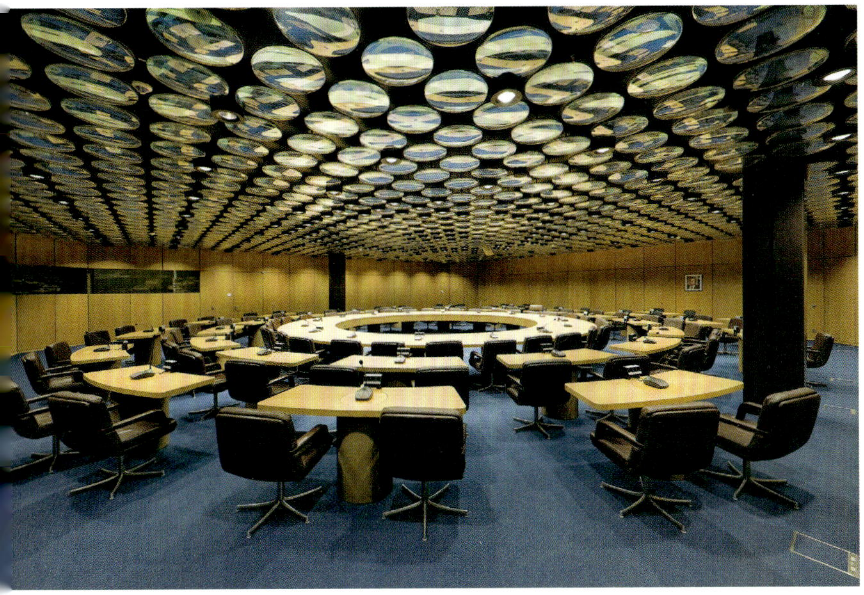

the special request of Helmut Schmidt, the Federal Chancellor of the time. For the artistic design of the interior, Adolf Luther (1912–1990) contributed a spatial sculpture for the foyer and a lighting ceiling for the conference room, consisting of 948 hollow mirrors with integrated lighting, transforming the so-called Nato Hall into a spatial artwork.

The pieces selected as art in architecture for the Federal Chancellery were all works of concrete art or op art, their non-figurative character reflecting the zeitgeist and political primacy of reserved gestures. However, not all contemporaries accepted it as an appropriately official complement to the architecture. The deliberately modest "centre of power" of the Bonn Republic only gained a certain metropolitan flair when the "Large Two Forms" (→ p. 114) by the internationally renowned British sculptor were added. The sculpture by Moore gave the Federal Chancellery its media hallmark, defining the image of the Federal Republic throughout the world until the government moved to Berlin. When the sculpture was presented in September 1979, the Federal Chancellor Helmut Schmidt, an art aficionado, recognised its symbolic power with respect to a divided Germany, stating: "Two parts that nevertheless intrinsically belong together".

COMMISSIONED ART BETWEEN PROGRAMME AND FREEDOM

Until the mid-1960s, abstract formal conceptions were not permitted as a means of artistic expression in major GDR state commissions since they were regarded as "cold aestheticism", "naked functionalism" and "lacking all popular character". This is demonstrated by the numerous murals in the style of Socialist Realism, which were commissioned with the intention of combining political, propaganda, educational or programmatic aims in an attempt to historically legitimise the GDR. By contrast, in the Federal Republic, artistic freedom had a high status, which is why thematic instructions were rarely included in awarding art in architecture commissions. Instead, abstract and concrete art was recognised as the expression of a free constitutional democracy.

Since the constitution of the GDR had confirmed the leadership of the SED in 1968, the Party's nomenclature permeated the three branches of state power, its legislative, executive and judiciary bodies. Thus the system was de facto a state under single-party rule. Party schools educated its comrades on the level of local districts, as well as the SED "Karl Marx" Party College in Berlin-Mitte, which was established in the building complex "Haus am Köllnischen Park". In 1971, an extension was built for the school, including a staircase that accommodated a commissioned work by Willi Sitte entitled "Proletarier aller Länder, vereinigt euch!" ("Workers of the world, unite!"(→ p. 116). Although Sitte had been criticised for many years for his painting style, which was orientated towards pre-war Modernity, he was able to establish himself as an artist through his political work, which gained him official recognition. In his artistic interpretation of the theme for the Party College, Sitte combined social and political intentions with the expressive representation of naked human bodies. From the outset, the mural never fulfilled political expectations, since Sitte neglected to focus sufficiently on the Soviet contribution to the development of Socialism and was therefore accused of "pan-Germanism". The artistic technique and the presentation of male nudes also led to the painting's rejection, which motivated

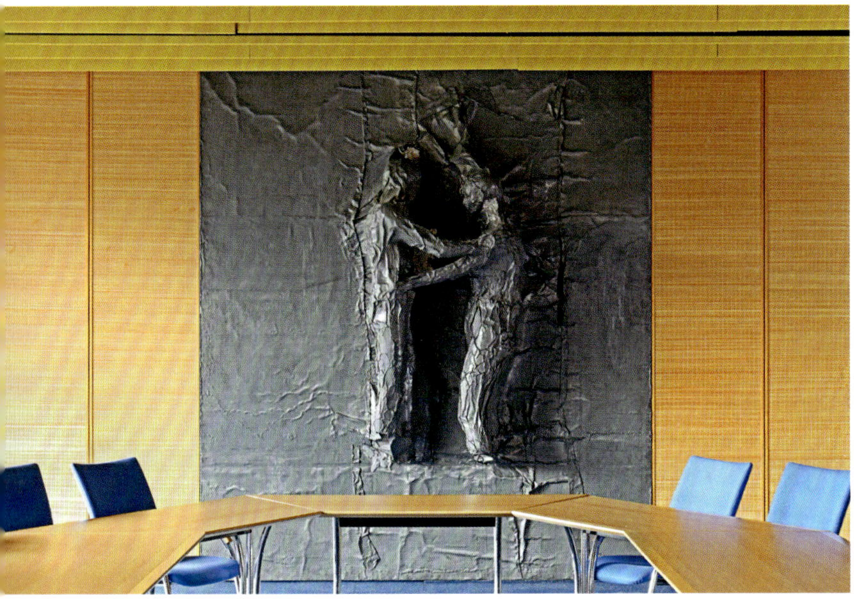

Wolf Vostell, “Der Dialog”, 1978, Federal Ministry of the Interior, Bonn

the Dean of the college, Hanna Wolf, to conceal the staircase artwork behind bands of curtain material.

In the 1970s, thematic instructions were not generally stipulated for art in architecture pieces in the new and extension buildings for federal ministries in Bonn. One exception was the Federal Ministry of the Interior in 1979, when two art in architecture competitions were announced for its new mess, with the themes “Freiheit im Schutz des Staates” (“Freedom under the protection of the state”) and “Kreislauf des Wassers” (“Water cycle”). In the first process, Erich Reusch (1925–2019) was selected with a four-part ground work consisting of round copper plates that were laid flush with the lawn. Gottfried Gruner (1923–2011) won the second competition with his design “Aquamobil”. Gruner’s piece reflects on contemporary aspects of the newly emerging environmental movement, which became relevant in the late 1970s. The “Supplementary fund for additional commissions to visual artists intended for federal building measures” financed further commissions dedicated to the theme of “Humanity and nature”, resulting in separate competitions for the fields of “Light”, “Earth” and “Sun (warmth)”. Since then, the three-part lead relief “Der Dialog” (“The dialogue”) by Wolf Vostell (1932–1998) has adorned the large meeting room in the mess and meeting building. The mural tapestry “Arachnura Celeste” by Gabriele Grosse (born in 1942) is located in the dining room and the wooden mural work by Ursula Sax (born in 1935) was installed in the cafeteria. While the latter two works were largely autonomous pieces with no specific local reference and could be exhibited in a different spatial context, despite the stipulated task, the lead relief by Vostell is integrated into the wall of the meeting room. Even more comprehensively integrated art in architecture pieces were installed in the new building for the Ministry of Agriculture in Bonn, where Otto Herbert Hajek (1927–2005) developed an enveloping exterior and interior art in architecture landscape. Similarly, Johannes Peter Hölzinger (born in 1936) produced a holistic art concept for the Ministry of Defence at the Hardthöhe: it included sculptures, façade designs and landscape gardening elements, as well as three-dimensional ceiling, floor and mural designs in the interior, achieving a synthesis between architecture and art.

Unlike art in architecture in the Federal Republic, funds in the GDR did not have to be spent on works relating to specific buildings, so that murals, mosaics, sgraffitos, reliefs and building sculptures were not only produced for individual edifices, but also for entire squares and outdoor spatial designs as art in urban space. From 1964 onwards, as Halle-Neustadt was being developed into the GDR's prototypical prefabricated housing city, efforts were made to achieve a synthesis of architecture and visual art, using art to communicate political aims and idealised images of society. With almost 150 works in public spaces, including sculptures, murals, fountains, surface designs, spatially structuring elements, structured walls and gable walls, Halle-Neustadt became the country's largest open-air gallery. In the new city, the visual programme was to enthuse the "new person" – a socialist persona – with technological optimism, solidarity within the collective and an overriding sense of harmony. Although the focus on propaganda was not dominant, the commissioned works can be regarded as programmatic art, as seen in the gable mural by Erich Enge (born in 1932) entitled "Lenins Worte werden wahr" ("Lenin's words come true", 1971) or the murals by

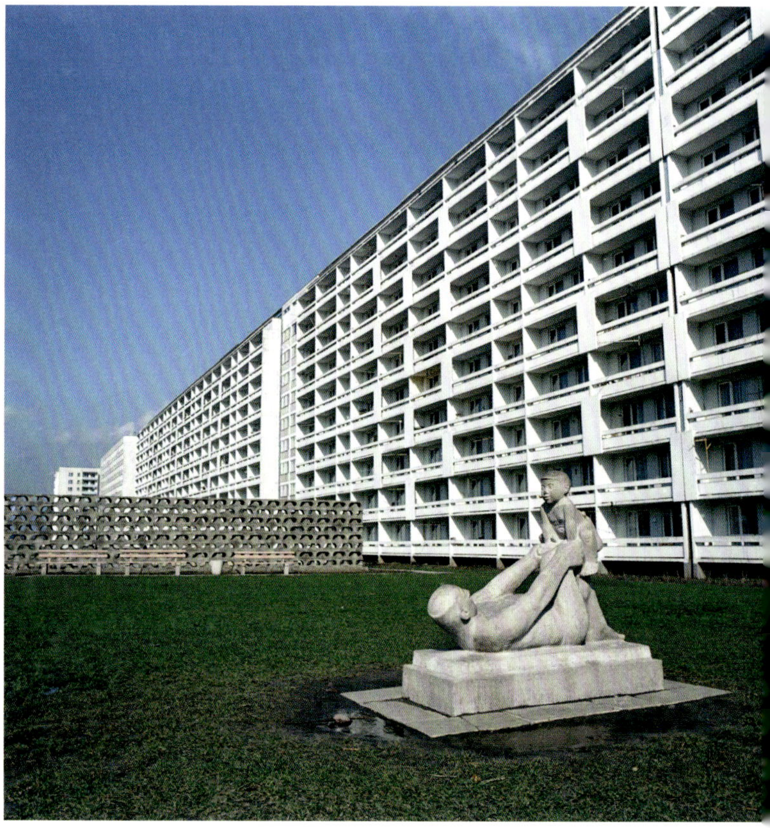

Urban spatial design with a sculpture by Rudolf Hilscher, "Vater und Sohn", 1964/1970, Halle-Neustadt

Hermann Glöckner, "Mast mit zwei Faltungszonen", 1976, Dresden

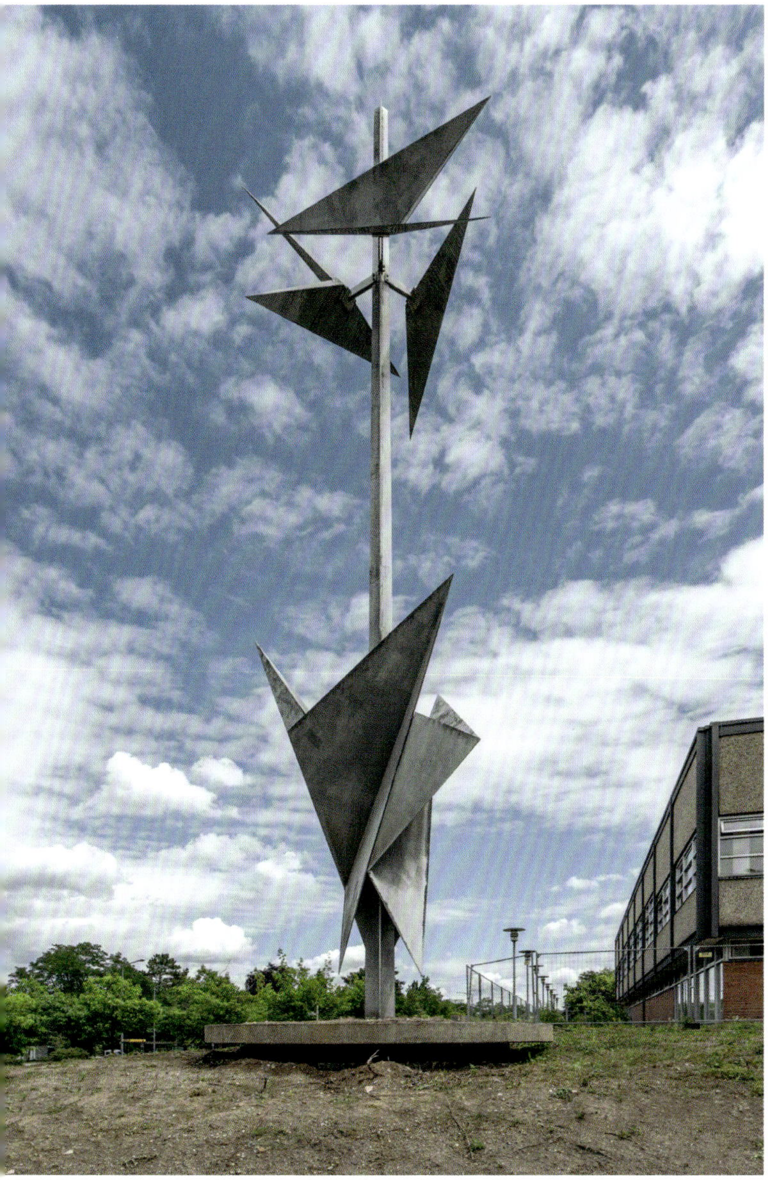

Josep Renau (1907–1982) "Die von Menschen beherrschten Kräfte von Natur und Technik" ("The powers of nature and technology harnessed by the people") and "Einheit der Arbeiterklasse und Gründung der DDR" ("Unity of the working class and foundation of the GDR", 1974) at the educational centre (→ p. 202). A considerable number of the works commissioned in Halle-Neustadt between 1964 and 1989 also served to structure and aestheticise the urban space, such as concrete structural walls for green and open areas or the design of walkways through buildings.

In 1957, the councils of Leipzig and Dresden first received their own funds from the Ministry of Culture to commission architecturally related art. A commissioning body organised awards to artists and controlled the implementation of designs. In 1976, the Dresden sculptor Hermann Glöckner (1889–1987) designed a "Mast mit zwei Faltungszonen" ("Mast with two folding zones"), for which he not only sought funding, but also an appropriate location in his home town. Glöckner's sculpture was strongly influenced by the Russian Constructivism of the 1930s. Thus his artistic stance was contrary to the state aesthetics of the National Socialists and the early GDR, so he only achieved public recognition in old age. Based on a proposal by the Office for Architecturally Related Art, Glöckner's design was to be produced in a newly developed housing estate. The reaction by the Social Council for Urban Development and Visual Art was mixed, leading to a delay in the search for an appropriate location. Finally in 1984, the Arts Committee of the Technische Universität Dresden managed to present it at a prominent location in front of the new canteen, making the abstract work of art legible as a visible symbol of social transformation towards greater artistic freedom and scope of action.

CONCLUSION BEFORE NEW BEGINNINGS: THE PLENARY HALL OF THE GERMAN BUNDESTAG IN BONN

In 1988, in parallel with the two major new buildings in Bonn for the Federal Ministry of Post and Telecommunications (1981–1988) and the Federal Ministry of Transport (1986–1989), the foundation stone was laid for the new Plenary Hall of the German Bundestag according to plans by Günter Behnisch. While it was being built, the Berlin Wall fell in 1989, followed by German reunification in 1990 and the decision to move the capital to Berlin in 1991. The Plenary Hall was nevertheless completed by 1992. Its art in architecture was selected in 1990 by a committee formed by the Bundestag Council of Elders, with the aim of awarding commissions to artists whose works reflected the self-perception of a reunified, democratically constituted Germany. Thus internationally renowned artists such as Nicola de Maria (born in 1954), Sam Francis (1923–1994) and Mark di Suvero (born in 1933) were invited to produce art in architecture pieces, while contemporary German sculptural works were also created by Rebecca Horn (born in 1944) (→ p. 120) and Olaf Metzel (born in 1952). These were complemented by posthumous pieces by two important German 20th-century artists: Joseph Beuys (1921–1986) from the West and Hermann Glöckner from the East. In 1992, the latter's sculpture "Durchbruch" ("Breakthrough") was placed in front of the Bundeshaus, which was based on a design from the 1930s. It consists of two diagonally positioned plates of corten steel that are intertwined in a way that makes them appear to penetrate each other. The fall of the Berlin Wall gave the piece additional symbolic meaning, contributing to the artwork's enduring fame today.

Olaf Metzel, "Meistdeutigkeit", 1996, Plenarsaal, Bonn

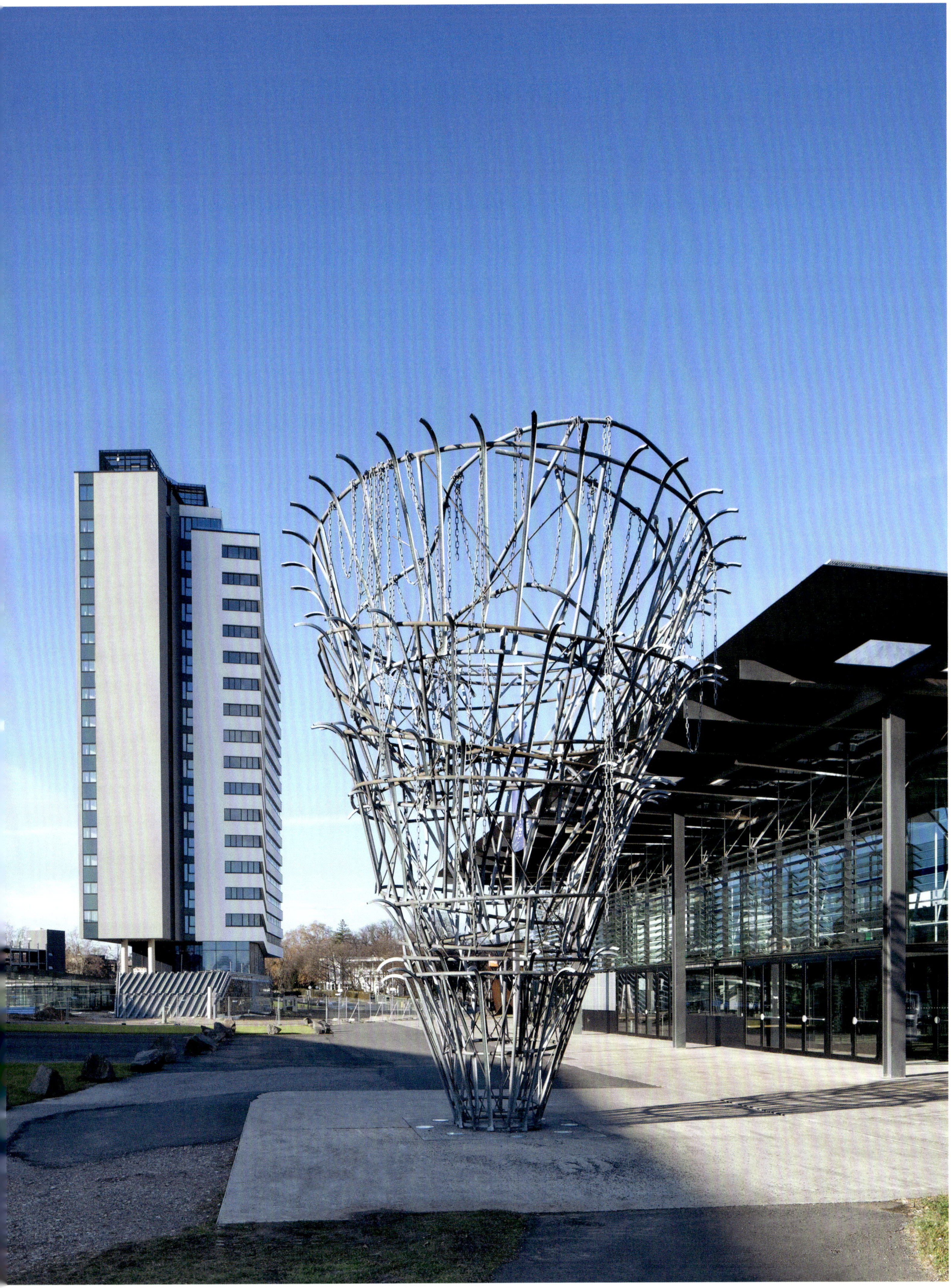

STAATSRAT BUILDING BERLIN

TODAY EUROPEAN SCHOOL OF MANAGEMENT AND TECHNOLOGY

Address:
Schlossplatz 1
10178 Berlin

Architecture:
VEB Berlin-Projekt,
collective led by Roland Korn,
1962–1964

Art in architecture:
Walter Womacka
and Günther Brendel,
Fritz Kühn

On the 15th anniversary of the foundation of the GDR, the Staatsrat moved into a programmatic new building at Marx-Engels-Platz 1, as it was known at the time, in the historical city centre of Berlin. The three-storey steel skeleton construction planned by the architects' collective led by Roland Korn has a prestigious official façade with banner-like areas of red granite, symbolising the red flag of the Socialist and Communist movements. It includes an integrated portal of the Berlin Palace, which was demolished in 1950, from where Karl Liebknecht had declared the Socialist Republic on November 9, 1918.

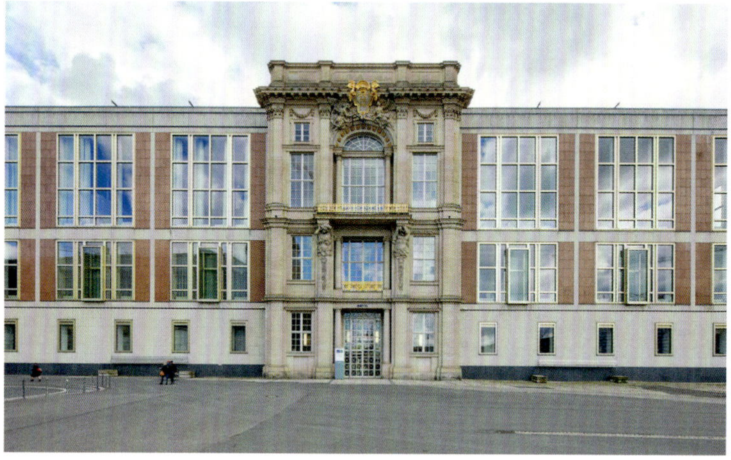

Walter Womacka (1925–2010) was contracted to carry out the artistic fittings of the foyer, with its building-high glass window, which was intended both as architectural decoration and as a political symbol. Entitled "From the history of the German workers' movement", it presents idealised life in the GDR in the form of a happy family surrounded by committed workers, as well as industrial and agricultural scenes. The centre is occupied by portraits of Karl Liebknecht and Rosa Luxemburg, above which the line of text "And whether we will still be alive when it is achieved, we live out our programme; it will rule the world of liberated humanity. Despite everything!" is written in German. It stems from an editorial for the Party body of the Communist Party, "Die rote Fahne" ("The Red Flag"), which Liebknecht had written shortly before being murdered.

The 180 square-metre glass artwork was not produced using a traditional stained glass window technique and instead consists of smaller colourful pieces of glass on a large-scale glass base plate, in order to make the colours shine and thereby express the propagated optimism of the state leadership.

WALTER WOMACKA
"Aus der Geschichte der deutschen Arbeiterbewegung" ("From the history of the German workers' movement"), 1964
Stained glass window
10 x 16.5 m

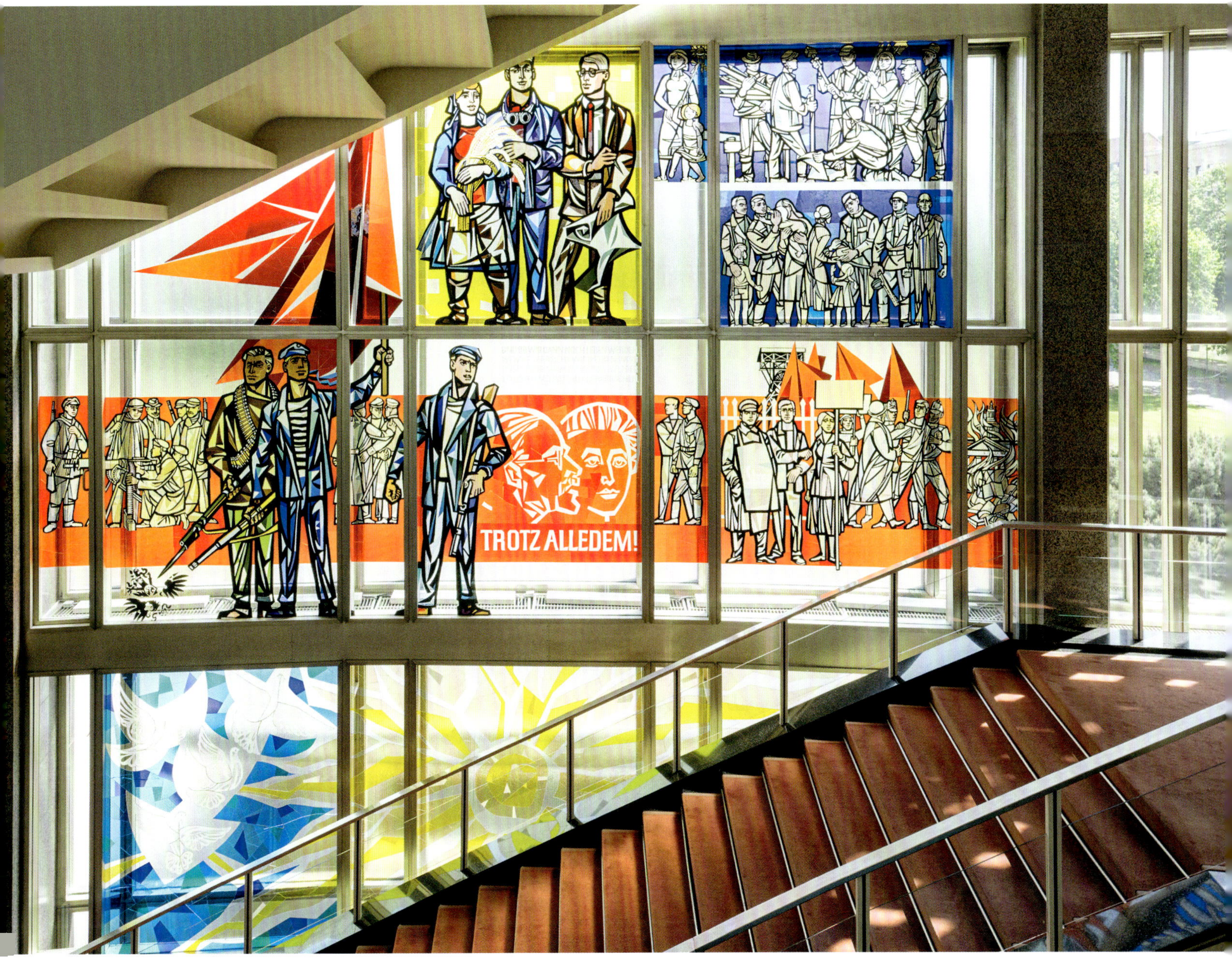

Womacka was a protagonist of Socialist Realism and one of the leading artists in the field of art in architecture. His election as Vice President of the Association of Visual Artists in 1959 consolidated his growing importance as a GDR artist, as confirmed by major art in architecture commissions for the staircase of the Humboldt-Universität zu Berlin and the mosaic frieze on the Haus des Lehrers at Berlin's Alexanderplatz, which were produced around the same time as the stained glass window of the Staatsrat building.

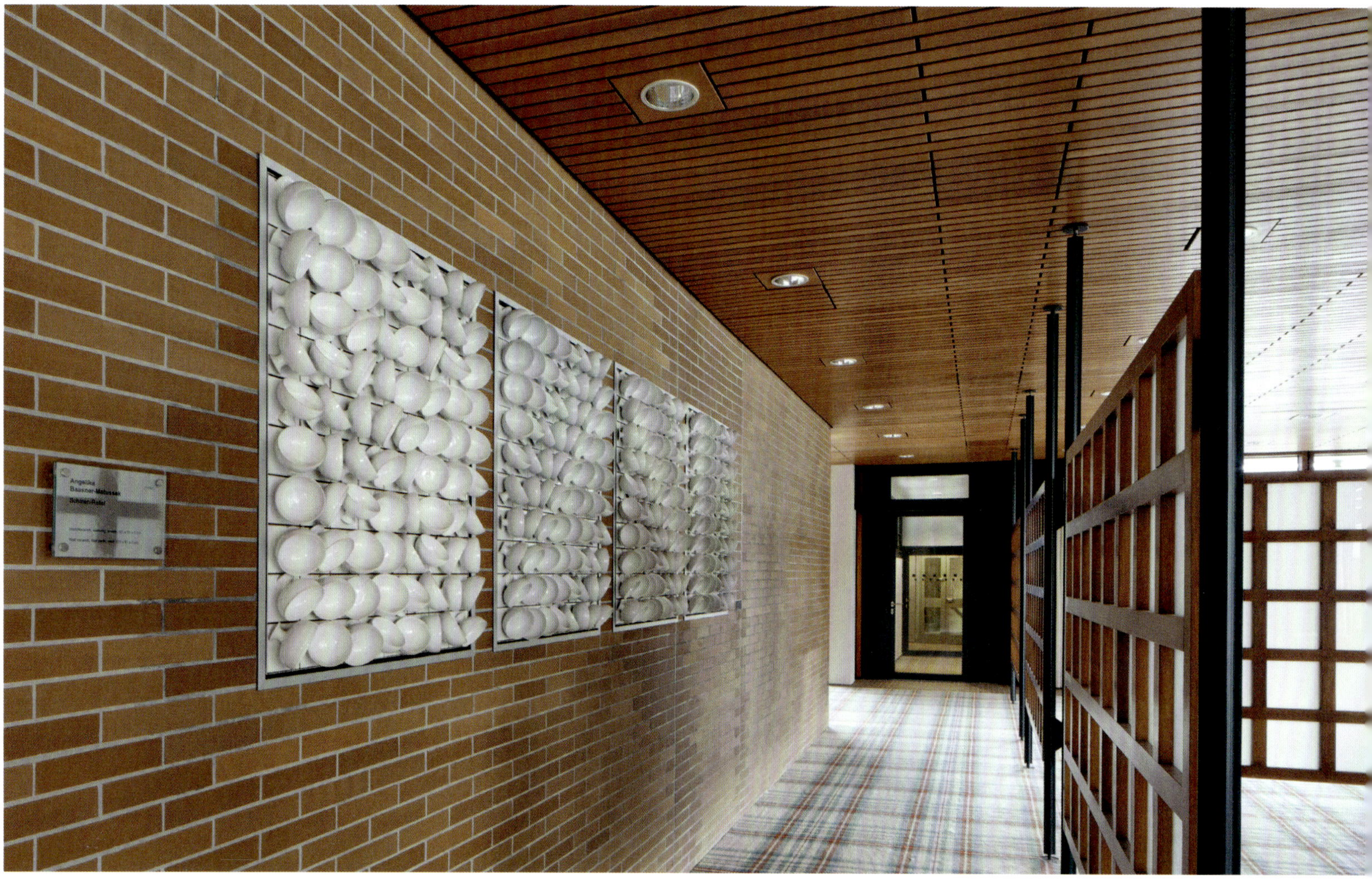

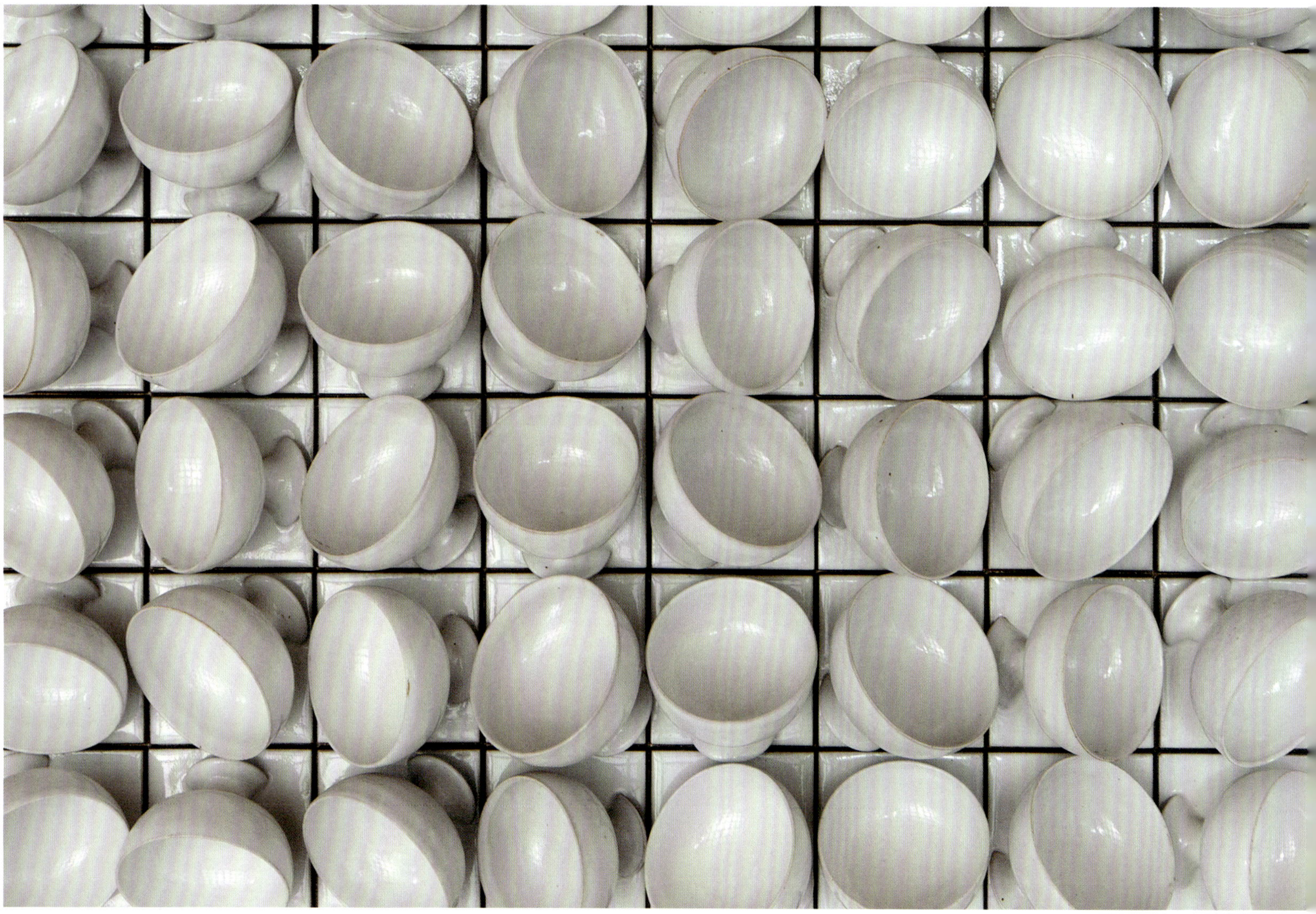

GERMAN BUNDESTAG PARLIAMENTARIANS' TOWER BONN

TODAY UN CAMPUS BONN

Address:
Hermann-Ehlers-Strasse 10
53113 Bonn

Architecture:
Egon Eiermann, 1966–1969

Art in architecture:
Angelika Baasner-Matussek and Alexander Camaro, HAP Grieshaber, Hans Kaiser, Fritz Koenig, Norbert Kricke, Georg Meistermann, Günter Ferdinand Ris, Lothar Schall, Emil Schumacher, Günther Uecker, Woty Werner

The new construction of the parliamentarians' tower between 1966 and 1969 marked the end of provisional buildings for the Bundestag in Bonn. Built by the internationally renowned architect Egon Eiermann, the tower with 30 floors and a height of 114 metres provided sufficient space for the parliamentarians' offices and meeting rooms. The modernity of the architecture reflected the new self-confidence of the young Federal Republic in every detail. Thus the "Langer Eugen", as it was called in a reference to the then President of the Bundestag Eugen Gerstenmaier, was a landmark in the city, not only due to its height. The prestigious, modern character of the architecture also needed to be expressed in the art in architecture. Together with Eiermann, the Federal Building Authority selected twelve artists for its artistic decoration, aiming to represent the entire spectrum of contemporary art movements with different techniques and styles, including op art, as well as informal, kinetic and concrete art.

Angelika Baasner-Matussek (born in 1941) was commissioned to conceive the artistic design for the restaurant on the top floor. She placed a four-part ceramic mural in the entrance area that is inserted flush into the brick wall. The portrait-format reliefs each consist of eighty white, hand-made bowls that are individually rotated to create a dynamic pattern, thereby achieving an aesthetically meaningful reference to the gastronomic services. Baasner-Matussek, who had trained as a ceramic artist at the Hochschule für Bildende Künste Berlin, applies a technique to her artwork that is known from 1960s Minimal Music: the composition consists of the repetition of very small, only slightly varying tonal units; the grid, module and variation form elements of the "Bowl relief", picking up on design principles of architecture.

ANGELIKA BAASNER-MATUSSEK
"Schalenrelief"
("Bowl relief"), 1969/1970
Ceramics, 4 fields
each 100 x 80 x 5 cm

HAUS DER STATISTIK BERLIN

TODAY USE NOT YET DECIDED

Address:
Otto-Braun-Strasse 70–72
10178 Berlin

Architecture:
Manfred Hörner, Peter Senf and Joachim Härter, 1968–1970

Art in architecture:
Ronald Paris
and Karl Hillert, Achim Kühn

In the 1960s, the urban planning of Alexanderplatz was redesigned under the auspices of the Chief Architect Joachim Näther to become one of the capital's central squares. In 1970, the GDR State Central Administration for Statistics moved into its new headquarters at the northern edge of the square. Its task was to plan and control the centrally steered economy on the basis of official statistics. The three-winged building was constructed as a reinforced concrete skeleton structure. Ronald Paris (born in 1933) produced a large-scale mural for the interior using dispersion colours with pigments on Rabitz, a wired form of plaster. The visual composition is based on the poem "Lob des Kommunismus" ("In praise of Communism") by Bertolt Brecht. His text is inserted into the presentation and begins with sentences that translate as "It is reasonable. You can grasp it. It's simple. / You're no exploiter, so you'll understand." The poem ends with the statement: "It is the simple thing / That's hard to do."

RONALD PARIS
"Lob des Kommunismus"
("In praise of Communism"),
1969/1970
Dispersion paint
with pigments on Rabitz
2 x 8.70 m
(now stored at
the GDR Museum, Berlin)

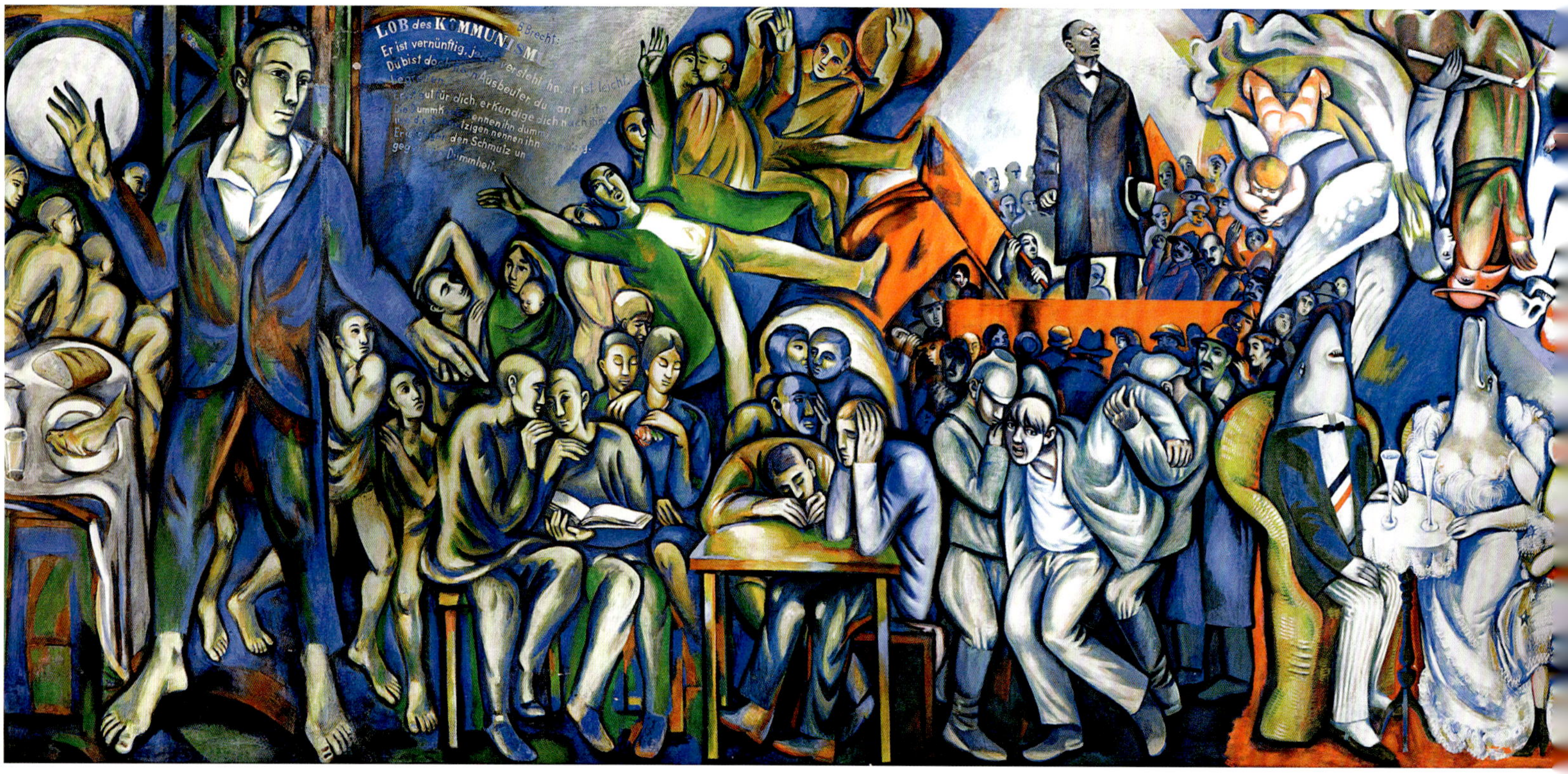

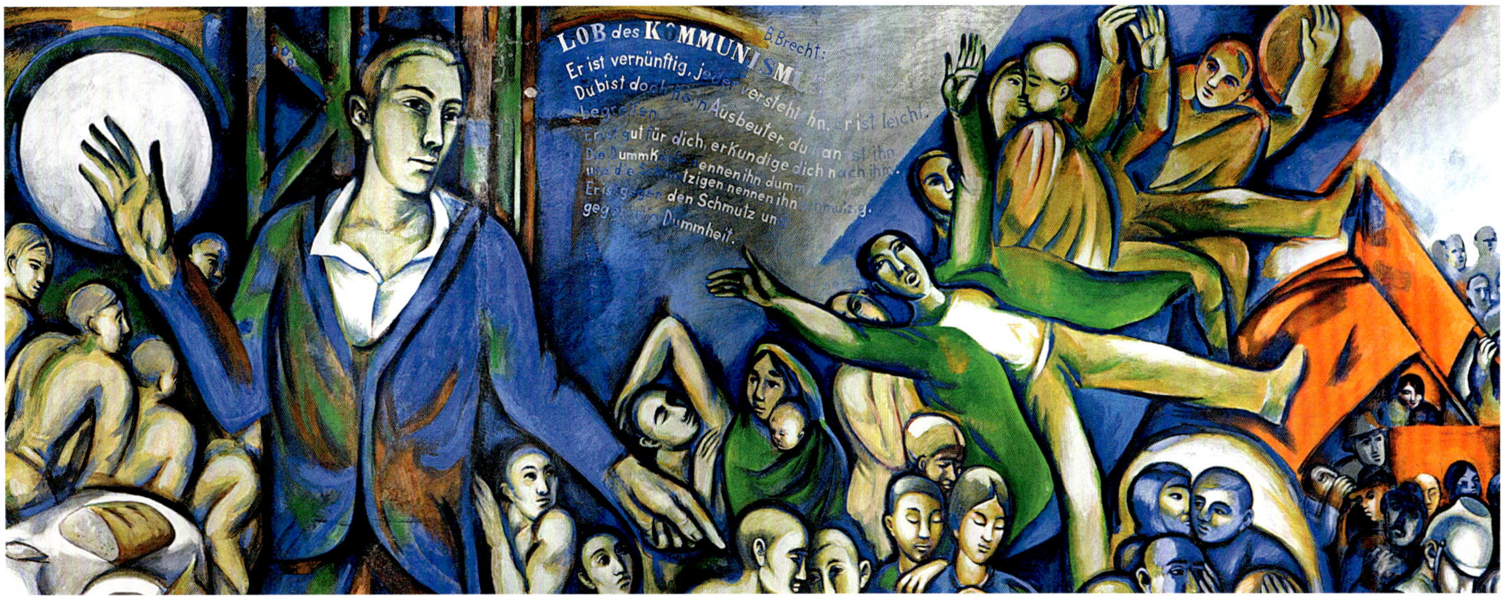

Although the GDR celebrated Brecht as its national poet, the artwork by Paris was almost cancelled due to the last lines of the poem, which were perceived as a criticism of Socialist development. The piece was only tolerated due to its non-public location in the conference hall. Paris uses glowing colours to demonstrate the superiority of the Communist world view, using scenic images of the oppressed struggling against the crimes of capital.

His style is orientated towards the powerful figures by Max Beckmann, presenting solitary individuals against the anonymous mass of the major city. Paris also transcends the typified representation of soldiers, reading workers and playing children by playfully adding figures with shark heads and crocodile tears that recall theatrical scenes. In 2010, the painting was added to the collection of the GDR Museum in Berlin.

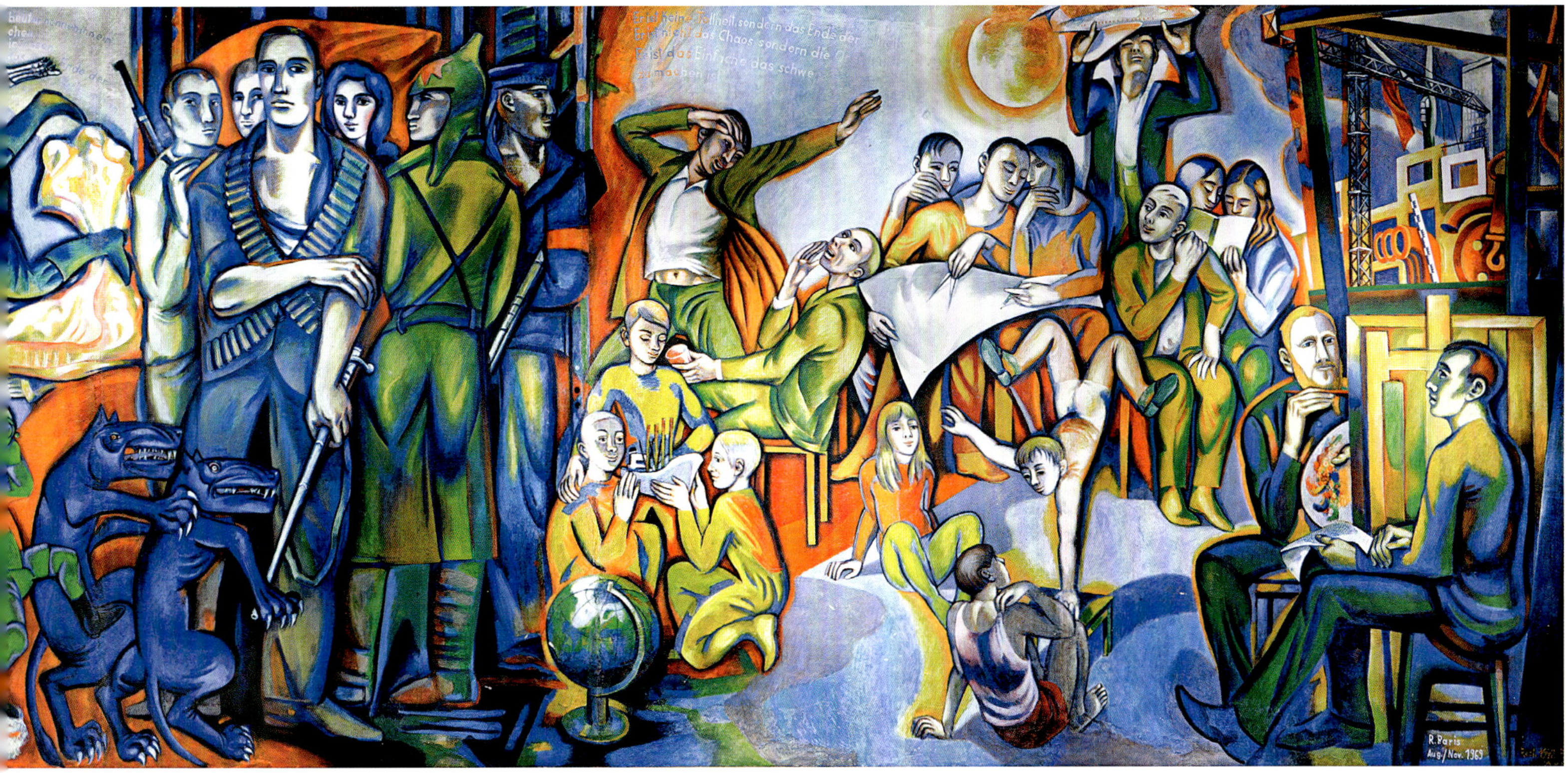

PALACE OF THE REPUBLIC BERLIN

Address:
Marx-Engels-Platz
10178 Berlin

Architecture:
Kollektiv der Bauakademie der DDR, led by Heinz Graffunder, 1973–1976
demolished 2006–2008

Art in architecture:
Wolfgang Mattheuer and Günther Brendel, René Graetz, Erhard Großmann, Bernhard Heisig, Jo Jastram, Arno Mohr, Willi Neubert, Ronald Paris, Reginald Richter and Richard Otfried Wilhelm, Kurt Robbel, Wolfram Schubert, Willi Sitte, Werner Tübke, Hans Vent, Matthias Wegehaupt, Walter Womacka, Lothar Zitzmann

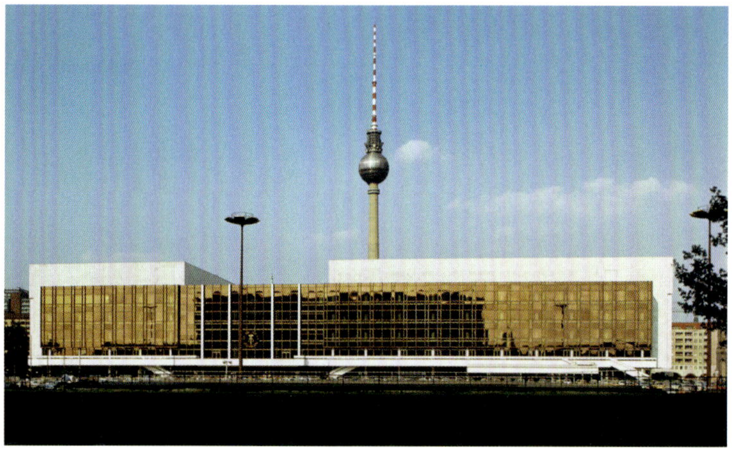

The Palace of the Republic was opened in 1976 after a construction period of only three years. It served as the seat of the GDR Volkskammer and as a cultural facility for the general public. In accordance with its uses, the elongated building was structured in two sections that were connected by a continuous glass façade. The art in architecture was to be integrated at any early stage of the building process by a committee led by the Chief Architect Heinz Graffunder and the consultant collective led by the sculptor Fritz Cremer (1906–1993), in a spirit of synthesising visual art and architecture. Ultimately, however, only the glass sculpture by Reginald Richter (born in 1931) and Richard Otfried Wilhelm (born in 1932) in the main foyer, the bronze relief by Jo Jastram (1928–2011) in the foyer of the Volkskammer and the porcelain mural designs in the restaurants and cafés were completed as part of the architectural concept, while the gallery exclusively received autonomous, contemporary paintings, including one by Wolfgang Mattheuer (1927–2004), making him one of the "16 high-profile painters" commissioned to produce artworks for the gallery. The Party and state leadership had originally stipulated the theme of "The struggle and victory of Socialism", but following considerable opposition from the artists, the Lenin quote "Are Communists allowed to dream?" was chosen instead. The doctrine of exclusively commissioning Socialist Realist artists was abandoned in favour of the idea of visualising the diversity of GDR art.

Mattheuer, who was appreciated for the interpretational openness of his motifs and the discursive nature of his paintings, created a scene that initially appears to be idyllic: the picture entitled "Guten Tag" ("Good day") presents three members of a family in front of a landscape that is flooded with light and stretches to the horizon. On closer inspection however, the scenery proves to be a sprawling industrial city with all the signs of damage to nature, only revealing lush vegetation beyond a dense lattice fence. The commissioned

WOLFGANG MATTHEUER
"Guten Tag" ("Good day)", 1975
Oil on hard fibre
280 x 281 cm
(now stored at the Deutsches Historisches Museum, Berlin)

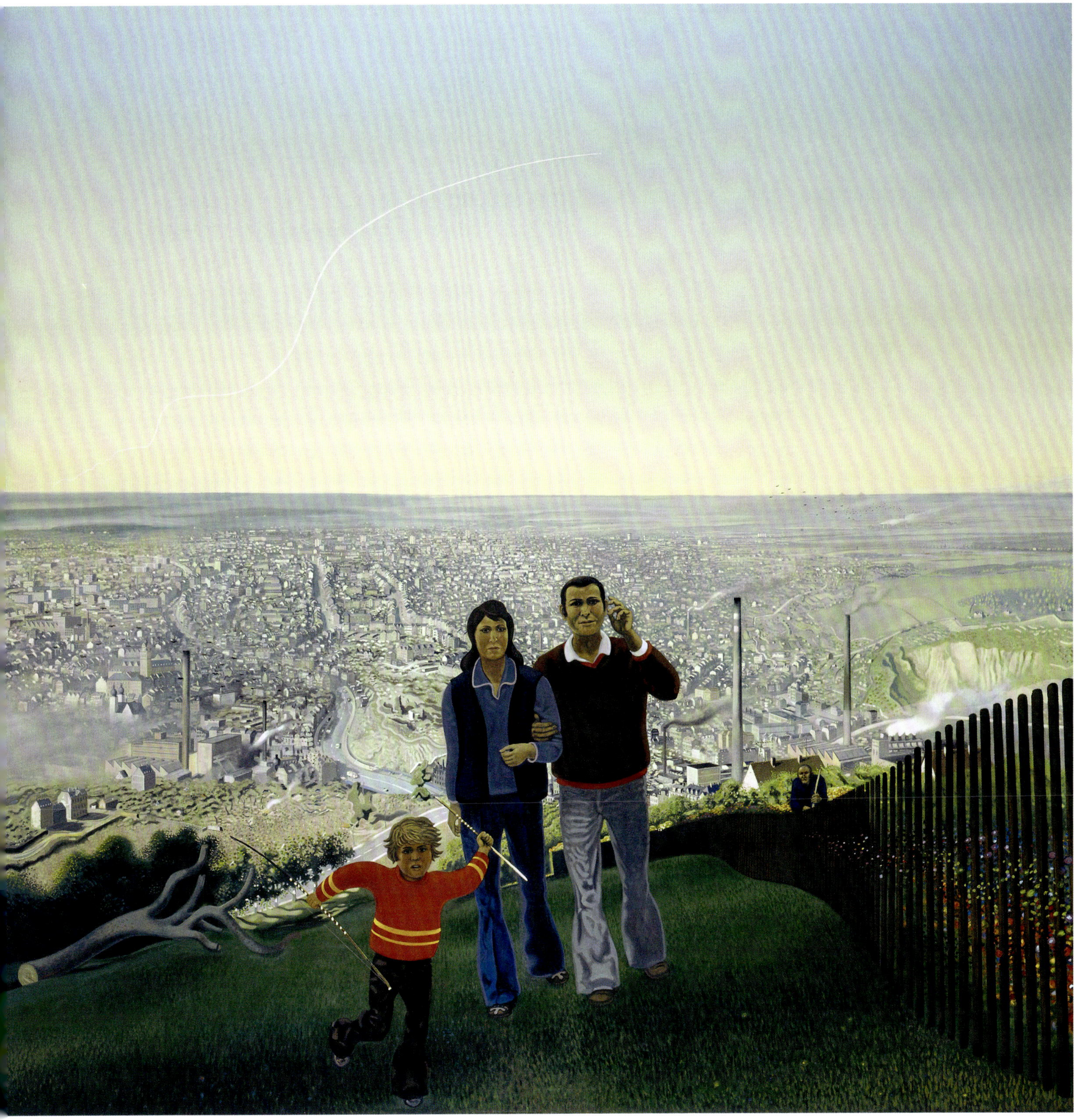

work negotiated a fine line between the political leadership's desire for prestige and international recognition on the one hand and the content-based quality of a symbolically laden, ambivalent composition on the other, which could also be interpreted as a criticism of the political situation and especially the opposition in the GDR between ideological goals and real life. Today, the painting has been loaned by the Federal Republic of Germany to the Deutsches Historisches Museum.

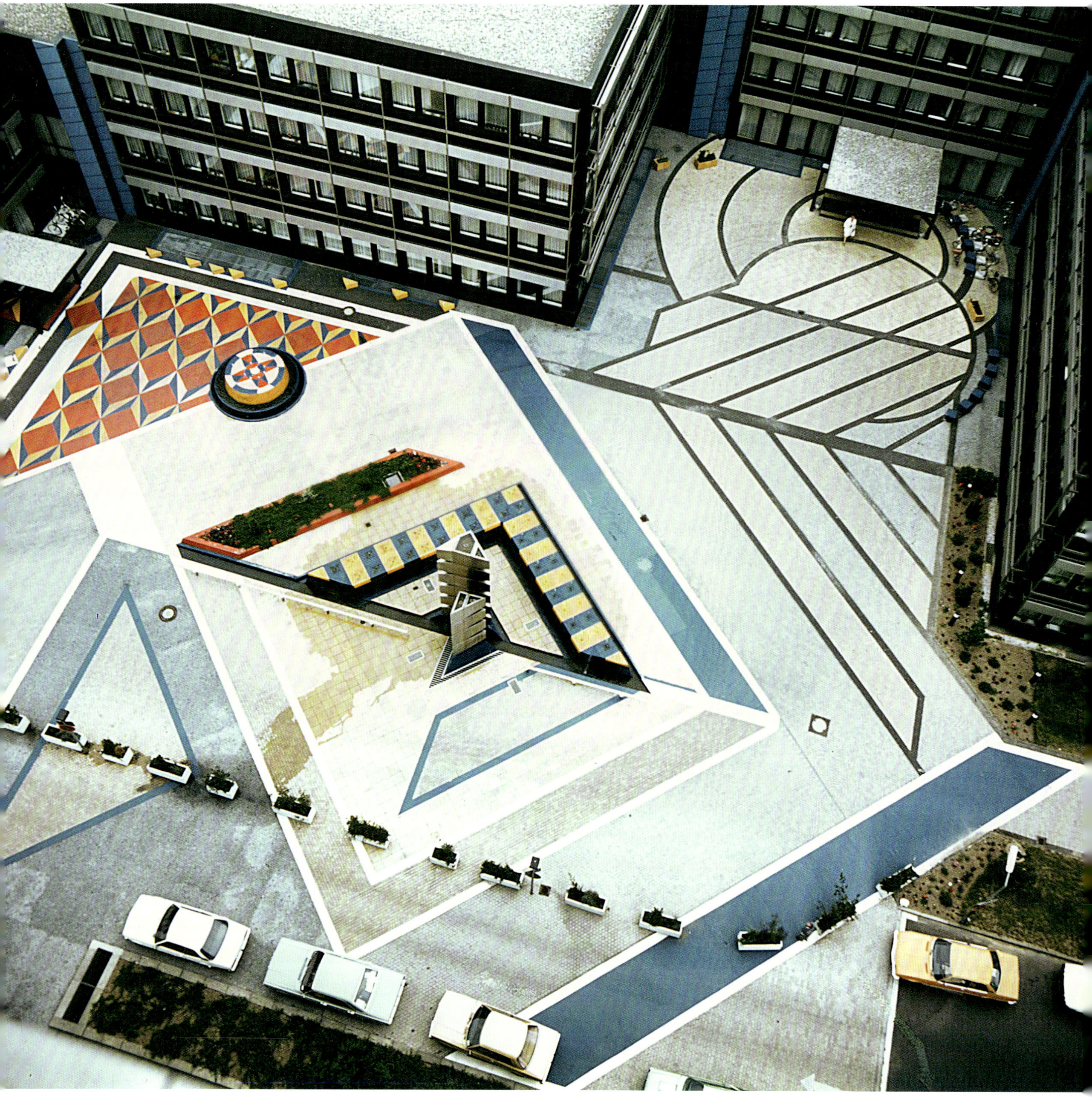

OTTO HERBERT HAJEK
Platzartikulation
(Spatial articulation), 1976
Square design, façade elements,
wall and floor designs

FEDERAL MINISTRY OF FOOD AND AGRICULTURE BONN

Address:
Rochusstrasse 1, 53123 Bonn

Architecture:
Federal Building Authority, 1974–1976

Art in architecture:
Otto Herbert Hajek and Bernhard Heiliger, Ansgar Nierhoff

On the grounds of the former Troilo Barracks, which were converted in 1949 for the Federal Ministry of Labour and Social Affairs, and the Federal Ministry of Food and Agriculture, a new building complex was constructed for the latter between 1974 and 1976. The four buildings, which each have four or five storeys, have a staggered arrangement to create an angle that frames a large square covering 2,500 square metres.

Otto Herbert Hajek (1927–2005) was contracted to conceive the square's artistic decoration and a number of interior areas. He was renowned for what he called his "spatial articulations" in the primary colours of blue, yellow and red. For the Ministry of Food and Agriculture, he developed an artwork with a direct reference to architecture by placing a sculptural fountain at the square's centre and combining it with geometrical floor mosaics and colour-contrasting building edges to form an overall concept. The geometrical patterns are also continued on the flooring and walls of the ministry corridors. Hajek combined a wide range of materials and techniques for this project: in addition to a carpet in a red, yellow, blue and white diamond pattern, he produced a wooden relief in brown, beige and petrol-blue colours, as well as a grey and black striped terrazzo, which was supplemented by diagonally running yellow wall panels and intersected by black stripes.

Hajek transcended the standard dimensions of sculpture and painting with his architecture-art-landscapes, making him internationally renowned. He produced several more of his spatial colour concepts for the Federal Government, including pieces for the German Embassies in Lomé (Togo) and Montevideo (Uruguay), as well as the Federal Ministry of Transport in Bonn.

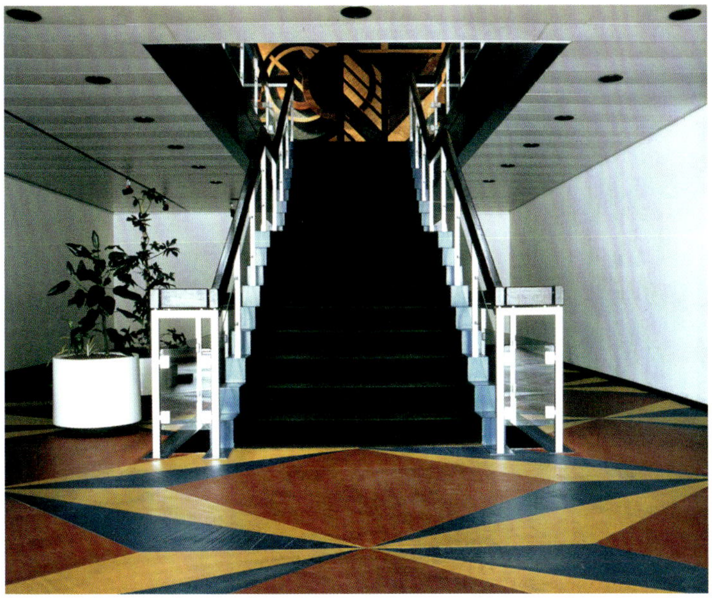

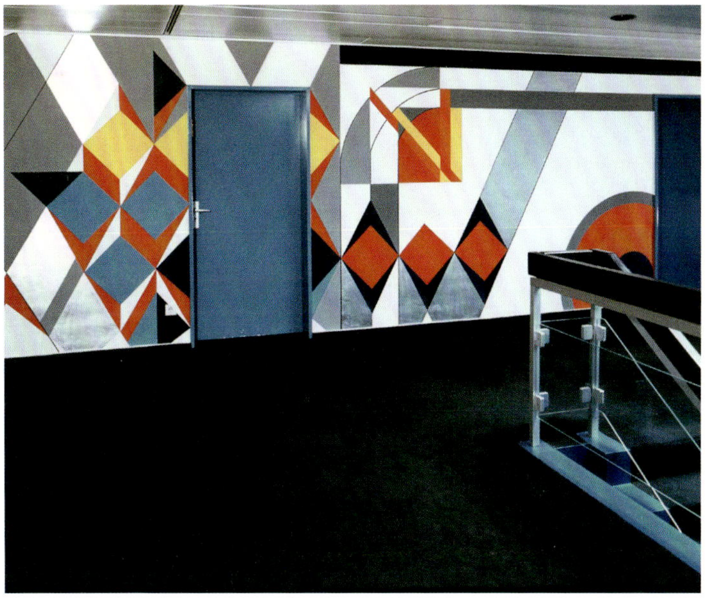

FEDERAL MINISTRIES OF JUSTICE, OF EDUCATION AND SCIENCE, OF RESEARCH AND TECHNOLOGY BONN

TODAY FEDERAL MINISTRY OF EDUCATION AND RESEARCH, AND THE FEDERAL RAILWAY AUTHORITY

Address:
Heinemannstrasse 2 and 6
53175 Bonn

Architecture:
Stieldorf Planning Group,
1969–1975

Art in architecture:
Ansgar Nierhoff
and Victor Bonato, Karl Dierkes, Gestaltungsgruppe für Farbe, Jürgen Hans Grümmer, Lutz Hatmann, Haus-Rucker Co, Erich Hauser, Heinz Mack, Matschinsky-Denninghoff, Eva Ohlow, Günther Ferdinand Ris, Ursula Sax, Robert Schwarz, Joachim Spies, Rolf Szymanski et al.

In 1968, planning began for a new ministerial district between Bonn and Bad Godesberg. Of the seven originally planned high-rise buildings, only two 12 and 15-storey buildings were constructed, their name "Kreuzbauten" (meaning "cruciform buildings") resulted from their crossed ground plan. The "provisional capital Bonn" had become the permanent government seat of the Federal Republic. In 1974, a two-stage competition was announced for the artistic design of the exterior grounds of the "Kreuzbauten". Ansgar Nierhoff (1941–2010) was one of the most famous sculptors in Germany at the time and produced numerous art in architecture pieces and works in public spaces during the 1970s. His competition proposal envisaged a work positioned in three different locations. The intended spatially definitive effect of the diagonally positioned disk elements was questioned during its preliminary assessment. Eventually, Nierhoff's piece "Plastische Kreuzung" ("Sculptural junction"), which had been presented at the *documenta 6* in Kassel in 1977, was purchased.

The sculpture, which was placed in one of the large inner courtyards, consists of two crossing hollow, rectangular stainless-steel volumes that pick up on the axes of the "Kreuzbauten" and repeat their basic form. The modulation of the ground is part of the artwork and consists of a depression directly beneath the junction of the stainless steel bodies, suggesting a soft, easily malleable material. Nierhoff often used this effect in his work, which requires a great deal of planning and effort during the processing stage and contradicts the qualities of the material. Despite their size, his sculptures never appear monstrous, since like "Sculptural junction", they refer to the surroundings into which they are integrated.

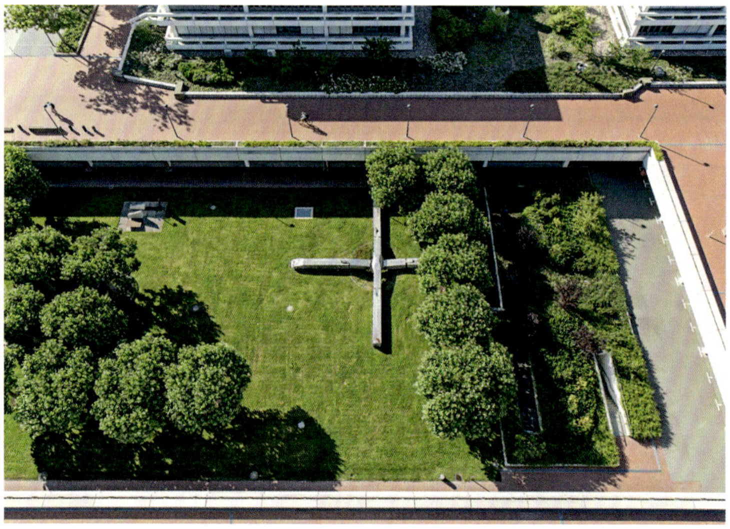

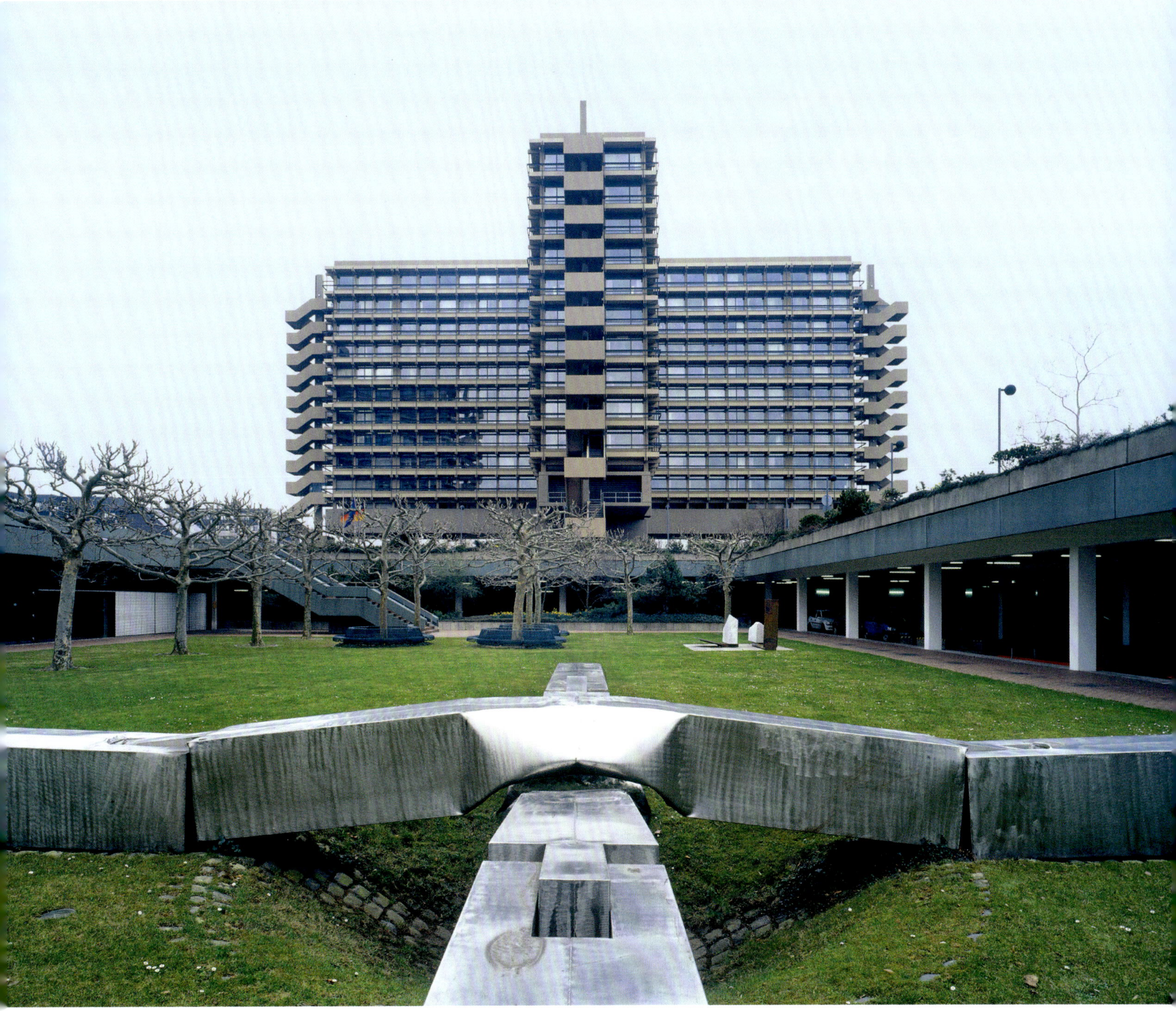

ANSGAR NIERHOFF
"Plastische Kreuzung"
("Sculptural junction"), 1977
Stainless steel
0.92 x 19.3 x 18.25 m

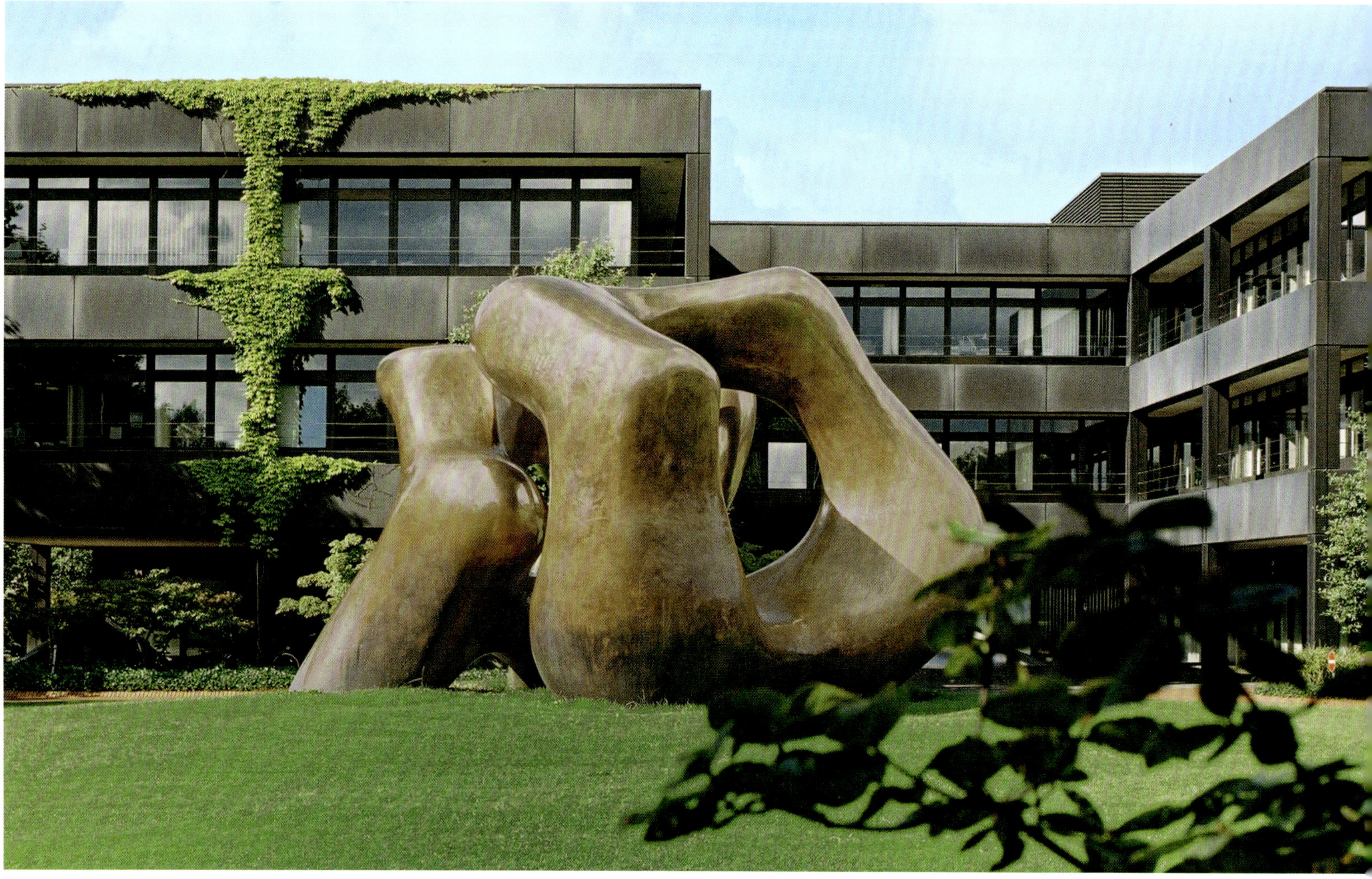

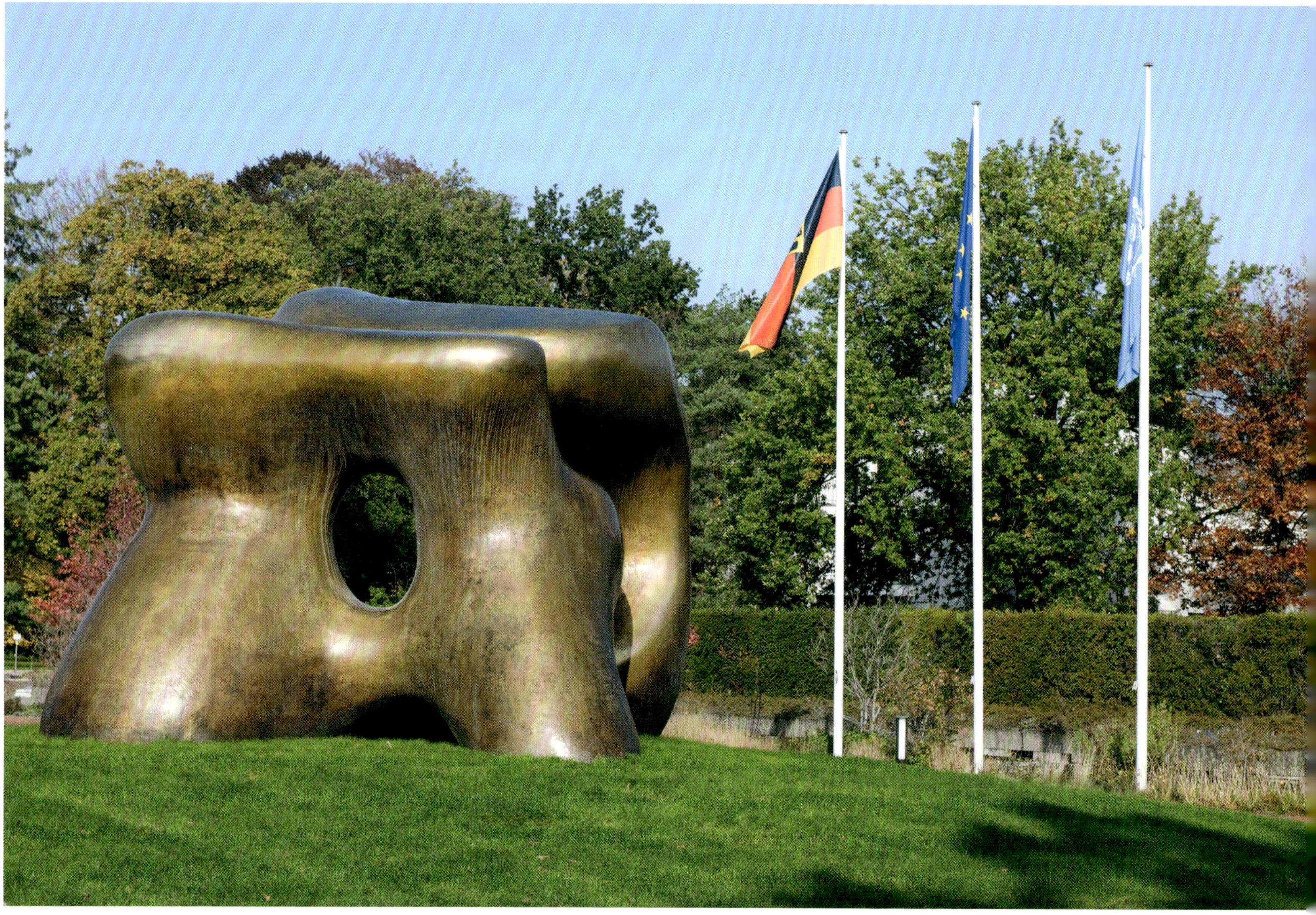

FEDERAL CHANCELLERY BONN

TODAY FEDERAL MINISTRY FOR ECONOMIC COOPERATION AND DEVELOMPENT

Address:
Adenauerallee 139
53113 Bonn

Architecture:
Stieldorf Planning Group, 1974–1976

Art in architecture:
Henry Moore
and Erich Hauser,
Günther Ferdinand Ris

The Federal Chancellor Helmut Schmidt is said to have compared the Bonn Chancellery building to the charm of a Rhineland savings bank, although the design by the Stieldorf planning group conformed entirely to the reserved official character of federal buildings of the time. In 1979, only three years after the building complex was completed, including its exterior grounds, Schmidt ordered the forecourt to be redesigned, installing a bronze sculpture by the British artist and personal acquaintance Henry Moore (1898–1986) on its lawn. In doing so, the Federal Chancellor deliberately ignored the result of an art in architecture competition for the Federal Chancellery in 1974. Thus the orb sculpture "Integration" by Hans Dieter Bohnet (1926–2006) was reinstalled on the bank of the Rhine.

Moore is one of the most important sculptors of the 20th century. His extensive work is characterised by studies on the human body, whereby mostly rounded female forms tread the line between figurative and abstract art. The monumental size of the two organic forms, which enter into a mutual relationship, makes the sculpture visible from afar. Its oval apertures create diverse perspectives that can also be seen in relation to their surroundings. Framed by the three-storey, flat building, with its dark brown aluminium façade, the surface of the bronze provides a clear counterpoint to the architecture. Schmidt interpreted the form as a sign of life, a symbol of human ties and also an expression of the human condition. With its central location, the bronze sculpture dominated the media image of the Federal Chancellery during the period of the Bonn Republic. Since the government's move to Berlin, the former Chancellery building in Bonn has been used as the headquarters of the Federal Ministry for Economic Cooperation and Development.

HENRY MOORE
"Large Two Forms", 1966–1969/1979
Bronze
365 x 400 x 610 cm

"KARL-MARX" PARTY COLLEGE OF THE SED BERLIN

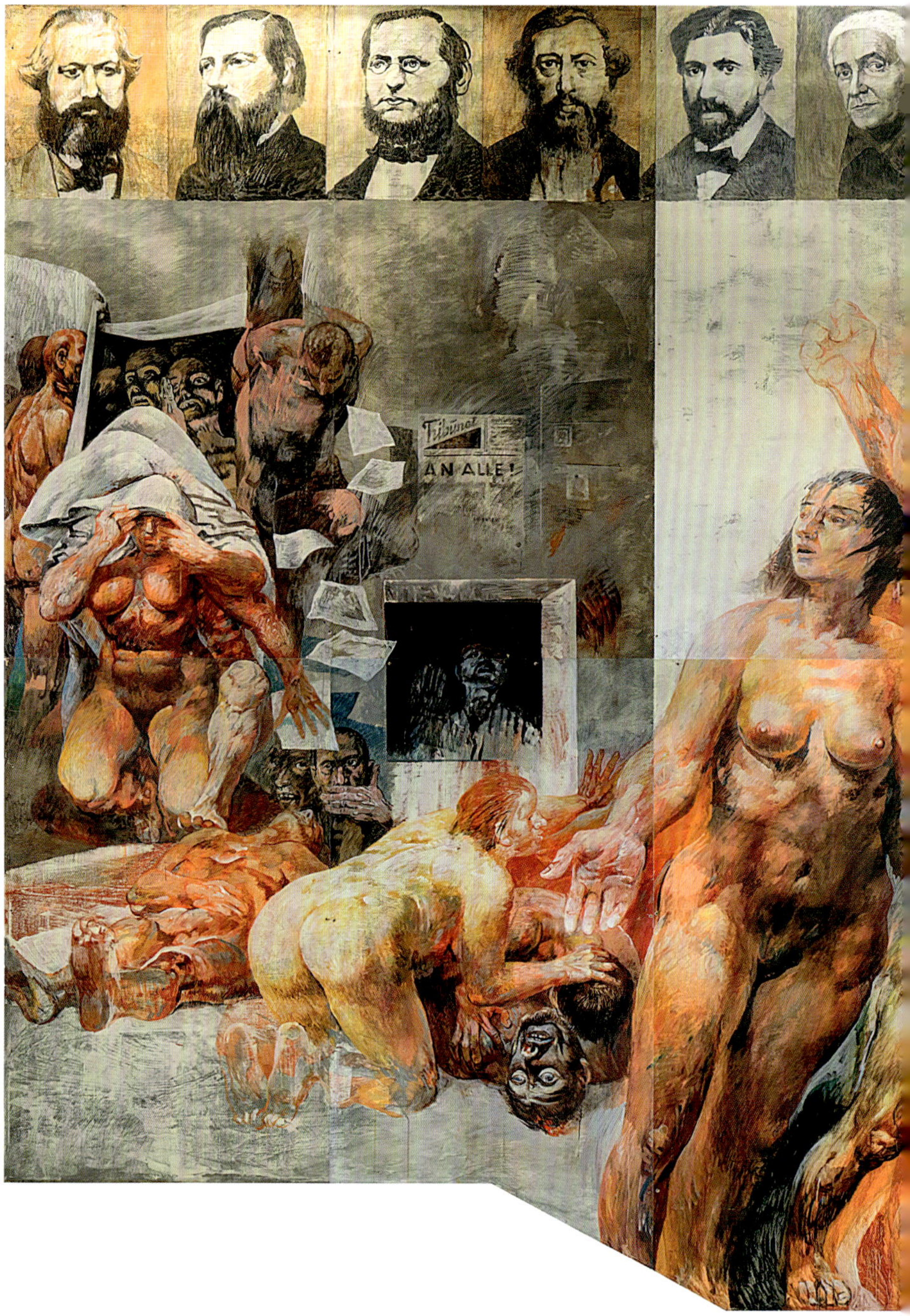

Address:
Rungestrasse 5
10179 Berlin

Architecture:
1971
demolished 2013

Art in architecture:
Willi Sitte

WILLI SITTE
"Proletarier aller Länder, vereinigt euch!" ("Workers of the world, unite!"), 1979
Mixed technique on hard fibre
2.32 x 18.71 m
(now stored at the Beeskow Art Archive)

When Willi Sitte (1921–2013) was commissioned to produce a mural for the "Karl Marx" Party College of the Central Committee of the SED in East Berlin, he had already had a chequered career as a painter. His individual painting style, which was orientated towards pre-war Modernity, had been criticised for many years. He was only able to establish himself as an artist in the GDR in the late 1960s, after active political work in the SED and an open avowal to Communism. In 1978/1979, when he produced the mural "Proletarier aller Länder, vereinigt euch!" ("Workers of the world, unite!") for the SED Party College, he had already been a member of the Volkskammer since 1976. His artistic interpretation combined social and political intentions with figurative representations, often in almost Baroque-like forms, while the expressive depiction of human bodies and the manifestation of social statements and political ideas were often provocative.

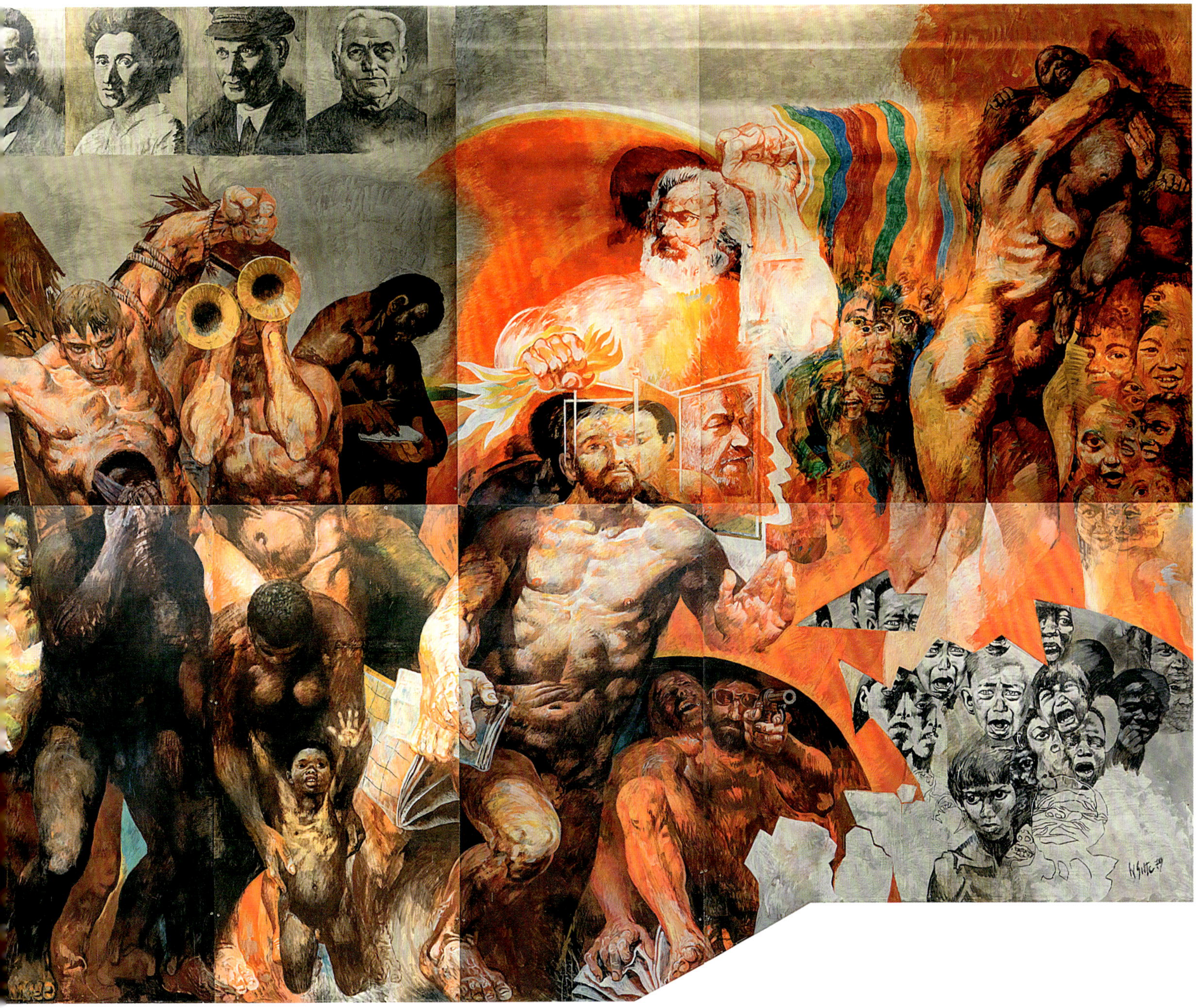

The mural for the new Party College building was situated on a staircase landing, from where the steps continue in both directions. At its centre, where anyone using the stairs would have inevitably looked, was a group of naked people, thronged together in "revolutionary forward movement". Above this group – like Zeus, the father of the gods – Karl Marx is enthroned with lightning in his hand. The allegoric presentation of the struggle for Communism is crowned by ten portraits of leaders of the German workers' movement. The portrayal of male genitals was a source of criticism, along with the lack of praise for the Soviet achievements, due to the exclusive depiction of German comrades. As a result, the Dean of the Party College, Hanna Wolf, felt it necessary to hide the painting behind bands of material. Today, the mural is stored at the Beeskow Art Archive.

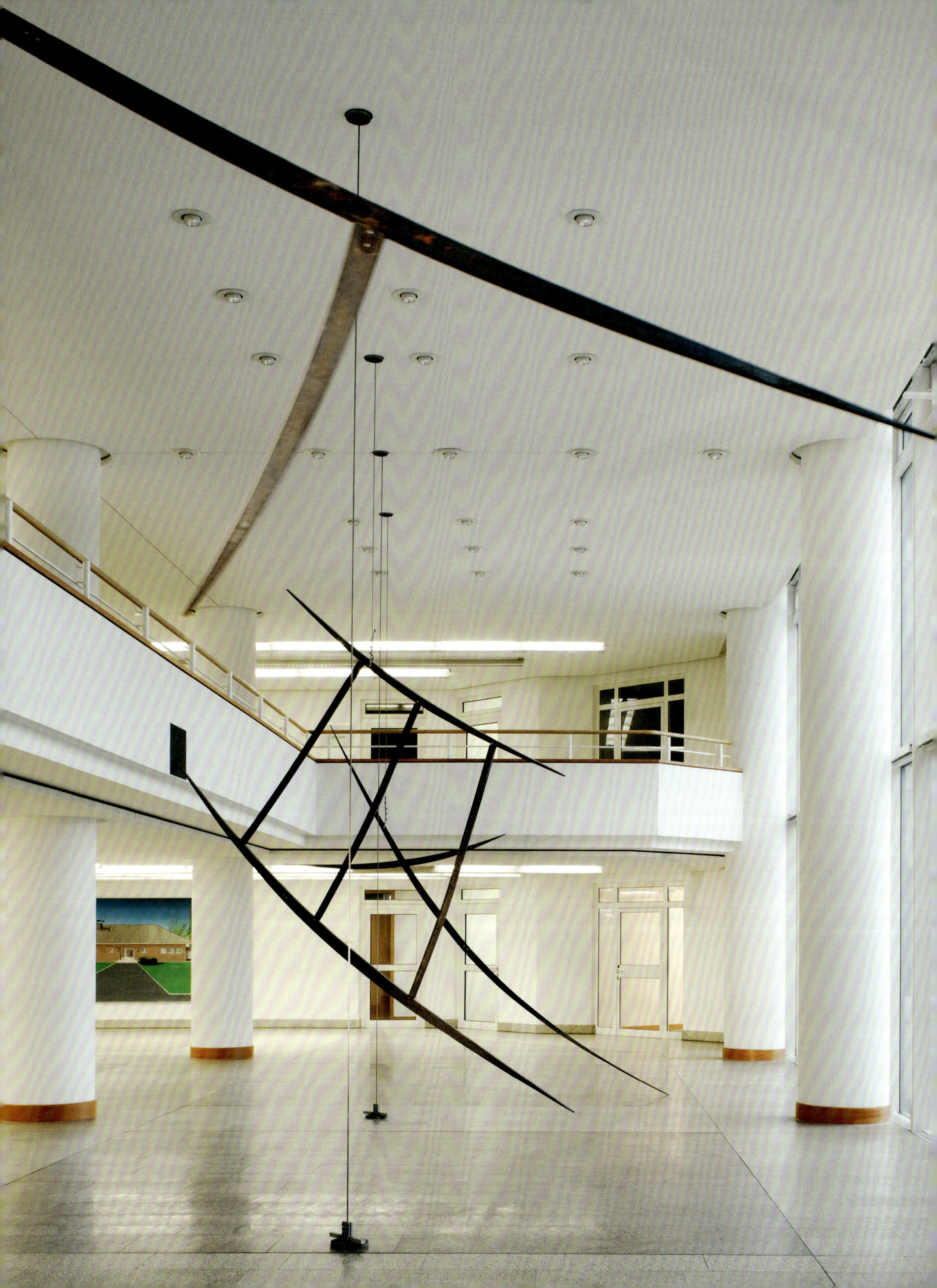

FEDERAL MINISTRY OF TRANSPORT BONN

Address:
Robert-Schuman-Platz 1
53175 Bonn

Architecture:
Deiß/Bargou Architekten and Architekturbüro Eller Maier Walter, 1986–1989

Art in architecture:
Wolfgang Nestler
and Joachim Bandau,
Otto Herbert Hajek

Before a six-storey new building was completed in 1989 according to plans by Deiß/Bargou Architekten, the Federal Ministry of Transport, which had been founded in 1949, had not had its own headquarters. The office wings of the new building are grouped in a star shape around a central, largely glazed entrance hall that opens out towards Robert-Schuman-Platz. The artistic installations were to refer to the ministry's tasks, as well as taking the specific spatial conditions into account.

Wolfgang Nestler (born in 1943) won the competition announced in 1988, with his design for a multi-storey installation in the entrance hall that covers two double floors, reflecting the artistic principle of the fragile balance of power between material and form. Above the entrance, two elliptical metal discs are suspended from the ceiling using steel cord, their form and type of suspension allowing them to remain in constant, minimal motion. Three metal objects on the middle hall level are screwed together out of steel bands and also hang from steel wire. A steel arch is positioned on the upper double-storey, which has been tensioned using steel cord. These objects inspire associations of crossing paths and transport networks, thereby referring to the ministry's responsibilities. The installation is only recognisable in its entirety from the exterior grounds through the window front, whereby the elements on the upper levels appear as an elegant drawing behind the glass façade. Inside the building, the observer can only gradually experience the art in architecture by walking through the floors and grasping the connections between the respective objects.

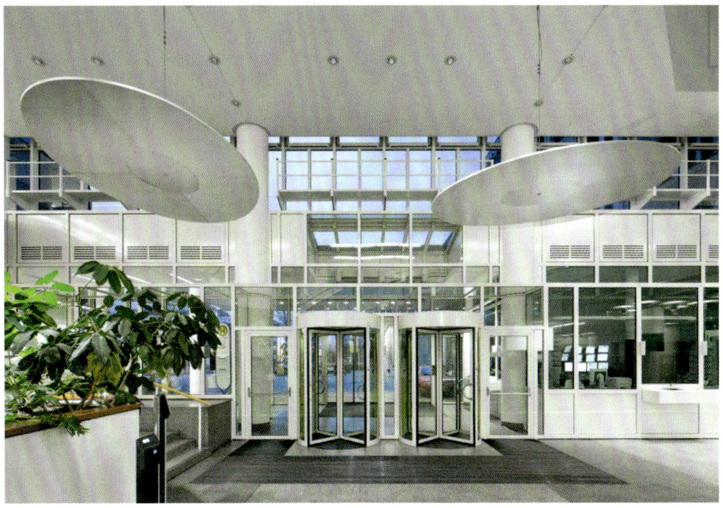

WOLFGANG NESTLER
Untitled, 1989
Various metal objects

GERMAN BUNDESTAG PLENARY AREA BONN

TODAY WORLD CONFERENCE CENTER BONN

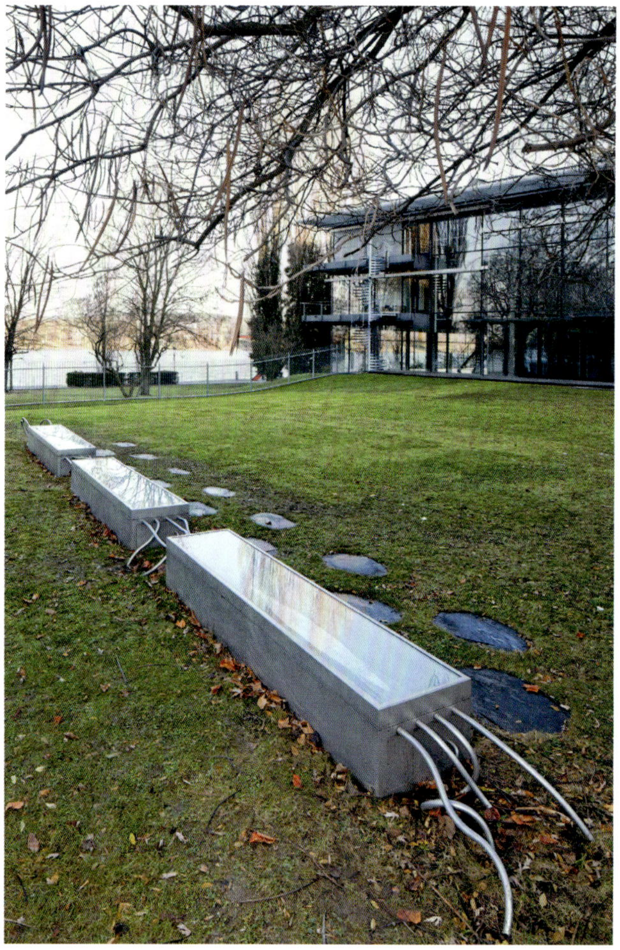

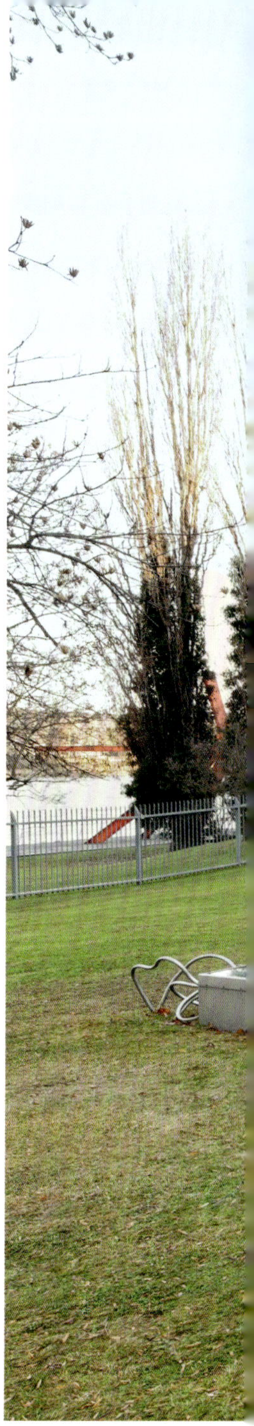

Address:
Hermann-Ehlers-Strasse 29
53113 Bonn

Architecture:
Behnisch & Partner, 1988–1992

Art in architecture:
Rebecca Horn
and Joseph Beuys, Sam Francis,
Hermann Glöckner,
Nicola de Maria, Olaf Metzel,
Mark di Suvero

REBECCA HORN
"Mondfluss" ("Moonflow"), 1997
Stainless steel, armoured glass,
mercury, motors
300 x 60 x 45 cm each

The new building for the plenary area designed by Günter Behnisch is the last building constructed for the German Bundestag in Bonn (1988–1992). It now accommodates the World Conference Center Bonn and is an architectural example of the principle of "transparent building", as Behnisch described it, meaning buildings without any symbols of status and power. The building, which was planned on the footprint of the predecessor building, consists of a steel and glass structure and is connected on the Rhine side to the former Bundeshaus by means of a glass-covered walkway. For the green area between the two buildings, the installation and performance artist Rebecca Horn (born in 1944) was invited by the Parliamentary Arts Committee to produce her sculpture "Mondfluss" ("Moonflow"). It consists of three flat stainless-steel boxes covered with armoured glass. These are

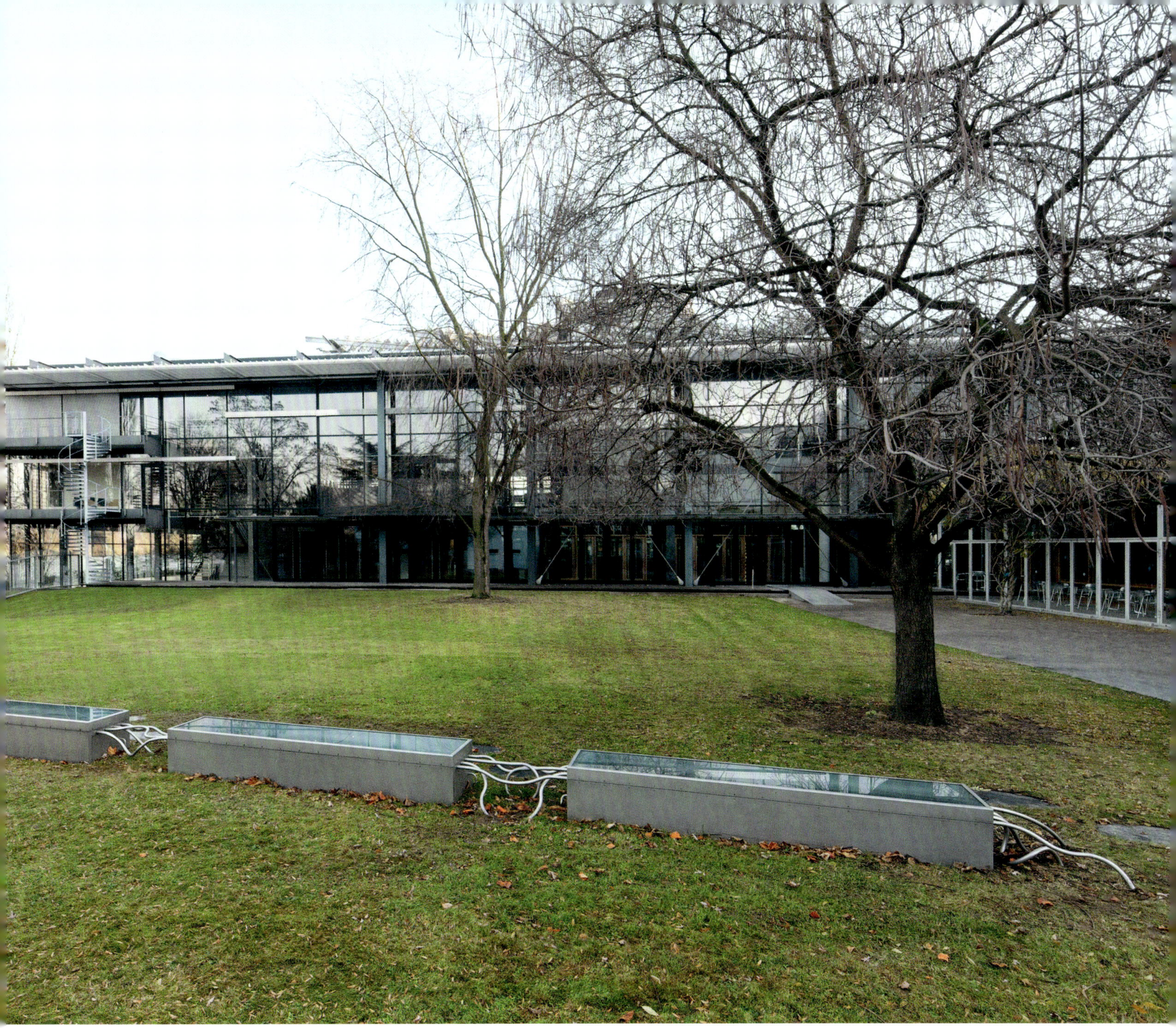

filled with mercury and made to vibrate by motors. Furthermore, dark stainless steel tubes between the basins, which are placed at a distance of one metre from each other, suggest a constant flow of mercury, the "moonflow", which forms a poetic counterpart to the Rhine in the direct vicinity.

In 1972, Rebecca Horn was the youngest participant at the *documenta 5* in Kassel, where she subsequently exhibited a further three times. Her work consists of films, installations, kinetic objects and sculptures that are never unambiguous and often develop an unsettling poetry, which has made the artist internationally famous. Horn produced several art in architecture works for the Federal Government, including pieces for the Bundesrat, the Federal Ministry of Transport in Berlin and the Deutscher Wetterdienst in Offenbach.

DEVELOPING

BERLIN
AFTER REUNIFICATION

THE CAPITAL

The reunification of Germany was rapidly followed by the question of its capital and the seat of government: the Berlin Wall fell in November 1989, German unification was officially declared in 1990, and in 1991, the Bundestag decided to move the parliament and seat of government from Bonn to Berlin. The move in the summer of 1999 was preceded by major debate and construction projects on a gigantic scale. In the no-man's land of the Spreebogen, where shortly before, the Berlin Wall had separated the two German states, the Reichstag building was prepared for the new German parliament. The government district was also developed there, including the Federal Chancellery and new buildings for the Bundestag. In Berlin-Mitte, existing buildings were renovated, adapted and expanded for the federal ministries.

Reunification was certainly a political, social and economic challenge, but also a challenge in terms of architecture and art. The initiated building work led to a stark increase in art in architecture projects, all the more so because Article 35 of the unification contract signed between the Federal Republic of Germany and the German Democratic Republic on August 31, 1990 had just described the equal importance of political, economic and cultural tasks for the new Federal Republic. The unification contract demanded no less from art and culture than to make an "autonomous and indispensable contribution to the process of unifying the German states, on the path to European unity". Culture therefore became a key factor in the search for a new national identity, and art in architecture was one of its most important instruments.

DEVELOPING THE CAPITAL – BERLIN AFTER REUNIFICATION

Martin Seidel

Apart from the Constitutional Court, the government move from Bonn to Berlin affected all of the highest state bodies of the Federal Republic. The Office of the Federal President received Bellevue Palace and a new building in the Tiergarten. The Bundestag moved into the converted Reichstag building and the large, new parliamentary buildings on the Spreebogen, as well as two buildings on Unter den Linden. The Federal Government moved into the newly built Federal Chancellery, while its ministries largely occupied existing buildings in Berlin-Mitte, as did the Bundesrat, which was accommodated in the former Prussian House of Lords.

As declared by Klaus Bußmann, the Director of the Westfälisches Landesmuseum für Kunst und Kulturgeschichte and Chairman of the Arts Council of the Federal Government, the art in architecture had the natural goal of "sending a clear signal of contemporaneity using present-day art". Like all art in architecture, the fixed points of planning measures were the architecture itself, its specific utilisation and the users. The aim was to enhance the building culture of edifices and spaces, as well as the Federal Government's self-presentation as a building client that played an even greater role following the Two-Plus-Four Agreement in 1990 and the full sovereignty of Germany. During Berlin's development as the new capital of both former German states, the aim was also to involve artists from the victorious powers of World War II, yet above all to consolidate the internal cohesion of Germany and therefore the participation of artists from the former GDR. Another no less important factor was that art in architecture in Berlin had to interact with four systems of reference with respect to politics, building history and cultural history: the old, especially Wilhelminian Berlin buildings, edifices constructed during National Socialist rule, developments during the GDR regime and new buildings. The art in architecture for the government move also differs from other art in architecture in terms of the necessary organisation. The Federal Building Authority (today's Federal Office for Building and Regional Planning, BBR) and the Bundesbaugesellschaft Berlin (Federal Building Society Berlin, BBB), which was founded in 1993 for the new Spreebogen developments and continued to operate until 2009, were both responsible for the measures. Furthermore, the highest state bodies – the Federal President, the Bundesrat, the Bundestag and the Federal Government – all formed arts councils. It was their task to investigate art locations, search for appropriate artists and also determine the selection process. The arts councils repeatedly decided against colloquia and the generally used competitions, in favour of direct commissions, thereby managing to gain internationally renowned artists for the most important projects. Nevertheless, competitions continued to be carried out even for more important projects, for instance for the Bundesrat, in parallel with the systematic purchasing of paintings and graphic designs.

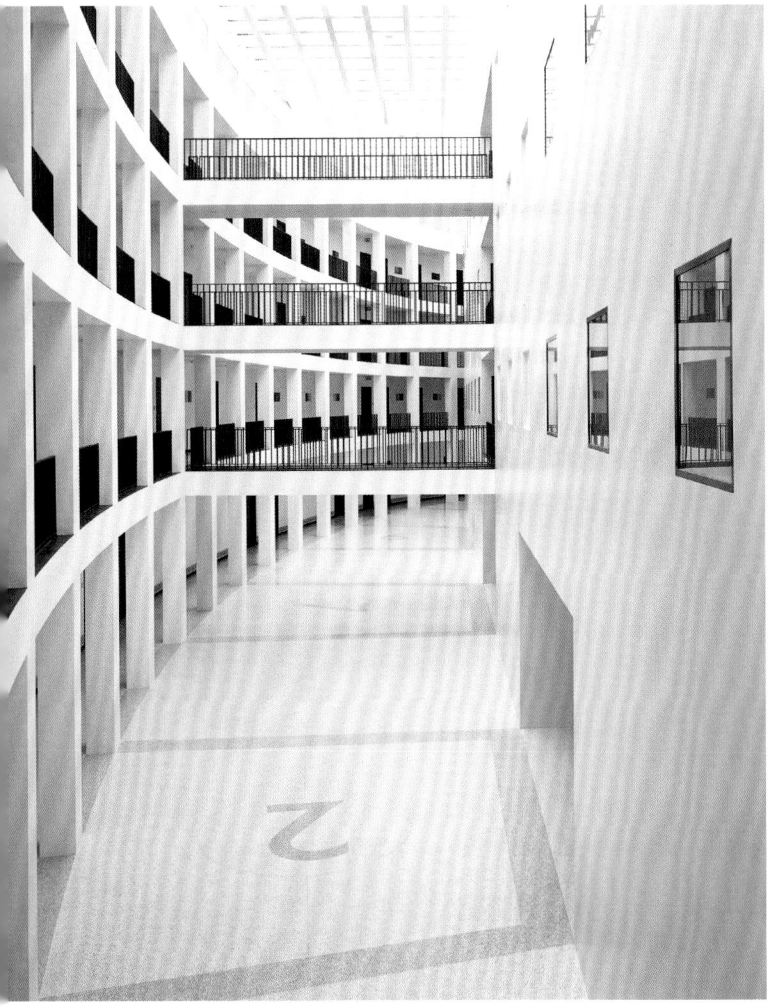

Lothar Baumgarten,
untitled, 1998, Office
of the Federal President,
Berlin

THE OFFICE OF THE FEDERAL PRESIDENT

In 1994, the then Federal President Richard von Weizsäcker represented the first state body to move its headquarters, leaving the Villa Hammerschmidt in Bonn and residing in Berlin's Bellevue Palace. Four years later, he was followed by the Office of the Federal President, which moved into a new building beside the palace. The office and the location in the district of Tiergarten required particular caution with respect to the architecture and its art. The architects Martin Gruber and Helmut Kleine-Kraneburg designed an elliptical building clad in black natural stone, its height dictated by the tree population at the site. For the art in architecture, the Arts Council of the Office of the Federal President recommended appropriate consideration and arranged a meeting between the architects and the artist Lothar Baumgarten (1944–2018), whose previous comparable commissions recommended him for the task. Following his direct commission, he designed a terrazzo floor with a grey-in-grey field of inlaid numbers. As a symbol of perfect balance, which is also characterised by the form of the building's ellipse, Baumgarten inscribed the floor with a numeric sequence of 1 to 9, the numbers' addition following the principle of a magic square, always resulting in the same sum and thereby expressing harmony. The second part of the art consists of 90 monochrome majolica panels inserted flush with the walls on the three upper levels. The colourscape is derived from the Romantic painter Caspar David Friedrich (1774–1840) and suggests landscape horizons in the windowless galleries of the interior space. In the Office of the Federal President, art and architecture form a unity, their aesthetic Hermeticism rejecting all potential for further design.

This focused mixture of determination and reserve in architecture and art represents a statement of self-confidence, equanimity and respect, forming a meaningful analogy to the self-perception of the office of the Head of State.

THE REICHSTAG BUILDING

The Office of the Federal President has a reserved location surrounded by trees and behind a fence, thus attracting little public attention in the Grosser Tiergarten park. The opposite is the case in the vibrant parliament district on the Spreebogen between Berlin's Central Station and the Brandenburg Gate. It is the location of the Reichstag building and the "Band des Bundes" ("Federal Band") that connects the Federal Chancellery, Paul Löbe House and Marie Elisabeth Lüders House in a straight line over the former border, thereby symbolising the reunification of Germany.

The heart of the parliament district is formed by the Reichstag building on the green Platz der Republik. Constructed between 1884 and 1894 according to plans by Paul Wallot, it is the archetypal symbol of German democracy. It has attracted masses of visitors ever since it was wrapped in a silver-grey plastic textile by the artist couple Christo and Jeanne-Claude in the summer of 1995 and subsequently converted by the British architect Norman Foster, who completed the task in 1999. Apart from the monumental architecture, the eye-catching element of the building is not the historical gable relief or the allegorical stone sculptures on the parapet zone, but Foster's new large, walkable glass dome, which is illuminated at night. The architectural intervention has already achieved a great deal in raising public awareness. By contrast, the art in architecture of the Reichstag building, which was anchored in the cultural task defined by the government's move and the country's unification contract, had different tasks and locations inside the building. The Arts Council of the Bundestag, which consists of ten members of parliament from all parties in proportion to their parliamentary representation, plus two art experts, awarded no fewer than 19 commissions for paintings, objects, installations, interventions and spatial designs, while also purchasing 6 further pieces. These enormous efforts required an increase in expenditure on art in architecture from 2 to 3 percent of the overall building and conversion costs. The conscious decision not to use competitions and colloquiums was based on the intention not only to commission less well known, young artists and especially female artists: there was also the aim of commissioning renowned artists, as well as those from the former GDR and the four allied protecting powers. The large entrance hall was reserved for two heroes of contemporary painting: Sigmar Polke (1941–2010), who installed five lightboxes presenting historical motifs, and Gerhard Richter (born in 1932), whose 21-metre high and 3 metre wide black, red and gold enamel glass panels exist on the periphery between pure painting and a symbol of sovereignty. Often large-scale, multi-part paintings, calligraphic paintings, objects, sculptures and media installations by established artists such as Hanne Darboven (1941–2009), Gotthard Graubner (1930–2013), Anselm Kiefer (born in 1945), Markus Lüpertz (born in 1941), Ulrich Rückriem (born in 1938), Emil Schumacher (1912–1999) and Katharina Sieverding (born in 1944) are distributed in various entrance areas, foyers, protocol, meeting and discussion rooms, the commemoration room, the cafeteria, the restaurant and the club room. As a representative of the Leipzig School, which was

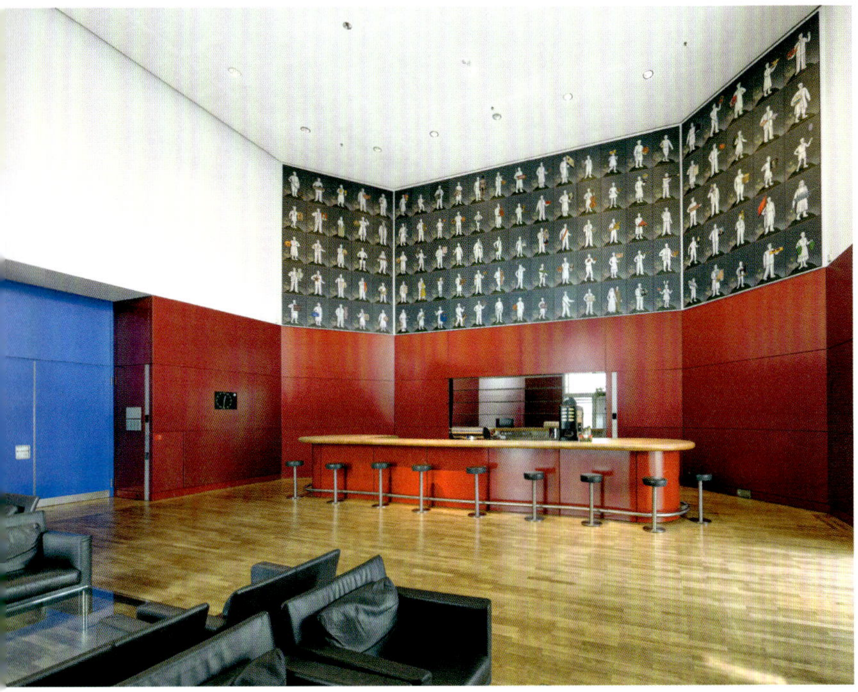

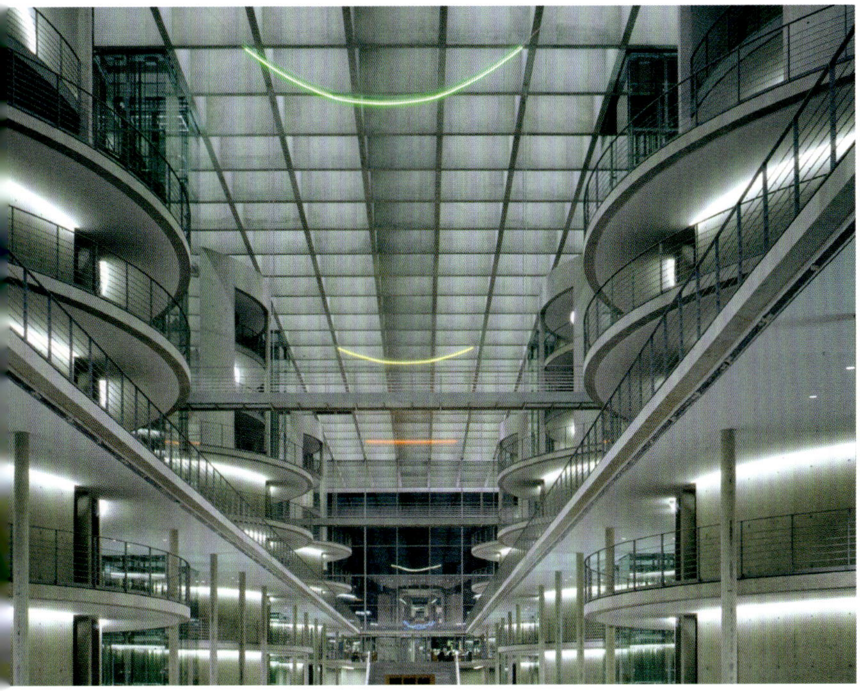

founded during the GDR period, Bernhard Heisig (1925–2011) was invited to produce an oil painting of a historical panorama. In a respectful gesture towards the allied protecting powers, the Frenchman Christian Boltanski (born in 1944), the Russian Grisha Bruskin (born in 1945) and the US artist Jenny Holzer (born in 1950) (→ p. 136) were also commissioned, producing spectacular installations.

Overall, the high proportion of moveable, two-dimensional art was due to the fact that Foster developed the architecture autonomously. Integral art in architecture was therefore initially impossible. However, one piece that continues to be controversial is the architecturally related and by now perhaps most famous work by Hans Haacke (born in 1936) in the building's northern inner courtyard (→ p. 168). Over a 21 x 7 metre green area, the concept artist installed the illuminated inscription "DER BEVÖLKERUNG" ("TO THE POPULATION"). The conscious break with the historical inscription "DEM DEUTSCHEN VOLKE" ("TO THE GERMAN PEOPLE") on the gable of the western portal gives the building a new level of meaning. This re-dedication also requires the cooperation of the parliamentarians, since they are called upon to aid the plants' growth by adding soil from their constituencies. It has become a historical chapter and an element of the work itself that both the content and the artistic concept led to an éclat among politicians, who only approved the artwork's implementation following a parliamentary vote with an extremely close outcome.

Nothing could better illustrate the placement plausibility of art in architecture and nothing could more clearly demonstrate the contrast to the art at the Office of the Federal President than this piece of contemporary criticism. However, the artworks' colourful

Grisha Bruskin, "Leben über alles", 1999, German Bundestag/Reichstag building, Berlin

François Morellet, "Haute et basse tension", 1999–2001, German Bundestag/Paul Löbe House, Berlin

diversity of genres, modes of expression and themes in the Reichstag building also makes a clear statement with respect to the location. Even the choice of artists was based on no artistic programme, instead attempting to reflect cultural-political proportions. Female artists were still very under-represented despite the good intentions. However, there is no doubt that the pluralism of the artistic positions fittingly expresses the pluralism of modern parliamentarianism. This choice reveals an analogy with the art at the Office of the Federal President on a structural level, since it is based on the same consideration for the profile of the buildings' use: in this case doing the opposite, namely focusing on only a single artistic position.

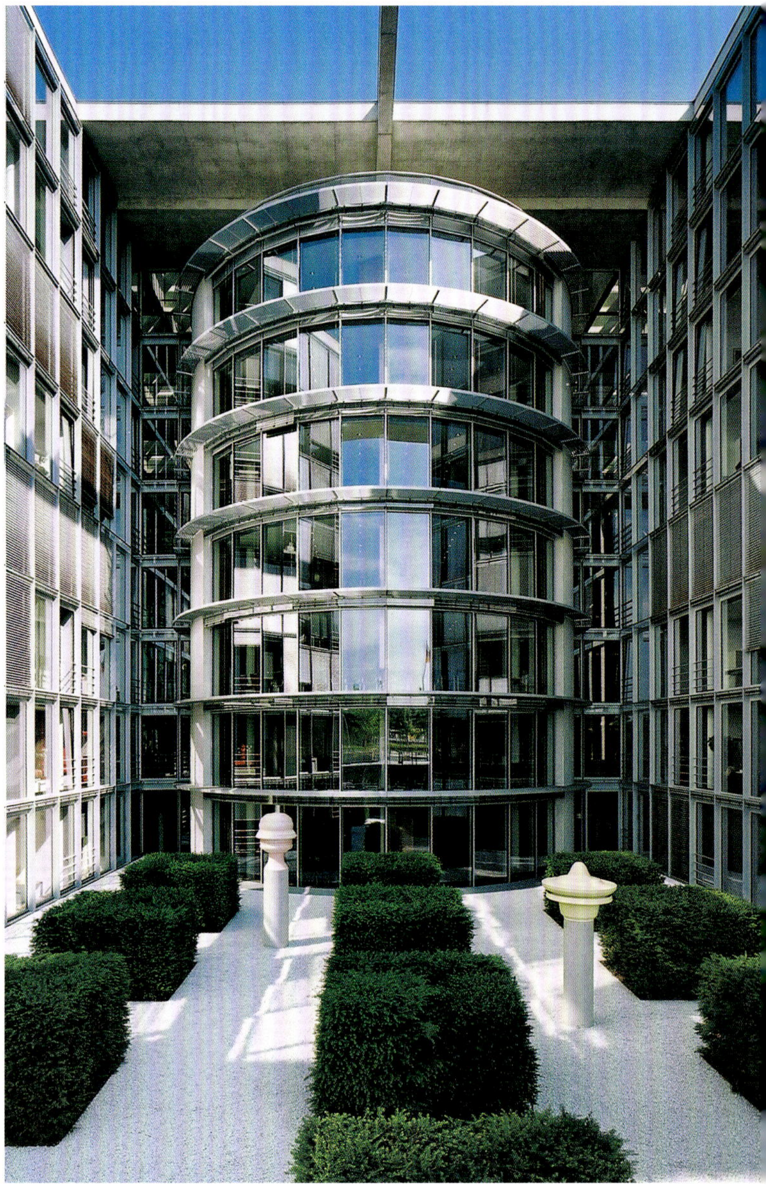

NEW BUILDINGS FOR THE GERMAN BUNDESTAG

The new functional buildings for the Bundestag in the government district on the Spreebogen – Paul Löbe House, Marie Elisabeth Lüders House and Jakob Kaiser House – differ from the Reichstag building in many ways, including the fact that they enthusiastically present their art in architecture to the outside world. Paul Löbe House and Marie Elisabeth Lüders House were both designed by the Munich architect Stephan Braunfels and form the eastern section of the 900-metre long "Band des Bundes" crossing the River Spree to create a unique ensemble of Berlin architecture. Paul Löbe House itself is 200 metres long, over 100 metres wide and 23 metres high. The architecture, which is characterised by strict circular and square forms, opens up with glass façades and is organised in five wings running in both directions from a continuous hall, their atria creating an open structure. The façade of Paul

(e.) Twin Gabriel, "Deutscher 1", "Deutscher 2", 1992/2001, German Bundestag/Paul Löbe House, Berlin

Neo Rauch, "Mann auf der Leiter", 1998/2001, German Bundestag/Paul Löbe House, Berlin

Julia Mangold, untitled, 1998/2003, German Bundestag/Marie Elisabeth Lüders House, Berlin

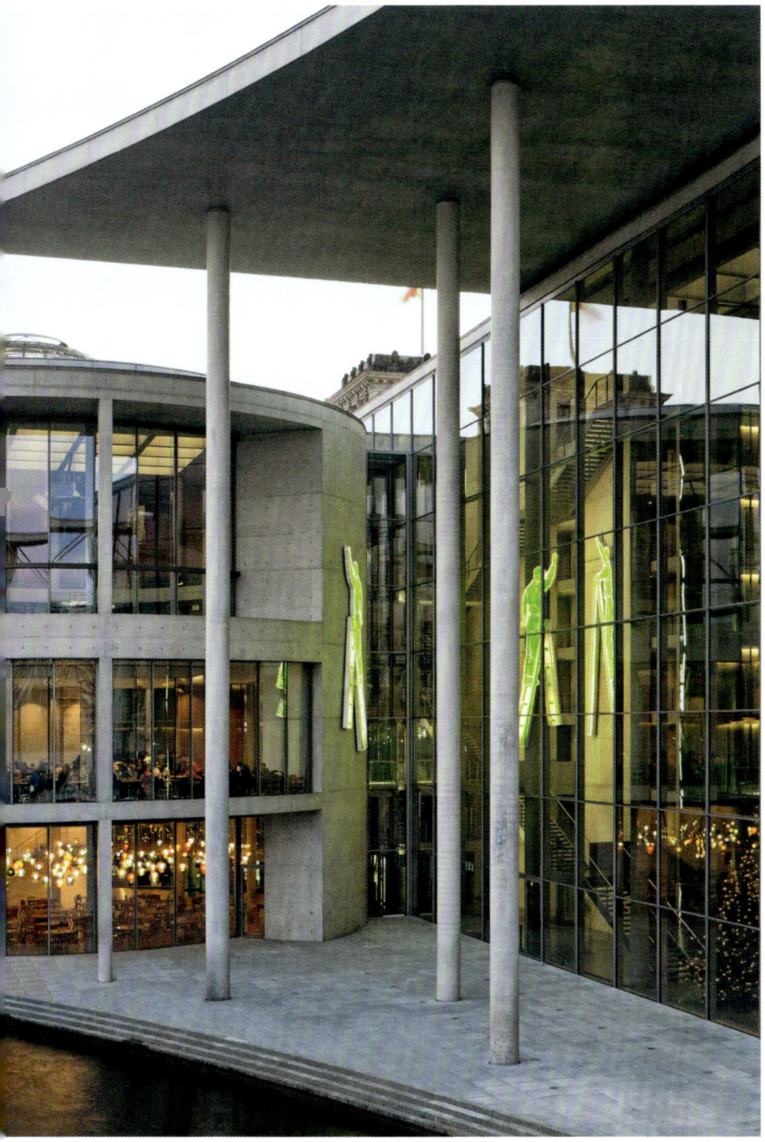

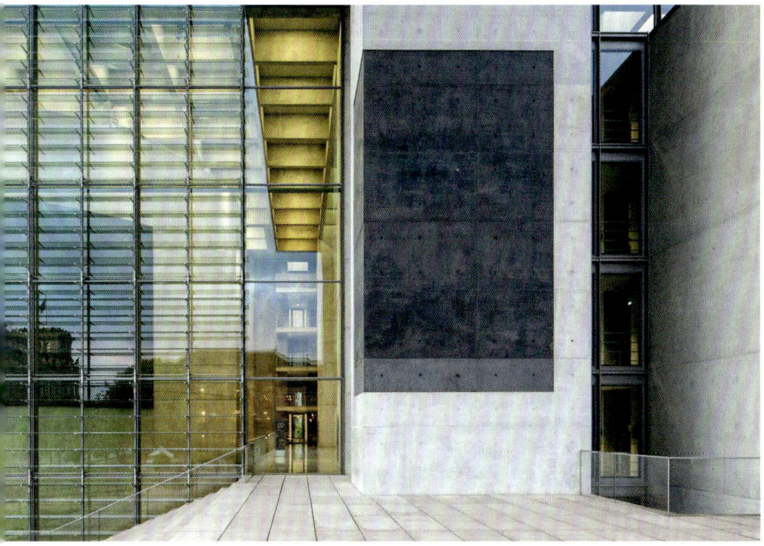

Löbe House reflects the image of the opposite Federal Chancellery; the art by Elsworth Kelly (1923–2015) is visible on the wall behind it: four large aluminium panels framed in blue, black, red and green add colour and rhythm to the fair-faced concrete surface. The hall also accommodates an artwork by François Morellet (1926–2016), consisting of four neon garlands suspended from the ceiling. In darkness, they radiate into the exterior space and transform the gigantic entrance area into an illuminated stage.

The lateral exterior courtyards also serve artistic purposes. The works installed there can have an interventional character, such as the building grid by Franka Hörnschemeyer (born in 1958), which reconstructs the former Berlin Wall structures of the GDR and today's Bundestag building. They can be educational or cautionary, as in the case of the 19 constitutionally defined articles of fundamental rights, which Dani Karavan (born in 1930) engraved onto glass steles that outline a courtyard of Jakob Kaiser House along the Spreepromenade. And they can also be joyful and humorous, as in the case of the rotationally symmetrical Teflon sculptures "Deutscher 1" and "Deutscher 2" ("German 1" and "German 2") by the artistic duo (e.) Twin Gabriel (Else Gabriel, born in 1962 and Ulf Wrede, born in 1968). Keen observers will recognise the profiles of Johann Wolfgang von Goethe and a German shepherd dog in the artworks.

From an urbanist perspective, one of the most appealing spots in all of Berlin is where Paul Löbe House and Marie Elisabeth Lüders House meet one another on opposite sides of the River Spree. They open up new perspectives from house to house, both from the riverbank promenades and from the excursion boats. Paul Löbe House radiates with the colourful lamps of the artistic restaurant design by Jorge Pardo (born in 1963), along with two illuminated figures by Neo Rauch (born in 1960) that are attached to the eastern façade. A bronze statue of a horseman by Marino Marini (1901–1980), which was not explicitly produced for that location, adorns the attractive open-air stairs of Marie Elisabeth Lüders House. Beside it, the sculptor Julia Mangold (born in 1966) produced a reserved and yet equally impressive piece of art in architecture, an 8 x 8 metre square concrete base at the platform pillar, with a rounded counterpart on the rotunda inside the building, creating an exciting relationship between the two pieces.

All three houses are characterised by magnificent artworks of all genres and styles. There is calligraphic art inserted into the walls and flooring. Pieces of art are suspended from the ceiling, such as the rowing boats by Christiane Möbus (born in 1947) (→ p. 148). An inner courtyard includes the four-storey architectural sculpture of an angular brickwork piece by Per Kirkeby (1938–2018). Another interesting artwork is the interactive installation by Angela Bulloch (born in 1966), which uses light signals to communicate between two separate sections of Paul Löbe House.

The success of the art in architecture at these locations is the direct result of the organisation and early coordination between the artists and the architect. The art concept for Jakob Kaiser House and the overall concept for Paul Löbe House and Marie Elisabeth Lüders House were each supervised by two renowned art experts, their respective reports having a definitive influence on the decisions taken by the Arts Council of the Bundestag. To a certain extent, one can even detect a curator's hallmark in the final choice of artworks. However, the balance of different and sometimes contradictory artistic positions and temperaments is not the result of personal preferences, but of the quality of the

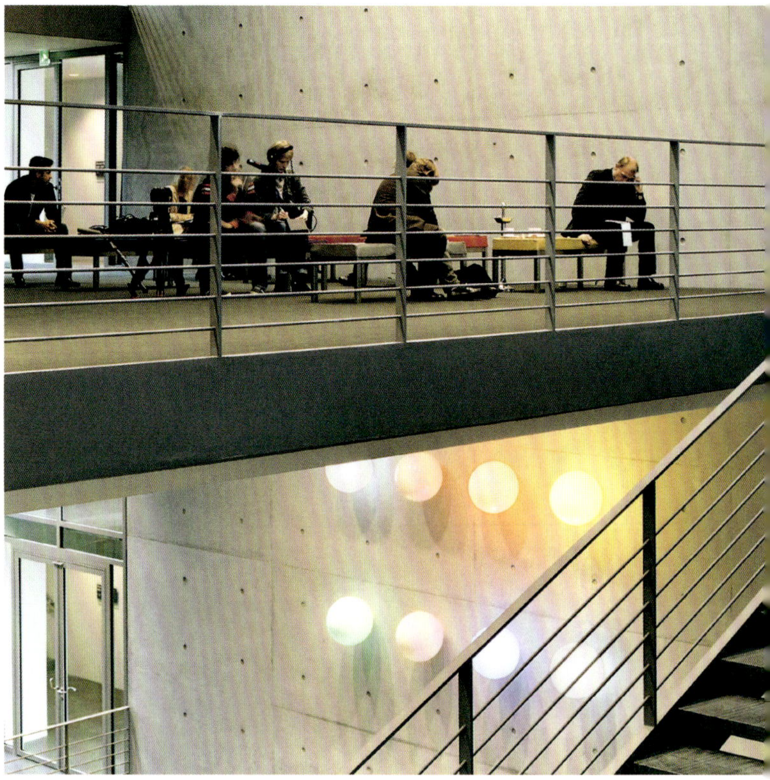

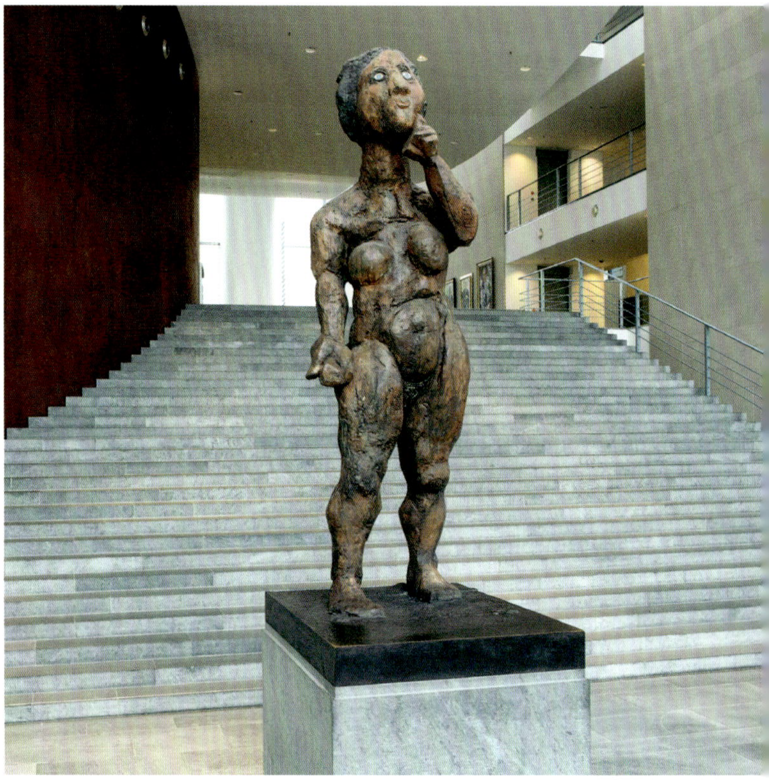

Angela Bulloch, "Seats of Power – Spheres of Influence", 1998/2001, German Bundestag/ Paul Löbe House, Berlin

Markus Lüpertz, "Die Philosophin", 1998/2001, Federal Chancellery, Berlin art itself, which is never arbitrary and yet – as is fitting for parliamentary buildings – diverse.

THE FEDERAL CHANCELLERY

Like the Reichstag building, the Federal Chancellery, which was designed by Axel Schultes and Charlotte Frank, is also a free-standing building. With its dynamic façade and the distribution of the building volume over its elongated wings, the building presents itself as the postmodern antithesis to the Wilhelminian Reichstag. While the Reichstag's glass dome symbolises transparency and modern democracy, the entire architecture of the Federal Chancellery, which was completed in 2001, fulfils the same purpose. The urbanist idea of the "Band des Bundes" also stands for a new beginning and the regained unity of Germany. The "Band des Bundes" is a further concept by Axel Schultes and Charlotte Frank. The axis lined by oak trees connects the Chancellery and the surrounding Kanzlerpark with Paul Löbe House, past the so-called Forum in between them and then continues to Marie Elisabeth Lüders House on the other side of the River Spree. The symbolism of this urban-planning connection between buildings over the former route of the Berlin Wall is stringent. However, the reunification becomes directly tangible with the over five-metre high Corten steel sculpture entitled "Berlin", which dominates the atmosphere of the visibly open Chancellery forecourt. The abstract forms of this two-part pillared sculpture, which was produced in 1999, with its outreaching and clasping cantilevers, unmistakeably express the theme of encountering and approaching (→ p. 138). The fact that this new symbol of national identification was produced by a foreign artist, the Basque sculptor and visual artist Eduardo Chillida (1924–2002), is in itself a significant aspect of the work.

In a strikingly visual way, Chillida's sculpture also encapsulates the transition from the Bonn Republic to the Berlin Republic. Its older counterpart, the bronze sculpture by Henry Moore in front of the former Federal Chancellery in Bonn, is comparable in terms of its size and the motif of two approaching forms. However, the organic character of Moore's piece has become hard-edged, geometrical and structural in Chillida's work. Unlike Moore, Chillida was commissioned to produce the sculpture and discussed it with the then Federal Chancellor Gerhard Schröder while it was being produced. It is difficult to estimate the extent to which Schröder influenced the form. However, it is unmistakeable that the "Berlin" sculpture is a firm statement and a self-confident symbol, seen in media images all around the world, of a Germany that has regained its international standing following reunification.

The Federal Chancellery positions itself very clearly towards the outside world through its architecture and Chillida's sculpture. Inside, not all concepts of the Chancellery's own art council were feasible. However, on its suggestion and in intense exchange with the Federal Chancellor, Markus Lüpertz (born in 1941) developed monochrome wall surfaces as art in architecture for the sweeping surrounding walls of the conference hall. In an analogy to the medieval teachings of virtues and temperaments, they draw a thematic parallel to the Chancellery by presenting an allegory of good government; it is joined by the bronze sculpture "Die Philosophin" ("The philosopher"), which was originally intended for the Ministry of Labour and was installed in the Chancellery's foyer following Schröder's personal intervention. In addition to an artistically conservative gallery of portraits of former Federal Chancellors, the other paintings and sculptures acquired through purchases or loans, representing almost a century of art history from Expressionism to the present day, were distributed around the entire building. For instance the Press and Information Room contains the famous works entitled "Augenbilder" ("Eye images") by Ernst-Wilhelm Nay (1902–1968), which have been provided as permanent loans. Art in architecture funds were used to purchase two photographic pieces by Jeff Wall (born in 1946). The Arts Council only dared to organise one art in architecture competition, namely for the Skylobby in 2001, which was dedicated to young art. The winning proposal consisted of large-scale paintings by Michel Majerus (1967–2002), Corinne Wasmuth (born in 1964) and Franz Ackermann (born in 1963). Generally, the art in architecture of the interior spaces of the Federal Chancellery does not focus on a contemporary aesthetic or the thematically critical aspect of the location. Instead, it represents a museum-like collection of high-quality and exceptional autonomous artworks.

FEDERAL MINISTRIES

In 1996, the then Federal Minister of Labour, Klaus Töpfer, founded the Arts Council for building measures of the Federal Government in Berlin to determine the art for the remaining government buildings. Its task was to develop a master plan for seven federal ministries, including art locations, appropriate artists and a selection process, which was modified by the Federal Office for Building and Regional Planning, and implemented until 2004. It is well known that art can occasionally encounter difficulties when dealing with ministries. Unlike the Federal Chancellery and the Bundesrat, the ministries were not involved in decision-making processes, which could and did lead to conflicts with the users, who were not always familiar with the forms of expression of contemporary art, or prepared for them. For instance, this resulted in the Federal Ministry of Labour rejecting the bronze statue "The philosopher" by Markus Lüpertz, which was considered provocative and thematically irritating. It was later installed in the Federal Chancellery.

In a controversial question concerning the government's move, namely whether to build something new or move into an existing building, the idea of the critical, continued use of existing buildings from the Nazi or GDR periods became established. The aim was to save costs and face up to history. However the artists and their clients were not always primarily interested in coming to terms with history. Many works completely ignore the buildings' former uses and pursue other interests. At the Federal Ministry for Labour and Social Affairs in the old government district around Wilhelmstrasse, no work explicitly engages with the building's past and uses, although it previously accommodated the Reich Propaganda Ministry and then the GDR Media Centre. The Federal Foreign Office moved into the former Reichsbank building, which was completed in 1939 and later used by the Central Committee of the SED. During the building's conversion, which was completed in 1999, the architect Hans Kollhoff ensured that the temporal layers of architecture stemming from the Nazi and GDR periods were preserved or even reconstructed, additionally designing a third, contemporary layer together with the artist Gerhard Merz (born in 1947), namely an integrative concept of large, neutral colour surfaces. The large Foreign Office extension building designed by Müller Reimann Architekten integrates

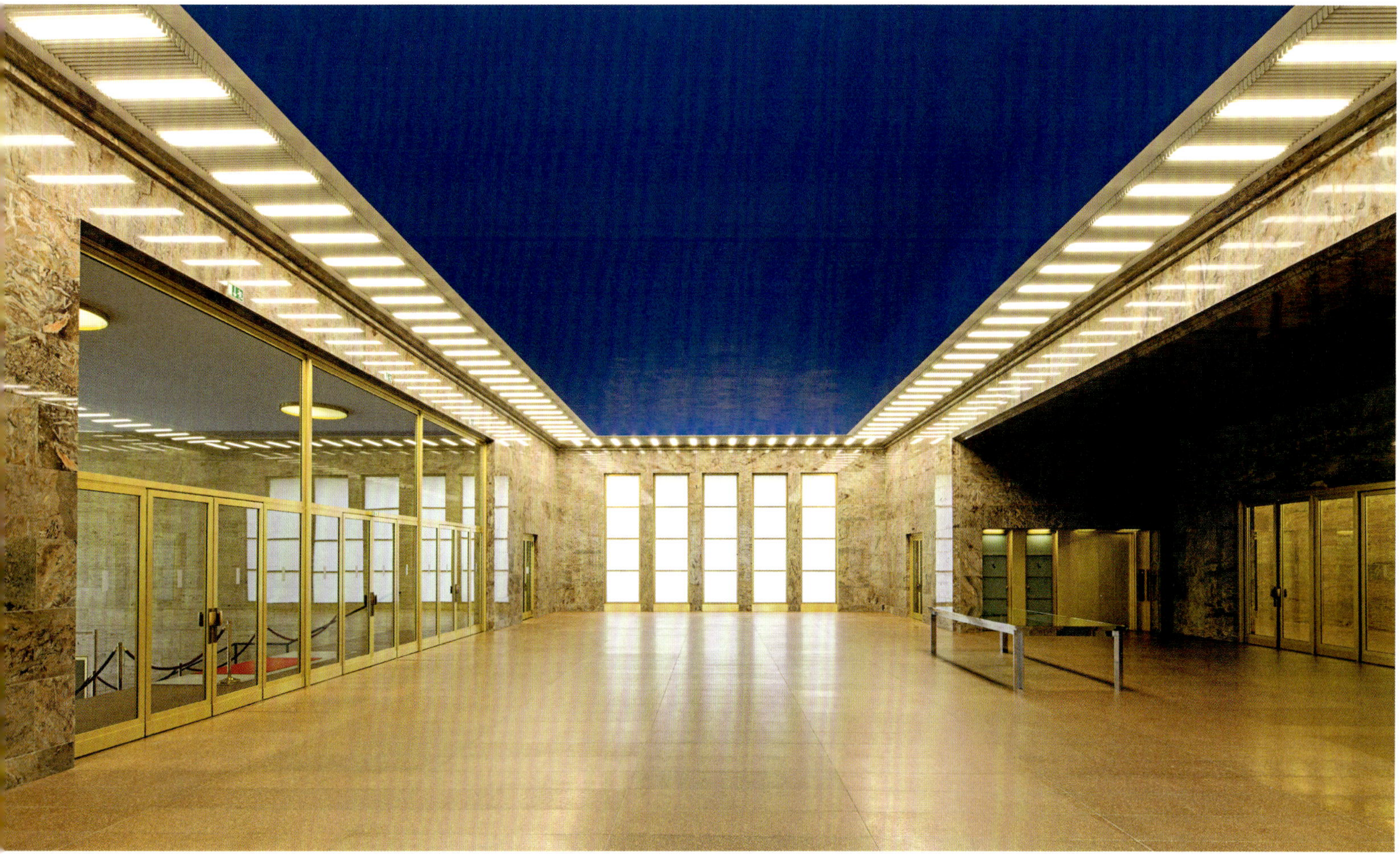

Gerhard Merz, colour-light concept, 1995/2000, Foreign Office, Berlin

a glass façade by the light artist James Carpenter (born in 1949). It defines the lighting conditions in the room and radiates out into the urban space. Together with the public accessibility of the foyer, the art in architecture symbolises the openness and transparency of a ministry that has closed the book on the existing building's past and focuses on the present and the future.

The Federal Ministry of Finance moved into the second major Nazi building in Berlin, the Reich Ministry of Aviation completed in 1936, which later served as the House of Ministries during the GDR period. The further conversion concluded in 1999 largely retained the character of the architecture. The installed art in architecture is a completely abstract artwork in the inner courtyard, with large steel sculptures by Robert Schad (born in 1953). The concept artist Jochen Gerz (born in 1940) sought to engage with the content of Schad's piece by means of a video interview he carried out with members of the ministry. Palimpsests were also produced for the building. For instance Michael Wirkner (1954–2012) used non-figurative paintings to react to originally existent Nazi and GDR symbols (→ p. 146). The "Soldatenrelief" ("Soldier relief") of the Nazi period had already been removed by the GDR government and covered with a ceramic mural by Max Lingner (1888–1959) in 1953. After the end of the GDR regime and reunification, a further recoding measure was carried out: in 2000, the artist Wolfgang Rüppel (born in 1942) adapted a photographic motif of the uprising on June 17, 1953 to create a floor installation with a length of 25 metres, which was funded by the State of Berlin and the Federal Government. This artwork adds a new chapter to the ideological history of the square.

When art in architecture becomes specific, it generally does not become insistent memorial art, as can be seen in the case of the "Roter Teppich" ("Red carpet") by Via Lewandowsky (born in 1963), which was produced following a commission by the Ministry of Defence (→ p. 170). In 1993, the ministry moved into its second headquarters in the Bendlerblock facility on Berlin's Reichpietschufer and had to take a stance with respect to the building's heavy historical burden.

There are some such examples, however. In today's Federal Ministry of Justice, an installation by Ulrich Schröder (born in 1954) that was inaugurated in 2000 and is visible from the street, recalls that the GDR International Press Centre once had its headquarters behind those walls. On November 9, 1989, the SED functionary Günter Schabowski held his famous press conference there, proclaiming that GDR citizens were free to travel.

When the former Permanent Representation of the FRG in the GDR was converted for the (former) Federal Ministry of Education and Resarch, an art in architecture competition for students was announced, for which Daniela Klein (born in 1974) converted the closed porter's lodge into a showcase. On its window, the reflected historical quote "Entscheidung mit den Füßen" ("Decision with one's feet") can be seen, referring to the fact that GDR citizens occupied the representation several times.

By 2004, the Federal Government had commissioned no fewer than forty art projects for its Berlin government buildings, reflecting all styles, genres and artistic stances. Fortunately for the art, memorial pragmatism was never the rule and only the exception.

THE BUNDESRAT

The Bundesrat, the chamber of the Federal States, also moved its headquarters to an existing Wilhelminian building in Berlin: the former Prussian House of Lords, which had been constructed between 1899 and 1904 according to plans by the architect Friedrich Schulze for the first Chamber of the Prussian Parliament. Part of the building was heavily damaged during World War II. It was subsequently used by the GDR Academy of Sciences, before being converted for the Bundesrat by the architectural office Schweger + Partner between 1997 and 2000. The measures especially made the opening of the walls and the light roof structure in the plenary hall understandable as an expression of today's democracy. On the façade towards Leipziger Strasse, the facility's Neoclassicism had largely remained undamaged. In the tympanum supported by six pillars, the allegory of the State of Prussia by the historicist sculptor Otto Lessing (1846–1912) survives

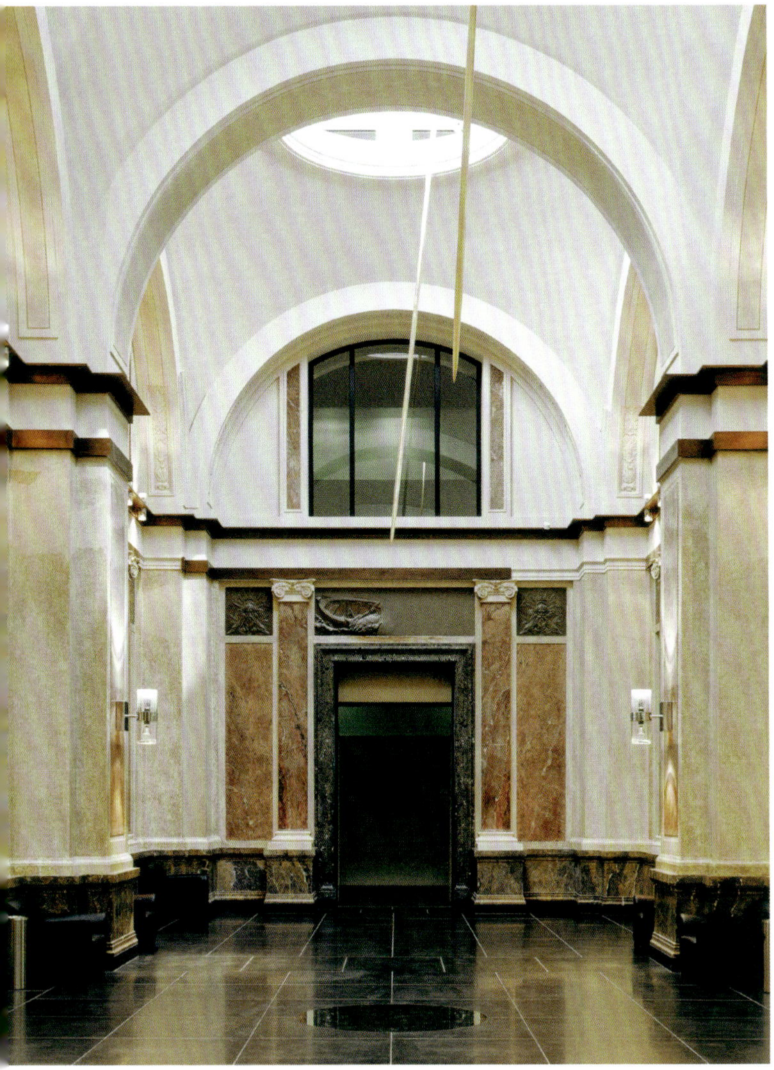

Rebecca Horn,
"Die drei Grazien", 2000,
Bundesrat, Berlin

to this day. Following a competition, the old decorative figures on the parapet, which were destroyed in the war, were replaced in 2000 by abstract bronze panels and bronze heads produced by the Danish artist, sculptor and architect Per Kirkeby (1938–2018) (→ p. 140). It represents a confident gesture of autonomous, contemporary art, its noblesse nevertheless respecting the existing structures.

The second art in architecture piece for the Bundesrat, a kinetic light installation by Rebecca Horn (born in 1944), refers to the institution in a more indirect way. Three 15-metre long brass rods hover above the floor of the foyer in front of the plenary hall. The circular movements of "Die drei Grazien" ("The three graces"), as the piece is called, catch the light of the glazed domes and guide it into the hall, where the mirror on the floor reflects it and creates new perspectives. The interaction between a clear number of elements and the symbolism of illumination and insight enter into a reserved relationship with the political nature of the Bundesrat. The extremely successful synthesis of art and architecture is also a credit to the forward-looking Arts Council, consisting of the art experts Carl Haenlein, Heinrich Klotz, Barbara Straka and Kari Tapio, as well as users' representatives and the architect Peter Schweger. The council defined the locations, invited ten artists to participate in a competition and made a selection early enough to enable this magnificent symbiosis of art and architecture. "The three graces" are a shining example of the potential of today's art in architecture in historical interrelationships. They are a further "clear signal of contemporaneity using present-day art" and a highlight of art in architecture, which has played such a major role in the development of Berlin as the capital of a reunified Germany.

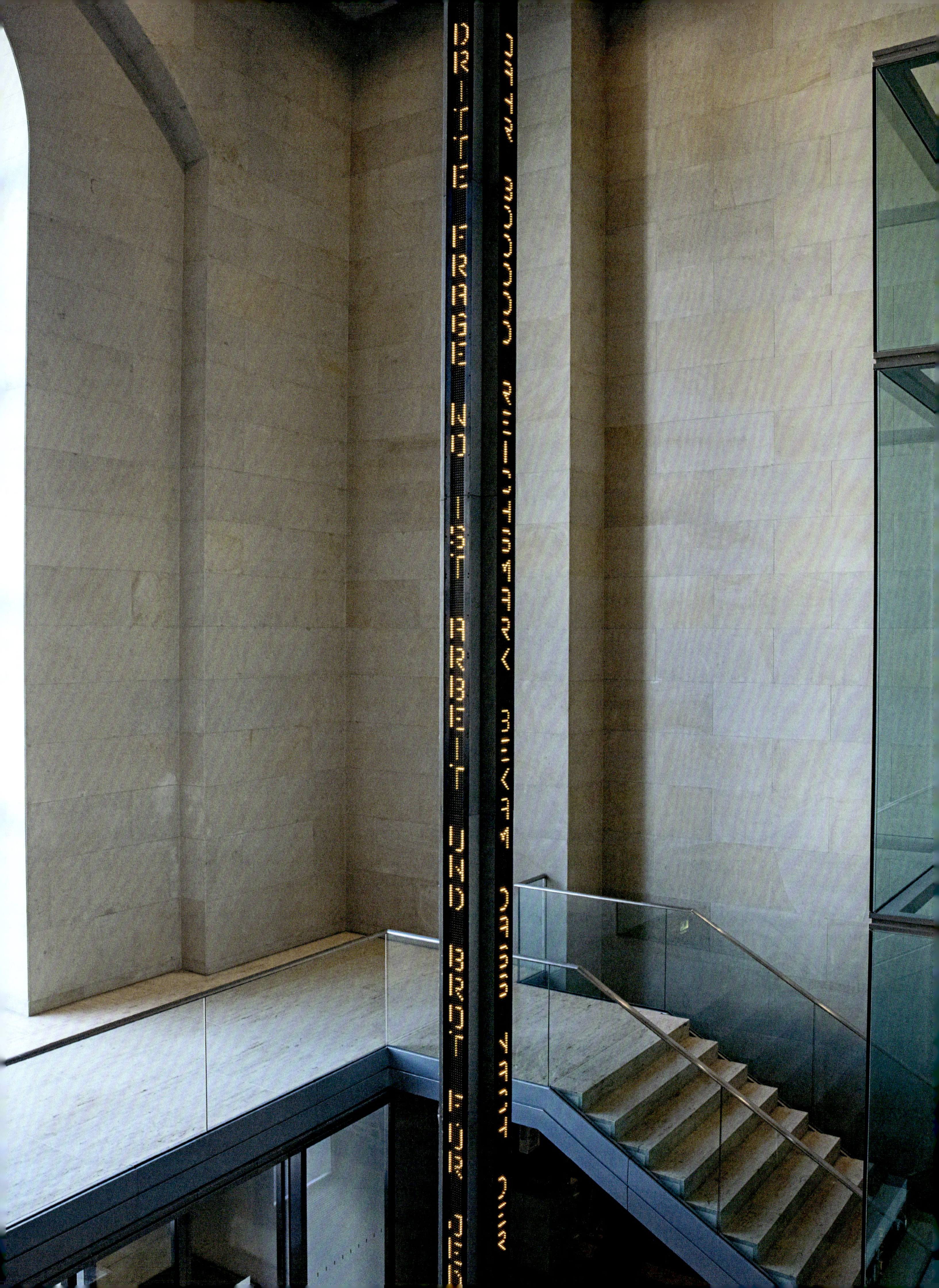
DRITTE FRAGE WO IST ARBEIT UND BROT

GERMAN BUNDESTAG REICHSTAG BUILDING BERLIN

Address:
Platz der Republik 1
11011 Berlin

Architecture:
Paul Wallot, 1884–1894
Reconstruction:
Paul Baumgarten, 1961–1972
Conversion:
Norman Foster, 1995–1999

Art in architecture:
Jenny Holzer
and Gerhard Altenbourg,
Georg Baselitz, Christian Boltanski,
Jürgen Böttcher-Strawalde,
Grisha Bruskin, Carlfriedrich Claus,
Christo and Jeanne-Claude,
Lutz Dammbeck, Hanne Darboven,
Rupprecht Geiger, Hermann Glöckner,
Gotthard Graubner, Hans Haacke,
Bernard Heiliger, Bernhard Heisig,
Anselm Kiefer, Carl-Heinz Kliemann,
Markus Lüpertz, Wolfgang Mattheuer,
Georg Karl Pfahler, Sigmar Polke,
Gerhard Richter, Ulrich Rückriem,
Emil Schumacher, Katharina
Sieverding, Walter Stöhrer,
Günther Uecker, Woty Werner

The Reichstag in Berlin is the archetypal, symbolic building of German democracy. Due to its importance, a specific art concept was developed for it prior to fitting it out as the seat of parliament of a reunified Germany, with funds for art in architecture increased from the usual 2 to 3 percent of the total building costs. The Arts Council of the German Bundestag and the two experts Götz Adriani and Karin Stempel selected works by 15 renowned artists from Germany and one work each from the protecting powers (whereby Norman Foster, the conversion architect, represented the United Kingdom).

The USA's representative, the concept and installation artist Jenny Holzer (born in 1950), contributed a media work for the publicly accessible northern entrance hall. The 14-metre high steel pillar is clearly visible from outside the building. Yellow LED words are continuously projected onto its four flanks, presenting texts from a total of 447 selected speeches by members of the Reichstag and the Bundestag, including interjections, which are represented by blinking.

The displayed texts are thematically coordinated. However, the intention of this art in architecture is not to communicate the content of the speeches. It takes around 20 days to run through them all. Instead, when viewing the artwork normally, the legible fragments of speeches condense into an image of a multi-vocal debate culture that becomes a visual pillar of parliamentarianism through the form of its presentation. The artistic attraction of Jenny Holzer's "Running Oral History" lies in the symbolism of the content, the visual effect of the flowing text and not least the aesthetics of the pillar, which appears to be drilling its way through the floor and ceiling as a narrow spatial axis.

JENNY HOLZER
Untitled, 1999
Steel stele with LED display
1,435 x 14.5 x 14.2 cm

FEDERAL CHANCELLERY BERLIN

Address:
Willy-Brandt-Strasse 1
10557 Berlin

Architecture:
Axel Schultes and Charlotte Frank,
1997–2001

Art in architecture:
Eduardo Chillida
and Franz Ackermann,
Rainer Kriester, Michel Majerus,
Markus Lüpertz, Jeff Wall,
Corinne Wasmuht

The “Berlin” sculpture on the forecourt of the Federal Chancellery in Berlin is one of the most famous and media-present art in architecture works of all. The Corten steel sculpture is five and a half metres high and weighs almost 90 tonnes, gracefully accentuating the entrance area, while in its perception, forming a unity with the extravagant prestige architecture.

One of the most celebrated 20th-century sculptors, Eduardo Chillida (1924–2002) produced the piece specifically for this publicly visible, prominent location. Placed upon an isle of grass, it creates references both to the architecture of the Federal Chancellery and to the history of the once divided Berlin. For example the mighty columns, with their projecting lateral elements that reach out at the centre, paraphrase the silhouette of the higher administrative building in the centre and the lateral office wings. At the same time, the symbolism of the unconnected, yet mutually reliant and associated columns also picks up on the underlying principle of the “Band des Bundes” (“Federal Band”), which was developed by the architects Axel Schultes and Charlotte Frank; the urban-planning axis is an image of the regained unity of Berlin and Germany, connecting the Federal Chancellery over the Spreebogen (the bend in the River Spree) to the Bundestag buildings situated in the former GDR territory, namely Paul Löbe House and Marie Elisabeth Lüders House.

Chillida’s “Berlin” also establishes an analogy with its famous predecessor, the bronze sculpture by Henry Moore entitled “Large Two Forms”, which stands in front of the former Federal Chancellery in Bonn. The fluent, soft, natural form of the bronze sculpture by Moore, which was produced between 1966 and 1969, is replaced by Chillida’s iron sculpture, a rational structure. While in the words of the then Federal Chancellor Helmut Schmidt, the sculpture in Bonn reflects the “natural gesture of a shared identity”, Chillida’s piece was described by the later Federal Chancellor Gerhard Schröder as a reference to, “the fate of our country: partition and reunification.”

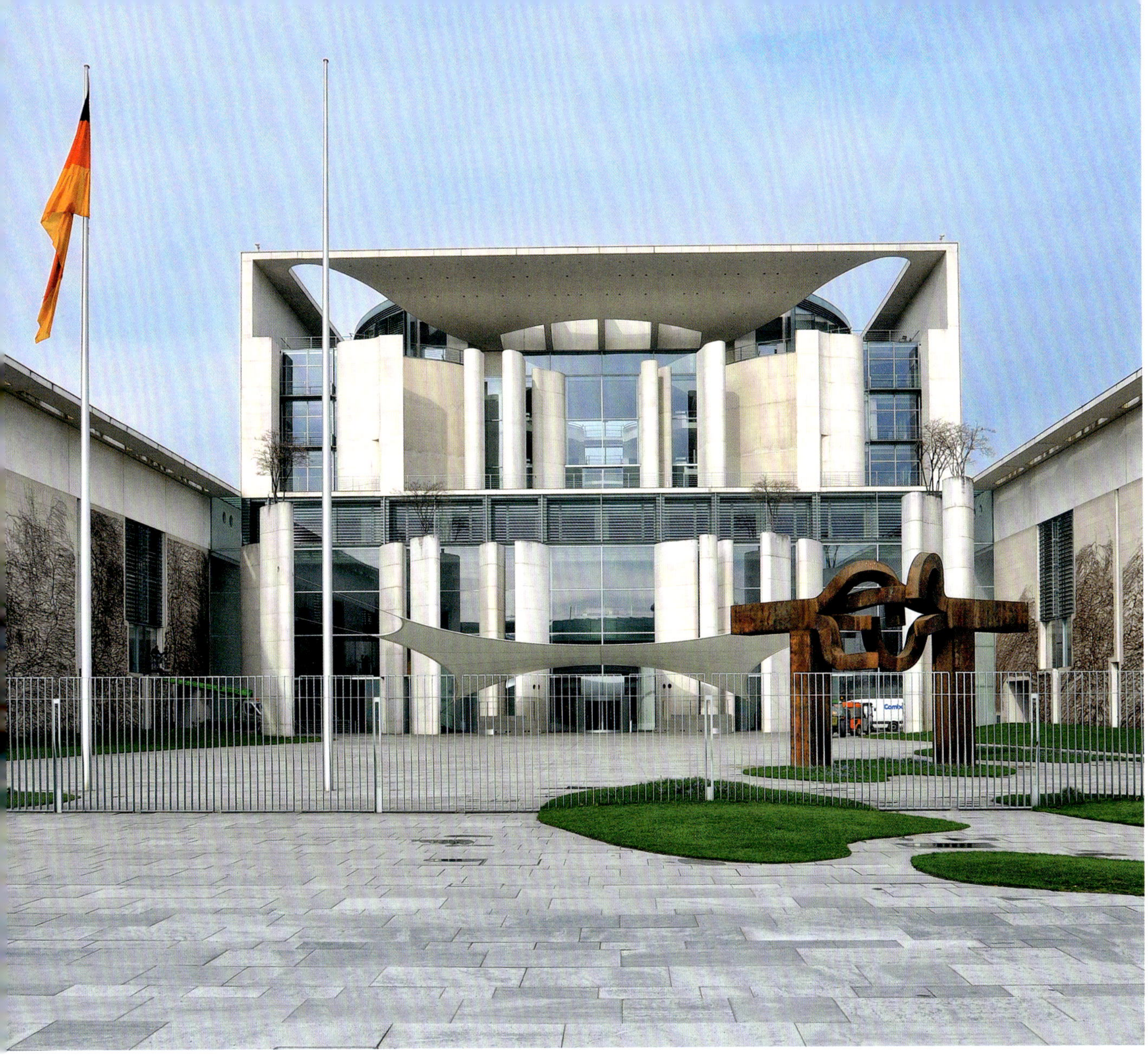

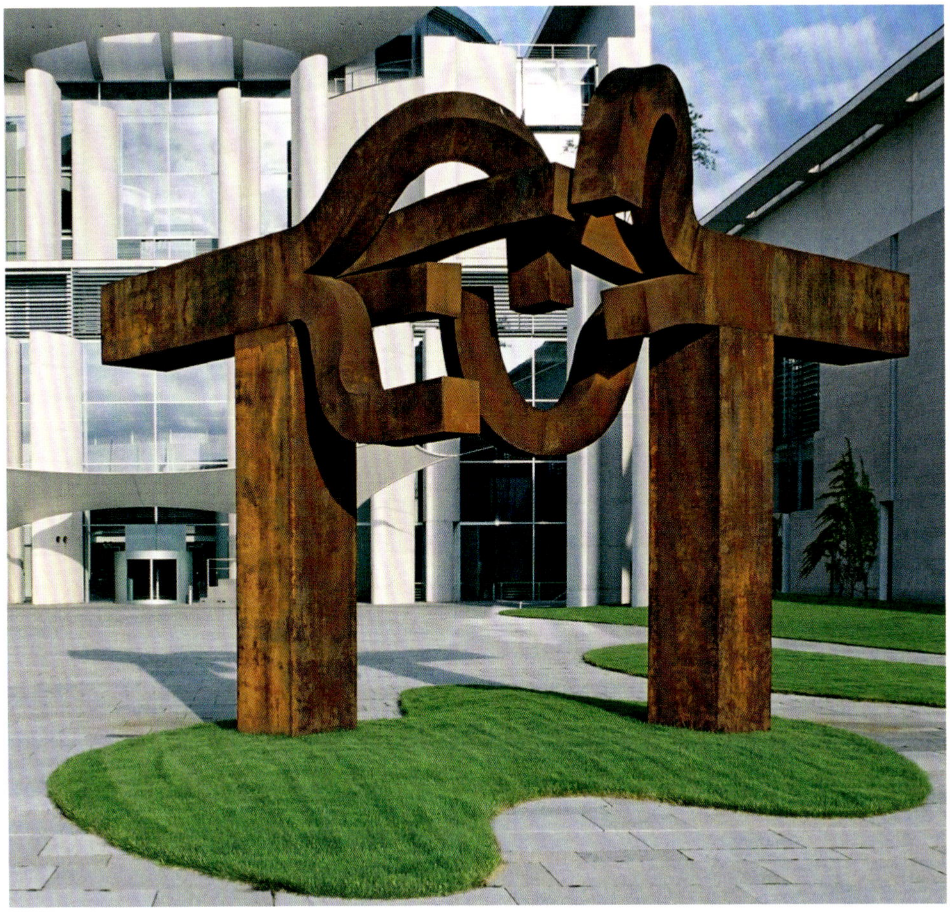

EDUARDO CHILLIDA
"Berlin", 1999
Corten steel
550 cm high

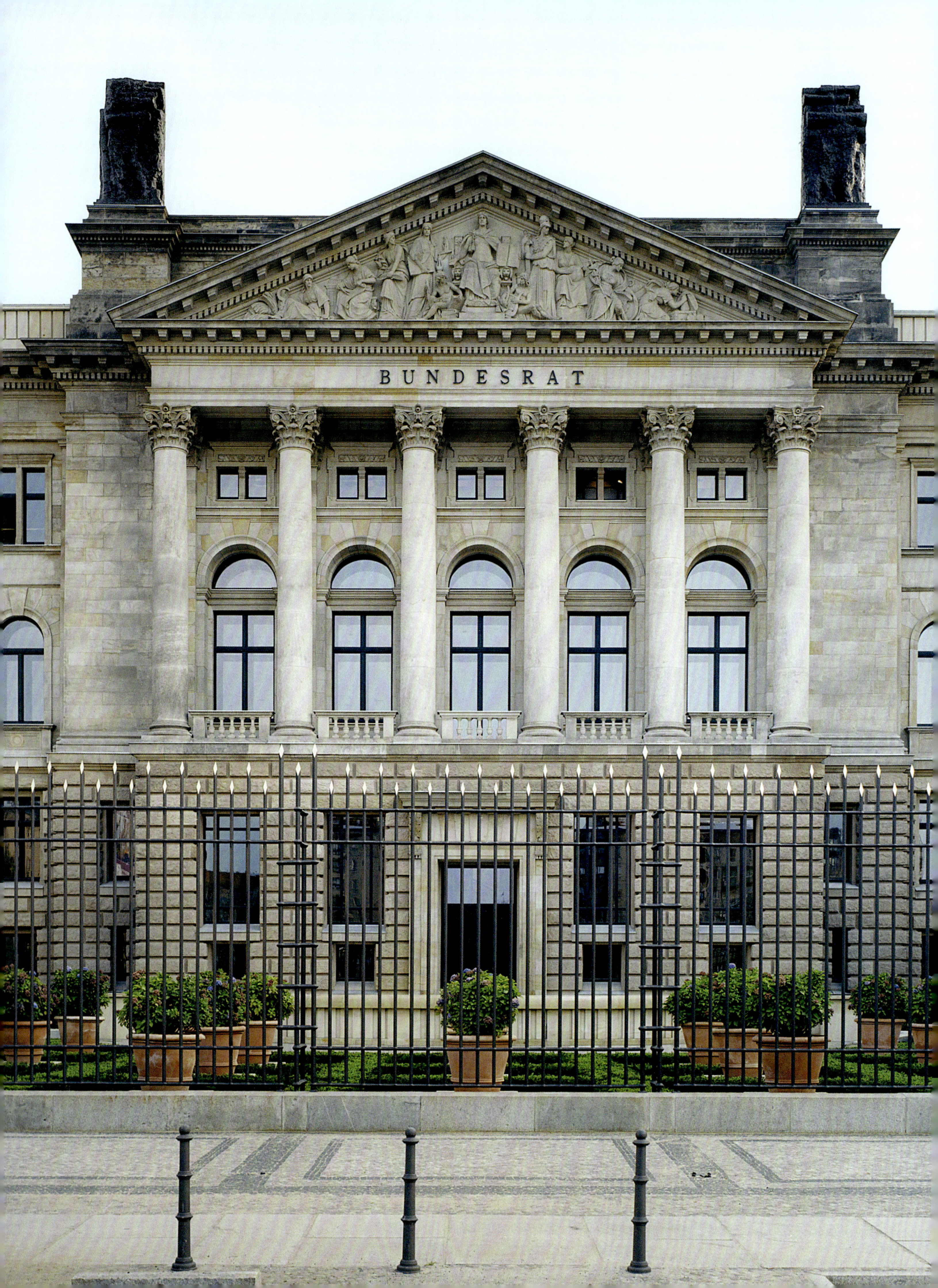
BUNDESRAT

BUNDESRAT BERLIN

Address:
Leipziger Strasse 3–4
10117 Berlin

Architecture:
Friedrich Schulze, 1899–1904
Conversion:
Schweger + Partner, 1997–2000

Art in architecture:
Per Kirkeby
and Rebecca Horn

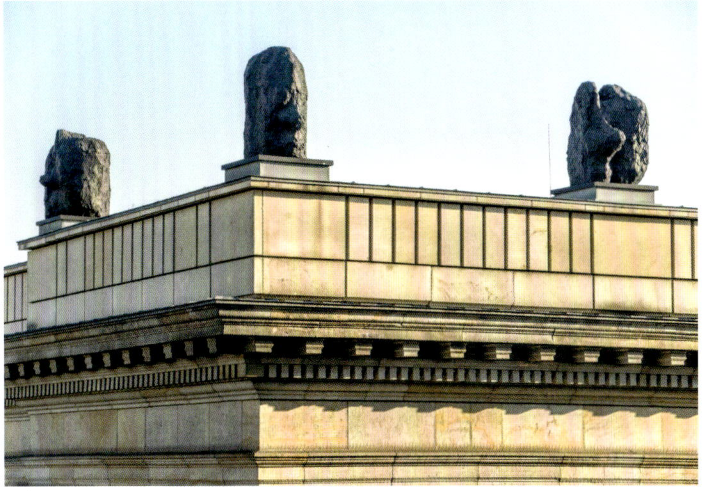

Since 2000, the Bundesrat has convened in the Prussian House of Lords in Berlin, which formerly housed the first Chamber of the Prussian Parliament. Despite severe wartime damage and conversions for the GDR Academy of Science and then for the Bundesrat, the neoclassical façade towards Leipziger Strasse has largely been preserved in its original condition. The pieces by the Danish sculptor Per Kirkeby (1938–2018) are new. Two roughly four-metre high and two-metre wide bronze sculptures, their form perhaps intentionally recalling tablets of law, crown the attica zone. They flank the tympanum, which is supported by six columns, depicting the historical personification of the State of Prussia by Otto Lessing (1846–1912). Kirkeby also produced three bronze pieces with black patina, resembling human heads, to accentuate each head-end building reaching directly up to the street.

Kirkeby's full and half sculptures replace allegorical stone sculptures that were destroyed during World War II. They therefore remain true to the *genius loci* and the decorative principles of the historical figurative ornamentation. However, this does not merely constitute aesthetic repair. Instead, Kirkeby's artworks are a supplement, the wonderfully proportioned and balanced sculptures updating the Wilhelminian visual programme. They transpose the thematic significance of the old (partially preserved) building sculptures, which were based on clear notions of order and power, into the diverse, democratic expression of powerfully associative abstract forms.

One artistically fine, but fundamental difference between the existing artworks and the additions lies in the fact that although Kirkeby's bronzes have monumental dimensions; they are formed plastic art, rather than stone sculptures. That subtle aesthetic counterpoint makes the break between the past and the present exciting and artistically valuable.

PER KIRKEBY
Untitled, 2000
Bronze 400 x 200 cm each
(panels in the attica zone)

FEDERAL MINISTRY OF LABOUR AND SOCIAL AFFAIRS BERLIN

Address:
Wilhelmstrasse 49
10117 Berlin

Architecture:
Karl Reichle, 1936–1940
Conversion:
Kleihues + Kleihues Architekten, 1997–2001

Art in architecture:
Katarína Zavarská
and Thom Barth, Daniel Buren, Peter Chevalier, Felix Droese, Eva Leitolf, Carsten Nicolai

The Berlin offices of the Federal Ministry of Labour and Social Affairs provided numerous points of reference for art in architecture, both in view of the architecture of the old and new buildings, and with respect to the history of their use. While the preservation-listed old building was fitted out, where once the Reich Propaganda Ministry and then the GDR Media Centre had been accommodated, the Arts Council of the Federal Government, in coordination with the Ministry of Labour and the architect, awarded three commissions, among others, for the lobbies of the corridors in the old building's wings, namely for four spaces situated above each other.

The Slovak textile artist Katarína Zavarská (1948–1999) produced six images for the southeastern axis beside the entrance hall. They are collages of dyed, printed pieces of felt and ironed-on textile fragments, graphics and photographs. Thematically, the portrait and landscape-format, rectangular, square and cruciform images relate in a clear, albeit generalising way to the varied history of the building, as well as the ministry's field of tasks. In the ground-floor lobby, two connected vedute panels entitled "Genius loci Berlin" recall the development of the city of Berlin. Two panels on the first floor use cut-out newspaper articles to address the theme of "Die sozialen Konflikte der Weimarer Republik und der Wirtschaftskrise" ("The social conflicts of the Weimar Republic and the economic crisis"). On the third floor, a portrait-format rectangle presents motifs of "Handwerk und Industrie" ("Craftsmanship and industry"). Finally, on the top floor, a portrait-format piece entitled "Musisches und schöpferisches Arbeiten" ("Artistic and creative work") uses texts and images to refer to great figures such as Johann Sebastian Bach, Johann Wolfgang von Goethe and Richard Wagner.

Zavarská's collages integrate texts, graphics and photographs as particles of reality into the cuboid image surfaces with the decided character of a painting, in which the basic forms and colours add striking accentuation. After the artist's death, her husband, the scenographer Ján Zavarský, completed the work.

KATARÍNA ZAVARSKÁ
"Genius loci, Berlin",
"Die sozialen Konflikte der Weimarer Republik und der Wirtschaftskrise" ("The social conflicts of the Weimar Republic and the economic crisis"),
"Handwerk und Industrie" ("Craftmanship and industry"),
"Musisches und schöpferisches Arbeiten" ("Aesthetic and creative work"), 2000
6 collages, dyed and printed felt on carrier plates

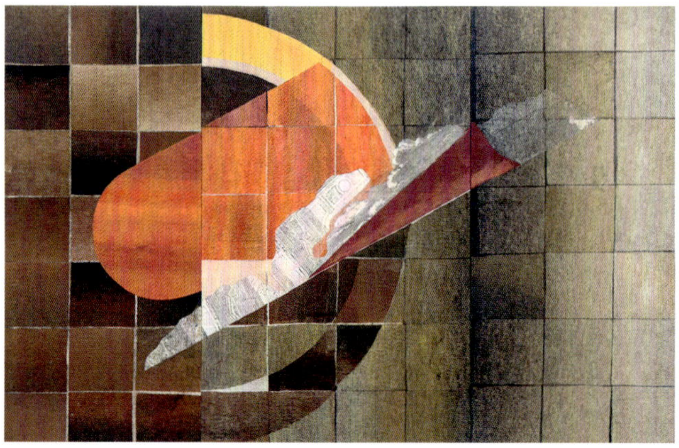

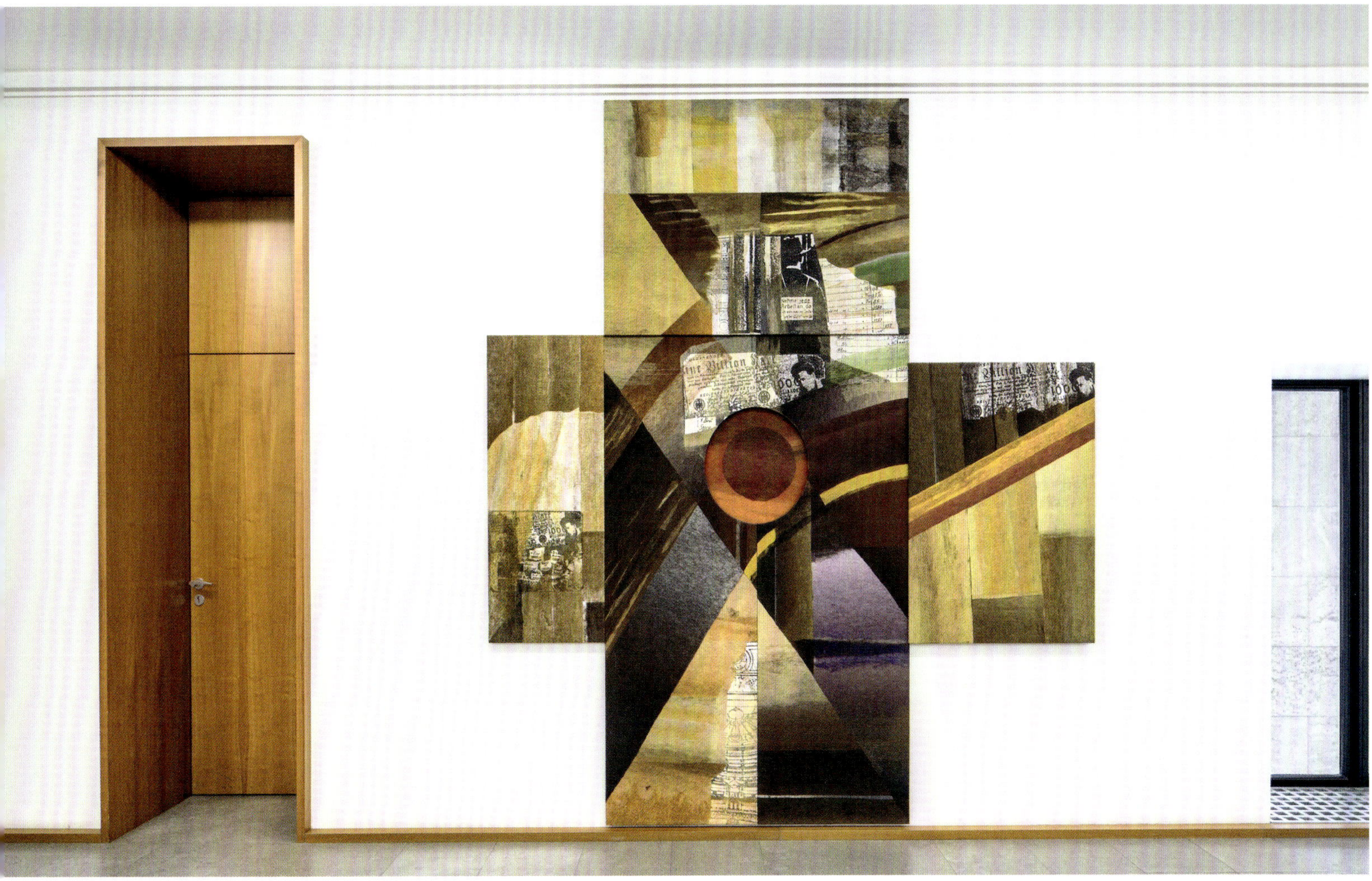

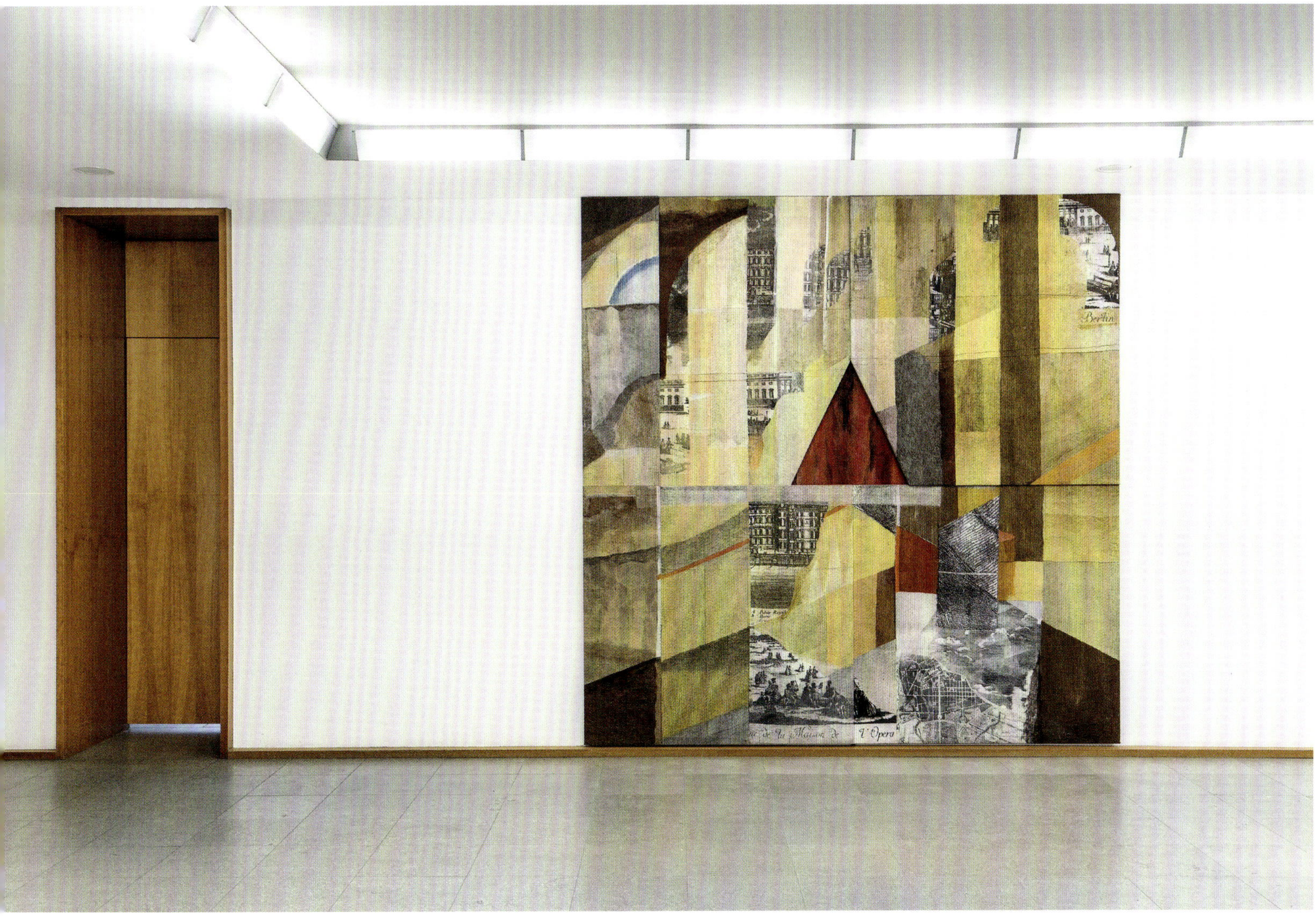
Berlin

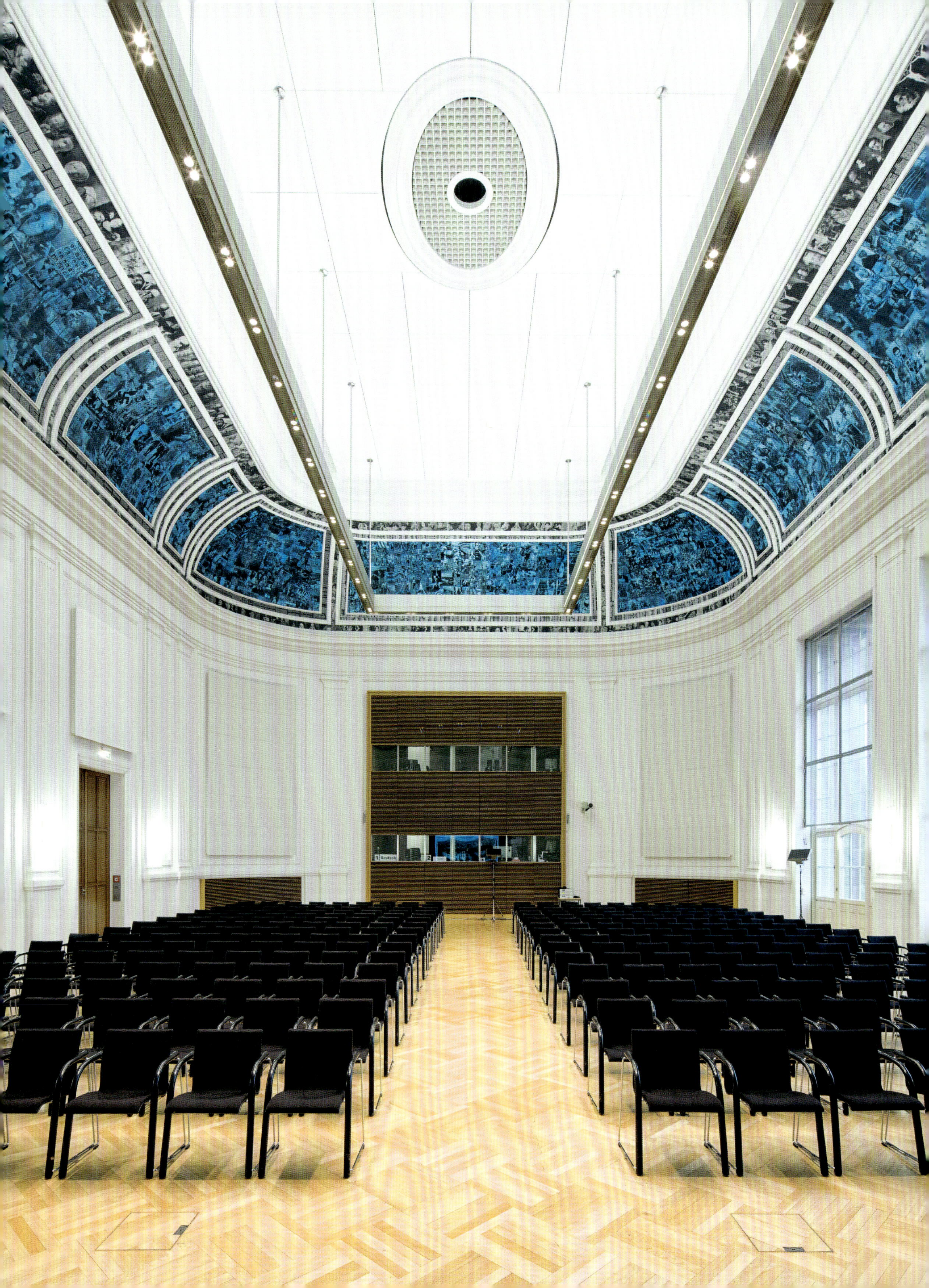

FEDERAL MINISTRY FOR ECONOMIC AFFAIRS AND TECHNOLOGY BERLIN

TODAY FEDERAL MINISTRY FOR ECONOMIC AFFAIRS AND ENERGY

Address:
Scharnhorststrasse 34–37
10115 Berlin

Architecture:
Invalidenhaus:
Isaak Jakob von Petri, 1746–1748
Kaiser-Wilhelms-Akademie:
Cremer & Wolffenstein 1905–1910
Conversion and extension:
Baumann & Schnittger, 1991–2000

Art in architecture:
Marcel Odenbach
and Moritz Götze, Angela Hampel,
Annette Sauermann

The headquarters of the Federal Ministry for Economic Affairs and Energy is an especially attractive piece of real estate situated between Hamburger Bahnhof and the Invalidenpark in Berlin-Mitte. It includes old and new buildings with interesting construction and use histories, as well as exceptional art in architecture interventions. The neoclassical hall of the ministry conference centre in the former Invalidenhaus is dominated by the large paper work "Als sähe ich im Himmel die Erde" ("As if I saw the Earth in the sky") by Marcel Odenbach (born in 1953). It is a collage of blue-coloured photocopies of media images, which the artist, who is renowned for his paper and video pieces, integrated as a surrounding frieze into the 16 vaulted areas between the ceiling and the wall.

The images refer to German history, including war, partition and reunification: they present famous figures, scenes and culture from the fields of the arts, entertainment and sport; or they refer to non-European continents as a reminder of Germany's role and responsibility throughout the world. There are also floral motifs, photographs of the lunar landing and famous artworks, as well as texts from the constitution, the Bible and political declarations. Black and white copies with extracts from famous portraits and historical paintings form the framework of this panoptical "mirror of the world" (M. Odenbach).

In its strict coffering and the pleasing tone of the images, the design follows the system and artistic aspiration of old ceiling frescoes, which combine in-depth content with decorative intentions. Thus, the texts in Odenbach's small-scale collage are not truly legible and cannot be pinpointed in terms of their content, while the wealth of images and text information impresses through its aesthetic force and medial power. The artwork presents a visual scope of collective memory that immediately inspires general interest.

MARCEL ODENBACH
"Als sähe ich im Himmel die Erde"
("As if I saw the Earth in the sky"), 2000
Paper, coloured photocopies

FEDERAL MINISTRY OF FINANCE BERLIN

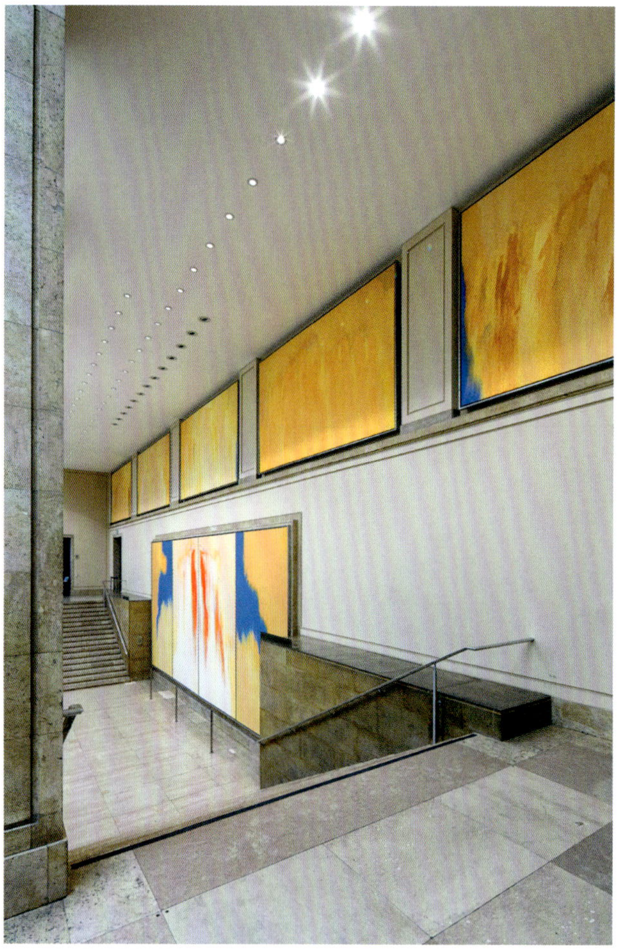

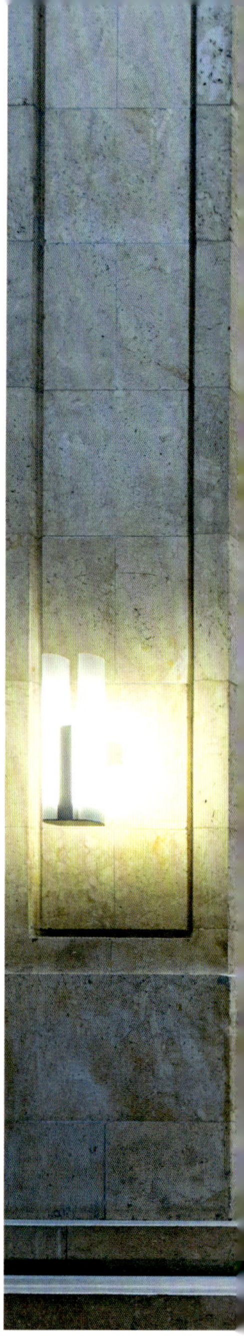

Address:
Wilhelmstrasse 97
10117 Berlin

Architecture
Ernst Sagebiel, 1935–1936
Conversion:
HPP Architekten, 1996–1999

Art in architecture:
Michael Wirkner
and Jochen Gerz,
Roswitha Josefine Pape,
Robert Schad

MICHAEL WIRKNER
Untitled, 2000
9 image panels, oil on canvas, wood

The enormous building of the Federal Ministry of Finance has had a highly contrasting use history. It was the first monumental building of the "Third Reich". Constructed for the Reich Ministry of Aviation, it served as the GDR House of Ministries from 1949 onwards. In 1992, the building accommodated the headquarters of the Treuhandanstalt, before ultimately being used by the Federal Ministry of Finance in 1999.

Naturally, the GDR replaced the old symbols of power, inscriptions and Hitler-artworks. When the building was again appropriated and realigned following German reunification, the art in architecture locations were selected in view of their historical connections and backgrounds. One especially important location in the original and therefore also in the new building concept was the stone hall, with its staircase leading to the large festive hall. An imperial eagle with a swastika and a Hitler quote that once overlooked the hall were replaced by the GDR state emblem and then later by the art

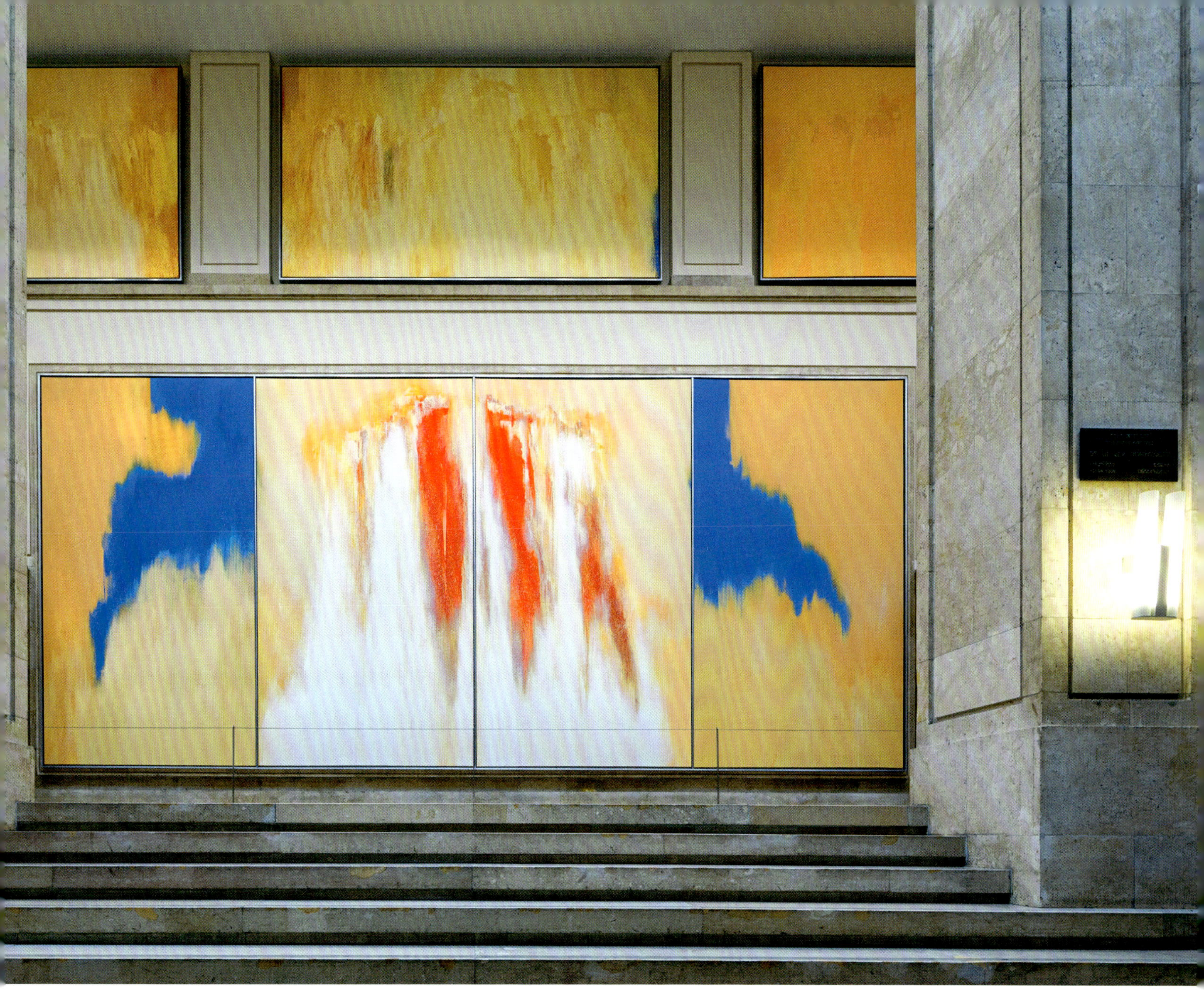

in architecture of the Federal Republic, a nine-part abstract painting by Michael Wirkner (1954–2012).

In the space where the eagle and the GDR emblem had once been installed on the lower cornice, Wirkner has inserted four upright rectangular panels. Five smaller horizontal rectangular paintings in light, warm colours were also placed in the wall niches above them. The large panels develop in a red and blue pattern to create a festive, sublime colour symmetry. The concept follows the lines of the architecture and was created to take it into account. This can be seen in the scale and alignment of the visual panels and also in the deliberately produced colour analogies. The abstract nature of the images is based on the history of the location and ultimately the artistic decision not to charge the location with yet more emblematic visual content and significance. The fact that Michael Wirkner described the images as "colour curtains" shows where their significance cannot be found, namely on surface appearances.

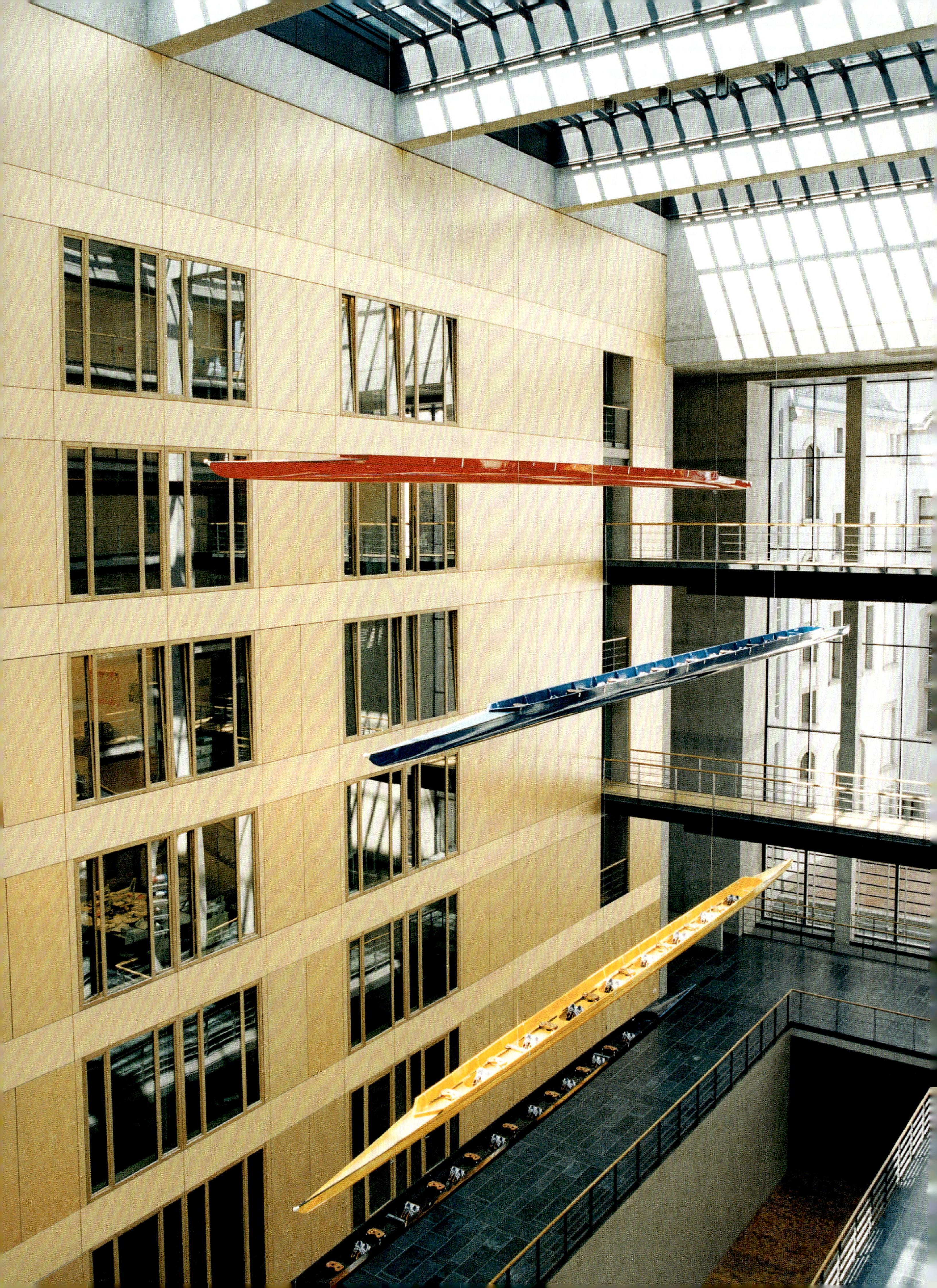

GERMAN BUNDESTAG JAKOB KAISER HOUSE BERLIN

Address:
Dorotheenstrasse 100/101
10117 Berlin

Architecture:
Schweger + Partner, 1997–2002

Art in architecture:
Christiane Möbus and Hans Peter Adamski, Hartwig Ebersbach, Ulrich Erben, Rainer Fetting, Lili Fischer, Günther Förg, Raimund Girke, Antony Gormley, Andreas Gursky, Peter Herrmann, Matthias Hoch, Karl Horst Hödicke, Matthias Jackisch, Dani Karavan, Axel Kasseböhmer, Per Kirkeby, Jürgen Klauke, Astrid Klein, Thomas Kohl, Carsten Nicolai, Martin Noel, Hans Peter Reuter, Bernard Schultze, Andreas Schulze, Max Uhlig, WES & Partner

Jakob Kaiser House, which is situated behind the Reichstag building on both sides of Dorotheenstrasse and accommodates offices for parliamentarians, is the largest building of the Bundestag. Although it is a coherent building complex, it is unlike the neighbouring Marie Elisabeth Lüders House and Paul Löbe House in that it consists of existing buildings plus eight new sections that were planned by four architectural offices. Based on that situation, the two art experts responsible for the art in architecture on the real estate, Manfred Schneckenburger and Evelyn Weiss, conceived an art concept that differs in each building.

The art in House 1 immediately makes a powerful statement. Four black, red, yellow and blue painted original eight-man rowing racing boats are suspended from the roof of the bright entrance hall. They are in permanent random vertical motion, controlled by a computer, thereby constantly producing new perspectives, as well as colour and height constellations.

The sculptor and object artist Christiane Möbus (born in 1947) has repeatedly worked with boats, also referring to the Oxford and Cambridge University boat race. Thus the boats in Jakob Kaiser House are a metaphor of fair political competition. However, the colours black, red, yellow and blue are those of Germany and Europe, rather than of political parties. To prevent all too limiting and overwhelming interpretations, Möbus herself suggested at least a "distant" connection to the "dimension of a ship lift" since the ground floor opens up towards the basement.

Regardless of such thematic components, an absurdly poetic range of associations is inspired by this gently moving intervention, as well as the formal elegance with which the vector-like, narrow boats in radiant colours are integrated not only into the architectural context of columns and galleries, but also the window and wall structures, giving the installation its aesthetic autonomy.

CHRISTIANE MÖBUS
"auf und ab und unterwegs"
("up and down and on the move"), 2001
4 eight-person racing rowing boats, sports shoes, steel wire, motor winches
17 m each

FOREIGN OFFICE BERLIN

Address:
Werderscher Markt 1
10117 Berlin

Architecture:
Heinrich Wolff, 1935–1939
Conversion:
Kollhoff Architekten, 1996–1999

Art in architecture:
Trak Wendisch
and Stephan Balkenhol,
James Fraser Carpenter,
Gisela Hachmann-Ruch, Hubert
Kiecol, Harald Klingelhöller,
Gerhard Merz, Maurizio Nannucci,
Jürgen Partenheimer

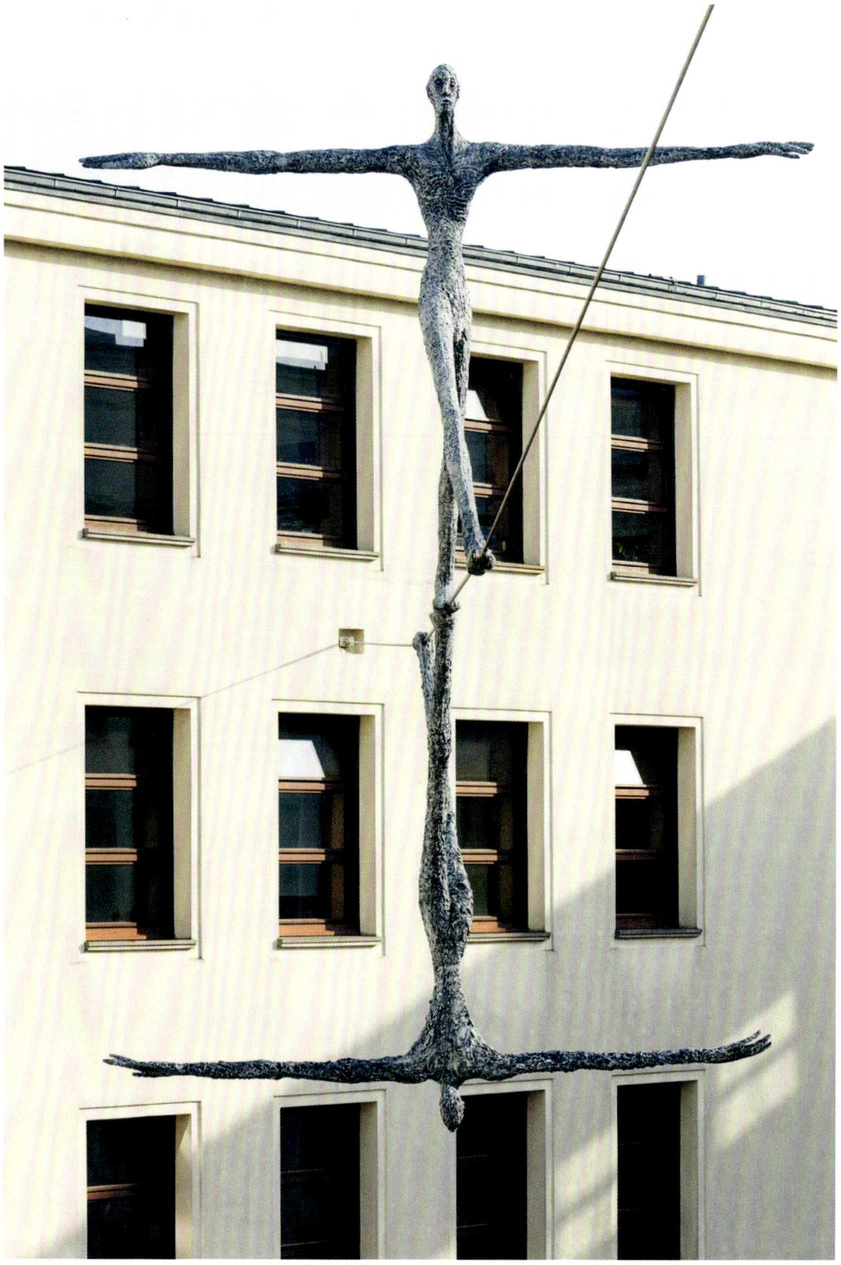

TRAK WENDISCH
"Seiltänzer"
("Tightrope walkers"), 2001
Cast aluminium
250 cm each

A main characteristic of the real estate of the Foreign Office by the Kupfergraben, diagonally opposite the former Staatsrat building, is its enormous dimensions. Equally characteristic is the critical proximity with which the cuboid extension building by Müller Reimann Architekten, completed in 1999, meets the large-scale architecture of the former Reichsbank dating back to 1939. The elongated, five-storey old building, with its steel skeleton, was used by the Berliner Stadtkontor after 1945 and then from 1949 by the GDR Ministry of Finance, as well as by the Central Committee of the GDR from 1959 onwards. Between 1996 and 1999, the office Kollhoff Architekten fitted the building out for the Foreign Office. During those measures, several art in architecture competitions were announced for the rooftop terrace. Above one of the seven inner courtyards, the painter and sculptor Trak Wendisch (born in 1958) spanned a tightrope with a surreal pair of tightrope artists that horizontally mirror each other. Both of the 2.5-metre tall, slim figures made of cast aluminium have an attractive, archaic appearance, with an aesthetically perfect (and statically necessary) balance of horizontal and vertical elements. Their focused stance gives the impression of being able to master the tasks ahead with secure confidence. The metaphor of a tightrope walk is quickly grasped in view of the historical background of the building's varying uses, as well as the history of the two states' rapprochement. The tasks of the Foreign Office can also be regarded as a tightrope walk, which can succeed with the visualised caution and attitude. Such symbolism is by no means unknown in art in architecture for the reunited Berlin – and is even evident in the urban-planning "Band des Bundes" ("Federal Band"), which places the Federal Chancellery and the Bundestag buildings along a single axis. The figures moving in opposite directions also preserve a fundamental aspect that expresses something of the *conditio humana.*

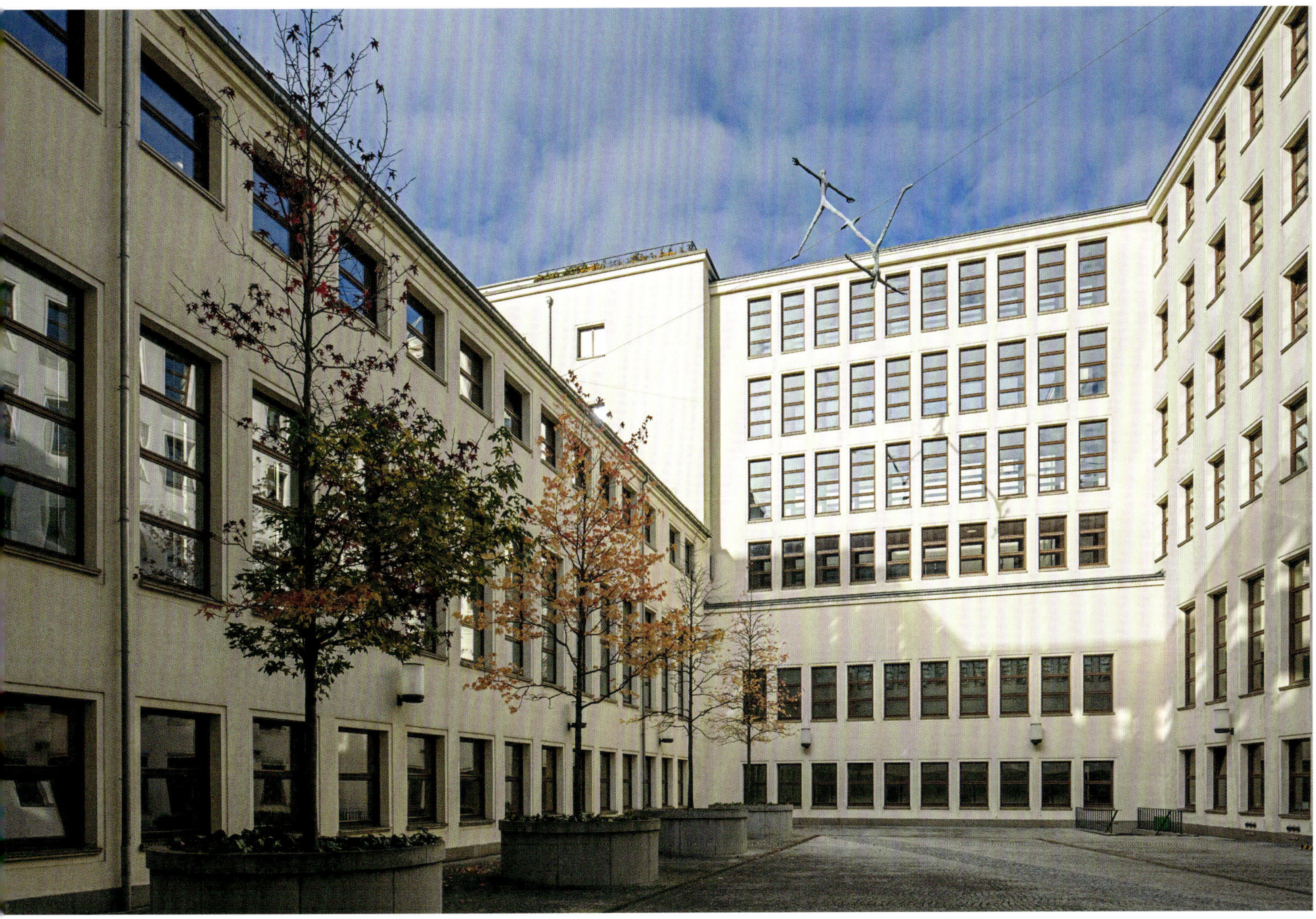

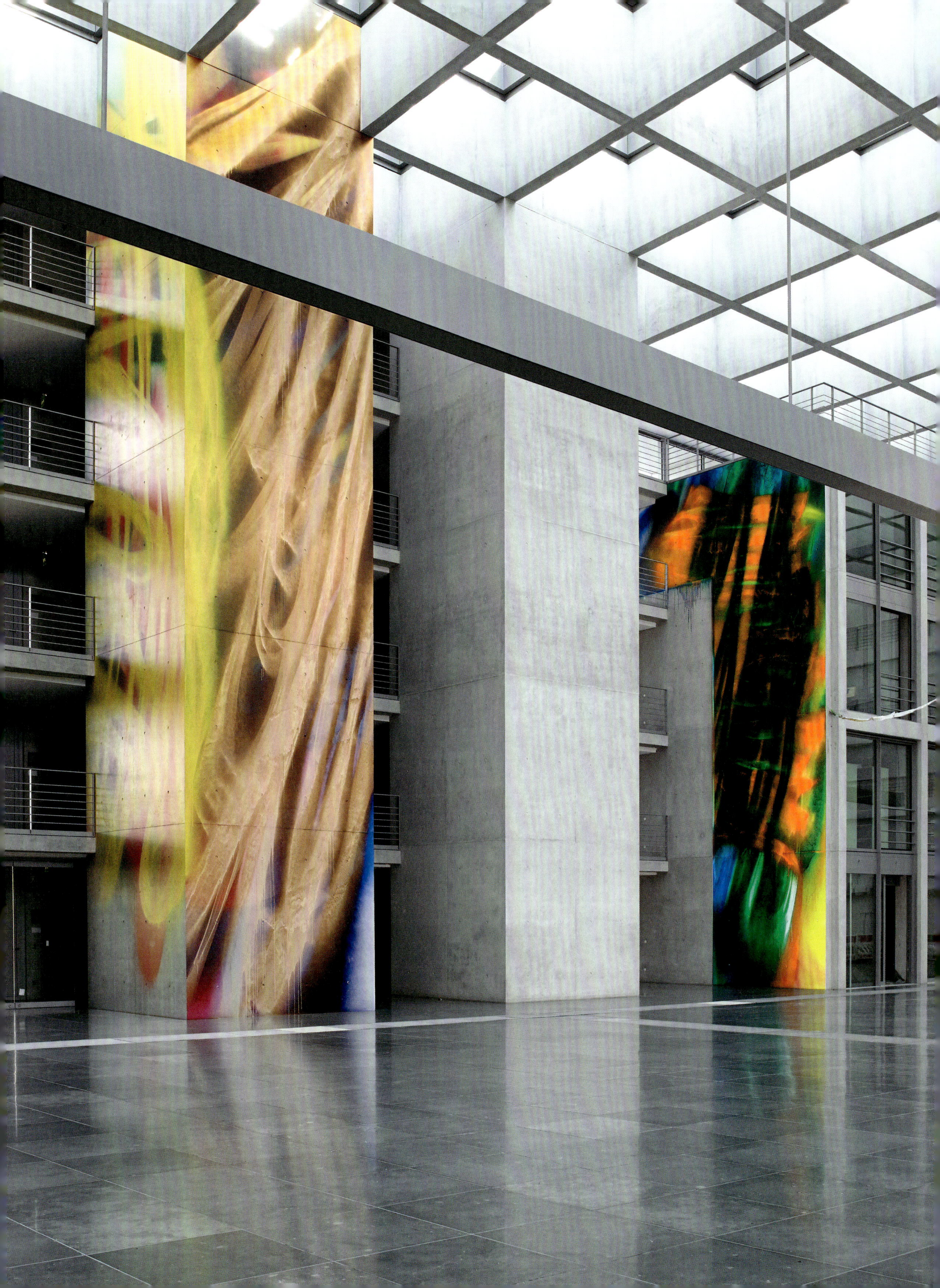

GERMAN BUNDESTAG MARIE ELISABETH LÜDERS HOUSE II BERLIN

Address:
Luisenstrasse 29–30
10117 Berlin

Architecture:
Stephan Braunfels, 1998–2003
Extension:
construction begun in 2010

Art in architecture:
Katharina Grosse
and Michel de Broin, Tony Cragg,
Bernhard Heiliger

Katharina Grosse (born in 1961) is one of the most successful artists of our time. Her "extended painting" goes beyond traditional image concepts and engages with space, mainly in locally related interventions, often with spectacular dimensions. In 2015, one of her works was installed in the extension to Marie Elisabeth Lüders House. Grosse placed five large fair-faced concrete surfaces on the longitudinal sides of the grand assembly hall, namely the sides of pillars and special elements, with a gestural acrylic painting and stark colours. The airbrushed paint creates moving colour spaces with overlaps, swathes and bands covering a total surface of 330 square metres. Despite the size of the work, some of which reaches up to the ceiling, the piece, which recalls street art in terms of its nature and technique, retains its character of spontaneity and directly involved corporeality. Large-scale spray painting interacts with the architecture with respect to proximity and distance, while refusing to achieve a synthesis. It is subordinate to the architecture by respecting its boundaries. At the same time, it also places itself above architecture in selecting which sections will be covered and to what extent, thereby appropriating the room with targeted measures. Thus the architecture no longer appears as a limiting counterpart. Instead, architecture and painting achieve an intermediary spatiality that produces its very own reality. In this way, the art in architecture becomes an existential experience and a form of self-affirmation for the people viewing it.

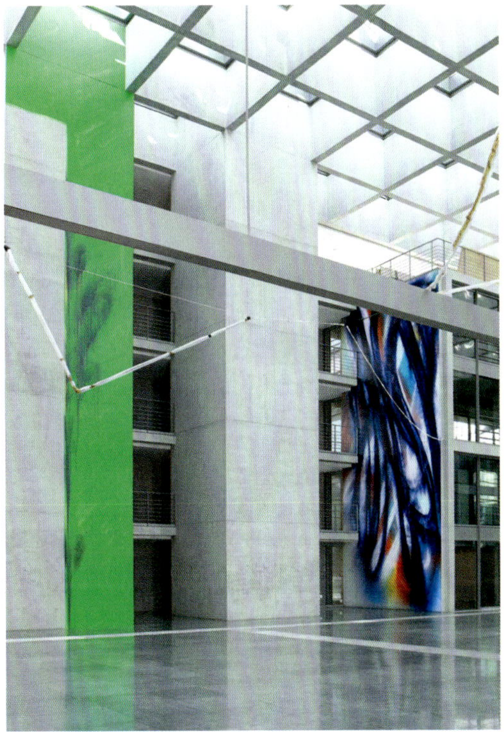

KATHARINA GROSSE
Untitled, 2015
Acrylic paints on fair-faced concrete
15.9 x 35 x 25 m

ART IN ARCHITECTURE

HISTORICAL AND CONTENT-BASED COMMENTARY

TAKES A STANCE

The form and content of architecturally related art is characterised by its special status as commissioned art. As such, art can also communicate a politically motivated image of society and an understanding of values. The respective political system influences the specific definitions, tasks and aims that art in architecture must address in its appearance and expression, which must also be considered in social and economic contexts. The cultural task and critical potential of art in architecture is especially evident when it comments on the location where it is installed and the location's history.

For instance after World War II, the two newly founded German states had to develop a stance towards their handling of architecture from the National Socialist period. The lack of undamaged buildings motivated the Federal Republic and the GDR to pragmatism in finding new uses for them; often, the alterations merely consisted of removing symbols of Nazi power. In subsequent years, however, a more differentiated stance towards historically burdened prestige buildings developed. The theme became controversial again after German reunification in 1990, when a number of GDR state buildings continued to be used by the newly united Federal Republic. While existing buildings were being fitted out, art in architecture was regarded by both clients and artists as a chance to comment on the history of the buildings and their representative functions in a multifaceted and visually powerful way. Thus, art in architecture positions the democratic stance of the institutions reusing historically burdened buildings. In addition to the important function of art in architecture as historical commentary, a series of artworks also refer to the tasks of the institutions for which they were produced. For instance, art in architecture can provide an aesthetic response to the current fields of operations, reflect on the institution's history, make a critical statement from the perspective of historical distance and raise awareness of politically responsible actions.

ART IN ARCHITECTURE TAKES A STANCE

Constanze von Marlin, Anna-Sophie Laug

Reich Ministry of Aviation, 1940, Berlin

Wolfgang Rüppel, "Denkmal zur Erinnerung an den Aufstand des 17. Juni 1953", 2000, in the background: Max Lingner, "Aufbau der Republik", 1953, Federal Ministry of Finance, Berlin

Handling buildings from dictatorships or with problematic former uses is essentially a question of the culture of memory. Since "architectural evidence" is very important in providing authentic locations, it is essential for commemorating the victims and critically engaging with one's own history. Thus it is also crucial to preserve buildings that were once used or constructed for reasons of prestige and ideology. For example in 1945, a British unit took over the sports area known as the Reichssportfeld, which had been expanded for the 1936 Olympic Games, including a wealth of ornamentation with heroic sculptures by Arnold Breker, Josef Thorak, Georg Kolbe, Willy Meller and others. Sports events were resumed there in 1946; from 1957, minimal denazification measures were carried out on the architecture and by 1966, the former Reichssportfeld was already included in West Berlin's preservation list. Other buildings from the National Socialist period also continued to be used for the same purpose as before: people lived in housing estates from the 1930s and taught in Hitler Youth homes and schools according to new democratic principles. Similarly, the Bundeswehr (Federal Armed Forces) is still partially accommodated in barracks constructed for the Wehrmacht.

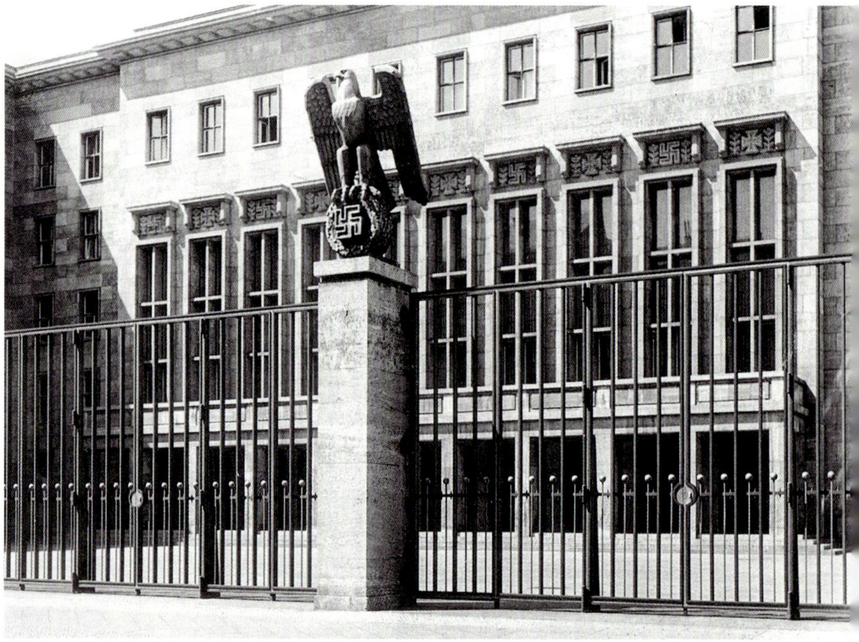

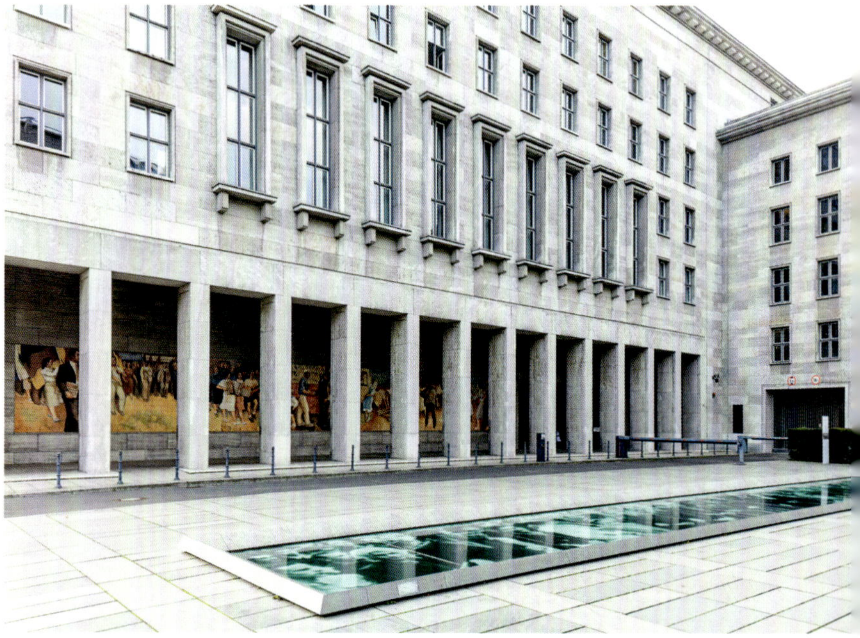

ASPECTS OF GERMAN HISTORY IN THE HOTSPOT BERLIN. ART IN ARCHITECTURE AS HISTORICAL COMMENTARY

Immediately after the end of World War II, the Soviet military administration, as the victorious power, moved into the former Reich Ministry of Aviation in Berlin, which had suffered only minor damage. The interim use of the building merely required the removal of Nazi symbols such as swastikas and the imperial eagle, as well as the so-called "Soldatenrelief" ("Soldier relief") by Arnold Waldschmidt (1873–1958). In 1947, the building accommodated the newly founded German Economic Commission, a central administrative organisation for the Soviet Occupation Zone. The GDR constitution was officially enacted in the building on October 7, 1949.

Following the foundation of the GDR, various ministerial departments were accommodated in the building, which was by then officially known as the Haus der Ministerien ("House of Ministries"). Its Nazi-related architecture was reprogrammed by means of sculptures and images. The mural "Aufbau der Republik" ("Building the Republic") by the painter and graphic designer Max Lingner (1888–1959) was explicitly applied to the wall that had previously been occupied by the 25-metre stone relief of marching Wehrmacht soldiers, with swastika flags flying in the wind, which Waldschmidt had produced in 1941 for the column hall in Leipziger Strasse (→ p. 74). From then on, the seat of the GDR government proclaimed an idealised social vision of a glorious future for the people in Socialist society.

Following German reunification, the Federal Ministry of Finance moved into the building in 1990, initially using it as a branch and then as its headquarters from 1999 onwards. The Federal Ministry addressed the challenge of the building's continued use by keeping its history alive as a commemorative warning for future generations. This was not only achieved by preserving the architecture (the building's demolition had already been approved and was subsequently retracted), but also by preserving several works of art in architecture that commented on the various temporal layers.

In 2000, instead of removing the mural by Lingner, an additional work by Wolfgang Rüppel (born in 1942) was installed in the building's forecourt. It is entitled "Denkmal zur Erinnerung an den Aufstand des 17. Juni 1953" ("Monument to commemorate the uprising of June 17, 1953"). Using the exact dimensions of the piece by Lingner, the glass image integrated into the floor of the forecourt presents a coarsely screened print based on an original newspaper photograph of the demonstration in 1953. On June 17, 1953, in front of the then House of Ministries, only a few months after the inauguration of Lingner's mural, a national uprising was crushed with great brutality by the Soviet military and the GDR Volkspolizei. It was the first ever mass demonstration in the Soviet Union's power bloc. The motif of striking workers enters into a tense relationship with the propaganda representations of a forward-looking Socialist society. The memorial piece by Rüppel gives the historical location of the former Reich Ministry of Aviation, the former GDR House of Ministries and today's Federal Ministry of Finance a new level of interpretation.

When the building was converted into the headquarters of the Federal Ministry of Finance (1996–1999), the concept artist Jochen Gerz (born in 1940), who was internationally renowned for his memorial projects against fascism and racism, was invited to produce an interactive video installation that addressed the theme of German history. Thus, he made the question "Das Geld, die Liebe, der Tod, die Freiheit – was zählt am Ende?" ("Money, love, death, freedom – what counts in the end?") move over the building and the façade of the inner courtyard in the form of a laser projection. He also addressed the theme by interviewing fifty ministry employees. Their replies are documented and can be accessed on two screens integrated into the fence between the pavement and the ministry, and are activated by passers by on the pavement at the touch of a button. Unlike the policy-dictated approach by Lingner, Gerz focuses on quintessential questions of life, which are personally important to everyone, thereby bridging the gap between the building's past and today's field of tasks.

By contrast, the painter Michael Wirkner (1954–2012) reacted to the building in a decidedly aesthetic and formalistic way. His abstract colour-filled painting neither forces content on the viewer, nor does it offer itself as an obvious field of interpretation. Instead, Wirkner's large-scale work in friendly colours overwrites the power symbols of the "Third Reich" and the German Democratic Republic that had formerly existed on the rear wall of the stone hall, thereby giving the space a completely new atmosphere (→ p. 146).

The decision in 1991 to restore Berlin as the capital city went hand in hand with a policy to consciously integrate the parliament and government buildings into the historically developed urban structure of Berlin-Mitte. As a result, numerous additional buildings for new parliamentary and ministerial uses had to be converted and fitted out. Above all for buildings with heavy historical burdens, art in architecture played an especially important role, requiring the development of specific art concepts. Artistic approaches were to pick up on references to the location both in terms of content and form, while addressing the building's complex history and the institution's new fields of tasks.

One outstanding example of comment on historically charged architecture by a piece of art in architecture is entitled "DER BEVÖLKERUNG" ("TO THE POPULATION") by Hans Haacke (born in 1936) and produced for the converted Reichstag building (→ p. 168). The artwork in the northern courtyard refers to the historical gable inscription "DEM DEUTSCHEN VOLKE" ("TO THE GERMAN PEOPLE"), which was only implemented twenty years after the building's completion because it was rejected by William II. The inscription conceived by the architect and industrial designer Peter Behrens was finally implemented in 1916, when the people threatened to withdraw their support for the Kaiser during World War I. Haacke's artwork consists of a plant box with an inscription in neon lettering reading "To the population". Members of parliament were asked and continue to be called upon to fill it with earth from their constituencies. Haacke's work investigates the historical dedication of the Reichstag building from the difficult early years of German parliamentarianism and today's self-perception as a parliament that is emancipated from authoritarian paternalism. Controversial discussion within and outside parliament before the design's installation focused on the question whether Haacke's neon inscription corrects the central gable inscription or is aimed at expanding the original sense, thereby initiating a thought process. The conflict even climaxed in a parliamentary debate, in which the supporters of Haacke's installation won by a narrow majority, allowing the artwork to be installed in the northern atrium of the Reichstag building in 2000.

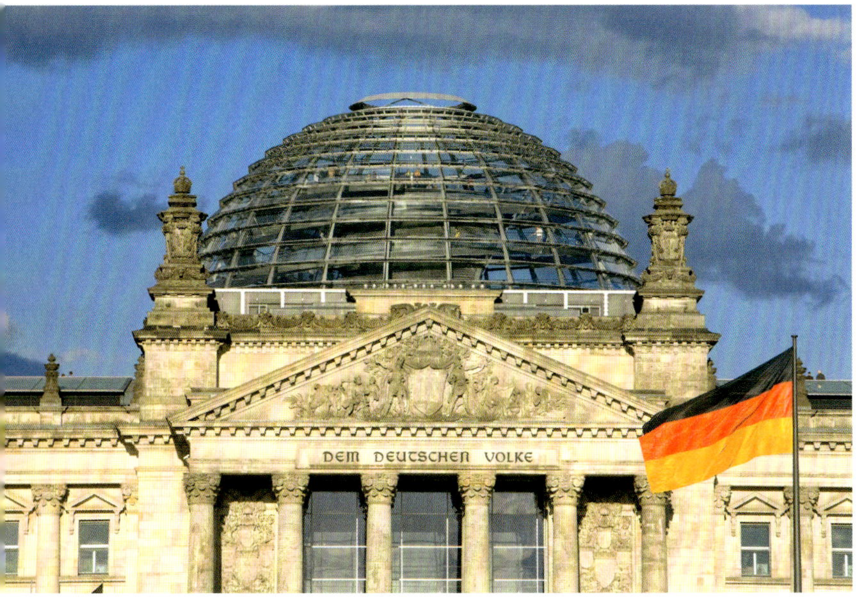

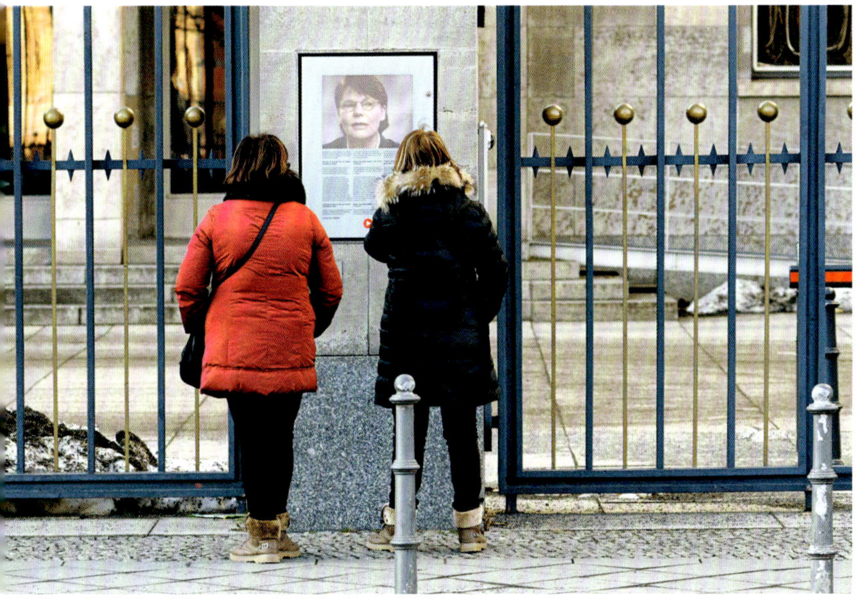

The Berlin headquarters of the Federal Ministry of Justice are situated in a building complex that comprises several clothing-factory buildings constructed around the turn of the century, including Haus Stern, which served as a press centre during the GDR period. At this historic location, Günter Schabowski, the GDR Government Spokesperson, announced immediate, unlimited freedom of movement between East and West Germany on November 9, 1989. Thus the building plays a key role in the fall of the Berlin Wall and German unity. The artwork "Die Verkündigung der Reisefreiheit" ("The announcement of travel freedom") by Ulrich Schröder (born in 1954), which was produced in 2000, addresses the theme of that historic occasion. Behind a large window – which is publicly visible from Mohrenstrasse – an installation with a sculptural appearance has been set up, consisting of chairs and a computer screen. The chairs have been attached to an angled floor plate and aligned towards a monitor displaying a video image of an expansive sea. The sloping floor plate can be interpreted as a reference to the "upheaval" of the political system, which was initiated by a peaceful revolution, while the sea indicates travel freedom and open prospects for the future.

Reichstag building, Berlin

Jochen Gerz, "Das Geld, die Liebe, der Tod, die Freiheit — was zählt am Ende?", 2000, Federal Ministry of Finance

EXTENDED FOCUS. CRITICAL ENGAGEMENT WITH HISTORICAL BUILDINGS IN GERMANY

Structural remains from the National Socialist period are also being reused outside Berlin and are similarly the subject of artistic commentary. As the "city of the Party rallies", Nuremberg became one of the most important locations of National Socialist propaganda. Evidence of this can still be seen today in monumental buildings such as the Reich Party Rally Grounds or the so-called Südkaserne ("South Barracks") from the 1930s. The accommodation building of the Schutzstaffel (SS) on the western edge of the Party Rally Grounds is a typical example of the architecture of power during the Nazi period and is preservation-listed today. Taken over by the US Army in 1945, it served as accommodation for forced labourers after the war, who were waiting to return to their home countries. From 1948, it was used as a barracks facility for the US Army. In 1992, the Americans handed the building over to Germany, allowing it to be used for new, civilian purposes. After its renovation and modernisation, the Federal Office for Migration and Refugees moved in, since the rising numbers of asylum seekers in the early 1990s demanded greater capacity for the institution. Not all employees supported the move into the former Südkaserne in Nuremberg in late 1996, due to its architecture. Like many buildings from the Nazi period, the key question was how to convert the historically burdened building. The Federal Office decided to actively engage with the history of the location in publications and guided tours, as well as through artistic intervention. The method of the winning competition entry by the Düsseldorf artist Manuel Franke (born in 1964) is excellently suited to that task. His approach is specific to the situation and combines the content level with formal references. Franke's sculptural-architectural measure "Zeitenklammer" ("Time clip"), which he produced in 1997, addresses the former barracks' use history by designing the newly created entrance area with contemporary references to the architectural relic (→ p. 166).

Gabriele Obermaier (born in 1957) also offers a direct commentary on existing Nazi architecture with her sculpture "Weiches Haus" ("Soft house"), which she developed in

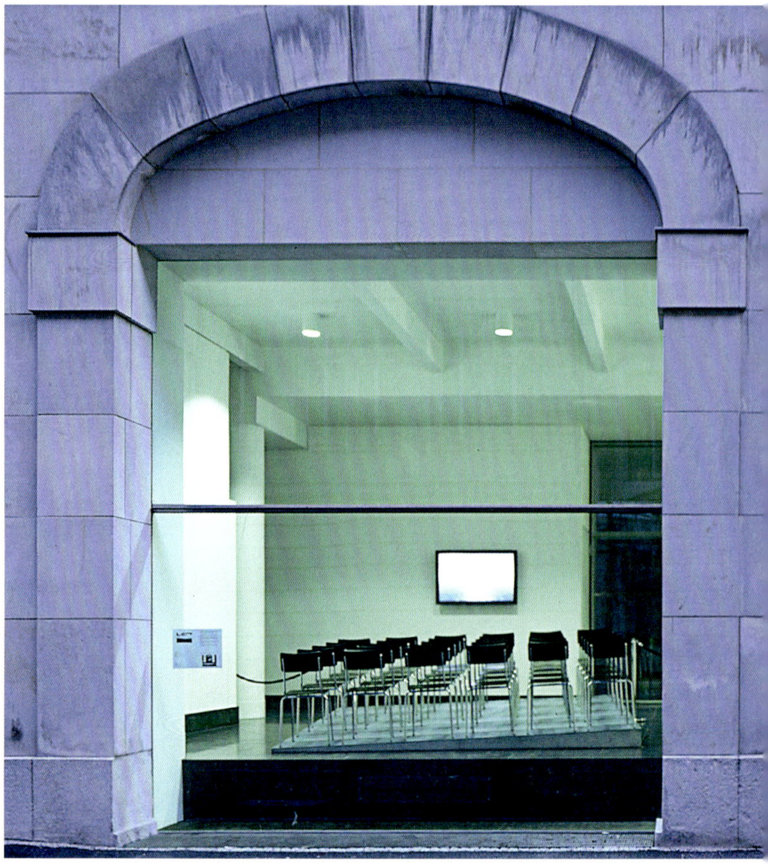

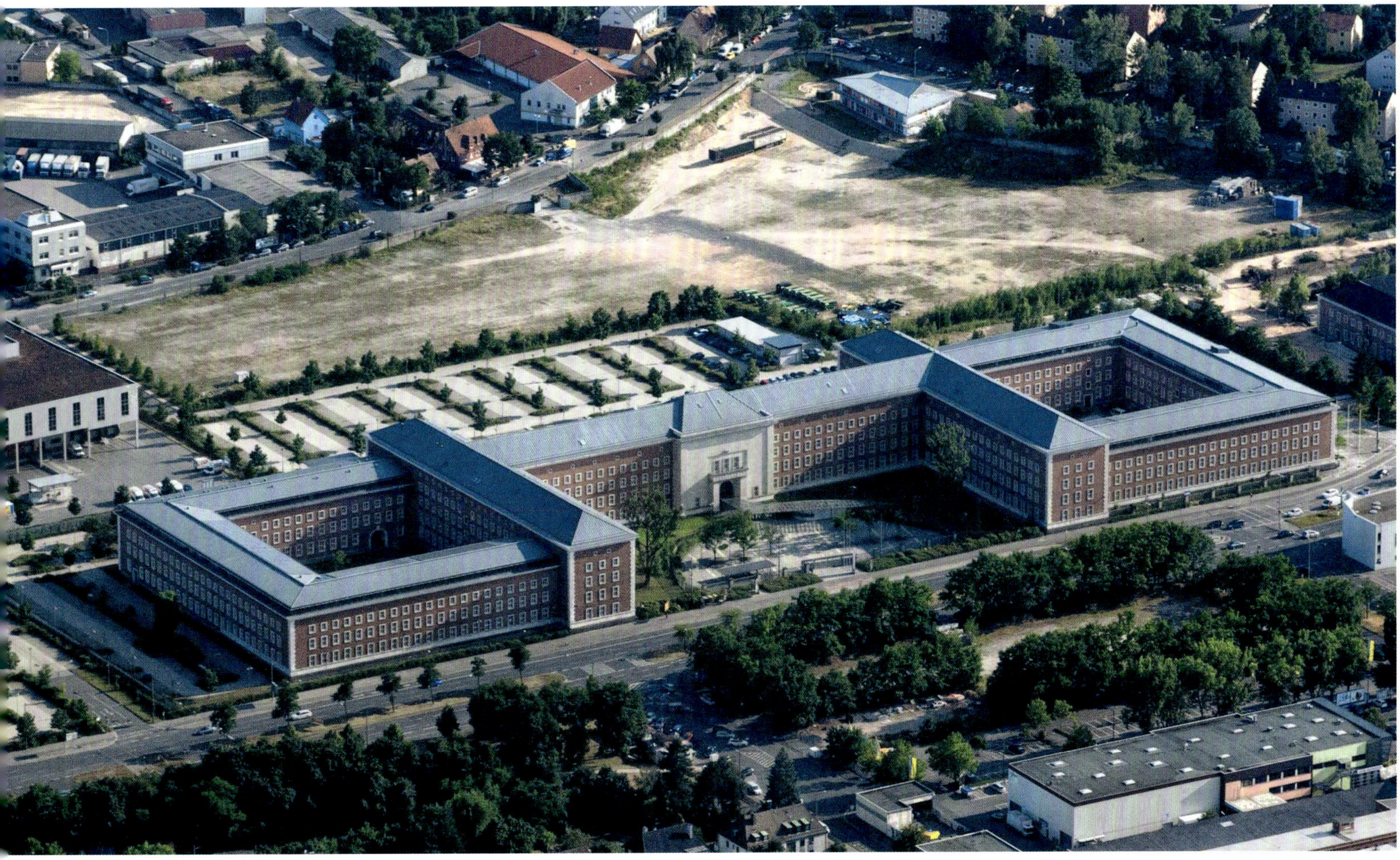

2009 for the Federal Social Court of Germany in Kassel. With her aluminium sculpture, the artist picks up on quintessential structural characteristics of the original court building, which was constructed in a neoclassical style between 1936 and 1938, and has accommodated the Federal Social Court of Germany since 1953. Obermeier deconstructs and humorously counteracts the rigid nature of the former National Socialist building – and therefore the ideology – by designing her art in architecture as a flexible and therefore slightly collapsing felt model in an aluminium mould.

Ulrich Schröder, "Die Verkündigung der Reisefreiheit", 2000, Federal Ministry of Justice,Berlin

Former accommodation for the Schutzstaffel (SS), today the Federal Office for Migration and Refugees, Nuremberg

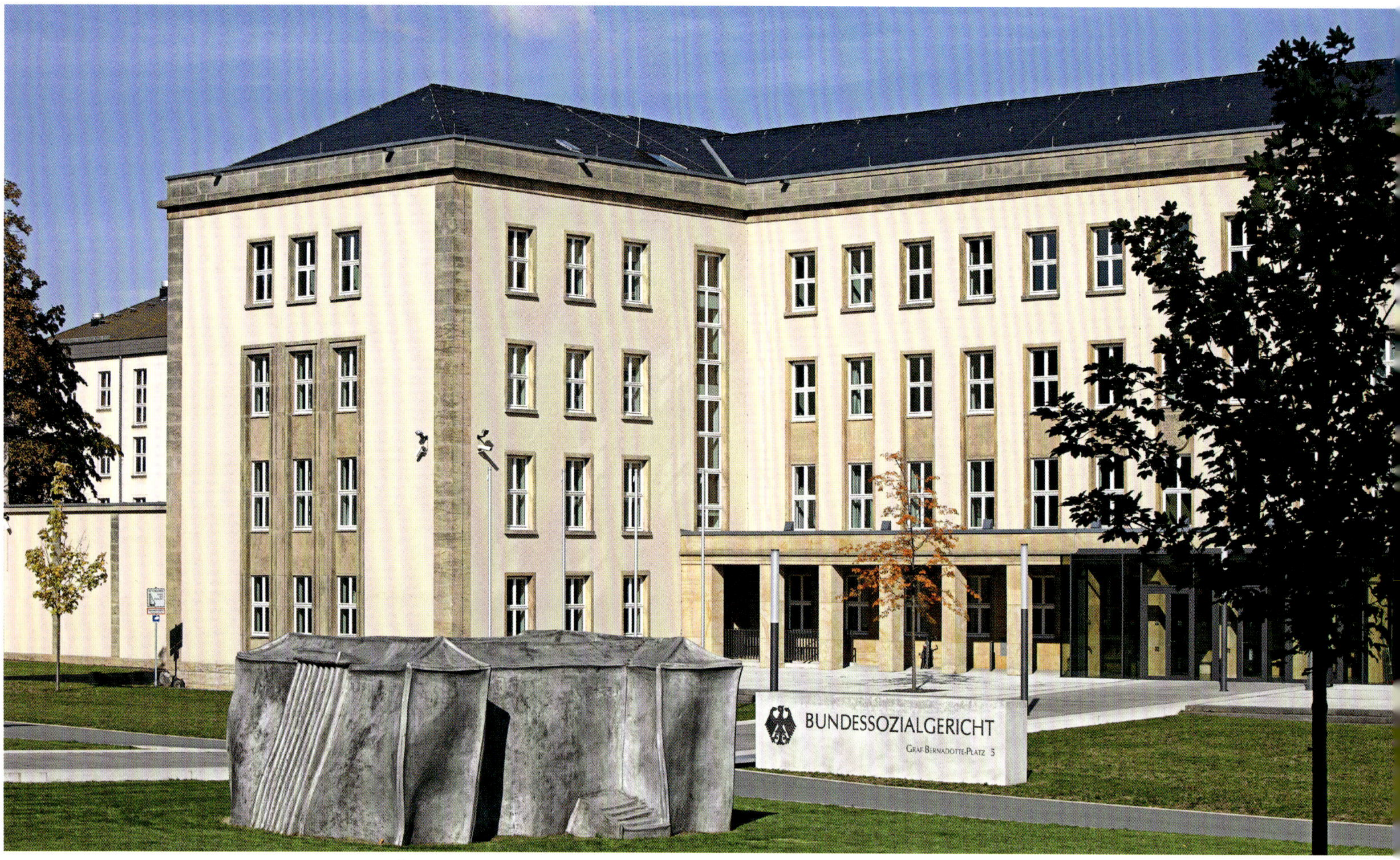

CONTENT-RELATED. ART IN ARCHITECTURE AS COMMENTARY ON INSTITUTIONAL TASKS

Unlike the reuse of many buildings from the Nazi period, the continuation of research work on the island of Riems had no problem with its legitimacy, nor did it need to distance itself from the past. Indeed several sculptural works by Waldemar Grzimek (1918–1984) exclusively referred to the institution's scientific alignment. In 1910, the Prussian Ministry of Cultural Affairs ordered Friedrich Loeffler to found the first Institute for Animal Health on the island of Riems near Greifswald, aimed at researching the foot-and-mouth virus. Initial building activity dates from the year of the institute's foundation. Over the decades, the institute was converted and extended several times. In the late 1950s, the two-storey main building of the research facility from the 1940s received new artworks: between 1957 and 1960, Hans Neubert (1924–2011) was commissioned by the GDR Deutsche Akademie der Landwirtschaftswissenschaften ("German Academy of Agricultural Science") to produce the ten-part mural cycle "Sinn und Praxis der Virologie" ("The purpose and practice of virology"). The cycle presents a detailed and comprehensive portrait of the institute researchers' tasks. Neubert's style is dedicated to classical modernity; thus, the influences of Max Beckmann are evident in the strong contouring and dense composition. The motifs chosen by Neubert for the mural cycle show no idealisation of the scenery, nor any clear alienation. Instead they realistically portray the professional working atmosphere.

In 2014, during the overall expansion of the location on the island of Riems, including new buildings for laboratories and stables, as well as an office building with a conference

Gabriele Obermaier, "Weiches Haus", 2009, Federal Social Court, Kassel

Hans Neubert, "Herstellung der Kristallviolett-Vakzine gegen Schweinepest", part of the the mural cycle "Sinn und Praxis der Virologie", 1957–1960, Institute for Animal Health, Greifswald, Island of Riems

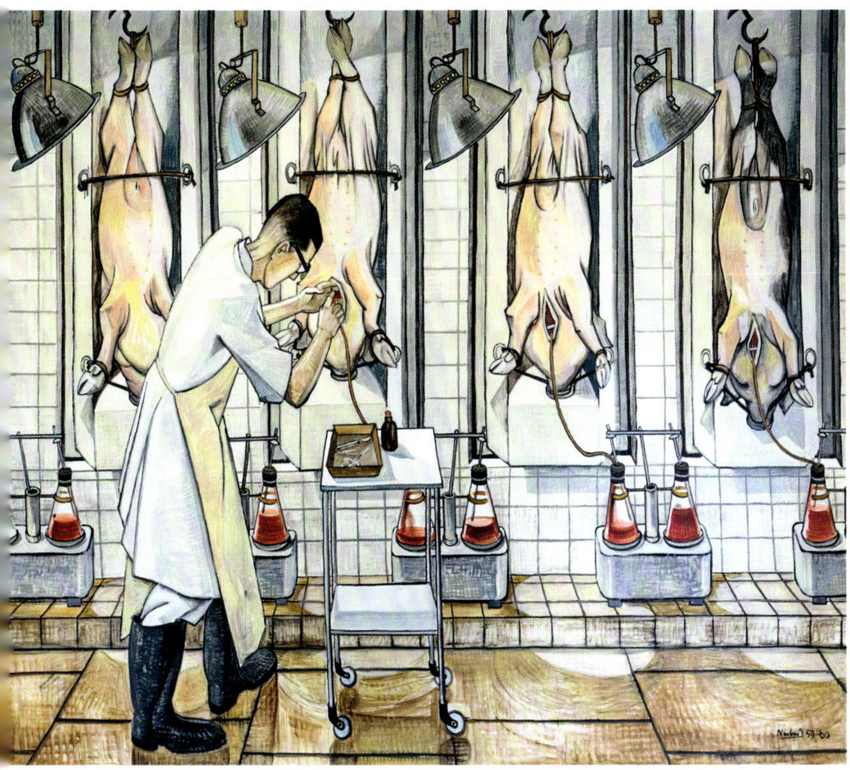

area, two art in architecture pieces were produced by Barbara Trautmann (born in 1966) and Matthias Geitel (born in 1962), which each address different aspects of the research institute. The exterior sculpture "Insulaner" ("Island dweller") by Trautmann consists of 189 icosahedra and refers to the scientific work with dangerous viruses (→ p. 214). The two murals by Geitel entitled "Grenzen und Ereignisse" ("Boundaries and events") and "Virusform" ("Virus form"), pick up on the ability of viruses to penetrate other organisms and cause global pandemics. With their content-based and formally successful implementation of the competition tasks, the artists refer to the facility's research challenges, while engaging with the content of earlier art in architecture works for the Friedrich Loeffler Institute.

Numerous art in architecture pieces were also produced for the buildings of the German Bundestag, as well as federal ministries in Berlin, which address the content of the responsibilities and tasks of the respective institutions. One visual commentary on the political and social history of Germany was produced by Marcel Odenbach (born in 1953) for the Federal Ministry for Economic Affairs and Energy (→ p. 144). The historical building section of the ministry, which was built as the Invalidenhaus between 1747 and 1748, and converted and expanded between 1991 and 2000, was used as a hospital and accommodated the Ministry of Health during the GDR period. Odenbach's ceiling frieze consisting of a blue-coloured photo collage is framed by text extracts from the constitution, the Bible and political manifestos, which combine to comment on German history.

Dani Karavan (born in 1930) also refers to the Federal Republic's constitution in his conceptual installation "Grundgesetz 49", which was produced in 2002 for the Jakob Kaiser House of the German Bundestag. It runs along the former inner-German border between East and West Berlin and recalls the difficult post-war period. Directly by the Spreepromenade, 19 panes of glass, each approximately three metres high, surround a courtyard of the Jakob Kaiser House towards the River Spree. At eye level, 19 articles of fundamental rights according to the 1949 constitution have been laser-engraved on the glass. In this way, the Israeli artist conceptually refers to the parliamentary location by focusing on the word of law. In addition to the historical bridge, a geographical connection to the old federal capital Bonn is also achieved, since it was there that from 1948 to 1949, the Parliamentary Council developed the constitution on the instructions of the three western occupying forces. One specific quality of art in architecture can be its functional integration into the architecture. The work by Karavan achieves this in a very elegant way by making the glass panes outline the property boundary, while their transparency creates a fluent public space. Karavan, who became internationally renowned with his expansive *Gesamtkunstwerke*, connects the architecture of Jakob Kaiser House to the surrounding landscape to achieve an aesthetic unity by integrating the existing elements, including six technically necessary ventilation chimneys. Furthermore, he adds new design elements such as the radial floor structure consisting of strips of lawn framed by bands of Corten steel. From the courtyard area, they run beneath the glass plates to the banks of the Spree.

The artistic marking of today's Stasi Museum in Berlin demonstrates a successful engagement both with the history of Germany and with the current tasks of the institution using the building. The art competition for

Matthias Geitel, "Grenzen und Ereignisse", 2014, Friedrich Loeffler Institute, Federal Research Institute for Animal Health, Greifswald, Island of Riems

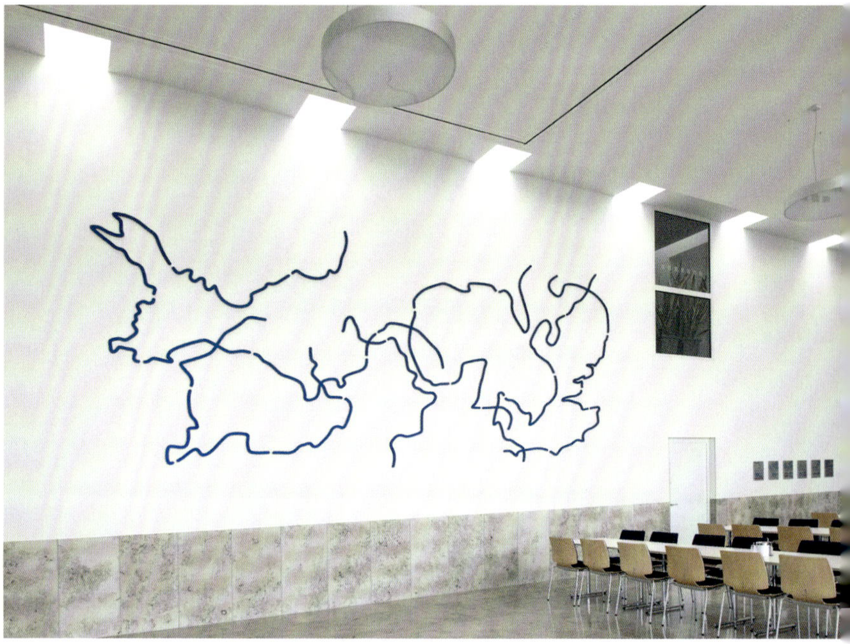

Dani Karavan, "Grundgesetz 49", 1998/2003, German Bundestag/ Jakob Kaiser House, Berlin

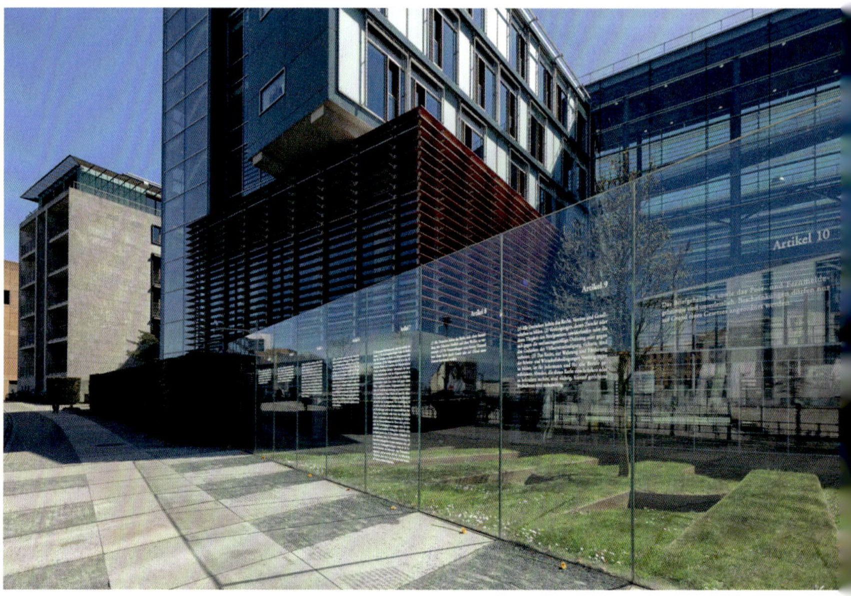

the exterior grounds of the documentation and education centre "Repressionen in der SED-Diktatur" ("Repression in the SED dictatorship") was won by the group raumlaborberlin with its idea of marking the building and the forecourt of the former Stasi headquarters with the inscription "EINGEGANGEN am…" ("REGISTERED on…") (→ p. 172). With its ambiguous statement, the art inspires people to consider the unjust system, which has now been overcome and had been hidden behind the bureaucratic façade of the State Security at this location. At the same time, the stamp marks the entrance to today's Stasi Museum.

Making historical events visible through art in architecture works is an essential aspect of the culture of memory in order to keep German history alive in politics and society. Art in architecture allows clients and artists to take a stance, handle the history of the buildings' construction and use, and comment on the former and current tasks of the institutions. The interaction between architecture and art creates several levels of significance and interpretation that provide viewers with a multifaceted perspective on the past and the present. The genre of art in architecture is able to transcend the aesthetic level and inspire spontaneous curiosity through artistic comment, as well as affording multilayered interpretative potential that can stimulate both critical reflection and identification with the built environment.

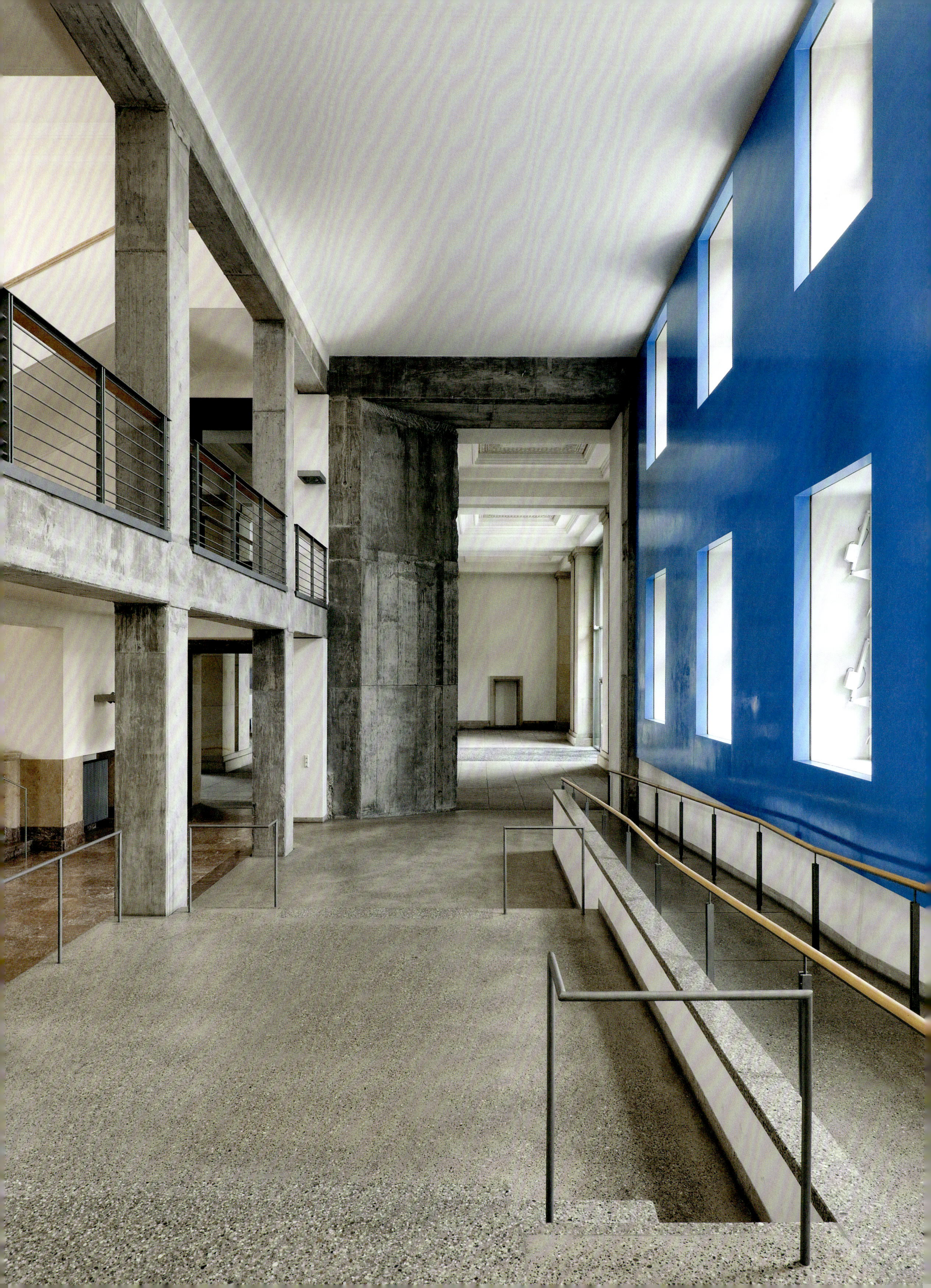

FEDERAL OFFICE FOR MIGRATION AND REFUGEES NUREMBERG

Address:
Frankenstrasse 210
90461 Nuremberg

Architecture:
Franz Ruff, 1937–1939
Conversion:
Grabow + Hofmann, 1993–1996

Art in architecture:
Manuel Franke

Since 2016, the Federal Office for Migration and Refugees has been accommodated in a barracks facility on the edge of the former National Socialist Party Rally grounds in Nuremberg. Along with Albert Speer, its builder Franz Ruff was one of the most prominent architects of the Nazi period, who consolidated the National Socialist claim to power with prestigious buildings. The art in architecture by Manuel Franke (born in 1964), a sculptural-architectural measure entitled "Zeitenklammer" ("Time clip"), engages with the building's historical use as a barracks facility, which was constructed for the Waffen-SS and used by the US Army for decades after the war. During that period, the visible natural stones were demonstratively covered in a blue resin varnish to give the monumental building a lighter character. After the departure of the American forces, this "neutralising layer" was removed from the by then preservation-listed building. The artistic measures by Franke include blue wall paint in the newly created entrance area, referring back to the former blue varnish. The original street paving on a raised foundation recalls the original transport route for soldiers of the Wehrmacht. Finally, the concrete load-bearing elements were kept in their raw condition in the new entrance hall, in order to explicitly highlight the architectural conversion of a military facility into a civilian administration with humanitarian tasks as a stark contrast to the prestige-laden architecture of National Socialism.

MANUEL FRANKE
"Zeitenklammer" ("Time clip"), 1997
Mural, plaster, synthetic resin varnish, sealant

GERMAN BUNDESTAG REICHSTAG BUILDING BERLIN

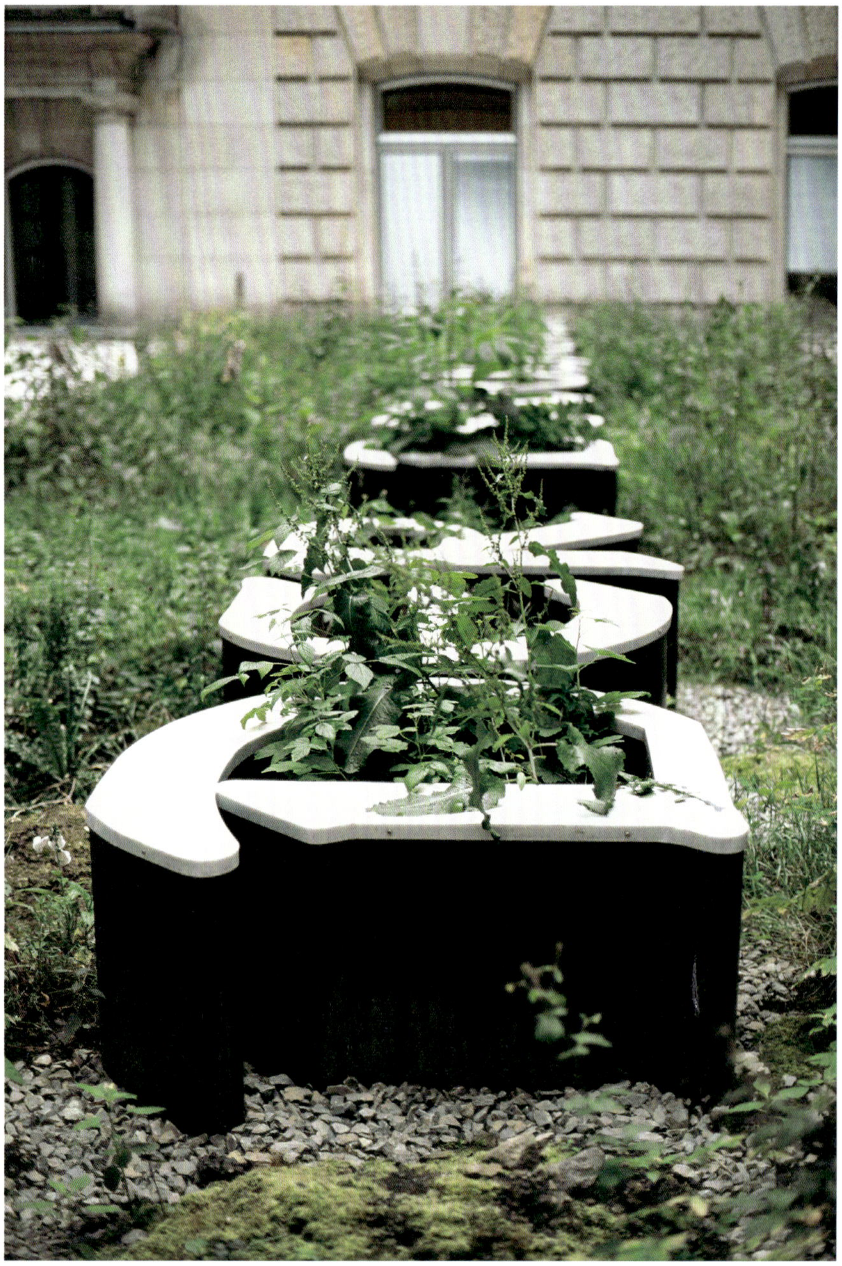

Address:
Platz der Republik 1
11011 Berlin

Architecture:
Paul Wallot, 1884–1894
Reconstruction:
Paul Baumgarten, 1961–1972
Conversion:
Norman Foster, 1995–1999

Art in architecture:
Hans Haacke
and Gerhard Altenbourg,
Georg Baselitz, Christian Boltanski,
Jürgen Böttcher-Strawalde,
Grisha Bruskin, Carlfriedrich Claus,
Christo and Jeanne-Claude,
Lutz Dammbeck, Hanne Darboven,
Rupprecht Geiger, Hermann Glöckner,
Gotthard Graubner, Bernard Heiliger,
Bernhard Heisig, Jenny Holzer,
Anselm Kiefer, Carl-Heinz Kliemann,
Markus Lüpertz, Wolfgang Mattheuer,
Georg Karl Pfahler, Sigmar Polke,
Gerhard Richter, Ulrich Rückriem,
Emil Schumacher, Katharina
Sieverding, Walter Stöhrer,
Günther Uecker, Woty Werner

HANS HAACKE
"DER BEVÖLKERUNG"
("TO THE POPULATION"), 2000
Wooden planks, neon lettering,
21 x 7 x 1.2 m

The Reichstag building was constructed between 1884 and 1894 by Paul Wallot for the Reichstag of the German Empire. In 1920, the first democratically elected Reichstag of the Weimar Republic assembled there. Following severe fire damage in 1933 and due to World War II, the Reichstag was reconstructed by Paul Baumgarten in the 1960s, although the building lacked a specific use until German reunification. After the comprehensive conversion of the Reichstag building (1995–1999) by the British architect Norman Foster, the German Bundestag moved into its new parliamentary seat in 1999. In accordance with the developed art concept, internationally renowned artists were invited to engage with the history of the building and its function as a "Forum of the Nation". Hans Haacke (born in 1936) developed a participatory piece of art in architecture for the Reichstag building, which refers to the historical inscription beneath the gable of the western portal: "DEM DEUTSCHEN VOLKE" ("TO THE GERMAN PEOPLE"). The neon lettering "DER BEVÖLKERUNG" ("TO THE POPULATION") radiates in a plant box that parliamentarians have been filling with earth from their constituencies since 2000. Haacke thereby recalls the disastrous consequences of the term "Volk" ("people" or "nation") and its connection to the "Blut und Boden" ("blood and earth") ideology of the National Socialists. A tense relationship is established between the lettering in the inner courtyard and the gable inscription on the Reichstag, inspiring viewers to consider and discuss the role and self-perception of the parliament, as well as the term "Volk". Since the decisions of the Bundestag affected all residents of the Federal Republic, the parliamentarians are responsible "not for a mythical nation, but for the population", as the artist stated. The design was only implemented in 2000 following a controversial debate in the Bundestag.

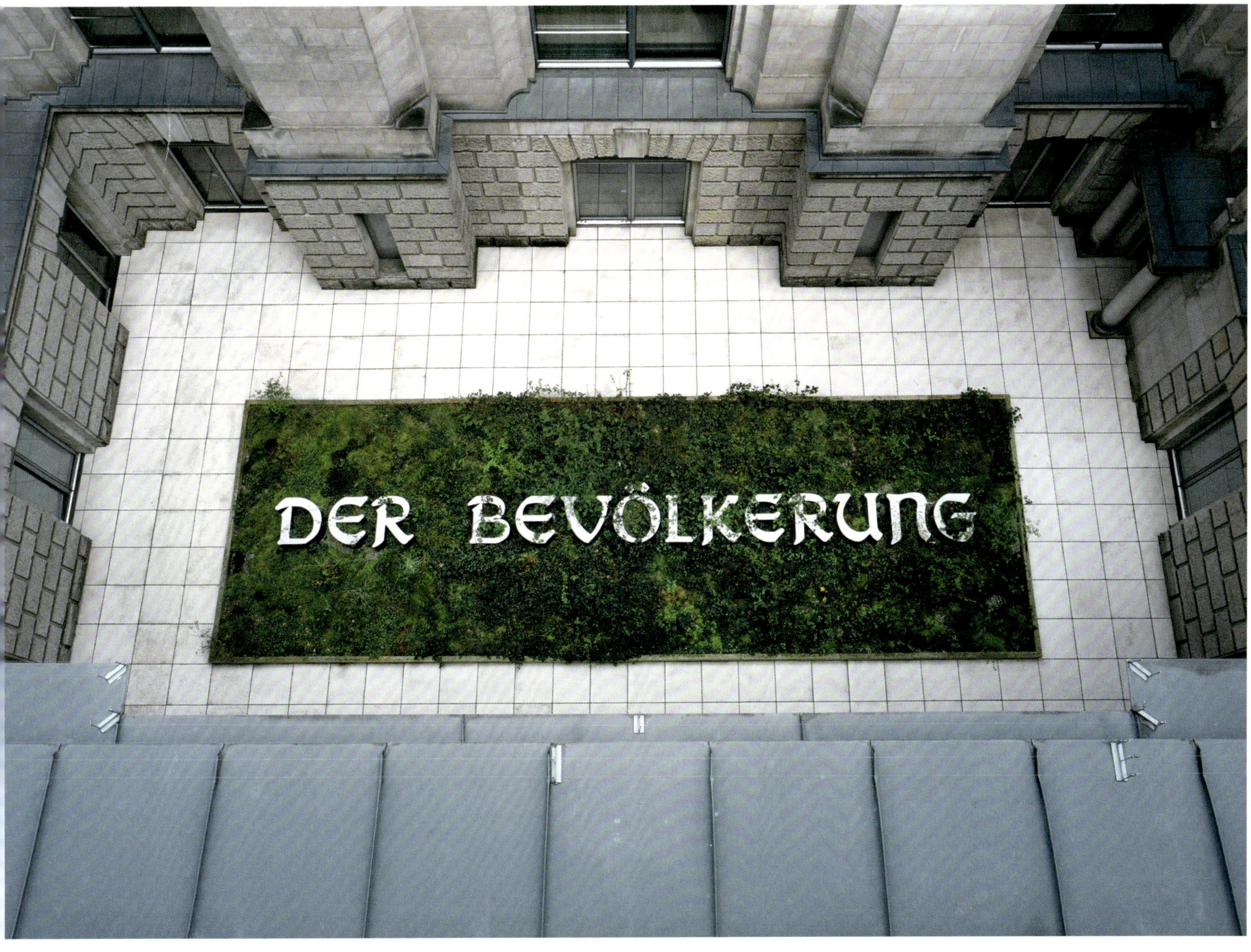

FEDERAL MINISTRY OF DEFENCE BERLIN

Address:
Stauffenbergstrasse 18
10785 Berlin

Architecture:
Reinhardt & Süßenguth, 1911–1914
Conversion:
Burckhardt, Emch und Berger GmbH, Berlin, 1997–2001

Art in architecture:
Via Lewandowsky
and Renate Anger

The building designed by the architectural office Reinhardt & Süßenguth with Neoclassical and Baroque Revival style elements was constructed between 1911 and 1914 as the highest Marine command headquarters. After World War I, it accommodated the Reich Ministry of Defence, before the National Socialists used it as the command headquarters of the Wehrmacht. While fitting out the building for the Federal Ministry of Defence, six artists were invited to participate in an art in architecture competition based on an art concept for the foyer developed by the Federal Government. The prize-winning entry was designed by the Berlin artist Via Lewandowsky (born in 1963), who conceived a floor piece for the entrance area of the ministry, which engages with the history of the location. His "red carpet", presented in the central column hall dominated by mighty pillars and balustrades, initially has a subtle effect. At first glance, the 5 x 10 metre textile work recalls the red carpet that is rolled out on special occasions to honour guests of state and famous people. On closer inspection, the glamour effect is quickly replaced by the insight that the carpet depicts an aerial photograph of the ruined district around Stauffenbergstrasse, destroyed by war. The artwork evokes associations of a "carpet bombing", the blood-red colour referring to the destruction and woe caused by war. In today's Federal Ministry of Defence, the image can be interpreted as a warning of the horrors of war.

VIA LEWANDOWSKY
"Roter Teppich" ("Red carpet"), 2002
Wool
5 x 10 m

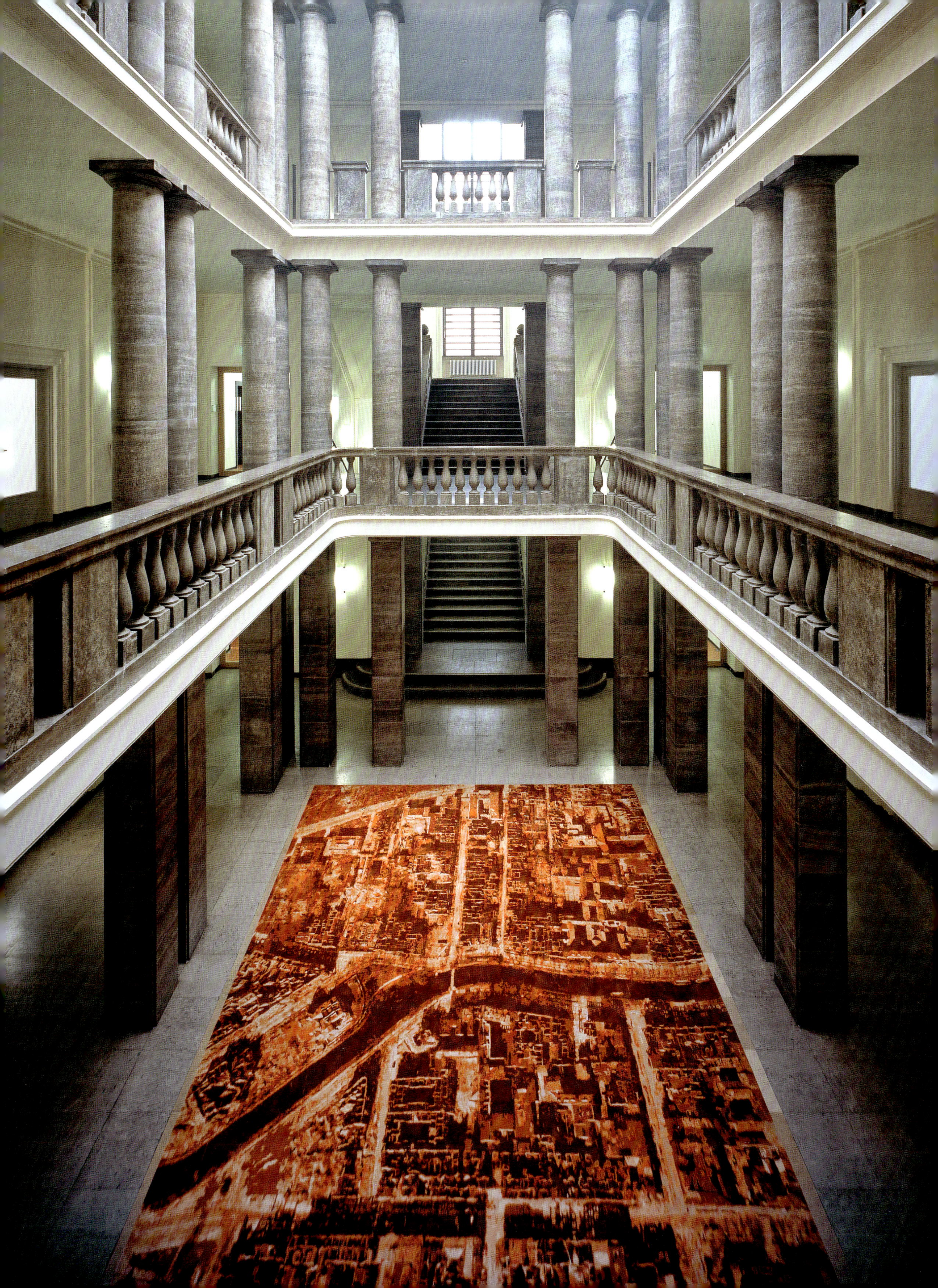

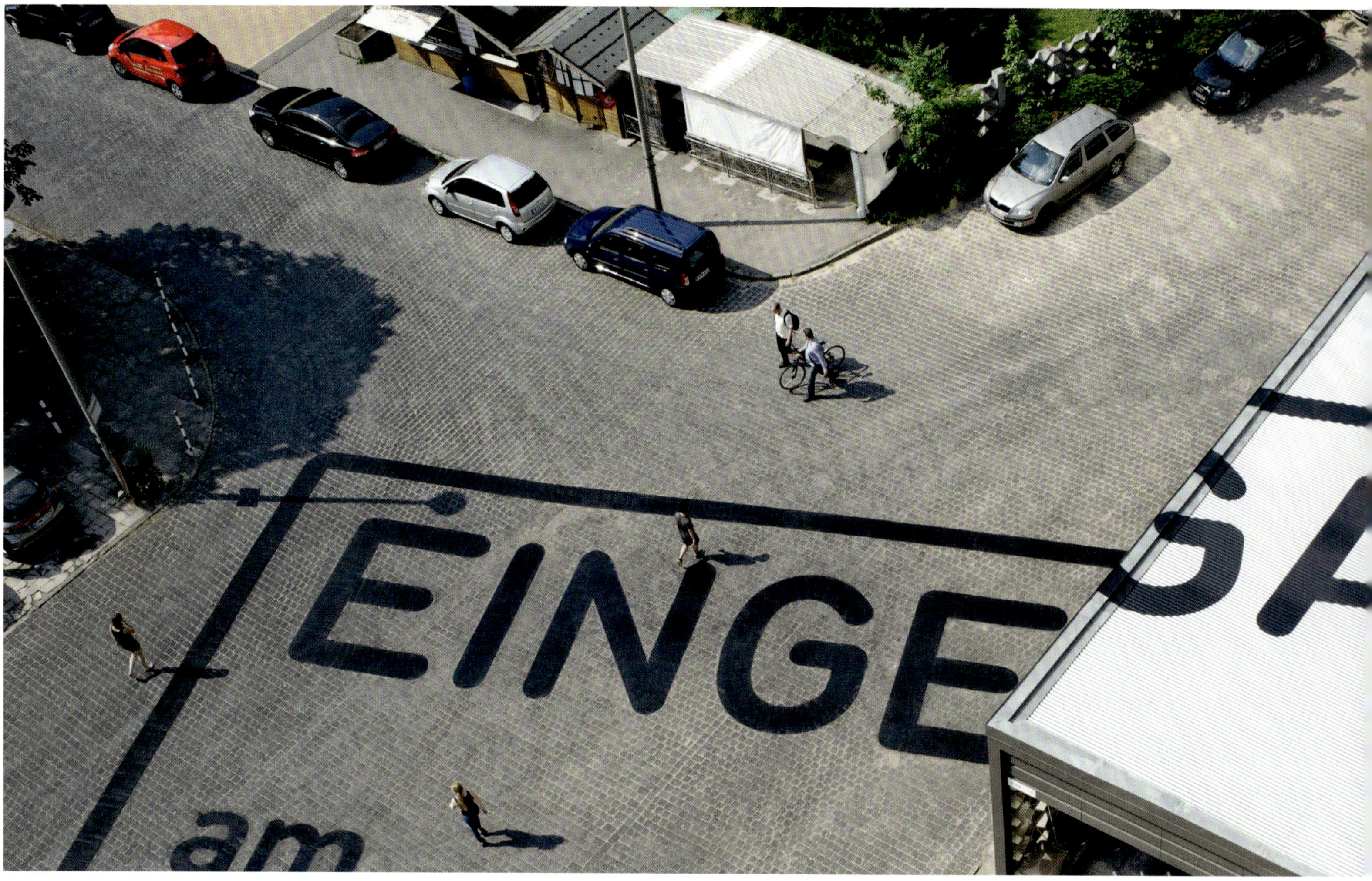
EINGE
am

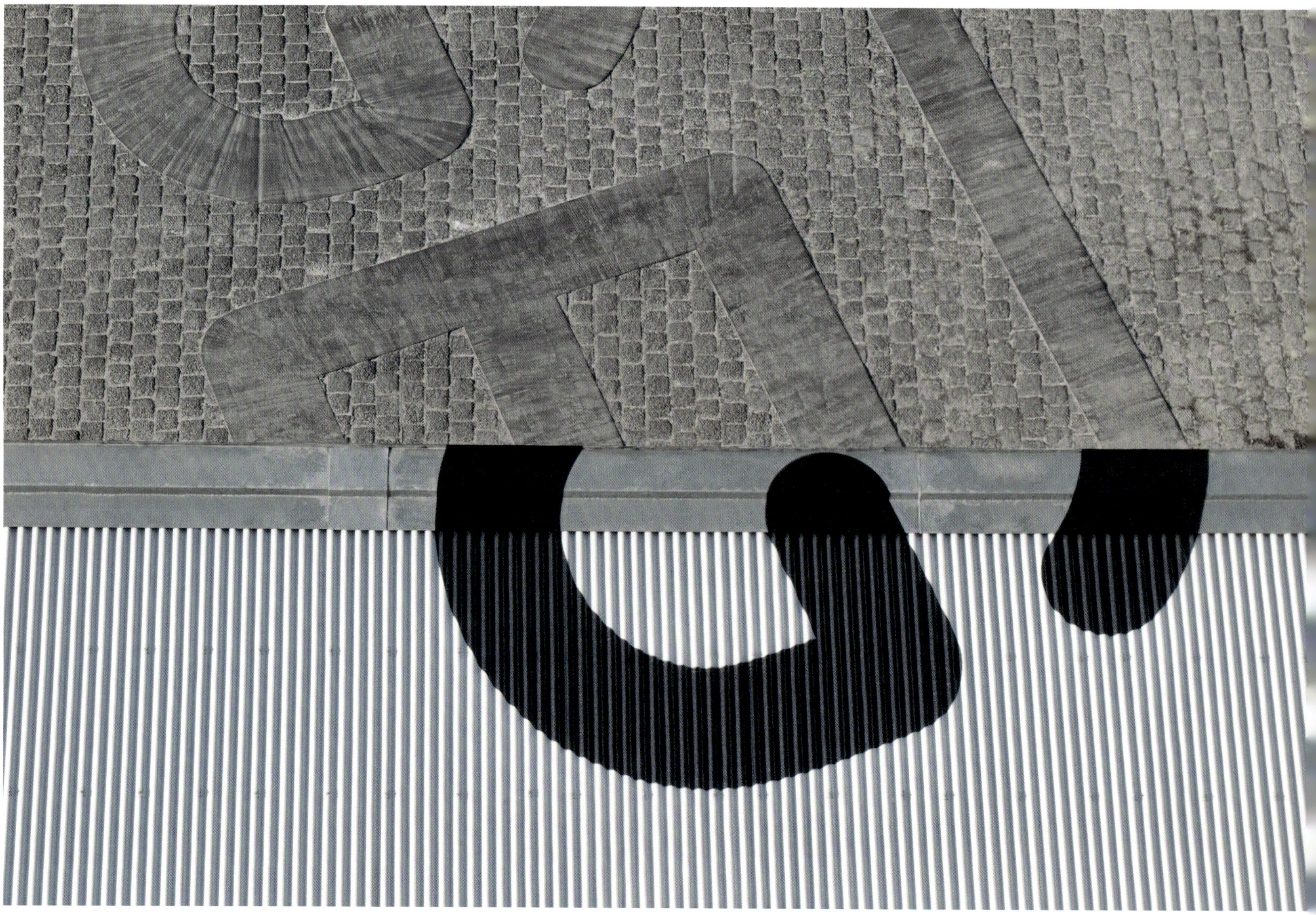

STASI MUSEUM BERLIN

Address:
Haus 1, Ruschestrasse 103
10365 Berlin

Architecture:
1961–1962
Conversion:
Arnold und Gladisch, 2010–2011

Art in architecture:
raumlaborberlin

The formerly heavily shielded entrance to the complex of the GDR Ministry of State Security now accommodates the Stasi Museum in its House 1. The exhibition communicates the atmosphere and spirit of the Stasi power apparatus. Founded in 1950, the ministry developed into a widely networked, high-personnel surveillance apparatus to repress the citizens of the GDR if there was any suspicion of political resistance against the SED, espionage or an attempt to flee the country. In 1989, the ministry had 91,000 full-time and between 110,000 and 190,000 unofficial employees.

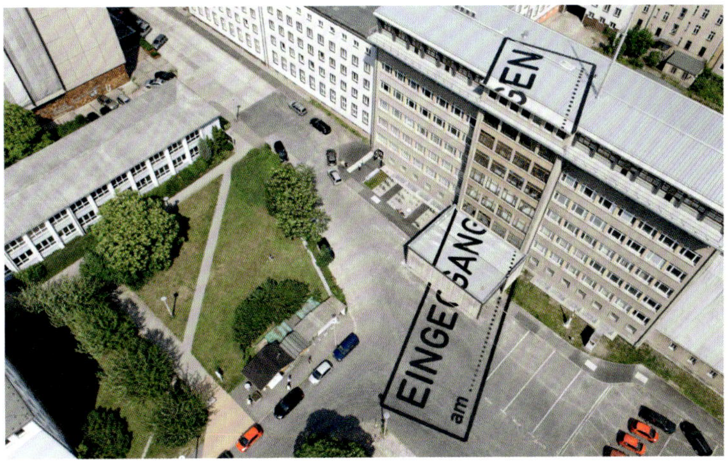

The group raumlaborberlin won the art in architecture competition for the exterior grounds, which had been announced as part of the conversion and fitting-out measures to the building to create a documentation and education centre. The aim of the process was an artwork that raises the external profile of the museum and improves the design of the exterior grounds. Today, an enormous stamp marks the forecourt, the canopy and the main roof of the former Stasi headquarters. “EINGEGANGEN am…” (“REGISTERED on…”) concisely encapsulates the madness with which the GDR developed its control and deterrent machinery over a period of decades, perfecting the Stasi surveillance system with exceptional bureaucratic thoroughness and zeal. The banal and everyday means that oiled the wheels of this bureaucratic apparatus were files, paper, typewriters, folders, indicews, filing cabinets, telephones, envelopes and stamps, such as “REGISTERED on…”. The stamp is also a pun, since the German word “eingegangen” also means “deceased”, thereby alluding to the fact that the GDR is now consigned to history.

RAUMLABORBERLIN
“EINGEGANGEN am…”
(“REGISTERED on...”), 2011
Marking material
13 x 47 m

FROM AUTHORITIES

STATE FACILITIES AND THEIR ART

TO SPORT

We encounter federal art in architecture everywhere. According to rough estimates, the Federal Government has commissioned around 10,000 works of art in architecture since the Federal Republic of Germany was founded. These are joined by architecturally related art from the GDR period. The large number was only achieved because the Federal Government has its own fields of responsibilities, despite the state's federal organisation. Its exclusive competences include all foreign affairs, goods transportation, aviation and railways, as well as postal services, telecommunication and the Federal Criminal Police Office. These competences grant the Federal Government, the country's highest executive level, jurisdiction over the buildings used not only by the constitutional bodies and the Federal Government itself, but also by the five highest courts. It manages buildings for cultural institutions, labour offices, internal security facilities, financial administrations and the transport sector, as well as buildings for science and technology, structures for Federal Armed Forces, allied stationed forces and supranatural institutions in Germany and abroad, and even the Bundeskunsthalle in Bonn.

In addition to the exclusive core competences of the Federal Government and the federal states, the federal structure requires that both national and regional governments share responsibilities for the sectors of transport, the expansion and new construction of schools, regional economic structural initiatives and educational planning. In the field of social and educational affairs, the Federal Government also presides over funding and supervises appropriate measures.

All of these tasks require buildings. Since the Federal Government implements art in architecture as a "fundamental necessity", as defined by the "Guideline on art in architecture", the relevant artworks are not just produced for prestigious, highly frequented locations. They are commissioned wherever the Federal Government is active as a building client – even in projects where the installed art can only be perceived by a few people at their workplaces.

FROM AUTHORITIES TO SPORT

Martin Seidel

The types and forms of art in architecture are extremely diverse, while its tasks go far beyond decoration. Naturally, art in architecture also plays an aesthetic role with respect both to the architecture and itself. It also adds a profile to locations, giving them depth and dignity. It represents the builder and the architecture's users, forms an image, plays a memorial and cautionary role and assumes identity-building and social functions. Last but not least, art in architecture supports artists and therefore art and culture as a key pillar of society and the state.

State art in architecture has such a high profile because the Federal Government treats all of its art in architecture projects equally. It makes no difference whether the measures are for a federal building in Berlin, in the capital city of one of the states, or in a small or medium-sized town. Equally, no distinction is made between a project for a research laboratory with a staff of at most a few dozen, or the Federal Intelligence Service with its 4,000 employees. The same quality criteria and artistic briefs are applied to art in architecture produced for a high-budget new government building as for art in architecture for a single-storey extension building for a civil service canteen. The only difference is the funds available for art, which are derived from the respective building costs. Thus, initially and in principle, there is no difference between art in architecture for a customs office at a border crossing or a music college; nor between an aeroplane maintenance hall on Federal Armed Forces grounds and an inner-urban labour office. A virological research institute in a prohibited zone receives the same attention as a Federal Armed Forces hospital that accommodates 20,000 patients, most of whom are civilians, and treats far in excess of 200,000 outpatients every year.

Art councils were established for the largest federal building measures during the government's move from Bonn to Berlin. Formally, however, the same planning criteria, selection processes and competition procedures apply to all art in architecture measures. One aspect that applies more to art in architecture for the Federal Republic than to architecturally related art produced in the GDR is the fact that every art in architecture project and its responsible body is free to decide how it wishes to handle the art, choose its specific locations, and determine the genres, styles, themes and artists themselves.

Numerous variables that combine to form endlessly new constellations determine the diversity of the art in architecture. One criterion that always has an undeniable effect is a very natural instinct concerning the "appropriateness" of the art in architecture, since it attempts to do justice to the functional, social, artistic and architectural requirements, while balancing out the interests of the clients, architects, artists and users. The quality of subjectivity, which is necessary and deliberately applied to every project, the variety of the buildings and their uses, and the pieces' artistic inventiveness are the great strengths of the resulting art in architecture and a main reason for its diversity.

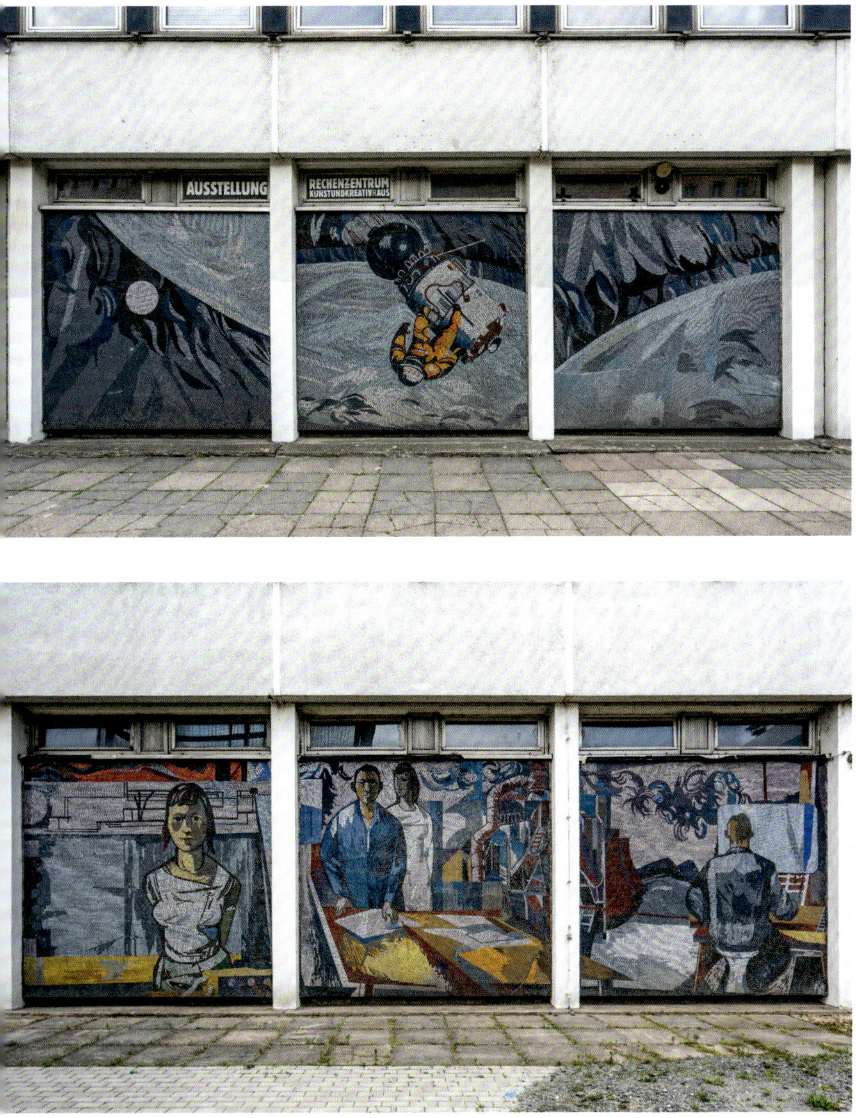

Fritz Eisel, "Der Mensch bezwingt den Kosmos", 1969–1972, VEB Maschinelles Rechnen, Potsdam

AUTHORITIES

Authorities form an important state body responsible for art in architecture, including not only the higher federal authorities, the Federal President's Office, the Bundestag administration, the Federal Chancellery, the Federal Constitutional Court and federal ministries, but also the subordinate federal authorities, higher, middle and lower offices, federal institutions and public corporations.

In terms of the architecture, authorities rarely form a class of their own, and never do so regarding their art in architecture. Instead, each authority is special on both an institutional and an architectural level. However, in the past, significant differences concerning the architecturally related art arose from the contrasting political systems and their expectations. For most of the period of its existence, the GDR used administrative buildings to propagate Marxist ideals, above all on the façades, using didactic visual programmes to unite the people, namely the workers, farmers and intelligentsia, while also consolidating the sense of the Socialist philosophy of progress.

The large copper relief by Walter Womacka (1925–2010) entitled "Der Mensch überwindet Zeit und Raum" ("Humanity overcomes time and space", 1971) is situated on the eastern façade of the Haus des Reisens (House of Travel). Its central theme of the cosmonaut uses the visual rhetoric of the state propaganda on technology and progress more than it refers to the building's use. Similarly, the eighteen-part glass mosaic cycle entitled "Der Mensch bezwingt den Kosmos" ("Humanity conquers the cosmos") was produced by Fritz Eisel (1929–2010) between 1969 and 1972 for the building of the former computer centre known as VEB Maschinelles Rechnen in the District of Potsdam. It reflects the political climate in which it was produced. Although the 70-metre long cycle refers to the building by portraying data processing, most of it presents motifs of exploring space, defending the country and agricultural production, as evidence of the Socialist victory over capitalism.

The qualities, expression and depth of art in architecture are always a question of the individual piece and never exclusively revealed in the fundamental decision in favour of figurative or abstract art. However, the approach to art in architecture in the Federal Republic of Germany was principally different. Above all in the 1970s and 1980s, art in architecture turned its back on literal visualisation and emblems, often preferring the interaction between non-figurative art and the architecture, including its surroundings.

In the case of the Federal Motor Transport Authority in Flensburg, a sequence of four minimalist structural steel sculptures by Karl-Ludwig Schmaltz (born in 1932) was placed in the green access area between the gate and the main entrance. The sensible organic counterpart to its dynamic structure is formed by a four-part group of stones by Leo Kornbrust (born in 1929), situated in the garden for employees' breaks. Both artworks address the themes of acceleration and slowing down. Thus they refer to the institution for which they were produced even more explicitly than the figurative works by Womacka and Eisel.

One can also descend a level in the administrative hierarchy without needing to fear any less ambitious art in architecture. Since 1999, the foyer of the Waterways and Shipping Office in Eberswalde, one of 304 federal authorities with a modest number of employees and visitors, has accommodated a poetic piece by the world-renowned light, video and performance artist Nan Hoover (1931–2008), consisting of

Karl-Ludwig Schmaltz, "Bodenkristallit Flensburg", 1977/1981, Federal Motor Transport Authority, Flensburg

Ulrich Brüschke, "0° Breite (Modified Cellular Towers)", 2012, Headquarters of the Federal Intellingence Service, Berlin

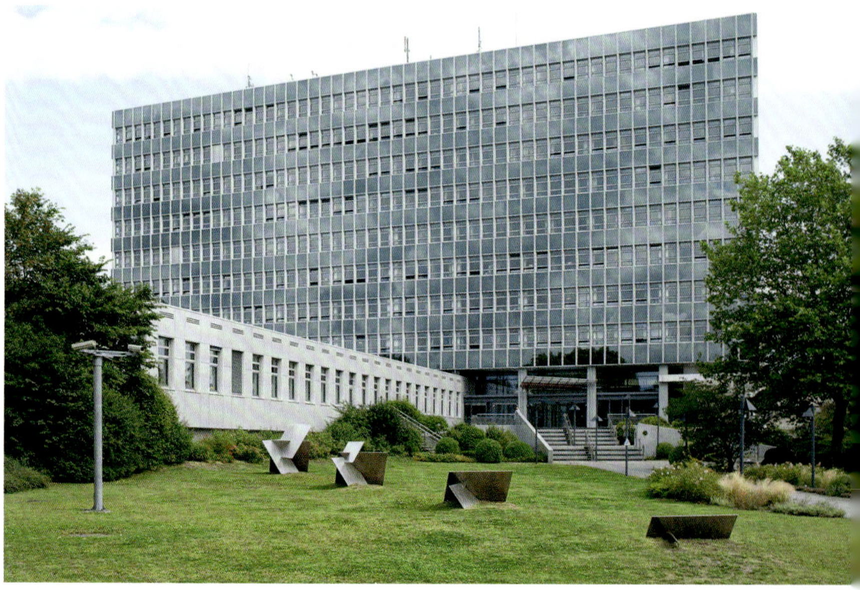

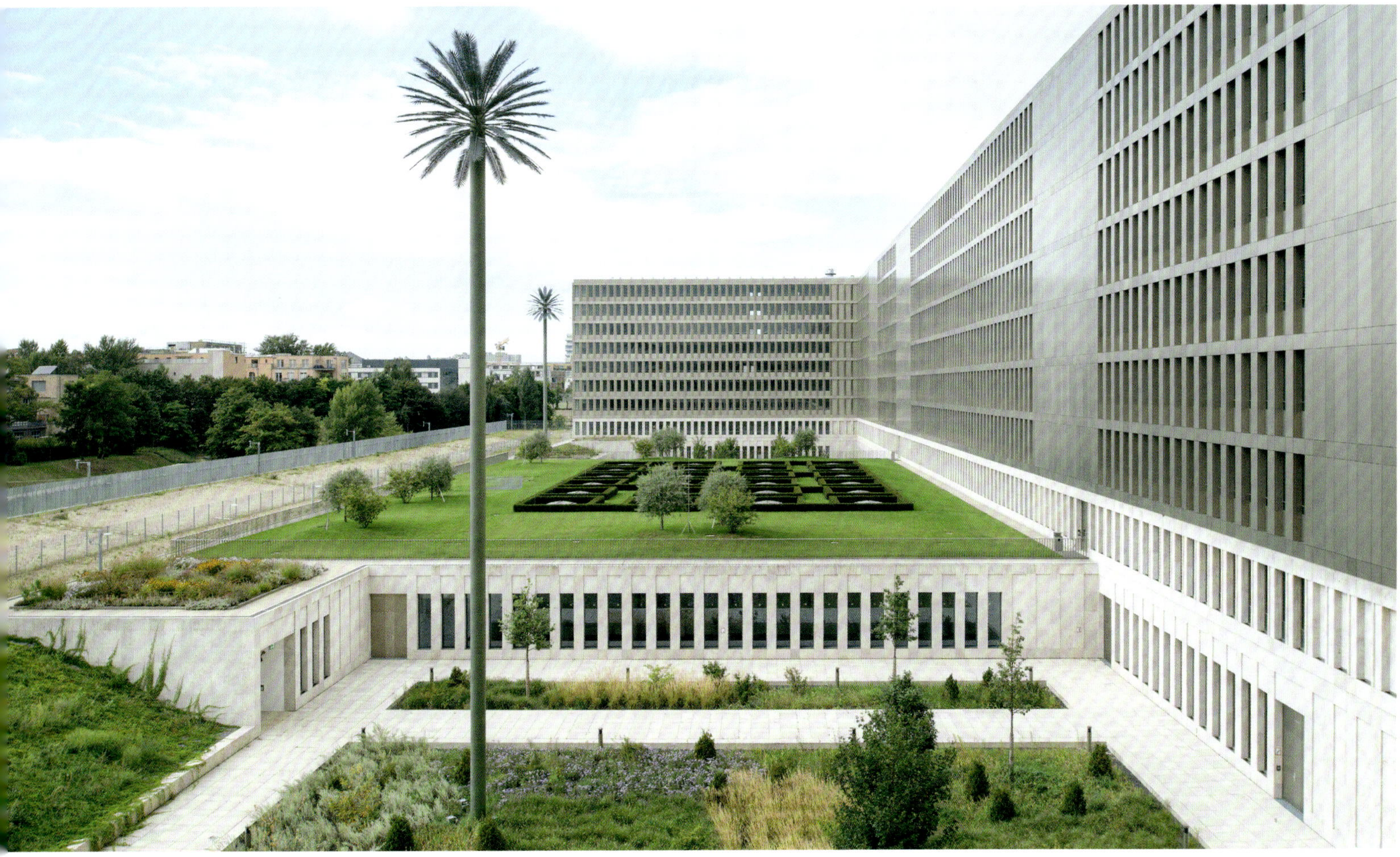

a video installation with black and white snapshots of water being moved by the wind and the sunlight reflected by the waves.

Naturally, the Federal Intelligence Service in Berlin can present art in architecture on a different scale. On its terraces, two palm trees made of steel and plastic by the artist Ulrich Brüschke (born in 1959) rise up around 25 metres into the Berlin sky; the drive is accentuated by an 18-tonne steel sculpture by Stefan Sous (born in 1964); artworks have also been installed in the interior areas. The efforts are not based on the notion that the Federal Intelligence Service, a federal authority, is subordinate to the Federal Chancellery. Instead, from the perspective of building culture, the principle of proportionality in the art in architecture regulations requires artistic formats and materials that are appropriate to the enormous 270 metre long, 160 metre wide and 30 metre high building.

The standing of the state art in architecture throughout the country experienced a geopolitical boost with the country's reunification. In 1992, following a decision by the Federalism Commission, numerous authorities moved from the former West Germany to the so-called "new federal states" in the East. For instance the Federal Labour Court was relocated from Kassel to Erfurt, the Federal Administrative Court from Berlin to Leipzig, the Federal Environment Authority from Berlin to Dessau and the Federal Waterways Engineering and Research Institute from Karlsruhe to Ilmenau. Advanced art in architecture concepts were developed at all of these locations – for example in Erfurt, for the Federal Labour Court (→ p. 212) – involving complex concepts and a wealth of renowned artists.

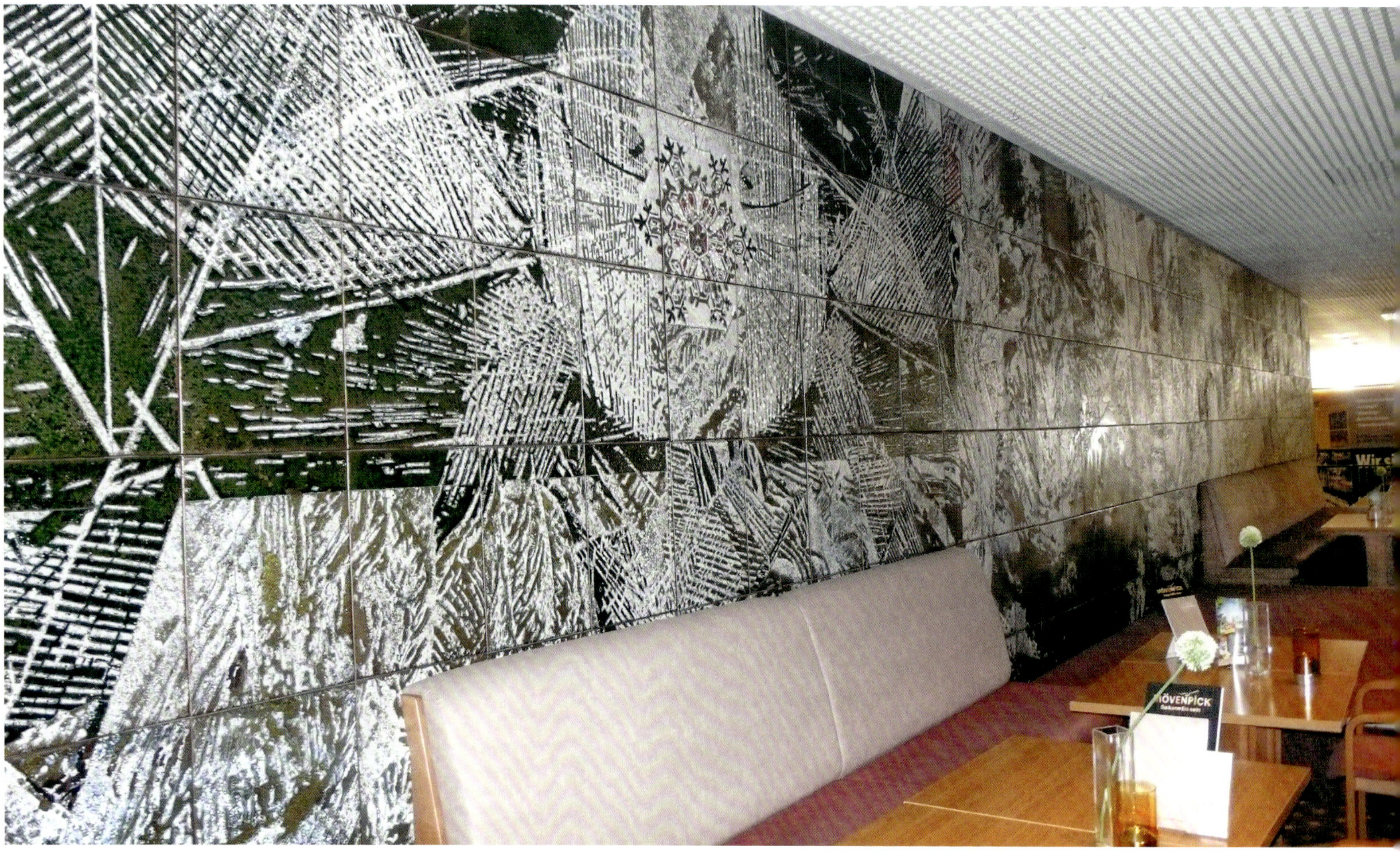

PUBLIC CORPORATIONS AND COMPANIES

State-owned businesses, be they production or service companies, play an important role for art and its perception outside museums, galleries and shows. These companies heighten the presence of art and enable encounters in places where art would otherwise not be installed.

One can find art in the state sectors of banking, transport, postal services, telecommunication and the housing sector. The commitment to art in architecture, which is connected to representative requirements, is often so considerable that several facilities employ special art officers. One such corporation is the KfW banking group, the world's largest national development bank, which owns large stocks of two- and three-dimensional artworks by respected contemporary

Helmut Humann, "Wind-Wetter-Wand", around 1976, FDGB holiday facility "Am Fichtelberg", Oberwiesenthal

artists installed in its branches in Berlin, Bonn and Frankfurt am Main.

The GDR supported architecturally related art with a programmatic brief for its state-owned companies (→ p. 198). The resignation of Walter Ulbricht as First Secretary of the SED and the succession of Erich Honecker in 1971 represented a significant political turning point that also affected the cultural and arts sectors in the GDR. The art produced for the holiday facility of the Freier Deutscher Gewerkschaftsbund (Free German Trades Union, FDGB) in Oberwiesenthal (1972–1975) used no propaganda at all in terms of Socialist Realism. Instead, five regional artists produced partially abstract partitioning elements, sculptures and murals for all public areas of the holiday facility. Their motifs and the materials refer to the local Ore Mountains.

HEALTHCARE SECTOR

In Germany, public hospitals are the responsibility of the states or the administrative districts – with the exception of the Federal Armed Forces hospitals, which are important for art in architecture. Since 2008, the number of such hospitals has fallen from thirteen in 1975 and fourteen at the time of German reunification to only five today. However all of them integrated art in architecture. The Arts Council chaired by the artist Max Bill was established at the Karlsruhe Regional Finance Office, which was also responsible for federal buildings. For the Federal Armed Forces Hospital in Ulm (constructed 1974–1979), it adopted the proposal by the architects Heinle, Wischer und Partner to develop a holistic art concept that remains remarkable to this day. It comprised the specially modelled exterior grounds including five large, blue painted sculptures by Georg Karl Pfahler (1926–2002) (→ p. 240), as well as the entrance hall with murals and sculptures by Alfonso Hüppi (born in 1935) and patient and staff rooms with panel paintings and graphic designs. The different interests complement each other perfectly: combining architectural, artistic, representative and – not least therapeutic aspects.

The federal art in architecture rules also apply to buildings supervised by the states, wherever the Federal Government carried at least 50 percent of the construction costs. For instance, the Federal Government has a stake in the art in architecture for the clinic Diagnostisch-Internistisch-Neurologisches Zentrum opened in Dresden in 2011. The artworks consist of visual, written and object installations by Eva Wilde (born in 1972), Judith Siegmund (born in 1965) and Nikolaus Koliusis (born in 1953). They brighten the atmosphere and heighten people's senses.

RESEARCH INSTITUTES

The Federal Government also operates research facilities. They include the German Weather Service, the Robert Koch Institute and the German Archaeological Institute, as well as federal institutions responsible for materials research and testing, transport and building sectors, food and agriculture, risk research, shipping, hydrology, health education, the labour market and vocational research, the environment, veterinary medicine, development policy and many other fields. These are joined by facilities where the Federal Government provided at least half the funding for the building costs in cooperation with the federal states – such as the Deutsche Forschungsgemeinschaft, the Fraunhofer Gesellschaft, the Max Planck Gesellschaft, the Leibniz

Institutes and the German Centre for Higher Education Research and Science Studies.

All these institutes create a network that ensures the presence and diversity of art in architecture throughout the country. In the field of research, art in architecture does the same as it does elsewhere: it remains true to its versatility and adapts to every individual task in accordance with the requirements of the architecture and building utilisation. Thus there are no pre-determined locations for the artworks. And all genres and techniques – murals, objects, sculptures, installations – are represented. Nor can they be classified as specific typologies: they are all selected according to the individual preferences of the clients and/or competition juries, as well as the architects and artists.

As in all fields, art in architecture for this sector naturally seeks strict formal references to the architecture and/or content-related references to the buildings' use. Around 1960, the Friedrich Loeffler Institute Greifswald, a virological institute situated at a remote location on the Baltic island of Riems in the former GDR, was equipped with art. The painter Hans Neubert (1924–2011) produced ten murals at the time, which meticulously illustrate the "Sinn und Praxis der Virologie" ("Purpose and practice of virology"). At the same time, the sculptor Waldemar Grzimek (1918–1984), who worked both in the East and in the West, made a clear, yet non-specific reference to the institute with his bronze sculpture "Äsendes Rind" ("Grazing cow"), as well as two animal steles. Half a century later, Barbara Trautmann (born in 1966) made that reference more concrete, producing an expansive ground installation inspired by a virus model for the exterior grounds (→ p. 214).

As was typical for the architecturally related art of the time in the GDR, the cycle by

Waldemar Grzimek,
"Äsendes Rind", 1960,
Institute for Animal Health,
Greifswald, Island of Riems

Norbert Kricke,
"Raumplastik", 1966,
Physikalisch-Technische
Bundesanstalt,
Braunschweig

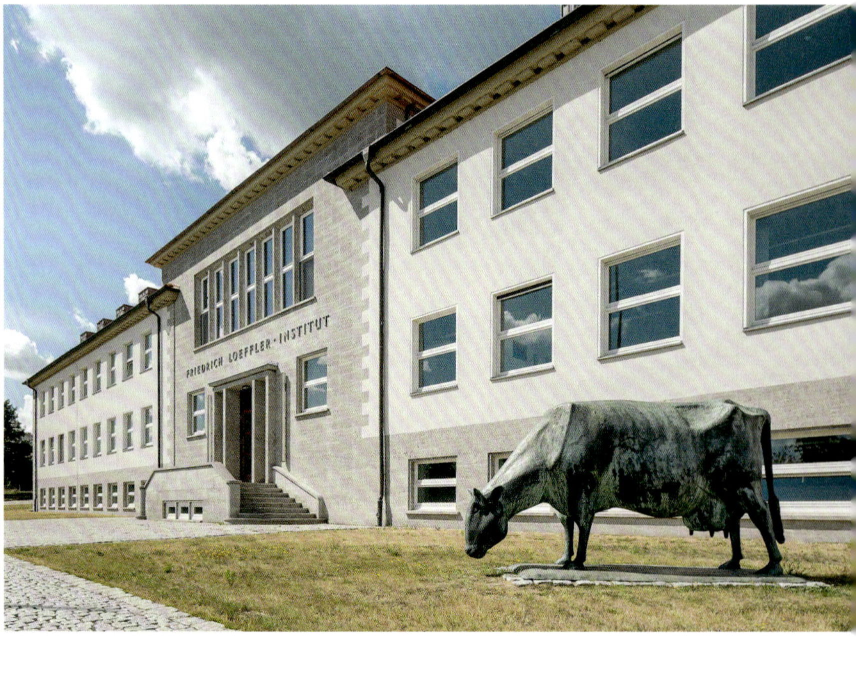

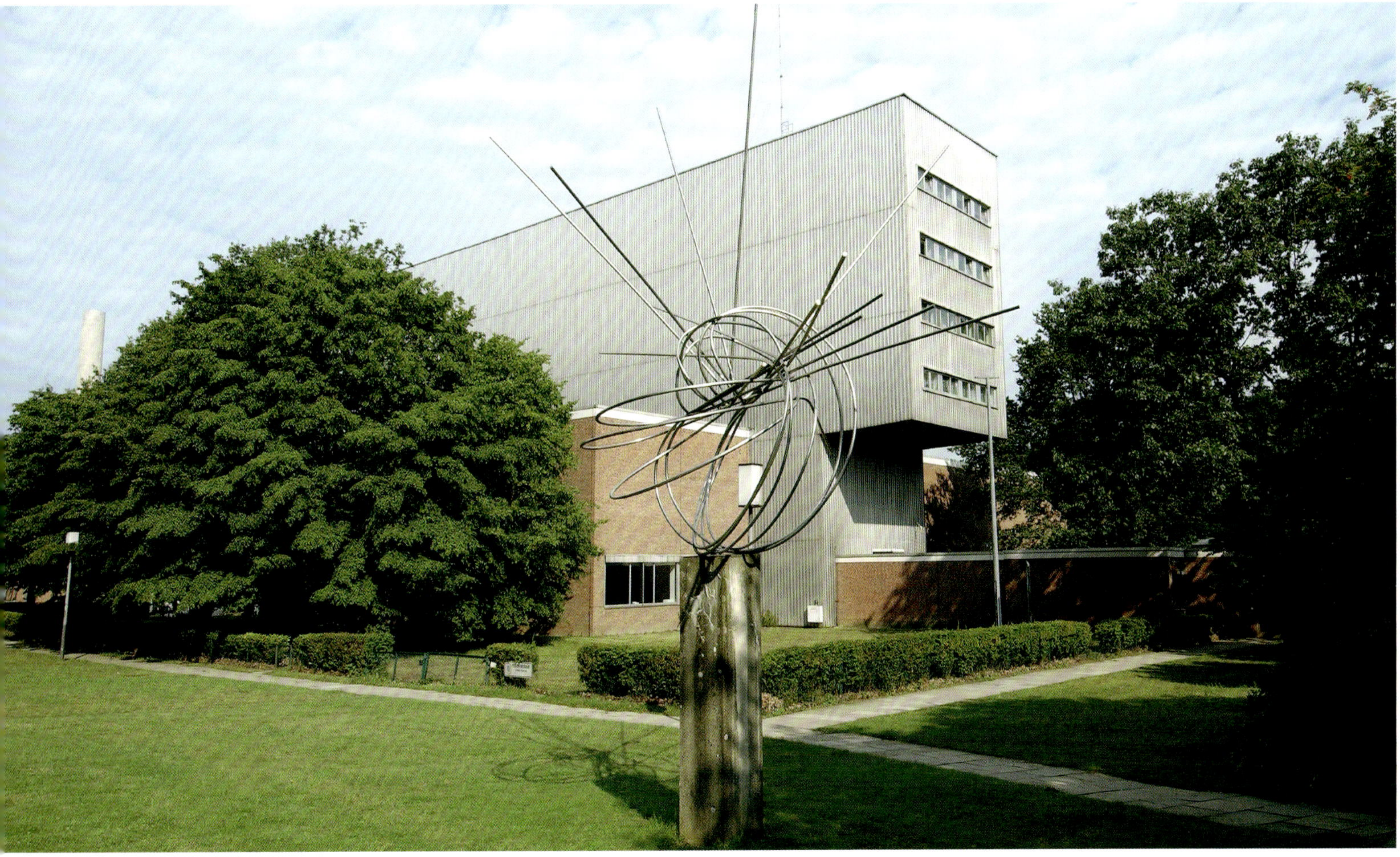

Hans Neubert focuses on the didactic aspects present in the Socialist Realism, while the cardinal artistic virtues of innovation and originality are secondary. One of the major new research facilities in West Germany was developed from the 1950s onwards: the Physikalisch-Technische Bundesanstalt (PTB) in Braunschweig. The principle of treating all building activities equally led to a situation where this decentralised research centre, with a very modest number of employees, nevertheless allowed them to enjoy their everyday working environment with pieces by famous artists such as Otto Herbert Hajek (1927–2005), Norbert Kricke (1922–1984), Ansgar Nierhoff (1941–2010) and Andrea Ostermeyer (born in 1961). Over 20 artistic positions – from an enamel mural relief to a conceptual large-scale steel sculpture on the exterior grounds – today cover a period from the 1950s to the 2000s, reflecting six decades of German art history on the highest level. Compared to the art's lack of publicity, the costs are certainly not justified by the argument that art in architecture is "art for all". Although it cannot always be "art for all", art in architecture is at least "art for many" and not simply art for experts and art collectors. Thus the efforts for the PTB are "worthwhile" from the perspective of a culturally-minded state and building culture, as well as supporting the arts and artists.

Many research facilities form a campus, often with organically developed artistic neighbourly relationships. For instance at its new locations at Nordufer and Seestrasse, the Robert Koch Institute in Berlin presents superb pieces by Ansgar Nierhoff, Herbert W. Kapitzki (1925–2005), Heinrich Brummack (1936–2018), Ursula Sax (born in 1935) (→ p. 302), Engelbert Kremser (born in 1938) and Rolf Szymanski (1928–2013). In 2014, new construction and renovation measures were carried out on two buildings, for which a mural design by the installation artist Nevin Aladağ (born in 1972) was commissioned. The Berlin-based artist Egill Sæbjörnsson (born in 1973) produced the institute's calling card for the location beside the main entrance, an almost seven-metre high concrete wall with a stone semi-sphere. As darkness descends, it is animated by projections, presenting constantly transforming image structures that recall bacteria, viruses, single-celled organisms and planets, all in the Berlin cityscape along the busy Seestrasse.

More recent art in architecture works – such as the installations at the ILT and IPT Fraunhofer Institutes in Aachen (→ p. 216) – demonstrate a certain affinity to technology. However, it is almost impossible to derive a specific reference to research institutes. As in other fields: no research facility, no research location and no architecture truly preempts the interpretation of its art in architecture. For instance in 2016, the renowned "all-round artist" Timm Ulrichs (born in 1940) produced a nine-part sculpture entitled "Wachsender Stein" ("Growing stone") for the interior and exterior spaces of the building for the high performance research computer at KIT – the Karlsruhe Institute for Technology. The progressive sequence of "stones" is based on one real stone and eight bronze sculptures that imitate the stone, while having different forms and sizes. The visually indistinguishable appearance of stone and bronze is the result of computer technology, yet evokes an archaic impression. In 2018, Leni Hoffmann (born in 1962) and Manuel Franke (born in 1964) created an environment for a different KIT building featuring a coloured concrete sculpture and a trapezoid profile, connected to a lawn section with some specially planted trees. It positions itself in an especially impressive way

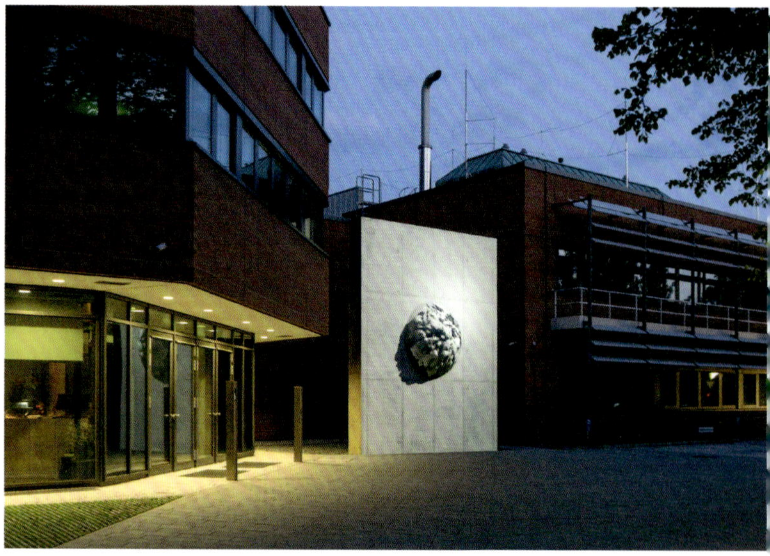

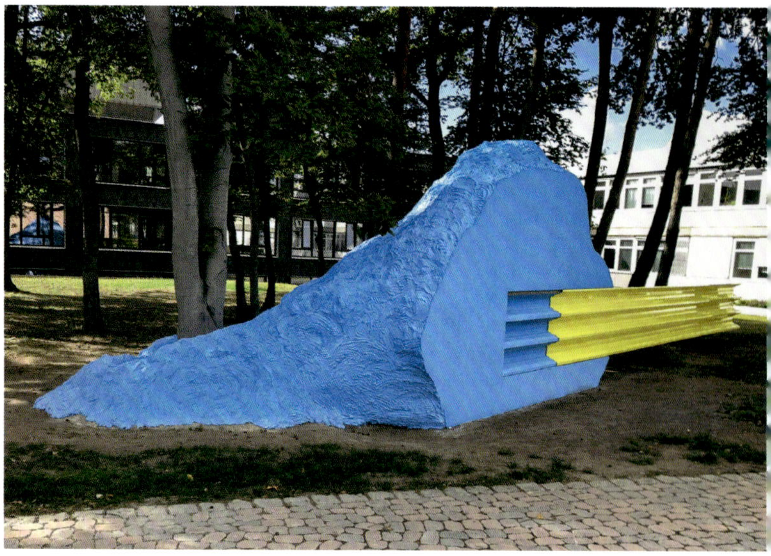

Egill Sæbjörnsson, "Steinkugel", 2014, Robert Koch Institute, Berlin

Leni Hoffmann, Manuel Franke, "warp", 2018, KIT – Karlsruhe Institute for Technology, Karlsruhe

Sebastian Stumpf, "Sleep #3", Kulturstiftung des Bundes, Halle (Saale)

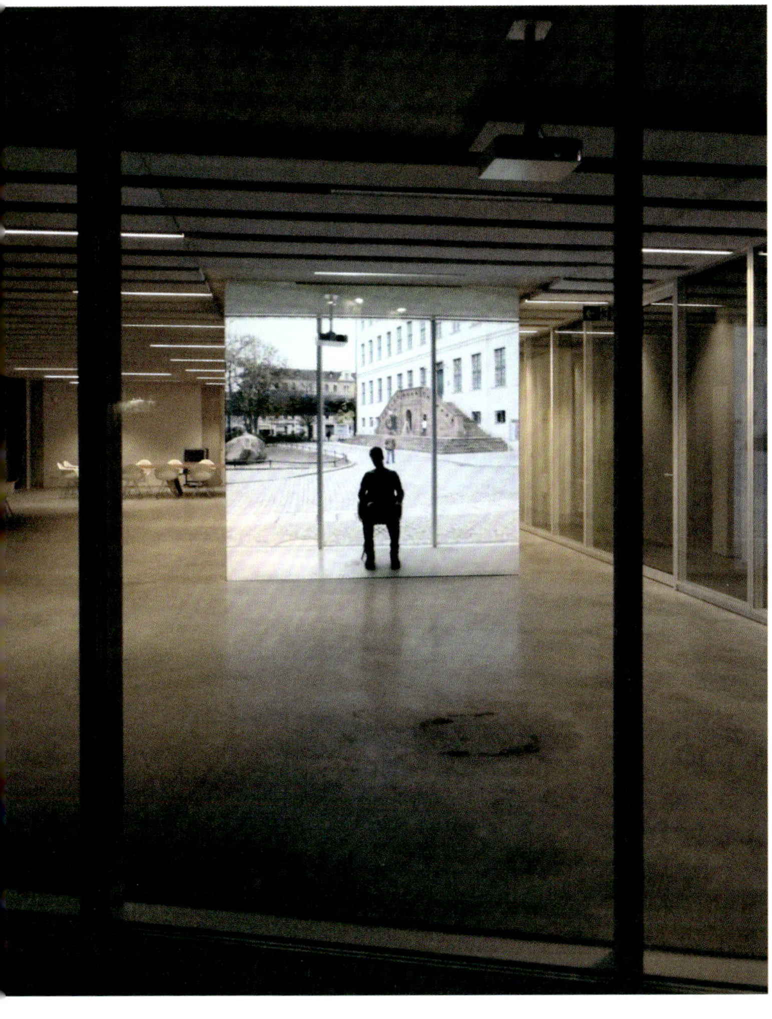

by doing without any technology despite the highly technological KIT environment.

CULTURAL FACILITIES

Cultural facilities form part of the core competences of the federal states, which is why the Federal Government takes a back seat. Nevertheless, it is also active on a national level in the field of constructing cultural buildings, and therefore commissioning art in architecture. In a divided Germany, the Federal Government supported Berlin as a city of education, science and art, above all the Stiftung Preußischer Kulturbesitz as the legal cultural inheritor of Prussia, as well as its new buildings, the Neue Nationalgalerie, the Gemäldegalerie and the State Library at the Kulturforum. In 1992, the Bundeskunsthalle was opened in Bonn, while in 2012, the new building of the Kulturstiftung des Bundes in Halle an der Saale included the video projection "Sleep #3" by Sebastian Stumpf (born in 1980).

As with all other art in architecture measures, no specific iconography or stylistic stance can be discerned. Instead, the responsible decision-makers work to the best of their knowledge and consciences in defining the underlying conditions of the planned art in architecture projects. They consider the magical relationship between art, architecture and building use, define the location(s) for the artworks and announce the competitions.

From a historical perspective, however, architects repeatedly played an important, sometimes even dominant, role in the production of art in architecture. For example, Hans Scharoun designed the Berlin Philharmonic (1960–1963), which is furbished with considerable art in architecture. He also provided the design for the State Library on Potsdamer

Strasse, developing ideas on the appearance of the intended art in architecture. Finally in the late 1970s, renowned artists – including Erich Fritz Reuter (1911–1997), Erich Hauser (1930–2004) (→ p. 204), Ansgar Nierhoff, Günther Uecker (born in 1930) and Bernhard Heiliger (1915–1995) – contributed murals, installations, window decorations and even floor designs, as well as exterior sculptures to create an impressive ensemble that brought together art and architecture in an integral concept.

Occasionally, the social responsibility of art in architecture involved complementing an institution's own artistic concepts, as is the case with the Neue Nationalgalerie, which was designed by Ludwig Mies van der Rohe between 1965 and 1968 and is situated opposite the State Library. Immediately after the completion of construction work, the client installed four large, abstract sculptures on the surrounding terrace, thereby sending a political signal of the West's free artistic language. The pieces by Alexander Calder (1898–1976), Henry Moore (1898–1986) and George Rickey (1907–2002) are gifts and studio purchases. The fourth work, a sculpture completed by Joannis Avramidis (1922–2016) in 1970 and entitled "Polis", was a commission funded by the art in architecture budget, although it was produced before its final location had been determined.

With the exception of the Neues Gewandhaus in Leipzig (→ p. 208), the GDR state always constructed cultural buildings as multifunctional halls. In doing so, the builder always focused the architecturally related art – at least during the more authoritarian period of Walter Ulbricht – on a perspective on global history and ideological proclamations. For instance since 1969, the western façade of the Kulturpalast Dresden has been covered by

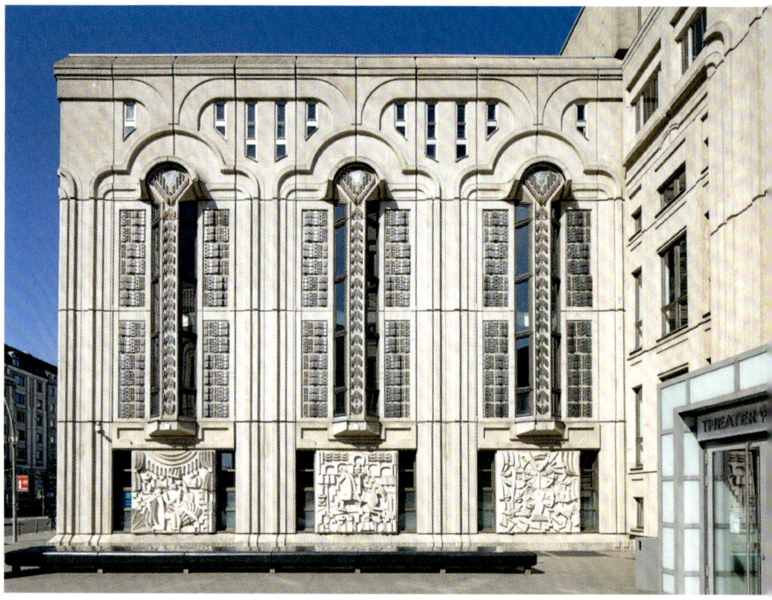

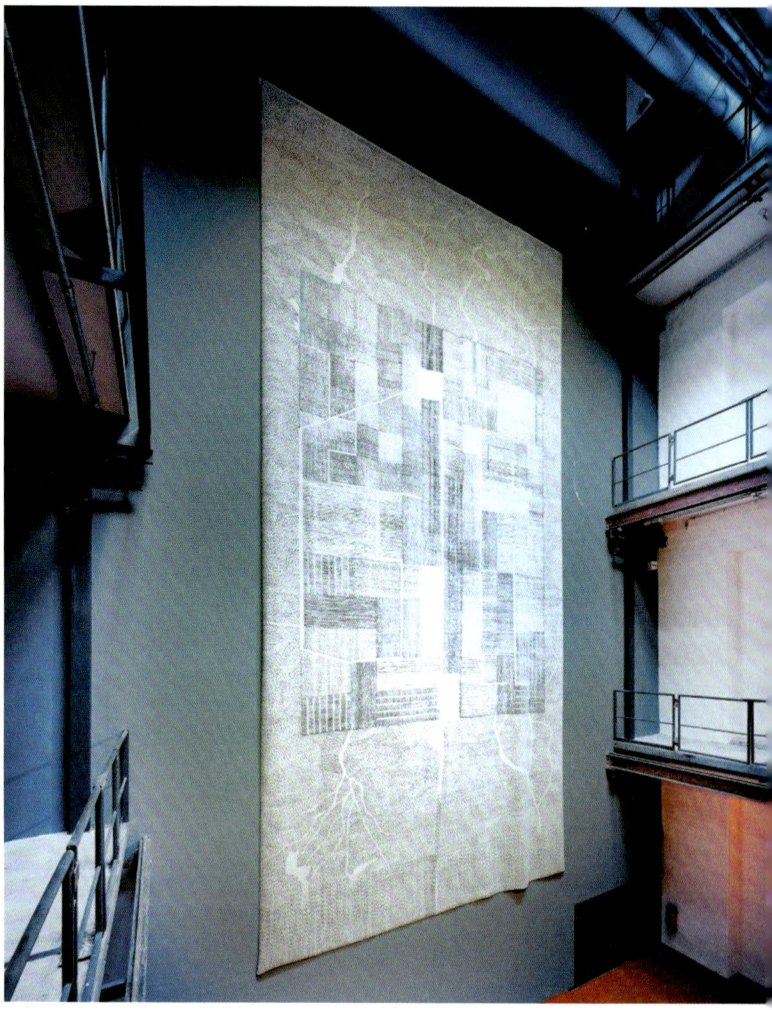

Emilia N. Bayer, "Theater Schumann, Zirkus Renz, Varieté", 1982–1984, Friedrichstadt-Palast, Berlin

Christine Meisner, "Rivers and Rights", 2017, Barenboim-Said Academy, Berlin

Sunkoo Kang, "Statue of Limitations", 2017–2020, Humboldt Forum, Berlin

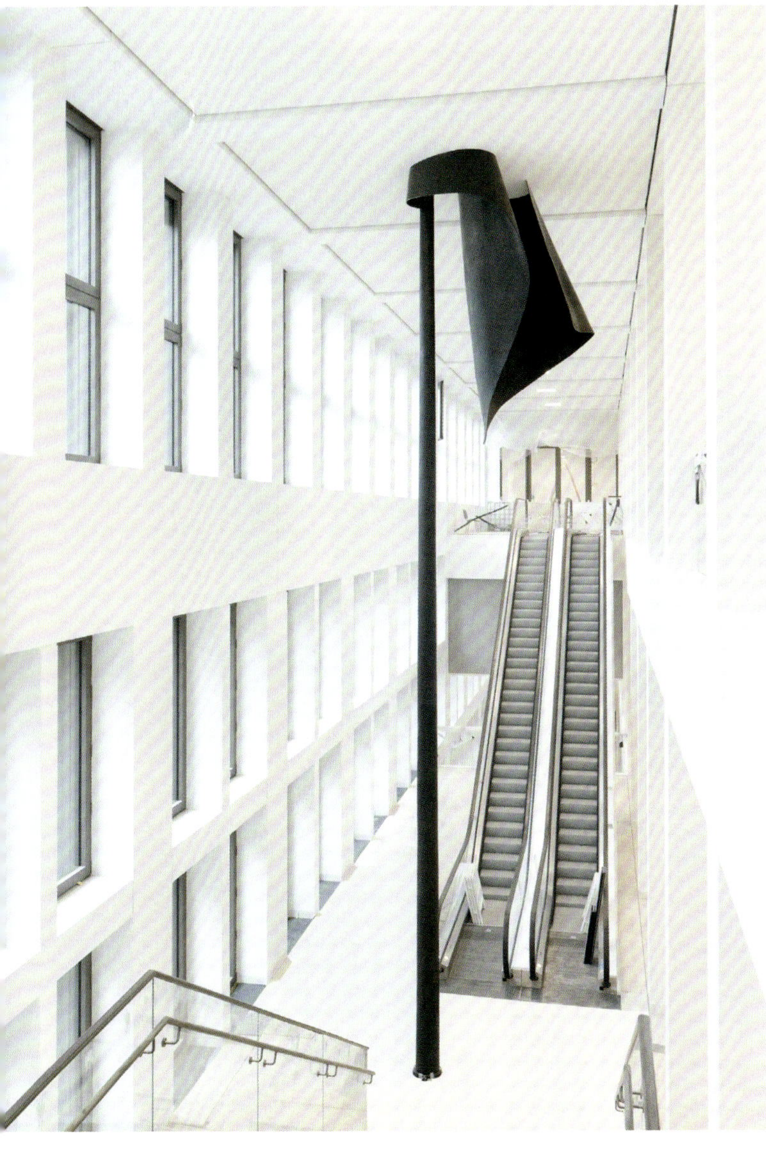

a 30-metre long mural "Der Weg der Roten Fahne" ("The way of the red flag") by Gerhard Bondzin (1930–2014). It presents a historical review, whereby its title and also its working title ("1849–1969: 120-year struggle for progress and Socialism by the city's revolutionary forces") already indicate that the artwork could equally have been applied to an administrative building (→ p. 304). By contrast, the Gewandhaus in Leipzig (→ p. 208) and the Friedrichstadt-Palast in Berlin, which was newly constructed between 1981 and 1984, reflect a changed cultural-political awareness. The 3 x 3 metre concrete reliefs on the Friedrichstadt-Palast by the sculptor Emilia N. Bayer (born in 1934) are dedicated to the *genius loci* without addressing the general public; on the northern and southern sides of the building, they reveal a quality of reserved abstraction in presenting the history of the Friedrichstadt-Palast as a circus, a playhouse and a variety theatre.

Such restraint also characterises today's art for the Barenboim-Said Academy music school, which was built in 2015 in a former depot of the Berlin State Opera at Unter den Linden. A six-metre high hand-woven tapestry of wool and silk by Christine Meisner (born in 1970) highlights the foyer of the Pierre Boulez Hall designed by Frank O. Gehry. The portrayed rivers of the Nile, Jordan, Euphrates and Tigris refer in fine lines, as well as great reserve and respect, to the school's alignment of bringing different nations together.

Recent art in architecture – for instance for the Humboldt Forum in the Berlin Palace – positions itself in many ways as a reflection on history and current political events in the mode of an appeal. The Berlin artist Sunkoo Kang (born in 1977) designed two complementary halves of one black flag at half mast, thereby recalling colonial history. The artwork has a high public profile since one half of the

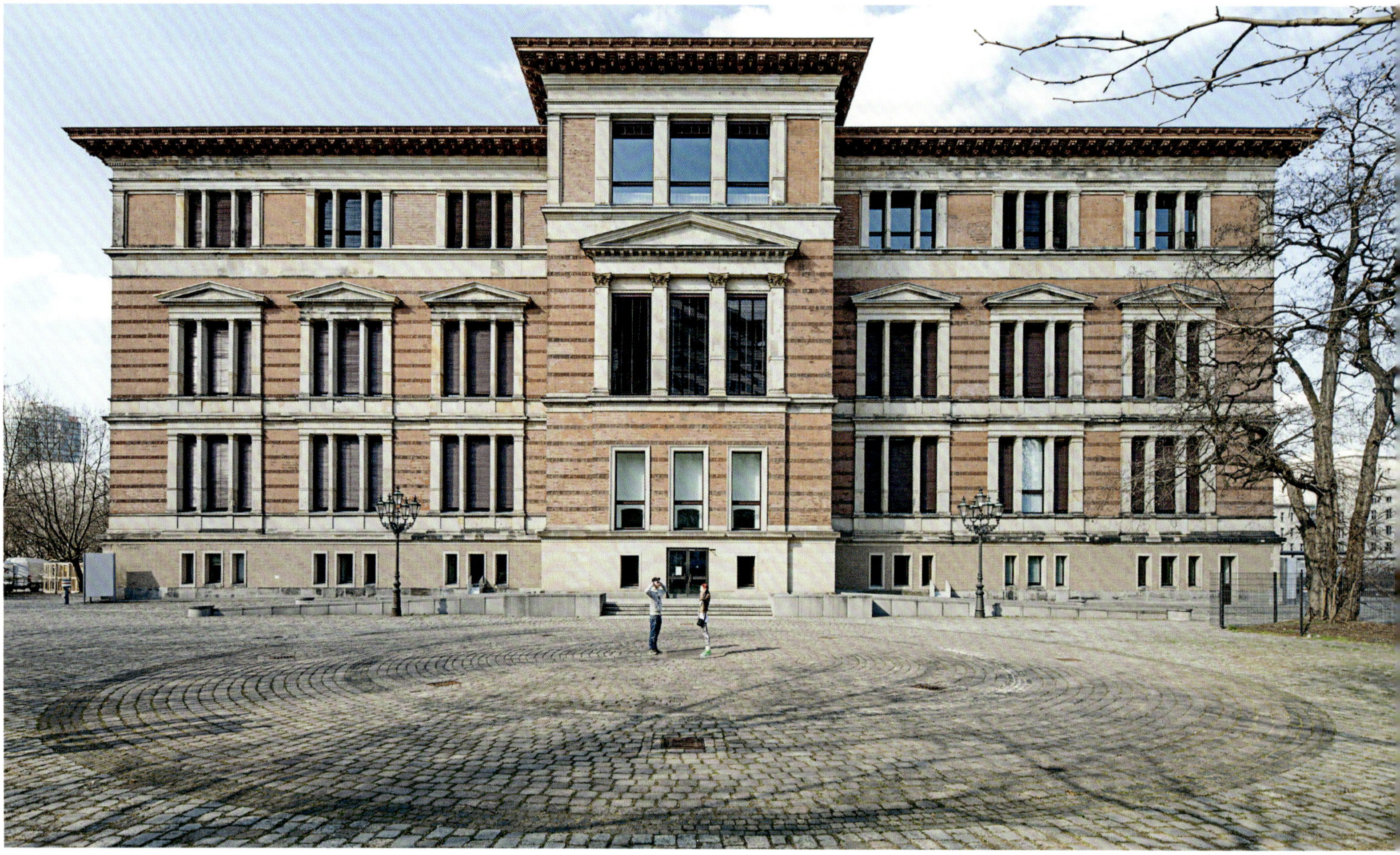

flag is installed in the central staircase of the Humboldt Forum and the other is placed on Nachtigalplatz, in what is known as the "African Quarter" of Berlin's Wedding district.

One piece of art in architecture should not be overlooked that was produced as part of the 2009 Economic Recovery Package II on building renovation, namely a "Pact for employment and stability in Germany to secure jobs, strengthen growth and modernise the country". On the paved square to the rear of the Martin Gropius Building in Berlin, Ina Geißler (born in 1970) and Fabian Lippert (born in 1972) installed the sound installation "Unterton" ("Undertone"). Depending on the movements and numbers of passers by, unsettling knocking sounds emanate from eight drain shafts. These inspire strong associations due to the direct vicinity to the former Gestapo headquarters, the Berlin Wall and the surveillance centre of the GDR State Security.

Ina Geißler, Fabian Lippert, "Unterton", 2011, Martin Gropius Building, Berlin

SPORT

The principle of treating all buildings equally and the cultural interest in encouraging art also outside museums, collections and galleries, as well as making the artworks accessible to everyone, also leads to encounters between state art and the world of sports. The Federal Government funds 18 decentralised Olympic sports centres, federal centres of excellence and over 200 federal sports centres. Thus, as a builder, it is also represented with art in architecture at locations and sports facilities that – like the Federal Wrestling Centre in Luckenwalde, Brandenburg – do not stand in the public limelight. Nevertheless, it is a location where art and building culture exist, as well as exemplifying efforts to give all facilities a dignified appearance as far as financial means permit, thereby using art to create identification symbols and an appropriate atmosphere.

Sports venues are also suitable as a means of presenting the state. However, this concept is hardly reflected in the supraporte mosaics that Wolfgang Frankenstein (1918–2010) designed in 1959 for the Dynamo sports hall at the Sportforum Berlin, in the East Berlin district of Alt-Hohenschönhausen. Instead, the elegant design shows almost pictographic restraint in focusing entirely on the characteristics of different sporting disciplines (→ p. 82).

By contrast, there was considerable desire to present the state and make a statement at the 1972 Olympic Games in Munich. For the still young FRG, the Games provided the ideal opportunity to portray the country as a cosmopolitan, peaceful member of the international community. The Olympic construction company commissioned renowned artists for the buildings co-funded by the Federal Government, the State of Bavaria and the City of Munich, both in and outside Munich. The aim was to use the architecture and its art to demonstrate how tolerant Germany had become. Furthermore, it was important to emphasise that, having been cut off from the international modern art scene by National Socialism, the country was in touch again and had regained its place among the elite of the international art world. The artists involved included Hermann Goepfert (1926–1982), Johannes Peter Hölzinger (born in 1936), Adolf Luther (1912–1990) and Otto Piene (1928–2014). No expense was spared, allowing Heinz Mack (born in 1931) to produce an extensive installation that used pumps to release clouds of steam over the Olympic lake. For the Olympic village, the architect and artist Hans Hollein (1934–2014) designed a fountain and so-called media lines as an "environmental design". The lines covered a total length of 1.7 kilometres in different heights, forming a guidance and lighting system, while also influencing the temperature throughout the Olympic village.

Such opportunities of self-presentation using art in architecture have been appealing to all political systems throughout history and in all locations. Only 36 years earlier, Nazi ideology had used art in architecture at the Olympic Games in Berlin to express the regime's physical ideals and present its racist doctrine. In 1972, the propaganda goal was to eradicate all of those impressions of 1936. However, abstract art in the 1970s was largely free of narrative, symbolic and even allusive aspects. It is clear that, in times of the Cold War, such art was also a political and aesthetic swipe at the Socialist Realism of the GDR and the Eastern Bloc. Thus art celebrated itself. And within it, the state staged itself before the eyes of the world as a supporter of the arts. West Germany was portrayed as an enabler of such art in the spirit of artistic and politically democratic freedom. The same stance is also recognisable in cultural buildings such as the Neue Nationalgalerie.

SUPRANATIONAL FACILITIES AND ALLIES

Art in architecture has many functions. One is the client's self-presentation. This is especially true for German buildings in foreign countries (cf. chapter entitled "Dialogue with the world", → p. 248 – 265), for embassies, schools, Goethe Institutes and other organisations where bilateral and international exchange occurs. Often, art in architecture in such contexts is aimed at encouraging international understanding and signalling friendship.

While architecture's means of expression are limited, it is easier for art to communicate. One method of doing so is demonstrated in the murals of the GDR's administrative buildings and cultural venues, with their repertoire of flags and symbols expressing peaceful intentions and a bond with the Soviet Union, as well as the peoples of the world. Another method is a free, non-figurative visual language that is independent of regional and national classification and connotation. As early as 1964, the artist Fritz Kühn (1910–1967), who was able to work in both parts of Germany, produced an accomplished example of such art. The piece designed for the (now demolished) Polish Embassy in the GDR's East Berlin, entitled the "Lindenblatt-Portal" ("Linden leaf portal"), presented a relief consisting of 224 serially arranged, stylised leaf motifs. The design referred to its location at Unter den Linden, expressing an elegant diplomatic understatement towards the Polish ally, instead of the usual visual rhetoric.

Hans Hollein, "Media-Linien", 1972, Olympic Village, Munich

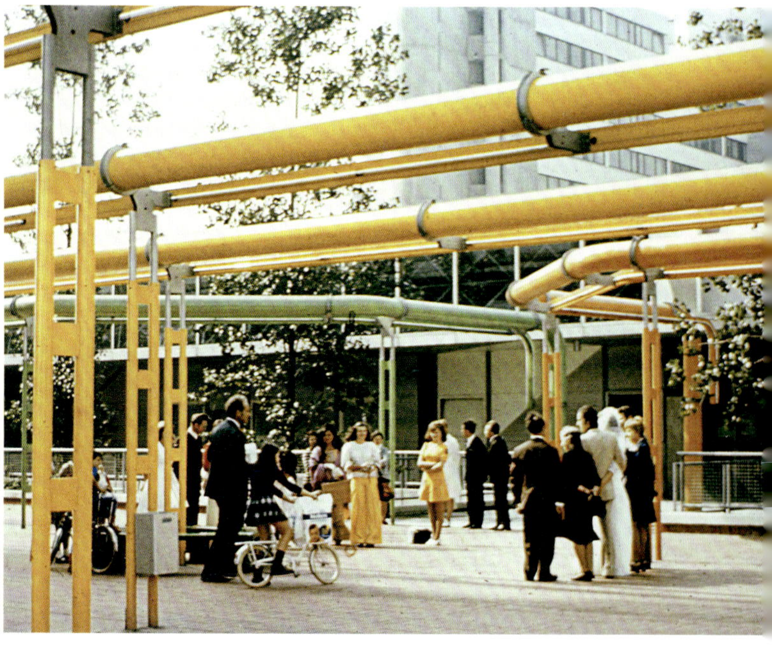

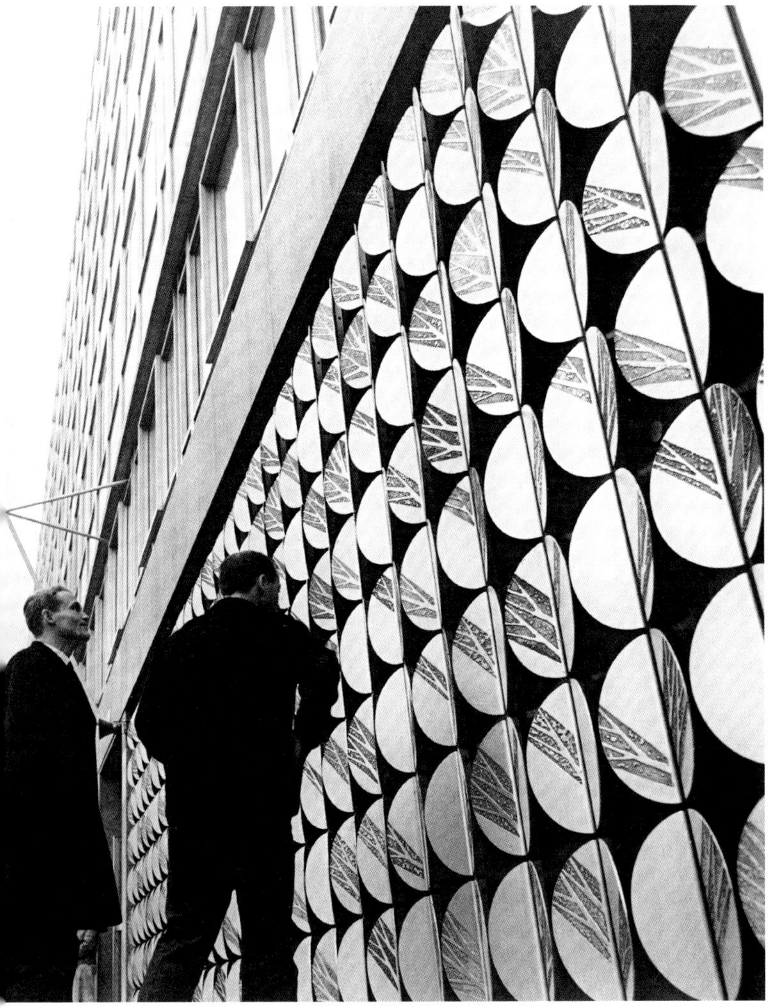

Fritz Kühn, "Lindenblätter", 1963/1964, Polish Embassy in the GDR, Berlin

In 1973, the FRG and the GDR became member states of the United Nations (UN). To mark the occasion, the GDR presented the UN the bronze sculpture "Aufsteigender" ("Rising man"), which was installed in the park of the UN headquarters in New York. Already produced in 1966/1967, the almost three metre high figure by the Communist sculptor Fritz Cremer (1906–1993) portrays a man in an easily legible, figurative style, who is releasing himself from the invisible, yet symbolically clear burdens and shackles of history.

By contrast, in the same year, the FRG commissioned the architect and designer Paolo Nestler (1920–2010) and the visual artist Günter Fruhtrunk (1923–1982) to design the "Quiet Room" for the UN headquarters. Irregularly shaped and diagonally applied mahogany, ebony and maple panels on the walls and ceiling, combined with rose-coloured tapestry areas, a light and dark grey carpet and the contrapuntal, perpendicular couches and tables, all merge "to form a visual continuum" (Nestler/Fruhtrunk). With this *Gesamtkunstwerk*, which is still impressive today, the commissioning Federal Republic was intent on preventing any risk that the form or content of its art might cause offence on the international stage.

Supranational facilities also exist in Germany. In accordance with its importance, the European Patent Office, which is based in Munich, owns more than a dozen pieces of high-quality art in architecture, which were produced by European artists to reflect the institution's international perspective. Similarly, the International Tribunal for the Law of the Sea in Hamburg made targeted efforts to involve international artists.

In 1994, the Berlin/Bonn Act stipulated the preservation of Bonn as a political location and the development of the former capital into a place of international and supranational institutions. As a result, 17 of the 24 UN offices based in Germany moved to Bonn. They are accommodated in the former plenary area of Bonn's federal district on the UN Campus and have taken over the art in architecture of the newly used buildings of the Langer Eugen tower, the Plenarsaal, the Bundeshaus and the Altes Wasserwerk. Three competitions were announced during measures to renovate the former parliamentarians' tower to accommodate the Secretariat of the United Nations Framework Convention on Climate Change. In its atrium, the artist Tadashi Kawamata (born in 1953) subsequently installed one of his famous "nests" as a ceiling installation made of larch wood boards. The Amsterdam artist Wafae Ahalouch el Keriasti (born in 1978) produced a symbolically laden, abstract work for the foyer wall consisting of murals, wooden elements and a light box, entitled "The Illuminator". Finally, Michael Sailstorfer (born in 1979) won the competition for the staircase-façade location. Since 2011, the thermometer installed there has been visible from afar. Like many art in architecture works produced since the late 1990s, especially as a result of the government's move from Bonn to Berlin, this piece reflects a shift towards more content-based aspects, acting as a cautionary and warning voice, demonstrating climate change in a highly prominent location, while referring to binding supranational responsibility.

TRANSPORT INFRASTRUCTURE

Art in architecture exists in administrative buildings of transport facilities, but also in transport buildings themselves. The transport infrastructure was a main task of

Tadashi Kawamata, "Nest", 2012, UN Campus, Bonn

Wafae Ahalouch el Keriasti, "The Illuminator", 2012, former parliamentarians's tower, UN Campus, Bonn

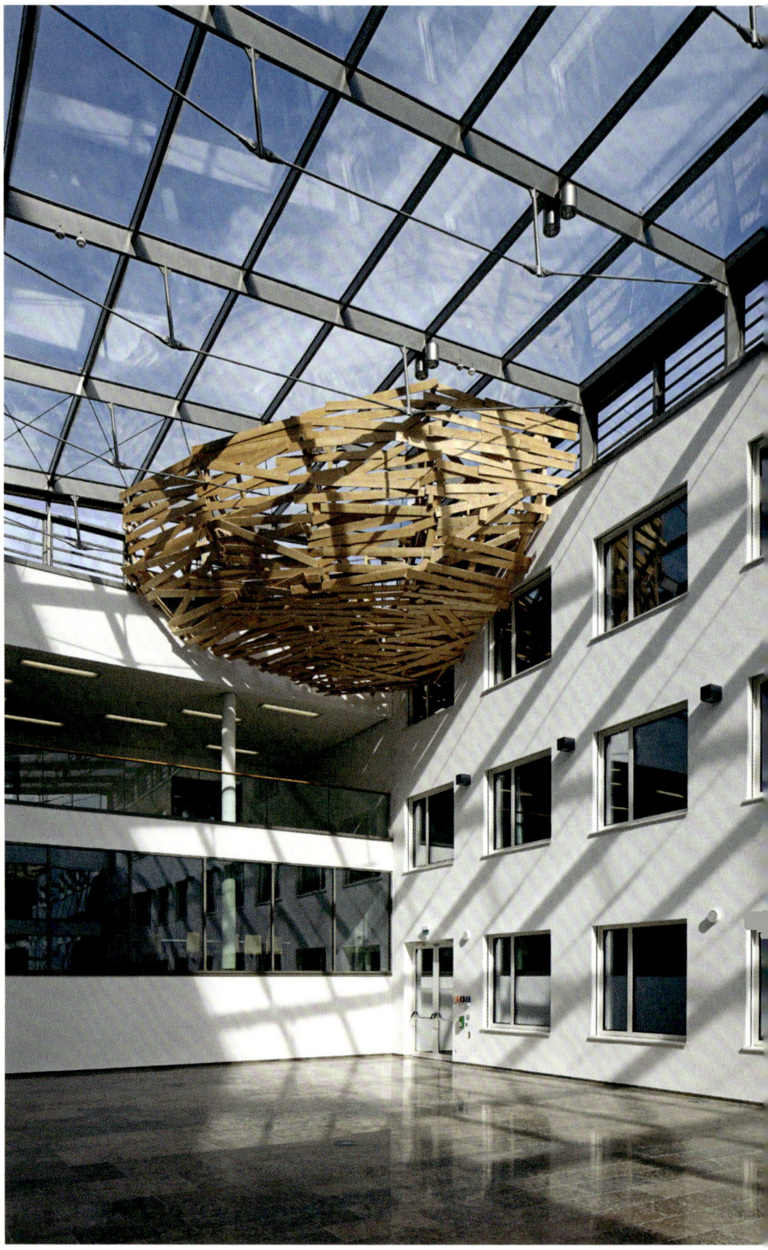

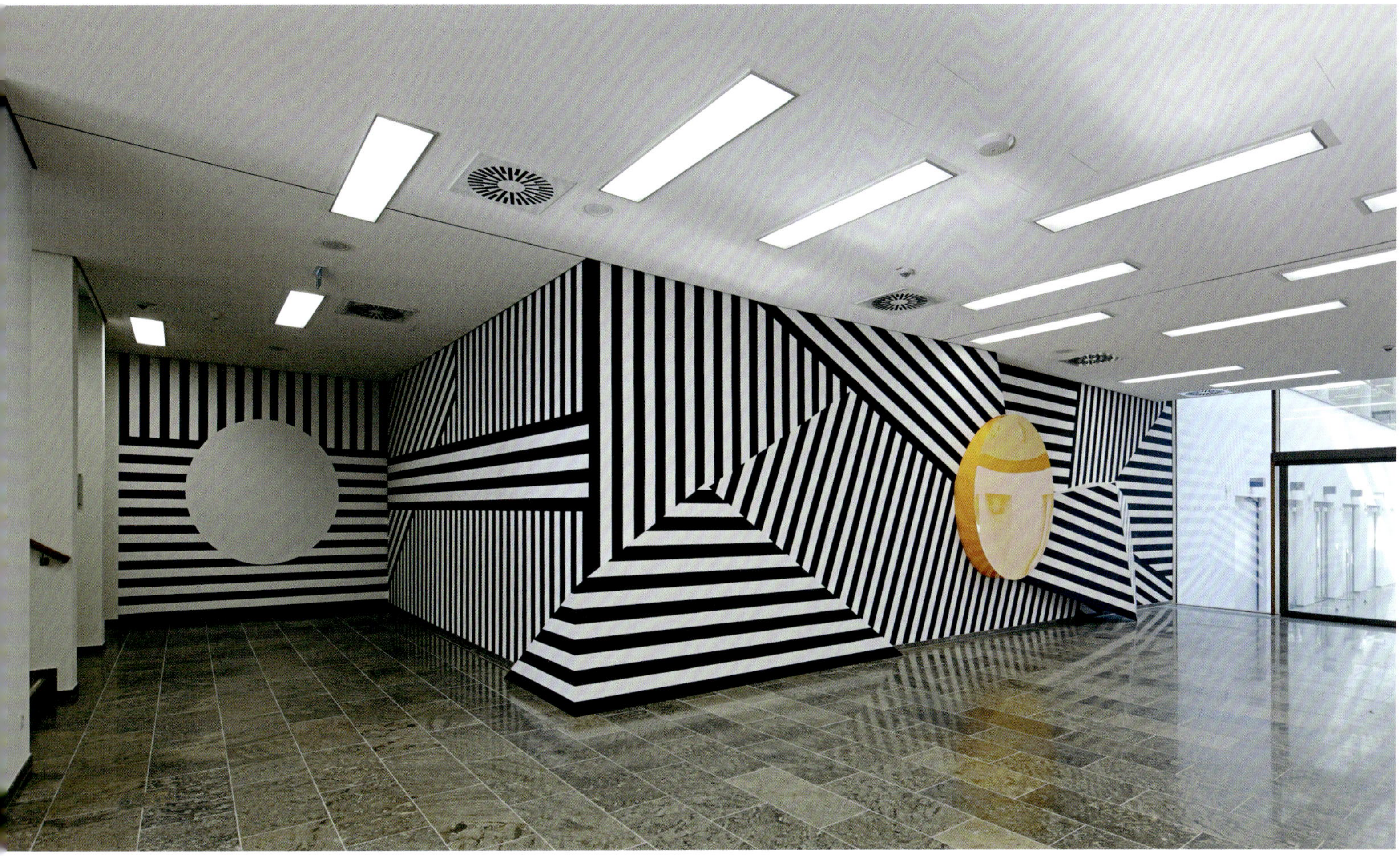

redevelopment work following World War II. New railway stations were built in both East and West Germany. For their spacious entrance halls, large-scale murals referred to the local geography and sightseeing attractions, as well as locally typical industries, professions and costumes. Such traditional themes and presentations were the rule – one example is the mural mosaic produced by the artist Wilhelm Schmied (1910–1984) for Sangerhausen Station in the GDR. However, one early, artistically powerful exception is the abstract plate relief behind the glass façade of Munich Station produced in 1951 by Rupprecht Geiger (1908–2009) (→ p. 72).

In the field of underground railways, municipal art programmes in Munich and Cologne led to pioneering projects. The Federal Government co-funded the Düsseldorf "Wehrhahnlinie", which opened in 2016, including six underground stations with elaborate artworks. As was the case for the major Berlin Brandenburg Airport project, the Federal Government ultimately plays the role of a patron of the arts. Often, art in architecture in highly condensed transport buildings is hindered not by a lack of sensitivity towards building culture or a disinterest in art, but by the greater allure of using the free spaces for advertising to achieve profits.

Federal major roads form one of the densest transport networks in Europe. The motorways inevitably require an appropriate number of motorway services, which are also decorated with art in architecture on their exterior grounds or in the restaurants. This has led to remarkable artworks. For instance in 1982, to mark the construction of the inner-German border-crossing facility near Gudow along the transit motorway between Hamburg and Berlin, not only was an abstract bronze sculpture by Fritz Koenig installed along the central reservation of the motorway: the Gudow Nord and Gudow Süd motorway services also received art in architecture pieces. For Gudow Süd, the Kiel painter Peter Nagel (born in 1941) created an almost eleven-metre wide oil painting. Produced in the style of "New Realism", which Nagel had co-founded, the painting "Auf der Brücke" ("On the bridge") (which now hangs in the Ministry of Transport in Kiel) reflects the inner-German border situation. The obvious symbolism of coming together is apparent in the bridge and other motifs. The composition was precisely tailored to the location, as the painted bridge railings started at the level of the benches in the guest room, creating the illusion of a boundary to the interior and transforming viewers of the work into viewed subjects themselves.

The Düsseldorf painter and sculptor Peter Brüning (1929–1970) produced a monument to road traffic itself for the *documenta 4*, presenting a model of rolled-up road lanes. In 1969, on the initiative of the Minister of Transport at the time, Georg Leber, and funded by the federally owned company "Gesellschaft für Nebenbetriebe" – the model was installed along the A 1 motorway near Wuppertal in the form of two multicoloured iron rings on a stone base with a height of over eight metres.

Border crossings and customs offices are also tried and trusted locations for art in architecture due to their transit function. The sculptures, which are mostly installed in the handling areas, can be abstract. However since 1957, the figurative Berlin Bear by Renée Sintenis (1888–1965) on the central reservation of the former border crossing at Dreilinden has attracted great attention. Fifty years later, the bizarrely painted bronze figure of a golem by Thaddäus Hüppi (born in 1963) on the joint German-Swiss customs office in Rheinfelden-Warmbach is a similar eye-catcher.

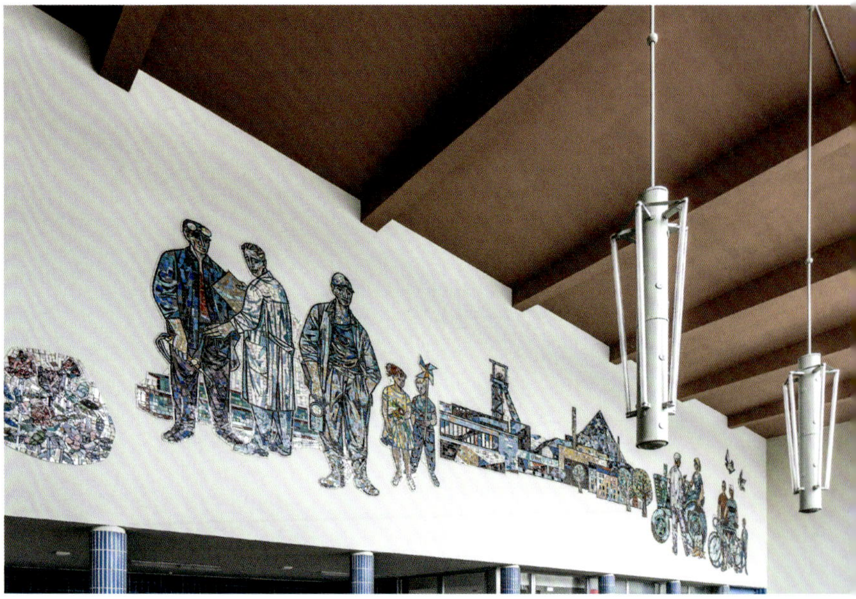

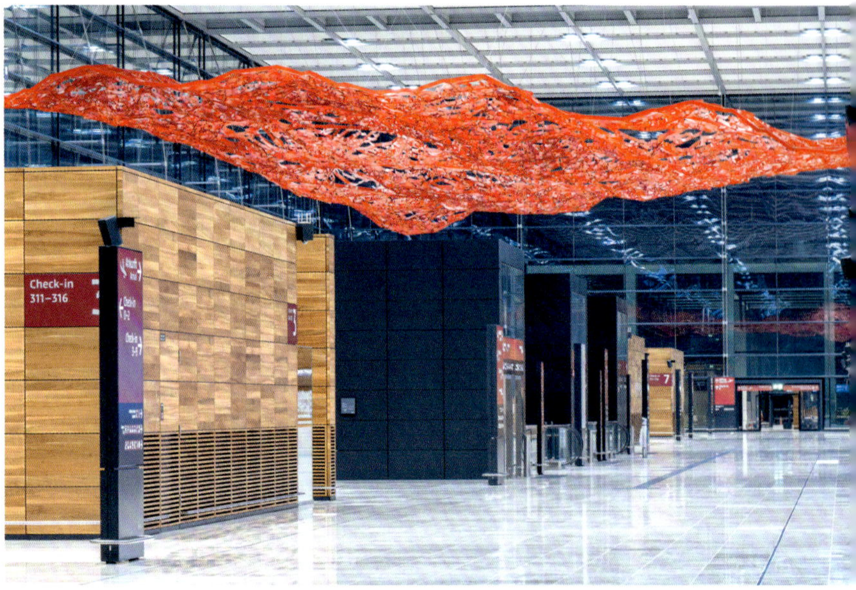

Wilhelm Schmied, "Landwirtschaft und Industrie im Kreis Sangerhausen", 1963, Sangerhausen Station

Pae White, "The Magic Carpet", 2012, Berlin Brandenburg Airport

The Main-Danube Canal, which was constructed between 1960 and 1992, should also be mentioned. It inspired a unique piece of art in architecture as land art, namely a sculptural major project by Hansjörg Voth (born in 1940) placed in the open landscape (→ p. 210).

HOUSING

Despite their relatively low profile, some municipalities and social housing companies continue to commission art relating to their building projects to this day. The Federal Republic also integrated art in architecture into its federal housing estates in Bonn in the late 1950s. The works have an idyllic tone: as the central journal of the building administration wrote in 1953, "Fountains and sculptures animate the estate's garden areas, creating beautiful, peaceful spaces in the city centre and shaping the experience of home." A more recent example is provided by the art in architecture for the housing development known as the "Serpentine", which was built on the Moabiter Werder in Berlin for civil servants and federal employees. The development was designed between 1997 and 1999 by the architects Georg Bumiller, Jörg Pampe and the Berlin architectural office Müller, Rhode, Wandert, as an extension of the "Band des Bundes".

The GDR also applied its programme for architecturally related art to the housing sector, especially with respect to the prefabricated architecture of the 1970s and 1980s. The need to somehow hide their architectural blandness led to a change of attitude towards geometrical, abstract surface designs, which had long been criticised as "Formalist", but went on to become a major factor.

PLURALITY AND DIVERSITY

In retrospect, how is the diversity of art in architecture achieved? Or in other words: what does art in architecture owe to the numerous federal institutions and construction projects? The double-edged answer is: not much and yet everything! The construction projects did not cause the diversity of the artworks' appearance. However, they produced such a large number of pieces. And they led to the extremely productive necessity of having to start afresh with each new project. The state regulation always assigns responsibility for individual projects to the construction project itself and the people involved. Thus, looking from building to building, it is clear that there are as many possibilities, forms of expression, artistic stances and approaches to appropriate art as there are buildings, architects, artists, designers, consultants, juries, contractors, users and occasions. Thus, the diversity of art in architecture is ultimately also the result of the multitude of state institutions and building projects.

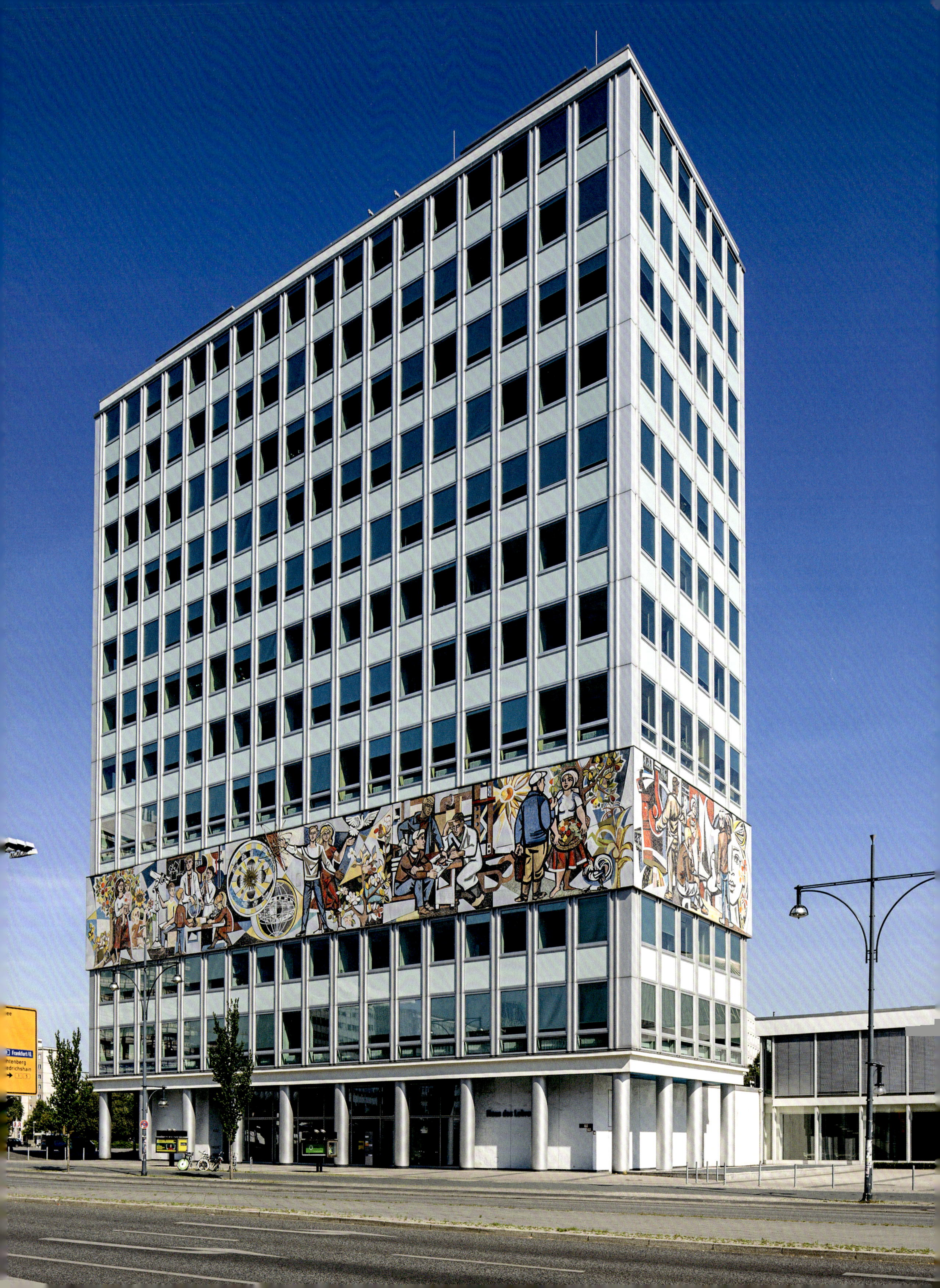

HAUS DES LEHRERS BERLIN

TODAY OFFICE USE

Address:
Alexanderstrasse 9
10178 Berlin

Architecture:
Hermann Henselmann, 1961–1964

Art in architecture:
Walter Womacka

The Haus des Lehrers ("House of Teachers") was the first high-rise building on Alexanderplatz, forming part of larger measures to redesign the square in the character of Socialist Modernity. In this long-term project, Walter Womacka (1925–2010) played an important role due to his political loyalty to the system, which often led to him being described as a "state artist". In 1970, he created the Brunnen der Völkerfreundschaft ("Fountain of international friendship"). A year later, he designed the copper relief on the Haus des Reisens ("House of Travel"), while also working with the support of an artist collective between 1962 and 1964 on the major mural "Unser Leben" ("Our life") on the Haus des Lehrers.

The twelve-storey high-rise building by Hermann Henselmann, the then Chief Architect at the Bauakademie's Institute for Special Buildings, was designed in an international style, its glass curtain façade providing no space for visual propaganda: such methods were used on a massive scale in public spaces in the GDR, inspired by the Muralismo of Mexican revolutionary painting in the 1920s. In his search for an alternative solution, the artist developed the idea of a surrounding frieze at the level of the third and fourth floors, where the library rooms were situated. Berliners nicknamed the artwork "the cummerbund".

Following a competition announced by the GDR Ministry of Culture, Womacka designed a seven-metre high mosaic for the area, covering a total length of 125 metres around the building. Conceived in simple colours and motif contours, the image on the western side facing the square is dedicated to everyday life in the GDR. The northern section presents the field of research and technology, while the eastern wall focuses on international friendship and the southern side portrays working life. The scenes framed as different genres combine to create a vision of a peaceful and advanced Socialist state. However, the commissioning body intervened in the artwork's development and rejected Womacka's early designs as "un-Marxist and metaphysical", resulting in today's visual programme and simplified design in accordance with the official art doctrine.

WALTER WOMACKA
"Unser Leben" ("Our life"), 1962–1964
Enamelled glass, ceramics, lead
Approx. 7 x 125 m

REICHSBAHNAUS-BESSERUNGSWERK COTTBUS

TODAY DB FAHRZEUGINSTAND-HALTUNG GMBH

Address:
Waisenstrasse 21B
03046 Cottbus

Architecture:
around 1968

Art in architecture:
Horst Ring

The painter and graphic designer Horst Ring (born in 1939), who has lived in Dessau since 1968, designed numerous architecturally related artworks for his home town and the local Lausitz region. Many of them were lost through the changing times. One mural has survived above the entrance of the double-winged administration building of the former railway works known as RAW Reichsbahnausbesserungswerk in the Cottbus district of Ströbitz. It is still used today by DB Fahrzeuginstandhaltung GmbH, a subsidiary of the national railway company.

Following a major fire in 1968, the railway works constructed in 1874 and known as RAW Reichsbahnausbesserungswerk Cottbus were largely rebuilt. This provided the opportunity to apply a mural to the administrative building to bring art closer to working people in accordance with official GDR cultural policy, above all presenting the social and political achievements and Marxist ideals of the Socialist state.

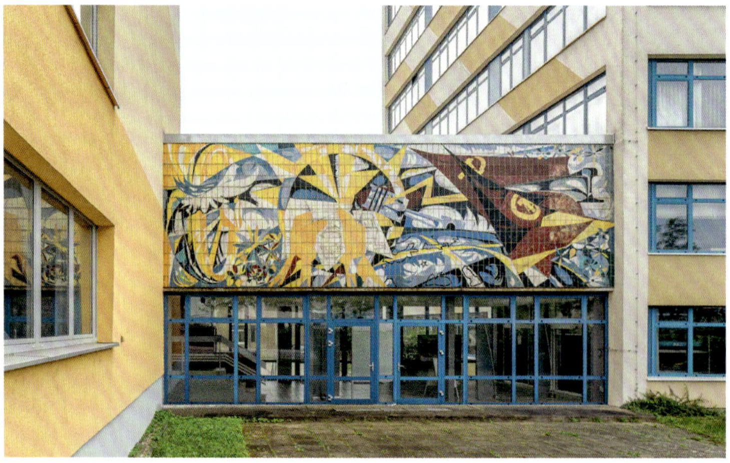

Using over a thousand painted tiles, Horst Ring created an expressive ceramic artwork with angular graphics in warm yellow and ochre tones combined with cool blue colours. The prismatic composition is defined by dynamic forms of circles, spikes, dome rods and rails. They combine with floral interjections, as well as the symbolic motifs of the dove to the left and the sun in the centre, creating a harmonious overall image. The central motif of a diesel locomotive construction sketch has a calming and sobering influence on the otherwise bright and lively composition, while referring to the professional activity at the railway works. The state flags of the GDR and the Soviet Union to the right of the picture address the theme of international friendship and the political bonds between the two states. While the title "Industrie und Arbeiterklasse" ("Industry and the working class") might lead one to expect more ideologically programmatic elements, the image expresses only restrained agitative propaganda.

HORST RING
"Industrie und Arbeiterklasse"
("Industry and the working class"),
1970
Painting on ceramic
290 x 830 cm

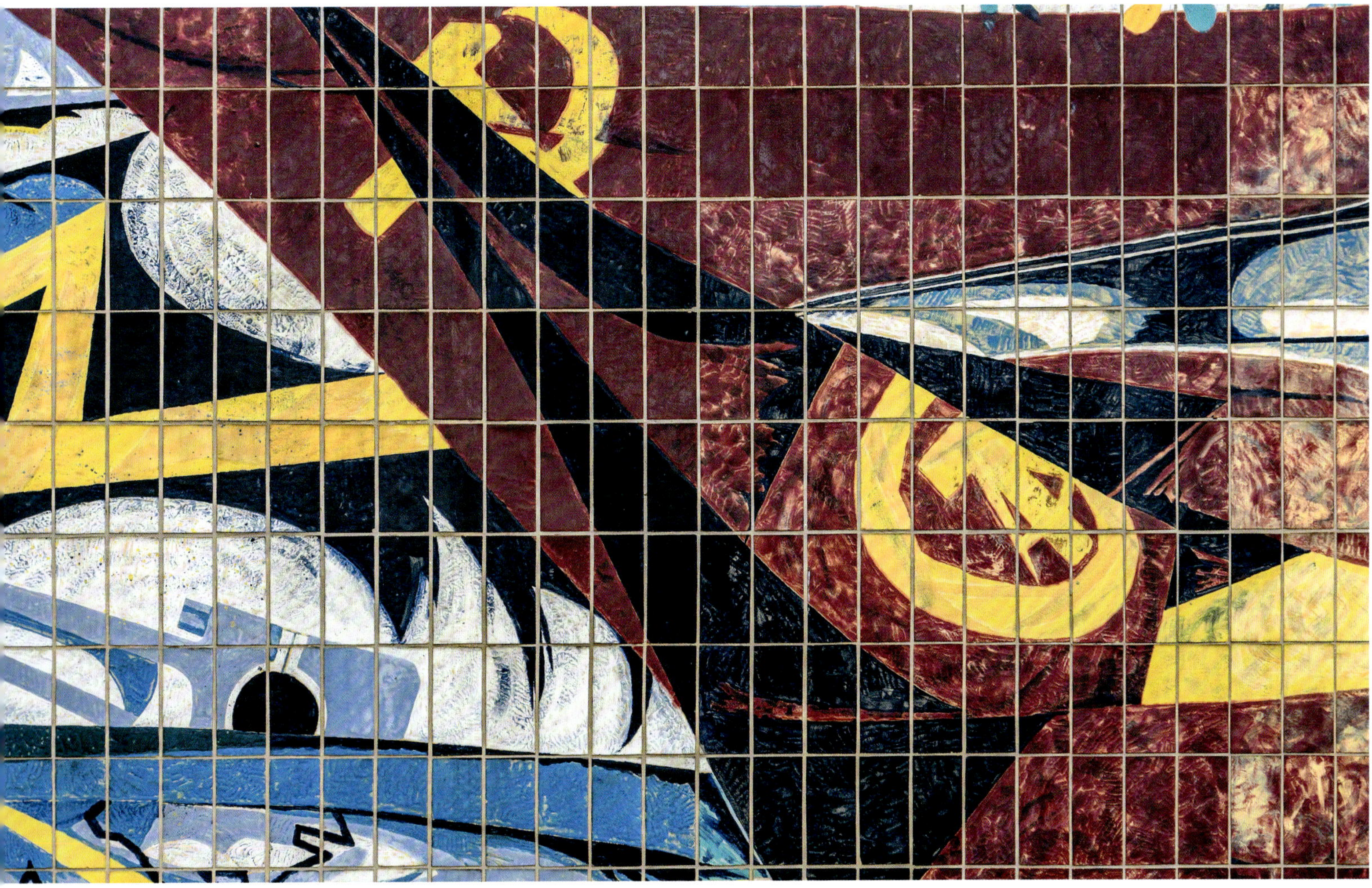
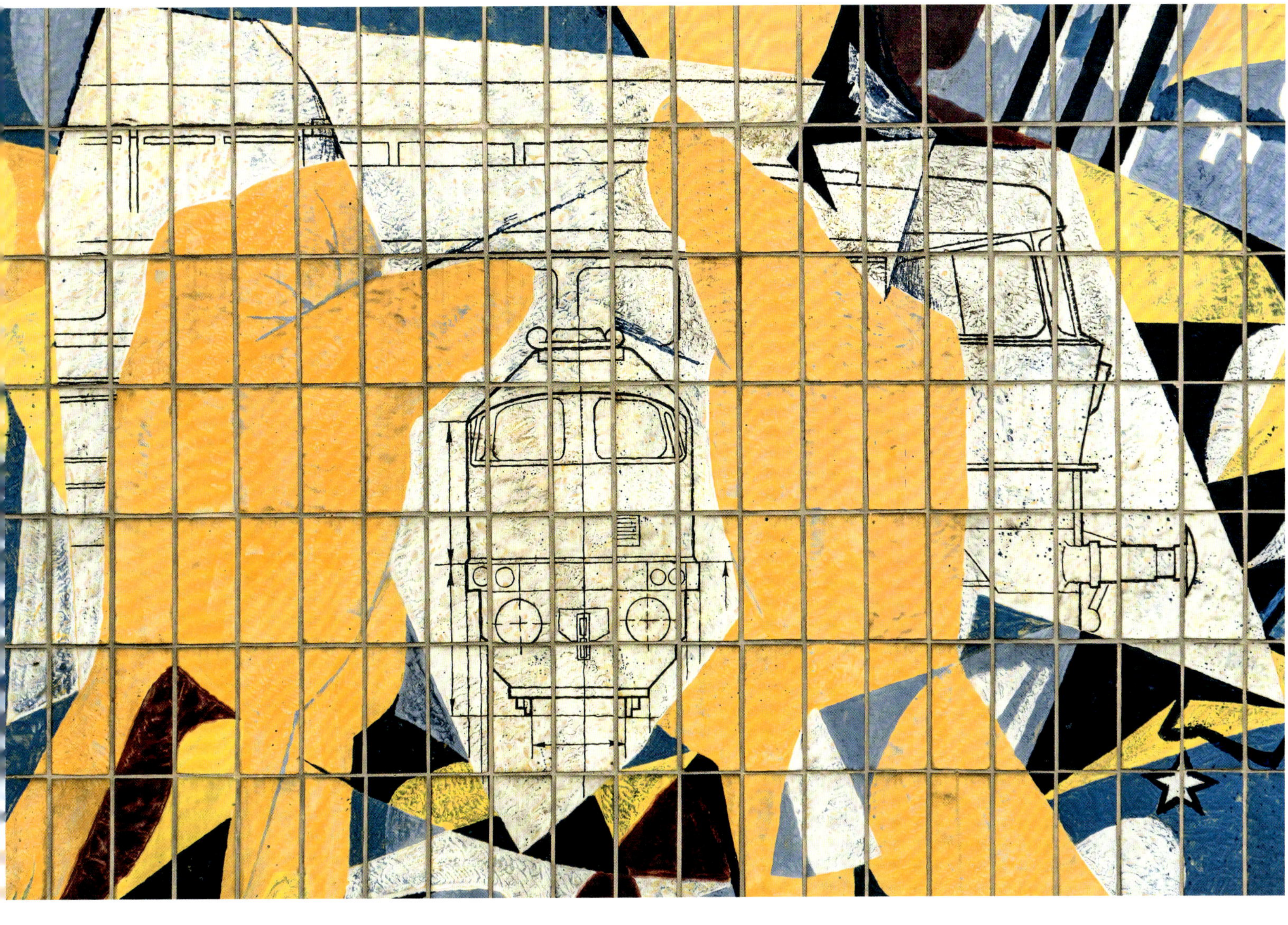

ADMINISTRATION CENTRE FOR THE FEDERAL LABOUR OFFICE NUREMBERG

Address:
Regensburger Strasse 104
90478 Nuremberg

Architecture:
Fischer, Krüder, Rathai Architekten, 1970–1973

Art in architecture:
Norbert Kricke
and Walter Ibscher, Adolf Luther, Günter Maas, Günther Uecker, Max Walter

Between 1970 and 1973, the administrative centre for the then Federal Labour Office was built in south Nuremberg. On a plot of 55,000 square metres, a star-shaped high-rise building distributes its substantial spatial requirements over three wings with varying heights. Its 18 floors and 57-metre height made it the city's tallest building at the time. Thus, the building measure also involved an appropriately large number of art in architecture projects. The Düsseldorf sculptor Norbert Kricke (1922–1984) produced an exceptional example of the new artistic awareness in post-war Germany. The "Großer Wasserwald" ("Large water forest"), with its 24 approximately two-metre high illuminated steles, is distributed over a flattened, green entrance area.

Kricke's installation thrives on the interaction between natural and technical phenomena: daylight and night light, the discreet translucence of the acrylic glass, the indirect electrical illumination and the water that rises inside the identical cylindrical forms, before flowing out along the exterior walls in ever-changing pools, drops and trickles. The steles form a closed water cycle and articulate an atmospherically dense artistic space between them, which neither narrates nor symbolises, but interacts with the changing weather and light conditions to create its moods.

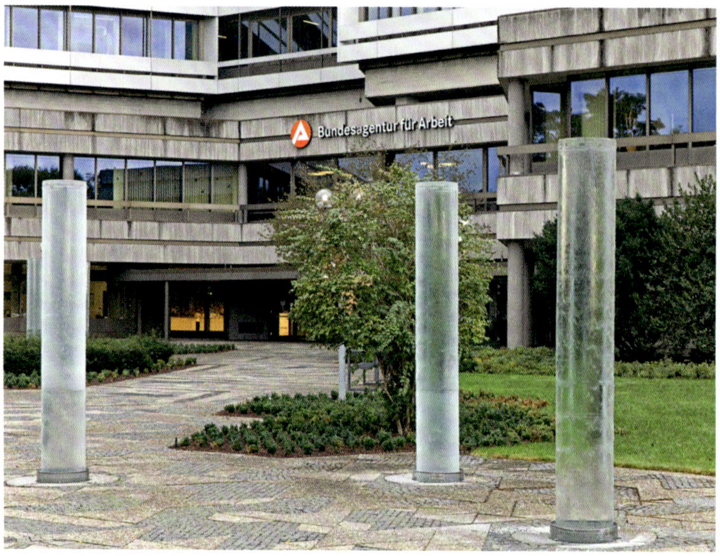

NORBERT KRICKE
"Großer Wasserwald"
("Large water forest"), 1973
24 steles, acrylic glass,
water, lighting

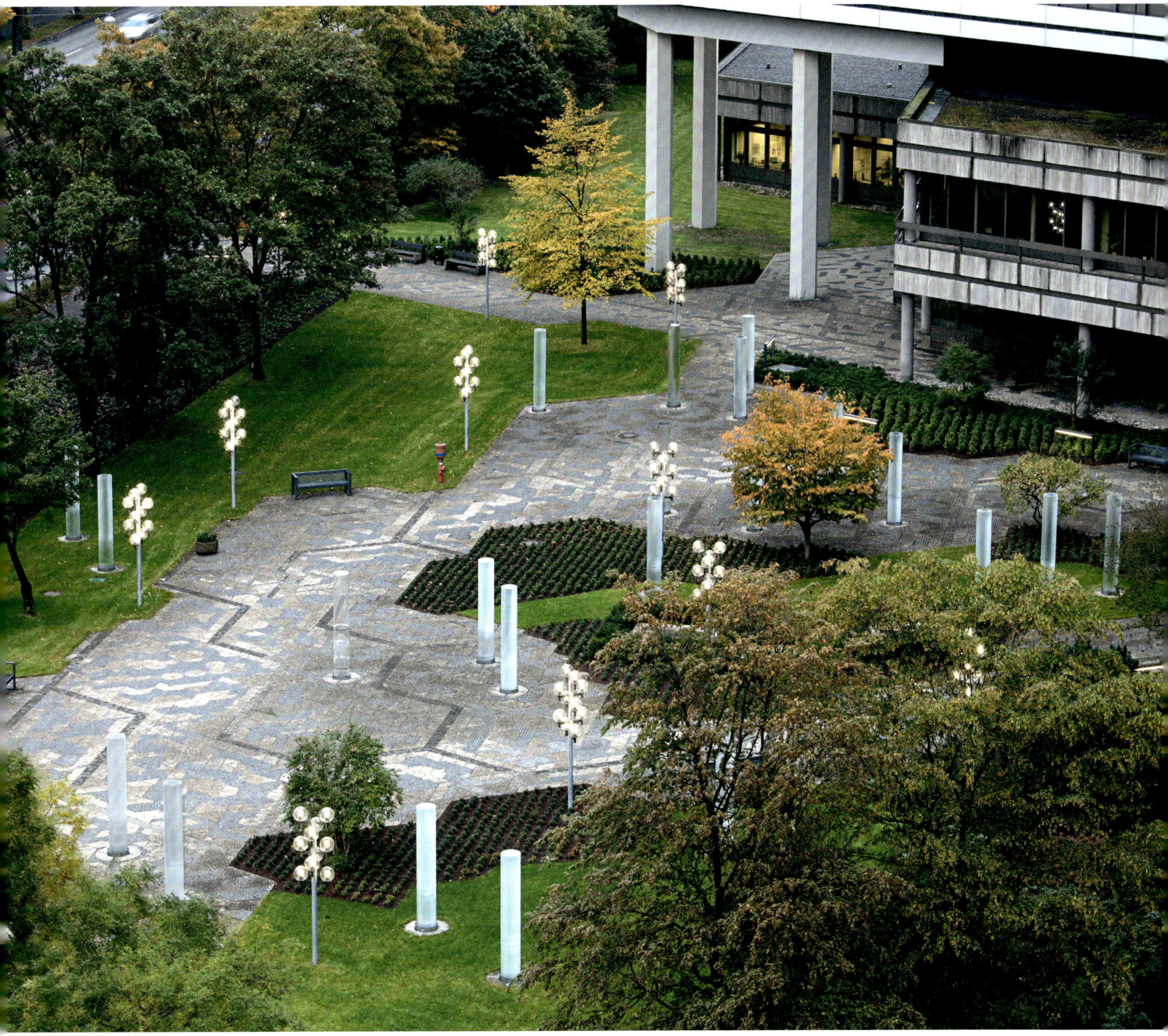

The "Water forest" represents a decentralised counterpart and an alternative to the large sculptures that Kricke himself often produced, which were installed in front of buildings as prestigious, address-forming, free-standing sculptures with maximum dimensions. As early as 1956, Norbert Kricke collaborated with the art critic John Anthony Thwaites to write the text *Forms of Water*. His artistically pioneering idea of a water forest also has its roots in the late 1950s and was implemented for the first time in 1964 for the bank Rheinische Girozentrale in Düsseldorf.

EDUCATION CENTRE HALLE-NEUSTADT

TODAY REGISTRATION OFFICE

Address:
Am Stadion 5/6
06122 Halle (Saale)

Architecture:
Richard Paulick, Chief Architect,
General Planning, 1964–1968

Art in architecture:
Josep Renau

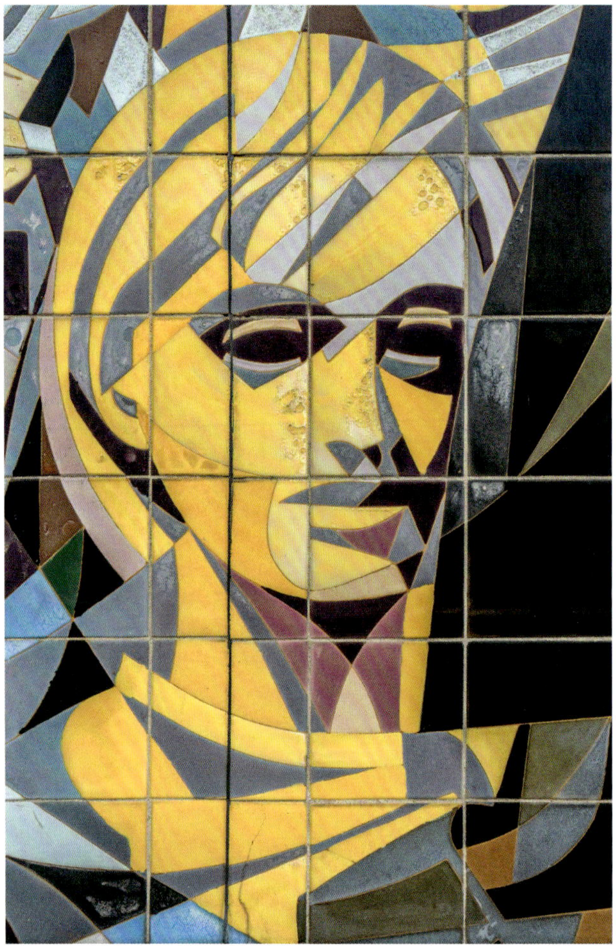

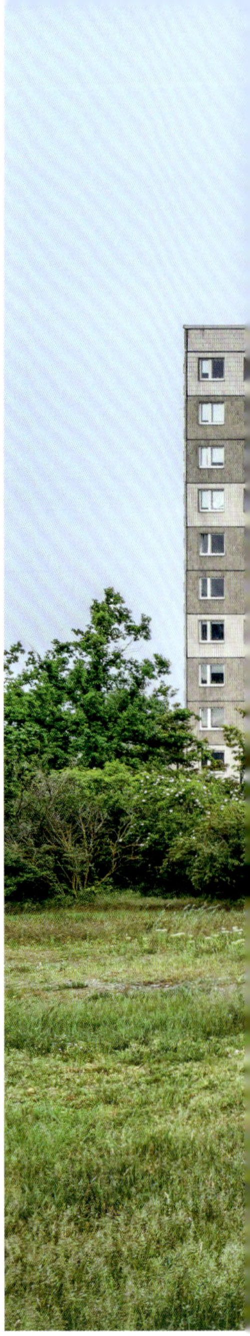

JOSEP RENAU
"Einheit der Arbeiterklasse
und Gründung der DDR" /
"Die von Menschen beherrschten
Kräfte von Natur und Technik"
("Unity of the working class and
foundation of the GDR" /
"The powers of nature and technology
harnessed by the people"), 1974
2 tile mosaics
37 x 7 m each

Halle-Neustadt was built out of nothing as the city of chemical workers from 1964 onwards and established as a Socialist model city. Within a very short time, apartments for several tens of thousands of people, kindergartens and crèches, secondary and vocational schools, shopping facilities and gastronomic services were developed there. The art was limited to figurative pieces in public spaces. They include two massive majolica murals for the staircase porches of the twelve-storey apprentice accommodation of the city's educational centre, which is now used by the Registration Office. Each piece is 37 metres high, 7 metres wide and was produced by Josep Renau (1907–1982) and his colleagues. The Spanish painter and graphic designer moved to the GDR in 1958 following an invitation from the government.

The artwork by the southern staircase is entitled "The powers of nature and technology harnessed by the people". Following the intervention of the local council for visual art and architecture, which

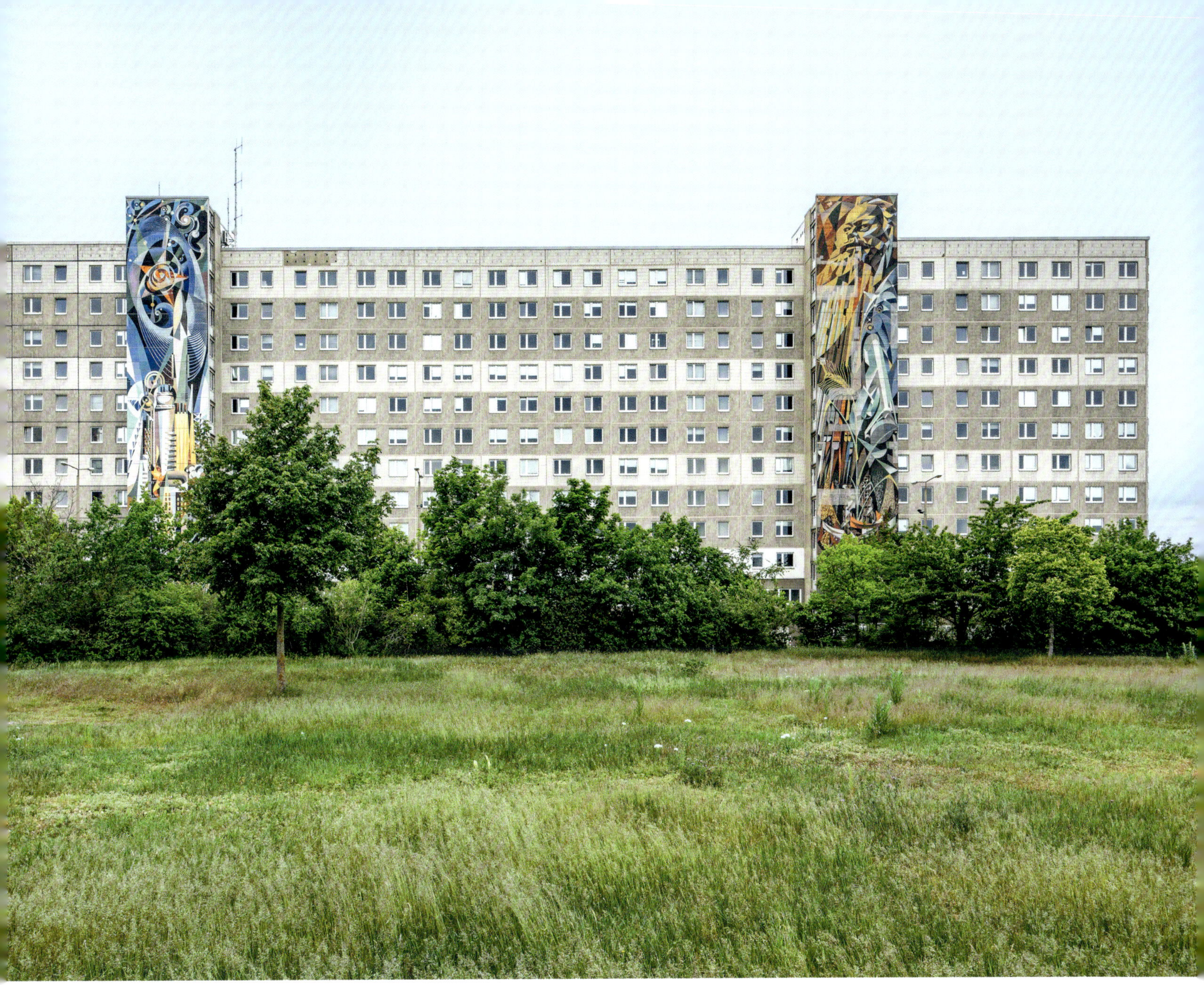

demanded a high-profile political stance, its northern counterpart is dedicated to the theme of "Unity of the working class and foundation of the GDR". The intended gable design was not implemented; a third tile image at the canteen entitled "March of the youth into the future" was lost when the building was demolished. The tried and trusted iconography and symbolism of high-rise buildings, a rocket, a handshake scene, ears of grain, a microscope, organ pipes and a portrait of Karl Marx form the content of the remaining two scenes. They present idealised images of Socialist society, while celebrating the achievements and progress of the GDR in the fields of agriculture, technology, science, research and the arts. The propagated concept of progress is reflected in a confidently mastered, futuristic visual language, conceived for viewing from both nearby and further away, and aimed at reaching and inspiring the viewer not only cognitively, but also emotionally.

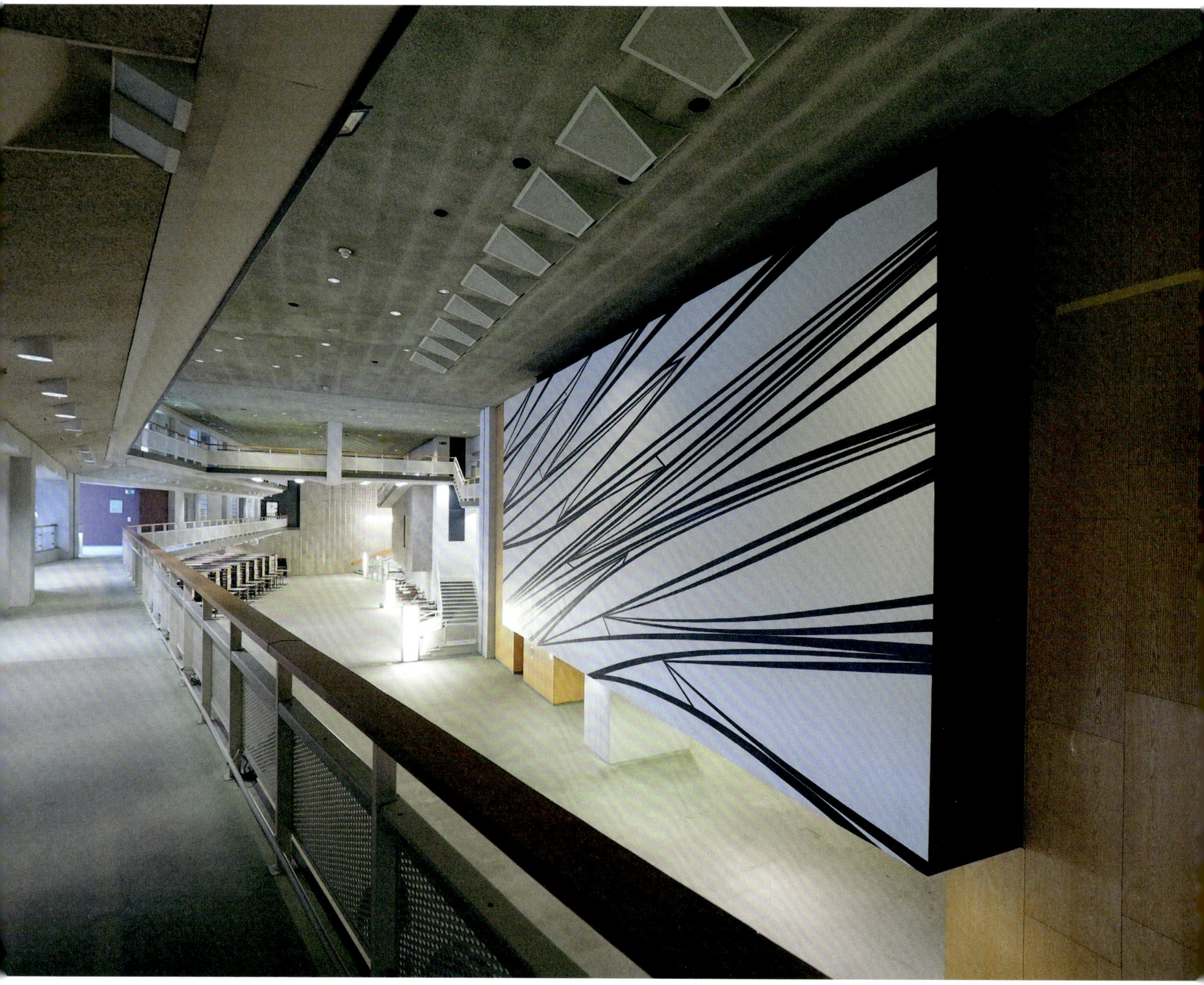

ERICH HAUSER

Flächenwand (Surface wall), 1977
Acrylic
132 x 635 cm

STATE LIBRARY BERLIN

Address:
Potsdamer Strasse 33
10785 Berlin

Architecture:
Hans Scharoun, 1967–1978

Art in architecture:
Erich Hauser
and Alexander Camaro,
Bernhard Heiliger,
Ansgar Nierhoff, Erich Fritz
Reuter, Günter Ssymmank,
Günther Uecker, Hans Wimmer

The design of the Berlin State Library's building in Potsdamer Strasse is significantly influenced by ship building, with richly structured and diversely accentuated features. Hans Scharoun and his colleague Edgar Wisniewski selected moving structures for the foyers, reading rooms and employee areas, using various ceiling and floor heights, galleries on several levels, varying walls and windows, as well as a diversity of building materials and, last but not least, art in architecture.

Hans Scharoun prepared the planning for the art in architecture. For the mural in the eastern foyer, he imagined something "like Schlemmer". However, following a competition, nothing was implemented that remotely resembled the Bauhaus artist's work. Quite the opposite: the winning artist, Erich Hauser (1930–2004) belonged to a later generation. The general focus of his work lay on abstract stainless steel sculpture, which, coupled with the artist's interest in informal painting, represented an advanced position at the time. He took the exceptional step of working as a painter for the intended wall space in the eastern foyer of the State Library, a cuboid structure with a canopy. His art remains abstract and retains the quality of a sculptor's sketch by its deliberate lack of colour, clearly defined lines and the spatially formative character.

The large "Flächenwand" (Surface wall) artwork painted in acrylic exploits the full dimensions of the elongated eastern foyer. It develops an apparently gestural painting that contributes to the dynamism of its atectonic visual art and counteracts the vertical-horizontal structure of the architecture, with its longitudinal and lateral galleries on two floors. In this way, despite its occasionally organic vivacity, the piece becomes the dominant impetus in experiencing the space, which is simultaneously a place of peace, a foyer and a transition area towards the reading rooms.

MAIN CUSTOMS OFFICE LÖRRACH – MOTORWAY CUSTOMS WEIL AM RHEIN

Address:
Lustgartenstrasse 1
79576 Weil am Rhein

Architecture:
Staatliches Hochbauamt
Radolfzell, 1980

Art in architecture:
Horst Hoheisel
and Walter Diederichs

In 1982, numerous paintings, drawings, watercolours, collages and graphic designs by local artists were purchased for the Weil am Rhein motorway customs facility. In 1985, they were joined by the figurative bronze sculpture "Wartender" ("Waiting man") by Walter Diederichs. These were all preceded in 1981 by the sculpture "Scharnier" ("Hinge") by Horst Hoheisel (born in 1944), who won an open competition involving 86 participants. It is an almost ten-metre long major Corten-steel sculpture, which was installed in front of the customs handling area on a green patch of Motorway 5 in its northbound direction.

Artists' interest in Corten steel, which was only produced in Germany from 1960 onwards, was extremely high at the time. Richard Serra, Wilfried Hagebölling, Heinz-Günter Prager, Franz Bernhard, Wolfgang Nestler, Ansgar Nierhoff and Erich Reusch – almost all of whom had, like Hoheisel, been born in the early 1940s – discovered the artistic potential of the weatherproof material. They were inspired by the shimmering patina and used the material to produce large-scale outdoor sculptures with structurally clear, often minimalist forms. The special aspect of Hoheisel's work for the German-Swiss customs facility is the connection between the design principles of such abstract sculpture and the narrative impetus that creates a relationship to the location where the art is installed: there is a clear logic connecting this "Hinge" to the customs on the border between two countries. It appears to be an obsolete remnant of past times that postulates not so much the breaking down of national borders as overcoming them. Despite its great symbolism, the artwork retains the autonomous aesthetics of abstract art.

For a long time, Horst Hoheisel has also focused his artistic work on the Holocaust and the culture of remembrance, producing numerous "negative memorials" – since 1995 in collaboration with the architect Andreas Knitz.

HORST HOHEISEL
"Scharnier" ("Hinge"), 1980/1981
Corten steel
370 x 950 x 460 cm

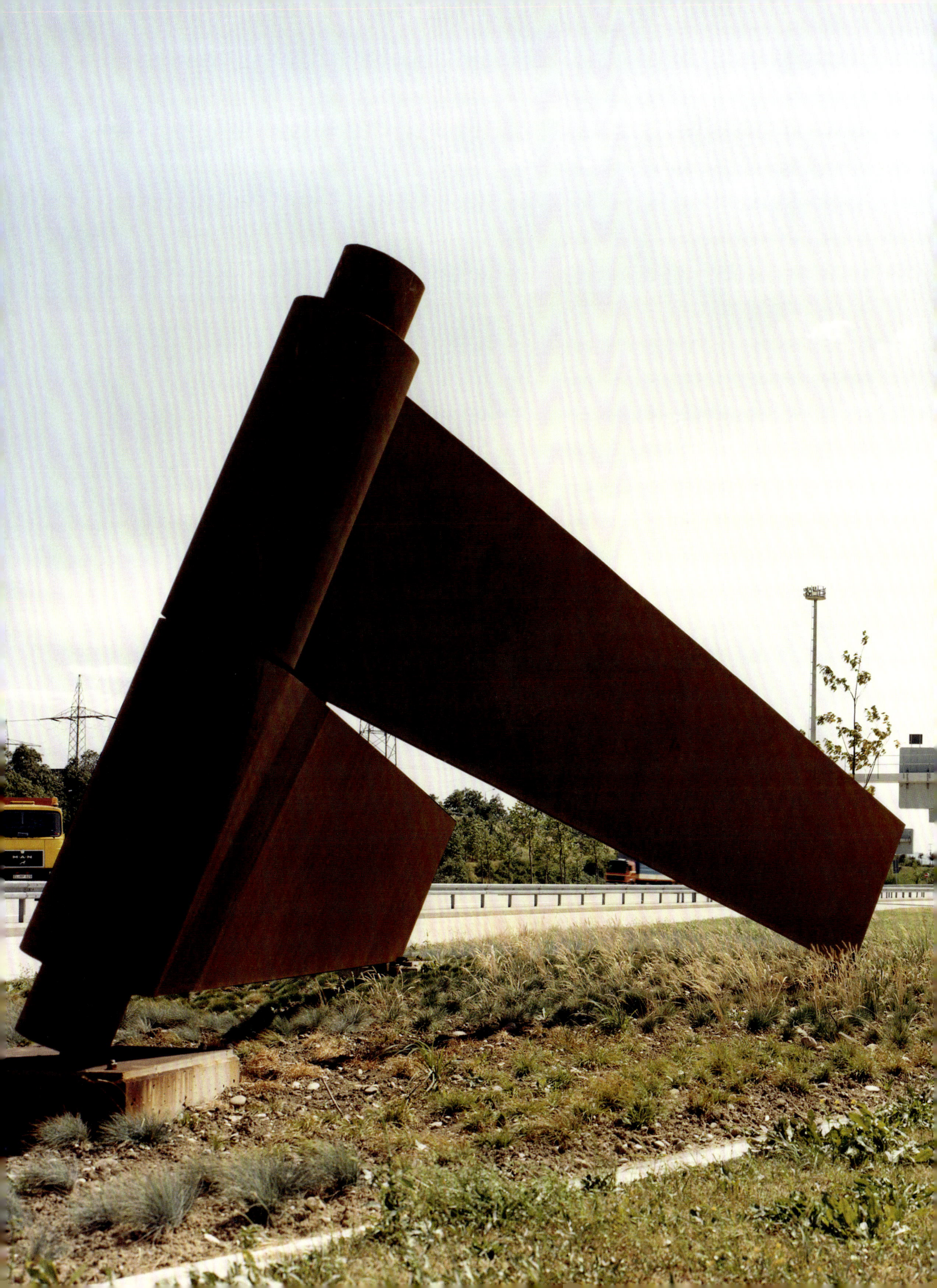

NEUES GEWANDHAUS LEIPZIG

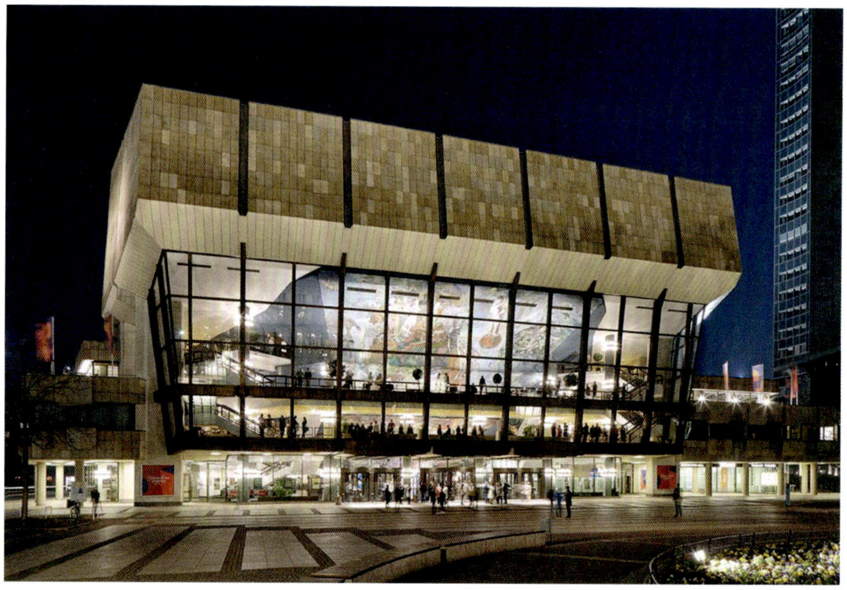

Address:
Augustusplatz 8
04109 Leipzig

Architecture:
Rudolf Skoda with Eberhard Göschel, Volker Sieg and Winfried Sziegoleit, 1977–1981

Art in architecture:
Sighard Gille
and Gudrun Brüne, Dietrich Burger, Ulrich Hachulla, Heidrun Hegewald, Susanne Kandt-Horn, Harald Metzkes, Ronald Paris, Nuria Quevedo, Arno Rink, Frank Ruddigkeit, Willi Sitte, Volker Stelzmann, Walter Womacka, Heinz Zander

The Neue Gewandhaus Leipzig is an impressive late Modern building with well-structured dimensions and a sloping glass façade that opens up towards Augustusplatz and the opera. The building has two notable characteristics, namely that it was the only pure concert-hall building in the GDR and that its art on the undersides of terraces in the main foyer, covering a 714 square metre area, is the largest of its kind in Europe. The urban-planning and architectural concept was developed by Rudolf Skoda, who was also the Chief Architect at the Development Section of the District of Leipzig Council. Following conceptual changes and controversial disputes, the Cultural Department of the District of Leipzig Council commissioned the painter Sighard Gille (born in 1941) to produce architecturally related art for the hall.

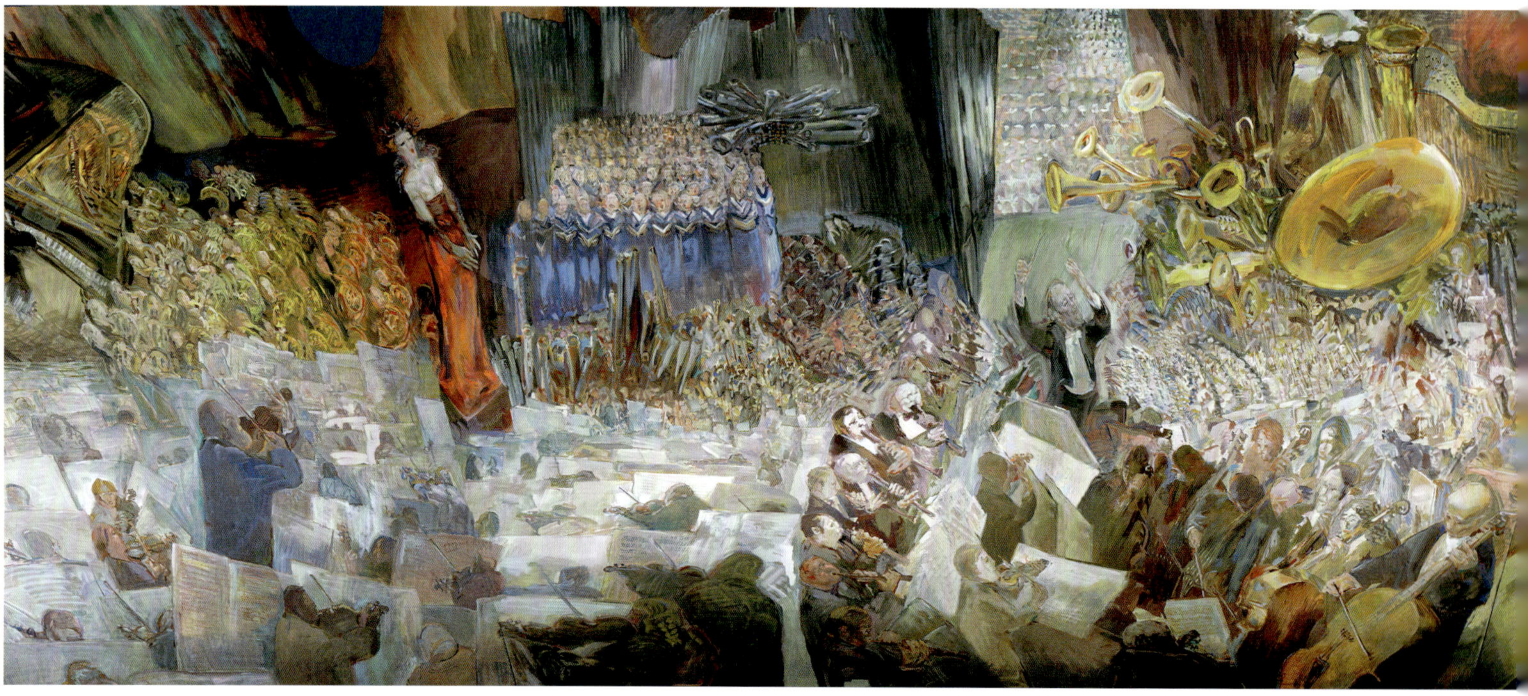

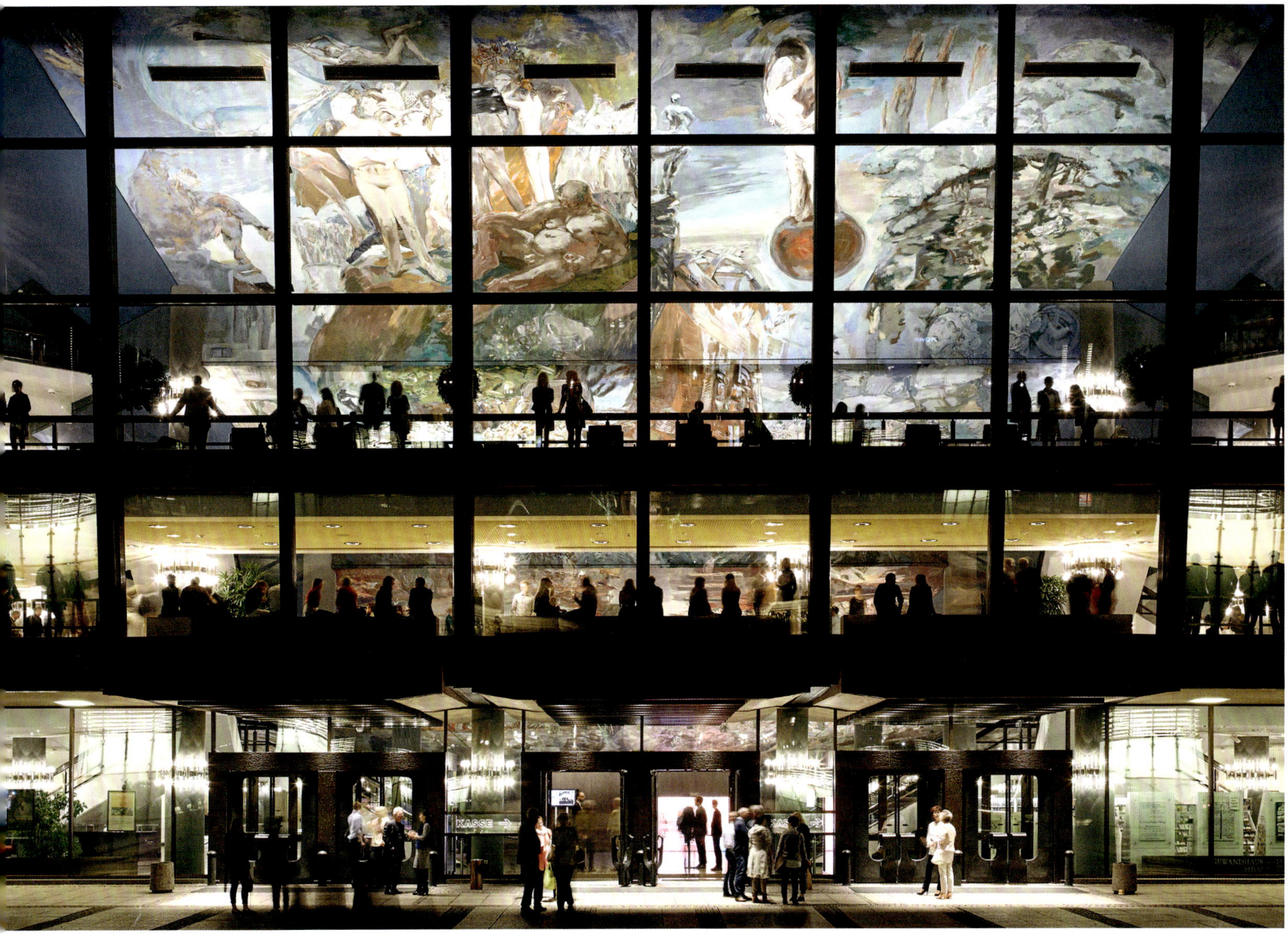

As a student of Bernhard Heisig, Werner Tübke and Wolfgang Mattheuer, and a teacher of Neo Rauch, Sighard Gille is a representative of the figurative, expressive Leipzig school of painters. His work, consisting of dispersion paint on plaster, completely covers the trapezoid undersides of the staggered terraces in the hall. It creates an immersive visual space that cannot be completely overviewed from a single perspective, projecting its mood further into the urban space through the glass façade. The commissioning authority required the "portrayal of human and Socialist musical creativity". Gille developed a visual programme that was distributed over the four defined corner zones. It begins at the bottom with a sweeping orchestral scene, in which the Musical Director at the time, Kurt Masur, is recognisable. Following the intermediary "Witches' frieze", the part entitled "Forces of darkness" depicts a dystopia with a wealth of motifs such as mourning and dead people, as well as fools. A further "Witches' frieze" separates this scene from the panopticon of modern cosmopolitan life, entitled "Lied der Stadt" ("Song of the city"), which smoothly develops into the "Lied vom Glück" ("Song of joy") – a bright vision of timeless happiness.

SIGHARD GILLE
"Gesang vom Leben"
("Song of life"), 1980/1981
Dispersion paint with Caparol
on smooth plaster
714 m² with a height of 31.8 m

MAIN-DANUBE CANAL HILPOLTSTEIN

Address:
Scheitelpunkt Main-Donau-Kanal,
Landschaft bei Pierheim,
91161 Hilpoltstein

Architecture:
Rhein-Main-Donau AG, 1960–1992

Art in architecture:
Hannsjörg Voth

A piece of art in architecture that is unique throughout the world is not situated in a building, but in the open landscape. The building measure to which the art owes its existence is the 171-kilometre Main-Danube Canal between Kelheim and Bamberg, which ensures a continuous shipping route between the North Sea and the Black Sea. The exact point of reference for the art cannot be seen with the naked eye. It is known as the canal summit ("Scheitelhaltung"), representing the highest point of a shipping canal. In the case of the Main-Danube canal, it covers 17 kilometres and crosses the Fränkische Alb region 30 kilometres south of Nuremberg near the middle-Frankish small town of Hilpoltstein as the main European watershed.

Towards the end of the long planning and building period between 1960 and 1992, Rhein-Main-Donau AG, a private infrastructure company under the auspices of the Federal Republic of Germany, invited twelve artists from the neighbouring countries to participate in an art in architecture competition, which was won by the Munich-based painter and sculptor Hannsjörg Voth (born in 1940). His piece, which can be classified as land art, is a straight-line landscape intervention consisting of two large, wedge-shaped granite walls. On the waterway, a wall section described by the artist as a sail is visible from afar.

As ships approach, the perspective and impressions change. When passing the gate-like situation, it becomes apparent that the 14-metre high sail sculpture is tapered on the narrower side facing the water, namely from 3 metres at the bottom to a few centimetres at the top. This perspective also establishes a correspondence with the second granite sculpture on the northern side, which is further away from the canal. From the land perspective, however, this exceptional art in architecture presents the view of two narrow edges, with a length of 144 and almost 44 metres respectively, receding towards the horizon as a slim line over the canal, thereby marking the juncture of the canal summit and the European watershed.

HANNSJÖRG VOTH
"Scheitelhaltung – Skulptur Europäische Wasserscheide"
("Canal summit – Sculpture of the European watershed"), 1990–1992
Two-part granite sculpture
144.2 x 14 x 3 m (south side)
and 43.40 x 14 x 2.80 m (north side)

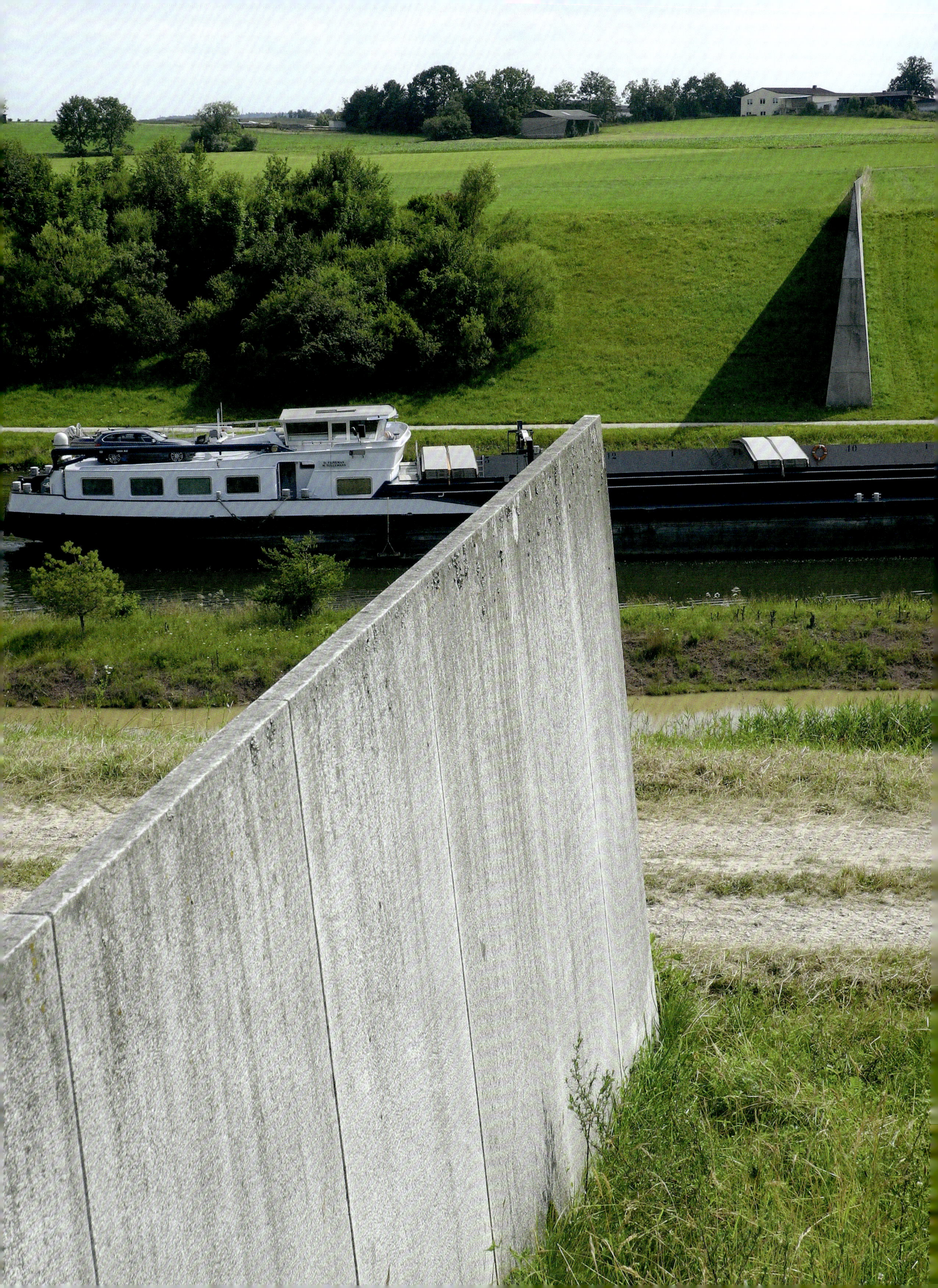

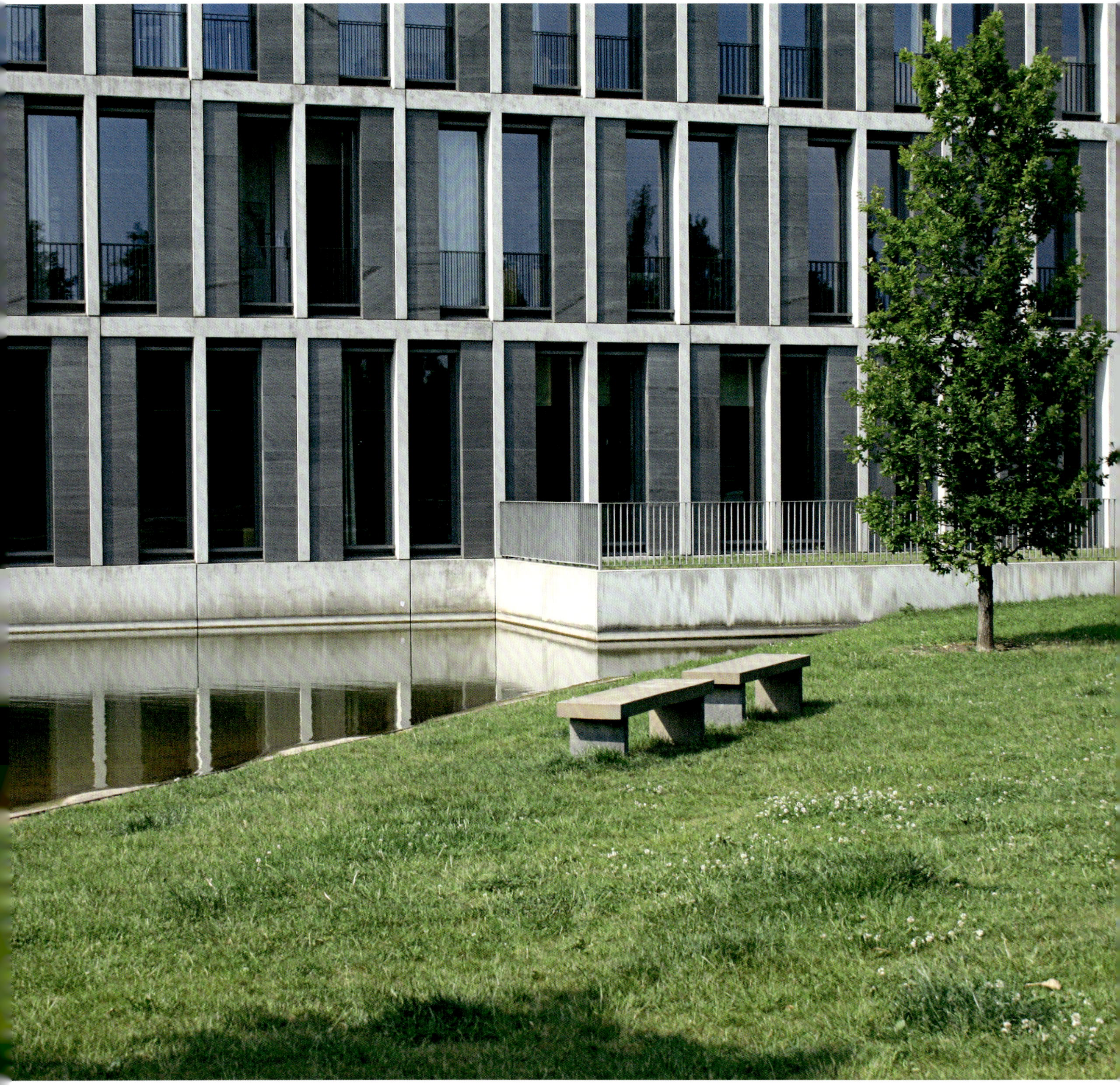

IAN HAMILTON FINLAY
Untitled, 1999
2 slate benches

FEDERAL LABOUR COURT ERFURT

Address:
Hugo-Preuss-Platz 1
99084 Erfurt

Architecture:
Weinmiller Architekten, 1996–1999

Art in architecture:
Ian Hamilton Finlay
and Ulrike Drasdo, Katharina Grosse, Veronika Kellndorfer, Klaus Kinold, Jürgen Partenheimer, Ricardo Saro, Rémy Zaugg

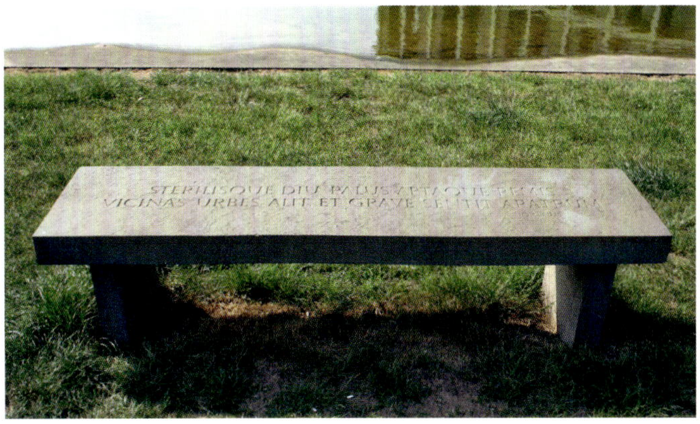

Following German reunification, the Independent Federal Commission decided in 1992 to move the seat of the Federal Labour Court from Kassel to the Thuringian capital Erfurt. For the new headquarters beneath the Baroque Zitadelle Petersberg, the Berlin architect Gesine Weinmiller designed a four-storey building made of fair-faced concrete and natural stone. Its remarkable aesthetics with abstract and minimalist tendencies are continued in the art in architecture. In the interior spaces, there are coloured aluminium panels by Katharina Grosse (born in 1961), oil paintings by Ricardo Saro (born in 1947), wall textiles by Ulrike Drasdo (1951–2017), photographic work by Klaus Kinold (born in 1939) and four written panels by Rémy Zaugg (1943–2005). Glass plates by Veronika Kellndorfer (born in 1962) are firmly fixed to the architecture as wall sections. The entrance courtyard accentuates a stele consisting of blue bronze cubes by Jürgen Partenheimer (born in 1947).

Reserve, concision and dignity are expressed not only by the architecture, but also by the open spaces of the Federal Labour Court. The Zurich landscape architects Kinast, Vogt und Partner designed a publicly accessible park with references to the Zitadelle fortifications. An additional art in architecture work is situated beside the eastern part of the pond: two slate benches without backrests stand beside each other. They were produced by the all-round artist Ian Hamilton Finlay (1925–2006). Verses by the Roman poet Horace are engraved upon one of them: "STERILISQUE DIU PALUS APTAQUE REMIS VICINAS URBES ALIT, ET GRAVE SENTIT ARATRUM"; the German translation is chiselled on the second bench: "DA, WO EHMALS RUDER / DIE HOHEN WELLEN / TEILTEN, DA LOCKERT / JETZT DER PFLUG DAS / LAND" ("WHERE OARS ONCE PARTED THE HIGH WAVES, NOW THE PLOUGH CLEAVES THE LAND"). Ian Hamilton Finlay marked many stones with words and placed them as "one word poems" in the famous garden of his home near Edinburgh. Like these, the lines by Horace inscribed on the benches, taken out of context, develop an autonomous poetic attraction, giving the art in architecture for the Federal Labour Court a deeper level of significance.

FRIEDRICH LOEFFLER INSTITUTE FEDERAL RESEARCH INSTITUTE FOR ANIMAL HEALTH GREIFSWALD

Address:
Südufer 10
17493 Greifswald – Insel Riems

Architecture:
1910
Extensions:
1919/1920, main building and additional laboratories 1938–1940
Itten+Brechbühl AG, Basel and Rauh Damm Stiller Partner, Greifswald, 2006–2012

Art in architecture:
Barbara Trautmann and Matthias Geitel

Both German states were also committed to art in architecture and architecturally related art in places that were not publicly accessible and therefore viewed either by few members of the general public or none at all, for instance in restricted zones. One such location is the Friedrich Loeffler Institute, a virology research facility built in 1910 on the island of Riems, which focuses on epizoology. The first artworks for the research facility were already produced in the 1920s. In the late 1950s, the painter Hans Neubert (1924–2011) realised ten murals on the theme of "Sinn und Praxis der Virologie" ("The purpose and practice of virology"). At the same time, the sculptor Waldemar Grzimek (1918–1984) added the bronze sculpture "Äsendes Rind" ("Grazing cow") as well as two animal steles. In 2014, as a result of building work following German reunification, these were joined by the installation "Insulaner" ("Island dweller") by Barbara Trautmann (born in 1966).

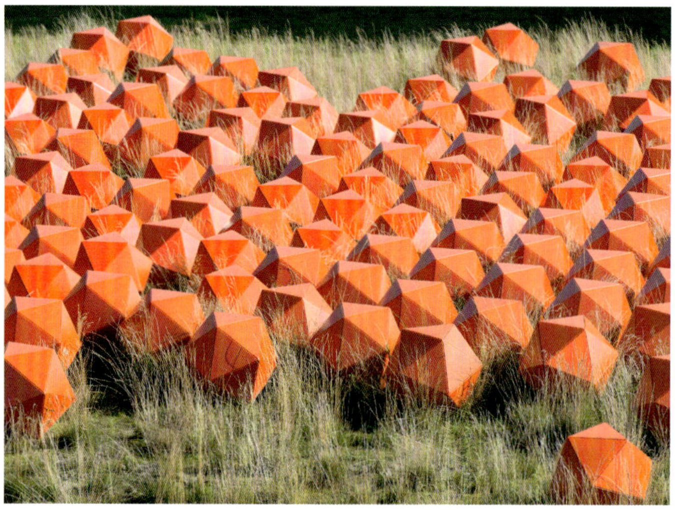

BARBARA TRAUTMANN
"Insulaner" ("Island dweller"), 2014
189 icosahedra, powder-covered steel sheeting

The artwork consists of 189 icosahedra, each made up of 20 identical, equilateral triangles, spread out over a horizontal area of around 400 square metres. The powerful reddish orange colour of the "Island dweller" on the meadow adds positive accentuation in the not entirely untroubled context of virology. As polygons that constantly appear to reform themselves, they also have an extremely enlivening effect on the heterogeneous, functional ensemble of old and new buildings. The installation offers ever new perspectives to the approximately 150 employees working at the facility today. Seen from the upper floors of the laboratory and conference building, one can also recognise the image of a virus model as seen through an electron microscope. Acting like a logo in this way, Barbara Trautmann's work makes a clear, memorable reference to the institution for which it was planned and commissioned.

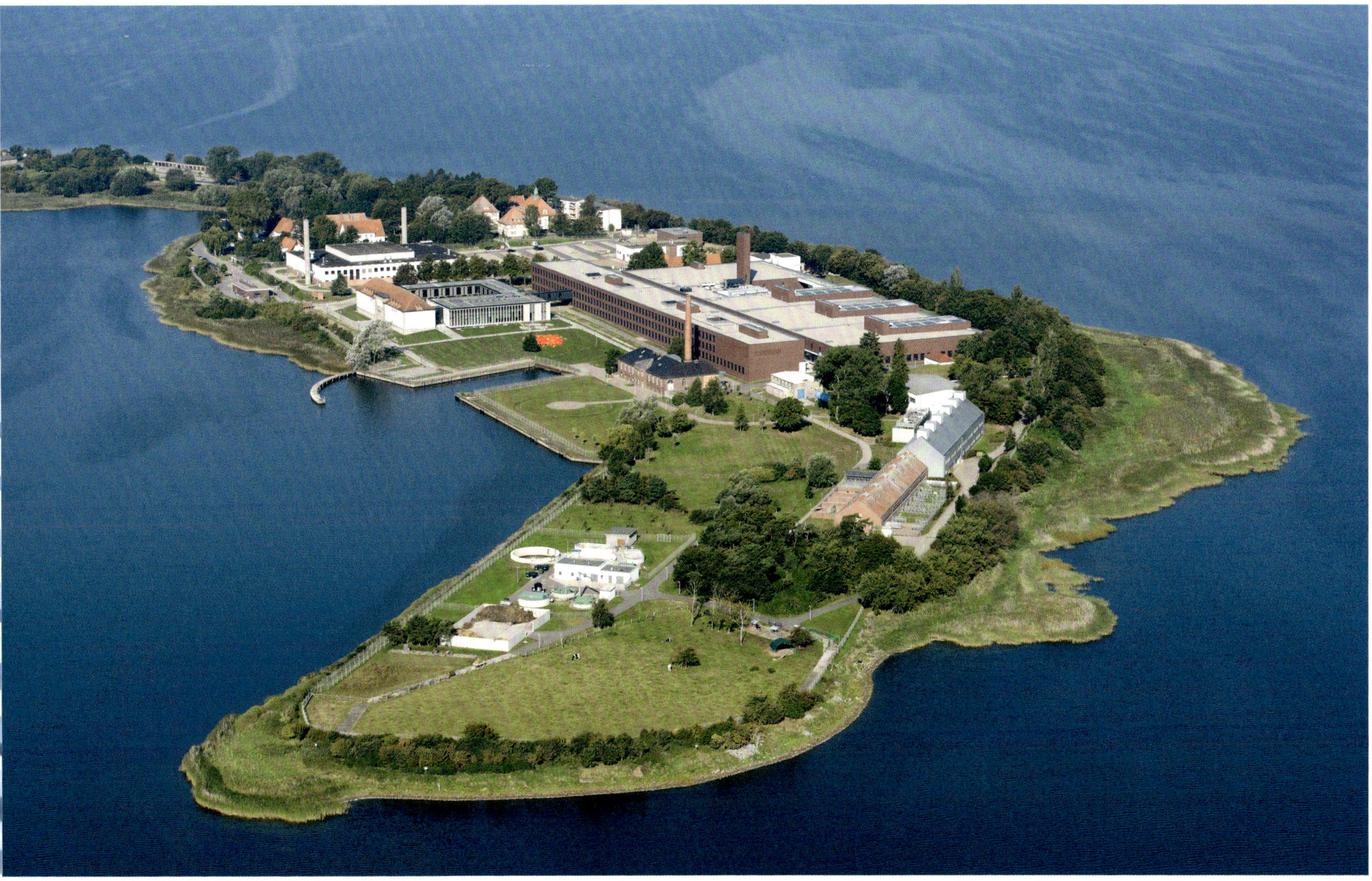

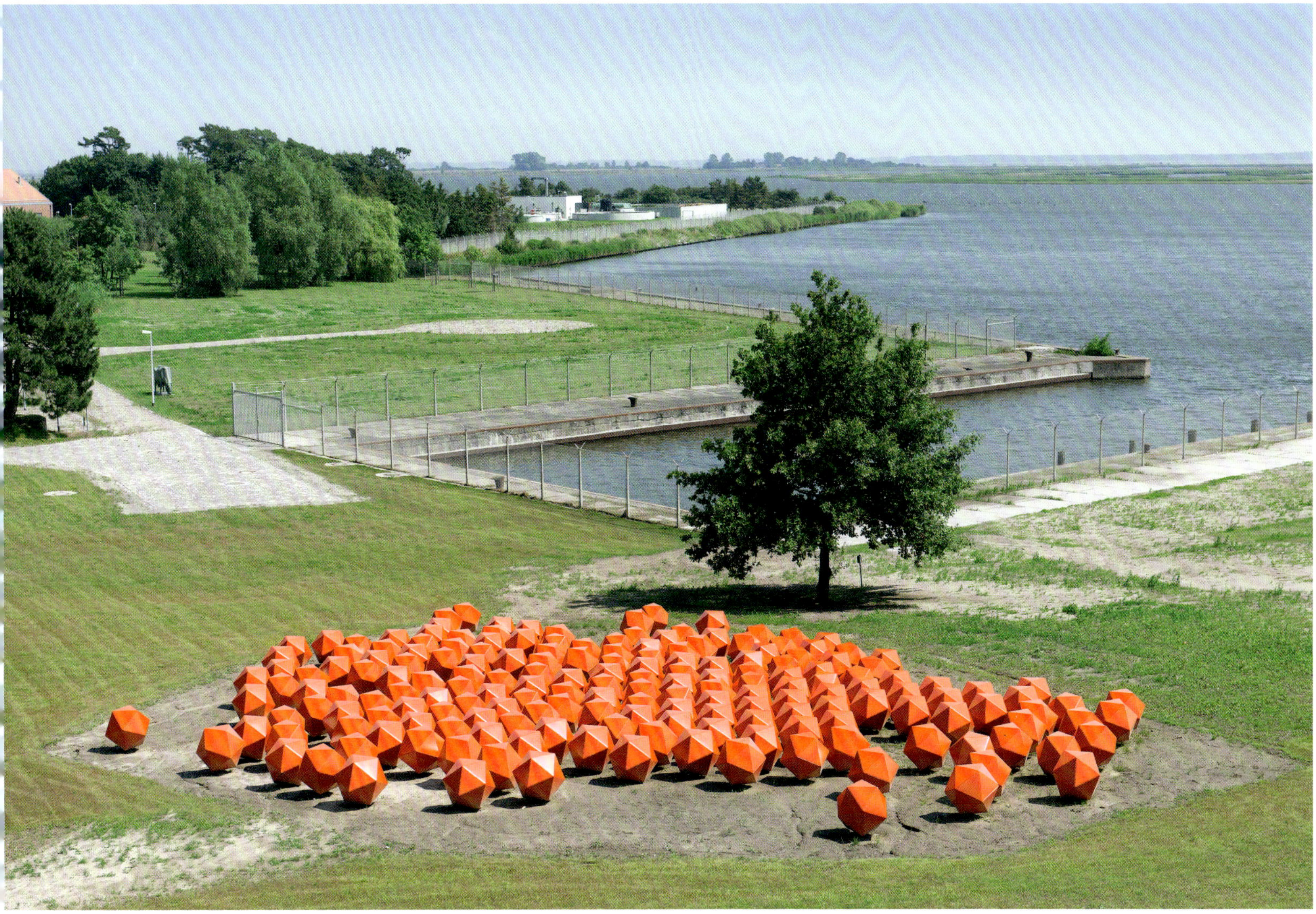

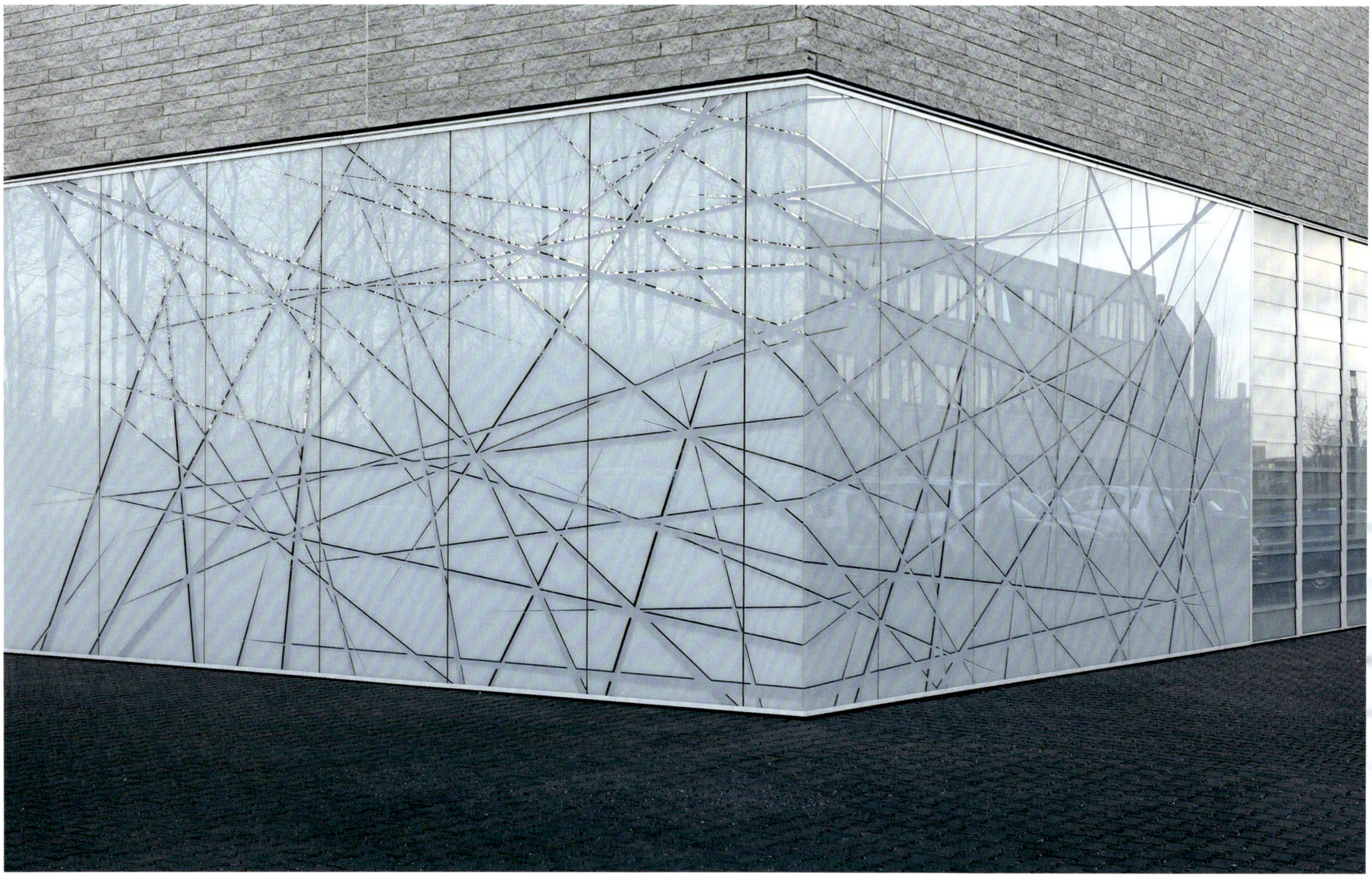

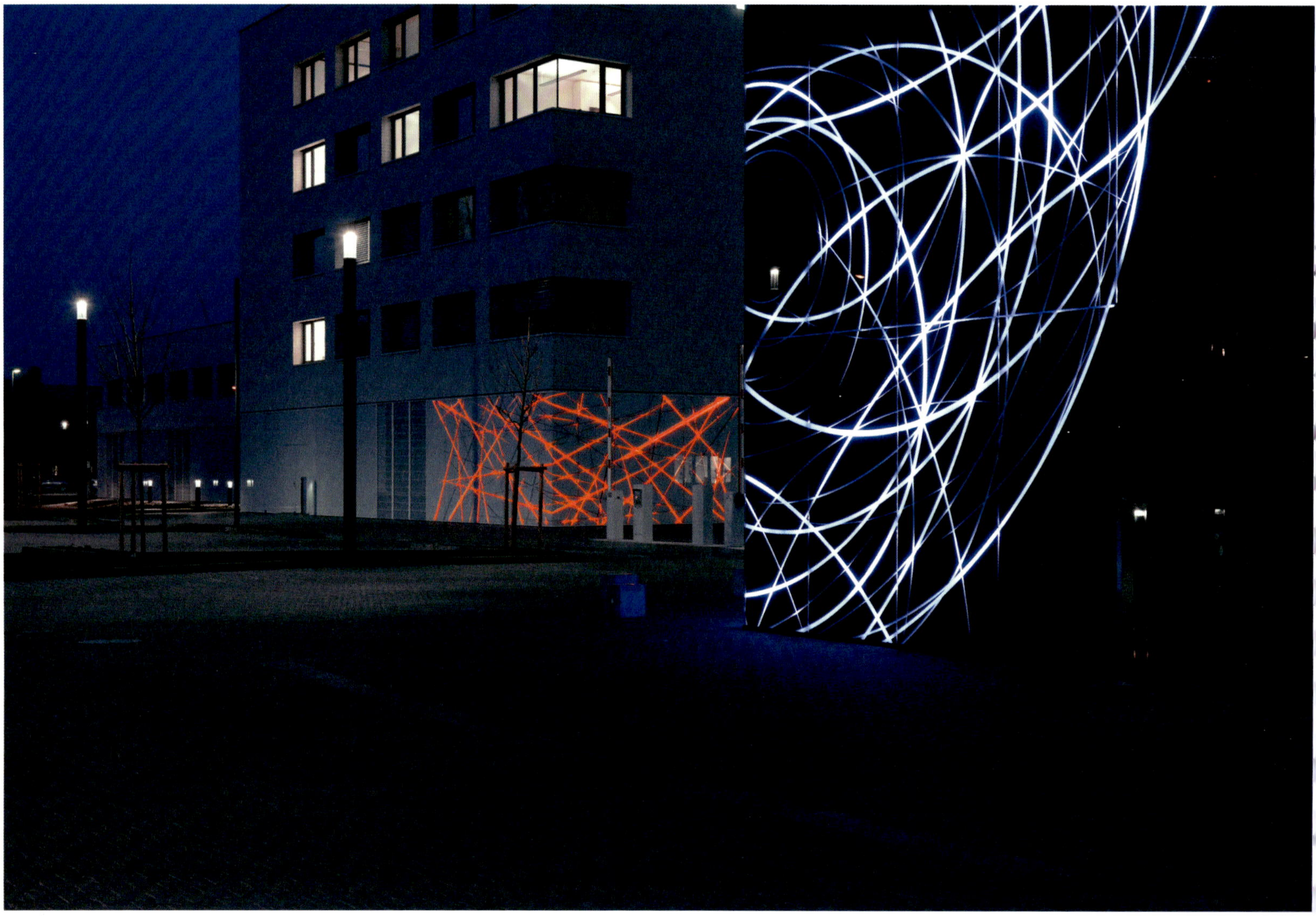

FRAUNHOFER INSTITUTE FOR LASER TECHNOLOGY ILT FRAUNHOFER INSTITUTE FOR PRODUCTION TECHNOLOGY IPT AACHEN

Address:
Steinbachstrasse 15 and 17
52074 Aachen

Architecture:
JSWD Architekten, 2009–2014

Art in architecture:
Annette Sauermann

In 2014, new buildings for the Fraunhofer Institute for Laser Technology ILT and the Fraunhofer Institute for Production Technology IPT were constructed on the Melaten Campus of RWTH Aachen University. The five- and six-storey head-end buildings of both complexes have similar architectural qualities, while still remaining very different. One consists of light-coloured concrete blocks, while the other has a façade with suspended three-dimensional aluminium panels.

The art in architecture by Annette Sauermann (born in 1957) establishes a relationship between the two neighbouring buildings, one that cannot be seen so clearly through the architecture itself. At the corners where the buildings face each other, the artist, in coordination with the architects, integrated large glass display surfaces into the façades, which are white and black respectively. The displays are animated with LED light designed in red for the ILT and slowly alternating white, green and blue for the IPT. The often overlapping LED lights are straight on the ILT and curved on the IPT. Clearly visible also during the day, they correspond with each other over the road, metaphorically suggesting a "network of knowledge" connecting the institutes on a professional level. The artist also connected the artwork to the intranets of both institutes, the increasing and fading light intensity of the art reflecting the volume of data transferred in the respective computer networks. Regardless of this symbolism, the installation is a vivid, pulsating artwork for everyone using the buildings or passing by. Annette Sauermann has implemented numerous light-based works of art in architecture, also for the Ministry of Economic Affairs in Berlin. In 2018, the artwork in Aachen was awarded the Deutscher Lichtdesign Preis (German Light Design Prize) in the category Light Art.

ANNETTE SAUERMANN
"Netzwerke des Wissens"
("Networks of knowledge"), 2015
Light colour ILT: red, light colour IPT: white/green/blue, slowly shifting
IPT: 5.46 x 23.76 m, ILT: 3.72 x 15.04 m

ART IN ARCHITECTURE

COMMISSIONED BY THE MILITARY

ON DUTY

The decision to rearm Germany after the end of World War II led to the foundation of the Bundeswehr (Federal Armed Forces) in the Federal Republic in 1955 and, the following year, to the establishment of the Nationale Volksarmee ("National People's Army", NVA) in the GDR. While the Bundeswehr is subordinate to the Federal Ministry of Defence, the NVA was led by the Ministry of National Defence under the tight control of the Central Committee of the Socialist Unity Party of Germany (SED). Thus the NVA was one of the most important commissioners of art in architecture in the GDR, its fixed visual programmes contributing to the political education of serving soldiers and the development of a Socialist state. By contrast, since its foundation, the guiding principle of the Bundeswehr's self-perception is the "citizen in uniform", which encourages cultural education and engagement with the arts in addition to military training. This naturally includes pieces of art in architecture for military facilities, which are otherwise primarily defined by practicalities and functionalism.

German reunification and the incorporation of the NVA into the Bundeswehr required a fundamental structural reform of the armed forces. It led to the closure of numerous military facilities throughout Germany, so that countless art in architecture works were placed in storage, relocated or even destroyed after buildings were converted or demolished. By contrast, other locations were expanded into major centres and received new art in architecture. The Federal Government's consistent application of art in architecture rules for military facilities is a prime example of the Bundeswehr's socio-political commitment to the holistic education of its soldiers and employees. Artists have reacted to the situation they encountered in a wide range of aesthetic ways over the past six decades, constantly finding new approaches to the theme of "defence", including the metaphorical presentation of a self-confident military and critical reflection on the destructive consequences of war.

ART IN ARCHITECTURE ON DUTY

Constanze von Marlin

After the foundation of the Bundeswehr on May 5, 1955 and the Federal Republic's membership of NATO a day later, military buildings became a major part of federal construction measures. They included administration, accommodation and service buildings for the Bundeswehr and guest forces, as well as computer centres, laboratory and training buildings, airports, navy locations, universities and hospitals. Within the Federal Government, several departments are responsible for military buildings: the Ministry of Defence, the Ministry of Building and the Ministry of Finance. The first two of these are responsible for carrying out the building measures, which are implemented by the federal and state building authorities. Their funding is provided by the Ministry of Finance and the ownership administration of the real estate through the Institute for Federal Real Estate, an institution under public law within the Ministry of Finance. Due to the buildings' military function and the often very limited public accessibility, art in architecture mainly plays a representative role with an inward perspective. Despite or perhaps even due to this fact, the Federal Ministry of Defence follows the cultural-political instructions of the German Bundestag by consistently planning the participation of artists in its building measures.

In the GDR, the Nationale Volksarmee was founded in 1956 under the control of the Soviet Union. It was led by the SED, initially as a professional force, but national service was introduced in 1962 following the construction of the Berlin Wall. In 1958, to strengthen the troops' political awareness, the NVA quickly implemented a decision at the 5th SED Party Assembly to enable the working class to scale the "heights of culture". However, mass cultural measures in the GDR armed forces were not regarded as a goal in itself and were instead used to consolidate the mental and moral maturity of recruits and "increase their combat readiness". For instance in 1960, the artists Christian Rost, Horst Schlossar and Harald Thiel were commissioned to establish painting and graphics groups in units of the 7th Tank Division of the NVA, which was stationed in Dresden. The resulting soldiers' paintings were presented in 1961 at the Haus der Deutsch-Sowjetischen Freundschaft ("House of German-Soviet Friendship") in East Berlin as part of the exhibition "Die Nationale Volksarmee in der Bildenden Kunst" ("The National People's Army in the Visual Arts").

POST-WAR PERIOD AND THE 1960s: DEVELOPMENT AND NEW CONSTRUCTION

In the 1950s and 1960s, a large number of art in architecture works were produced both in the Federal Republic and the GDR in connection with new and converted buildings for military facilities, including many barracks originally built for the Wehrmacht (the German army under National Socialism), such as the Hohenberg Barracks in Horb am Neckar, the Ernst von Bergmann Barracks in Munich and the Steigerwald Barracks in Erfurt. Unlike in the later Federal Republic, the 1960s saw a pragmatic approach to politically burdened architecture in both parts of Germany.

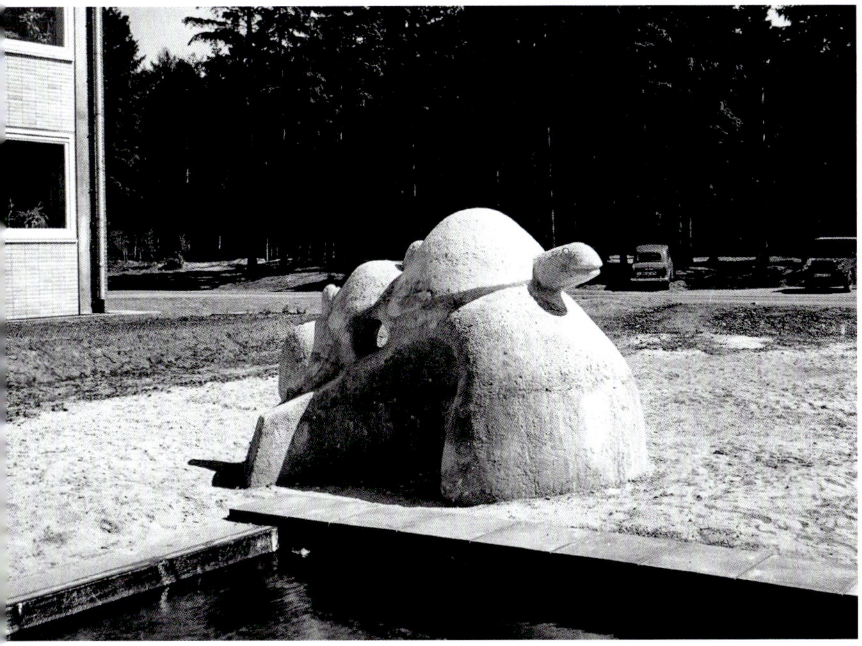

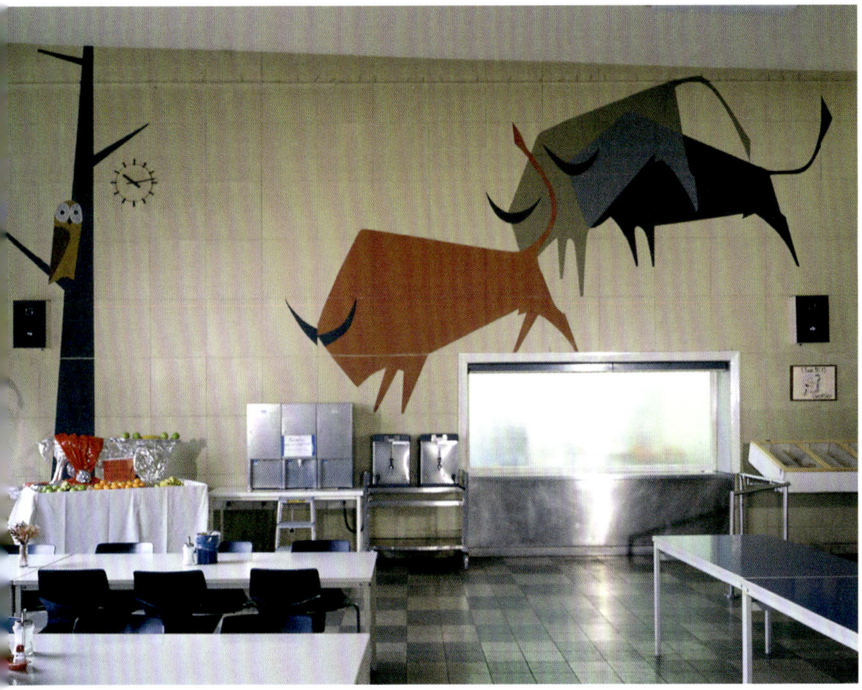

Anatol Buchholtz, "Schildkröten", 1958, Freiherr von Boeselager Barracks, Federal Armed Forces, Munster

Wilhelm Keudel, "Tiere im Angriff", 1958/1959, Gneisenau Barracks, Federal Armed Forces, Wolfenbüttel

Similarly, the art in architecture was not used to address the problems of the past. Instead, it was expected to refer to military tasks in a more general way.

The artworks produced for barracks in the Federal Republic until the late 1960s are characterised by a conservative artistic stance, a limited range of motifs and traditional artistic materials and techniques, such as bronze, natural stone, sgraffito, mosaics, steel strips and inlays. Industrial raw materials and products were also used, including concrete or Novopan chipboards. One popular motif was the presentation of animals, often symbolically referring to military tasks through the qualities attributed to the species. For instance in 1958, the artist Anatol Buchholtz (1927–2011), who mainly worked in and around Braunschweig, produced a concrete sculpture for the Freiherr von Boeselager Barracks in Munster consisting of a line of three tortoises, one directly behind the other. The presentation can be interpreted as a visual translation of military tasks, since the tortoise is armoured and its slow movement can be seen as a metaphor for heavy military machinery.

While sculpture was preferred for the exterior grounds of barracks, murals were popular for their interiors. For the newly constructed Gneisenau Barracks in Wolfenbüttel, which was built in 1956 for the 22nd Tank Grenadier Battalion and used by the Bundeswehr until 1994, the artist Wilhelm Keudel (1913–1972) produced the mural "Tiere im Angriff" ("Animals on the attack", 1958/1959). The entire head-end wall of the team dining room was clad in Novopan chipboards, on which three man-sized bulls are presented, their heads lowered in an attacking pose. In the line of their sight and the direction of their attack, a tree acts as a haven of peace; an owl is perched on its branch. The artist compares the bulls' spontaneously driven aggression to the considered wisdom of the owl, thereby creating an allegory of *furor* and *ratio*, military and diplomacy, war and peace.

Many of the sculptural works for barracks present naturalistic or slightly stylised human figures that refer to the facility's military use. The range includes Karlheinz Goedtke's (1915–1995) bronze sculpture "Stabbieger" ("Staff benders", 1959) for the Rantzau Barracks in Boostedt, which formally echoes works by Wilhelm Lehmbruck and Gerhard Marcks, as well as Jean Sprenger's (1912–1980) "Drei Krieger mit Schild" ("Three warriors with shields", 1959) for the Steuben Barracks in Achim (→ p. 232). Although the design of the three warriors cannot deny its origins in early 20th-century art, the materiality of the concrete sculpture expresses the drive towards modernisation and the desire for new post-war developments.

The murals and reliefs also include occasional abstract artworks. Produced in 1959, the natural stone mosaic by Alfons Klein (1905–1983) for the façade of the utilities building at the school for the Signal Corps in Feldafing fluctuates between abstract and figurative art. By contrast, Ursula Sax (born in 1935) produced a purely formal solution. In 1963, she developed a double door made with hammered copper sheeting for Building 7 of the Laupheim army airport. The artwork's bulges and recesses only faintly inspire associations with a shoal of fish, yet it provides the otherwise reserved barracks building with a special highlight. Between 1965 and 1969, Gerlinde Beck (1930–2006), an important representative of Minimalism in Germany, produced the sculpture "Double stele" for the Wilhelmsburg Barracks in Ulm, consisting of stainless steel sheeting that offers an aesthetic counterpoint to the functional architecture of the barracks

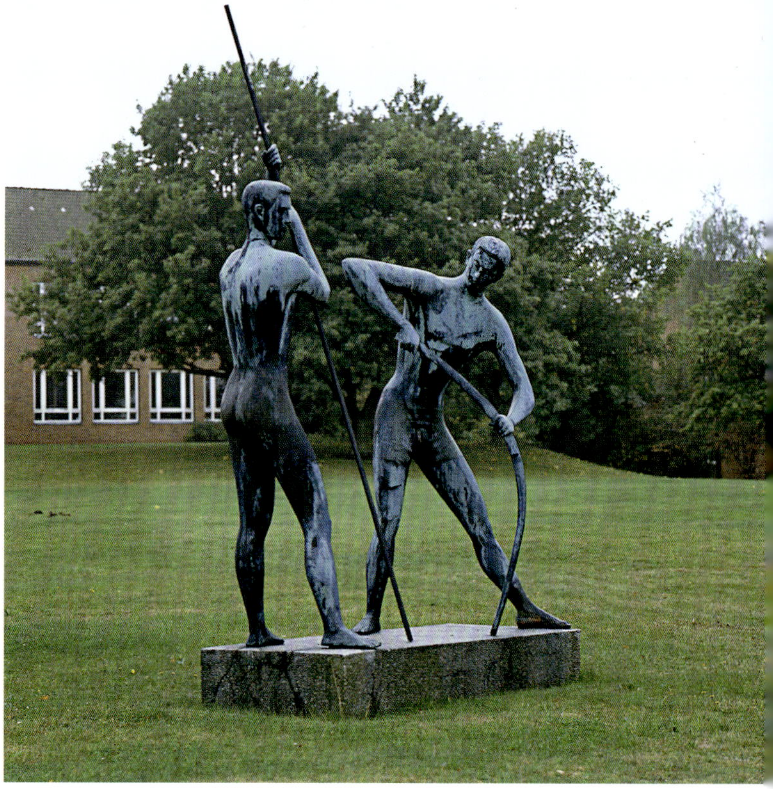

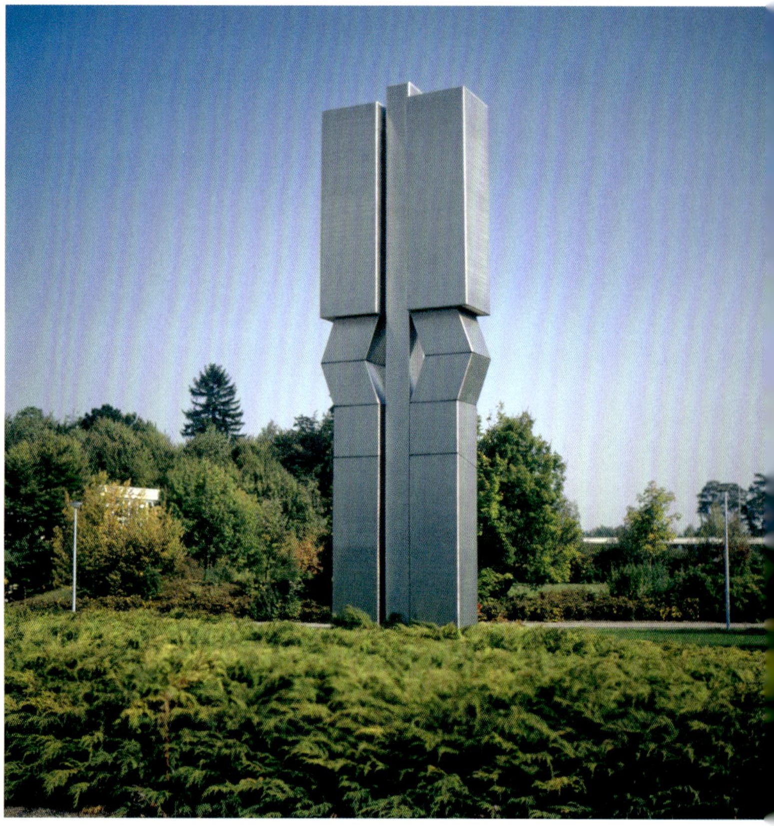

Karlheinz Goedtke, "Stabbieger", 1959, Rantzau Barracks, Federal Armed Forces, Boostedt

Gerlinde Beck, "Doppelstele", 1965/1969, Wilhelmsburg Barracks, Federal Armed Forces, Ulm

Hans Eickworth, "Denkmal eines Soldaten", 1967, GDR military headquarters, Berlin

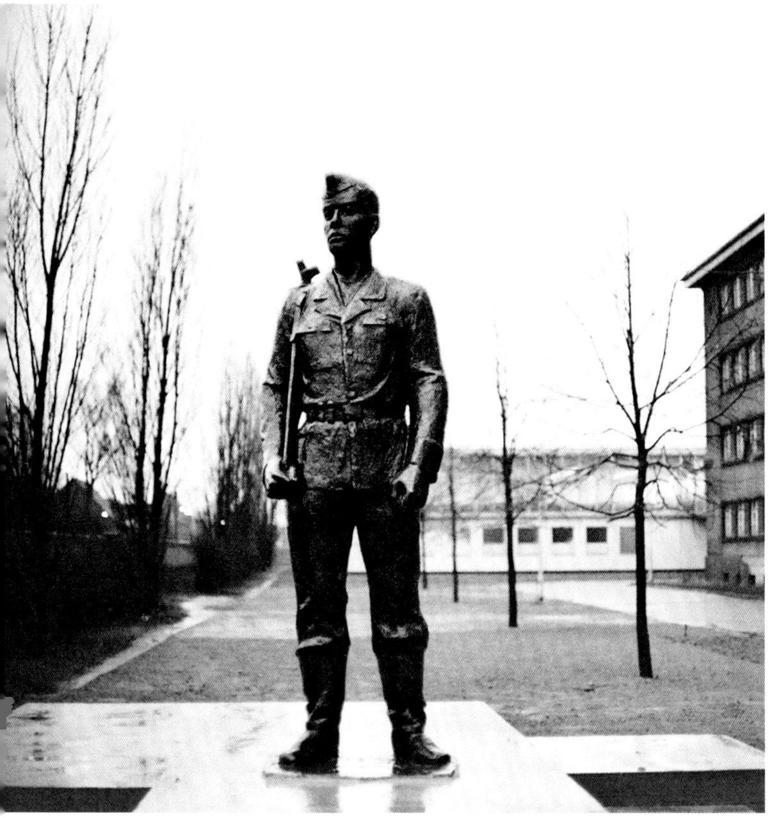

in terms of its dimensions and materiality. The jury praised the harmonious, balanced form, which alludes to the themes of tension and discipline, as well as a certain mobility and freedom.

Art in architecture also formed a natural element of buildings produced for the GDR's armed forces, which were founded in 1956. However, the artworks were aimed at educating the soldiers on a national duty to become "Socialist soldier personalities". One of the earliest works commissioned by the NVA is the monumental painting "Fahneneid" ("Oath of allegiance") produced by Harald Thiel (1931–2002) in 1962 for the 7th Tank Division (→ p. 234). It refers to a new oath of allegiance introduced in 1962, which not only confirmed the duty to defend the GDR and unquestioning loyalty to one's military superiors, but also included the oath to fight alongside Soviet and allied armies against all enemies of Socialism.

The extent to which the NVA continued to develop into a key pillar of GDR society can be seen in the numerous prestigious bronze statues of armed soldiers that were placed in public spaces in the 1960s and 1970s. One such example is the 1967 monument by Hans Eickworth (born in 1930) of a soldier in front of the East Berlin military headquarters: the soldier is characterised as a member of the NVA border troops, shouldering a Kalashnikov rifle, which had been standard issue in the Red Army since 1949.

The largest and most important NVA location was in Strausberg, Brandenburg, which had already been a major Prussian garrison town since the 18th century. From 1954 onwards, a former air base of the Wehrmacht in Strausberg Nord was used as the headquarters of the Volkspolizei ("People's Police") barracks. In 1956, it was converted and expanded to accommodate the GDR Ministry of National

Defence. At the same time, the Hugo Eberlein Guard Regiment was stationed in the south of Strausberg. It was responsible for the military security of the Ministry of National Defence and later in 1957 also the command centre of NVA air defence forces. The extension of the Lambert Horn Barracks (today's Barnim Barracks) included the installation of a bronze group of figures entitled "Waffenbrüder" ("Brothers in arms", 1970) by Gerhard Thieme (1928–2018), a motif that was widespread in a similar form at many other NVA locations, demonstrating the GDR's solidarity with the Soviet Union (→ p. 236). The artwork presents a conversation between a German and a Russian pilot, as is recognisable through their uniforms. The Russian officer uses a sweeping gesture to describe a landing manoeuvre to the GDR pilot.

THE 1970s: INTERNATIONALISATION

The 1970s were largely defined by a policy of détente between the two power blocs. Very soon after taking office as Federal Chancellor, Willy Brandt's symbolic kneeling gesture in Warsaw ushered in a new alignment of German policy towards the East, with the aim of easing tensions with Moscow and other Warsaw Pact states. There was also a recognisable transformation in the field of art in architecture for military facilities in the Federal Republic during this period: in the 1970s, internationally active artists were increasingly selected for central Bundeswehr facilities with a national status, thereby reflecting the Bundeswehr's self-perception as an army for peace that is integrated within the NATO alliance. The guiding principle of a "citizen in uniform" had applied since the Bundeswehr's foundation,

Günter Fruhtrunk, untitled, 1976, Bundeswehr University Munich, Neubiberg

Tomitaro Nachi, untitled, 1977, "am Fliegerhorst" Bundeswehr Air Force Officer Training School, Fürstenfeldbruck

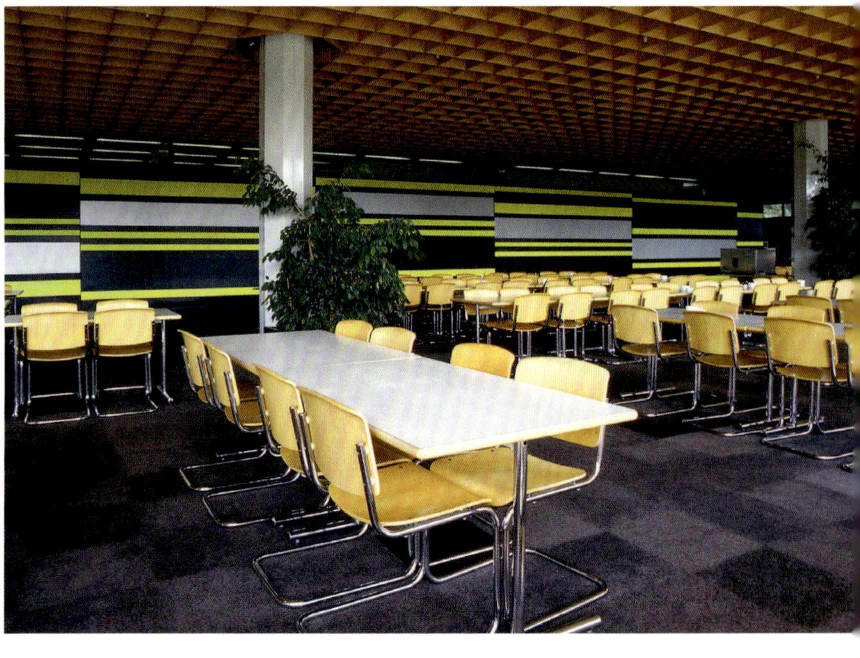

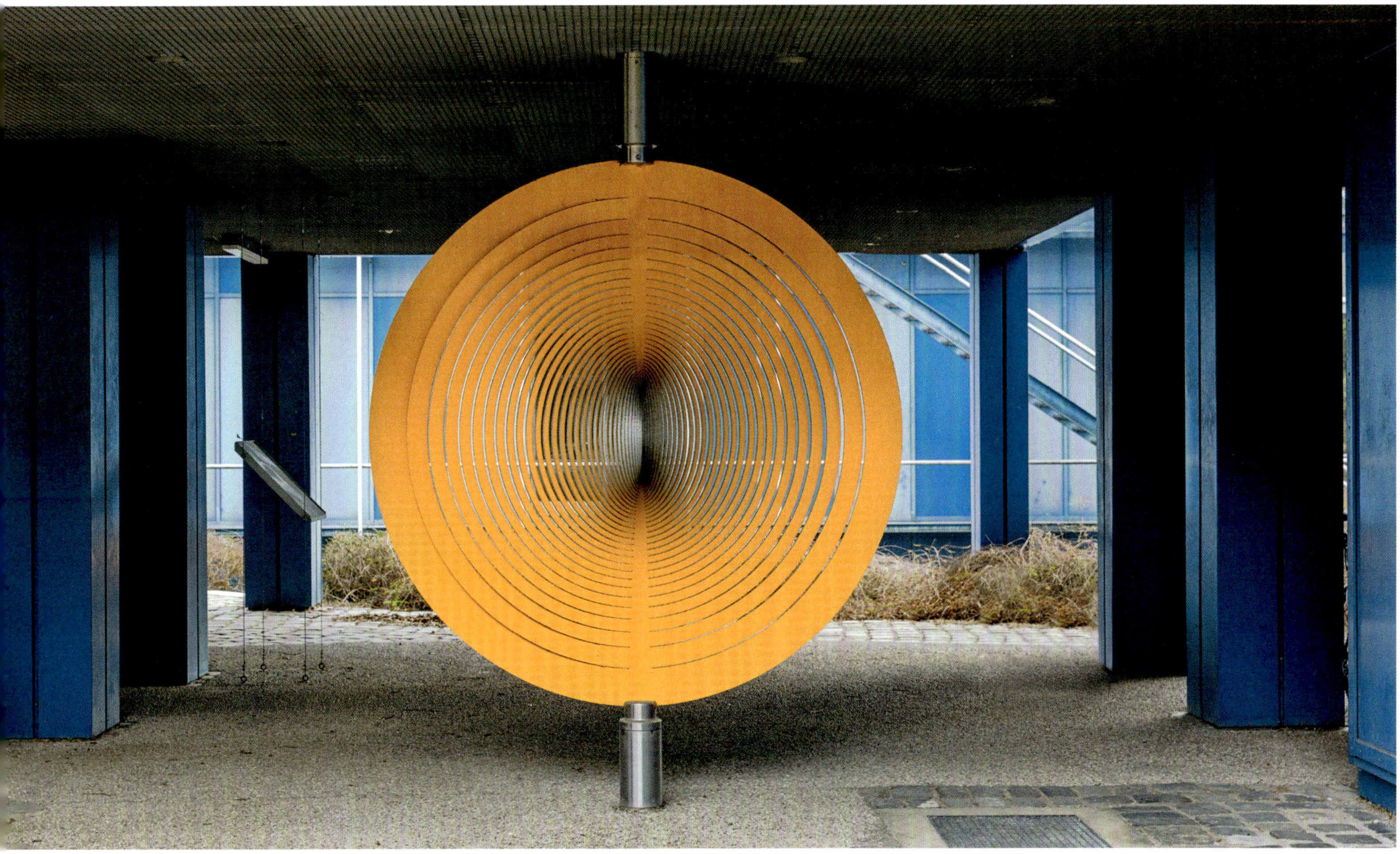

because the role of the Wehrmacht during World War II had shown that soldiers must not be blind recipients of orders and should instead follow their consciences, acting with insight and conviction. Helmut Schmidt, the Defence Minister of the time, believed that military training had to be combined with communicating humanist values and cultural education, thus initiating the foundation of the two Bundeswehr universities in Hamburg (1973–1977) and Munich (1974–1978). Both were decorated with an "educational collection" of high-profile graphic art, as well as receiving art in architecture by renowned artists in an effort to educate the training soldiers in contemporary artistic positions.

When selecting art in architecture, in addition to the educational aspect, public awareness of the artistic programme also played an important role. Many of the artists had presented works at the *documenta* in Kassel or the Biennale in Venice, were professors or had won international prizes. Above all, the contemporary style of concrete art characterised the art in architecture for the Bundeswehr universities, which received works by renowned artists such as Günter Fruhtrunk (1923–1982), Erich Hauser (1930–2004), Alf Lechner (1925–2017), Heinz Mack (born in 1931), François Morellet (1926–1916) (→ p. 238), Georg Karl Pfahler (1926–2002) and Kenneth Snelson (1927–2016). Important pieces by renowned national and international protagonists of contemporary art movements were also implemented elsewhere in the FRG. For instance the Japanese artist Tomitaro Nachi (1924–2007) produced several innovative kinetic sculptures for the Air Force Officer Training School in Fürstenfeldbruck (1975–1977), while the Belgian Panamarenko (1940–2019) created a flying object, the Swiss Karl Gerstner (1930–2017) produced a coloured steel sculpture and the Ulm-based artist Herbert Oehm (born in 1935) developed a land-art piece for the building.

Land art was often implemented for military buildings, including the large-scale art landscape developed by Georg Karl Pfahler in 1979 for the Bundeswehr hospital in Ulm (1974–1979) (→ p. 240). Another example from 1978 is the land-art piece entitled "Connection" by James Reineking (1937–2018) for the Military Police School and the Bundeswehr's administrative offices in Hanover.

The location of the Federal Ministry of Defence at the Hardthöhe in the south of Bonn was developed over a period of 40 years. The core of the facility is the barracks building, which was originally constructed in 1956 as a "1000-Mann-Kaserne" ("Barracks for 1,000 men"). It is orientated towards the local housing, both in terms of its architecture and its urban planning, thereby entirely conforming to the new principles of democracy at the time. In 1960, when the Ministry of Defence moved from the Ermekeil Barracks in the south of Bonn to the Hardthöhe, the barracks began being converted into a ministry location. It received its functional centre with the construction of the central area between 1979 and 1987 according to plans by Planungsgruppe Groth Lehmann Walter. The new building for the southern mess and ministry wing was constructed between 1986 and 1997 by the architect and artist Johannes Peter Hölzinger (born in 1936), thereby concluding the measures. In 1989, Hölzinger also developed a visual wayfinding system for the expansive central area, giving each of the eight building sections, which were grouped around three inner courtyards, a colour from the spectrum blue-green-yellow and yellow-red-violet. These tones acted as pure colour markings, but also combined with objects consisting of angular, wavy,

Johannes Peter Hölzinger, visual wayfinding system (angular, wavy, half-shell and spiral forms and combinations), 1989, Federal Ministry of Defence, Bonn

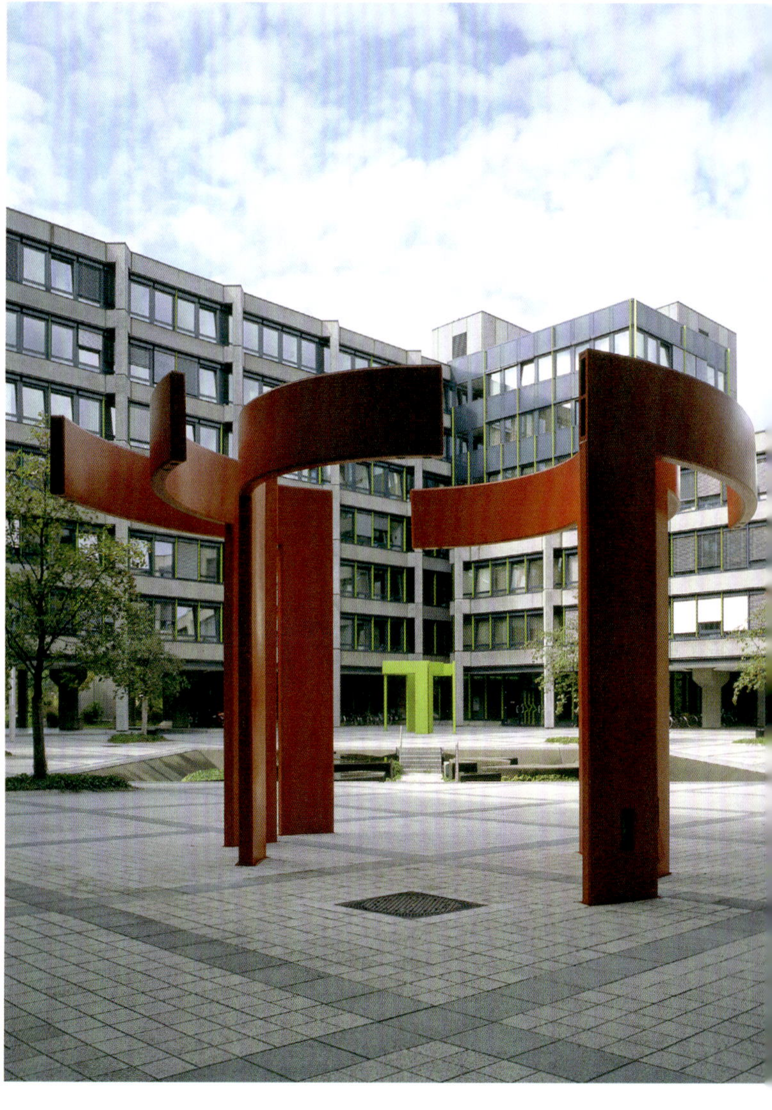

half-shell and spiral forms to improve orientation on the grounds. Hölzinger also developed an overall artistic concept that defined specific places for art in architecture, especially to support functional references such as guidance to specific facilities. The result is a collaboration between Johannes Peter Hölzinger and the competition winners Eberhard Fiebig (born in 1930), Leonardo Mosso (born in 1926), Norbert Müller-Everling (born in 1953), Ansgar Nierhoff (1941–2010) and the artist group Formalhaut led by Ottmar Hörl (born in 1950), as well as the architects Gabriela Seifert and Götz Stöckmann. It achieves an exceptional artistic interaction between art, architecture and the landscape to create a "synthèse des arts".

THE 1980s AND 1990s: FROM THE NEW PEACE MOVEMENT TO REUNIFICATION

In 1979, the NATO double-track decision to expand its nuclear arsenal while also making an offer to the Warsaw Pact to limit its nuclear weapons, introduced a decade that saw peace protests throughout Europe and North America. The themes of "war" and "peace" were also reflected in the art in architecture of the 1980s, whereby artists increasingly produced figurative, narrative works. Examples include the "Friedensbrunnen" ("Fountain of peace", 1982) by Jürgen Goertz (born in 1939) for the Bundeswehr Technical College in Karlsruhe, and the piece "Steinzeitung, Ruhende Nachricht" ("Stone newspaper, dormant news", 1982) by the artist couple Wolfgang Kubach (1936–2007) and Anna Maria Kubach-Wilmsen (born in 1937) for the exterior grounds of the Cambridge Dragoon Barracks in Celle. In 1981/1982, Eberhard Linke (born in 1937) produced a group of sculptures entitled "Gespräch zwischen den Blöcken" ("Dialogue between the blocks") for the Heinrich der Löwe Barracks in Braunschweig that visually expressed communication during the Cold War (→ p. 242). The sculpture "Mann mit abwehrender Geste" ("Man with defensive gesture", 1982) by Waldemar Otto (born in 1929) in front of the Theodor Körner Barracks in Lüneburg presents a naked, unprotected man, reflecting the precarious condition of human existence.

During this period, in addition to figurative sculpture, there was also a trend towards artworks that became an integral part of their environment. An art in architecture competition announced in 1980 for the Federal Academy for Defence Administration and Defence Technology in Mannheim required a concept for the artistic design of the forecourt, entrance area and foyer of the large lecture theatre, creating "a system of artistic objects [...] to compose a spatially permeating score". Erich Hauser (1930–2004) was successful with his proposal for a two-piece work consisting of an arrow-like form made of Corten steel on the forecourt and its artistic counterpart on the glass foyer roof. The two sculptures comment on the architecture in contrary ways: one appears to deconstruct the building, while the other almost merges with it. Furthermore, they enter into a dialogue with the work on the forecourt. Hauser, who became renowned above all through his steel sculptures in public spaces, created a complex and multifaceted work in Mannheim.

A wide range of integral works were also conceived for interior areas, such as the piece by Georg Engst (born in 1930) produced in 1986 for the dining room of the Feldwebel Lilienthal Barracks in Delmenhorst-Adelheide. It consists of a large-scale tectonic ceiling relief made of geometric forms, giving the room a sculptural character. On the other hand, numerous functional designs were also produced, for instance in 1988/89 for the Hohenberg Barracks in Horb am Neckar, where Mathias Ohndorf (born in 1934) designed an area at the centre of the barracks with large geometric patterns in white and yellow tones in tarmac, a bitumen-like road surface. In doing so, Ohndorf combined the utilisation of a helipad, where soldiers also paraded, with the aesthetics of an artwork, artistically moving towards an aesthetic environmental design.

Until national service was abandoned in 2011, the district recruiting offices in the Federal Republic had the task of providing replacement personnel for the Bundeswehr. Produced in 1987, the free-standing sculpture by Rainer Stiefvater (born in 1943) in front of the district recruiting office in Freiburg vividly depicts the role model of a citizen in uniform. 26 figures made of cast concrete are arranged in a quadrant, some individually and others grouped together more tightly. The disk-shaped figures gradually differ from one another, as the process of change progresses. Starting with the presentation of a man with a hat and a briefcase, the figures gradually develop in 24 stages into a man with a helmet and a rifle. The attributes define the first figure as a private person and the last figure as a soldier. The title "Metamorphose" ("Metamorphosis") refers to the transformation of a civilian into a "citizen in uniform", and inversely the transition of a soldier into a civilian.

One of the last major building measures by the NVA before the dissolution of the GDR was the new construction of the International Conference Centre of the Ministry of National Defence in Strausberg. Numerous artworks were commissioned for the development, including the large-scale mural consisting of painted Meissen porcelain by Volkmar

Erich Hauser, untitled, 1980/1981, Federal Academy for Defence Administration and Defence Technology, Mannheim

Georg Engst, ceiling sculpture, 1986, Feldwebel Lilienthal Barracks, Federal Armed Forces, Delmenhorst-Adelheide

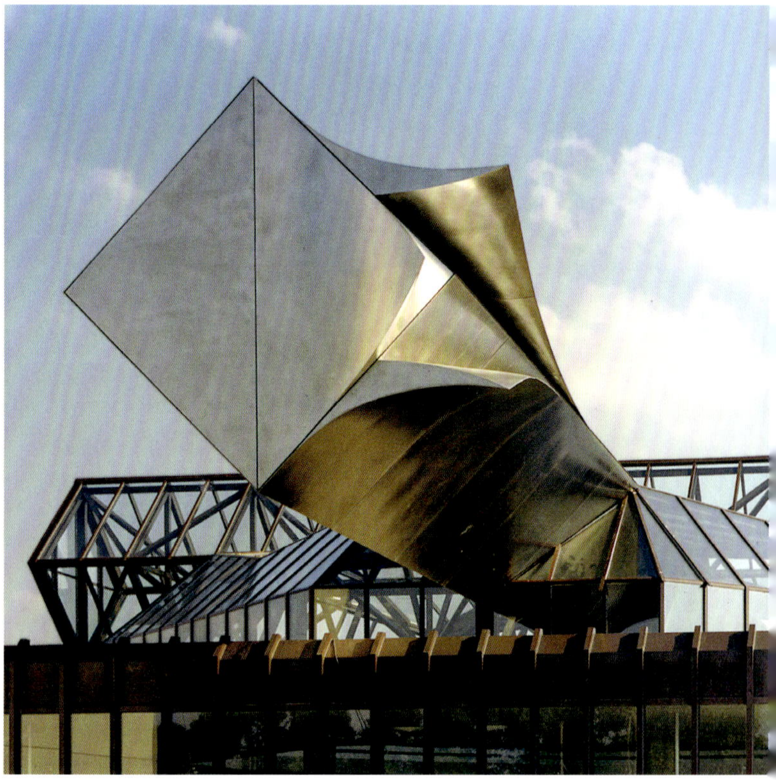

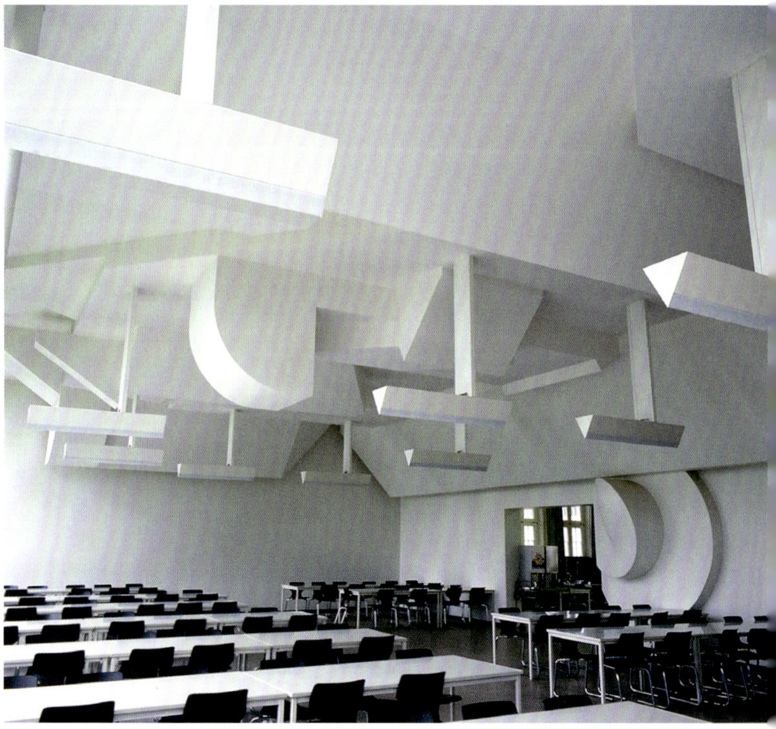

Bretschneider (born in 1930) and Heinz Werner (1928–2019), which was produced in 1985 and is not only impressive due to its 3 x 9 metre dimensions. Against the backdrop of a red flag that envelops the world, the founding fathers of the official GDR state ideology, Karl Marx, Friedrich Engels and Vladimir Ilyich Lenin, remind soldiers of their "Socialist conscience" and the importance of defending "Marxism-Leninism".

Following German reunification, the NVA was dissolved on October 2, 1990 and its personnel, equipment and real estate was incorporated into the Bundeswehr. However, the Two-Plus-Four Agreement of 1990/1991 stipulated a defence force in the united Germany of no more than 370,000 soldiers, leading to a fundamental structural reform of the armed forces. This not only led to a rigorous reduction in personnel, but also to the closure of numerous military facilities. The situation became even more acute when national service was abandoned in 2011. Thus, little new art in architecture has been produced for military buildings since 1990. Two important artworks were commissioned as part of the government's move to the capital, where the Federal Ministry of Defence established its second headquarters: the photo installation by Renate Anger (born in 1947) entitled "Ein Falter" ("A butterfly", 2002) and the "Roter Teppich" ("Red carpet", 2003) by Via Lewandowsky (born in 1963) (→ p. 170) specifically engage with the historical architecture and the tasks of the ministry.

As a result of the Bundeswehr's new orientation since 1990, there has been an increasing trend towards establishing focus centres. For instance the Kommando Spezialkräfte (Special Commando Forces, KSK) were stationed in Calw, Baden-Württemberg (→ p. 244), while Rostock was developed to become the

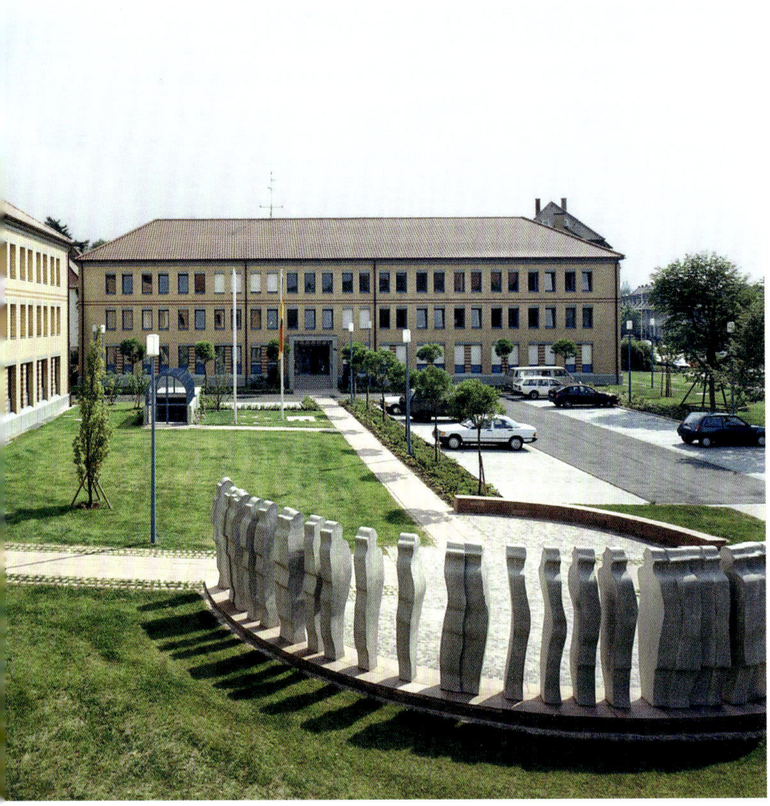

Rainer Stiefvater, "Metamorphose", 1987, District Recruiting Office, Freiburg

navy headquarters. The "Walter Steffens" navy school in Parow near Stralsund was transformed into the largest and most modern training facility of the German Navy, making it the Bundeswehr's most extensive investment project in the region of the former GDR. A large-scale, Europe-wide, open art in architecture competition was announced for the Navy Technical College, which was built in three stages until 2003. The winning entry from among the 250 participating artists was proposed by the artist group Inges Idee, consisting of Hans Hemmert (born in 1960), Axel Lieber (born in 1960), Thomas A. Schmidt (born in 1960) and Georg Zey (born in 1962). In 2001, they developed two pieces that take an ironic, humorous stance towards the tasks of a navy school: an oversized toy boat is placed on the lawn in front of the officers' mess, as if stranded. For the interior, a collection of mineral water bottles is exhibited in display cases like ships in a bottle.

Other locations were closed or converted, such as the Steigerwald Barracks in Erfurt, which has accommodated the Behördenzentrum des Bundes (Federal Administration Centre) since 2015. The measures involved renovating the original 1930s building and improving its energy performance. The art in architecture for the main customs office was produced by Daniel Priese and is entitled "Nebelhörner/Foghorns". The piece was the winning entry from among 101 proposals in a national, open art competition.

The art in architecture for military buildings is characterised by high artistic value that need not shy away from comparison with art in architecture for civilian federal buildings. Above all with respect to their thematic statements, formal accomplishment and spatial references, the artists have continuously provided impressive artistic responses to the given situations, thereby enhancing the architectural experience and strengthening identification with the institution. While figurative works dominated in the 1950s and 1960s, the 1970s reflected the ascendancy of the internationally prevalent abstract art movements. In the 1980s, strongly narrative works were produced in the context of Postmodernism, while integral art projects were also implemented. Since the 1990s, diverse conceptual artworks have been realised with a strong connection to the structural and institutional environment, as well as the people who work there.

Inges Idee, "Im selben Boot", 2001/2003, Parow Navy Training School, Kramerhof

Daniel Priese, "Foghorns", 2014, Federal Administration Centre "am Steigerwald", main customs office, formerly Steigerwald Barracks, Erfurt

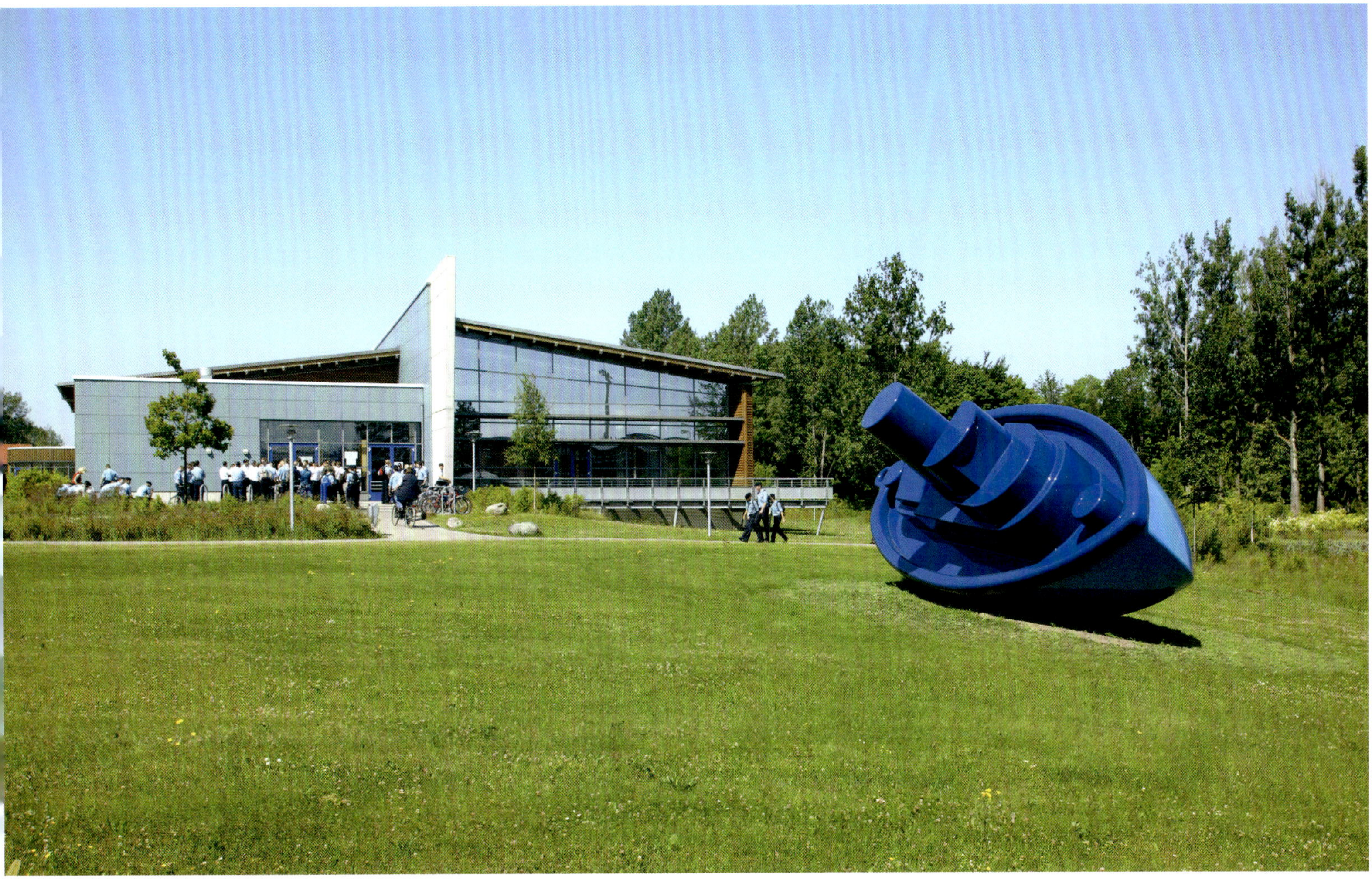

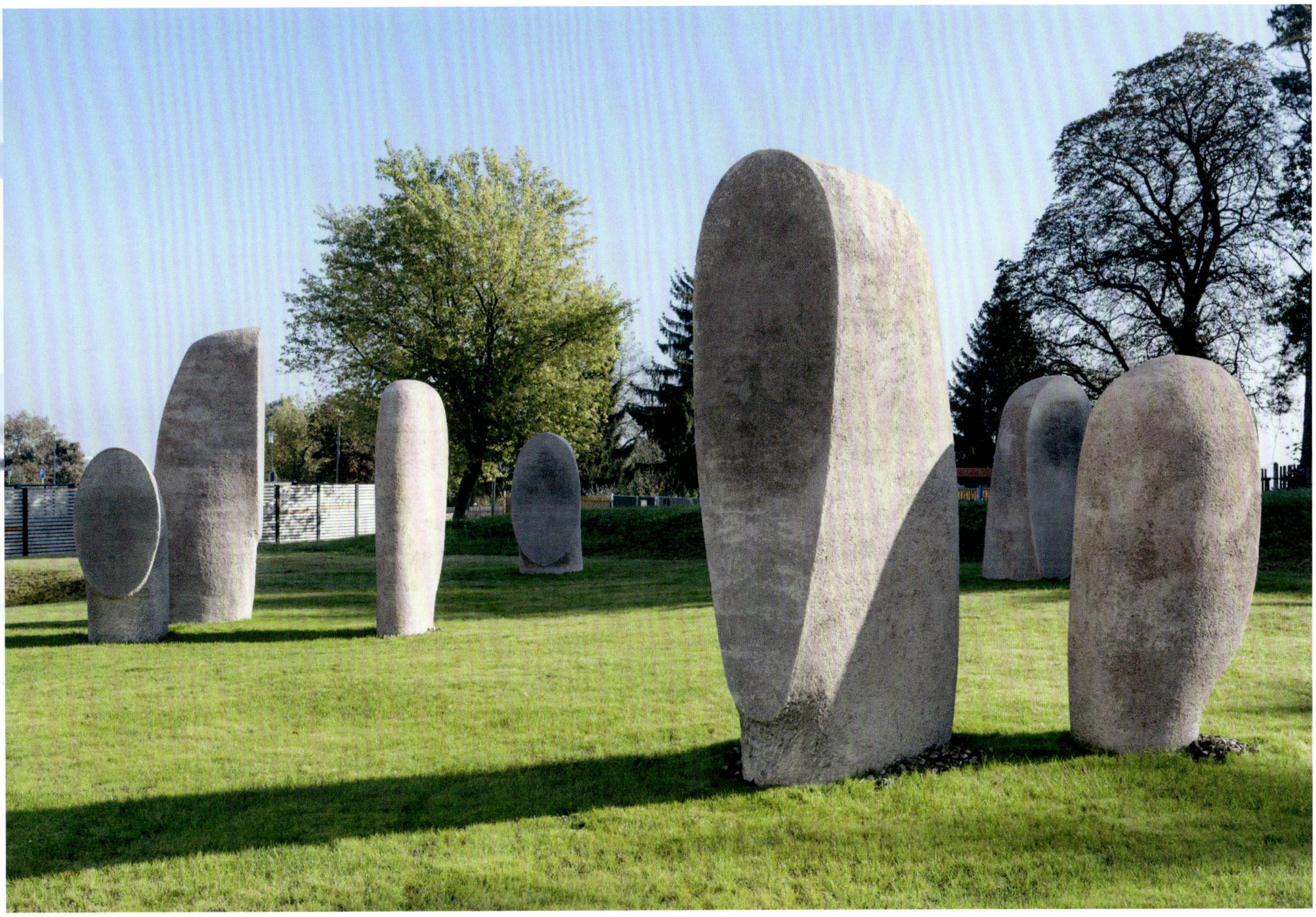

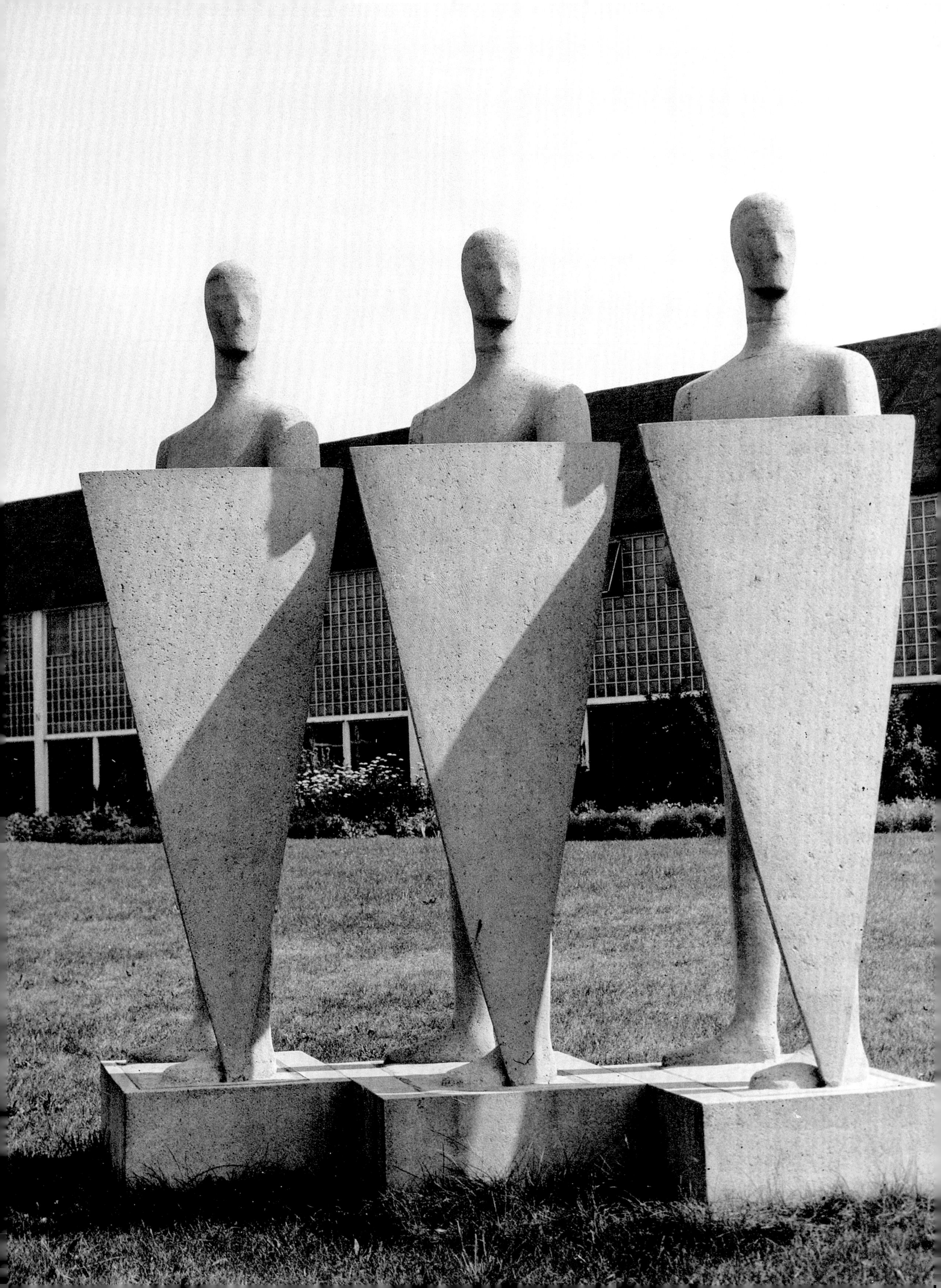

STEUBEN BARRACKS BUNDESWEHR ACHIM

TODAY HOUSING ESTATE

Address:
28832 Achim

Architecture:
Landesbauleitung Hannover, Bauleitung Achim, 1956–1959

Art in architecture:
Jean Sprenger

The former Steuben Barracks are located at the site of the old fuel oil stores for the Imperial Navy during World War I. Between 1956 and 1959, the existing buildings were extended by two three-storey pavilions for the Bundeswehr. During those measures, a free-standing sculpture by the artist Jean Sprenger (1912–1980) was installed on the exterior grounds in 1959. Standing upright and looking into the distance, the "Three warriors with shields" herald the beginnings of the still young Bundeswehr in a new era following the end of National Socialism. Their upright body language is enhanced by the triangular shields, points to the ground, which are held in a protective gesture. The sculptor thereby expresses both self-defence and vulnerability, as symbolised by the nakedness of the male figures. Although the mode of presentation has its roots in the naturalism of the early 20th century, the sculpture's style and cement material also conveys modernity and contemporality.

Sprenger became renowned for his design of the music theatre in Gelsenkirchen and his portrait busts of famous figures from the worlds of economics, politics and sport, including Konrad Adenauer and members of the family Krupp von Bohlen und Halbach.

JEAN SPRENGER
"Drei Krieger mit Schild"
("Three warriors with shields"), 1959
Cement

7TH TANK DIVISION NATIONALE VOLKSARMEE DRESDEN

TODAY
ONGOING CONVERSION

Address:
Albertstadt Barracks
01099 Dresden

Art in architecture:
Harald Thiel

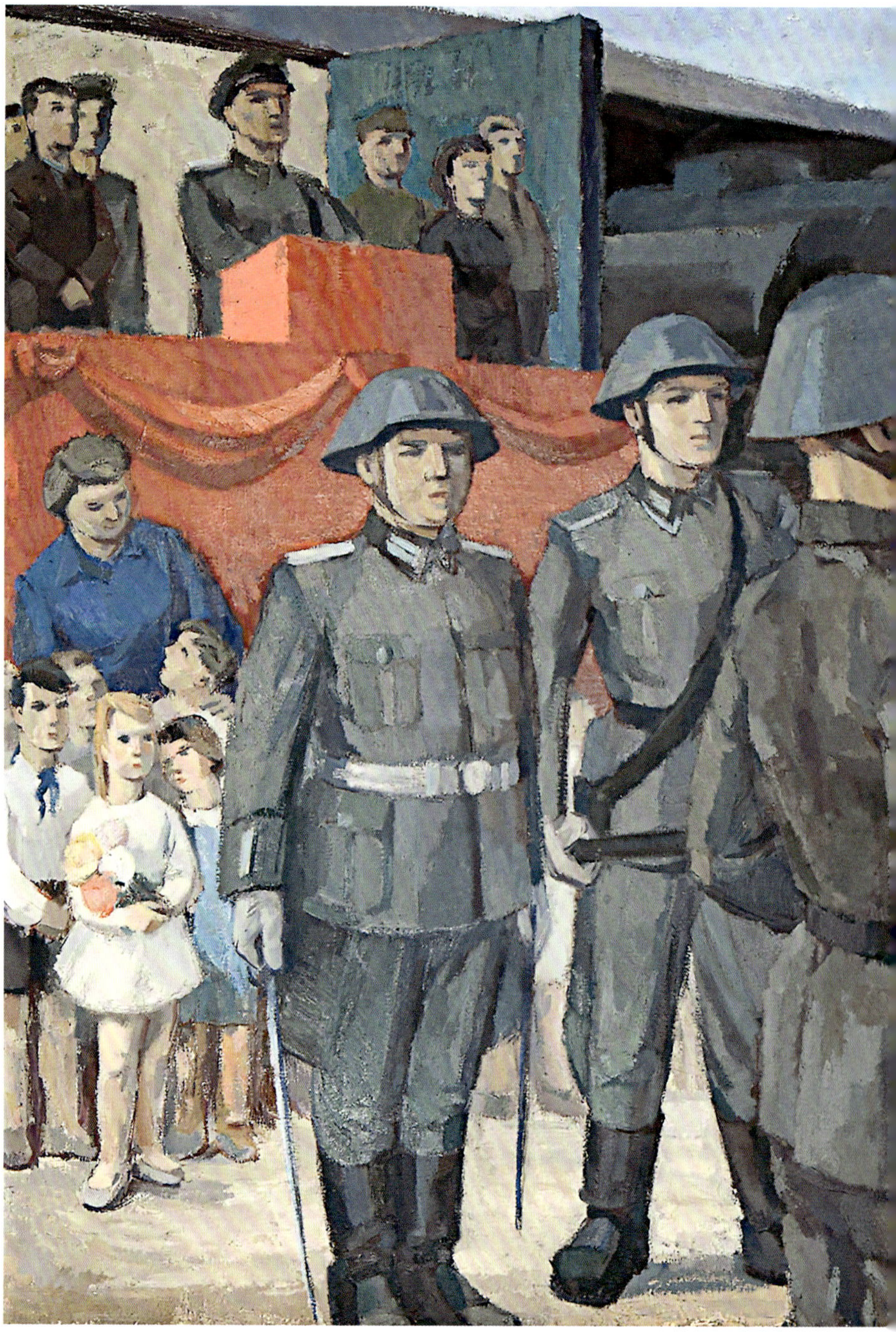

HARALD THIEL
"Fahneneid"
("Oath of allegiance"), 1962
Oil on canvas
165 x 320 cm
(now stored at the Militär-historisches Museum Dresden)

The Socialist Unity Party of Germany (SED) not only used the Nationale Volksarmee, the GDR's armed forces, to defend the country, but also to consolidate its own claim to power. The armed forces in East Germany were led and controlled by the SED, which expected a high awareness of ideological duty from its soldiers. Since the 19th century, one of the largest barracks complexes had existed in the Dresden district of Albertstadt, which is named after King Albert I of Saxony. The Nationale Volksarmee used it to station the staff of its 7th Tank Division, which played a pioneering role within the armed forces and was the first NVA unit for which art in architecture was commissioned. When the painter and graphic designer Harald Thiel (1931–2002) presented the piece entitled "Fahneneid" ("Oath of allegiance") to the 7th Tank Division in April 1962, the shock and indignation at the Berlin Wall's construction

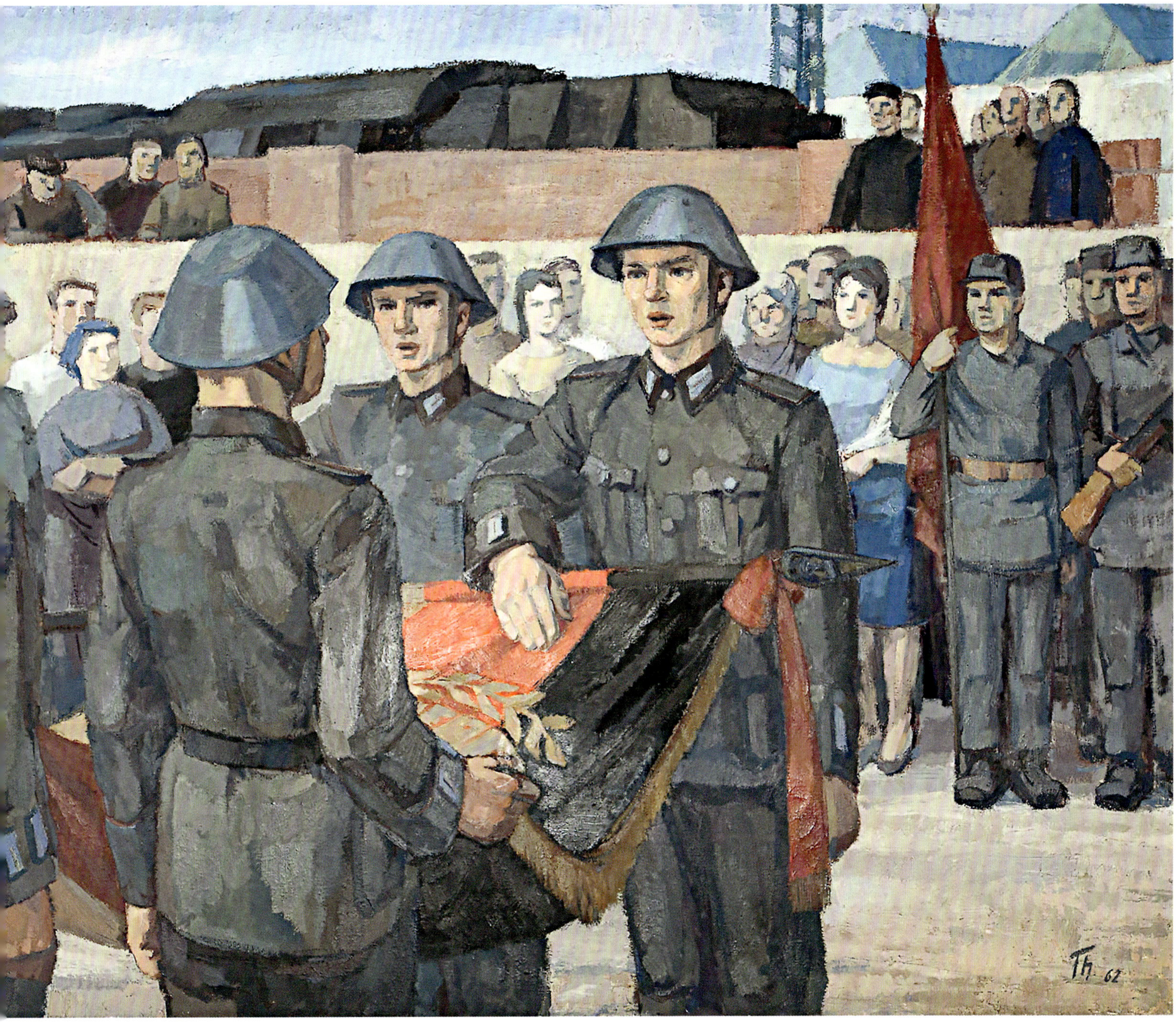

in August 1961 was still fresh in people's minds. Thus the ceremony of the "oath of allegiance" by four NVA soldiers was all the more significant as a guiding image for unconditional submission to the regime. Thiel programmatically set the realist scene in a public space that is observed by party functionaries on a grandstand, as well as a group of children and workers. The painter thereby expresses the armed forces' integration into society, which had been an ongoing socio-political theme since the introduction of universal military service in January 1962. After the NVA was incorporated into the Bundeswehr, the painting was added to the collection of the Militärhistorisches Museum in Dresden.

AIR FORCE AIR DEFENCE COMMAND CENTRE NATIONALE VOLKSARMEE STRAUSBERG

TODAY BARNIM BARRACKS BUNDESWEHR

Address:
Lambert Horn Barracks
(today's Barnim Barracks)
15344 Strausberg

Art in architecture:
Gerhard Thieme

The Nationale Volksarmee was established in the GDR in 1955 under the auspices of the Soviet Union. From the 1960s onwards, it developed into one of the most important state commissioners of visual arts in the GDR. The aim of the policy was to educate combat-ready Socialist "soldier personalities". In terms of content, commissions focused on martial themes such as military solidarity with the Soviet Union, alluding to the importance of the military alliance, as well as the value of the Soviet contribution to the development of the GDR.

The larger-than-life figures of a German and a Soviet pilot were produced by Gerhard Thieme (1928–2018) for the Lambert Horn Barracks in Strausberg, where officers of the air force and the NVA air defence were placed under a single command. The German pilot can be recognised through his pressure suit and a helmet with raised visor. An officer in breeches stands to the right, the star on his cap clearly indicating he is a member of the Soviet armed forces. In the spirit of "Learning from the Soviet Union means learning to win!", he describes a flying manoeuvre with a demonstrative gesture. Thieme repeatedly used the theme of people carrying out their work as the basis for his sculpture. His numerous major works for public spaces in Berlin include figurative representations of an "Aufbauhelferin" ("Development helper"), 1963, a "Bauarbeiter" ("Builder"), 1968, and a "Stahlwerker" ("Steel worker"), 1970, who were presented as symbolic personnel for the development of a Socialist society.

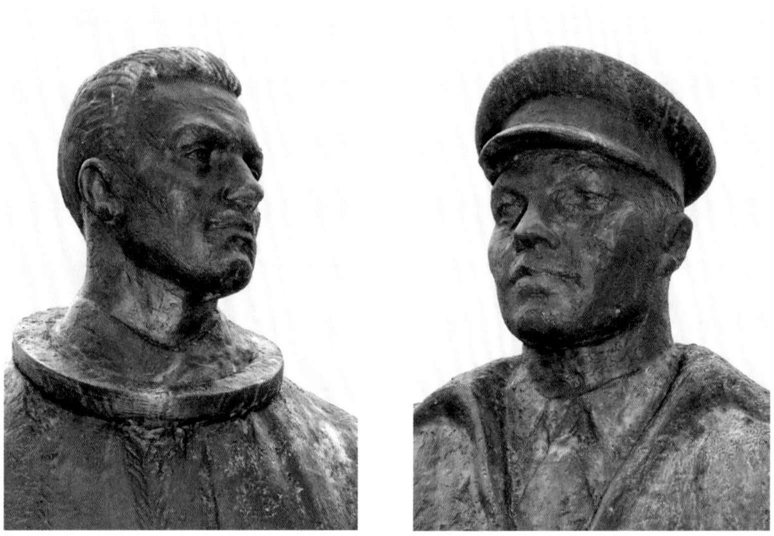

GERHARD THIEME
"Waffenbrüder"
("Brothers in arms"), 1970
Bronze, 250 x 112 x 50 cm
(now displayed at
the Militärhistorisches
Museum Gatow)

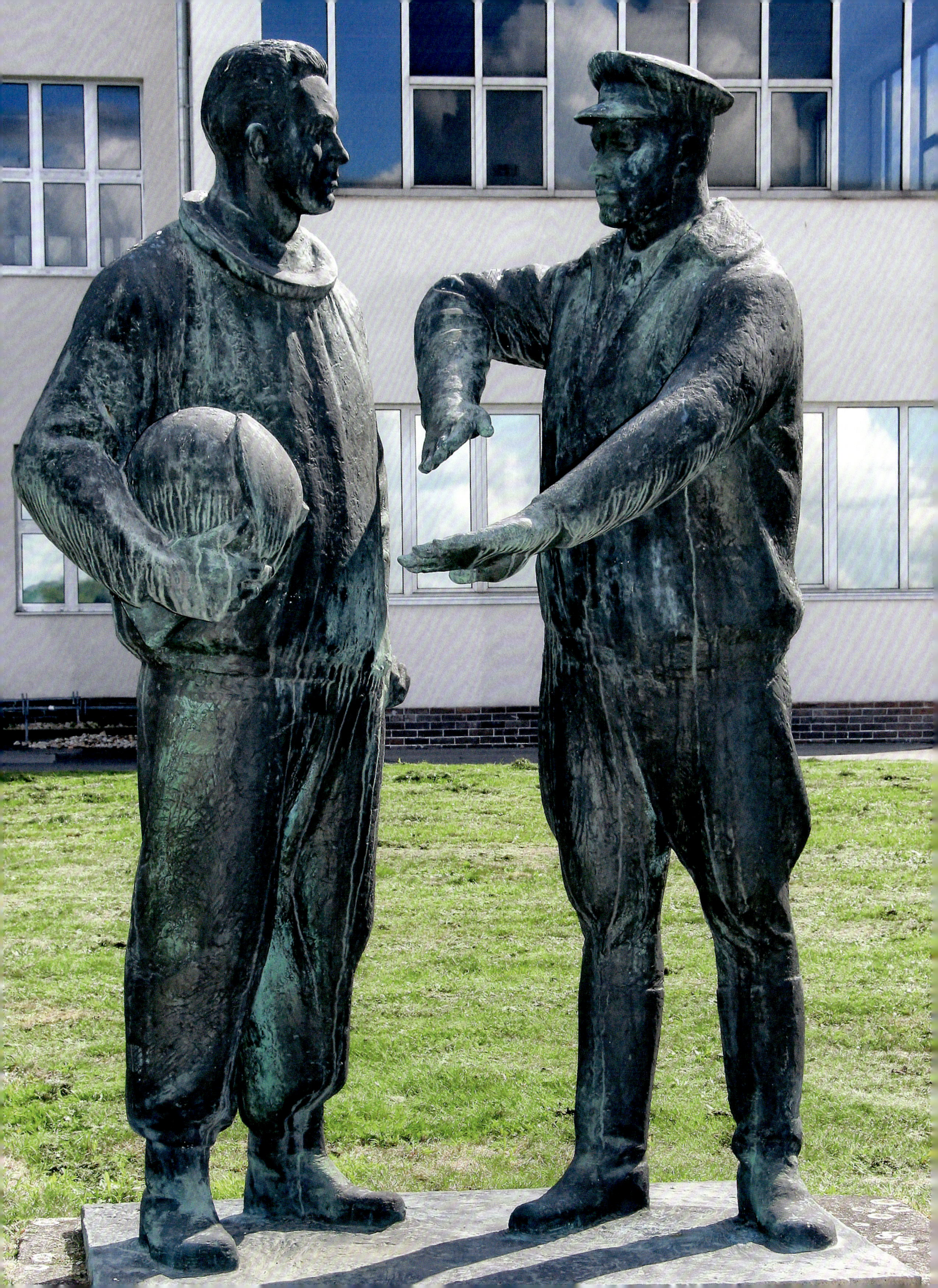

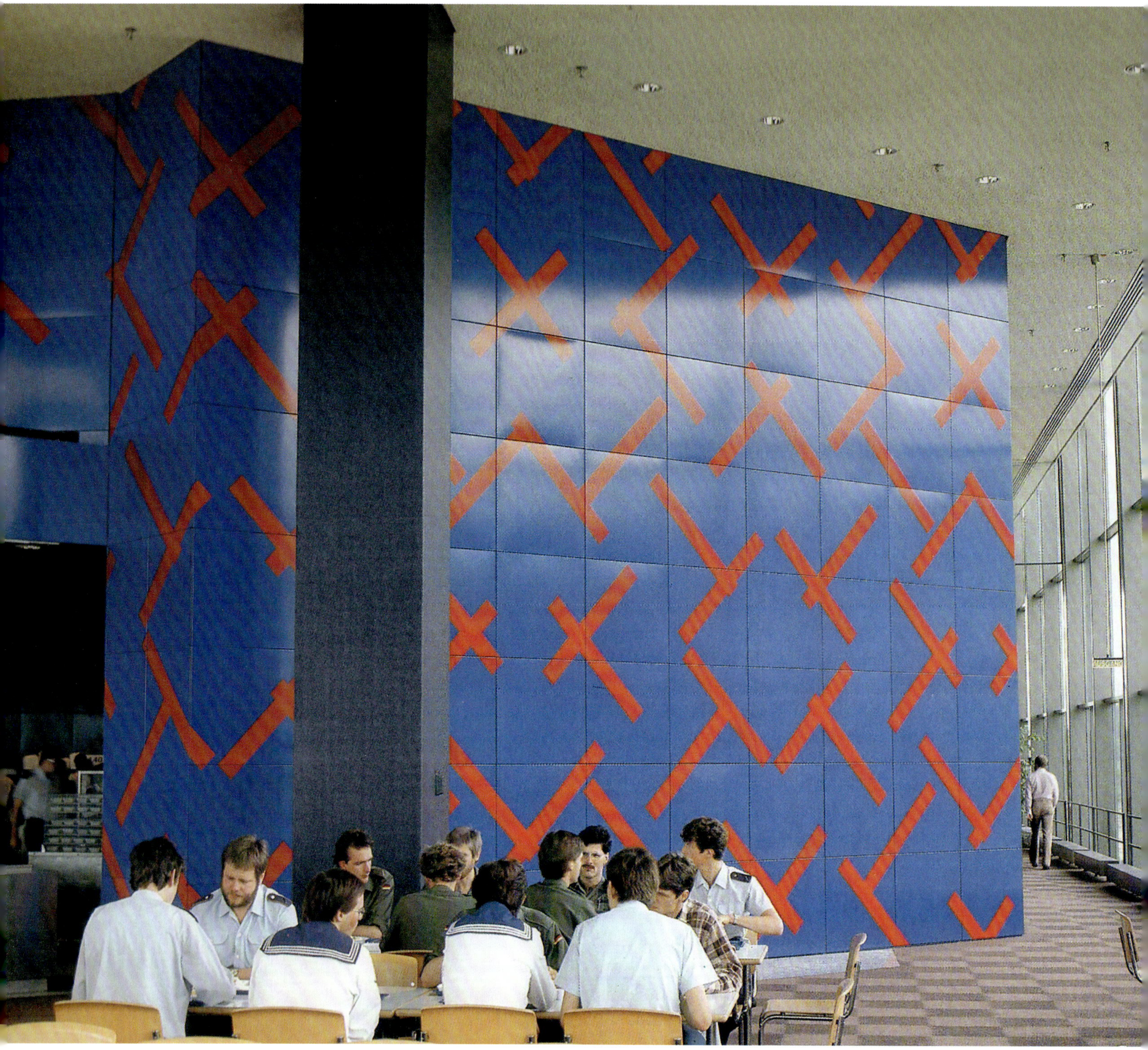

FRANÇOIS MORELLET
All-Over Strukturen
(All-over structures), 1976
Enamel

BUNDESWEHR UNIVERSITY HAMBURG

TODAY THE HELMUT-SCHMIDT-UNIVERSITÄT / UNIVERSITÄT DER BUNDESWEHR, HAMBURG

Address:
Holstenhofweg 85
22043 Hamburg

Architecture:
Heinle, Wischer und Partner, Stuttgart, 1973–1977

Art in architecture:
François Morellet and Alf Lechner, Ansgar Nierhoff, Erich Reusch, Kenneth Snelson

As Minister of Defence, Helmut Schmidt initiated the foundation of two Bundeswehr universities in Germany, which began their academic teaching in Hamburg and Munich in 1973. With this educational offensive, Schmidt picked up on the guiding principle of the internal leadership of the Bundeswehr since its foundation in 1955, namely to define soldiers as "citizens in uniform". A fundamental reorientation of the officers' training, as well as political and ethical education for the armed forces, was aimed not only at promoting autonomous thought and actions, but also at facilitating the fixed-term officers' return to the civilian labour market.

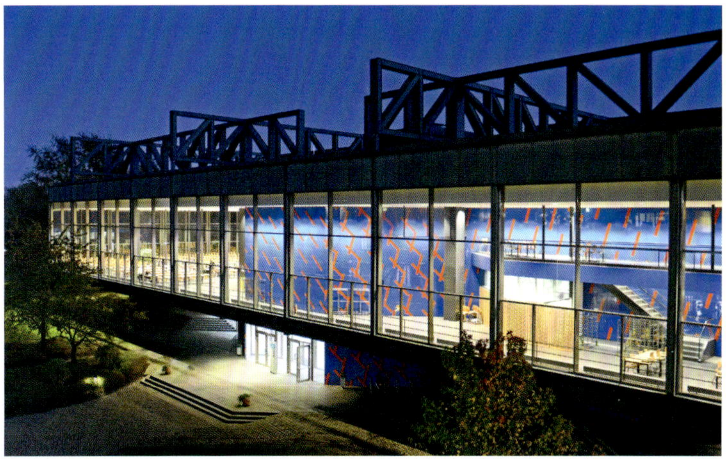

For the Hamburg Campus, the architectural office Heinle, Wischer und Partner designed an ensemble of 16 pavilions embedded in a large-scale, publicly accessible green area. The striking roof construction of the pavilions, with its exterior load-bearing structure, enables a form of architecture without walls, thereby reflecting the university's principles of openness and transparency. Through the floor-level windows of the canteen in one of the pavilions, one can already see the striking blue and red interior design from outside. The wall cladding made of enamelled steel sheeting by François Morellet (1926–2016) addresses the context of the all-over principle, with which the artist continuously experimented from 1950 onwards. The renowned French protagonist of concrete art developed various systems of stringing together, overlapping and fragmenting forms and surfaces out of potentially infinite structures that extend beyond the limits of the image. The design by Morellet for the Hamburg university impressed the competition jury through its translation of the architecture's orthogonal and octagonal elements in a unique rhythm that enables a wide range of visual impressions in the dining hall.

BUNDESWEHR HOSPITAL ULM

Address:
Oberer Eselsberg 40
89081 Ulm

Architecture:
Heinle, Wischer und Partner, Stuttgart, 1974–1979

Art in architecture:
Georg Karl Pfahler and Alfonso Hüppi, Christa Rembold-Hauff, Max Schmitz

The Bundeswehr Hospital in Ulm, which was built according to plans by the Stuttgart architectural office Heinle, Wischer und Partner, provides out- and inpatient treatment to members of the Bundeswehr and civilian patients, while also being used to train the Bundeswehr's medical personnel. The Federal Ministry of Defence provided DM 1.5 million for its art in architecture. The art concept was developed by the Art Committee of the Oberfinanzdirektion Karlsruhe, which was chaired by the artist Max Bill, based on a proposal by the planning architects. Works by Georg Karl Pfahler (1926–2002) and Max Schmitz (born in 1936) were installed on the exterior grounds. The theme of the "Swabian Jura", with its gentle slopes and sweeping forms, had already been defined during the building's construction and inspired Pfahler to conceive a piece of land art. He inserted five landscape-related, cast concrete sculptures into the modelled grounds, covering them with blue acrylic paint. The objects are two and a half metres high and between eight and 20 metres long. The colours and forms of the sculptures are inspired by natural features such as clouds, rivers and mountains. At the same time, they retain their autonomous aesthetics through the striking blue and green colour contrast.

In the 1960s, Georg Karl Pfahler became internationally renowned as a hard-edge painter. From 1965 onwards, he focused on spatial colour projects and switched from fictitious colour areas on a two-dimensional level to real, three-dimensional spaces. For the hospital in Ulm, he developed this idea into a walkable, tangible colour space that directly addresses the specific target group of patients and visitors.

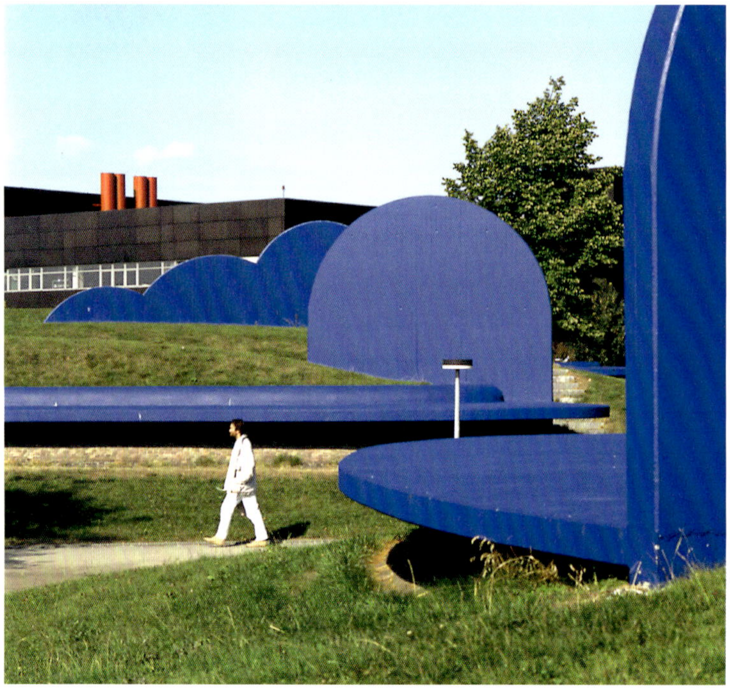

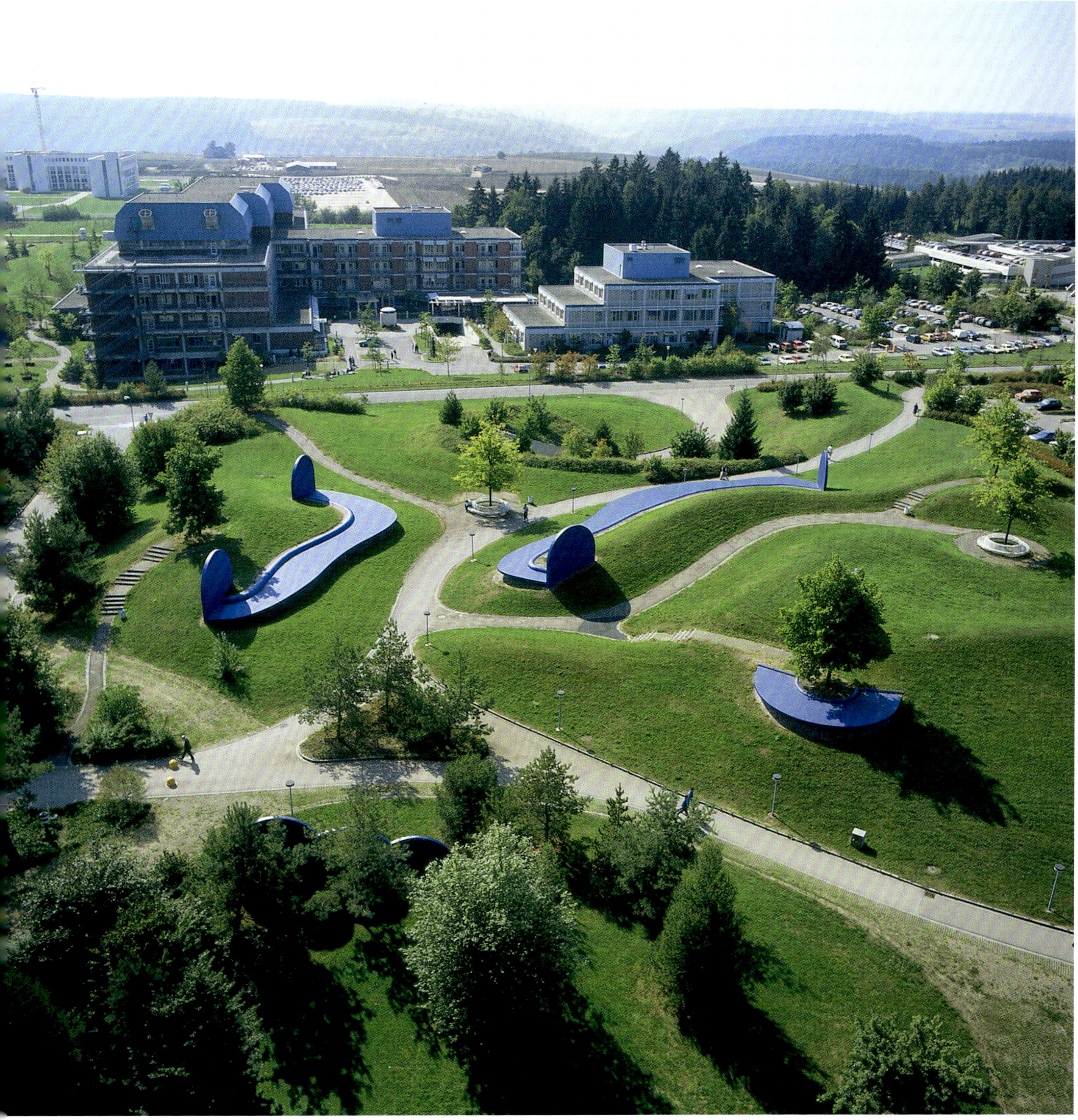

GEORG KARL PFAHLER
Untitled, 1979–1982
Cast concrete with blue acrylic paint

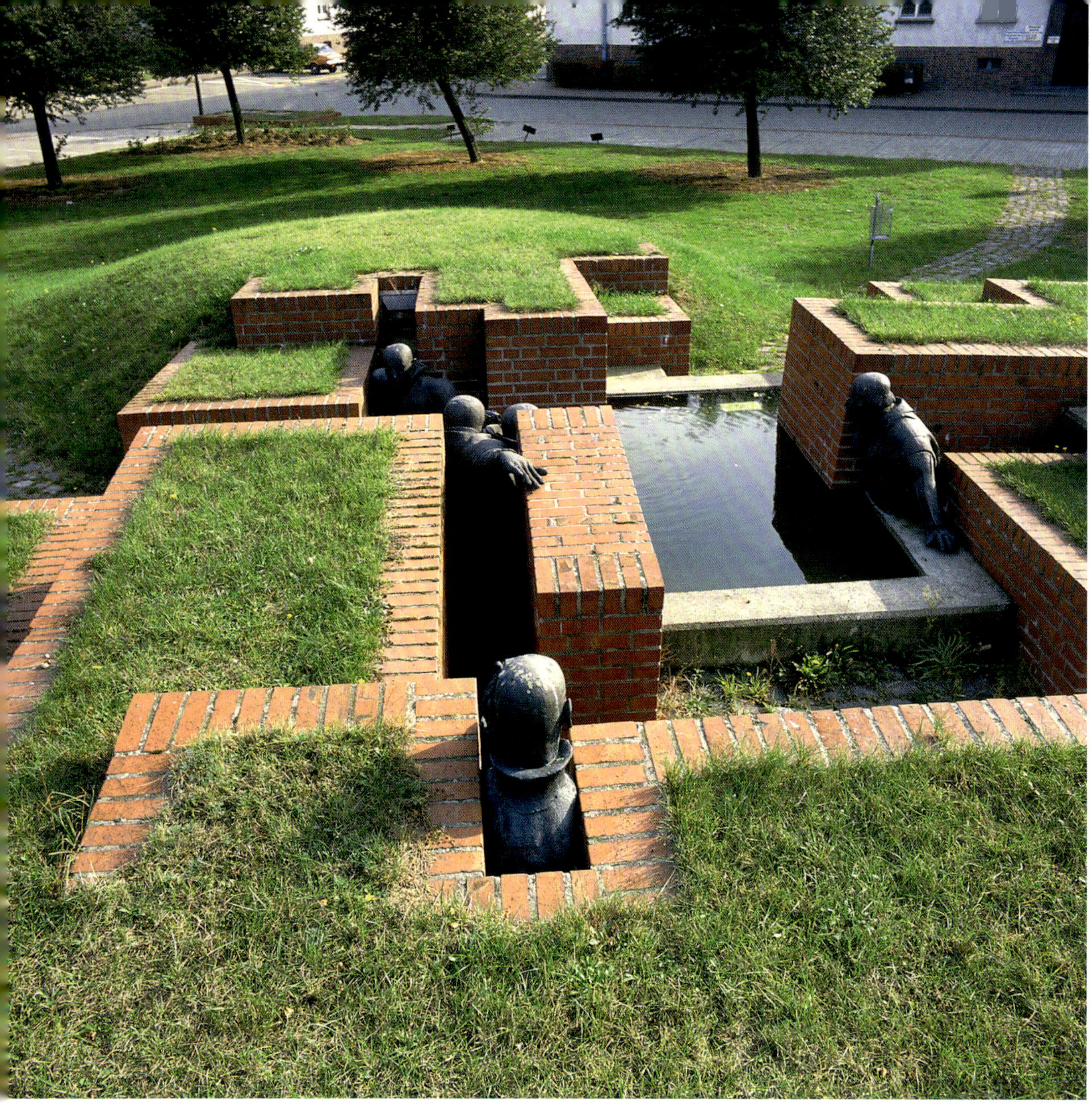

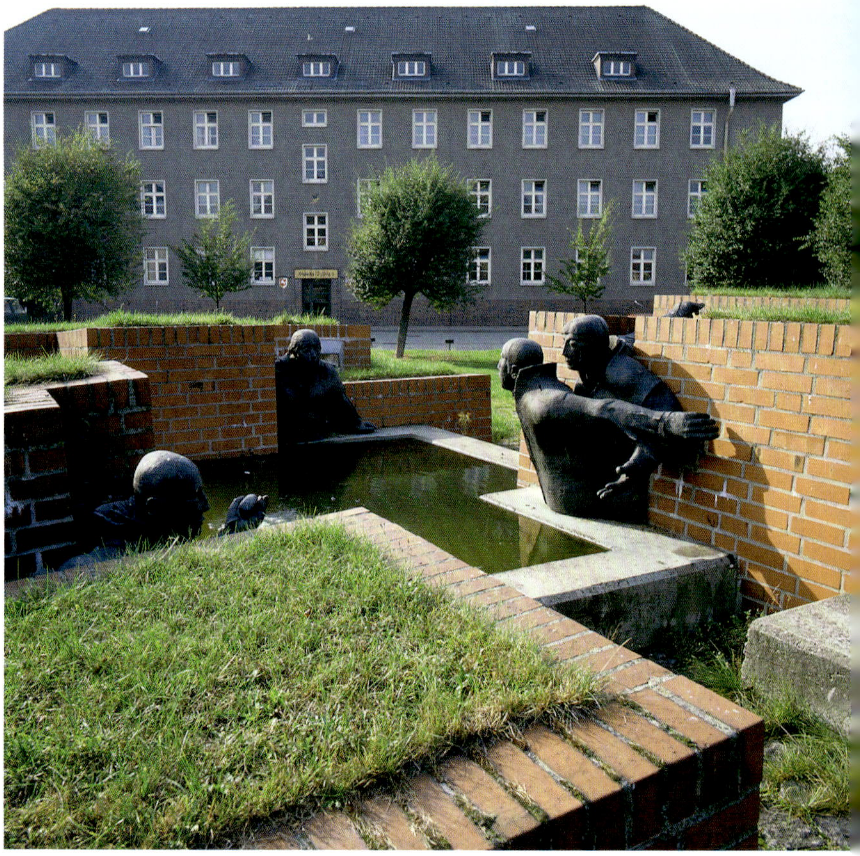

EBERHARD LINKE
"Gespräch zwischen den Blöcken"
("Dialogue between the blocks"),
1981/1982
Brick, bronze
approx. 10 x 10 m

HEINRICH DER LÖWE BARRACKS BUNDESWEHR BRAUNSCHWEIG

TODAY DEVELOPMENT AREA

Address:
Braunschweiger Strasse 1
38126 Braunschweig

Architecture:
1935

Art in architecture:
Eberhard Linke

In the 1930s, there were plans to transform Braunschweig into a National Socialist model city. The subsequent new development measures included the construction of the Heinrich der Löwe Barracks. After World War II, the British army initially took over the location, before the Bundeswehr used the facility between 1958 and 2003. In 1981/1982, Eberhard Linke (born in 1937) was commissioned to produce an artistically designed fountain for the exterior grounds, using means from the Supplementary Art in Architecture Fund. "Gespräch zwischen den Blöcken" ("Dialogue between the blocks") consists of a water basin surrounded by a labyrinth of brick walls with different heights. Five bronze half-figures are crouched in the niches and passages. The men warily look around in various directions. Their body language is cautious, making them resemble soldiers hiding in trenches, carefully making contact with their counterparts above the waterline.

The sculptor Linke from Lower Saxony repeatedly addressed aspects of international security in his works. For instance his sculpture "Mensch mit Schirm und Schild" ("Man with screen and shield") picked up on the US President Reagan's proclamation that the planned US missile defence shield (the German word "Raketenschirm" literally means "rocket screen") made his country invulnerable. The piece "Gespräch zwischen den Blöcken" ("Dialogue between the blocks"), refers to the climax of protest by the German peace movement against the Cold War arms race, recalling the oppressive, dangerous situation of the frontline, as well as the necessity of dialogue between the power blocs during the Cold War.

GRAF ZEPPELIN BARRACKS BUNDESWEHR CALW

Address:
Graf-Zeppelin-Strasse 22
75353 Calw

Architecture:
Baden-Baden
State Construction Authority,
1997–1999

Art in architecture:
Elisabeth Wagner

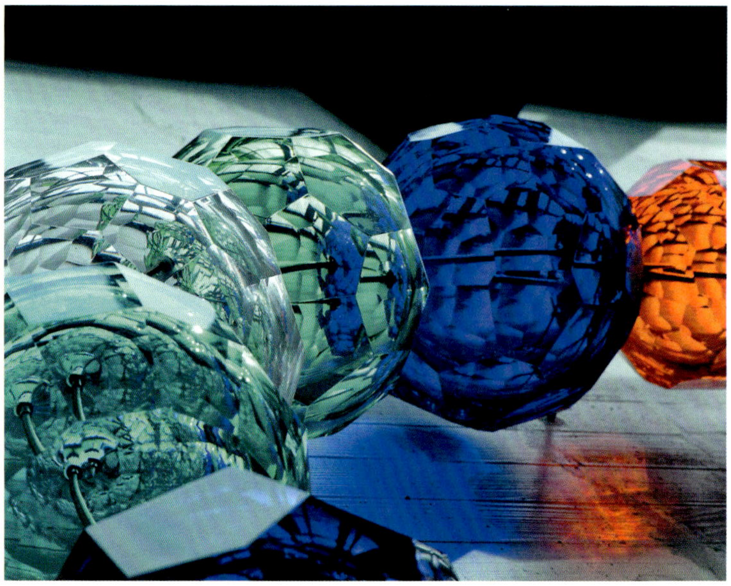

The Cold War finally ended in 1991 with the dissolution of the Warsaw Pact, thereby changing the underlying conditions for Germany's security policy. Disarmament, the reduced size of the armed forces and the merger between the Bundeswehr and the Nationale Volksarmee led to the foundation of the Kommando Spezialkräfte (Special Commando Forces, KSK), a special military unit with a deployment focus on education, counter-terrorism, rescue, evacuation and recovery, commando combat and military consultancy.

The KSK have been stationed in the Graf Zeppelin Barracks in Calw since 1996. The art in architecture competition for the new utilities and support building was won by Elisabeth Wagner (born in 1954), a sculptor who works with a wide range of materials. Her piece provides a perfect complement (German: "Pendant") to the sober architecture of steel, glass and concrete, as well as the institution that uses the ensemble: on the north wall of the entrance hall, she suspended an oversized string of pearls made of 42 coloured Murano glass orbs, their fragility, transparency and bright colours apparently contrasting with the tasks of KSK soldiers, yet also addressing the theme that "every chain is only as strong as its weakest link" – a fact that especially applies to special forces, who need to rely on their comrades during the missions. The title "Pendant" also plays on the responsibility of art in architecture to react to its environment. The required precision, perfection and discipline in a military context is complemented by the necessary addition of artistic aspects such as beauty, playful elegance and lightness.

ELISABETH WAGNER
"Das Pendant"
("The pendant"), 2000
Murano glass
470 x 210 x 40 cm

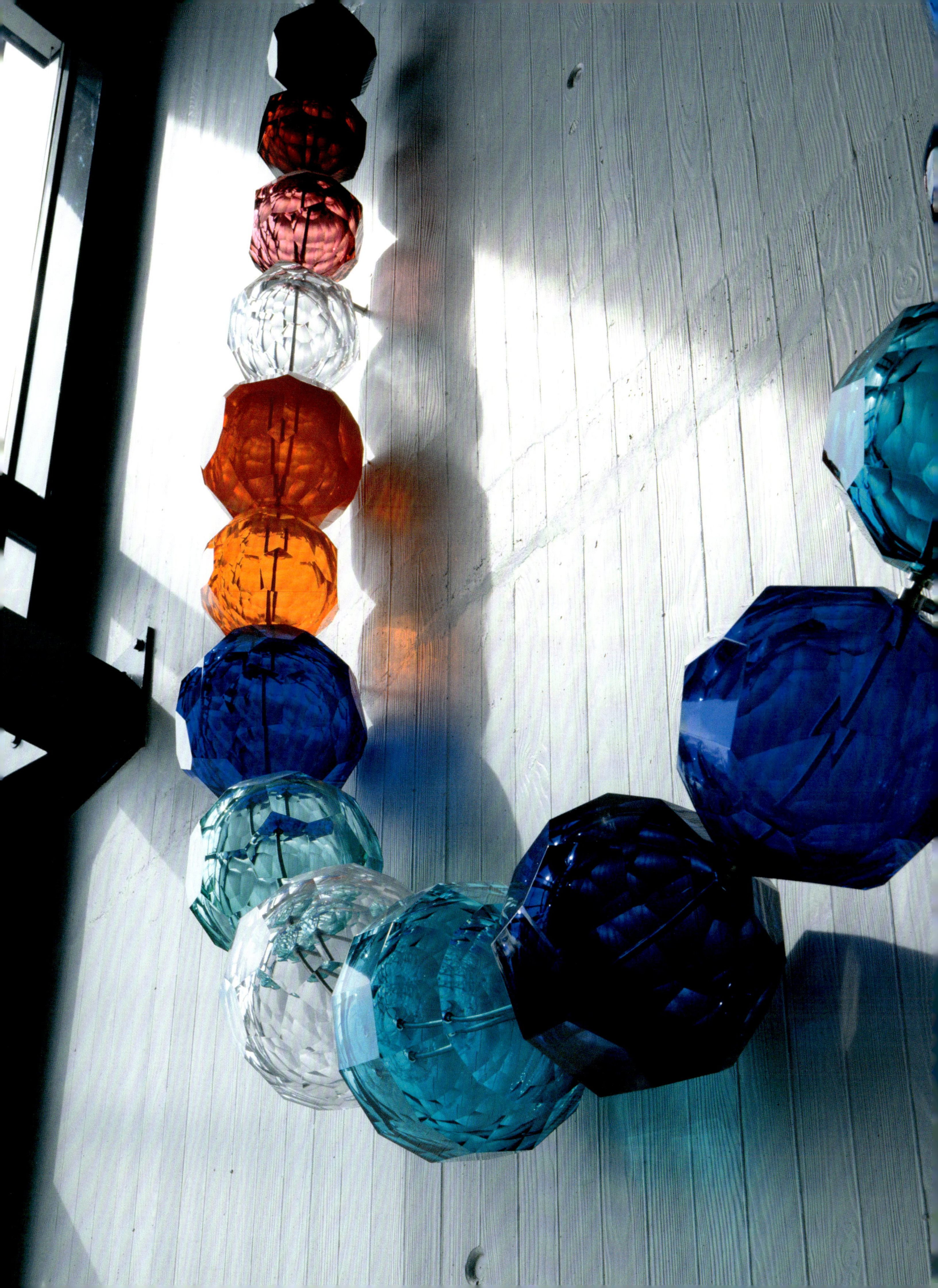

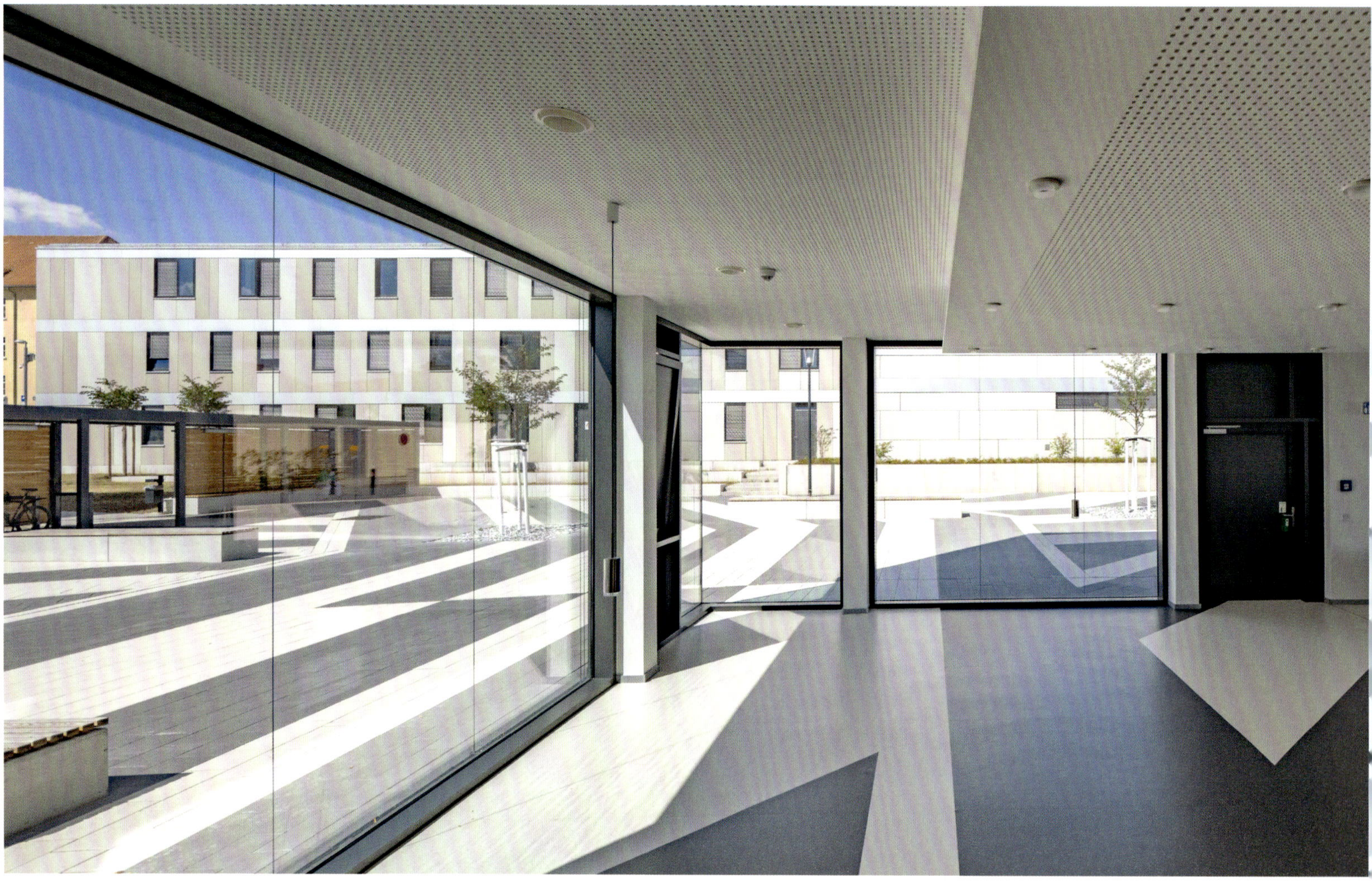

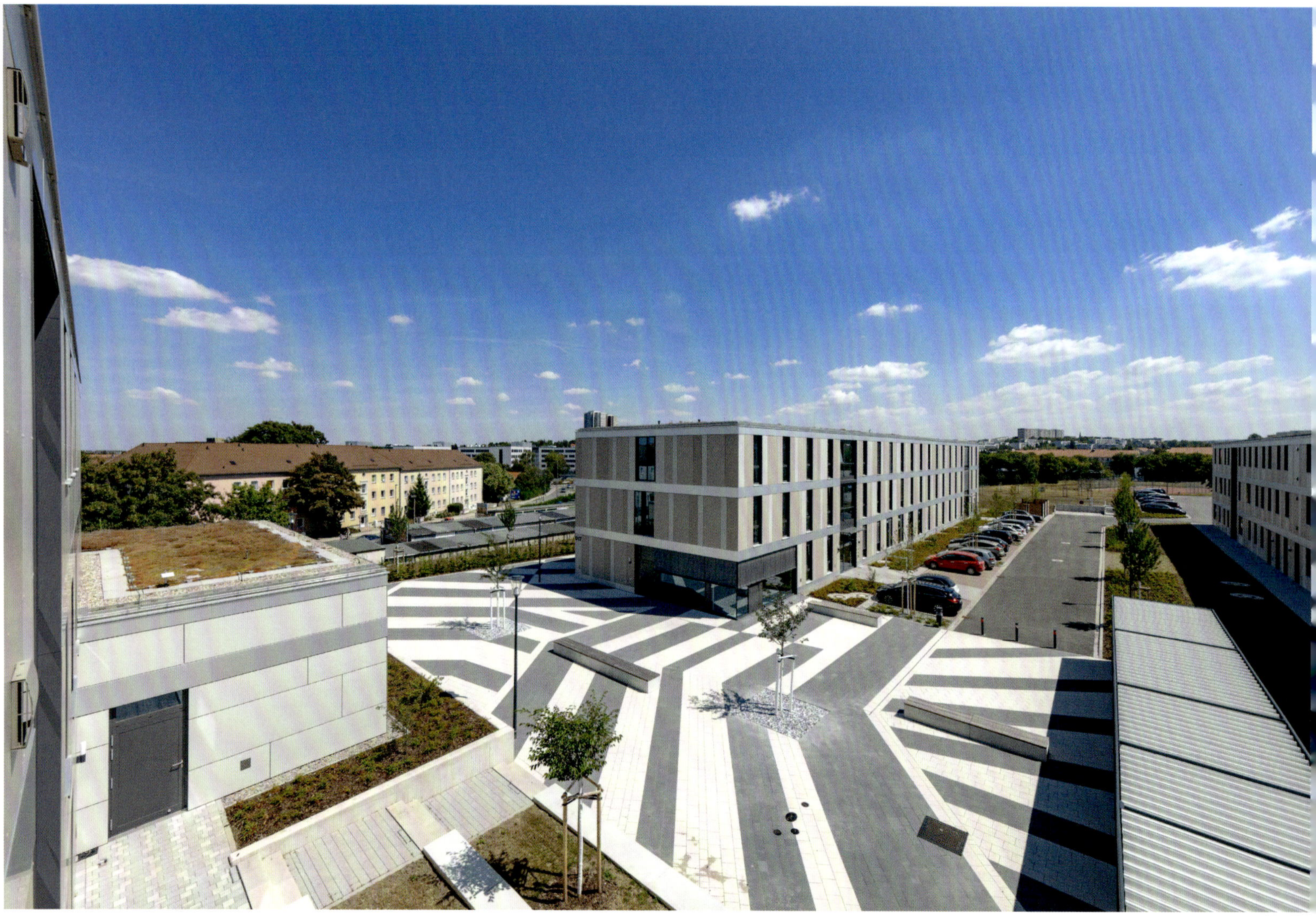

LÖBERFELD BARRACKS BUNDESWEHR ERFURT

Address:
Zeppelinstrasse 18
99096 Erfurt

Architecture:
hks Architekten, Erfurt, 2017–2018

Art in architecture:
Michael Sailstorfer

The most recent art in architecture for a Bundeswehr location was produced by Michael Sailstorfer (born in 1979), who won the national competition during extension measures for the Löberfeld Barracks in Erfurt. The jury selected his design "Dazzle" from among the 91 entries for installation in the street space between the three new barracks buildings. He designed a pattern of black and white paving blocks that continue into one of the building foyers. The pattern consists of irregular stripes that change direction and have contrasting breadths, thereby articulating the square. Sailstorfer often picks up on everyday objects as the starting point for background transformation in his sculptures and installations. His Erfurt artwork was inspired by markings on British World War I warships. The irregular camouflage pattern was known as "dazzle", describing the desired effect of confusing the enemy by optical illusion. The idea was conceived by the British artist Norman Wilkinson (1878–1971), who was primarily renowned for his marine artworks. While serving in the British navy during World War I, he witnessed numerous attacks by German submarines in the English Channel. One of his camouflage principles stipulated that port and starboard sides were always painted differently, while lines never ran in parallel to the actual contours of the ship, thereby visually dissolving the ship's outline into several individual forms. In Erfurt, the adapted camouflage pattern adds dynamism to the rectangular ground plan of the square and marks it as a meeting place.

MICHAEL SAILSTORFER
"Dazzle", 2017
Concrete paving
808 m^2

IN DIALOGUE WITH

ART IN ARCHITECTURE FOR BUILDINGS ABROAD

THE WORLD

Initially after World War II, neither of the two newly founded German states had foreign sovereignty. In the Federal Republic, the main focus was on constructing consulates from 1950 onwards, above all for its western allies in London, New York and Paris. After its status as an occupied country was rescinded in 1955, the FRG focused on systematically developing its foreign relations, especially with newly founded republics in Asia and Africa. The German Democratic Republic, which struggled for a long time to gain international recognition, initially only maintained foreign representations in the Soviet Union and other member states of the Warsaw Pact. Worldwide missions were only established after the Basic Treaty between the two German states was signed in 1972 and after the GDR became a member of the United Nations in 1973.

There are currently 227 Foreign Service representations abroad, consisting of 153 embassies, 54 consulates general, 7 consulates, 12 multilateral representations and one representative office. They are joined by 159 Goethe Institutes, 140 state-recognised German schools and scientific facilities such as the German Archaeological Institute or the German Historical Institute.

The institutions fulfil diverse political and cultural tasks. The embassies sustain economic interests, support German nationals locally and are involved in developing bilateral cooperation in the fields of research and technology, as well as social, agricultural and development policy. All political and cultural facilities have extensive representative functions. They are regarded as a "calling card" and the "eyes, ears and voice" of Germany. The diversity of the real estate and art in architecture significantly contributes to the image of Germany in its host countries and throughout the world.

IN DIALOGUE WITH THE WORLD

Martin Seidel

The Vienna Congress of 1814/1815 redrew the map of Europe. The subsequently cooperating major powers of France, Great Britain, Austria, Prussia and Russia established the first embassies in the capital cities of the other respective countries. In the period before 1914 and the outbreak of World War I, Germany's legations in Italy, Spain, Turkey and the USA were transformed into embassies as the country's political importance increased. Similarly, diplomatic representations were expanded further during the interwar years.

After World War II, the Federal Republic of Germany's far-reaching sovereignty was recognised in 1955 and it was admitted into the North Atlantic Treaty Organisation (NATO), leading to the resumption of old and the establishment of many new international relations. The Goethe Institute had already been founded in 1951 to encourage German language education abroad, maintain international cultural cooperation and communicate a comprehensive image of Germany. Similarly, a large number of German schools were established abroad during the 1950s.

The German Democratic Republic was only able to develop its diplomatic contacts on a worldwide scale following the Basic Treaty between the two German states in 1972 and the GDR's acceptance to the United Nations in 1973. Ultimately, it operated 72 embassy residences and 118 chancelleries, as well as other facilities. Most of them were accommodated in rented buildings rather than specially constructed state buildings, as was the case for the especially important embassies in Moscow, Budapest and Pyongyang. Eventually, the GDR nevertheless owned an immense amount of real estate abroad, which has hardly been researched from the perspective of the history of art and architecture, and became the property of the Federal Republic following reunification in 1990.

The diversity of architectural forms and art is a characteristic of all state building. However, buildings abroad differ from domestic buildings in two ways: firstly, they have a duty to suitably represent Germany abroad. Secondly, the wealth of artistic genres, forms and content is the result of locations with sometimes entirely contrary political, historical, cultural, urban and climatic conditions.

BETWEEN TRADITION AND INNOVATION

Due to historical developments, only few embassies are currently accommodated in their original, historical buildings. The development of diplomatic relations around the world after World War II led to busy construction activity for new German facilities abroad, especially in newly independent former colonies in Asia and Africa.

Like the other embassy buildings for Canberra (1956–1958), Tokyo (1956–1960) and the Consulate General in Rio de Janeiro (1956–1961), the first new building for a foreign diplomatic representation of the Federal Republic of Germany, namely the combined residence and chancellery in New Delhi, had to find an architectural language that demonstrated a break with the state buildings of the National Socialist past and reflected the new democratic

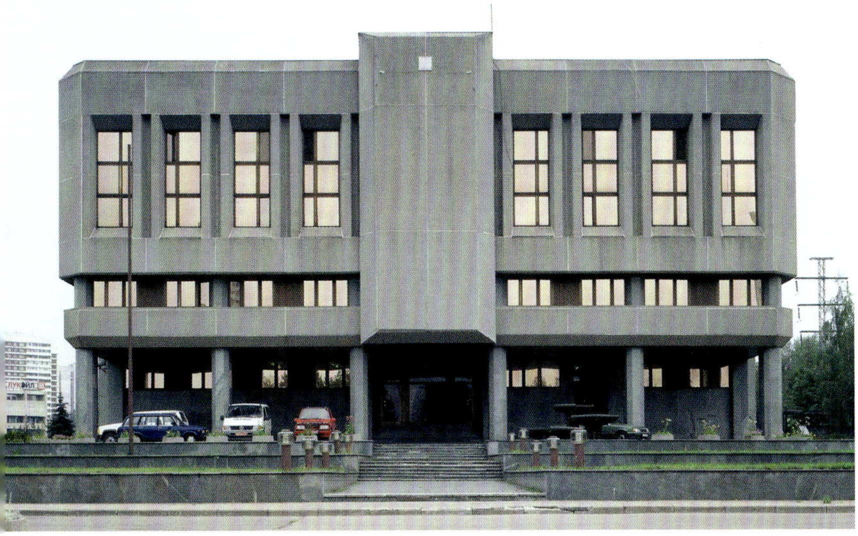

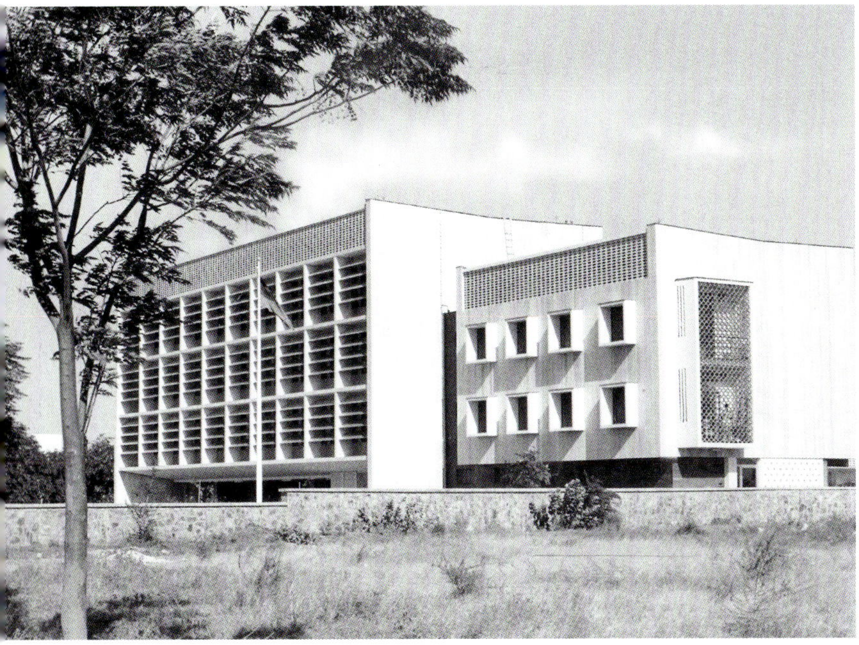

ideals of lightness, openness and transparency. At the same time, typical local building traditions and geographical specifics had to be taken into account. For instance the open ground floor of the embassy in New Delhi, which was planned by Johannes Krahn and the Federal Building Authority and completed in 1962, reveals the influence of Le Corbusier. By contrast, the local climate prevented the use of steel and glass for the façades and led to the design of sunblinds. The renowned sculptor Karl-Heinz Krause (1924–2019) conceived an elegant supraporte for the post-war modern architecture, namely the bronze relief "Fliegende Kraniche" ("Flying cranes") for the reception hall. A batik artwork with landscape motifs by the textile artist and carpet designer Edith Müller-Ortloff (1911–1995) was installed in the dining room, while a knotted carpet entitled "Die völkerverbindende Macht der Musik" ("The power of music to unite the nations") was placed in the reception hall. It also contained mosaic tables by Heinz Diekmann that referred to the seasons. The works installed in the embassy address the themes of homeland, travel and encounter, are figurative despite their abstract elements and express an edifying character. The presentation of themes, techniques and materials clearly reflects the conservative tendencies of the Adenauer period.

However, the Federal Building Authority, which represented the Federal Republic of Germany as the client, repeatedly preferred non-figurative, abstract art, especially for building projects abroad. At the time, in the deeply divided ideological and artistic debate, abstract art was considered progressive and able to demonstrate openness to the world, thereby expressing the new Germany's desire to leave its National Socialist past behind and keep abreast with the standards

GDR Embassy,
Moscow, USSR

FRG Embassy,
New Delhi, India

of international centres of art. Thus Krause's "Fliegende Kraniche" was only produced because the artist, as he later revealed in confidence, had not adhered to the abstract art requested by the competition brief.

By contrast, the large, at the time breathtakingly modern fountain sculpture by the Spanish sculptor Andreu Alfaro (1929–2012), which was commissioned by the Federal Republic for the German School in Valencia (→ p. 266), is a programmatic avowal to international avant-garde abstraction.

In an international context, architecture and art are always subject to strategic considerations. In 1963, the Federal Republic signed the Élysée Treaty with the major power of France, focusing on German-French cooperation. The same year, the chancellery building in Paris was completed according to plans by the Federal Building Authority. It was an unembellished, eight-storey steel-skeleton structure with side wings. The radical, abstract bronze mural by Bernhard Heiliger (1915–1995) integrated into the foyer could hardly be more contrasting. It retains the autonomy of a mobile relief through its bold, informal expression, while also creating imposing spatial relationships. It even attracted the attention of the Berlin daily newspaper *Der Tagesspiegel*, describing the work as the "first truly important piece of German contemporary art" that "fulfils representative functions in an embassy".

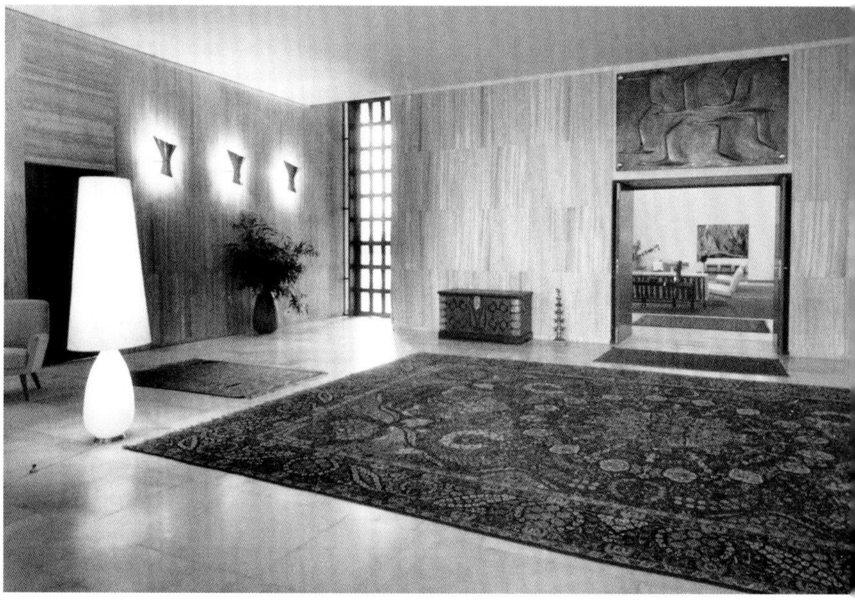

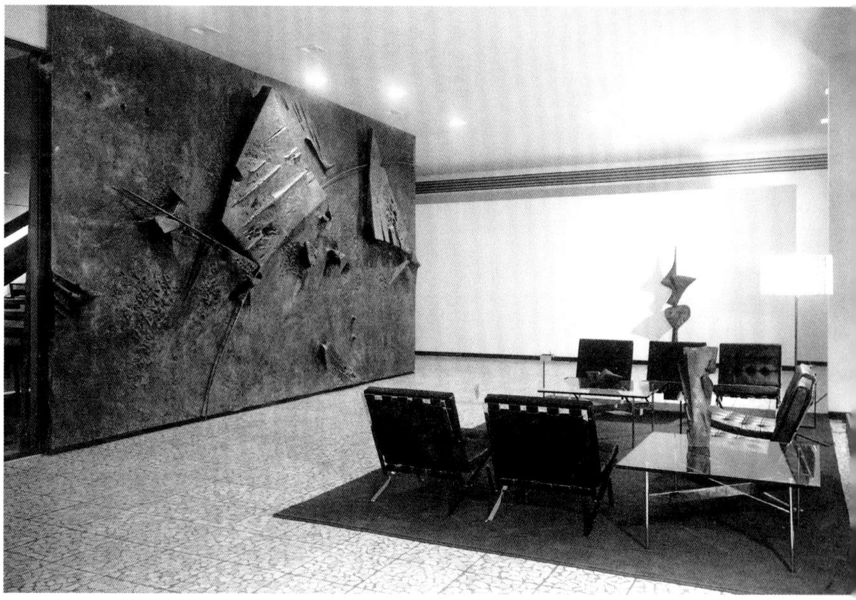

EXPANSION AND INTEGRATION

Art in architecture evades linear historical developments and simple schemes. One such example is the chancellery of the German Embassy in Washington (1962–1966). Its architect was Egon Eiermann, who had previously designed the German pavilion at the

Karl-Heinz Krause, "Fliegende Kraniche", 1959, FRG Embassy, New Delhi, India

Bernhard Heiliger, "Panta Rhei – alles fließt", 1964, FRG Embassy, Paris, France

FRG Embassy, Washington, D.C., USA

Blasius Spreng, inner courtyard design with water basin, fountain head and stone carpet, 1965, FRG Embassy, Vienna, Austria

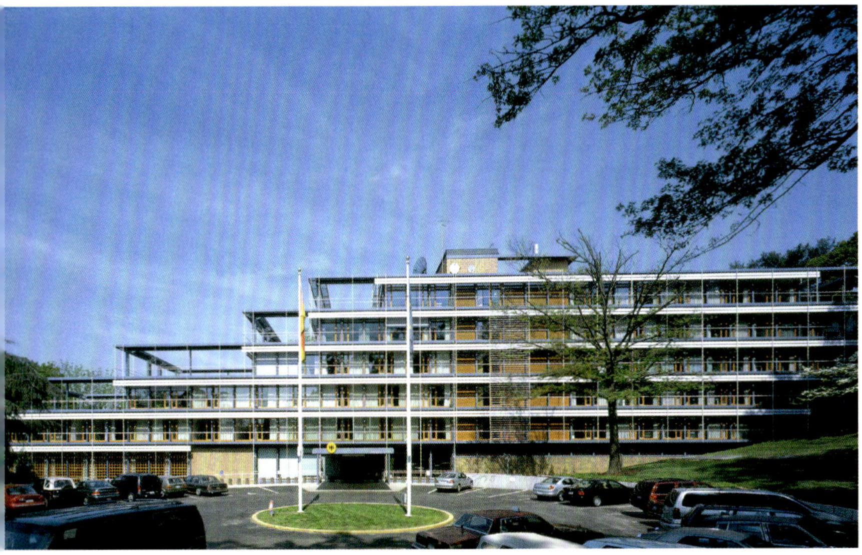

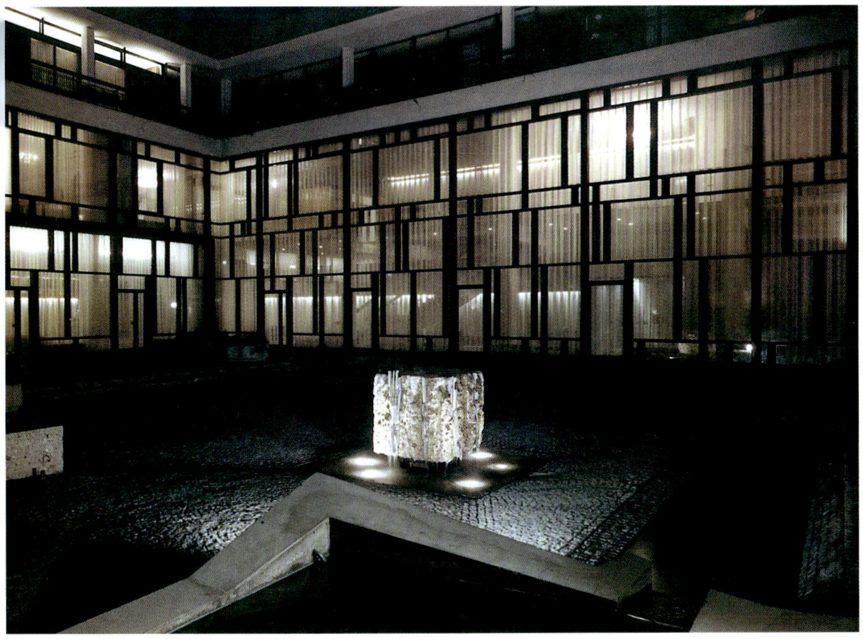

1958 Brussels Expo together with Sep Ruf. In Washington, Eiermann impressed with a building made of steel and glass that is integrated into the terrain as a horizontally defined, non-hierarchical terrace house. The unpretentious appearance of the model building of federal democracy was widely recognised among experts in the United States, the Federal Republic's most important ally, winning several architectural awards. The art for the building, which was chosen by Eiermann himself, could scarcely reflect the consistence of the architectural language: in the entrance hall, the abstract bronze sculpture "Große gerahmte Figuren" ("Large framed figures") by Fritz Koenig (1924–2017), a bronze bust by Erich F. Reuter (1911–1997) in the auditorium and, for the Ambassador's office, a small-scale abstract marble sculpture by Karl Hartung (1908–1967) that resembles growth forms. The three artworks were abreast with the times, but the plinth sculptures remained exhibits that were subordinate to the architecture.

By contrast, the artist Blasius Spreng (1913–1987) resumed his regular direct collaboration with the architect Rolf Gutbrod in working for the German Embassy in Vienna, producing an integral art concept that connected the interior and exterior spaces. A water basin, a free-standing fountain head, a stone seating group and a sculpture that was highly modern at the time, consisting of a concrete stele and applied aluminium cubes to create a "Blütenzweig" ("Flowering twig"), corresponded with the steel relief panels and an abstract mosaic on the floor of the entrance hall. The art in architecture's elegantly reserved nature allowed it to enter into a wonderful interaction with the architecture, which in turn impressed not least with its suspended shell limestone and quartzite slabs, although the building subsequently had to make way for a new, larger edifice.

FORMING AN ADDRESS

Otto Herbert Hajek, "Zeichen für Montevideo", 1974, FRG Embassy, Montevideo, Uruguay

Fritz Koenig, "Große Flora", 1977/1978, FRG Embassy, London, UK

Like buildings in Germany, the locations of real estate abroad are a definitive factor for the art in architecture. There is a great difference between a facility abroad that is established in a densely developed urban context, in a high-rise building (such as the chancellery of the German Embassy in Tel Aviv) or in new buildings as part of a newly developed diplomatic quarter. To be perceived properly, unornamented architecture and also urban development contexts that have an anonymising effect regularly require exceptional characteristics to achieve differentiation, make them stand out and enhance identification with the building.

For instance an artwork can mark an entrance situation: in Vienna, the successful integration of art and architecture for the former embassy building was achieved by the Viennese artist Christa Neumann with an almost two-metre high sandstone sculpture. The free-standing, traditionally autonomous sculpture not only creates an effective complementary contrast to the façade and the residency's system of supports, but also assumes the function of forming an address along the drive to the residency.

In this way, artworks can gain the status of landmarks. When the chancellery in London was extended by Walther and Bea Betz, the sculptor Fritz Koenig (1924–2017) produced a version of his so-called flora-sculptures for the architecture. The bronze sculpture develops fine references to the building, while its slim height of six metres makes it an immediate eye-catcher, allowing it to act as a signpost.

Naturally, free-standing artworks are just one way of forming an address. Other examples were regularly provided by Otto Herbert Hajek (1927–2005), one of the most

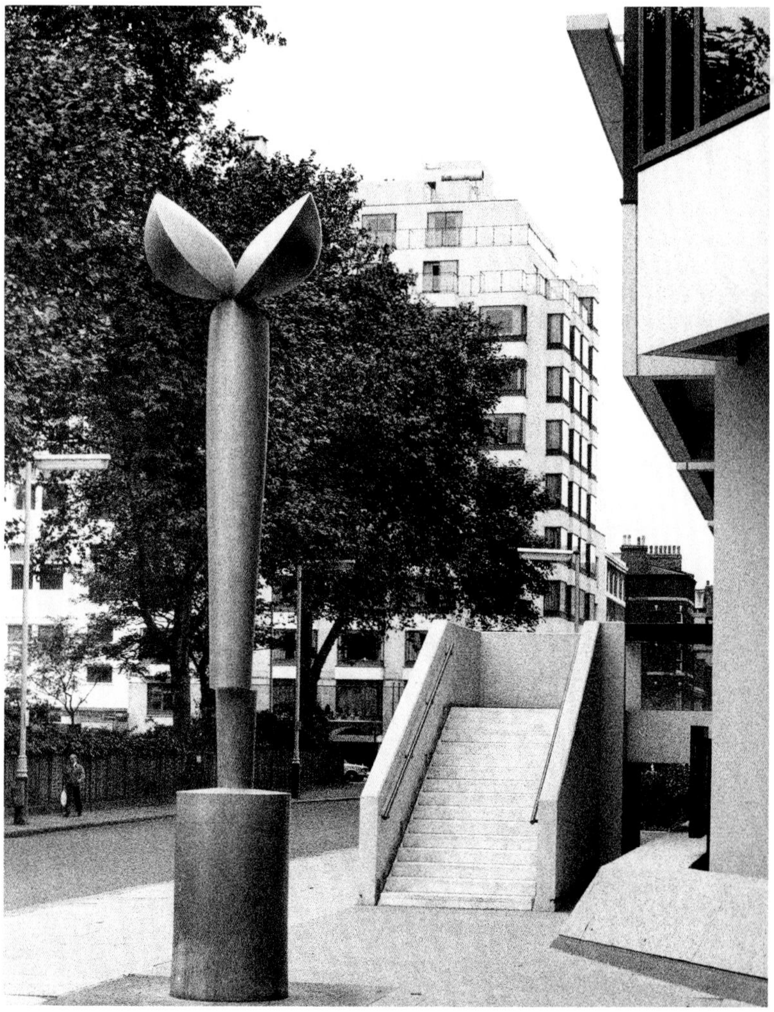

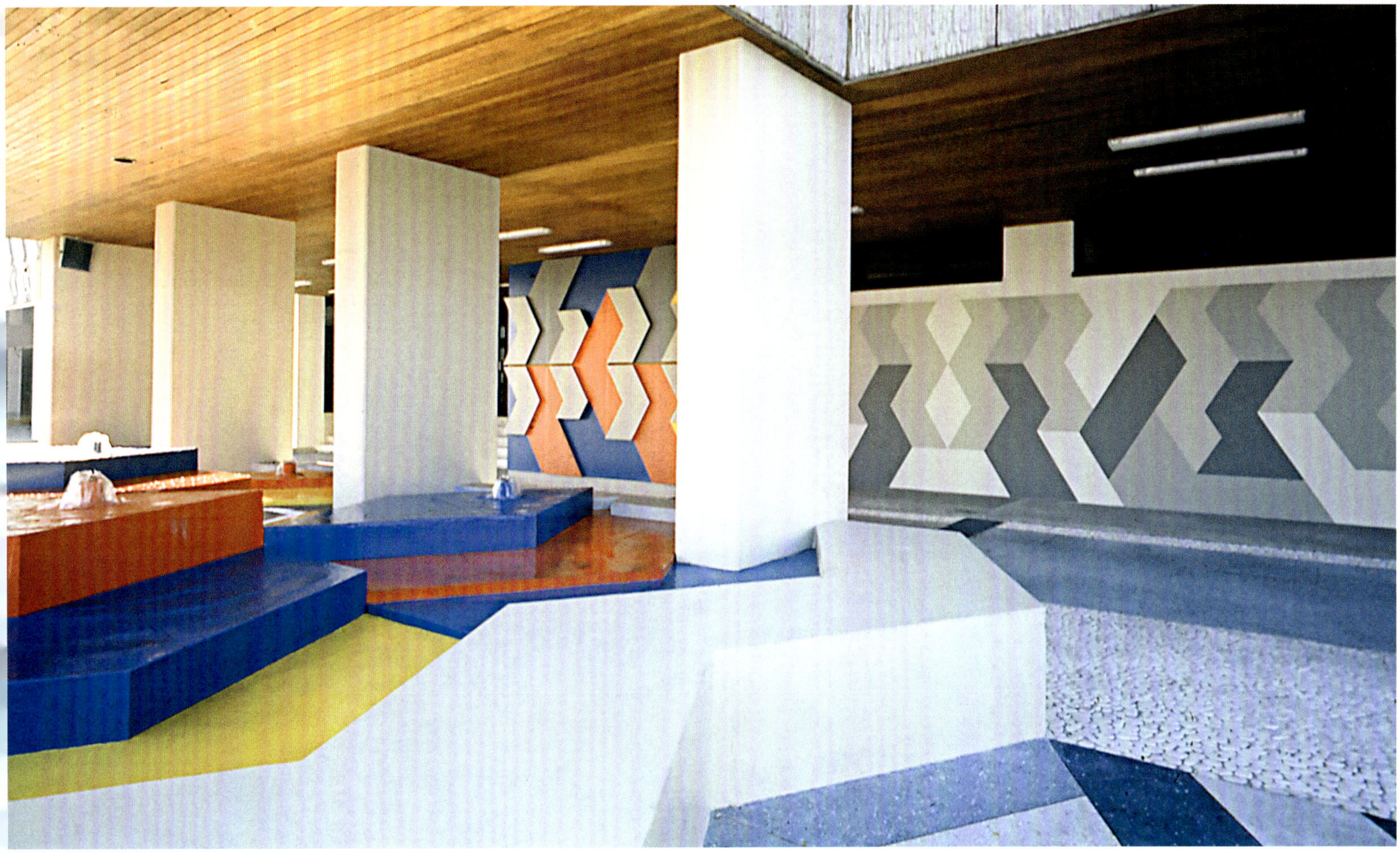

sought-after art in architecture artists of his time. Hajek also received commissions abroad. His work for the chancellery of the Montevideo Embassy (1974) combines paving and a fountain in the entrance drive with a concrete stele and striking surface designs on the walls. The art, with its prominent basic forms and colours, takes complete possession of the building and its surroundings. Hajek regarded the approach as an act that goes beyond the building, "humanising the environment". As with other installations by Hajek, the Montevideo project stands out as a "democratic monument" for individuality, tolerance and a more liveable shaping of the environment. Hajek's striking, indeed extravagant artistic approach was widely applauded, although it also encountered opposition. The fact that the Federal Building Authority even allowed Hajek's emancipatory art to find its way onto the diplomatic scene is therefore evidence of the FRG's will to make a new start in the decades following World War II.

AESTHETIC SELF-PORTRAYAL

The most important German architects and artists have always been involved in the largest, most politically significant buildings abroad. Architecture and art "made in Germany" have established themselves as a brand.

Hans Scharoun, the architect of the Berlin Philharmonic and the Berlin State Library on Potsdamer Strasse, planned only one development outside Germany, namely the ensemble for the German Embassy in Brazil's new capital (1968–1971). The powerfully expressive, but unpretentious exterior, the sweeping ground plans and the fluent spatial concepts are a fascinating reflection of the great conceptual transformation of the time. The art in architecture by Günter Ferdinand Ris (1928–2005) is no less impressive. His "Wasser-Licht-Stelen" ("Water-light steles") in the basin in front of the residency are based on industrial forms and the use of new materials. They combine with the light to embody progress, modesty, openness and transparency as social and aesthetic ideals of the new liberal-minded Federal Republic (→ p. 270). Ris's art was highly respected both in Germany and abroad, for instance demonstrating socio-political transformation in Germany at the "Expo '70" in Osaka.

The importance of architecture and art in a state's self-representation can also be seen in the first embassy building constructed for the GDR, namely the chancellery in Budapest (1965–1968). The architect Heinz Graffunder, who was commissioned to design the building, played a similarly important role in the East as Egon Eiermann and Hans Scharoun had done for Modernity in the West. The aesthetic appearance, the building size and the structural logic using prefabricated elements were all aimed at demonstrating the performance of the GDR state's building sector. No expense was spared with respect to its fitting out. The main entrance consisted of an informally designed aluminium portal according to plans by Fritz Kühn (1910–1967) (→ p. 268). He also designed a fountain for the garden courtyard. Above all, Kühn was an artistic blacksmith who was highly regarded both in East and in West Germany, his works including a spatial grid wall for the German pavilion at the Brussels Expo in 1958, as well as the famous acoustic wall, which was produced in 1964 for the former GDR Staatsrat building. A high, glass fountain by Reginald Richter (born in 1931) adorned the broad atrium of the Budapest chancellery. Other artworks included a tapestry by Dieter Gantz (1932–2018) in the conference hall, depicting dramas by Bertolt Brecht, as well as a map of

GDR Embassy, Budapest, Hungary

Reginald Richter, glass fountain, 1966, GDR Embassy, Budapest, Hungary

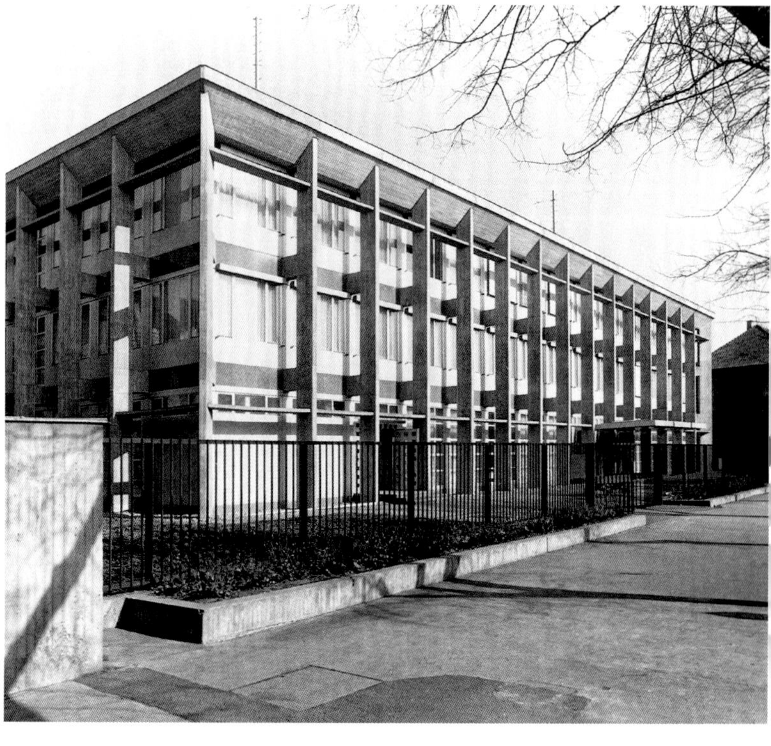

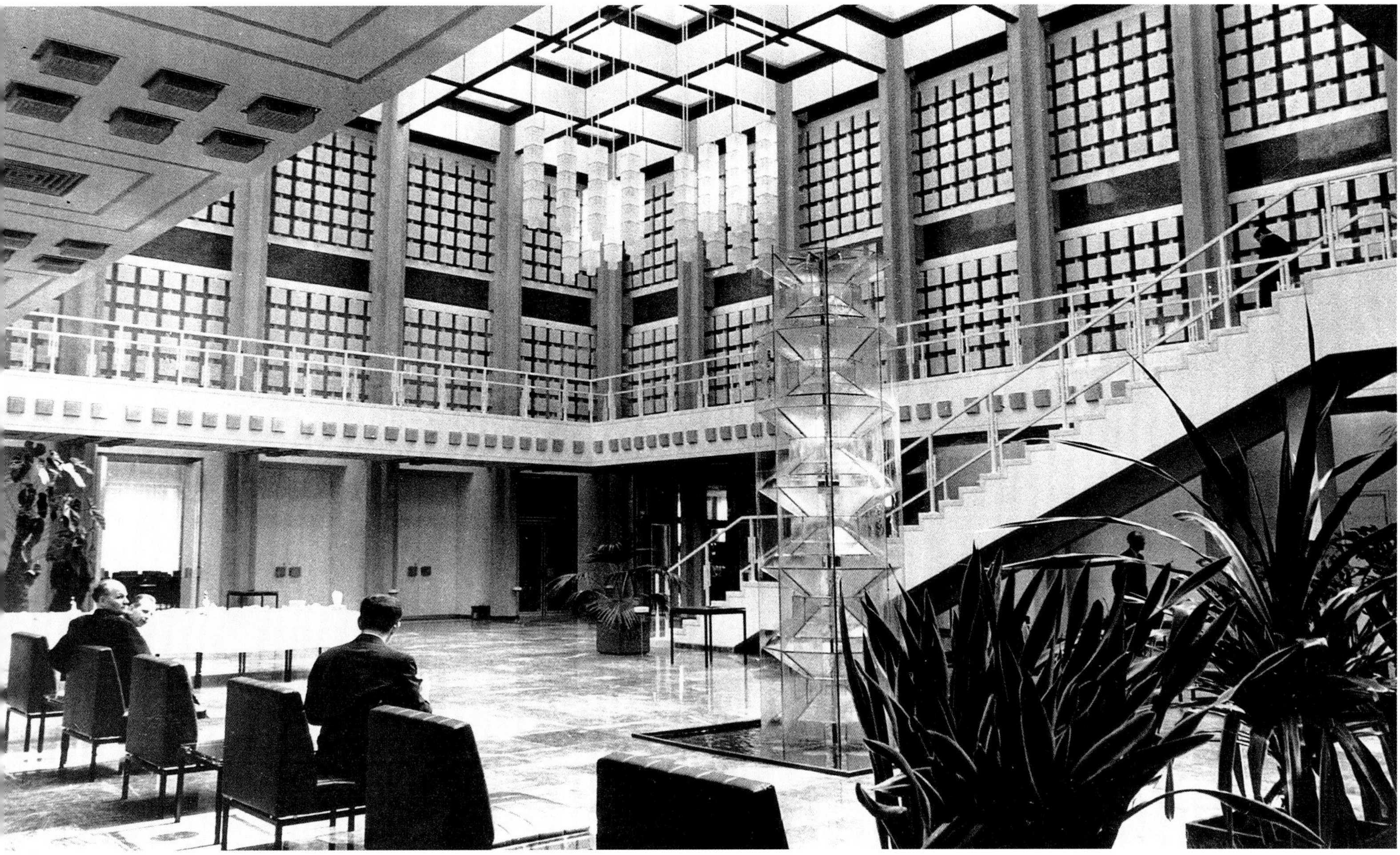

the GDR made of Meissen porcelain, which was produced by Eduard Gerhard Clauß (1906–1966) for the antechamber of the Trade Department. To maintain artistic standards, collective building-cultural responsibility remained with the architects and artists regarding the designs for the lamps, textiles and furniture. In doing so, the chancellery blurred the boundaries of art, design and crafts – in complete conformity with the state's "Regulation on the artistic design of administrative buildings" (1952).

By contrast, the similarly large GDR embassy in Pyongyang (1967–1973) had nothing more to offer aesthetically than a glass image with the GDR emblem in the chancellery staircase, thematically addressing the friendship between the two states using their respective national colours.

PROTOCOL DEMANDS

In both German states, artistic and aesthetic self-portrayal was always connected to political and ideological stances and interests. When the Federal Republic became a member of the United Nations (UN) in 1973, the Federal Building Authority commissioned the painter Günter Frühtrunk (1923–1982) and the architect and designer Paolo Nestler (1920–2010) to design the "Quiet Room" at the UN Headquarters in New York. The abstract, geometric all-over design of walls, the ceiling, the floor and furniture was purely aesthetic – thereby precisely reflecting the etiquette and political alignment of the Federal Republic, which aimed to act with caution on the stage of the United Nations.

The GDR was accepted into the UN at the same time, but remained true to its perspective on art, presenting the UN with a figurative bronze sculpture entitled "Aufsteigender"

("Rising man") by Fritz Cremer (1906–1993). It was installed in the park on the grounds and is dedicated to the "peoples' struggle for freedom", without succumbing to any overt political agitation.

In a majority of cases, art for buildings abroad is a question of political, social and aesthetic self-representation. Old stately villas in foreign countries are highly desirable as residencies, such as the palais of the Schuylenburch family in The Hague, which was built in a Louis Quatorze style in 1715, or the extremely ornate Palais Beauharnais in Paris.

Since residences accommodate the ambassadors, but are primarily locations of diplomatic receptions, it is often the case that even new buildings use artworks with traditional aesthetic qualities with respect to their genres, styles, themes and techniques, ensuring a more liveable and refined elegance in the buildings. Above all, tapestries experienced a typical boom in such buildings abroad; even the GDR integrated a tapestry by Dieter Gantz in its Budapest chancellery "as an especially beautiful and sumptuous technique".

From the outset, the most architecturally and artistically ambitious embassies nevertheless fitted the foyers, festive halls, corridors and gardens of their residences with textile works, small sculptures, supraporte reliefs and wrought iron sundials, thereby referring to traditional artistic forms of sovereignty, even when choosing advanced design approaches. For example in 1975, the textile artist Ingeborg Schäffler-Wolf (1928–2015) produced specifically for the reception hall of the Teheran residence two over six-metre high abstract mural tapestries that adapted the old medium to the new conditions of art in architecture.

Whether the impetus behind the building's fittings was innovative or conservative, state buildings abroad and especially foreign

Günter Fruhtrunk, PaoloNestler, "Quiet Room", 1978, UN Headquarters, Secretariat Tower, New York, USA

Fritz Cremer, "Aufsteigender. Den um ihre Freiheit kämpfenden Völkern gewidmet", 1966/1967, UN Headquarters, New York, USA

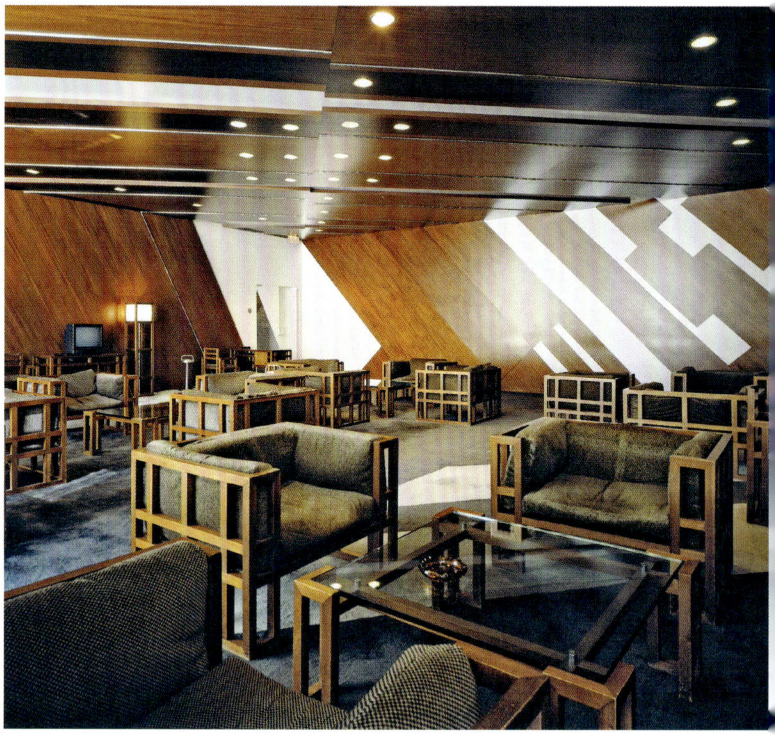

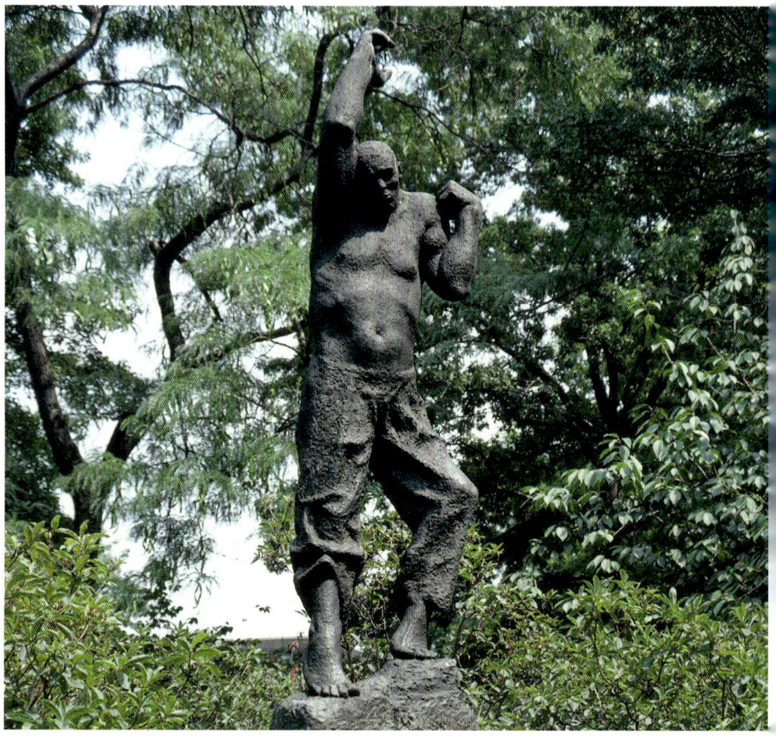

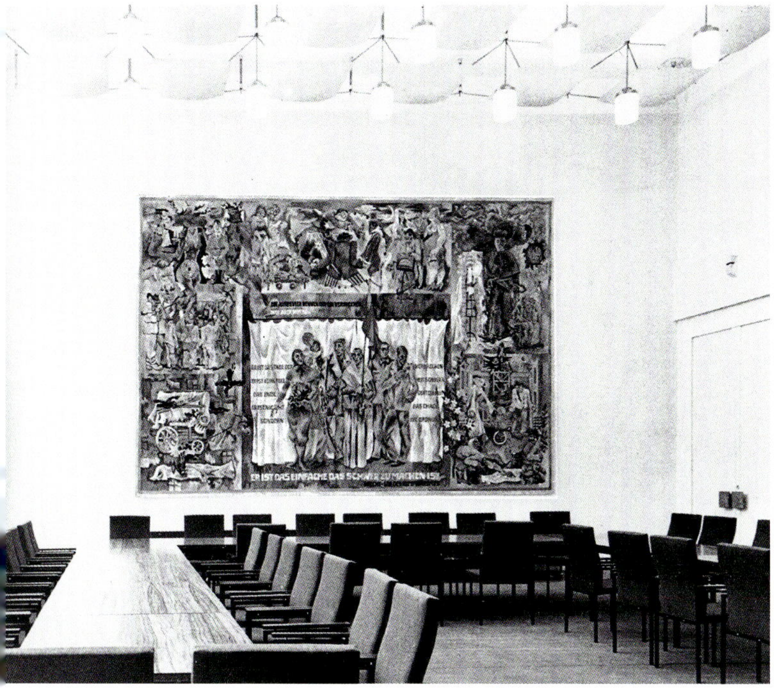

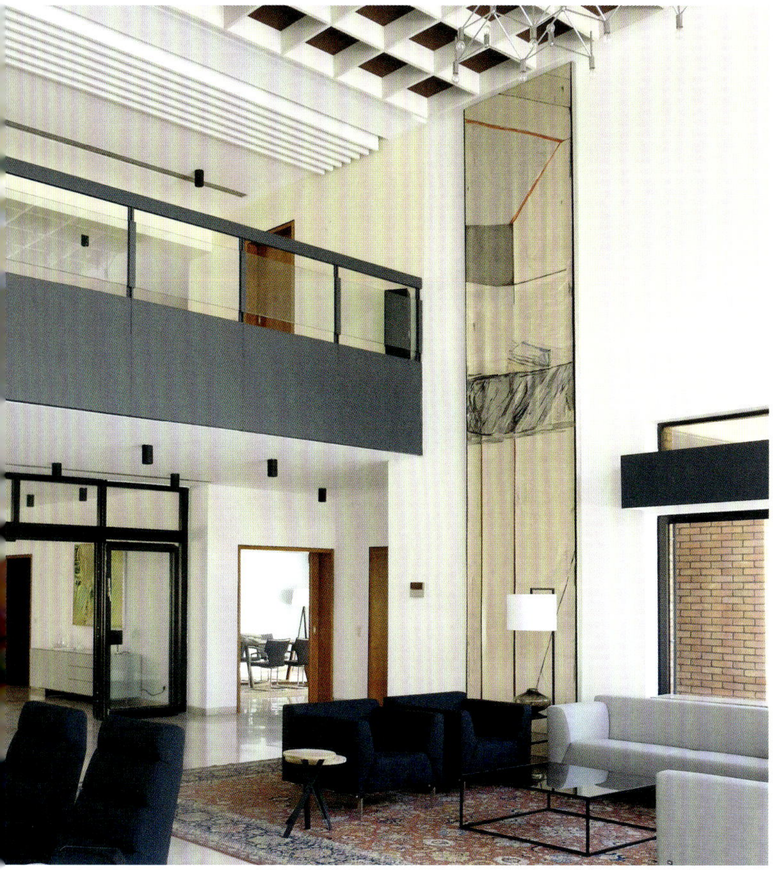

Dieter Gantz, tapestry, 1968, GDR Embassy, Budapest, Hungary

Ingeborg Schäffler-Wolf, mural tapestry, around 1975/1976, FRG Embassy, Teheran, Iran

representations cannot be thrown into one basket. A German school is different from a consulate, which in turn is unlike an embassy. Similarly, an embassy residence has different demands compared to its chancellery. A facility's location in a developing country differs from one in an emerging country, or in a G20 or G7 state.

The Vatican has a special status. In the German Embassy at the Holy See in Rome, the Federal Republic presents itself with a striking ensemble of reddish-brown facing-brick buildings constructed between 1980 and 1984. With its historicising elements such as a battlement crown and balustrade, the architecture by Alexander von Branca demonstrates a stance that, in view of the buildings' location and use, upholds the ideals of festivity, permanence and reliability. A conservative spirit also inspired the residency fittings, with depictive tapestries and paintings from the 18th and 19th centuries, as well as art in architecture. The ceiling paintings by Peter Schubert (born in 1929) in the reception hall and the study, as well as the frescoes by Hann Trier (1915–1999) in the dining room and breakfast room, are informal and abstract, while Trier's pieces are characterised by rhythm, tempo and direct physicality. However, as art in architecture, these paintings, which create the illusion of blurring the spatial boundaries, are dedicated to the location and the notion of achieving a respectful, or even sacred atmosphere.

Fundamentally, the political importance and, correspondingly, the size of a building in a foreign country are key factors when planning its architecture and art. This is nowhere clearer than in the residency of the German Embassy in Washington. In the direct vicinity of Egon Eiermann's chancellery, which is regarded as a prime example of a democratically aligned, modest architectural language, the residency, which was planned thirty years later by Oswald Mathias Ungers and completed in 1994, ascends on a slope as a white free-standing building with a great abstract formal character, recalling a stately mansion. The series of columns and the portico alone express architectural confidence and a sense of mission. Ungers subjected the building to an omnipresent module of squares, consistently defining everything from the art in architecture down to the lights, chairs and crockery. Immediately at the entrance hall, two large murals by Gerhard Merz (born in 1947) appear as fixed elements of the architecture; the module also required the Parsifal panels by Markus Lüpertz (born in 1941) in the entrance hall to assume an unusual square format; eight informal oil paintings by Christa Näher (born in 1947) are also subordinated to the structural stipulations in the study, as is the case in the boudoir with a ceiling painting and a tapestry by Rosemarie Trockel (born in 1952), who also designed a set of mocha crockery for the room. Overall, the residency in Washington represents a unique special case, architecture in which the desire for aesthetic self-projection goes far beyond the requirements of political representation.

The largest German building project in a foreign country, aside from the residency in Washington, was the new building for the chancellery of the German Embassy in Moscow. The building complex was planned during the Cold War by the Hamburg architects Hans Mensinga and Dieter Rogalla, and was completed in 1992, including a chancellery, a multifunctional building, residential buildings and a kindergarten. The architecture and art for the chancellery necessarily have a different expression from the embassy residency eight kilometres away, which was constructed in a Renaissance style in 1912, with appropriately elegant furnishing.

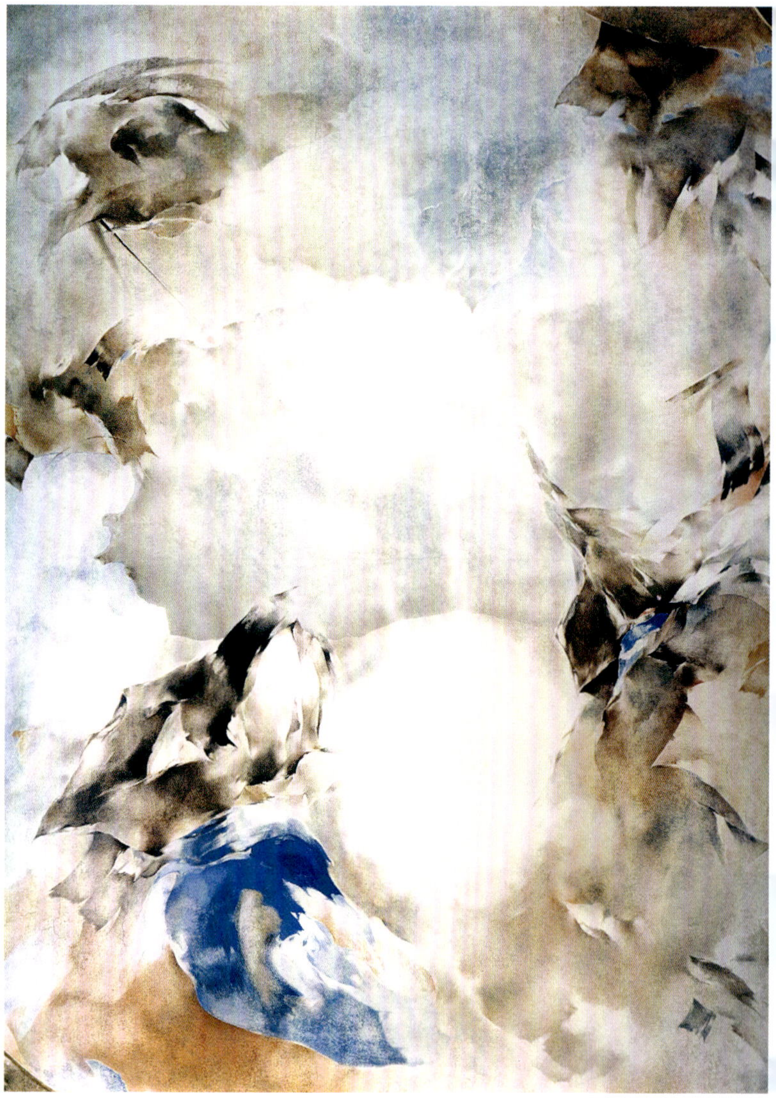

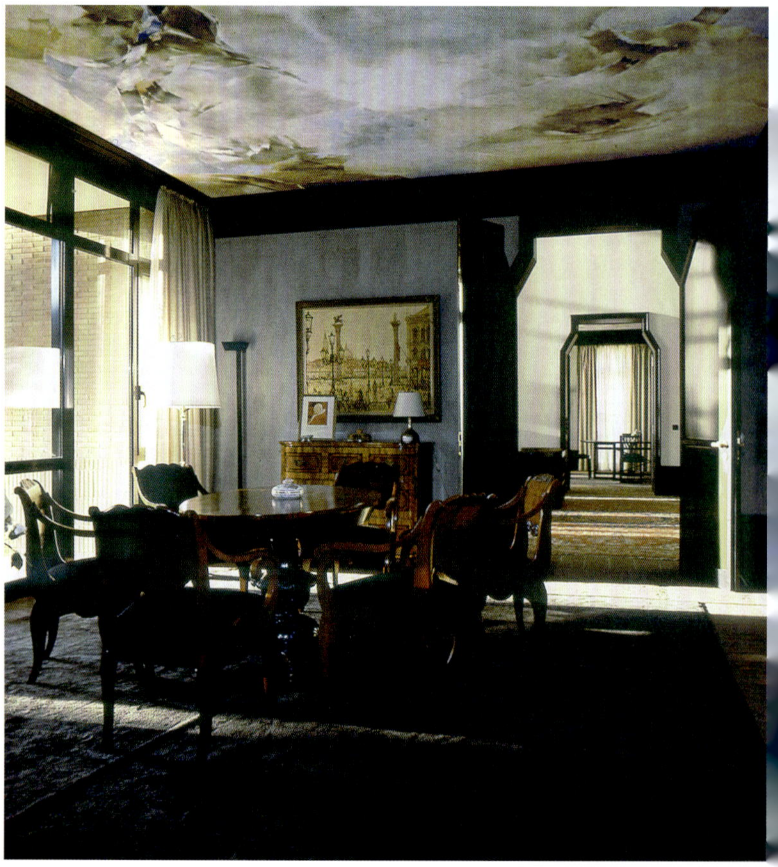

Peter Schubert, ceiling fresco, 1981, FRG Embassy, Holy See, Rome, Italy

Peter Schubert, ceiling fresco, 1981, FRG Embassy, Holy See, Rome, Italy

Markus Lüpertz, "Parsifal", 1992–1994, German Embassy, Washington, D.C., USA

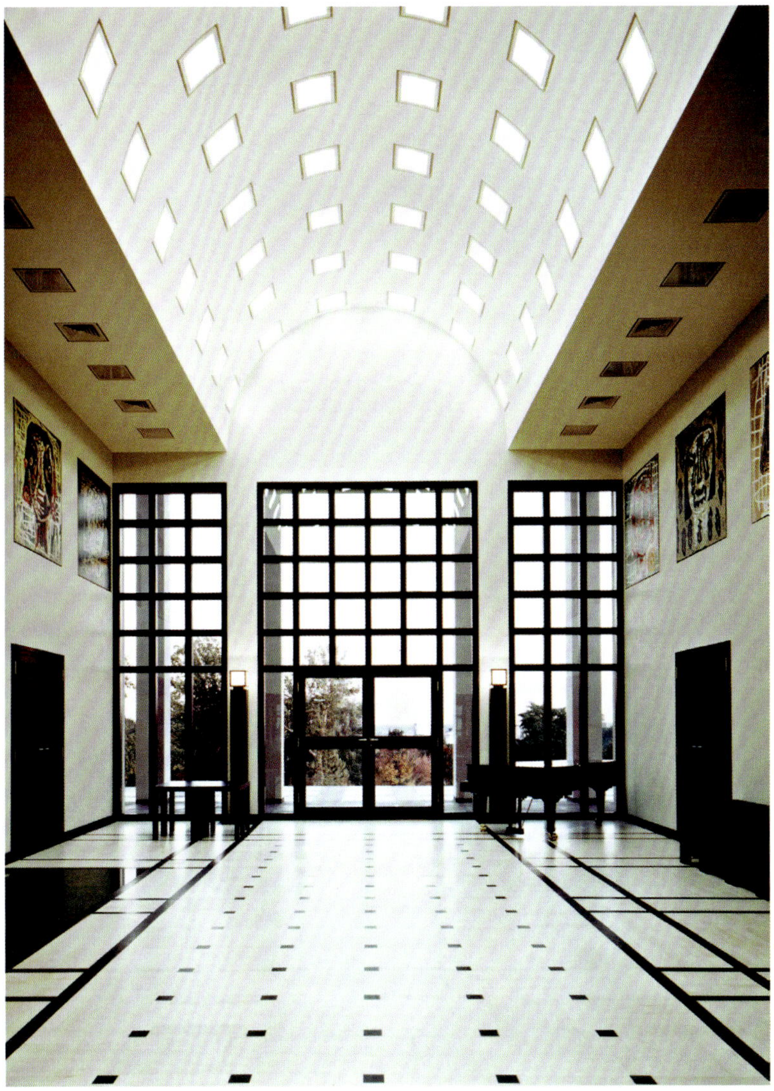

The entrance area of the chancellery is dominated by an almost four-metre high, mighty, yet finely balanced "head" sculpture by the sculptor Franz Bernhard (1934–2013), which is made of Corten steel sheeting. It embodies an awareness of art that prefers the authenticity of form and content to the prestigious sheen of surfaces. However, although the aesthetics of the nuanced rust were highly contemporary at the time, there were pragmatic reservations. The Ambassador noted that in Moscow, "rust is a symbol of economic decline" and is "the least suitable material to represent German art, especially in the entrance area".

The four-part, abstract sculptural ensemble produced by Robert Schad (born in 1953) and installed in the green area of a residential courtyard did not initially receive a warm welcome from the Foreign Office, due to its aesthetics. Yet it is remarkable that the upright and lying, welded rectangular steel profiles could inspire so many associations. They may resemble watch towers, security grates and lighting masts, or perhaps trees, a collection of people, a herd of animals or many other things. The artist himself described the potential variety of associations as the most important aspect of the work, thereby referring to German-Soviet post-war history. Thus, the artist neither intended a one-dimensional interpretation of the content, nor are the sculptures legible in this way. For instance, tips and angular forms have a repellent character. However, their whimsical formation reveals lighter components. In any case, the broad spectrum of associations remains a diplomatically progressive statement that becomes particularly forceful in view of the fact that the USSR had been one of the two superpowers until its dissolution in 1991.

In choosing art for the German House New York, the headquarters of the permanent representation at the United Nations and the consulate general, the Federal Building Authority was aware of the potentially delicate task of artistic missions. Between 1996 and 1998, it took the precaution of awarding a direct commission for figuratively designed spatial partitions in the restaurant to the sculptor Stephan Balkenhol (born in 1957), who was highly regarded in the USA at the time. According to the Federal Building Authority files: "The outward, prestigious self-representation of Germany faces particular risks, especially in New York, due to the extremely sensitive and critical public opinion." Balkenhol used poplar wood panels that were glued, hewn and colourfully framed to create a seven-part screen with concave reliefs, depicting women and men, as well as thematically and ornamentally arranged ants.

Robert Schad, "Im (Weiten) Sinn", 1992, German Embassy, Moscow, Russia

Stephan Balkenhol, untitled, 1996–1998, German House, New York, USA

Horst Antes, "Kopf für Dakar", 1980, FRG Embassy, Dakar, Senegal

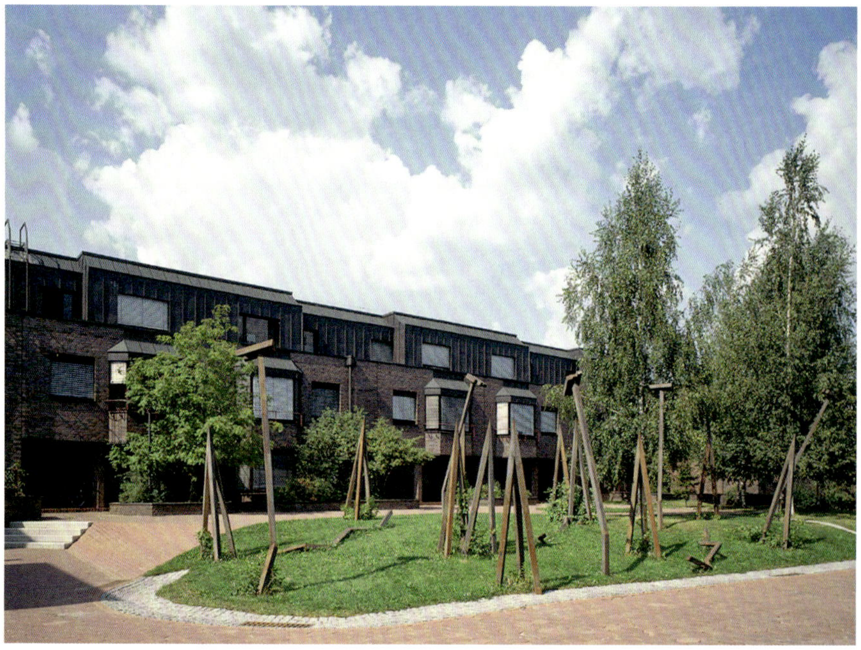

DIPLOMATIC TASKS

Figurative art caused certain problems on a number of occasions. One example was produced in 1980, namely "Kopf für Dakar" ("Head for Dakar") by the sculptor and painter Horst Antes (born in 1936). In view of German history, the Foreign Office expressed its concern at "the associations of the brown Corten steel bust with rather pronounced lips", coupled with the fact that the piece was to be installed outside the embassy premises, locating the art in architecture in a public space. However, despite these reservations, the Senegalese President Léopold Sédar Senghor received the work positively and even expressed his joy at the echoes of African stylistic elements.

For a long time, authorities responsible for art in architecture had tended to reject aspects of figurative art. Times change, however. After German reunification and the collapse of

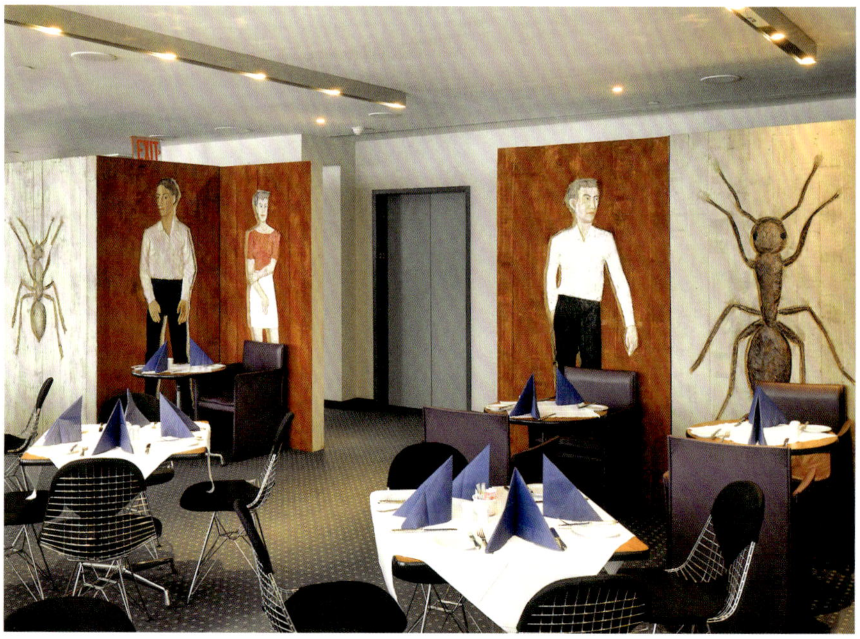

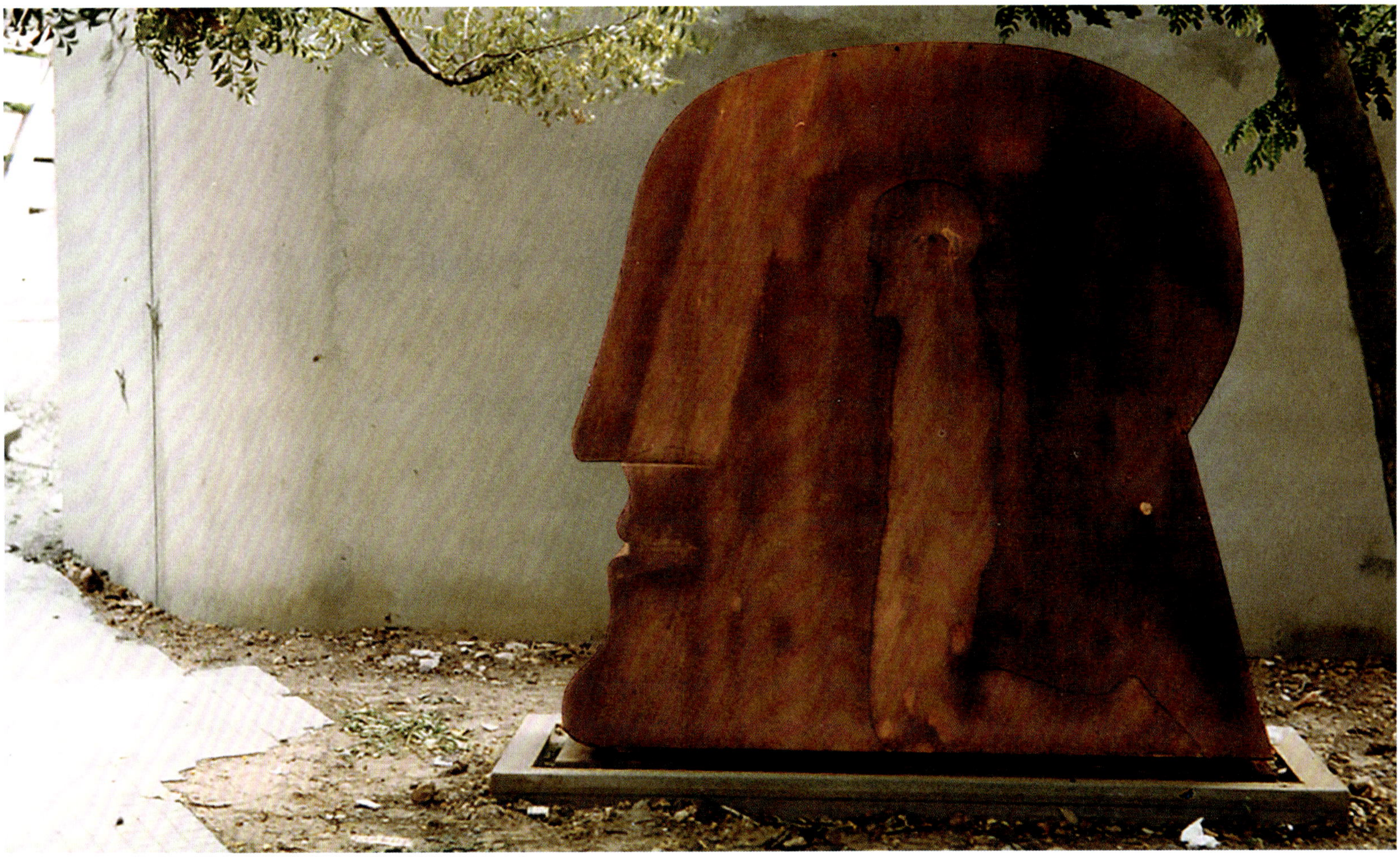

the Soviet Union, a new world order emerged. This had a diverse effect on art. Art was also affected by postmodernism and, from the 1980s onwards, increasingly began to present symbols and legible content again. After a period in which abstraction had dominated, art for newly constructed buildings in foreign countries reopened itself up to content. The themes and motifs of art began to comment and reflect on the state's missions of friendly, bi- and multilateral relations. In the case of murals, objects and sculptures for the German School in Beijing (1999), as well as the embassies in Tokyo, Mexico City (→ p. 274) (both constructed in 2005) and Dushanbe (2005–2008), themes clearly focus on coming together, hospitality and international relations.

Nevertheless, every art in architecture project has its own individual history. The embassy in Warsaw is a good example. The building designed by Holger Kleine and completed in 2008 was the first public German building constructed in Poland since World War II. That was also a challenge for art in architecture, for which three prizes were awarded in the competition. The sculptor Birgid Helmy (born in 1957) won 1st Prize with her proposal to install a sculpture of two skaters as an appeal for friendship and international understanding. The 3rd-Prize winning entry by the artists Stefka Ammon (born in 1970) and Veronike Hinsberg (born in 1968) proposed a bronze sculpture of a potato and an annual German-Polish potato feast, thereby also addressing the theme of coming together. However, the Foreign Office requested the ultimately implemented winner of the 2nd Prize, entitled "reflecting pool", by the Berlin artist Rainer Splitt (born in 1963). Although the title refers to the reflecting pools of memorial sites, giving the piece a deep significance, the blue coloured cast structure, which visibly spreads over the garden lawn, is also an abstract artwork. The Ambassador in Warsaw at the time, Michael Gerdts, differed from the jury in focusing on the aspect of bringing nations together, stating: "Fundamentally, I warmly welcome the instrument of art in architecture to support German artists and as a calling card for German cultural creativity abroad. However, I believe the selection of pieces should primarily focus on establishing a communicative bridge with our host countries […]."

The most recent art in architecture projects reflect their great artistic freedom. A collage by the artist couple J&K (Janne Schäfer, born in 1976, and Kristine Agergaard, born in 1975) for the two-storey foyer of the Goethe Institute in Cairo interweaves motifs of Egyptian mythology with photographic fragments of the Arab Spring in 2011 to create a polemic piece entitled "Glory to the Unknown" (→ p. 276).

By contrast, the work for the German Embassy in Belgrade refrains from any memorial, cautionary or didactic content. The Berlin group of artists and architects known as realities:united (Jan Edler, born in 1970, and Tim Edler, born in 1965) designed an installation for the ground floor and the staircase area on the first floor, consisting of two square and two round mirrors shaded in a monochrome tone. In recommending the piece for implementation, the jury of the art in architecture competition stated that the width and shading of the space created by the mirrors inspire, "associations ranging from a fashion show and a cat walk to a royal hall of mirrors, [thereby evoking] a certain elegance [that] can do no harm to Germany's international image."

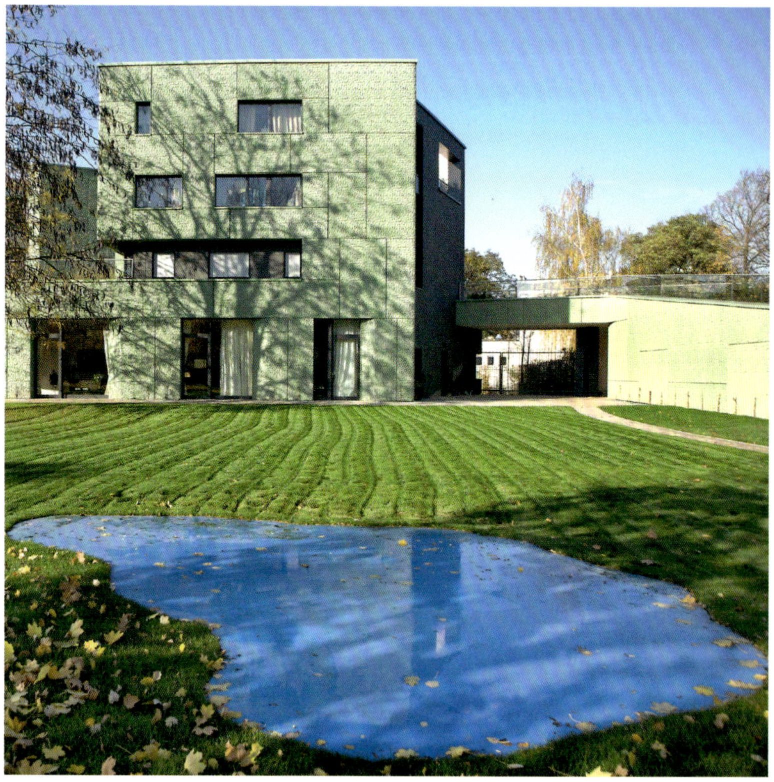

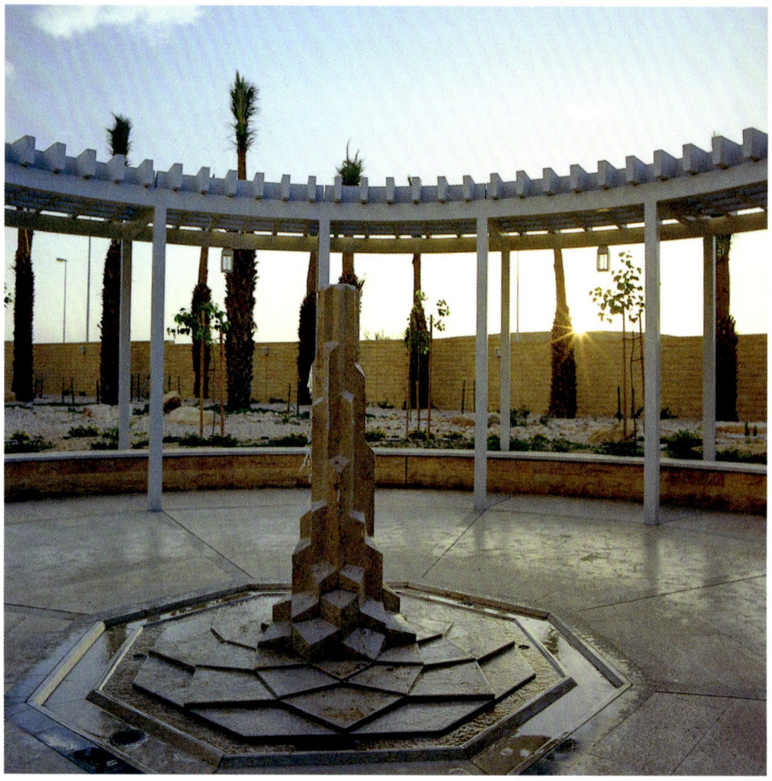

Rainer Splitt, "Reflecting Pool", 2007, German Embassy, Warsaw, Poland

Karl Schlamminger, fountain, stone cascade 1986, FRG Embassy, Riyadh, Saudi Arabia

BETWEEN ART AND DIPLOMACY

The almost 70 years of art in architecture for buildings in foreign countries demonstrate that there are as many approaches, possibilities, forms of expression and stances as there are buildings, representatives of building administrations, architects, artists, juries and users. External factors and underlying conditions, such as security requirements, measures to improve orientation or noise insulation, and, last but not least, the indoor climate, can all play a role. For instance for climate reasons, fountains and artworks involving the use of water are very popular as art in architecture for some buildings abroad: the German Embassy in the Saudi Arabian capital Riyadh, which was designed by Kurt Schentke and completed in 1987, is surrounded by a desert and therefore exists in a very hot climate. Thus, the art in architecture funds were invested to produce not one, but two fountain facilities. In the open staircase of the chancellery, Erich Reusch (1925–2019), who at the time held the Chair of Integrating Art and Architecture at the Kunstakademie Düsseldorf, designed a (no longer operative) three-tiered fountain system. Reusch combined the functional requirements of humidifying the dry desert air and binding the dust with a design consisting of bronze plates and projecting dripping pins, varying the principles of his important pioneering work in the field of wall and floor sculptures. The fountain in the residency garden is also a reaction to the local climate. However, its sculptor Karl Schlamminger (born in 1935) explained the design of the sculpture, which resembles a stalagmite formation, in reference to Islamic architecture, making specific connections to local traditions, thereby fulfilling both artistic and diplomatic functions, as is expected of exemplary art in architecture for buildings abroad.

GERMAN SCHOOL VALENCIA

Address:
Carrer de Jaume Roig, 16
46010 Valencia, Spain

Architecture:
Federal Building Authority,
Carl Mertz and Peter Müller,
1959–1961

Art in architecture:
Andreu Alfaro
and Heinrich Schwarz

Completed in 1961, the German School in Valencia is a building complex that is situated in the city centre, surrounded by high-rise buildings. It groups the elongated, five-storey main school building, sports hall and kindergarten around a large schoolyard. In 1996, not least due to the eye-catching ornamentation of the school façade and the concrete grid of the sports hall, the ensemble was added to the international association Docomomo's list of remarkable and preservation-worthy buildings and urban-planning ensembles of Modernity. The school's art in architecture is still striking today.

The spiral-shaped fountain sculpture "Espacio para una fuente" (literally "Space for a fountain") by the Valencian sculptor Andreu Alfaro (1929–2012) consists of an immense spatial volume with its elegant curves and sweeping lightness. The sculpture, which affords a wealth of different perspectives, was produced at a time when sculptors such as Alfaro often chose to demonstrate the diversity of artistic forms that were possible using new industrial materials such as steel.

The spatial and structural references impressively outline the sculpture against the overt grid of the classroom building and also against the small-scale, square fair-faced concrete grid of the sports hall, achieving a clear accentuation on the expansive schoolyard. Furthermore, they very practically form an attractive location for pupils to gather, with a high quality of stay.

The work also shows how important an art in architecture commission can be for an artist's career: "Espacio para una fuente" was the first monumental piece by Alfaro, who was one of the few local artists to receive a commission for art in architecture for German buildings abroad, and later became famous around the world, winning many awards.

ANDREU ALFARO
"Espacio para una fuente", 1960
Steel

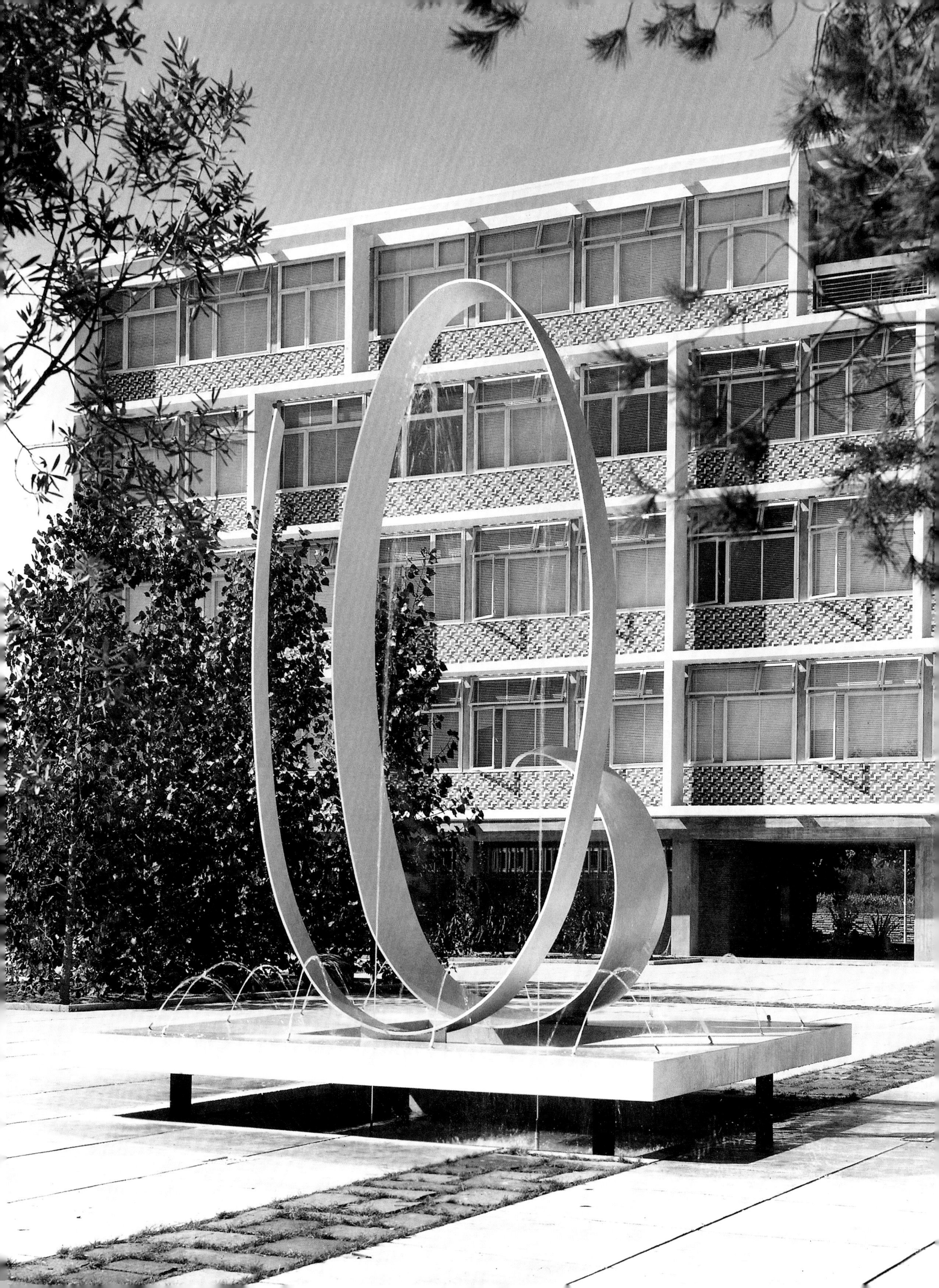

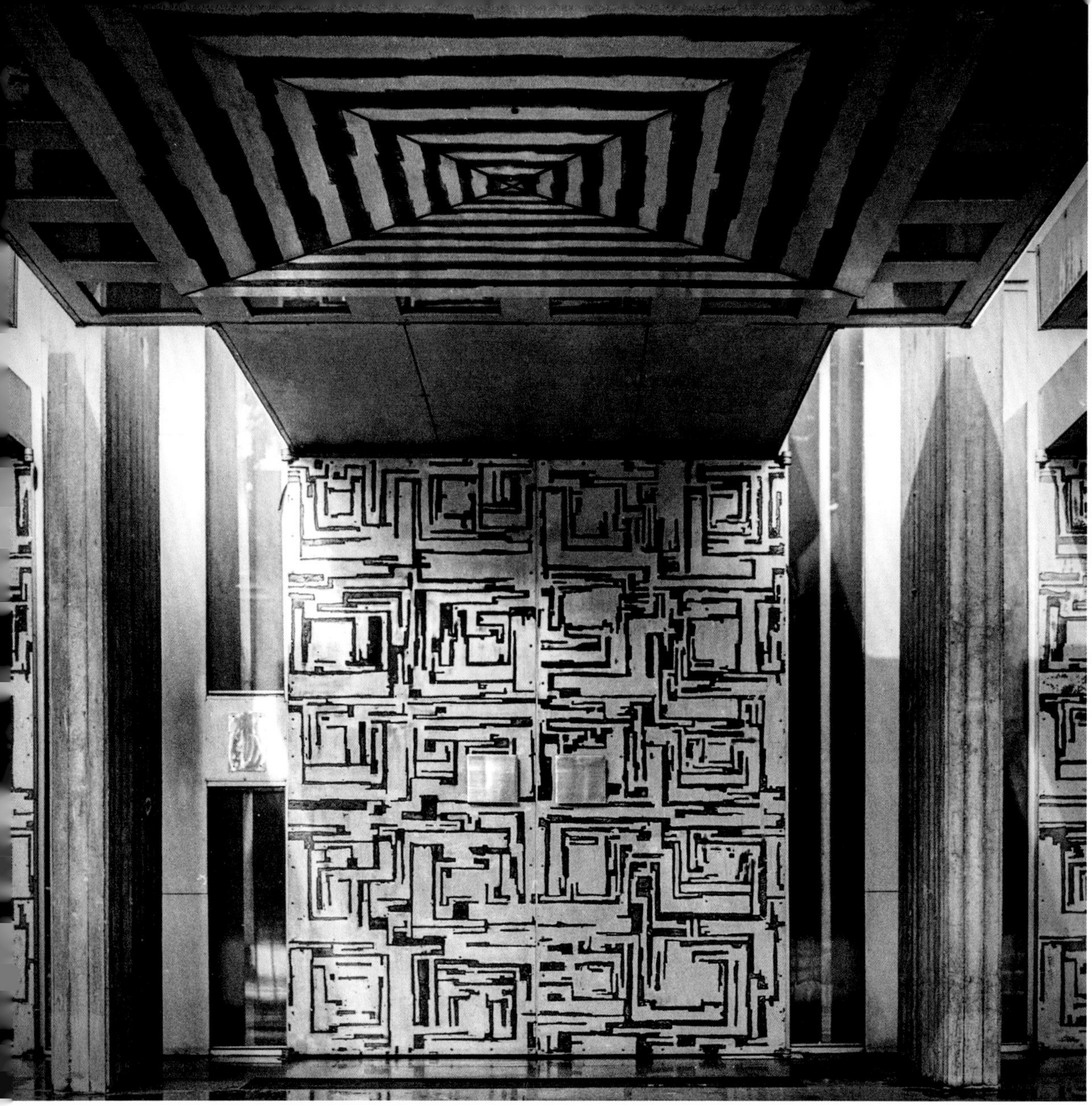

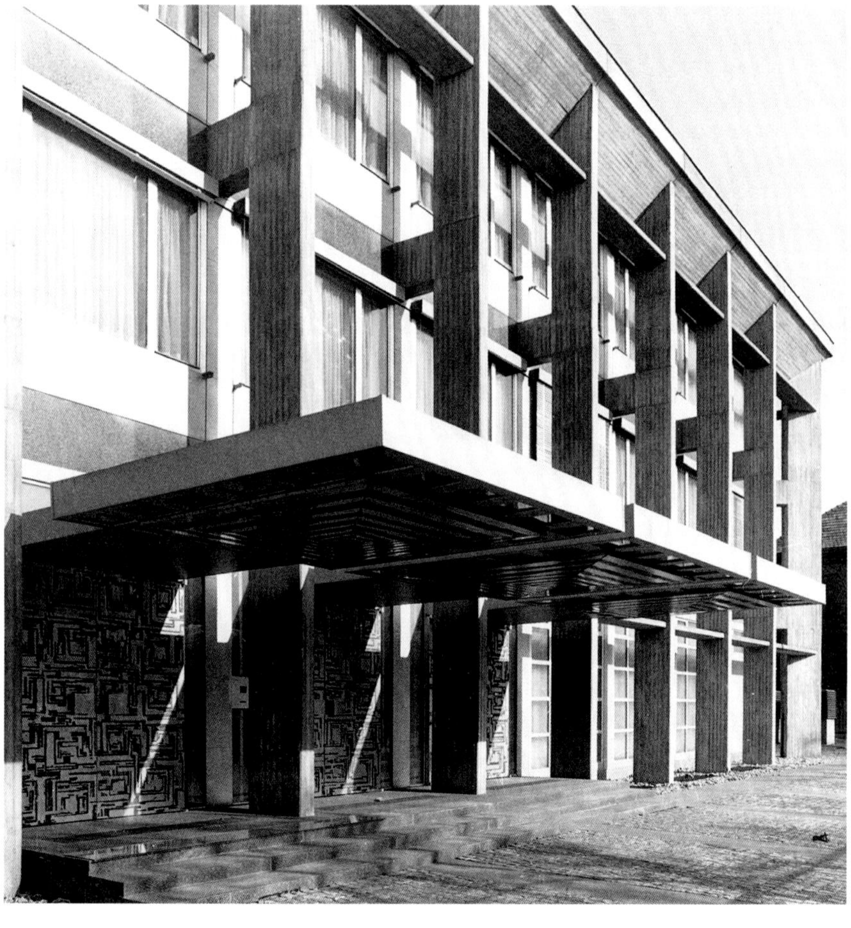

FRITZ KÜHN
Untitled, 1967
3 doors and canopies, aluminium
(no longer existent since its sale and conversion between 2007 and 2008)

GDR EMBASSY BUDAPEST

TODAY OFFICE USE

Address:
Stefánia út 101–103
1143 Budapest, Hungary

Architecture:
Heinz Graffunder and collective,
1965–1968

Art in architecture:
Fritz Kühn
and Eduard Gerhard Clauß,
Dieter Gantz, PGH Glasgestaltung
Magdeburg, Ute Putbrese,
Ernst Schwarz

Constructed between 1965 and 1968, the chancellery in Budapest was the first new embassy building for the GDR, which was still striving for recognition as an independent state at the time. The architect Heinz Graffunder already stressed the prestigious importance of the massive cube, which was far larger than the surrounding urban-planning scale. It was also striking through the modernity of the visible reinforced concrete structure and its slanted cornice, as well as through the use of prefabricated elements, demonstrating the performance of the state building sector. The prestigious effect of the building for the GDR is also expressed in the fact that the artists involved also continued to work with Graffunder and his collective on the Palace of the Republic (1973–1976).

One of them was the artistic blacksmith Fritz Kühn (1910–1967), who received important commissions in both East and West Germany. His works include a spatial grid wall for the German pavilion at the 1958 Expo in Brussels, the famous acoustic wall for the former Staatsrat building of the GDR (1964), as well as the metal doors for the Lower Saxony Parliament in Hanover (1962) and the Berlin City Library (1965), among others. Kühn conceived a fountain with many parts for the garden courtyard of the Budapest chancellery. For the prominent location of the main entrance, he also designed an aluminium portal consisting of three double-doors, each with its own canopy. For this piece, Kühn appropriated a strictly quadratic architectural grid and transformed it into an ornament of corroded, angled forms dyed in steel blue, which was repeated on the sixty panels of the doors. Thus the informal décor was developed as an autonomous visual wall, without becoming obtrusive or striving to contradict the architecture's concise quality.

FRG EMBASSY BRASÍLIA

Address:
SES Avenida das Nações,
Quadra 807, Lote 25
70415-900 Brasília DF, Brazil

Architecture:
Hans Scharoun, 1968–1971

Art in architecture:
Günter Ferdinand Ris
and Hans Theo Baumann,
Fritz Koenig, Adolf Luther,
Herbert Oehm, Lothar Quinte,
Emil Schumacher

The Federal Building Authority commissioned Hans Scharoun, a renowned protagonist of modern German architecture, to construct the German Embassy in Brazil's newly founded capital city. The architect's famous buildings include the Berlin Philharmonic and the Berlin State Library at Potsdamer Platz. For the embassy in Brasília, Scharoun's only foreign construction project, he continued to apply the principles of organic building and developed the architecture out of the construction task. Thus the four-storey embassy and the two-storey residency buildings connect with the adjoining housing section to form a rich sequence of structures. The new concept of mutually adjacent and enveloping buildings for prestigious, working and residential purposes, as well as fluent interior spatial concepts and not least the decision against using a residency canopy, which had hitherto been obligatory, express a changed notion of esteem and new architectural ideals.

New concepts were also reflected in the art in architecture. The selected artist, Günter Ferdinand Ris (1928–2005), was a sculptor who had already become renowned through his presentations at the *documenta* and biennales. One of the dominant themes of his art was his exploration of "forms of water". For the project in Brasília, Ris designed three "water-light steles" that ascend out of the residency fountain. The idea of combining stainless steel cylinders of different heights with Perspex rings and cascading water was revolutionary, as was the artistic emancipation of industrial materials and forms he used. The concept and design principles of the "water-light steles" was – like Scharoun's architecture – inspired by a quality of modesty, transparency and a willingness to experiment that reflected the mood of new beginnings in the ascendant Federal Republic during the so-called "Brandt-Scheel" era.

GÜNTER FERDINAND RIS

"Drei Wasser-Licht-Stelen"
("Three water-light steles"), 1970
Stainless steel, Perspex, lighting

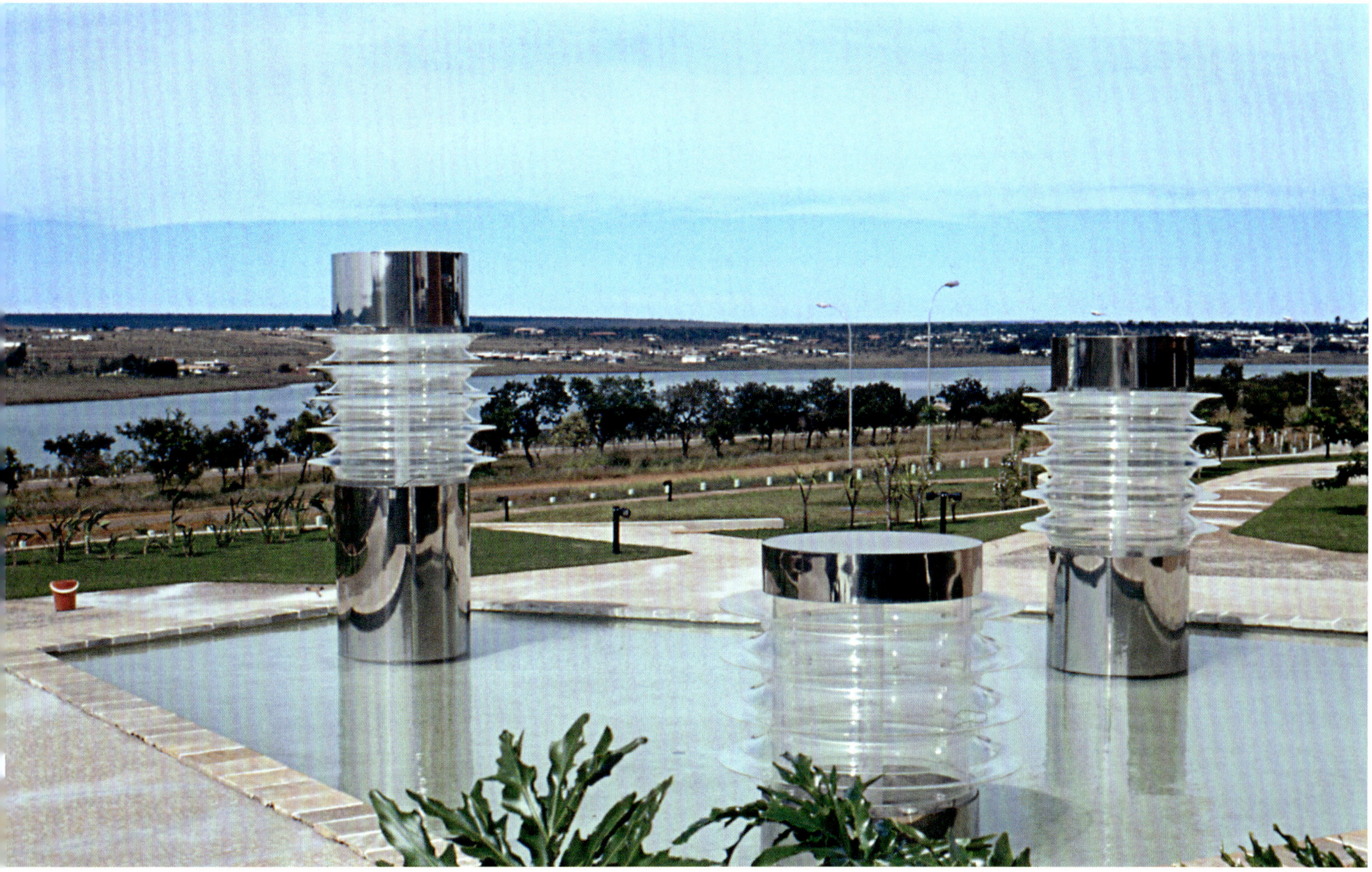

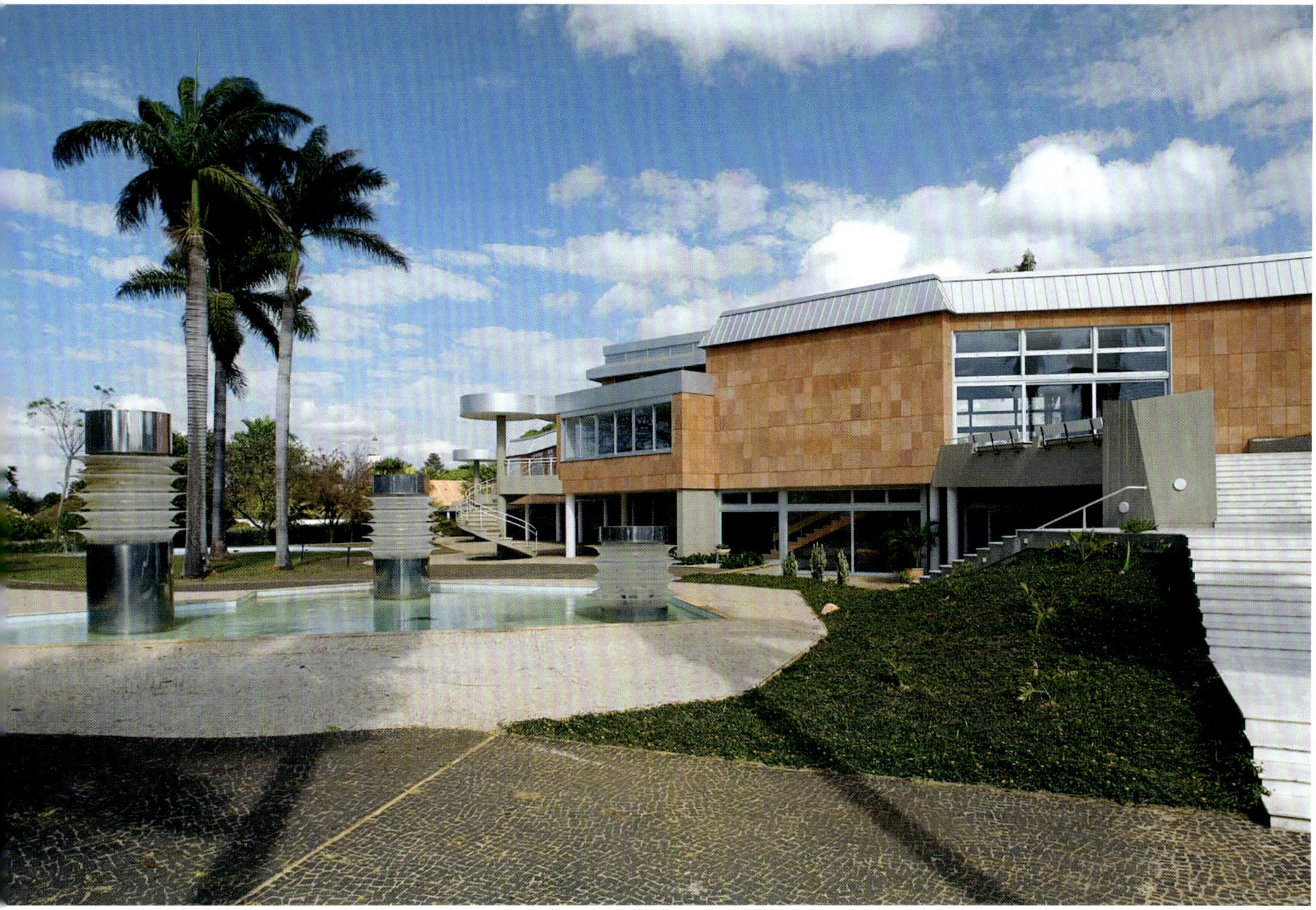

GERMAN EMBASSY HELSINKI

Address:
Krogiuksentie 4b
00340 Helsinki, Finland

Architecture:
Juha Leiviskä, Helsinki, 1990–1993

Art in architecture:
Frank M. Zeidler and Edgar Gutbub, Leo Kornbrust

The German Embassy in Helsinki on the island of Kuusisaari, eleven kilometres outside the city centre, is one of the Federal Republic's most attractive foreign representations. Its appeal is not simply based on its superb situation on the Gulf of Finland. It is also due to the architect Juha Leiviskä's efforts, whose exquisitely fine structures and lively architecture react to the privileged location. Like the building's exterior appearance, the modern, white interior spaces excel through the light conditions and an openness towards the surrounding area. In the garden, the concrete structural sculptures by the artists Leo Kornbrust (born in 1929) and Edgar Gutbub (1940–2017) make a key contribution to the overall impression of the embassy. One special aim was decorating the residency rooms. Prior consideration by the architect and a competition resulted in an abstract cycle of paintings produced by Frank M. Zeidler (born in 1952). Six large panelled paintings vary in black and white tones and inspire associations with clouds and water landscapes, especially when combined with the title "Doppelhorizontal-lichte Sechs" ("Double horizontal light six"). In a sphere between inner and outer observation, the images thereby continue the dialogue with the exterior space, the garden, the sky and the sea, while also picking up on the architecture and the openness of the rooms. Each painting retains the independence of an autonomous panel, at the same time providing references beyond its autonomy. The pieces' formal and content-related coherence, the constant height of 2 metres and their installation 40 centimetres above the ground connects the spaces, making the cycle an irreplaceable example of spatial effect. The solution that the artist originally strived for, namely binding the images even more closely to the architecture by inserting them into the walls, was impossible for constructional reasons.

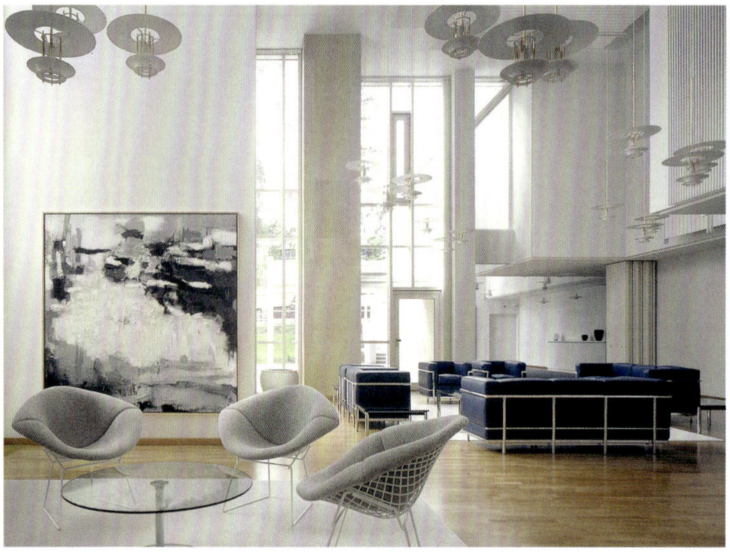

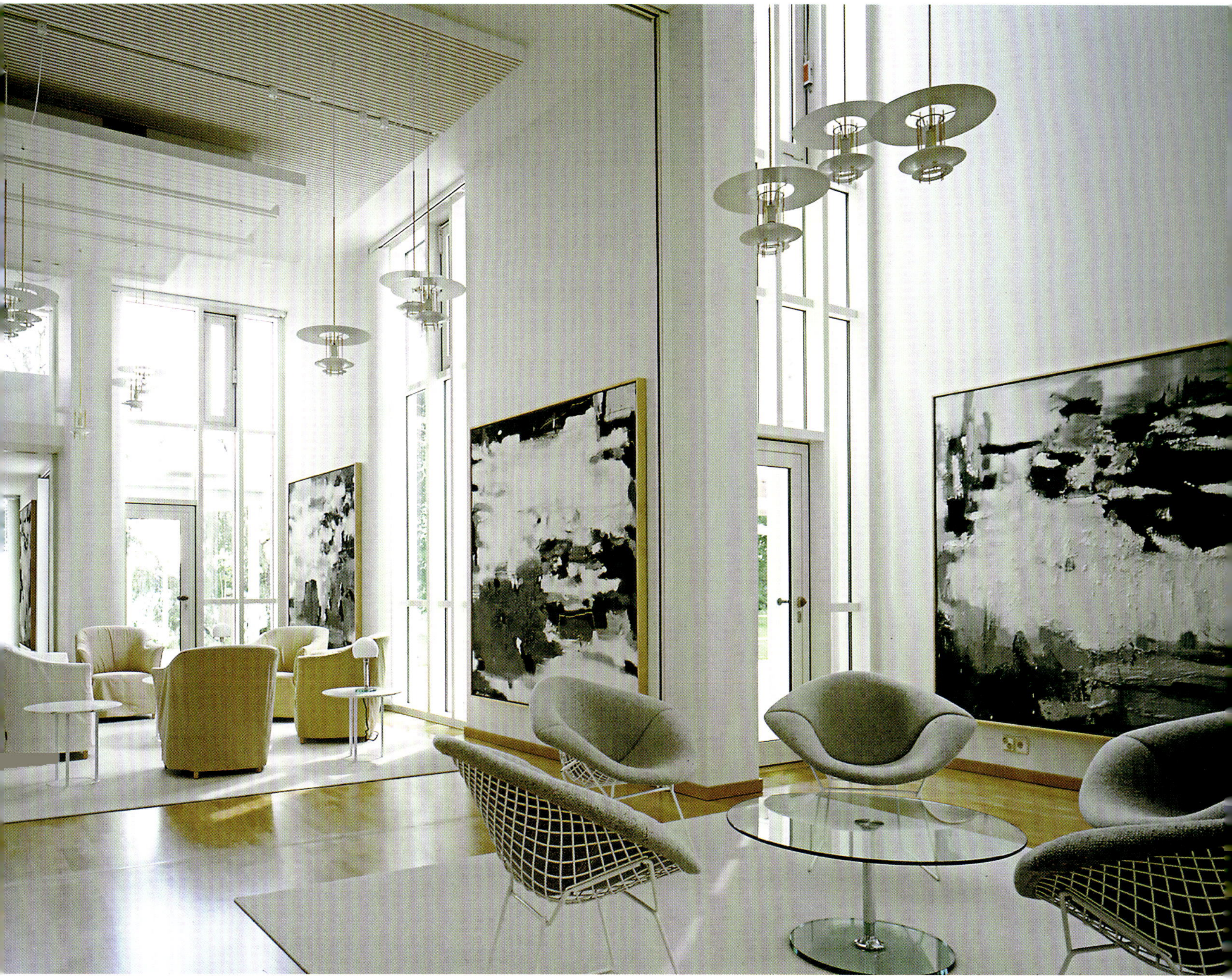

FRANK M. ZEIDLER
"Doppelhorizontal-lichte Sechs,
Helsinki–Berlin 1992"
("Double horizontal light six"), 1993
6 paintings, mixed technique
on canvas
200 cm high

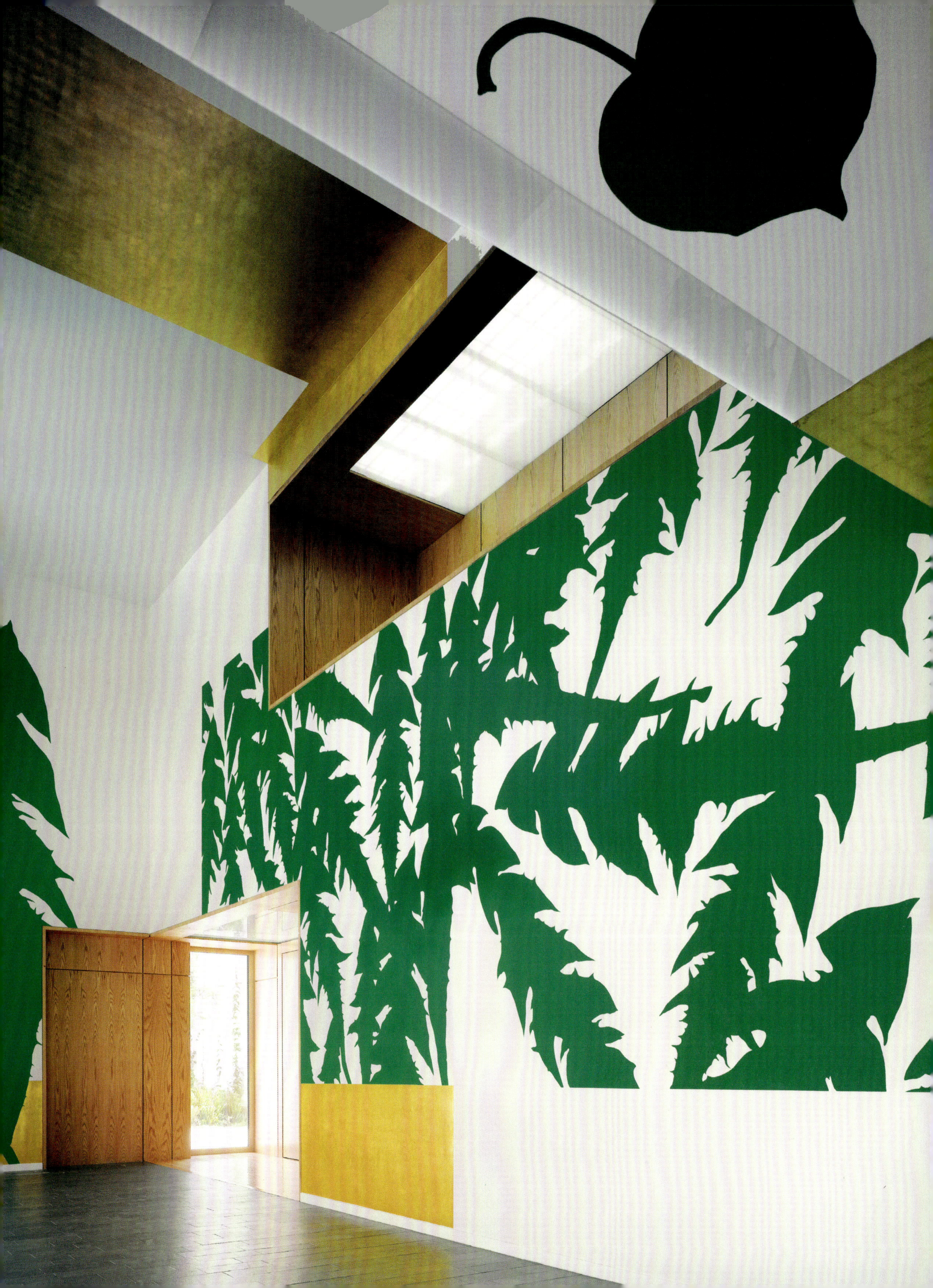

GERMAN EMBASSY MEXICO CITY

Address:
Avenida Horacio 1506
11510 Mexico City, Mexico

Architecture:
Staab Architekten, 2005–2007

Art in architecture:
Renate Wolff

Between 2005 and 2007, the new chancellery of the Federal Republic was constructed in Mexico City on the centrally located corner plot of the former GDR Embassy. The two-storey cuboid building was designed by the Berlin architect Volker Staab, its purist, reduced formal language clearly expressing the building's representative character – despite the security wall and limited visual relationships from and into the city. The common second characteristic of federal buildings abroad, namely to engage with local building traditions, can be seen in the design with three inner courtyards, the use of reddish brown lava stone for the façades and a sand-coloured natural stone inside the building.

The designer of the lobby art in architecture, the Berlin-based artist Renate Wolff (born in 1956), establishes even clearer references to the country of residence. Stylised impressions of dandelion, oak, apple tree and pear tree leaves, as well as light green and golden coloured areas cover the entire two-storey space, including the single-storey corridor area. On an artistic and design level, geometric-abstract and organic-figurative elements combine to achieve a balance between the aesthetic experiences of a non-ornamental Modernity and a decorative counter-Modernity. The colours and motifs not only create a pleasant, friendly atmosphere: the German vegetation and the gold leaf, which echoes Mexico's Inca past, also symbolise the encounter between two cultures. In intense interaction with the closed areas, wall apertures and joists in the foyer, Renate Wolff's paintings create an appropriate continuum based on the real location and a spiritual, associative space.

RENATE WOLFF
"Große Reise"
("Great journey"), 2006
Acrylic paint, gold leaf

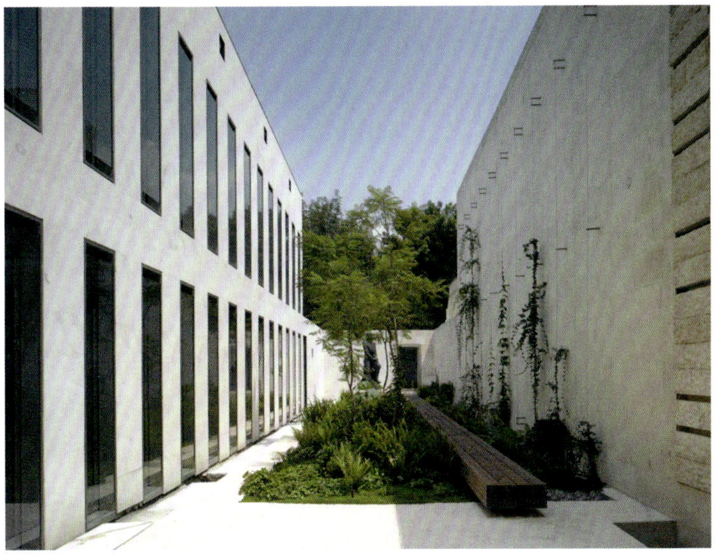

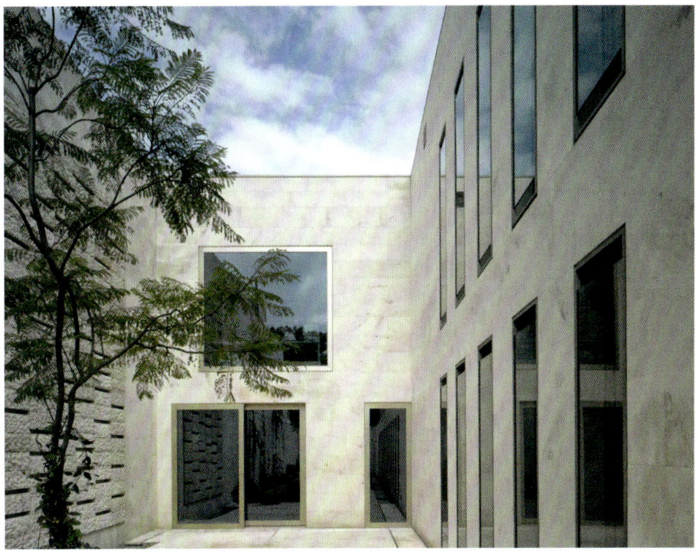

GOETHE INSTITUTE CAIRO AND GERMAN ACADEMIC EXCHANGE SERVICE CAIRO

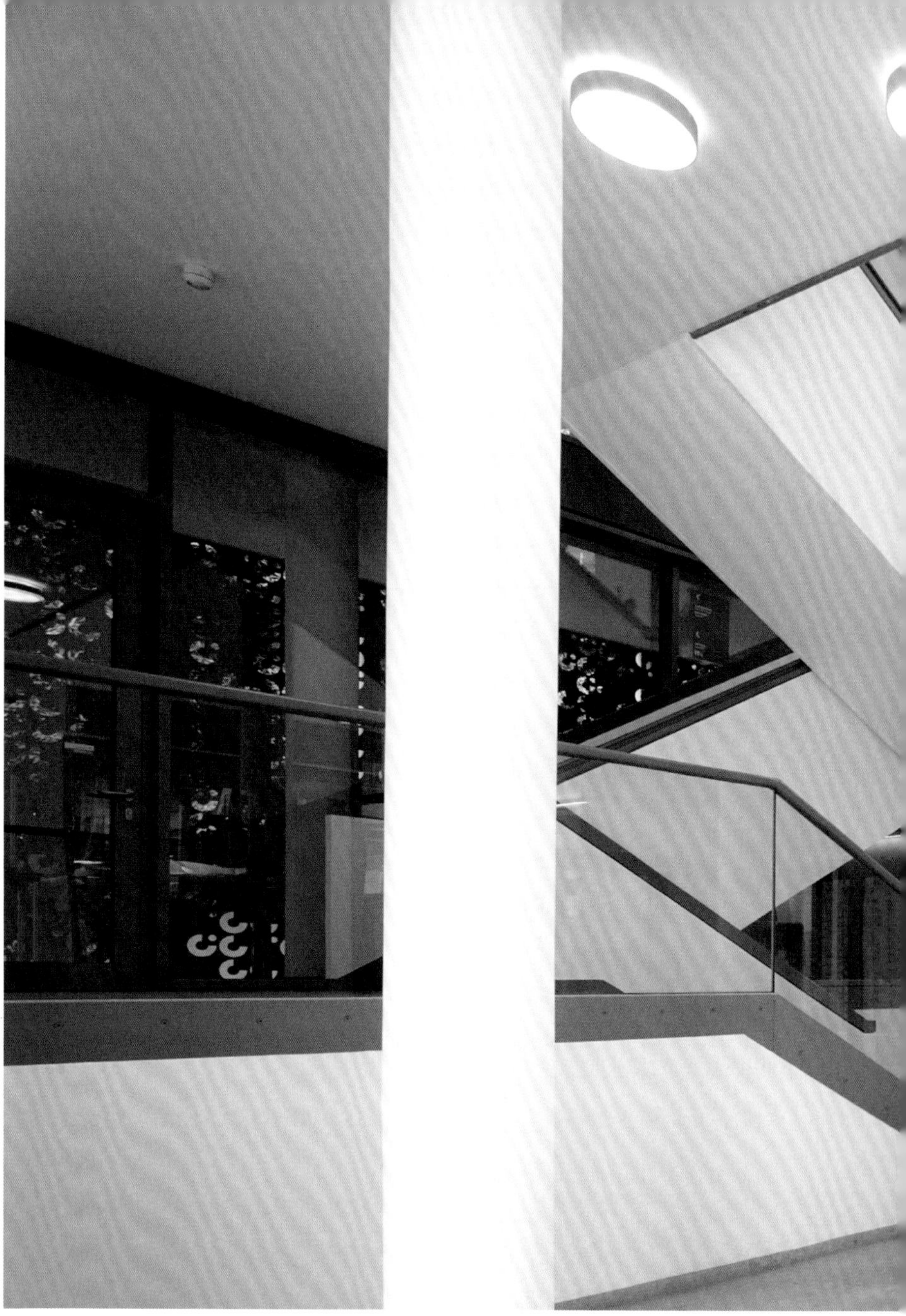

Address:
Sharia Hussein Wassef 17
11518 Cairo, Egypt

Architecture:
Worschech Architekten, 2012–2016
(1st construction stage)

Art in architecture:
J&K (Janne Schäfer and
Kristine Agergaard)

J&K
"Glory to the Unknown", 2016
Digital photo collage,
9-part mural relief
310 x 840 x 9 cm

For a long time, the facilities of the Goethe Institute Cairo, which was established as a regional centre, were distributed over several locations. In 2016, they and the Cairo branch of the German Academic Exchange Service were pooled onto two neighbouring but unconnected properties in the Cairo district of Dokki. As a result, a new main and entrance building was constructed for the Goethe Institute. The white-plastered, largely glazed, cuboid structure was conceived by the Leipzig office Worschech Architekten. Despite its unmistakeable western, modern characteristics, the structure surrounding the garden and the use of metal elements with an Arabic-style perforation reveals references to the local architecture. The architecturally initiated dialogue is transformed into a surreal historical review in the art in architecture.

In the publicly accessible foyer, which adjoins with the event hall and library, the two artists J&K (Janne Schäfer, born in 1976, and Kristine Agergaard, born in 1975) installed a collection of nine collage

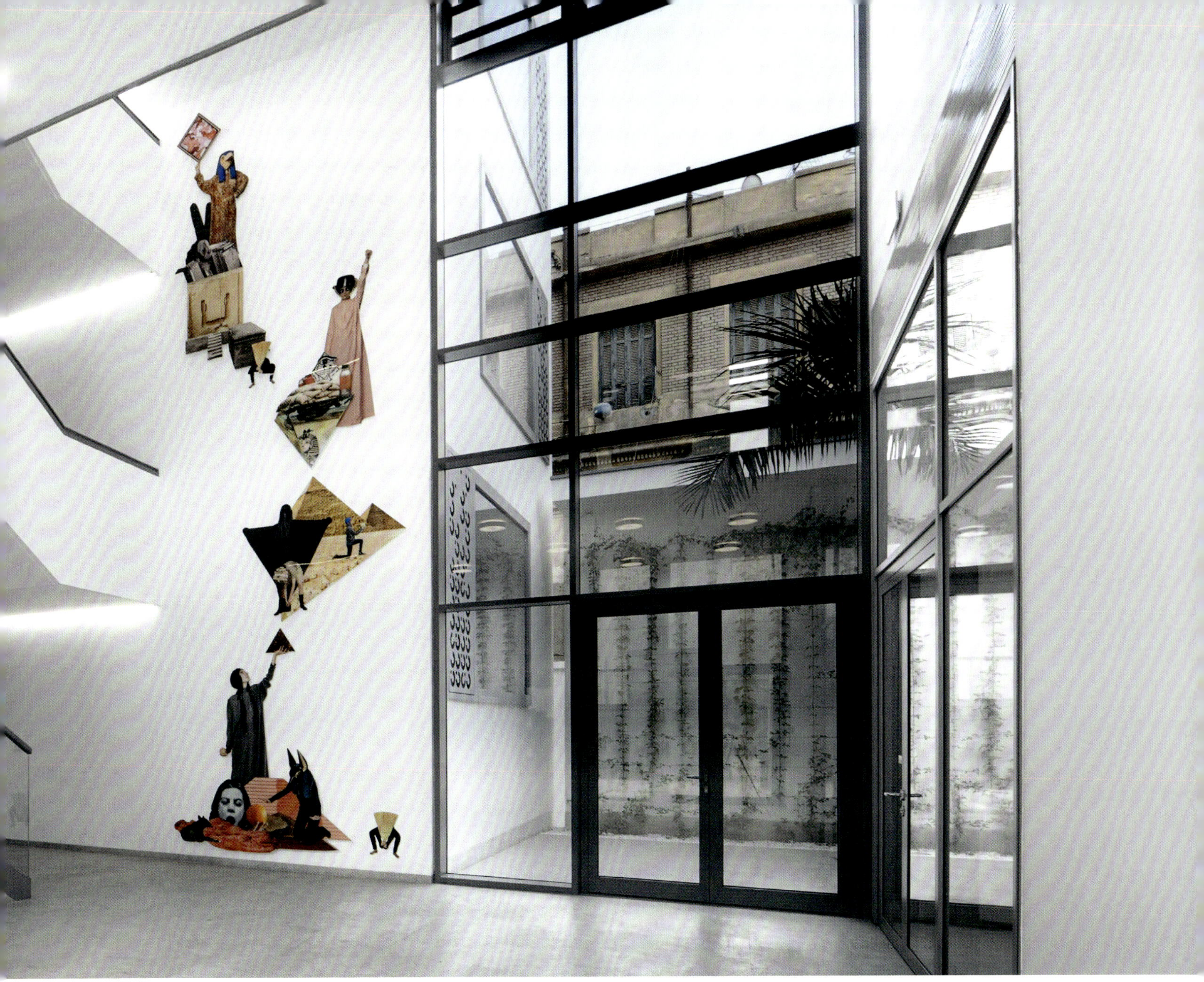

photo reliefs covering two storeys. Topoi of ancient Egyptian mythology and motifs of the 2011 Arab Spring revolution are combined in a colourful, quirky mixture.The collages are based on photos taken by the artists themselves and found on the Internet. In surreal dramatisations, with strange costumes and postures of triumph, submission and resistance, Cleopatra, the god of death Anubis and Tutankhamen appear beside demonstrators in the 2011 revolution. These characters encounter pyramids, hieroglyphs, archaeological fragments of sculptures, visual portfolios, along with victory signs and barricade-sandbags. Derived from the writing on a plastic bottle, the dance of images has a title that sheds a critical light on contemporary Egypt and supports the victims of the revolution: "Glory to the Unknown".

STEP BY STEP

STAGES OF
ART IN ARCHITECTURE

TO ART

Art in architecture for federal buildings is produced following a state commission as part of a building measure. In line with its self-perception as a cultural nation, the Federal Republic of Germany fulfils its exemplary role in supporting architecture and art. The starting point and therefore the beginning of every process to produce art in architecture is the building. Depending on the amount of the building costs, between 0.5 and 1.5 percent of the building measure's budget are allocated to art.

Commissions for artworks are usually the result of competitions organised by the relevant building administration. In the case of open competitions, artists submit proposals directly. Following preliminary assessment, the artworks are evaluated by a jury according to previously defined criteria. In the case of two-stage competition processes, the artists first apply with references, on the basis of which they are selected by a committee to participate in the competition.

The competition announcement describes the process, the building in the context of the real estate, the users, the specific art locations and the brief for competition participants. Art in architecture can refer thematically to the history of the location, the architecture or the building's use. Unlike museum art, which is generally mobile, art in architecture must take a wide range of underlying conditions into account. For instance, they include functional requirements, fire-safety regulations and statics.

The jury that decides on the submitted competition proposals consists of expert jurors (artists and art historians) and jurors representing the client, the building administration and users. It selects the most suitable piece from among the anonymously entered and presented proposals, awards 1st Prize to the artwork and provides implementation recommendations. Once a contract has been closed with the artists, specific plans are developed to integrate the selected artwork's implementation into the ongoing construction process. The aim is to present the completed building and the art in architecture simultaneously to the users.

STEP BY STEP TO ART

Beate Hückelheim-Kaune

For 70 years, art in architecture has had a firm place in federal building tasks. The Federal Government assumes responsibility not only for prominent building projects with nationally relevant functions, but also for art in architecture, going beyond architectural design, thereby fulfilling its exemplary role in supporting building culture. Thus, the "Guidelines for implementing federal building tasks" (RBBau) includes Section K7, regulating the participation of visual artists. Since 2005, these regulations have been adopted in a "Guideline on art in architecture" ("Leitfaden Kunst am Bau"), which also stipulates specifications and offers help in implementing federal procedures. The guideline, which was published by the Federal Ministry of Building, is based on experiences of the Federal Office for Building and Regional Planning (BBR), which has organised numerous competition processes, and was developed in coordination with the Federal Ministry of Finance. It also contains regulations on handling already existent art in architecture.

FORMS OF COMMISSIONING

The underlying basis for all commissions is the rule of general transparency and equality. In the case of design competitions, and therefore also art in architecture, the rule is above all guaranteed through the anonymity of artists participating in a competition. In the majority of cases today, open and limited-open competitions are organised. Artists learn about the competitions through announcements in art journals and on the websites of artists' associations and building administrations. The competition announcement contains all the conditions and above all additional information on the building, the real estate, the users, the task and the artwork's location; it can generally be downloaded from the building administration following appropriate online registration.

In open competitions, regardless whether they are implemented in one or two stages, all artists can participate directly with a specific competition entry for the announced art location. This above all offers the chance for younger, as yet unknown artists to impress with their anonymous proposals. In the case of limited, open competitions, there is a prior application process in which interested artists must apply to take part and are professionally selected on the basis of their references.

What influences the quality of a good decision? Experience shows that it is the type of process, its compatibility with the task, the quality of implementation, the members of the jury and their collaboration. The criteria for the jury in deciding on the competition are the project's guiding principle, the artistic quality of the design and its feasibility during the building process, also taking the defined budget into account. One essential aspect is the common will of everyone involved to produce high-quality, contemporary art that is allowed to polarise and refer to current themes with a critical stance.

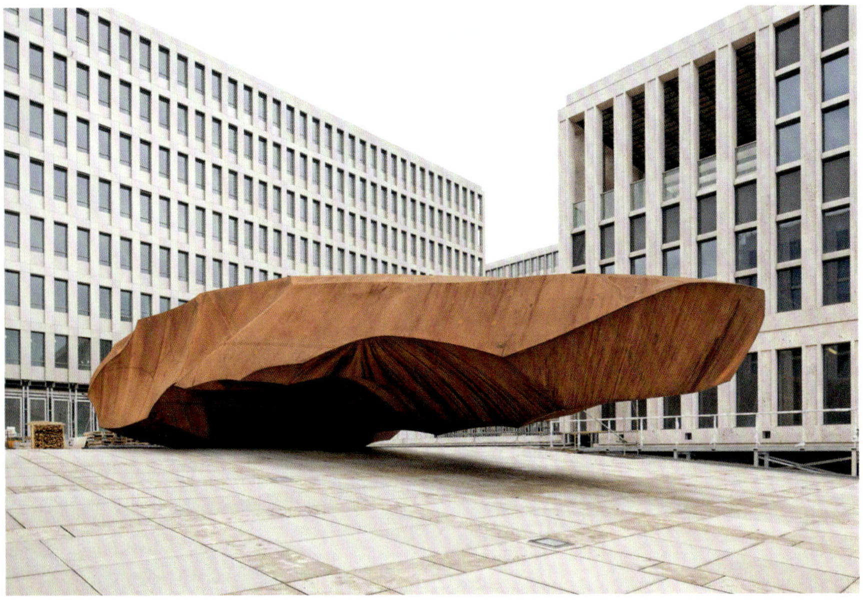

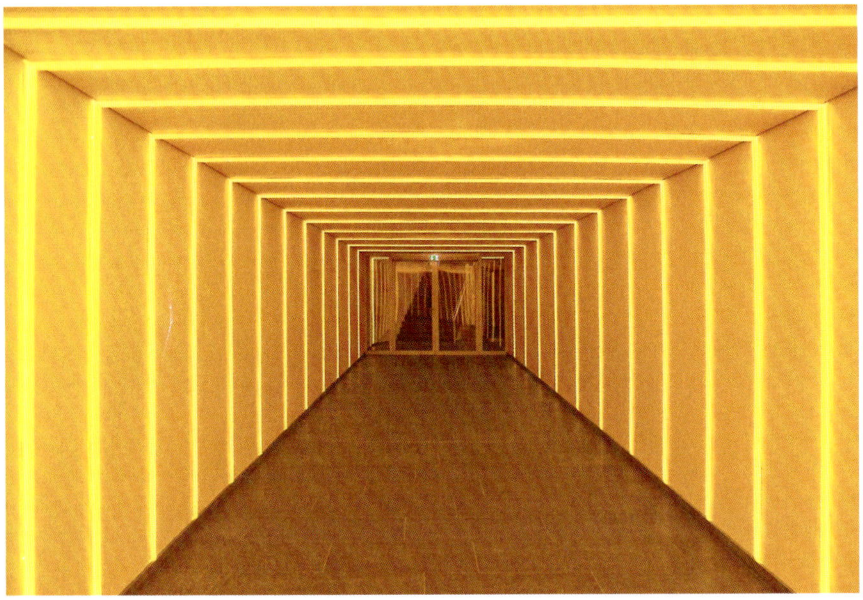

THE FREEDOM AND CONDITIONALITY OF ART IN ARCHITECTURE

A piece of art in architecture should be specifically produced for the respective building task. As an autonomous artistic contribution, it can refer to the history of the location, the building's use or the architecture. The reference to the locality or the edifice consolidates its address and strengthens the users' identification with the building or the real estate. If the artwork is publicly accessible or visible, passers by become more aware of the relevant institution and its tasks. In any case, the work should not be arbitrary and instead enable sustained reception.

All art professions and lasting forms of expression are possible in principle. They vary depending on the context of the task and its location. The diversity is clear when looking at examples of implemented federal art in architecture in 2012: a gigantic sculpture made of Corten steel by Stefan Sous (born in 1964) for the entrance drive of the Federal Intelligence Service in Berlin, the video installation "Sleep #3" by Sebastian Stumpf (born in 1980) in the glazed foyer of the German Federal Cultural Foundation in Halle an der Saale, the spatially definitive lighting installation "Raum – Struktur – Rhythmus" ("Space – Structure – Rhythm") by Gunda Förster (born in 1967) in an underground connecting tunnel for the German Bundestag, and a visual wallpaper designed as a graphic novel, entitled "Comic vs. Hitec" by Robert Patz (born in 1981) for the Max Delbrück Center for Molecular Medicine in Berlin-Buch.

To fulfil federal policy goals, the "Guideline on art in architecture" does not exclusively apply to federal building measures and is also used for publicly co-funded building

Stefan Sous, untitled, 2012, Headquarters of the Federal Intelligence Service, Berlin

Gunda Förster, "Raum – Struktur – Rhythmus", 2012, Wilhelmstrasse underground walkway, German Bundestag, Berlin

measures in which the state covers at least half the costs, owing to the considerable public interest such projects involve. One such example is the above-mentioned artwork on the campus of the Max Delbrück Center in Berlin-Buch, which is receiving expert supervision from the Federal Office for Building and Regional Planning. The research centre announced a limited, anonymous competition for students at the Weissensee Academy of Art Berlin and the Berlin University of the Arts, in which 27 young artists participated following prior internal selections by the art schools. As preparation, the students had the opportunity to see the work of the scientists in the building. Finally, the winning artwork by Robert Patz was implemented. On the walls of the inner core of the research building for ultra-high magnetic resonance, covering three floors in varying perspectives, a graphic novel tells the fictional story of an apprentice who disappears in a tomography machine. The most important criteria of art in architecture, namely that it is produced for the specific location, is conceived as a lasting presentation and enters into a clear relationship with the building in terms of content and space, were excellently fulfilled in this case. The competition process only for students also increased awareness of art in architecture among the young artists.

Who decides on the result of the competition process? Basically, federal art competitions should involve a jury with a majority of voting jury members who are art experts, such as art historians, curators or artists, while the builder is represented by the client, the users, the building administration and the architectural office.

Competitions are proven instruments to find several concrete solutions for one artistic task, from which the best can be selected

Robert Patz, “Comics vs. Hitec”, 2012, Max Delbrück Center for Molecular Medicine, Berlin

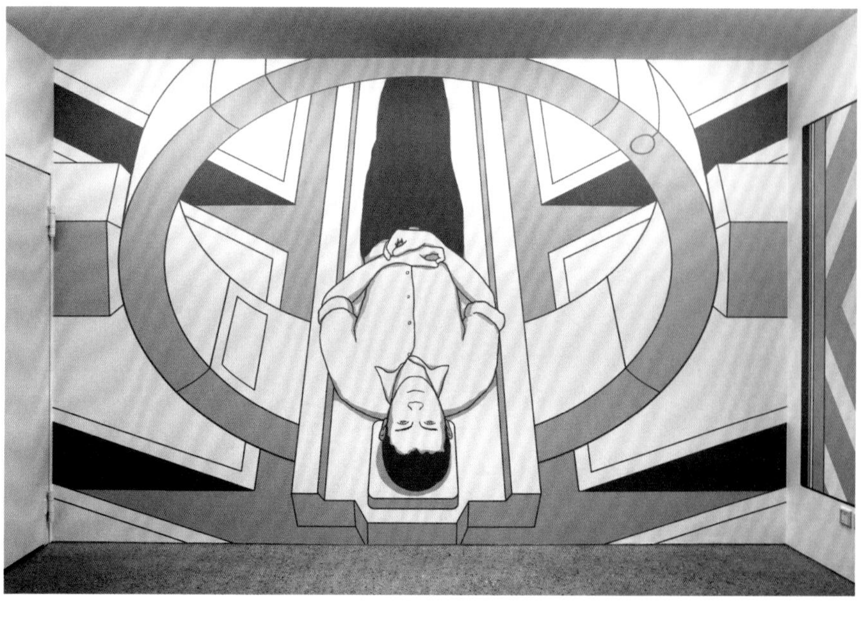

Dörte Michaelis, “Der Traum vom Fliegen”, 2006, Federal Armed Forces training centre, Warbelow

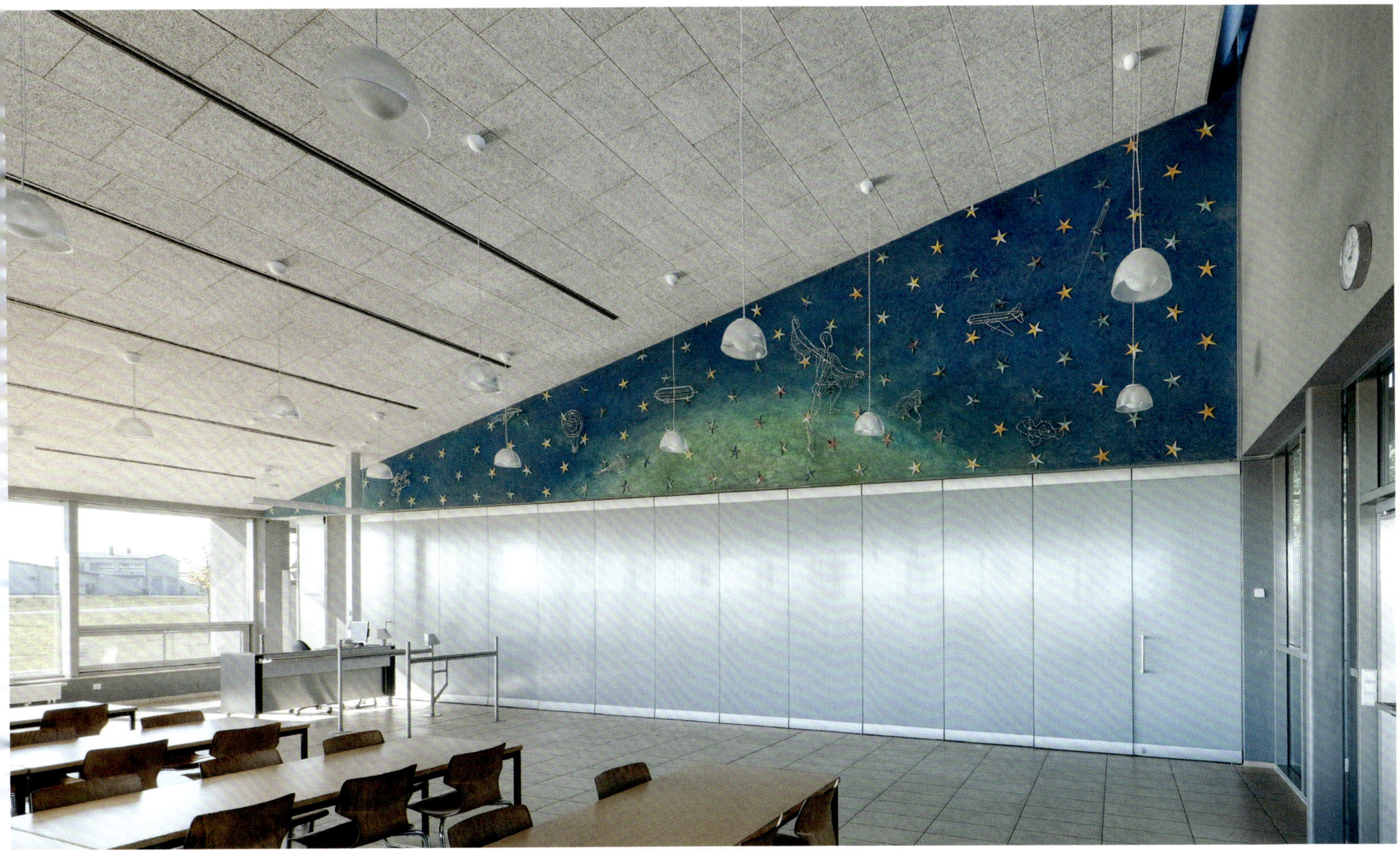

for the relevant situation and implemented. During the process, the designs are assessed with respect to their conceptual, aesthetic and craftsmanship qualities. Adherence to the stipulated budget is equally assessed, as well as possible follow-up costs, since federal buildings must be planned sustainably, with long-term, low-maintenance and cost-effective use.

If only low budgets are available, a purchasing process may be sensible. In individual, justified cases, it may also be viable to award a direct commission. For instance a new service building was constructed in 2005–2006 for the Friedensausbildungsstelle Warbelow (a military training centre). The client, in coordination with the responsible ministry, decided to commission Dörte Michaelis (born in 1957) directly. She had won 2nd Prize in two previous art in architecture competitions. The artist worked together with the commanding officer of the facility's anti-aircraft squadron in developing a mural on the theme of "Der Traum vom Fliegen" ("The dream of flying"), presenting an encyclopaedic depiction of the history of aviation.

During building measures for the state broadcaster Deutsche Welle in Bonn (1997–2002), the Federal Office for Building and Regional Planning cooperated with art experts to develop a concept involving artists from the regions where the broadcaster is active, so that five works were produced by artists from Africa, Asia, Central and Eastern Europe, and the Middle East, including the sculpture "Fest für Neptun" ("Feast of Neptune") by the Nigerian sculptor Sokari Douglas Camp (born in 1958).

In rare exceptional cases, close collaboration between architects and artists can lead to a direct commission, as in the case of the Alfred Wegener Institute in Bremerhaven (2000–2004). The sculptor Erich Wiesner had already successfully collaborated for years with the architect Otto Steidle, for instance on the colour design of the university in Ulm (1992). In Bremerhaven, Wiesner and Steidle proposed a joint, integrated design for the façade, whereby materials and the arrangement of the coloured, varnished clinker bricks were combined to create an integrative concept. After its completion, the façade became an architectural attraction and an identifying symbol for the harbour area.

The underlying conditions for art in architecture's implementation are as diverse as the appearances and manifestations of the works themselves. In 2015, the new building for the Federal Ministry of the Interior in Berlin was completed according to plans by Müller Reimann Architekten. In 2016, an open, two-stage implementation competition was announced for the exterior grounds. The two potential locations on the south-eastern corner of the building were to be accessible for ministry employees and visible from the public footpath and the commuter railway. They are also situated in the direct line of sight of the conference zone, which is frequented by German and international guests. Neither the artistic genre nor a stipulated content limited the design potential, although considerable security aspects had to be taken into account.

At the first jury meeting, ten designs from among the 77 anonymously entered proposals were selected for a second, in-depth evaluation process. Following a concluding discussion, the jury recommended the design by Roland Fuhrmann (born in 1966) entitled "Zusammenhalt" ("Cohesion"), reflecting one of the key tasks of the ministry, namely supporting social cohesion, while also requiring an active stance by the viewer. The spectrum of other designs was diverse, ranging from abstract pieces by the sculptor Michael Sailstorfer (born in 1979) to a fence by Dietrich

Sokari Douglas Camp, "Fest für Neptun", 2004, Deutsche Welle, Bonn

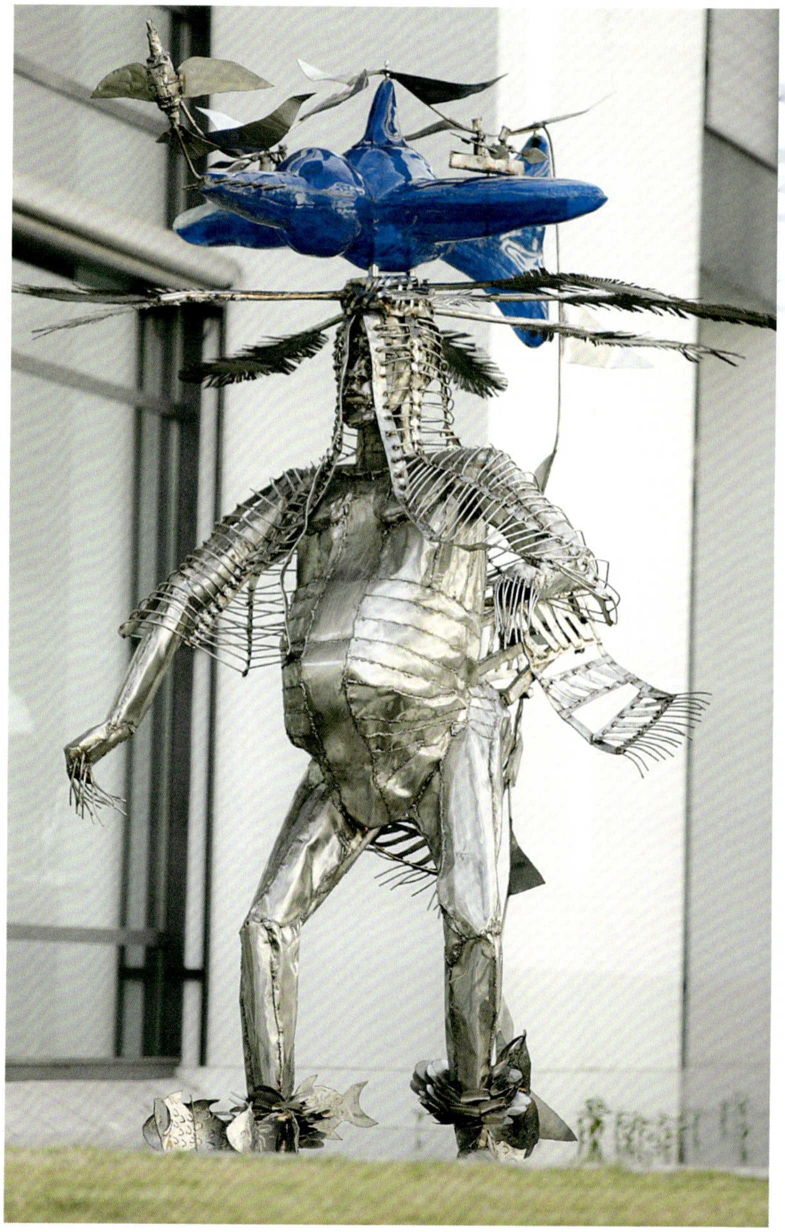

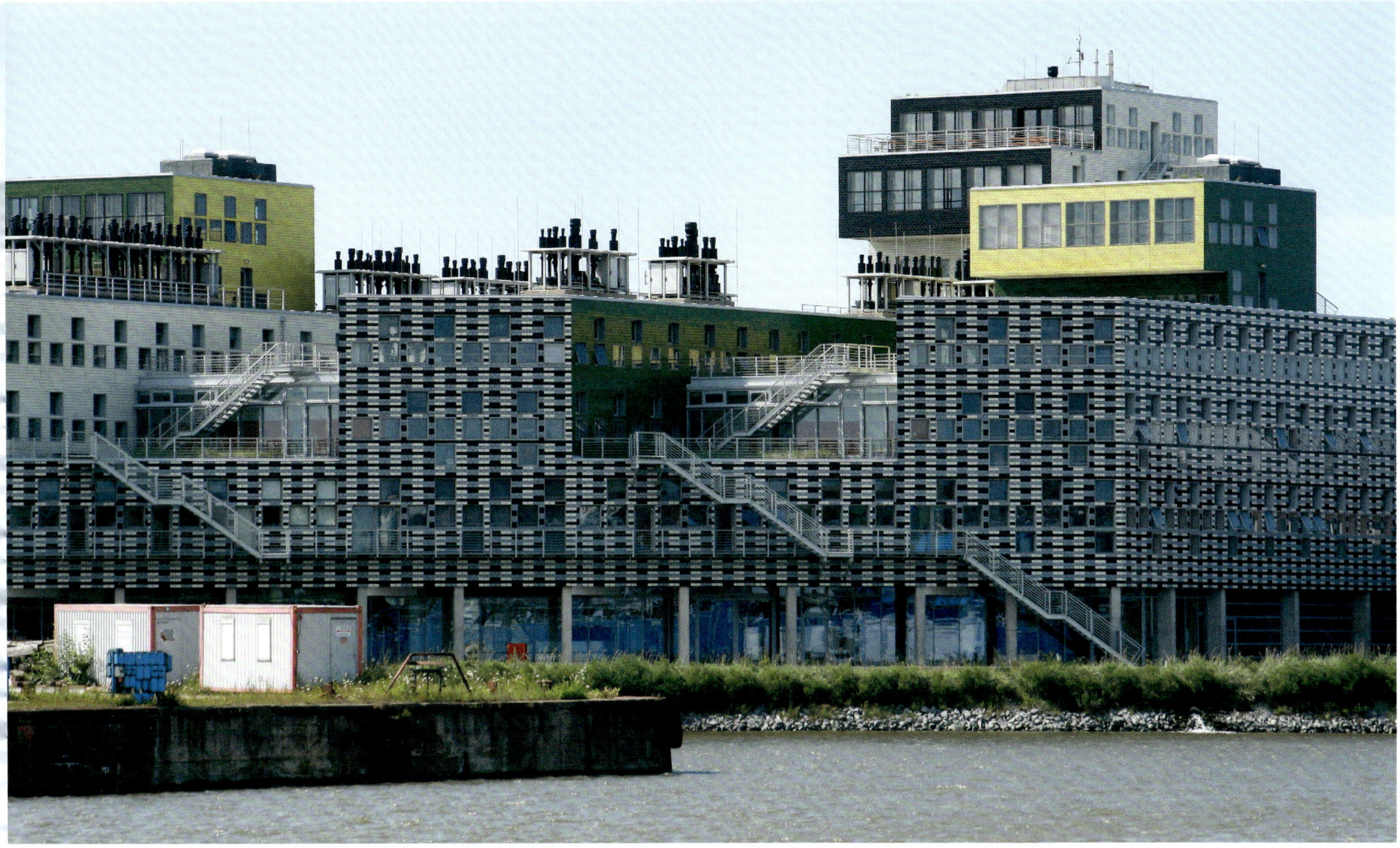

Erich Wiesner,
colour concept, 2002,
Alfred Wegener Institute,
Bremerhaven

Förster (born in 1959) or concrete replicas of interior furniture by David Mannstein (born in 1958) and Maria Vill (born in 1956), while two other proposals focused on the theme of security.

The artist duo missing icons | knobloch + vorkoeper proposed a concept entitled "Innere Sicherheit (Gefahrenmuster)" ("Internal security (patterns of risk)"), which envisaged covering the windows of two conference rooms with patterns resembling broken glass, provoking associations of violence through gun shot or blunt tools, as well as force majeure such as stone and hail impacts. All motifs are recognisable as images due to their enormous enlargement and graphic abstraction. The jury decided that the design focused too heavily on the aspect of security. Furthermore, it was felt that its dramatic accentuation did not take the long-term confrontations of employees and guests into account.

Such considerations reflect the special nature of art in architecture, which – unlike contextually independent museum art that is temporarily consumed by visitors on a voluntary basis – must always take the long-term requirements of the building's users and their everyday professional lives into account.

missing icons | knobloch + vorkoeper, "Innere Sicherheit (Gefahrenmuster)", 2016, unimplemented competition design for the new building of the Federal Ministry of the Interior, Building and Community, Berlin

Dietrich Förster, untitled, 2016, unimplemented competition design for the new building of the Federal Ministry of the Interior, Building and Community, Berlin

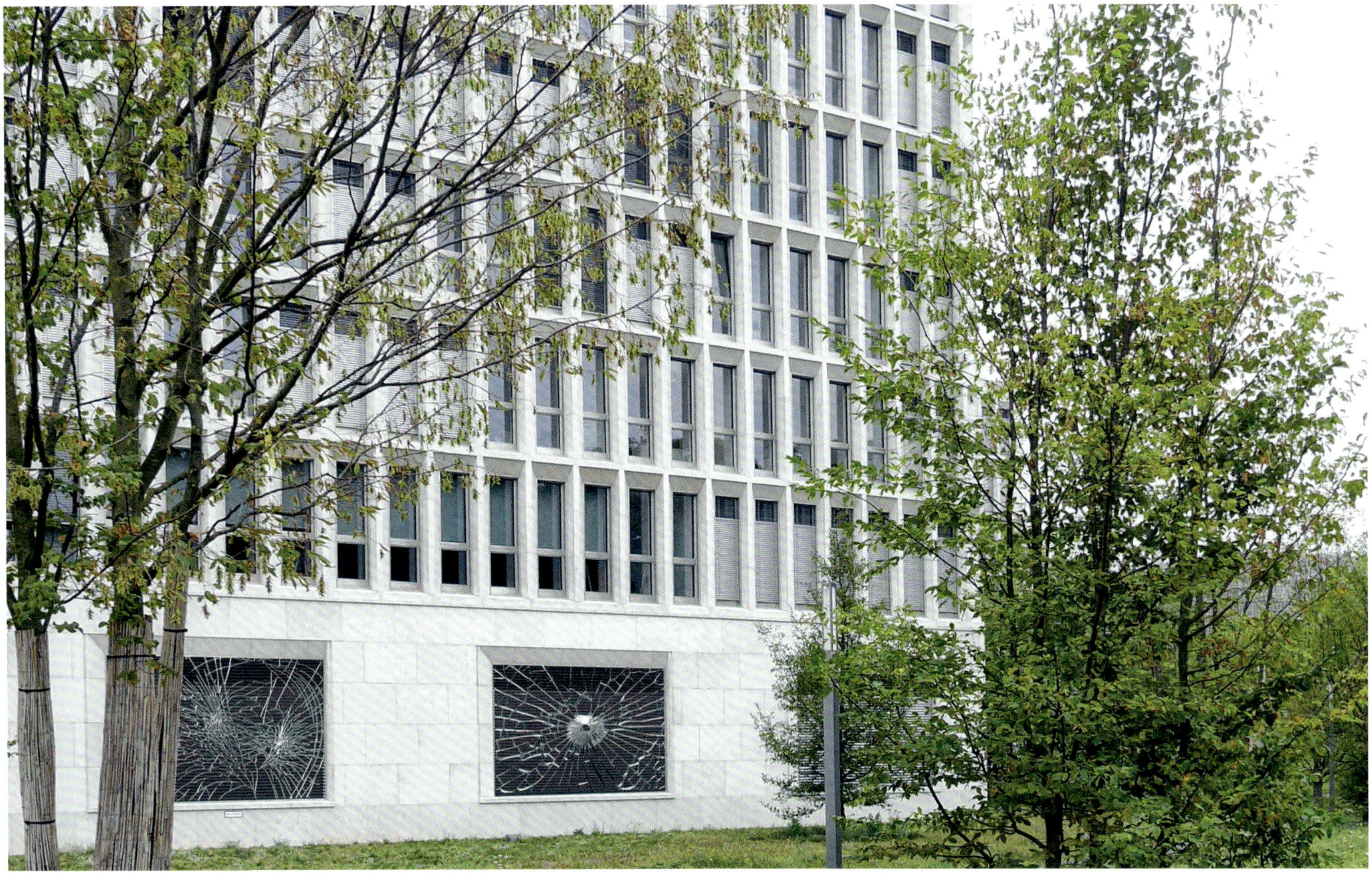

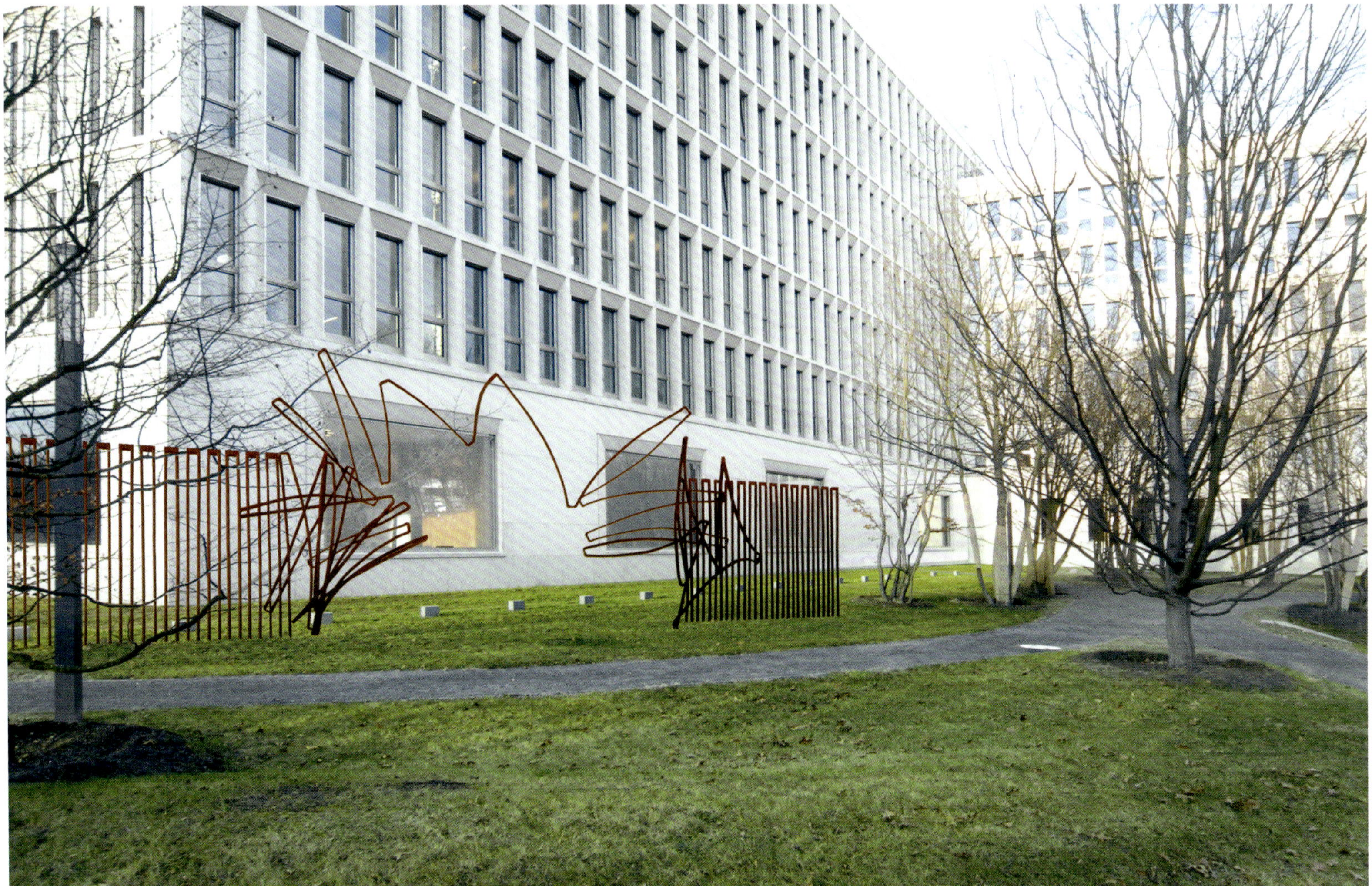

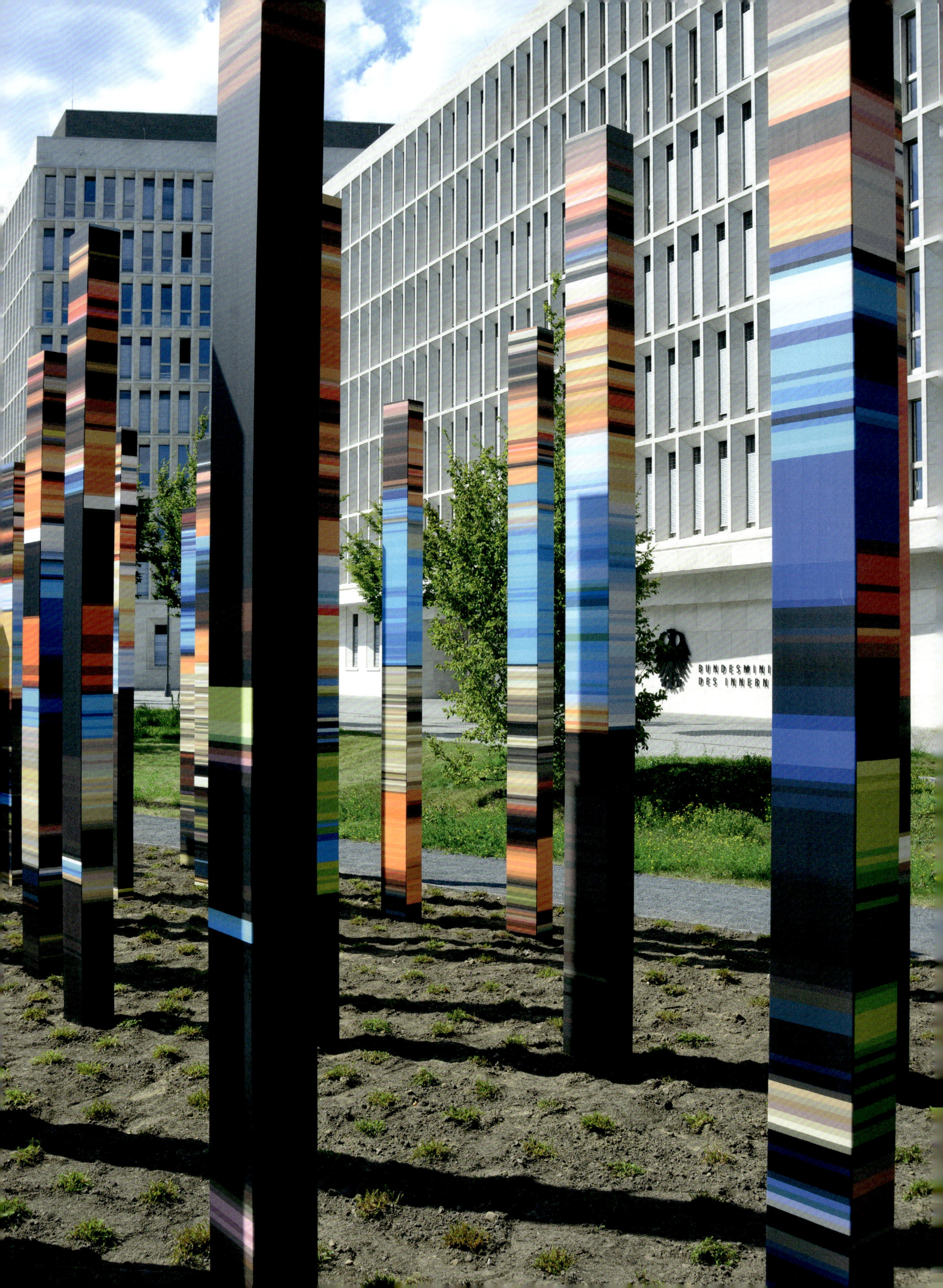
BUNDESMINI
DES INNERN

FEDERAL MINISTRY OF THE INTERIOR, BUILDING AND COMMUNITY BERLIN

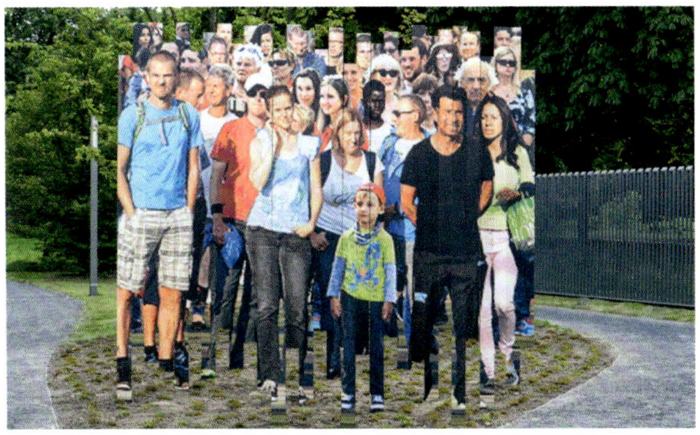

Address:
Alt-Moabit 140
10557 Berlin

Architecture:
Müller Reimann Architekten,
2012–2015

Art in architecture:
Roland Fuhrmann
and Sunkoo Kang

The new building for the Federal Ministry of the Interior is situated in the direct vicinity of the Federal Chancellery. Constructed according to plans by Müller Reimann Architekten, the Z-shaped, staggered building is surrounded by a generous green area. Roland Fuhrmann (born in 1966) impressed the jury in the art in architecture competition for the exterior grounds with his artistic concept "Zusammenhalt" ("Cohesion"), since one of the ministry's key tasks is to strengthen cohesion within German society.

The sculpture "Zusammenhalt" consists of thirty metal steles. Sections of a photographic motif have been applied to each of the steles' front sides. From a specific perspective, the sections combine to create the image of a group of people of different ages and genders, and from different cultural backgrounds, reflecting the diversity of the German population in a single snapshot. Starting with the coloured edges of the front side, a striped pattern envelopes the rest of the steles like a barcode. The art in architecture thereby visualises how statistical data recording and bar charts are based on real people – the pillars of society. The interplay between figuration and abstraction, depending on the viewer's perspective, allows the artwork to symbolise both the cohesion of society and its potential collapse. Only when seen together from a specific perspective do apparently isolated elements form a coherent unity, just as social cohesion represents the result of the perspective and engagement of each individual.

Fuhrmann has produced a large number of art in architecture works, including for the Chemistry Institutes and the Institute for Hydrology at the Technische Universität Dresden, for the Center for Regenerative Therapies TU Dresden (CRTD) and for the Max Planck Institute for Microstructure Physics in Halle (Saale). His artistic approach is characterised by an intensive study of the relevant institutions' work.

ROLAND FUHRMANN
"Zusammenhalt" ("Cohesion"), 2017
Stainless steel, pigment print
Height: 280–440 cm,
11–21 x 25 cm each

LONG IN

THE MAINTENANCE, PRESERVATION AND LOSS OF ART IN ARCHITECTURE

THE TOOTH

Article 14 of the German constitution states that “with property comes responsibility”. In that sense, the Federal Government also assumes long-term responsibility for the maintenance and preservation of the art in architecture it commissions. The owners and building administrations work hand in hand with the institutions that use the real estate to present and preserve works appropriately. The lasting quality and future maintenance costs of art in architecture are already taken into account when commissioning artists.

One special challenge is the non-museum environment of the artworks: light, dirt and humidity can be as damaging as unwanted external influences or natural ageing processes. Above all, outdoor art in architecture locations can pose a wide range of challenges, such as the weather, plant growth and vandalism. Thus regular checks are required to ensure the stability of the artworks and discover any damage at an early stage.

Cleaning and restoration measures are standard maintenance procedures on art in architecture, for instance to remove dust and graffiti, treat corroded surfaces, update software in the case of new media or exchange faulty elements. If a building needs to be substantially changed or sold, it is sometimes no longer possible to keep an artwork at its original location. In coordination with the artists, an appropriate new location within the same real estate is sought wherever possible. Alternatively, if the building’s user moves to another address, the art in architecture can be moved to the institution’s new location and preserved in this way. Great efforts are made to prevent the loss of an artwork through destruction. In addition to the maintenance and protection measures, scientific documentation and communication services raise public awareness of the value and importance of art in architecture.

LONG IN THE TOOTH

Anna-Sophie Laug

Most art in architecture is conceived in an architecturally related or locally specific way and designed by the artist for a very particular location, depending on the conditions there. This has both benefits and disadvantages: on the one hand, the art in architecture's immobility as a result of its format, weight and anchoring protects it from being easily replaced or removed, but on the other, it is almost inseparably connected to the building and its development.

Art in architecture is implemented in a context and during building measures intended to fulfil clear requirements in terms of their use and functions; the real estate's users – such as the Federal Government, federal ministries, federal authorities, research institutes and embassies – have specific demands on their buildings, sometimes forcing the art into a subordinate role. Conversion, reuse and even demolition plans, which for instance occur when federal buildings are restructured or vacated, can also influence whether artworks can remain at their current locations, thereby posing the question of the possibility of their preservation.

Artworks situated on exterior grounds are also exposed to environmental influences and must cope with wind and weather effects, which not every material manages to the same degree. Negative manual effects caused by people, for instance wearing down walkable and touchable artworks, as well as vandalism through graffiti or other intentional damage, are further potential risks for art in architecture, along with pests and unwanted plant growth.

These and a wide range of other challenges are addressed by the users of the buildings, as well as their owners, above all the Institute for Federal Real Estate (Bundesanstalt für Immobilienaufgaben) and building administrations with special responsibilities for the maintenance of artworks. In accordance with Section 9 of the "Guideline on art in architecture", they must also ensure that the art in architecture is presented in a respectful way that is compatible with the artistic idea. Like all artworks, art in architecture is subject to copyright law, requiring artists to approve any changes to the piece, the (built) environment and the location. The overriding goal, however, remains to preserve the artwork in its original condition and established environment.

MAINTENANCE

Day-to-day business on the maintenance and upkeep of artworks includes checking and ensuring their stability, as well as cleaning them. In the simplest cases, this entails removing particles such as dust, while more difficult measures include the removal of graffiti, stickers and moss. These tasks are assumed by the institutions using the real estate, while restoration and building measures are ordered by the owner and implemented by the responsible building administration. To ensure adequate maintenance, it is necessary to receive full documentation for an artwork when it is completed. Such information includes data sheets on the materials used and their appropriate care, as well as cleaning instructions and photographs of the piece's completed condition; in 2012, the procedure was defined in

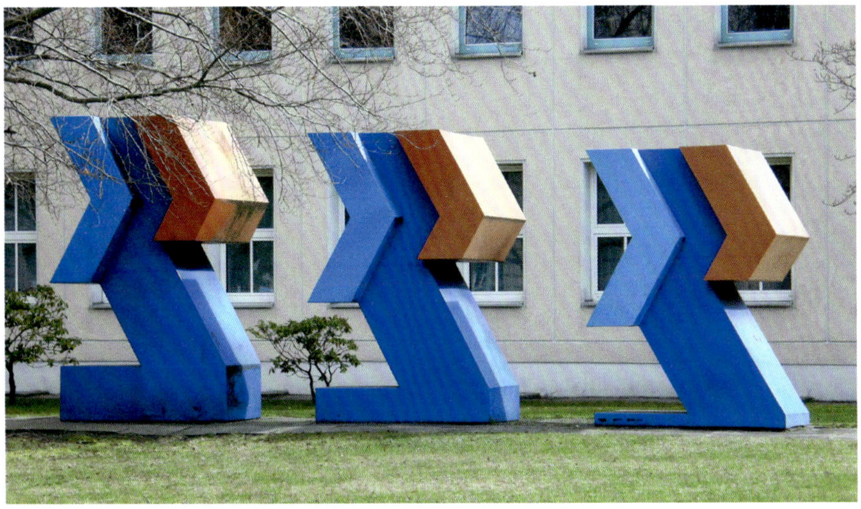

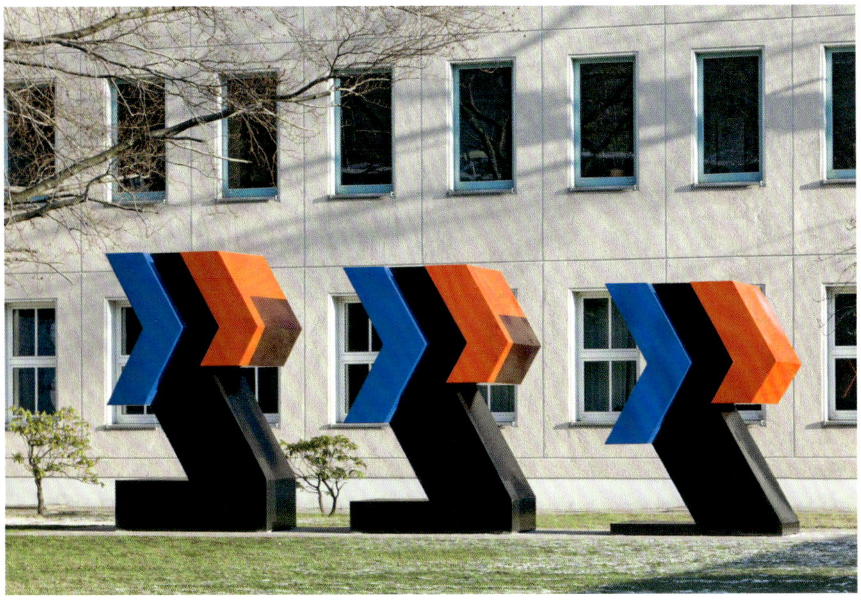

Otto Herbert Hajek, "Zeichen im Stadtraum", 1980, former Federal Building Authority, Berlin, and after restoration in 2012, Institute for Federal Real Estate, Berlin

the updated "Guideline on art in architecture" in Section 10 entitled "Documentation".

Classic up-keeping measures include restoration. For instance, the work "Zeichen im Stadtraum" ("Signs in urban space", 1980) by Otto Herbert Hajek (1927–2005) required restoration over thirty years after its installation in front of the former Federal Building Authority (Bundesbaudirektion) in Berlin. In 2011, the seven free-standing sculptures covered in red, black and blue received a general overhaul under the auspices of the Federal Office for Building and Regional Planning (Bundesamt für Bauwesen und Raumordnung), the successor organisation of the Federal Building Authority. Over the years, the paint had not only lost its intense colour, but had also partially flaked from the surface. There was also corrosion damage. Based on the restoration finds, combined with photographs and archive material, it was possible to recreate the original colour quality using a light-resistant paint. The artwork's stability was ensured in the long term by new steel anchors sunken into the concrete base, allowing the sculptures, which were designed as an artistic guidance system, to again highlight the building entrance from afar.

The great identity-enhancing potential of art in architecture and thus the willingness to maintain it even in non-federal buildings can be seen in the restoration of "Der Weg der Roten Fahne" ("The way of the red flag", 1969). The mural, which covers over 300 square metres on the façade of Dresden's Kulturpalast, was produced by a collective of artists led by the then Professor at the Dresden University of Fine Arts, Gerhard Bondzin (1930–2014). In 2001, it gained the status of a cultural monument (→ p. 304). The restoration work was commissioned by the City of Dresden and was carried out in 2016, again with the involvement of the university and its students.

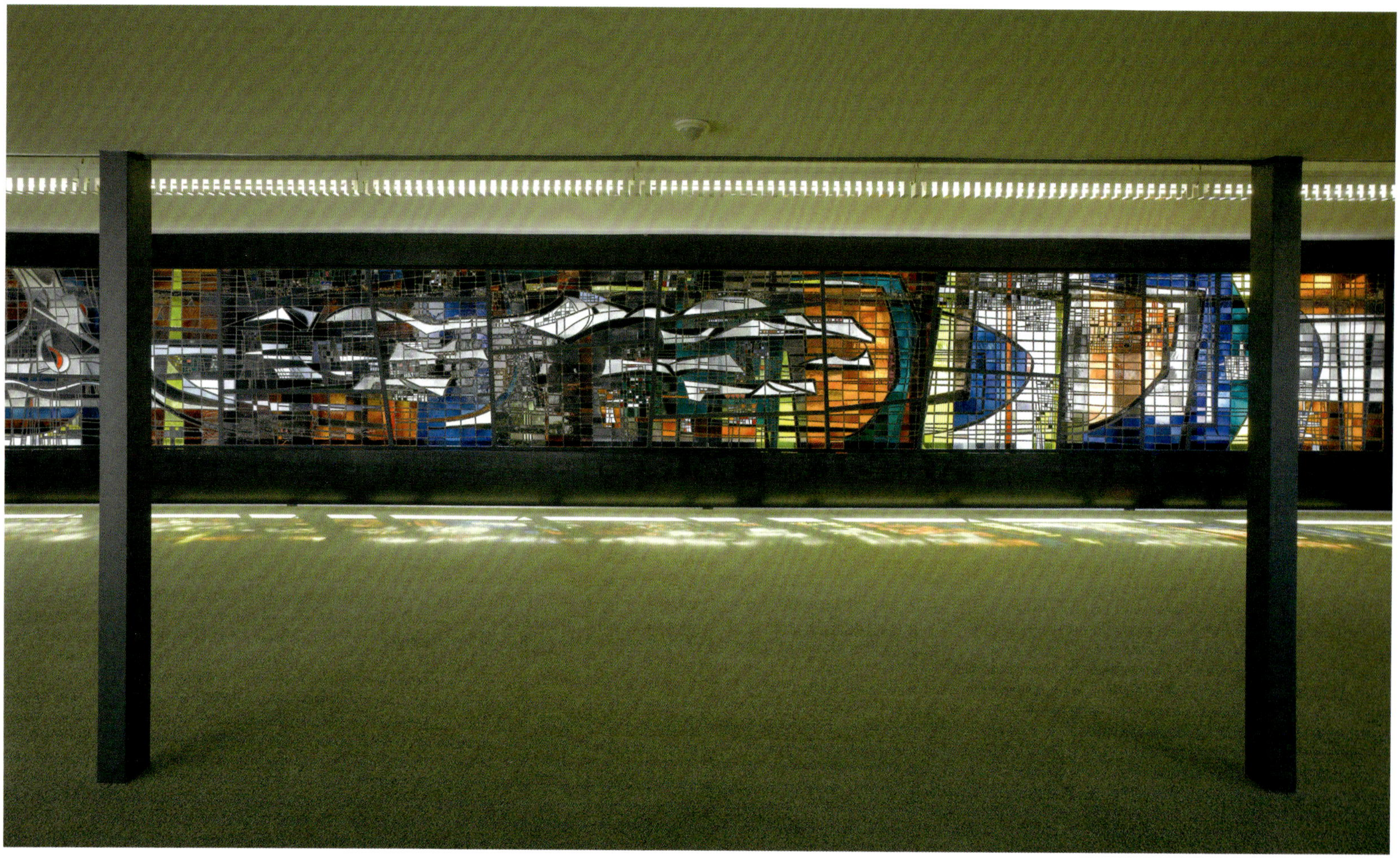

A change of user or owner can also provide an opportunity for art in architecture, as seen in the example of a glass window by the artist Clara Kress (1899–1971) from 1961. It was originally produced for the staff building of Detachment 1 of the Bundeswehr Air Force Division in Karlsruhe and presents flight impressions on coloured glass surfaces. In 2008, when the Federal Constitutional Court selected the former staff building of the General Kammhuber Barracks as its interim location, the artwork was cleaned and missing pieces of glass and cementing were replaced while the real estate was being converted. Unlike its previous presentation in front of a large, transparent window, the work was framed at the same location by a structural "passepartout", concentrating the light incidence on the artwork and thereby considerably enhancing its radiance.

In addition to traditional materials such as natural stone, wood and metal, new media are increasingly being used for art in architecture. Over time, these can deteriorate not only physically, but also digitally, for instance when the required hardware and programmes rapidly become antiquated. A committed IT team tackled such an ageing process with the video piece "Proposal", 1999, which was installed in the foyer of the main building of the Wasser- und Schifffahrtsamt (Waterways and Shipping Office) in Eberswalde. The technicians managed to configure an operating system that allowed the films by the artist Nan Hoover (1931–2008) to be presented again on three displays integrated into the wall.

However sometimes, changes and natural processes with respect to art in architecture can be intended and desired. For instance, since 2000, the artwork "DER BEVÖLKERUNG" ("TO THE POPULATION") by Hans Haacke (born in 1936) in the northern inner courtyard of the Reichstag building

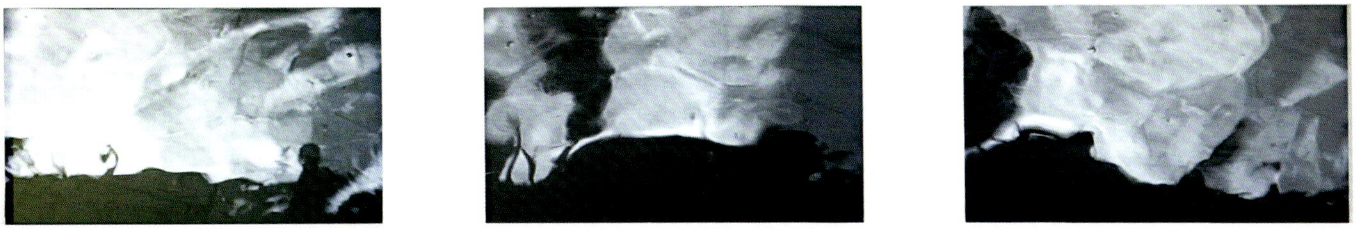

has invited members of parliament to scatter earth from their constituencies over the area of the installation (→ p. 168). Since the piece is intentionally left unmanaged by a gardener and new earth is regularly added, a surprising diversity of vegetation has grown on the soil and continues to do so. In this way, Haacke visualises natural growth and withering in his consciously participatory piece of "process art", rather than requiring conformity.

Clara Kress, stained glass window, 1961, former General Kammhuber Barracks, Federal Armed Forces, today Federal Constitutional Court, Karlsruhe

Nan Hoover, "Proposal", 1999, Waterways and Shipping Office, Eberswalde

PRESERVATION

The government's move from Bonn to Berlin, including many ministries, the privatisation of formerly federal institutions such as the post office and the railways, as well as structural transformations with respect to employment agencies, customs and the Federal Armed Forces, led to changed spatial requirements and ownership relationships. Numerous buildings were vacated, extended, converted or demolished to make way for new real estate. The priority in handling art in architecture lies in preserving it wherever possible. However, it is not always possible to retain an artwork at its original location, forcing it to be relocated. The "Rasterbild mit Vögeln" ("Raster image with birds") by Ursula Sax (born in 1935), which had been produced in 1982, needed to be moved from the cafeteria of the Federal Health Authority's former Institute for Drugs and Medical Devices in Berlin, with clear benefits: although the mural of white steel struts had to be removed from its originally planned environment in front of a brick wall, the foyer of the newly converted lecture theatre for the building's subsequent user, the Robert Koch Institute, provided a prominent area to install the artwork (→ p. 302). In coordination with the artist, it was even possible to smoothly integrate the surface intended for the piece's reinstallation into the colour concept developed by the office Henn Architekten, which had been contracted to implement the conversion measures.

Sometimes, an adequate new location must be found for artworks of exceptional quality, such as "Kosmos 70", which was produced by Bernhard Heiliger (1915–1995) between 1963 and 1969 and originally installed in the western foyer of the Plenarsaal designed by Paul Baumgarten in the Reichstag building, remaining there from 1970 until the building's fit-out in 1994. A rotunda in the entrance hall of the extension building for Marie Elisabeth Lüders House by Stephan Braunfels has therefore been planned for "Kosmos 70", where it will once again develop all of its radiant attributes (→ p. 306). Willi Sitte's (1921–2013) large-scale painting "Proletarier aller Länder, vereinigt euch!" ("Workers of the world, unite!",

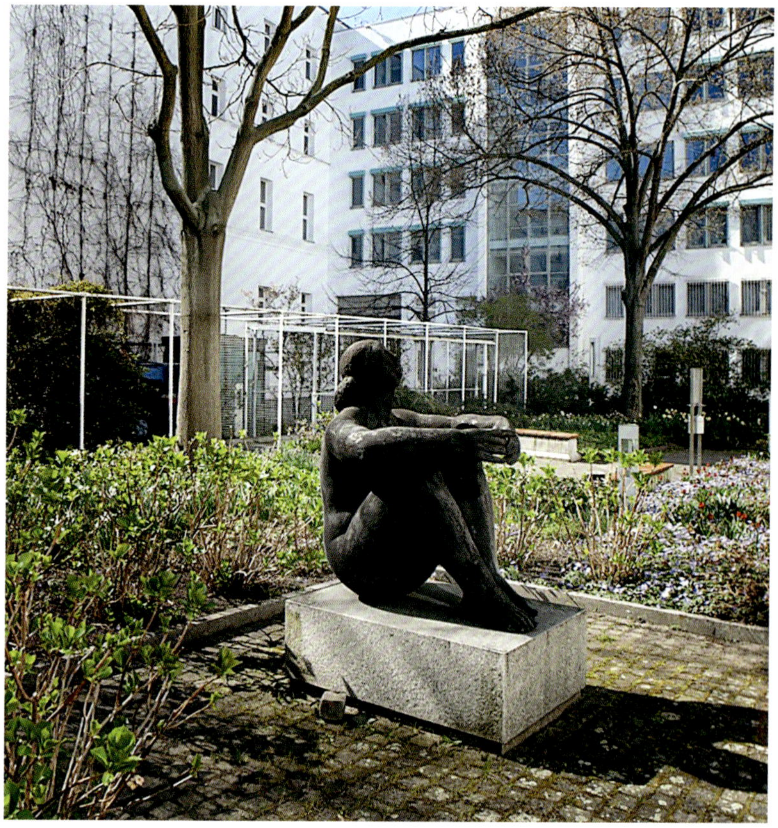

Wieland Förster, "Sich Sonnende", 1965, German Bundestag/ Unter den Linden 71, Berlin

Peter Nagel, "Auf der Brücke", 1982, originally Gudow Süd motorway services, relocated to the Ministry of Economic Affairs, Transport, Employment, Technology and Tourism, Kiel

Peter Nagel, "Auf der Brücke", 1982, Detail

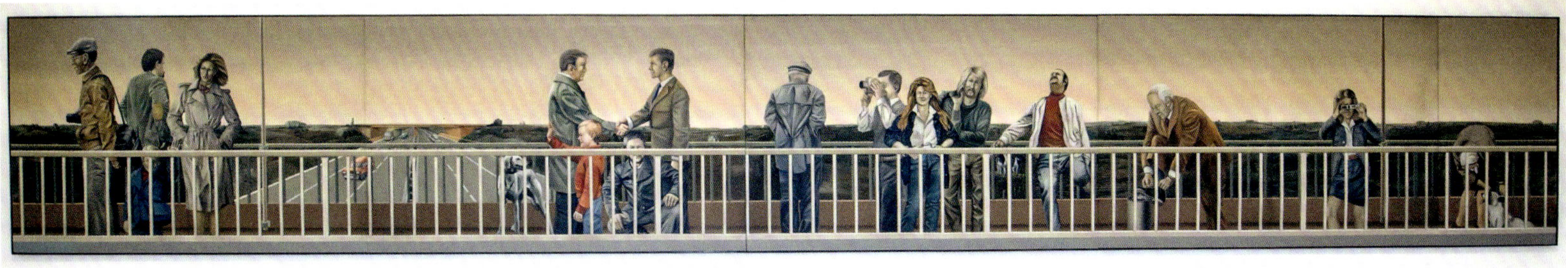

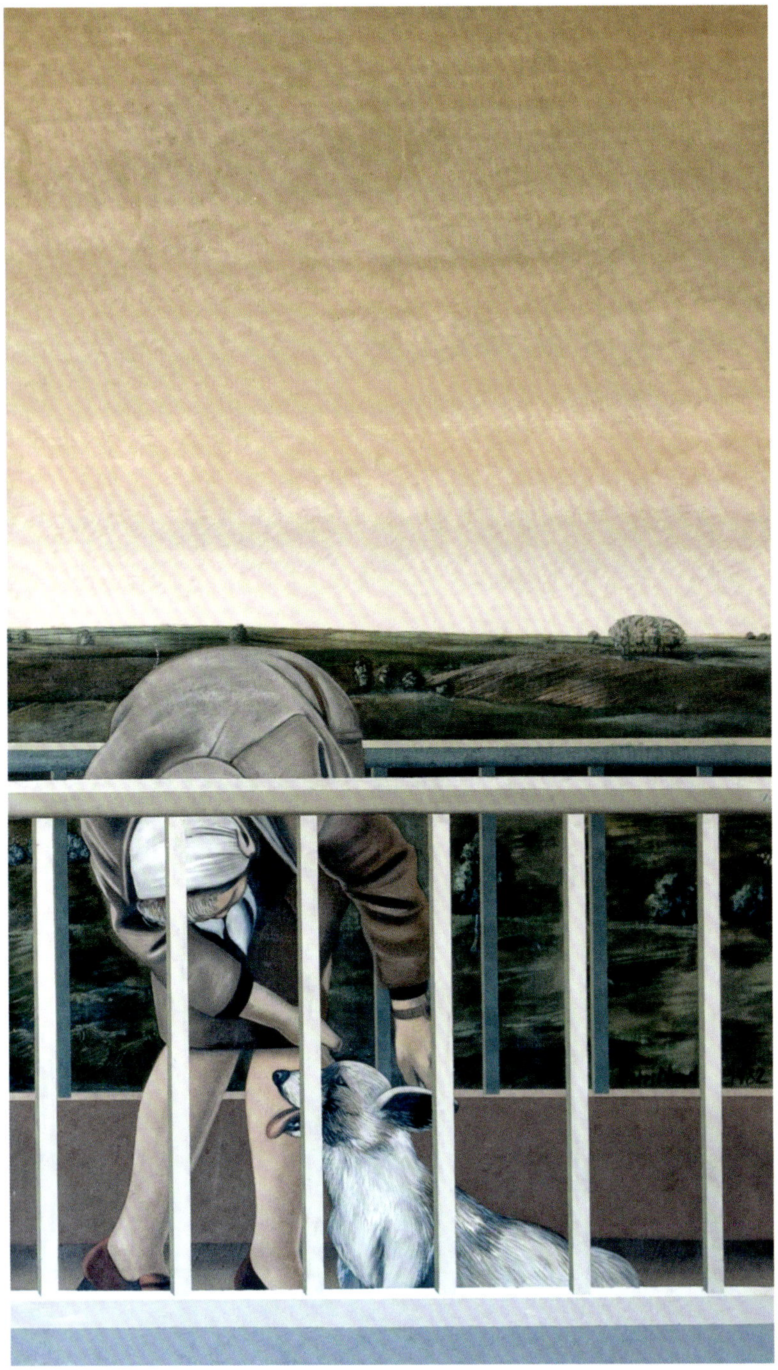

1978/1979), which was produced for the staircase of the Karl Marx SED Party College in Berlin (→ p. 116) and has been kept in storage in the depot of the Beeskow Art Archive since 1994, is still waiting for a new location that is appropriate to its monumental nature and multifaceted historical quality. The bronze sculpture "Sich Sonnende" ("Sunbather") by Wieland Förster (born in 1930), which was produced in 1965 for the garden facility of the GDR Ministry for Foreign Trade in Berlin, was already relocated to the inner courtyard of the parliamentarians' offices of the German Bundestag at Unter den Linden 71 in the late 1990s. Another example of an artwork finding a new home is the five-part oil painting "Auf der Brücke" ("On the bridge", 1982) by Peter Nagel (born in 1941). Its elongated view of a motorway with passers by perfectly suited its original location, both formally and in terms of its motif, since it was installed at the Gudow Süd motorway services, part of the border control facility for the Berlin-Hamburg transit motorway. After the facility's privatisation, the art in architecture was heavily compromised by changes to the interior decoration. The artist campaigned for his work, bought it back for a nominal sum and, in early 2016, achieved its new installation in the large meeting room of the Ministry of Transport in Kiel, where "On the bridge" is excellently placed, both in terms of its content and the presentation space.

Often, users themselves propose taking art in architecture with them when they move, since the identification factor of artworks specially produced for the institutions can be very high. When the German Embassy in Tokyo had to be demolished in 2003, its employees urgently requested the relocation of their mural mosaic (from around 1960) by Hedja Luckhardt-Freese (1905–1988) to the larger, earthquake-proof new building designed by the Stuttgart architects Mahler, Günster, Fuchs. After the Rantzau Barracks in Boostedt, Schleswig-Holstein, were vacated, the bronze sculpture "Stabbieger" ("Staff benders") by Karlheinz Goedtke (1915–1995), which was produced in 1959 and presents two male figures spanning a bow, was relocated to the Preußer Barracks in Eckernförde, which accommodate the navy battalion of Deployment Flotilla 1. The practice is common for military facilities when the real estate is vacated. The relocation of "Bundesadler" ("Federal Eagle", 1953) by Hans-Oskar Wissel (born in 1925), from Frankfurt am Main to Bonn also reflects the powerful bond with an artwork and its symbolic value, in this case the symbol of sovereignty of the Federal Audit Office. Its building was one of the first major federal construction projects outside Bonn and was erected in Frankfurt between 1951 and 1953. The institution later moved into the existing building of the former Post Ministry in Bonn in 2000. When changing an artwork's location, it is essential to preserve its inherent integrity and integrate it into its new structural and institutional context.

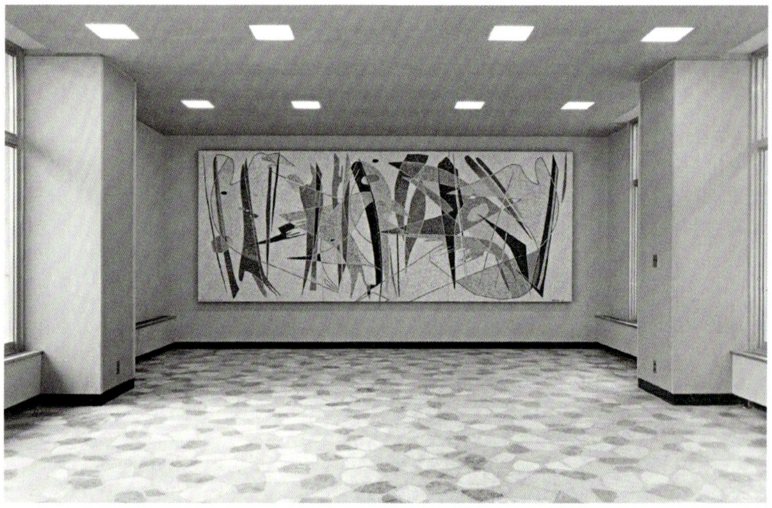

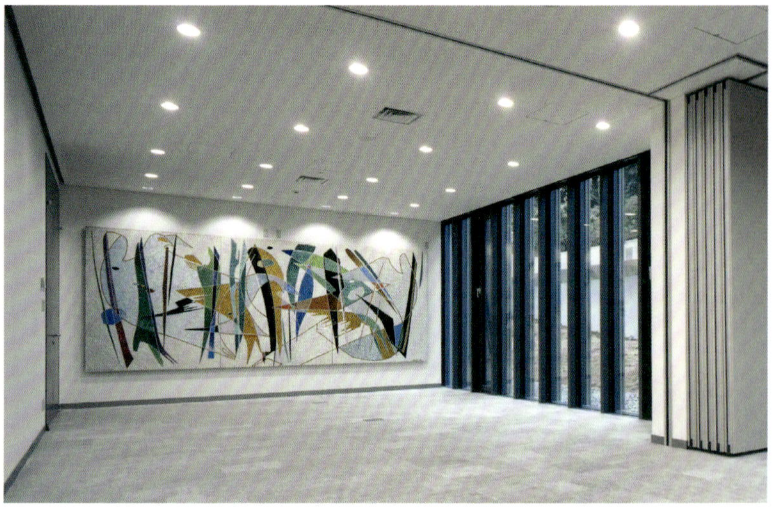

LOSS

The most painful experience in handling art in architecture is the complete loss of the artwork. Although its destruction is permitted by copyright law under specific circumstances, it is always the "ultima ratio", the last resort for everyone involved. External factors sometimes make it impossible to prevent the loss

Hedja Luckhardt-Freese, untitled, 1959, FRG Embassy, Tokyo, Japan, relocated to the new embassy building

Reinhard Omir,
"Kinetische Säule",
1972/1973, FRG Embassy,
Kabul, Afghanistan

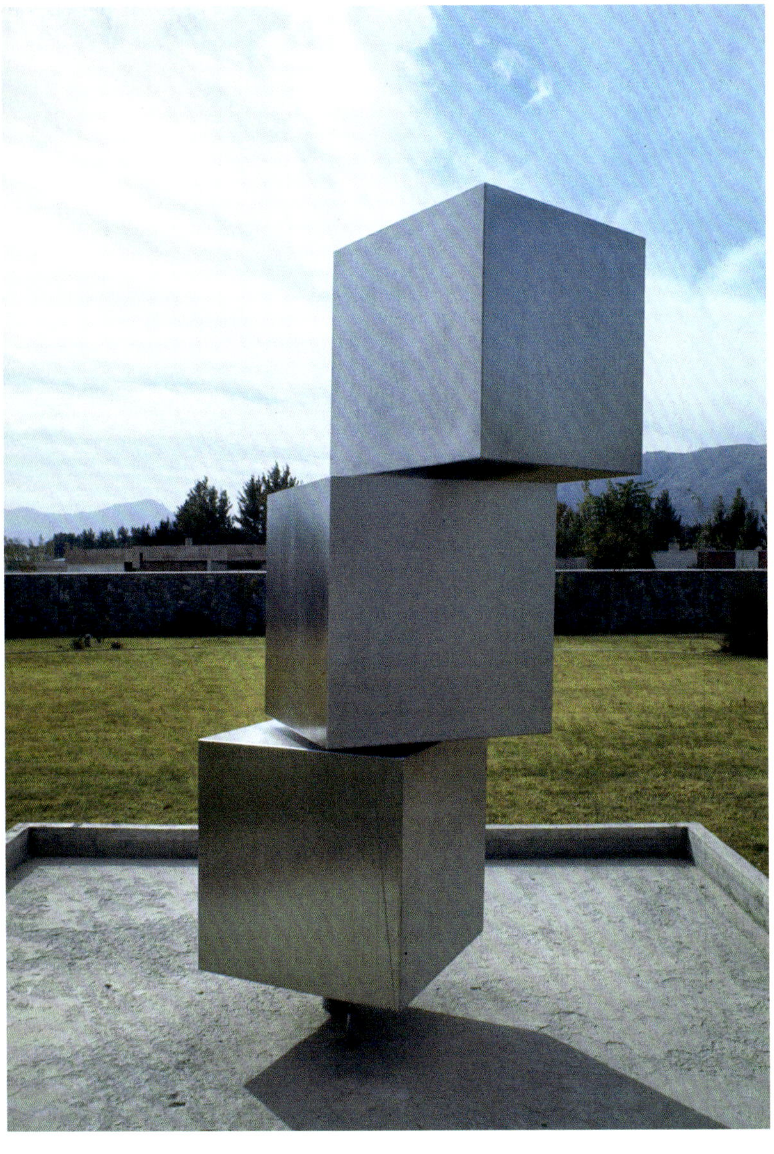

of an artwork. For instance "Kinetische Säule" ("Kinetic column") by Reinhard Omir (born in 1938), which was produced in 1973 for the German Embassy in Kabul, Afghanistan, was destroyed in 1979 in the turmoil of the beginning war. The fountain sculpture, consisting of three stainless steel cubes that used internal motors to rotate on their axes in a kind of dance, had originally existed in the two-storey residency's back garden, in front of the terrace.

If it is impossible to preserve or relocate an artwork, the options of selling it or returning it to the artist can be considered. The tapestry "Zweistromland" ("Mesopotamia") was produced in 1977 by Sigrid Wylach (born in 1941) for the restaurant of the Bundespresseclub (Federal Press Club) in Bonn, which was accommodated in an old building situated in the Gronau villa colony, serving as a meeting place for politicians and journalists. The Bundespresseclub was disbanded when the government moved from Bonn to Berlin and the building was ultimately sold. The tapestry was returned to Wylach in 2015; in this way, art in architecture may have been lost for the contexts for which it was originally intended, but it can still continue to exist as an autonomous piece.

Multi-part art in architecture works are especially endangered by partial loss. When the German Embassy in Vienna, which had been built between 1962 and 1965 according to plans by the architect Rolf Gutbrod, was set to be demolished in 2019, the art in architecture by Blasius Spreng (1913–1987) needed a new location. Around 1965, he had designed the inner courtyard with a fountain, a stone springhead, a stone carpet and the sculpture "Blütenzweig" ("Flowering twig"), as well as creating nine ornamental steel relief panels and a floor mosaic for the residency's main hall. Since it was only possible to install some parts of the works in the new building, the remaining panels were returned to the artist's family.

Mobile and water-related artworks such as fountains are especially at risk of losing their function. The latter can suffer from plant growth, erosion or leakage, while the permanently required water supply makes them maintenance-intensive and costly to run. Thus, fountains are sometimes explicitly excluded in competition briefs, while some already existent examples have been taken out of service. For instance the "Großes Wasserrelief" ("Large water relief"), which is two storeys high and was produced by Heinz Mack (born in 1931) in 1987 for the building of the former Federal Ministry of Post and Telecommunications in Bonn (now used by the Federal Ministry for the Environment, Nature Conservation and Nuclear Safety), no longer has any flowing water. The same fate was suffered by the water basins for the "Lesewald" ("Reading forest", 1989) by Ferdinand Kriwet (1942–2018): the water basins, which have since been drained, are situated in the same building and originally referred to the significance of communication for the commissioning institution. To prevent such measures in future, the current "Guideline on art in architecture" stipulates that the jury for an art in architecture competition must be able to assess the proposed artworks with respect to their life cycles, as well as their structural and technical consequences, including subsequent costs.

Losses usually occur when the real estate containing the immobile art in architecture changes ownership. However, the documentation process for federal art in architecture works, as initiated by the then Federal Ministry of Transport, Building and Urban Development and the Federal Office for Building and Regional Planning, has also led to the rediscovery of artworks that were considered lost.

Sigrid Wylach, "Zweistromland", 1977, Bundespresseclub, Bonn

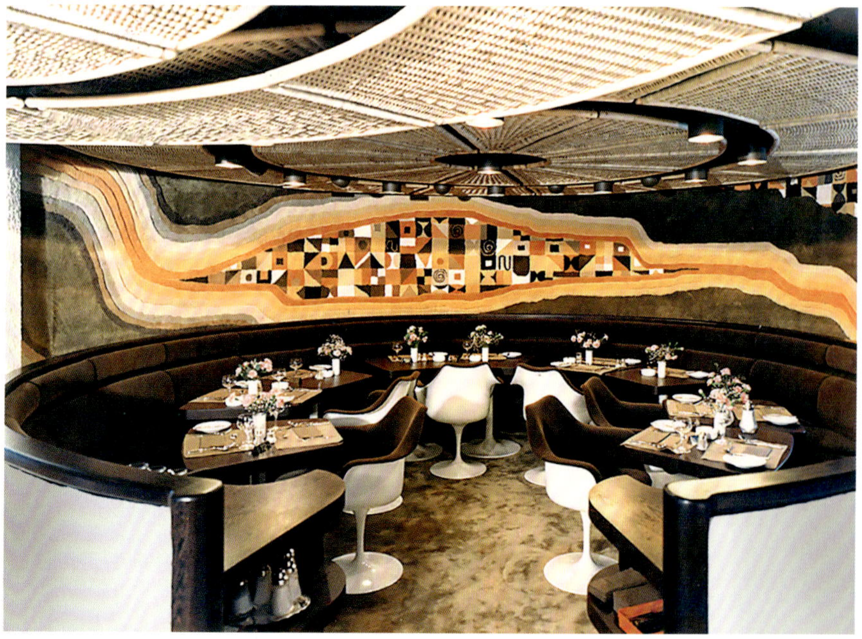

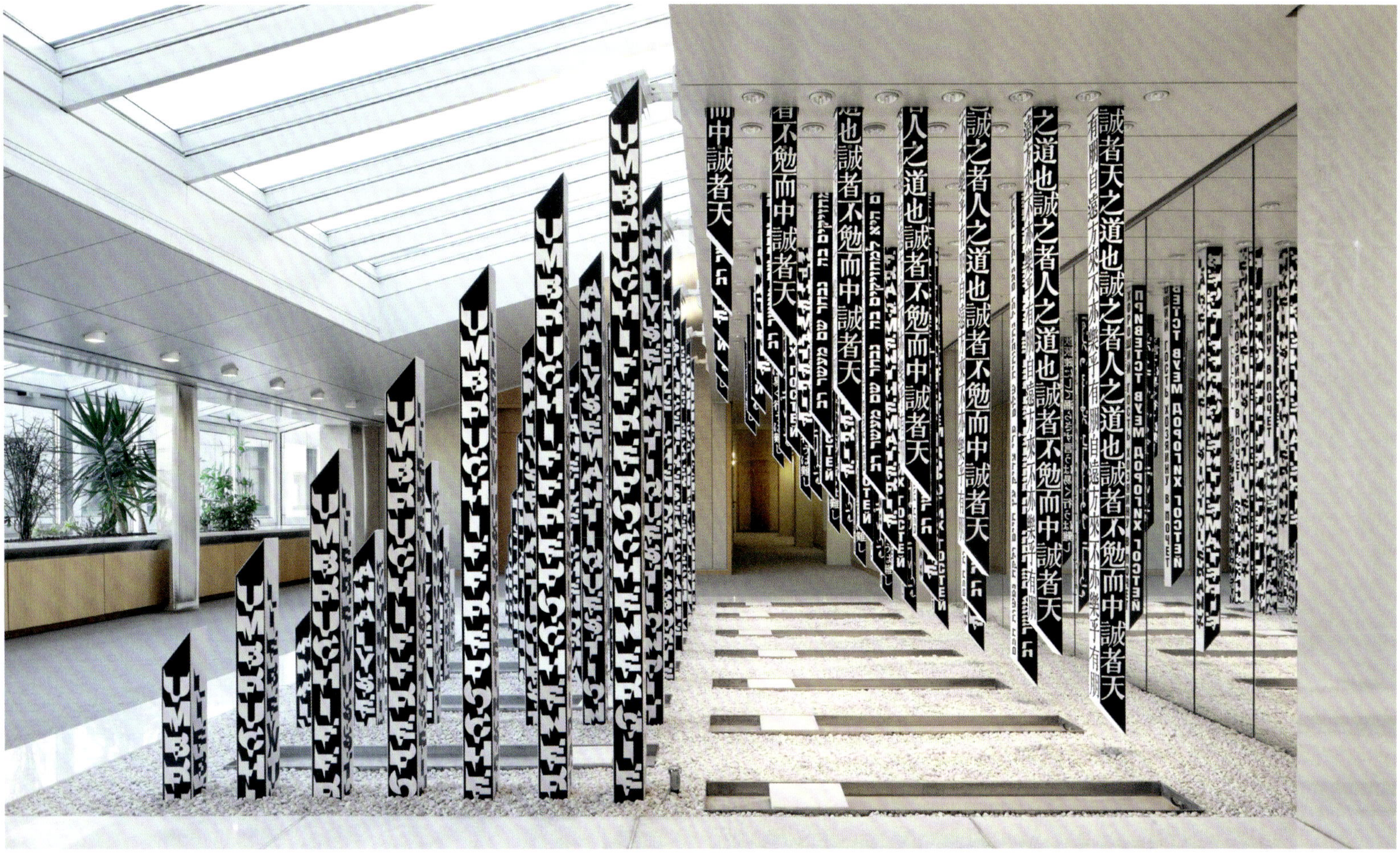

Furthermore, publications, workshop discussions, symposia and educational events on art in architecture play a key role in raising awareness of the works, the artists and the genre of art in architecture. In this way, experts and amateurs alike receive support in recognising and understanding the qualities and value of architecture and its related artworks, thereby providing added protection against the art being forgotten, neglected or lost.

Ferdinand Kriwet, "Lesewald", 1988, Federal Ministry of Post and Telecommunications, Bonn

ROBERT KOCH INSTITUTE BERLIN

Address:
Seestrasse 10
13353 Berlin

Architecture:
Architektengemeinschaft
Fritz Bornemann, Mathias Boyse,
Friedrich Karl Borck,
Dietrich Schaefer, 1978–1982
Conversion:
Henn Architekten, 2010–2013

Art in architecture:
Ursula Sax
and Nevin Aladağ,
Egill Sæbjörnsson

Between 1978 and 1982, a four-storey laboratory and office building with striking window bands was designed for the Federal Institute for Drugs and Medical Devices at the Federal Health Agency in Berlin according to plans by a team of architects consisting of Fritz Bornemann, Mathias Boyse, Friedrich Karl Borck and Dietrich Schaefer. Then between 2010 and 2013, comprehensive renovation work was carried out for the real estate's new user, the Robert Koch Institute: the facility's laboratories, offices, lecture theatre and cafeteria in House 5 were modernised by Henn Architekten and an additional building (House 6) was constructed.

During these measures, the cafeteria's structure was changed so substantially that the mural developed for it, entitled "Rasterbild mit Vögeln" ("Raster image with birds") by Ursula Sax (born in 1935) could no longer be mounted there. As is the case with many of her works, Sax, who has produced a large number of pieces for public spaces and art in architecture, created "Rasterbild mit Vögeln" in a way that inspired interaction with the surroundings and the architecture. With her mural, which consists of white varnished steel squares connected by rings to create a mobile network, the artist picked up on the regular brickwork of the cafeteria wall, before playfully breaking with the pattern. Pairs of trapezes inserted into the network recall the wings of stylised birds.

In coordination with the artist, a new location for the artwork was found in the foyer of the newly fitted lecture theatre. "Rasterbild mit Vögeln" was given a new painted-wall background that harmonises with the architectural colour concept. Both the contrast created in this way between the mid-grey paint and the white mural work, and its prominent new location in the foyer highlight the effect of the artwork, especially since it had been partially obscured by dining tables at its original location.

URSULA SAX
"Rasterbild mit Vögeln"
("Raster image with birds"), 1983
Steel, stove-enamelled
260 x 555 cm
Translocated in 2013

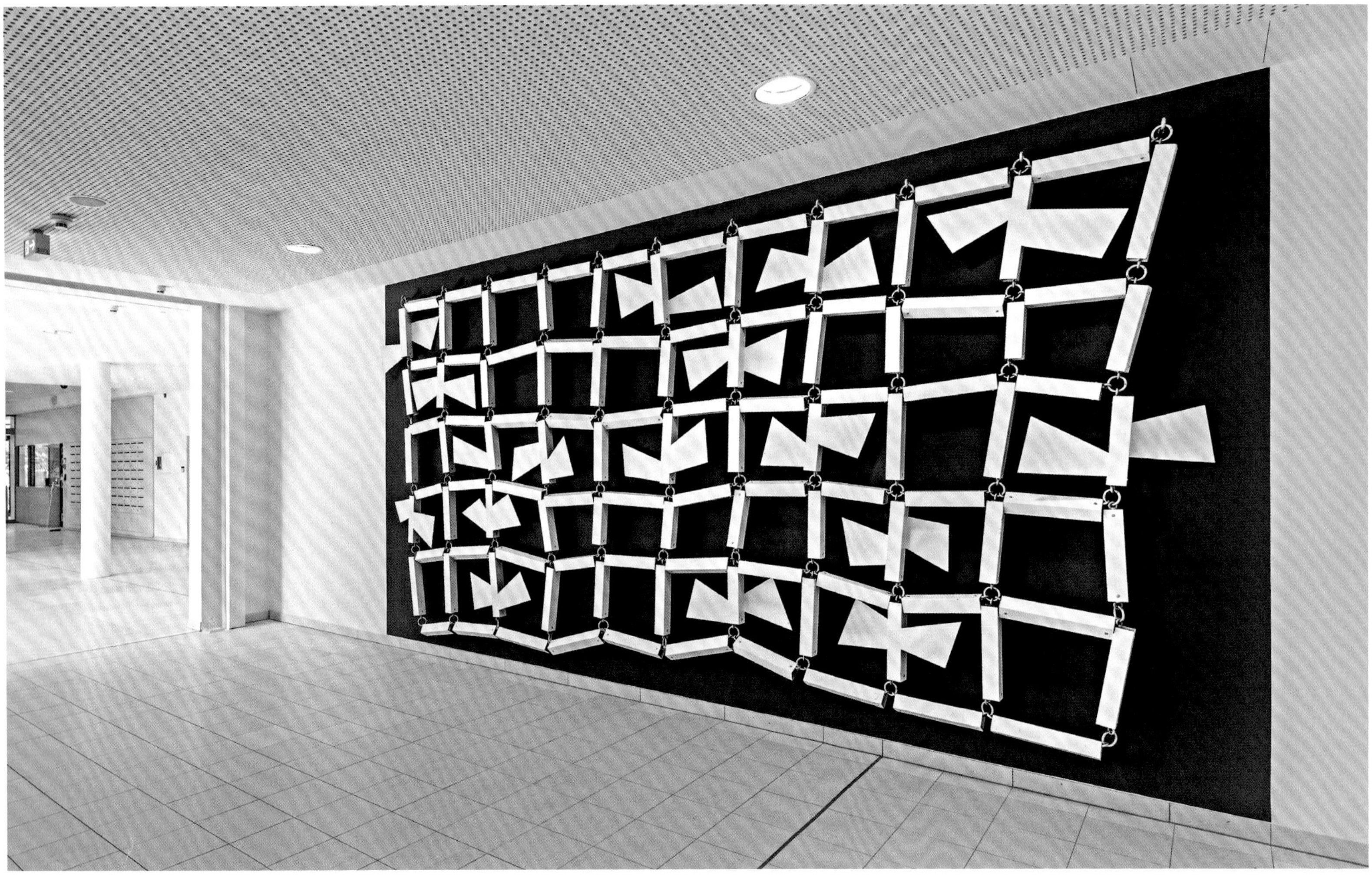

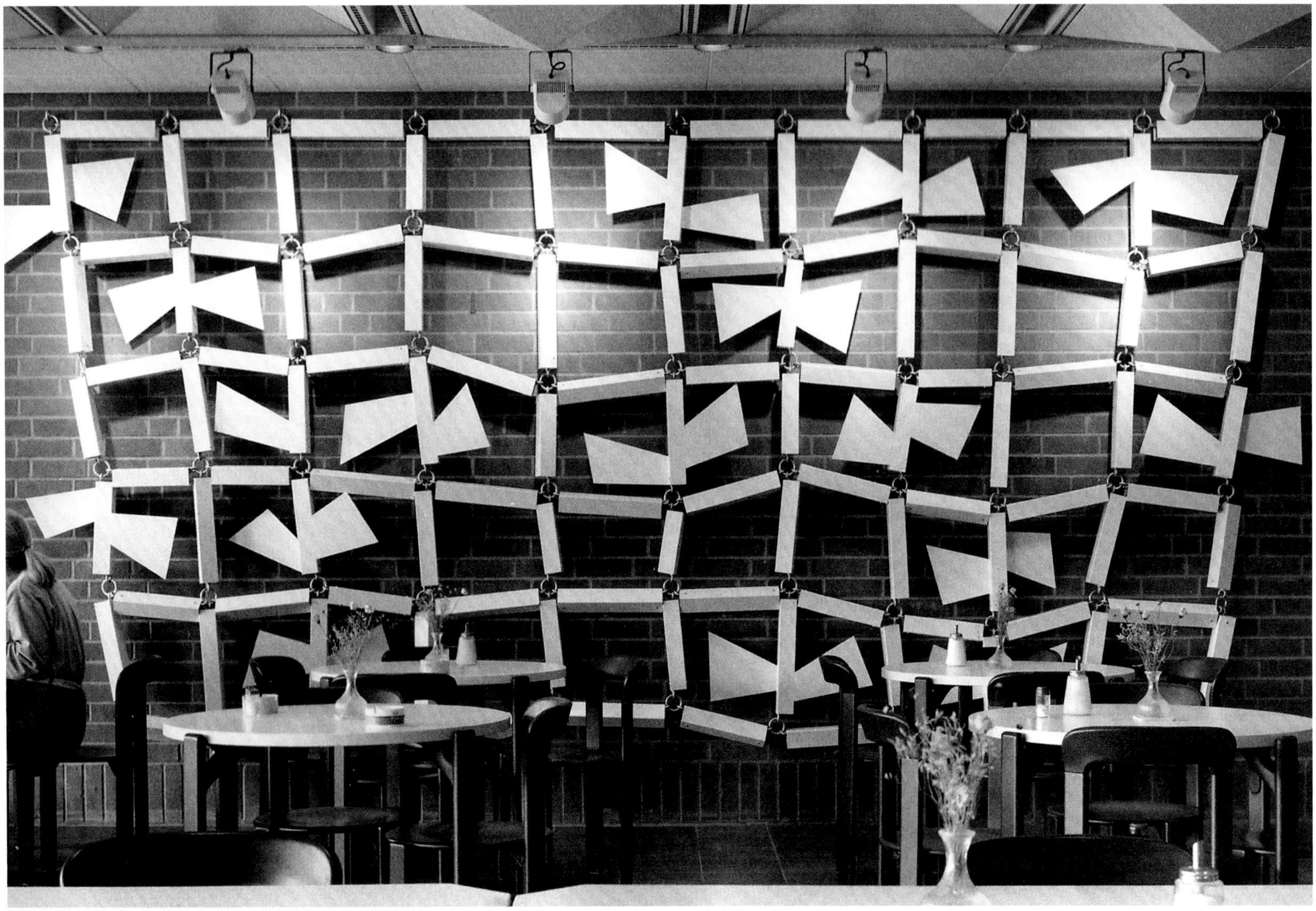

KULTURPALAST DRESDEN

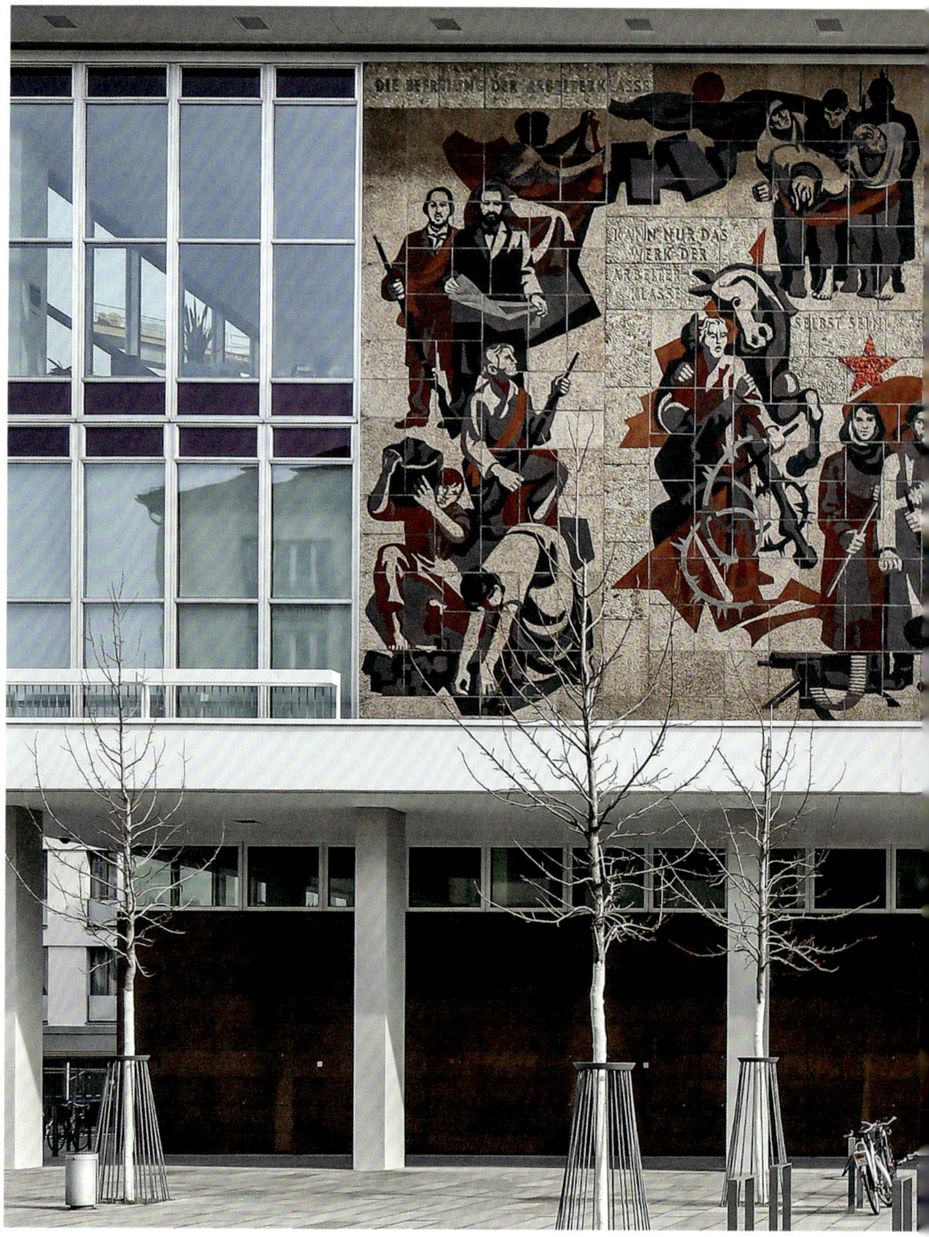

Address: Schlossstrasse 2,
01067 Dresden

Architecture:
Wolfgang Hänsch, 1967–1969
Refurbishment:
gmp – Architekten von Gerkan,
Marg und Partner, 2013–2017

Art in architecture:
Gerhard Bondzin
and Lüder Baier, Heinz Drache
and Walter Rehn,
Christa Engler-Feldmann,
Gerd Jaeger

The Kulturpalast in Dresden was designed by Wolfgang Hänsch in the style of international Modernity. It was constructed to celebrate the 20th anniversary of the GDR and named "Haus der sozialistischen Kultur" ("House of Socialist Culture"). Between 1967 and 1969, the three-storey reinforced concrete skeleton construction with a flat roof, glass façade and a plinth clad in natural stone was developed as part of the newly emerging Dresden city centre, representing one of the most important ideological building tasks of the GDR. After the original mural design by Rudolf Sitte (1922–2009) was rejected by the Dresden City Council, a direct commission for a mural on the western façade of the Kulturpalast was awarded to Gerhard Bondzin (1930–2014), Dean of Dresden University of Fine Arts.

Teachers and students at the Dresden University of Fine Arts formed a collective led by Bondzin, which was a typical working mode in the GDR, jointly creating what is now one of the GDR's most famous murals, "Der Weg der Roten Fahne" ("The way of the red flag").

GERHARD BONDZIN
Gerhard Bondzin
"Der Weg der Roten Fahne"
("The way of the red flag"), 1969
Coloured glass layers on concrete
11 x 30 m

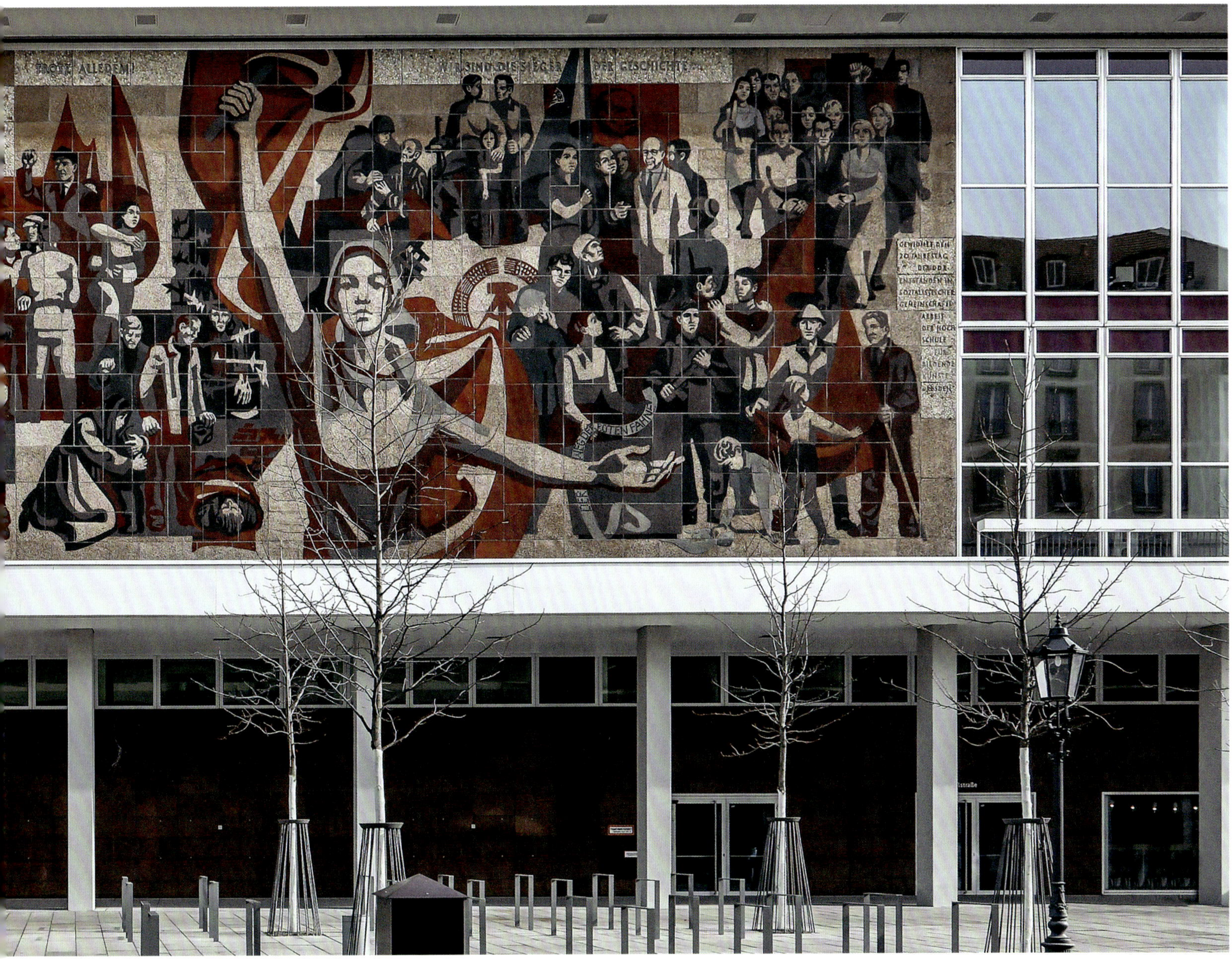

Covering 466 concrete panels that were coated in a layer of coloured glass using a process developed for industrial housing construction, the mural tells the story of the development of Socialism, depicting episodes of the workers' movement in Germany since 1848. A young female worker stands at its centre, holding up the eponymous red flag as a sign of the Communist Party and the Socialist idea. Around her, various scenes are depicted, including the Great Socialist October Revolution of 1917 and people in discussion with Walter Ulbricht, who was the leader of the Central Committee at the time.

The mural, which has been preservation listed since 2001, was restored in 2016 following a commission by the City of Dresden, which also involved students at the university. Such commitment shows the great identification potential of art in architecture and the willingness of states and municipalities to commit to the maintenance and preservation of the artworks.

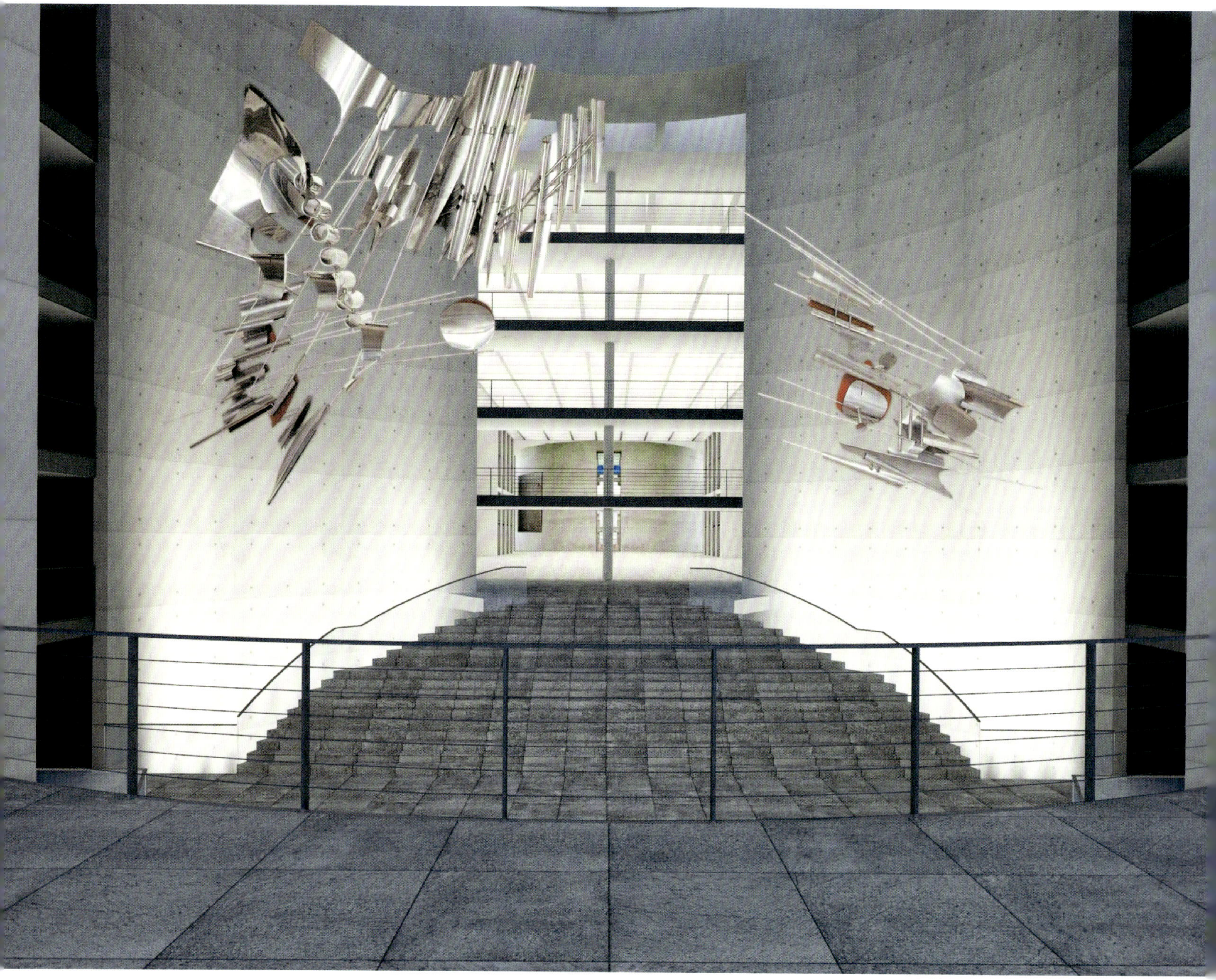

BERNHARD HEILIGER
Kosmos 70, 1963–1969
Aluminium
900 x 180 x 400 cm
New installation after the Marie Elisabeth Lüders House extension is completed

GERMAN BUNDESTAG MARIE ELISABETH LÜDERS HOUSE II BERLIN

Address:
Luisenstr. 29–30
10117 Berlin

Architecture:
Stephan Braunfels

Art in architecture:
Bernhard Heiliger and Michel de Broin, Tony Cragg, Katharina Grosse

When completed, the extension of Marie Elisabeth Lüders House, which was begun by Stephan Braunfels in 2010, will conclude the "Band des Bundes" developed according to an urban-planning design by Axel Schultes and Charlotte Frank. It consists of a row of new buildings in the government district that symbolically and architecturally connects the formerly separated districts of East and West Berlin. It will be defined by a 40-metre high tower that will serve as a new main entrance to the parliamentary building.

The two-part suspended sculpture "Kosmos 70" by Bernhard Heiliger (1915–1995) will find its new location in the rotunda of the entrance hall, with its large free-standing stairs. From 1970 to 1994, the artwork was situated in front of the Plenarsaal ("Plenary Hall") designed by Paul Baumgarten, which was located at the centre of the Reichstag building by Paul Wallot. Both monumental and intricate, "Kosmos 70" hung in the western foyer in front of the grid-structured window front of the Plenarsaal, allowing its interpretation as a political appeal for reunification. Indeed the internal workshop title of these two structures, which strive to come together, was "Posaunen von Jericho" ("Horns of Jericho"). Furthermore, Heiliger's artwork also demonstrated the liberality of western art compared to the official, state-indoctrinated art of the GDR. The artwork was placed in storage during the Reichstag's conversion to accommodate the German Bundestag. Following a decision by the arts council, Stephan Braunfels conceived the rotunda for the extension building in a way that provides sufficient space to present "Kosmos 70". Above the staircase, the artwork will welcome visitors to the publicly accessible gathering area.

Heiliger is one of the most renowned sculptors of the Federal Republic of Germany, producing commissioned pieces for the Federal Government, including artworks for the German Embassy in Paris and the Brussels Expo in 1958.

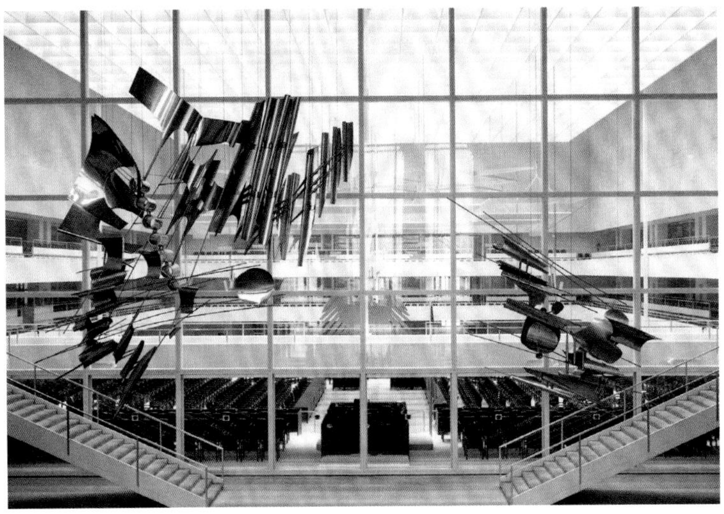

INDEX OF ART IN ARCHITECTURE PROJECTS

LOCATIONS

ARTISTS AND ARCHITECTS

PHOTO CREDITS

(by page number)

4 Photo: BBR/Cordia Schlegelmilch, **Art:** Hannes Schulz-Tattenpach; **11 Photo:** Archiv Horst Bredekamp; **12 Photo:** Deutsches Archäologisches Institut; **13 Photo:** Till Niermann, CC BY-SA 3.0; **14 Photos top and centre:** Comune di Siena; Fondazione Musei Senesi; **14 Photo bottom:** Rijksmuseum Amsterdam/ Dennis Hogers, CC BY-SA 3.0; **16 Photo top:** Jörg Bittner, CC BY-SA 3.0; **16 Photo bottom:** The National Gallery, London; **17 Photo top:** Uffizien, Florenz; **17 Photo bottom:** Hans Bug, CC BY-SA 3.0; **18 Photo:** British Library's collections, CC BY-SA 3.0; **21 Photo:** DBT/Jörg F. Mueller, **Art:** Gerhard Richter, 2020 (01102020); **22 Photo top:** DBT/Werner Huthmacher, **Art:** Günther Uecker, VG Bild-Kunst, Bonn 2020; **22 Photo bottom:** DBT/Julia Nowack, **Art:** Stiftung Gerhard Altenbourg, Altenburg/VG Bild-Kunst, Bonn 2020; **23 Photo:** DBT/Werner Huthmacher, **Art:** Carlfriedrich Claus, VG Bild-Kunst, Bonn 2020; **24 Photo:** DBT/Junophoto, **Art:** Moritz Götze, VG Bild-Kunst, Bonn 2020; **25 Photo:** BBR / Cordia Schlegelmilch, **Art:** Angela Hampel, VG Bild-Kunst, Bonn 2020; **27 Photo:** DBT/Stephan Klonk, **Art:** Bernhard Heisig, VG Bild-Kunst, Bonn 2020; **29 Photo:** Stadtmuseum Dresden, SMD_SP_1981_09152a, **Art:** Wilhelm Lachnit; **32 Photo:** Winckelmann-Museum Stendal, WM-VI-b-h-59, **Art:** Thomas Ranft, VG Bild-Kunst, Bonn 2020; **33 Photo:** Schmidt Kunstauktionen Dresden OHG, **Art:** Jürgen Schieferdecker, VG Bild-Kunst, Bonn 2020; **34 Photo:** Fritz Kühn Gesellschaft e.V., **Art:** Fritz Kühn; **35 Photos:** Lindenau-Museum Altenburg/Archiv der Photonegative von Ralf-Rainer Wasse, **Art:** Clara Mosch; **36 Photo:** SLUB Dresden/Deutsche Photothek/Christian Borchert 1981.10; **41 Photo top:** BBR/ Werner Huthmacher; **41 Photo bottom:** BBR/Werner Huthmacher, **Art:** Sam Francis Foandation, California/ VG Bild-Kunst, Bonn 2020 **43 Photo:** BBR/Cordia Schlegelmilch, **Art:** Ellsworth Kelly; **45 Photo:** Staatsbibliothek zu Berlin – PK, Ralf Stockmann, **Art:** Alexander Camaro, VG Bild-Kunst, Bonn 2020; **46 Photo:** DBT/Jörg F. Müller, **Art:** Jorge Pardo; **48 Photo:** DBT/Stephan Erfurt, **Art:** Franka Hörnschemeyer, VG Bild-Kunst, Bonn 2020; **49 Photo:** BBR/Cordia Schlegelmilch, **Art:** Beat Zoderer, VG Bild-Kunst, Bonn 2020; **50 Photo:** Josefine Günschel, **Art:** Josefine Günschel, VG Bild-Kunst, Bonn 2020; **51 Photos:** _ideazione./Sebastian Fischer, **Art:** Christian Boltanski, VG Bild-Kunst, Bonn 2020; **52 Photo**: Michael Jäger/Martin Duckek, **Art:** Michael Jäger, VG Bild-Kunst, Bonn 2020; **53 Photo:** BBR/Cordia Schlegelmilch, **Art**: Jan Theissen; **55 Photo:** BBR/Cordia Schlegelmilch, **Art:** Hans Uhlmann; **59 Photo:** BArch Bild 183-N0705-410/Ulrich Kohls; **60 Photo:** BArch B 145 BildF010266-0004/Christoph Müller; **62 Photo:** Martin Maleschka, **Art:** Alfred Hesse sowie Erich Gerlach, VG Bild-Kunst, Bonn 2020; **63 Photo:** Wüstenrot Stiftung/Philipp Lohöfener, **Art:** Arno Mohr; **65 Photos:** Archiv BBR, **Art:** Edith Müller-Ortloff; **66 Photo:** Stadt Frankfurt am Main, Denkmalamt, **Art:** Eberhard Schlotter; **67 Photo:** BBR/Cordia Schlegelmilch, **Art:** Will Sohl; **68 Photo:** BBR/Bernd Hiepe, **Art:** Charles Crodel; **70 Photo:** Architekturmuseum der Technischen Universität Berlin in der Universitätsbibliothek/Werner Harting, **Art:** Hermann Kirchberger; **71 Photo:** BBR/Martin Maleschka, **Art:** Hermann Kirchberger; **73 Photos:** BBR/Cordia Schlegelmilch, **Art:** Rupprecht Geiger; **74/75 Photos:** BBR/Cordia Schlegelmilch, **Art:** Max Lingner; **76 Photo top:** Bandesregierung/Doris Adrian; **76 Photo bottom:** Archiv BBR, **Art:**Hannes Schulz-Tattenpach; **77 Photo:** BBR/Cordia Schlegelmilch, **Art:** Hannes Schulz-Tattenpach; **79 Photo:** BBR/Cordia Schlegelmilch, **Art:** Bernd Krimmel; **80/81 Photos:** BBR/Anja Schlamann, **Art:** Hans Wimmer; **82 Photos:** BBR/ Martin Maleschka, **Art:** Wolfgang Frankenstein, VG Bild-Kunst, Bonn 2020; **86 Photo:** BArch Bild 183-C1001-0001-005/Hans-Günter Quaschinsky, **Art:** Fritz Kühn; **88 Photo:** Bernd Hiepe, **Art:** Walter Womacka, VG Bild-Kunst, Bonn 2020; **89 Photo:** Kunstverwaltung des Bundes/Michael Magnor, **Art:** Bert Heller; **90 Photo:** BBR/HG Esch; **91 Photos top:**

BBR/Werner Huthmacher, **Art:** HAP Grieshaber, VG Bild-Kunst, Bonn 2020; **91 Photo bottom links:** BBR/Werner Huthmacher, **Art:** Woty Werner; **91 Photo bottom rechts:** BBR/Werner Huthmacher, **Art:** Günther Uecker, VG Bild-Kunst, Bonn 2020; **93 Photo top:** Archiv BBR, **Art:** Haus-Rucker Co, VG Bild-Kunst, Bonn 2020; **93 Photo bottom:** Stephan Baumann, bild_raum, Karlsruhe, **Art:** Hans Kindermann; **94 Photo:** bpk/Gerhard Kiesling, **Art:** Reginald Richter, Richard Otfried Wilhelm; **95 Photo top:** Bandesregierung, Richard Schulze-Vorberg; **95 Photo bottom:** BBR/Bernd Hiepe, **Art:** Adolf Luther, VG Bild-Kunst, Bonn 2020; **97 Photo:** BBR/Cordia Schlegelmilch, **Art:** Wolf Vostell, VG Bild-Kunst, Bonn 2020; **98 Photo:** ddrbildarchiv.de/ Siegfried Gebser, **Art:** Rudolf Hilscher; **99 Photo:** Martin Maleschka, **Art:** Hermann Glöckner; **101 Photo:** BBR/Werner Huthmacher, **Art:** Olaf Metzel; **102 Photo:** BBR/Cordia Schlegelmilch; **103 Photo:** BBR/Cordia Schlegelmilch, **Art:** Walter Womacka, VG Bild-Kunst, Bonn 2020; **104 Photos:** BBR/Werner Huthmacher, **Art:** Angelika Baasner-Matussek; **106/107 Photos:** DDR Museum, **Art:** Ronald Paris, VG Bild-Kunst, Bonn 2020; **108 Photo:** bpk/ Gerhard Kiesling; **109 Photo:** Deutsches Historisches Museum/A. Psille, **Art:** Wolfgang Mattheuer, VG Bild-Kunst, Bonn 2020; **110/111 Photos:** Archiv BBR, **Art:** Otto Herbert Hajek, VG Bild-Kunst, Bonn 2020; **112 Photo:** BBR/Cordia Schlegelmilch, **Art:** Ansgar Nierhoff, VG Bild-Kunst, Bonn 2020; **113 Photo:** Michael Goergen, **Art:** Ansgar Nierhoff, VG Bild-Kunst, Bonn 2020; **114 Photo top:** Bandesregierung, Engelbert Reineke, **Photo bottom:** BBR/Bernd Hiepe, **Art:** Henry Moore, reproduced by permission of The Henry Moore Foandation; **116 Photo:** Martin Maleschka, **Art:** Willi Sitte, VG Bild-Kunst, Bonn 2020; **118/119 Photos:** BBR/Werner Huthmacher, **Art:** Wolfgang Nestler; **120/121 Photos:** BBR/Werner Huthmacher, **Art:** Rebecca Horn; **125 Photo:** BBR/Stefan Müller, **Art:** Lothar Baumgarten, VG Bild-Kunst, Bonn 2020; **127 Photo top:** DBT/Stephan Klonk, **Art:** Grisha Bruskin; **127 Photo bottom:** DBT/Roland Halbe, **Art:** François Morellet, VG Bild-Kunst, Bonn 2020; **128 Photo:** DBT/Stephan Erfurt, **Art:** (e.) Twin Gabriel; **129 Photo top:** BBR/Werner Huthmacher, **Art:** Neo Rauch; **129 Photo bottom:** DBT/Jörg F. Müller, **Art:** Julia Mangold; **130 Photo top:** DBT/ Stephan Erfurt, **Art:** Angela Bulloch; **130 Photo bottom:** BBR/Sandra Wildemann, **Art:** Markus Lüpertz, VG Bild-Kunst, Bonn 2020; **133 Photo:** BBR/ Cordia Schlegelmilch, **Art:** Gerhard Merz, VG Bild-Kunst, Bonn 2020; **135 Photo:** BBR/André Kirchner, **Art:** Rebecca Horn, VG Bild-Kunst, Bonn 2020; **136 Photo:** BBR/ Cordia Schlegelmilch, **Art:** Jenny Holzer, VG Bild-Kunst, Bonn 2020; **139 Photo top:** BBR/Sandra Wildemann, **Photo bottom:** Bandesregierung/Bernd Kühler, **Art:** Eduardo Chillida, VG Bild-Kunst, Bonn 2020; **140 Photo:** BBR/Florian Profitlich, **Art:** Per Kirkeby; **141 Photo:** Bandesrat/ Christian von Steffelin, **Art:** Per Kirkeby; **142/143 Photos:** BBR/Cordia Schlegelmilch, **Art:** Katarína Zavarská; **144 Photo:** BBR/Cordia Schlegelmilch, **Art:** Marcel Odenbach, VG Bild-Kunst, Bonn 2020; **146/147 Photos:** BBR/Cordia Schlegelmilch, **Art:** Michael Wirkner; **148 Photo:** DBT/Stephan Erfurt, **Art:** Christiane Möbus, VG Bild-Kunst, Bonn 2020; **150/151 Photos:** BBR/Cordia Schlegelmilch, **Art:** Trak Wendisch, VG Bild-Kunst, Bonn 2020; **152/153 Photos:** Nic Tenwiggenhorn, VG Bild-Kunst, Bonn 2020, **Art:** Katharina Grosse, VG Bild-Kunst, Bonn 2020; **156 Photo top:** BArch Bild 146-2006-0118/ Heinz Pollmann; **156 Photo bottom:** BBR/ Cordia Schlegelmilch, **Art:** Wolfgang Rüppel; **159 Photo top:** BBR/Sandra Wildemann; **159 Photo bottom:** BBR/ Cordia Schlegelmilch, **Art:** Jochen Gerz; **160 Photo:** BBR/Antonia Weiße, **Art:** Ulrich Schröder; **161 Photo:** Nico Hofmann, CC BY-SA 3.0; **162 Photo:** BBR/Cordia Schlegelmilch, **Art:** Gabriele Obermaier; **163 Photo:** Friedrich-Loeffler-Institutl/ Mandy Jörn, **Art:** Hans Neubert; **164 Photo top:** Matthias Geitel, **Art:** Matthias Geitel, VG Bild-Kunst, Bonn 2020; **164 Photo bottom:** BBR/Cordia Schlegelmilch, **Art:** Dani Karavan; **166 Photo:** BBR/Bernd Hiepe, **Art:** Manuel Franke, VG Bild-Kunst, Bonn 2020; **168 Photo:** DBT/Stephan Erfurt, **Art:** Hans Haacke, VG Bild-Kunst, Bonn; **169 Photo:** BBR/Stefan Müller, **Art:** Hans Haacke, VG Bild-Kunst, Bonn; **171 Photo:** BBR/Volker Kreidler, **Art:** Via Lewandowsky, VG Bild-Kunst, Bonn 2020; **172/173 Photos:** BBR/Werner Huthmacher, **Art:** raumlaborberlin; **177 Photos:** Martin Maleschka, **Art:** Fritz Eisel; **178 Photo:** BBR/Jan Petersen, **Art:** Karl-Ludwig Schmaltz; **179 Photo:** BBR/Alexander Obst, Marion Schmieding, **Art:** Ulrich Brüschke; **180 Photo:** Daniela Spiegel, **Art:** Helmut Humann; **182 Photo:** Friedrich-Loeffler-Institut/Mandy Jörn, **Art:** Waldemar Grzimek; **183 Photo:** PTB Bildstelle, **Art:** Norbert Kricke; **184 Photo top:** BBR/Cordia Schlegelmilch, **Art:** Egill Saebjörnsson; **184 Photo and Art bottom:** Leni Hoffmann, Manuel Franke, beide VG Bild-Kunst, Bonn 2020; **185 Photo:** Michael Fischer; **Art:** Sebastian Stumpf; **186 Photo top:** BBR/Cordia Schlegelmilch, **Art:** Emilia N. Bayer; **186 Photo bottom:** Ulrich Schwarz, **Art:** Christine Meisner; **187 Photo:** SHF/David von Becker, **Art:** Sunkoo Kang; **188 Photo:** BBR/Cordia Schlegelmilch, **Art:** Ina Geißler, Fabian Lippert; **190 Photo:** Privatarchiv Hollein, Franz Hubmann, **Art:** Hans Hollein; **191 Photo:** BArch Bild 183-F0102-0301-001/Heinz Junge, **Art:** Fritz Kühn; **192 Photo:** BBR/Cordia Schlegelmilch, **Art:** Tadashi Kawamata; **193 Photo:** BBR/Cordia Schlegelmilch, **Art:** Wafae Ahalouch el Keriasti; **194 Photo top:** Martin Maleschka, **Art:** Wilhelm Schmied, VG Bild-Kunst, Bonn 2020; **194 Photo bottom:** Flughafen Berlin Brandenburg GmbH/Günter Wicker, **Art:** Pae White; **196 Photo:** BBR/Cordia Schlegelmilch, **Art:** Walter Womacka; **198/199 Photos:** Martin Maleschka, **Art:** Horst Ring; **200/201 Photos:** BBR/Cordia Schlegelmilch, **Art:** Norbert Kricke; **202/203 Photos:** Martin Maleschka, **Art:** Josep Renau; **204 Photo:** BBR/Jens Andreae, **Art:** Erich Hauser, VG Bild-Kunst, Bonn 2020; **207 Photo:** Archiv BBR, **Art:** Horst Hoheisel; **208 Photo top:** Jens Gerber, **Photo bottom:** Christoph Sandig, **Art:** Sighard Gille, VG Bild-Kunst, Bonn 2020; **209 Photo:** Jens Gerber, **Art:** Sighard Gille; **211 Photo:** BBR/Johannes Stahl, **Art:** Hannsjörg Voth; **212/213 Photos:** BBR/ Martin Seidel, **Art:** Ian Hamilton Finlay; **214/215 Photos:** Alexander Obst, Marion Schmieding, **Art:** Barbara Trautmann; **216 Photos and Art:** Annette Sauermann; **221 Photo top:** Archiv BMVg, **Art:** Anatol Buchholtz, VG Bild-Kunst, Bonn 2020; **221 Photo bottom:** Archiv BMVg, **Art:** Wilhelm Keudel; **222 Photo top:** Archiv BMVg, **Art:** Karlheinz Goedtke; **222 Photo bottom:** Archiv BMVg, **Art:** Gerlinde Beck;

223 Photo: ddrbildarchiv.de/Burkhard Lange, **Art:** Hans Eickworth; **224 Photo:** Archiv BMVg, **Art:** Günter Fruhtrunk, VG Bild-Kunst, Bonn 2020; **225 Photo:** BBR/ Cordia Schlegelmilch, **Art:** Tomitaro Nachi; **226 Photo:** BBR/Dieter Leistner, Johannes Leistner, **Art:** Johannes Peter Hölzinger; **228 Photo top:** Archiv BMVg, **Art:** Erich Hauser; **228 Photo bottom:** Archiv BMVg, **Art:** Georg Engst, VG Bild-Kunst, Bonn 2020; **229 Photo:** Archiv BMVg, **Art:** Rainer Stiefvater; **231 Photo top:** BBR/ Jens Ziehe, **Art:** inges idee, VG Bild-Kunst, Bonn 2020; **231 Photo bottom:** Kay Zimmermann, **Art:** Daniel Priese; **232 Photo:** Archiv BMVg, **Art:** Jean Sprenger; **234 Photo:** David Brandt, **Art:** Harald Thiel, VG Bild-Kunst, Bonn 2020; **236/237 Photos:** MHM Berlin-Gatow/Heldenmaier, **Art:** Gerhard Thieme; **238 Photo:** Archiv BMVg, **Art:** François Morellet, VG Bild-Kunst, Bonn 2020; **239 Photo:** HSU/Reinhard Scheiblich, **Art:** François Morellet, VG Bild-Kunst, Bonn 2020; **240/241 Photos:** Archiv BMVg, **Art:** Georg Karl Pfahler; **242 Photos:** Archiv BMVg, **Art:** Eberhard Linke; **244/245 Photos and Art:** Elisabeth Wagner, VG Bild-Kunst, Bonn 2020; **246 Photos:** Thüringer Landesamt für Bau and Verkehr/Matthias Frank Schmidt, **Art:** Michael Sailstorfer, VG Bild-Kunst, Bonn 2020; **251 Photos:** Archiv BBR; **252 Photo top:** Archiv BBR, **Art:** Karl-Heinz Krause; **252 Photo bottom:** Archiv BBR, **Art:** Bernhard Heiliger, VG Bild-Kunst, Bonn 2020; **253 Photo top:** BBR/Reinhard Görner; **253 Photo bottom:** BBR/Lucca Chmel, **Art:** Blasius Spreng; **254 Photo:** Archiv BBR, **Art:** Fritz Koenig; **255 Photo:** Archiv BBR, **Art:** Otto Herbert Hajek, VG Bild-Kunst, Bonn 2020; **256 Photo:** Archiv BBR; **257 Photo:** Archiv BBR, **Art:** Reginald Richter; **258 Photo top:** UN Photo/Andrea Brizzi, **Art:** Günter Fruhtrunk, VG Bild-Kunst, Bonn 2020, Paolo Nestler; **258 Photo bottom:** UN Photo/ Milton Grant, **Art:** Fritz Cremer; **259 Photo top:** Archiv BBR, **Art:** Dieter Gantz, VG Bild-Kunst, Bonn 2020; **259 Photo bottom:** Archiv BBR, **Art:** Ingeborg Schäffler-Wolf; **260 Photos:** Archiv BBR; **Art:** Peter Schubert, VG Bild-Kunst, Bonn 2020; **261 Photo:** Archiv BBR, **Art:** Markus Lüpertz, VG Bild-Kunst, Bonn 2020; **262 Photo top:** Archiv BBR, **Art:** Robert Schad, VG Bild-Kunst, Bonn 2020; **262 Photo bottom:** Archiv BBR, **Art:** Stephan Balkenhol, VG Bild-Kunst, Bonn 2020; **263 Photo:** Archiv BBR, **Art:** Horst Antes; **264 Photo top:** BBR/Hanns Joosten, **Art:** Rainer Splitt, VG Bild-Kunst, Bonn 2020; **264 Photo bottom:** Archiv BBR, **Art:** Karl Schlamminger; **267 Photo:** Archiv BBR, **Art:** Andreu Alfaro; **268 Photo top:** Achim Kühn, **Photo bottom:** Archiv BBR, **Art:** Fritz Kühn; **270 Photos:** Archiv BBR, **Art:** Günter Ferdinand Ris; **272/273 Photos:** BBR/Arno de la Chapelle, **Art:** Frank M. Zeidler, VG Bild-Kunst, Bonn 2020; **274/275 Photos:** BBR/Christian Richters, **Art:** Renate Wolff, VG Bild-Kunst, Bonn 2020; **276 Photo:** S. Genge, Worschech Architekten, **Art:** J&K, VG Bild-Kunst, Bonn 2020; **281 Photo top:** BBR/Ulrich Schwarz, **Art:** Stefan Sous, VG Bild-Kunst, Bonn 2020; **281 Photo and Art bottom:** Ganda Förster, VG Bild-Kunst, Bonn 2020; **282 Photo and Art:** Robert Patz; **283 Photo:** BBR/Bernd Hiepe, **Art:** Dörte Michaelis; **284 Photo:** Deutsche Welle/Frank Liesegang, **Art:** Sokari Douglas Camp, VG Bild-Kunst, Bonn 2020; **285 Photo:** BBR/Martin Seidel, **Art:** Erich Wiesner; **287 Photo and Art top:** missing icons | knobloch + vorkoeper; **287 Photo and Art bottom:** Dietrich Förster; **288 Photo and Art:** Roland Fuhrmann, VG Bild-Kunst, Bonn 2020; **289 Photo:** Henning Schacht, **Art:** Roland Fuhrmann, VG Bild-Kunst, Bonn 2020; **293 Photos:** BBR/Werner Huthmacher, **Art:** Otto Herbert Hajek, VG Bild-Kunst, Bonn 2020; **294 Photo:** Roland Halbe, **Art:** Clara Kress; **295 Photo:** BBR/Cordia Schlegelmilch, **Art:** Nan Hoover; **296 Photo:** DBT/ Junophoto, **Art:** Wieland Förster, VG Bild-Kunst, Bonn 2020; **297 Photos:** Imke Lüders, **Art:** Peter Nagel, VG Bild-Kunst, Bonn 2020; **298 Photo top:** BBR Archiv, **Photo bottom:** BBR/Nikken Sekkei Ltd., **Art:** Hedja Luckhardt-Freese; **299 Foto:** BBR Archiv, **Art:** Reinhard Omir; **300 Foto:** BBR Archiv, **Art:** Sigrid Wylach; **301 Foto:** BBR/Werner Huthmacher, **Art:** Ferdinand Kriwet; **303 Foto top:** BBR/ Cordia Schlegelmilch, **Foto bottom:** BBR Archiv, **Art:** Ursula Sax, VG Bild-Kunst, Bonn 2020; **304 Foto:** Martin Maleschka, **Art:** Gerhard Bondzin; **306 Foto:** Matthias Hamel, Stephan Braunfels Architekten, **Art:** Bernhard Heiliger, VG Bild-Kunst, Bonn 2020; **307 Foto:** BBR Archiv, **Art:** Bernhard Heiliger, VG Bild-Kunst, Bonn 2020

IMPRINT

EDITORIAL DEPARTMENT:
Bundesministerium des Innern,
für Bau und Heimat (BMI)
Referat BW I 5 – Bauingenieurwesen,
Nachhaltiges Bauen, Bauforschung
Alt-Moabit 140, 10557 Berlin
Bundesamt für Bauwesen und
Raumordnung (BBR)
Referat A 2 – Projektentwicklung,
Wettbewerbe, Zuwendungsmaßnahmen
im Inland
Straße des 17. Juni 112
10623 Berlin

PROJECT MANAGEMENT:
Beate Hückelheim-Kaune,
Dr. Ute Chibidziura and
Michael Kasiske, BBR, Referat A 2

CONCEPT AND EDITORIAL BOARD:
Dr. Ute Chibidziura, BBR
Dr. Constanze von Marlin,
schmedding.vonmarlin.
with Dr. Anna-Sophie Laug and
Ella Becker

TRANSLATION:
Benjamin Liebelt, Berlin

PROOFREADING:
Tatyana Pugacheva, Berlin

LAYOUT AND GRAPHIC DESIGN:
StudioKrimm, Berlin

LITHOGRAPHY:
hausstætter Herstellung

PRINTING AND BINDING:
optimal media GmbH, Röbel/Müritz
Print run: 900

PUBLISHING:
Deutscher Kunstverlag
GmbH Berlin Munich,
Lützowstr. 33, 10785 Berlin
www.deutscherkunstverlag.de
www.degruyter.com

The German National Library
records this publication in the
German National Bibliography;
detailed bibliographical data can
be accessed online at http://dnb.dnb.de.

Lützowstr. 33, 10785 Berlin
Part of Walter de Gruyter GmbH
Berlin Boston
www.deutscherkunstverlag.de
www.degruyter.com
ISBN: 978-3-422-98623-7